Contents

Section C:
Some promising developments   *373*

Section D:
Appendices   *393*

List of Tables

List of Figures

Acknowledgements

First and foremost, my thanks go to the very many individuals, families, staff and support groups I have worked with, talked to and learnt from over the past 30 years. They have enriched my knowledge of this fascinating area by allowing me to learn from and share with them.

I have been fortunate over the course of my career to have learnt from and worked with a great many able clinicians and researchers who have taught me much about different relevant areas, such as infant and child development; developmental neurology; developmental psychopathology; neuroscience; genetics; and the field of autistic spectrum disorder (ASD). My thanks go to all of those mentioned below for helping me to my current level of understanding and for enabling me to convey, I hope, some of the rich complexity and excitement of work in this field. Any omissions, errors of fact or of interpretation are entirely my own.

My interest in the area of developmental psychology was stimulated by my long-time mentor and colleague Colwyn Trevarthen, whose dual interests and expertise in neuroscience and child development kindled my own. I was also fortunate in my early studies in psychology to have many excellent teachers, including John Beloff, Tom Bower, Margaret Donaldson, John Marshall, Lynne Murray, Jennifer Wishart and Peter Wright, who did much to channel and direct me. In philosophy, my thanks go particularly to Roy Bhaskar, the late Larry Briskman and Neil Tennant, all of whose views on philosophy of science and logic did much to sharpen my understanding of research method.

I have been fortunate to work with or under, and to be taught by, a number of leading clinicians in the area of ASD and developmental neuroscience, including Keith Brown, John Clements, Patricia Howlin, Marcel Kinsbourne, Robert Minns, Michael Rutter, Lorna Wing and the late Sula Wolff. I have also had the good fortune to attend taught courses by Jean Aicardi and Henri Hecaen, and to have studied early neurobehavioural development with Heidelise Als, Berry Brazelton, Victor and Lilly Dubowitz and Kevin Nugent.

I have discussed many of the issues raised here with a range of colleagues, including Simon Baron-Cohen, Tom Berney, Adrian Bird, B.J. Casey, Mary Coleman, John Corbett, Christopher Gillberg, James Harris, Bruce McEwen, John Menkes, Sid Shapiro, the late Walter Spitzer, Helen Tager-Flusberg and Philip and Oznat Teitelbaum. *The Biology of the Autistic Syndromes* (Coleman and Gillberg 1985) sparked much of what has become a lifelong fascination.

My interest in dietary and gastrointestinal factors has been stimulated by discussion with many clinicians and researchers, including Karoly Horvath, Simon Murch, Karl Reichelt, Bernie Rimland, Paul Shattock and Paul Whiteley; in immunology through discussions with Paul Ashwood, Jonathan Brostoff, Jack Marchalonis and Ivan Roitt;

and in fatty acid metabolism by Gordon Bell, the late David Horrobin, Basant Puri, Alex Richardson and Marion Ross.

My interest in genetics began many years ago through discussions with Conrad Waddington, and in behavioural genetics through contact with David Fulker, Robert Hinde and Aubrey Manning. This interest has extended steadily through my involvement in groups such as the Society for the Study of Behavioural Phenotypes, Sackler Foundation Neuroscience Think-tank meetings, the Scottish Autism Research Group and the International Society for Autism Research, and through discussions with clinical colleagues such as Martin Bax, Peter Baxter and Greig O'Brien.

Prelude

The only real voyage of discovery consists not in seeking new landscapes but in having new eyes. (Marcel Proust, 1871–1922)

Getting a diagnosis of autistic spectrum disorder (ASD) can be a major hurdle and a major achievement for families. Waiting lists can be lengthy, the number of clinicians adequately trained to use appropriate diagnostic assessments is still worryingly small, and attempts to address this problem have been piecemeal at best. Once a diagnosis has been given, you start thinking something like: 'Now we know what is wrong, we can start to sort it out.'

The diagnosis typically gives access to a lot of very general information about the ASDs – that the person may have a range of difficulties/differences which are part of what is talked about as 'the triad of impairments': problems with social interaction; problems with communication; and restricted repetitive and stereotyped patterns of behaviour, interests and activities. It can also lead to help from a range of services and interventions aimed at improving communication, supporting families and improving quality of life. Access to appropriate education, services and support is a major part of what is needed for anyone with an ASD and can be immensely helpful. These are general aspects of what is required, and apply to many people with an ASD, but they are not the focus of this book.

Getting a diagnosis can open up access to practical help over educational and vocational issues, respite care and financial support. Simply having an ASD diagnosis provides little information about the nature of the individual, why they are the way they are, or whether they will require such help and support.

A diagnosis can also be helpful in engaging with charities and support groups, many of which require an 'official diagnosis' as a condition for working with families. (A list of many of these groups is provided at the back of the book.)

The range of differences that can lead to a diagnosis of ASD means that you can be tall, medium or short; slight, average or heavily built; have a large head, a regular sized head or a small head; be learning disabled, of normal IQ or of high intelligence. You may or may not have epilepsy; you may or may not have immune abnormalities; you may or may not have sensory problems; you may or may not have gastrointestinal problems; you may or may not have any of a wide range of associated metabolic differences or difficulties. You might or might not benefit from any of a range of specific treatments, supplements, therapies or other interventions. There has been concern expressed over the broad range of presentations which come under the umbrella of ASD, and whether divisions into groupings based on cause, or into 'primary' and 'secondary' autism, might make things more manageable (Benaron 2003).

In this volume we discuss the wide range of genetic conditions that have been reported in association with a diagnosis of ASD. In so doing we fully acknowledge that this 'blueprint' is likely to alter as larger and better studies clarify where such links are robust and where they are chance associations; where there is a specific behavioural phenotype and where there is a wide variation in presentation. (See Moss and Howlin 2009 for further discussion of these important issues.)

Individual differences are often due to differences in genetic makeup. Establishing the nature of the genetic basis in an individual can be just as important for effective care and management as obtaining the initial diagnosis of ASD itself (Robin 2006). Simply getting the diagnosis of an ASD does not clarify our understanding about any of the above factors; however, knowledge about all of these factors may be important or even critical in providing the best help for someone with an ASD, or highlighting areas of additional need or difficulty. Often these differences within ASD are not adequately considered or properly assessed. Sometimes they are ignored on the basis that, if they are not autism-specific, they are not relevant to management.

It is this gap in understanding, where increasing knowledge of the differences within autism is often as important as recognizing the commonalities among those with the diagnosis, that forms the focus of this book.

The constant media barrage of information on the latest craze in miracle cures, and the claims that this or that treatment can work for anyone with autism, do little to help. An undirected search of the Internet usually does more to confuse than to sort things out. Many 'weird and wonderful' treatments can be found, some of which, no doubt, are effective for some people with ASD, some of which do neither good nor ill to most, while some are dangerous to many and a few, tragically, can be fatal.

All too often, treatments are advocated that are marketed because they are available rather than because they work. Sometimes evidence is presented that one person has changed dramatically (with the implication that, if it worked for them, it might work for you or your child). It is easy to be convinced when the wish for help is coupled with a good sales pitch from someone anxious to assist, or in some cases, more cynically, from someone keen to make a profit.

In this volume I have tried to provide comprehensive information covering as many as possible of the published papers on ASD in genetic conditions.

Some conditions are discussed in significantly more detail than others – for Down syndrome, for example, there is a large amount of information both on the condition and on interventions, as it was one of the earliest recognized genetic conditions. There is a large body of literature on, and there has been considerable controversy over, the possible benefits of alternative therapies. There is also a large literature on the biology and genetics of the muscular dystrophies, neurofibromatosis, Joubert and Williams syndromes, while for a number of the other conditions the literature is more sparse.

As many people reading this book are likely to investigate things that they hope might help, I have tried to provide some understanding of why some people with certain of these conditions may benefit from certain treatments, where others with the same blanket

ASD diagnosis would not. I have also tried to provide information on how to access a broad range of resources and support groups and keep informed of new developments. Many of the approaches that are discussed under specific genetic conditions are at an early stage in their evaluation and are highlighted to develop awareness of developments that are beginning to have an effect on clinical management.

Important note. Where biomedical treatment and management issues are discussed this is for information and guidance only. Treatments/interventions should never be considered lightly, and not without appropriate consultation with trained clinicians who have responsibility for the individual concerned.

It may be just as irresponsible to deny use of a treatment or approach where there is good evidence to support it, as it would be to begin a treatment that cannot be justified.

Kenneth J. Aitken
Edinburgh
November 2009

Introduction

For some, being on the autistic spectrum is how they are, it is how they always want to be, and it is something that carries no associated problems. For those fortunate people, this book may help to reach a clearer understanding of why they are as they are, without having much further effect on their lives. This is just like taking a course in human biology or psychology, which may help any one of us to come to a different view of why we feel and act as we do.

We will be looking at some of the differences between individuals with ASDs, not trying to illustrate what they have in common. These variations can be vast, and many exceptional people may have had an ASD – Isaac Newton, the polymath; Charles Darwin, the 'father' of evolutionary theory; Ludwig Wittgenstein, the philosopher; Albert Einstein, the physicist, discoverer of relativity and 'father' of the atomic bomb; Paul Erdos, the mathematician; Samuel Beckett, the playwright and poet; Erik Satie, the jazz musician; and L.S. Lowry, the 'matchstick-man' painter, have all been thought, by some at least, to have had ASDs. (For more detailed discussion of the putative association between creativity and ASD, see Fitzgerald 2004, 2005; Treffert 2006; Walker and Fitzgerald 2006.) Similar propositions have been made for a link between creativity and various other conditions, including schizophrenia (Horrobin 2001) and manic-depression/ bipolar disorder (Jamison 1993).

The expanding panoply of gifted individuals who were thought to have been on the spectrum seems somehow at odds with the fact that ASDs are usually seen as a set of conditions associated with communication difficulties, problems with social understanding, learning problems, and often with a host of associated medical issues. 'Savant skills' (isolated areas of extreme ability) are found in some individuals with ASDs, but are by no means typical or even common in this group. This illustrates the variation across those with ASDs rather than suggesting some key common factor.

Widespread public awareness of ASD is often dated to Dustin Hoffman's portrayal of an autistic savant in the film *Rainman*, a character based loosely on a real autistic 'mega-savant', Kim Peek (Peek 1997; Peek and Hanson 2007). This character has led to the general expectation that anyone with an ASD will have some spectacular ability.

This book provides a discussion of a complex area, aimed at a broad range of people – at affected families, at those on the spectrum, and also at clinicians and researchers who need an introduction to the genetics of the ASDs. It fills some of the gaps in basic knowledge – about whether genetic and epigenetic factors can cause or contribute to autistic conditions and about how and why they should be assessed. Where there is sufficient evidence it also suggests what can and could be done to help. I hope that, at the very least, this will make many people dealing with the ASDs stop and think.

I was interested to see the public reaction to the announcement of a study aiming to intervene *before* diagnosis with infants at 'high risk' of becoming autistic (born into families who already have an autistic child). Many of those who commented on the study and who themselves have ASDs said that they would much prefer to be as they are, than to have been denied that opportunity as a result of early intervention. (See http://seattlepi.nwsource.com/1#ocal/345823_autism03.html and comments.)

For many others with an ASD, their condition, rather than exclusively an asset, is associated with problems that they would much rather not have – problems such as epilepsy, anxiety, depression, gastrointestinal difficulties, immune sensitivities, learning problems, sleep problems and dietary sensitivities. For these people, and for their carers, this book may offer insight and help.

The past decade has seen a revolution in our ability to both detect and understand genetic and epigenetic conditions. Where it had previously been assumed that specific genetic disorders were rare in autism (perhaps seen at most in one to three per cent of cases), developing technologies have allowed us to examine DNA in ever finer detail. The focus, for several years, was on identifying the specific set of genes that were thought to be abnormal in most people with ASD. We now know that genetic abnormalities are relatively common in ASD. There is currently little support for a common set of affected genes, but rather there appear to be a large number of genetic factors, each sufficient to increase the risk. Equally, we are coming to realize that there are ethnic differences in the genetics of disease that may have important implications for screening and care:

> …the genetic variants predicted to underlie common disease are often not common across populations with different ancestry or differ significantly in frequency among such populations. (Bamshad and Guthery 2007)

As we shall see, a number of these conditions are much more common in certain ethnic groups than in others.

In the past, twin concordance levels were used to argue for a common genetic mechanism in autism. The reason for high levels of concordance in identical twins – where both twins are similarly affected – is typically that both share the same core genetic makeup (although for some things it could be due to having the same exposure, as we would see if both twins had been exposed to the same toxin or disease). If one pair of identical twins share a genetic difference that predisposes both of them to develop ASD, it does not, however, necessarily mean that they will share this same makeup with the next pair of concordant identical twins. Because one pair of identical twins who both have fragile-X syndrome are both autistic, this does not mean that another pair of identical twins who are both autistic will both also have fragile-X.

There is a flaw in the argument for common heritability that can be highlighted if we look at the following.

Most people would claim to follow the logic by which the first two statements (a) and (b) lead to their conclusion (c):

a) All men are mortal

and

b) Socrates is a man.

Therefore

c) Socrates is mortal.

That (a) + (b) leads to (c) seems clear and logical, but it is not a necessary conclusion. By following the same line of argument, you could also reach the following conclusion:

c) All men are Socrates.

– which most of us would see as clearly false (although it would be true if Socrates was the only man). A similar logical error seems to be made with ASD. The reasoning typically runs as follows:

a) All ASD has a genetic cause

and

b) Fragile-X is a genetic cause of ASD.

Therefore

c) All ASD is caused by fragile-X.

This conclusion would be correct only if ASD were caused by fragile-X, *and* ASD had only a *single* (genetic) cause. The following conclusion would be more sensible:

c) Fragile-X is *a* genetic cause of ASD.

There are many syndromes and conditions that have been associated with ASDs – some are more common in the families of those with an autistic spectrum disorder; others are genetic conditions that have been found more often than expected in those who are on the spectrum. Some of these findings may turn out to be fortuitous associations, reported because they looked significant at the time. Some people may have more than one genetic difference.

A single polygenic cause could lead to a high monozygotic (MZ; genetically identical), low dizygotic (DZ; genetically non-identical) concordance rate (i.e. if there was a single genetic cause then it would be more likely that both would be affected in identical than non-identical twin pairs); however, a number of independent but sufficient genetic causes could equally give rise to a high concordance rate if a number of genetic and/or environmental causes were independently sufficient.

Twin studies bring their own complexities. Being born a twin increases risks of a range of problems – you are typically born smaller and have a higher than normal risk of a range of perinatal difficulties. There has been considerable debate over whether being born a twin increases your risk of developing ASD (Betancur, Leboyer and Gillberg

2002 and Ho, Todd and Constantino 2005 both suggest that it may, while Hallmeyer *et al.* 2002 suggest that it does not). For certain conditions, such as Goldenhar syndrome [38], there does appear to be an increased risk of being autistic associated with being an identical (MZ) twin (Wieczorek *et al.* 2007).

Most people who have to come to terms with, and try to understand the nature of, someone with an ASD have little knowledge of these sorts of scientific argument. This will be the case for many parents trying to understand their child's difficulties or differences. They are presented with someone whose behaviour can be perplexing. When reading to try to understand the condition, they encounter a bewildering array of terms – for assessments, behaviours, disorders, treatments and interventions. These are almost guaranteed to confuse anyone looking into the area for the first time: What are linoleic acid and linolenic acid? What are 'omega-3', 'omega-6' and 'omega-9', and how does one differ from the others? What is the difference between negative punishment and negative reinforcement? Do I need to know about strange-sounding things like aquaporins, transdermal glutathione or hyperbaric oxygen treatment? How can he have autism if he has a diagnosis of (for example) muscular dystrophy – aren't they different...? The list of confusing questions can go on and on.

This book provides a tool which can help to improve the quality of life of many people with ASDs, and to encourage the view that gaining a better understanding of what underlies differences in ASD (both differences from the 'neurotypical' and differences within the autistic spectrum) can help to develop more effective methods of providing support for those who need it.

The aim here is not to say what should be done – the study of ASDs is an area of accelerating research interest, and of continuing changes in 'best practice'. Many ideas on genetics are constantly being reworked to accommodate new developments in our understanding. As we will discuss, conditions that a few years ago were seen as genetic and therefore unchangeable are now seen as genetic but modifiable, because we now have a better understanding of how they operate and how these techniques can affect development. The major change in our understanding of genetics has come from our increasing understanding of how genetic mechanisms are affected by non-genetic factors like parental behaviour and diet.

Schizophrenia, a condition in which there have now been over 700 candidate genes proposed and some 1,300 association studies carried out, still seems far from any resolution of its genetic underpinnings; it has not been shown to have a simple genetic basis but a large number of genetic factors appear to be involved (Collier 2008; Crow 2008; Need *et al.* 2009; O'Donovan; Craddock and Owen 2008; Sullivan 2008b).

There is a regular stream of new reports on possible associations between genetic conditions and ASD (see Chugani *et al.* 2007; Kanavin *et al.* 2007; Mefford *et al.* 2008; Neves-Pereira *et al.* 2009; Poo-Arguelles *et al.* 2006; Zafeiriou *et al.* 2007; Zannolli *et al.* 2003, for several examples), and of rare conditions co-morbid with ASD, such as Danon disease (Burusnukul *et al.* 2008) and Kabuki syndrome (Sari *et al.* 2008), where a gene mechanism has still to be identified. How do you work out if any of these are important (for you) and what they mean?

There are regular reports of new techniques that make possible the detection and study of smaller and smaller differences in our genetic makeup, the latest being the use of 'cytogenetic arrays' to detect small copy number variations resulting in microdeletions and duplications. The majority of these differences were virtually unknown even five years ago. A short readable introduction to this issue can be found in a *New England Journal of Medicine* editorial (Ledbetter 2008).

It is important to understand that because something has a genetic basis this does not necessarily mean that it is unchangeable; in the same way as understanding that the history of events that resulted in a fear or depression does not mean that it is untreatable. Understanding why is the first step to successful intervention (where this is needed) because knowledge of the mechanisms involved gives an idea of the ways in which they may be altered.

Where to start?

Typically, families are beginning to ask questions about whether their child is developing normally by the middle of their second year (De Giacomo and Fombonne 1998). Once concerns have been raised (typically to the health visitor, family doctor or paediatrician) by parents, grandparents or early carers, things often move slowly to first base after a long wait and much effort.

An Atlanta study (Wiggins, Baio and Rice 2006) found that, on average, diagnostic assessments were only begun when the child was around 48 months, with diagnoses typically being made when they were approximately 61 months – over a year later.

In England and Wales, the National Autism Plan for Children (NAP-C) gave a target of 8.5 months from initial concerns to diagnostic formulation and feedback to families (NIASA 2003). It has rapidly become apparent that achieving this target has been impossible in many areas (Preece and Mott 2006; Sharma, Chandrakantha and Mold 2007). Waiting lists seem to be going up and up and in most places services are hard pushed to meet demands. As criteria have been broadened, more families now wait considerable periods for diagnostic assessment, even when their child does not have an ASD, delaying both their access to more appropriate services and increasing the waiting time of those with ASDs. Where emphasis has been placed on cutting waiting times for diagnosis, there are few resources left for the increasing numbers of children being diagnosed.

After a diagnosis has finally been made, various things are likely to be put in place – perhaps a behavioural intervention programme is instituted, and some basic screening tests suggest that there is no obvious metabolic or genetic problem. Where clinically indicated, a brain scan may be carried out – this will typically show that the brain is 'grossly structurally normal' – and perhaps an EEG will be conducted, and this will also typically be reported as normal or as showing only some 'non-specific immaturities'. Once things have proceeded this far, what could or should happen next?

This book is about helping people to get past this basic level of understanding and investigation to reach second base with the minimum of stress. It should, I hope, also help with identifying problems and patterns that can lead to further investigations and, for some, to targeted and more effective treatments.

There is a palpable frustration in the lay literature, expressed by informed parents of affected children, some with basic medical qualifications, over the apparent lack of progress in identifying causal mechanisms and scientifically based approaches to treatment (see, for example, Fitzpatrick 2008; Nadesan 2005). A simple fallacy in much of this literature is the assumption that ASD is a single, ill-understood condition, with the implicit expectation that there may be a single approach that will be likely to help all, once the biological basis has been better understood. A corollary to this is the assumption that, in the meantime, anything that has been shown to be unhelpful in group studies will not be helpful to anyone on the autistic spectrum.

The continuing cause of frustration for many parents is the apparent assumption amongst many professionals that, as parents, they were given a 'user manual' and know the right questions to ask, or the right things to mention. It is probably even more frustrating when, having spent a long time trying to understand a particular aspect of the ASD, their ideas or concerns are dismissed out of hand.

Parents often go into clinic wondering things like:

- Is it important for our doctor to know that he walks on tiptoes a lot? That she has blank spells when she seems to be in a daydream? That he passes a lot of wind?

- Should I go into detail about the diet/behaviour/my worries?

- Will I get a hostile reaction if I mention that we thought he showed a bad reaction to a vaccination/infection…?

Any of the above may be important. Particular 'behavioural phenotypes' present as ASD, and can often be linked to particular genetic conditions. Many of those currently known are detailed in later sections of this book. Children with particular genetic differences predisposing to ASD can show worse reactions than others to natural infections or to particular treatments (see Poling *et al.* 2006; Towbin K.E. 2003b).

A wide range of clinical disorders are common in those with ASDs, and more and more of these are being linked to specific genetic conditions, to previously undescribed genetic factors or metabolic differences (see Aitken 2008; Cohen 2003; Gillberg and Billstedt 2000; Gillberg and Coleman 1996; Sykes and Lamb 2007).

Often there are delays in accessing appropriate assessments and treatments, as no one has thought to ask for them, or because of lack of demand when they are asked for, or when a developmental history has not focused on questions that would have led to the right tests, or where those tests are not currently available to clinicians. In addition, our knowledge of causation is as yet only fragmentary. Depending on whether initial concerns are over communication, development, behaviour and/or medical factors, different clinicians become involved and different avenues are pursued.

It is important to understand that much of the progress being made in understanding the ASDs comes from approaches (for example, knock-in and knock-out animal genetic models, molecular epidemiology and studies of epigenetic factors) that are not part of the academic training of the majority of clinicians who work with ASD, most of whom will have a medical, clinical psychology or paramedical background. Progress requires a cross-disciplinary perspective that is lacking from much of the clinical literature and is not provided in the 'evidence-based medicine' (EBM) model that forms the basis for current health approaches. EBM has revolutionized our healthcare systems by focusing the research evidence on what works (for a basic introduction see Goldacre 2009, and for a proper discussion see Straus *et al.* 2005). Methods have been developed to evaluate what works, how well and with whom. EBM relies on access to good, well-conducted research on agreed conditions. The approach is inherently sound, but only effective where there is research on an agreed condition. The major problem in much clinical practice is that there is poor agreement on the nature of the condition and/or little research evidence, but a need to do something (Horrobin 2003).

As ASDs can arise for a range of possible genetic reasons, some with treatment implications and some without, we need to develop much better research models to tease out what approaches might work with which conditions and why (a point frequently made by Fitzpatrick 2008).

There are a number of ways in which ASDs can present with obvious physical and developmental differences that are probably genetic in origin, but for which, as yet, we have no knowledge of the likely genetic basis. For example, Snape and colleagues (Snape *et al.* 2006) described a nine-year-old child with intellectual disability and autism in combination with an unusual skull shape and long fingers with contracted ligaments, but without the gene defect in FBN2 typically seen in this type of skeletal problem. Harry Chugani *et al.* (2007) in Detroit have reported on four children with autism and unilateral facial port-wine staining. (Such facial colouration is typically seen in Sturge-Weber syndrome, accompanied by cortical damage to the opposite side of the brain.) None of these children showed evidence of brain atrophy on MRI imaging, and their metabolic profiles differed from other children with autism reported by the same group (but see the discussion in section [59] below).

For several of the conditions included here the evidence to date suggests a link with ASD, but has so far been described by only one clinical or research group. Now that (in the USA at least) there is a network of research centres collaborating on collecting data (one such group being the CPEA – Collaborative Program for Excellence in Autism – and another the PARIS – Paris Autism International Sibpair Study group), getting such replication of findings should become easier. So far, lack of replication often arises, as certain centres pursue specific interests that are not researched in other centres, or use techniques that are not used elsewhere.

Some conditions such as congenital adrenal hyperplasia [25] have been included here because they have been frequently cited as possible factors, and the biological reasoning behind this may be important, but the current evidence does not suggest that they are important in the pathogenesis of ASD.

Although confirmation of the same finding by other researchers is taken as a benchmark for the likely importance of any finding in clinical science, this convention has become blurred in ASD for several reasons. Interesting associations may be truly causally related but, if untested by other groups, lack the 'independent replication' typically relied on in modern clinical science. This results in an apparent 'false negative' – lack of replication because replication has not been attempted, rather than because it has been attempted and has not been achieved.

As multicentre and multinational research collaborations have developed, data from several genetic and tissue databanks (such as the Autism Genetic Resource Exchange (AGRE), the Simons Foundation Simplex collection, and the EuroBioBank network) are now commonly used by numbers of different researchers, and 'confirmation' of findings is sometimes based on analyses of samples taken from, or data submitted on, the same individuals as those in the publications that reported the initial findings. Where part of the same material from the same subjects is looked at by several centres, or where several databanks have material from the same subjects, this could lead to misleadingly impressive agreement, since everyone finds the same thing because they are all looking at the same subset of people. This type of mistake can lead to 'false positive' results – drawing the conclusion either that an association is present where none in fact exists, or, where an association does exist, that it is stronger than it actually is. We now have numerous examples where a significant association found by one study or group cannot be replicated elsewhere. PON1, a gene that codes for an arylesterase (one effect of which is the oxidation of the insectide parathion), is one such example: the higher use of such compounds in North American farming may explain why there is a link between a defect in this gene and ASD in Noth America but no such link in Europe (D'Amelio *et al.* 2005).

There are various problems with the current research framework.

1. There is a reluctance to fund independent replication of research. Once a finding is already in the literature, it loses novelty and is less attractive as a fundable research project. Assuming that the right questions are addressed, the move to multicentre studies should reduce the problems inherent in this; however, there is a concomitant cost increase in such exercises.

2. Whether funded by government or charity, most research has been driven by a small number of individuals with particular views of what is sensible to pursue. These tend to be senior figures whose fondly held views often lag behind current scientific thinking and delay the investigation of less 'mainstream' hypotheses.

3. In some areas, such as the extent and nature of gastrointestinal involvement, for example, political expedience and a potential public health issue appear to have been major factors in driving the research agenda, rather than the clinical merit or otherwise of the ideas involved.

For these reasons a heavy emphasis is placed in this book on providing the information and tools for keeping up to date: how to search the clinical and research literature; what research and support groups are available and how to contact them; and generally how to look further into particular areas. I would doubt that for any of the conditions discussed here our current knowledge is as good as it will get, and for some areas what now seems true may be overturned by future studies.

Some people reading this book, especially those without or with only a limited science or biology background, may find it helpful to go through the text alongside a more general overview of terminology (such as Neisworth and Wolfe 2005), a basic genetics primer (like the excellent if slightly dated one by Bonthron *et al.* 1998), and an up-to-date medical dictionary or online resource. A more general introduction to genetics might be useful (such as Guttman *et al.* 2002), as well as a simple overview of some of the newer genetic techniques (such as Gibson and Muse 2004). A glossary of terms has been included at the back of the book.

For simplicity the term 'autistic spectrum disorder' (ASD) has been used with reference to those who meet the criteria for an ICD-10 or DSM-IV ASD diagnosis throughout. ICD-10 (the tenth revision of the *International Classification of Diseases*) is the World Health Organization's system for classifying medical conditions. DSM-IV Tr is the text revision of the fourth edition of the American Psychiatric Association's *Diagnostic and Statistical Manual.*

The main genetic conditions that have been reported in association with ASD diagnoses are discussed in Section B. For a number of these there is a clinical literature associated with a particular name, and where it appears that it may be synonymous with another condition (as we see, for example, with the various conditions linked to the 22q11.2 region of chromosome 22), more than one entry may appear. Each condition is given a separate section, with relevant information for linking it to any other possible names. It may be that for a genetic condition identified several years ago more recent developments in our understanding have changed our knowledge about how it operates.

Because I am Scottish, I have used UK spellings like 'paediatric', 'behaviour' and 'centre' rather than the more widely used American versions 'pediatric', 'behavior' and 'center'. I use the term 'learning disability' in the UK and European sense of a person with a global cognitive difficulty, rather than in the American sense of someone who has a more discrete impairment, which in the UK would be called a 'specific learning impairment'. The equivalent American term for 'learning disability' would be 'intellectual disability' (Harris 2006).

I frequently use 'aka' ('also known as'), since many of the conditions discussed can be referred to by multiple terms and it may be helpful for you to know, for example, that 'XXY syndrome' is also known as 'Klinefelter's syndrome'. An alphabetical list of syndromes is provided at the end of the book to help with this. Where a condition that is mentioned is treated in a separate section of the book, the number of the relevant section is given in square brackets for ease of cross-referencing, for example, Apert syndrome [12].

An important point to be aware of is that searching, say, PubMed (the National Institutes for Health (USA) database of medical references) using UK or US spellings will typically unearth different literatures – see 'Searching for further information' in Section D. Always remember to search on the alternative spellings of a term, or names for a condition, if you are trying to be comprehensive in locating publications.

A note on genetic terms

We will refer to the 'gene locus' for particular conditions. Genes, as we know them, are studied in a particular state of cell development known as *metaphase*, when DNA compacts into chromosomes. At this stage, the DNA is tightly wound around 'histones', almost like thread around a bobbin, and bound up inside 'scaffolding proteins' ready for cell division. At this point the chromosomes can be seen under a light microscope, and look the way most people see them in biology textbooks at school or university. They can be photographed and the pairs of chromosomes sorted into a *karyogram* (a diagram representing a Karyotpe – a map of the layout of the individual chromosomes in the nucleus of a living cell).

An area called the *centromere* can be seen on each chromosome (a narrower band of material seen some way along the chromosome, to which 'spindle fibres' attach during cell division itself, and along which each chromosome separates into two, usually identical, halves). In Figure 1 the centromere is the narrow 'waist' signified by the two short bars between the ellipse and the main body of the chromosome.

What do the numbers given as the 'gene locus' tell us? Where we discuss adenylosuccinate lyase (ADSL) deficiency, for example, you will see that it is linked to a particular gene locus:

22q13.1

In humans, males have an X and a Y sex chromosome and females have two X chromosomes. The other 22 pairs of chromosomes are the same in both sexes and are called *autosomes*. The autosomes are numbered in descending order of size, so chromosome 22 is the smallest autosome pair found in human DNA. This chromosome has over 800 genes. Genes are coding sequences of DNA that result in the production of proteins.

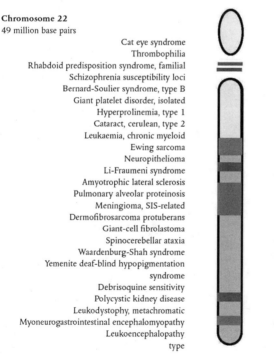

Chromosome 22
49 million base pairs

Cat eye syndrome	DiGeorge syndrome
Thrombophilia	Velocardialfacial syndrome
Rhabdoid predisposition syndrome, familial	Schindler disease
Schizophrenia susceptibility loci	Kanzaki disease
Bernard-Soulier syndrome, type B	NAGA deficiency, mild
Giant platelet disorder, isolated	Epilepsy, partial
Hyperprolinemia, type 1	Glutathioninuria
Cataract, cerulean, type 2	Opitz G syndrome, type II
Leukaemia, chronic myeloid	Ubiquitin fusion degradation
Ewing sarcoma	Transcobalamin deficiency
Neuropithelioma	Heme oxygenase deficiency
Li-Fraumeni syndrome	Manic fringe
Amyotrophic lateral sclerosis	Leukaemia inhibitory factor
Pulmonary alveolar proteinosis	Sorsby fundus dystophy
Meningioma, SIS-related	Neurofibromatosis type 2
Dermofibrosarcoma protuberans	Menigioma NF2-related, sporadic
Giant-cell fibrolastoma	Schwannoma, sporadic
Spinocerebellar ataxia	Neurolemmomatosis
Waardenburg-Shah syndrome	Malignant mesothelioma, sporadic
Yemenite deaf-blind hypopigmentation	Deafness, autosomal dominant
syndrome	Colorectal cancer
Debrisoquine sensitivity	
Polycystic kidney disease	Cardiocephalomyopathy, fatal infantile
Leukodystophy, metachromatic	Adenylosuccinate lyase deficiency
Myoneurogastrointestinal encephalomyopathy	Autism, sucinylpurinemic
Leukoencephalopathy	Glucosse/galactose malabsorption
type	Benzodiazepine receptor, peripheal
	Methemoglobinemia, types I and II

Figure 1: Schematic of chromosome 22

The letters p and q are used in the gene locus term when a more precise location on the chromosome is known. The p, standing for petit (or small), signifies the shorter length of chromosome from the centromere and the q signifies the longer section. The numbers after p or q indicate how far from the centromere the region lies: the higher the number, the further from the centromere. 22q12 is closer to the centromere than 22q13, and 22q13.1 is closer than 22q13.2.

This means that the gene difference identified as being present in those with ADSL deficiency is found on chromosome 22. (As the autosomes are numbered in descending order of size from 1 to 22, the difference is on the smallest autosome.) Further, it is on the q or longer section of chromosome 22, and at a site which is labelled 13.1, which tells us how far along the section from the centromere the difference is found.

Schematically, chromosome 22 looks like the diagram above. The diagram shows some of the clinical conditions that have been linked to changes in this chromosome and their approximate locations within chromosome 22. The area where the defective gene that results in adenylosuccinate lyase (ADSL) deficiency [9] is found is close to the bottom horizontal band on the diagram in Figure 1.

Figure 1 is adapted from an image produced by the US Department of Energy Genome Program, and, along with images for all of the nuclear chromosomes and similar lists of associated conditions, the original can be accessed from their website http://genomics. energy.gov.

SECTION A

Focus on the autistic spectrum disorders

head measurements to check how fast the head is growing. For North America and the UK, there is only good data on head growth, but only over the first three years of life. Ideally, therefore, such measures should be taken early, because the correct diagnosis may be important for understanding the problem and for providing appropriate therapy. Some investigations, such as neurotransmitter imaging, may only be warranted where a specific genetic/metabolic diagnosis has been clarified. (For developments in this area, see Lee W.T. *et al.* 2009.)

In general terms, we know that growth is different in many of those with ASD (Whiteley *et al.* 2004; Xiong *et al.* 2007). A recently described but as yet unreplicated association with physical overgrowth is with MOMO syndrome (where there is a combination of macrosomia, obesity, macrocephaly and ocular abnormalities) (Giunco *et al.* 2008).

You don't need to worry about autism just because your child has a big head. Many children with big heads are perfectly normal. There is a clinical term – 'benign familial megalencephaly' – for the situation where big heads run in your family and everyone is developmentally normal (Day and Schutt 1979). There is a group of other 'overgrowth' conditions which can also give you a big head and which have not as yet been linked to ASD: Beckwith-Wiedemann syndrome; hemihyperplasia; Klippel-Trelaunay syndrome; Maffucci syndrome; PEHO syndrome; Perlman syndrome; Parkes Weber syndrome; Simpson-Golabi-Behmel syndrome type 1; Sturge-Weber syndrome; and Weaver syndrome (this last may be the same condition as Sotos syndrome [68]). These also have particular developmental issues associated with them – epilepsy in Sturge-Weber, for example – so differentiating between conditions can be important in providing the best care and support.

Many other factors have different developmental trajectories in the ASDs when compared to controls – for example, differences in the development and maturation of cortical serotonergic neurotransmitter pathways (Chandana *et al.* 2005).

Help and treatment: does one size fit all?

If the evidence suggested that the same approach was best for helping everyone with an ASD, whatever the cause, then teasing apart the various causes and conditions that can result in ASD might be of academic interest but wouldn't be of much further use to clinicians or families.

A number of clinical papers have reviewed the evidence on treatments from the perspective that ASD is a single condition. These have all come to the same general conclusion: the evidence for beneficial effects of most treatments is limited at best (Herbert, Sharp and Gaudiano 2002; Howlin 1998, 2003; Levy and Hyman 2005; Lilienfeld 2005). This conclusion ignores those cases where improvement resulted from a clearly documented treatment but where the findings could not be repeated with other people with an ASD. This is not because these results are being ignored, but because of the assumption that the same underlying cause affects everyone and that therefore the same treatment should be equally beneficial to all. To illustrate this point, I will take a little time to discuss one 'alternative' autism treatment that was popular in the late 1990s but that has largely fallen out of favour – secretin. Secretin is a compound produced from S-cells near the top of the small intestine, usually in response to food leaving the stomach. It triggers the release of alkaline fluids from the pancreas to neutralize the hydrochloric acid produced by the stomach lining. If this did not happen, stomach acid would inflame, and then begin to digest, the walls of the intestine, and would imbalance the gut bacteria, leading to dysbiosis. Secretin has been used for many years as a test of pancreatic function.

In 1998, three autistic children were reported to have made huge improvements in their development and social and communicative function after being given secretin infusions as part of a routine gastrointestinal assessment (Horvath *et al.* 1998). (Prior to Horvath *et al.'s* report, secretin had never been used as a treatment, and to date it has never been licensed for use as a treatment, but only for use in clinical investigation.) In the USA, media coverage of the 'wonder cure' led to a clamour for secretin infusions by parents of autistic children and, very quickly, to a total exhaustion of world supplies. (At that time secretin was only produced in small amounts by the Scandinavian company Schering, whose secretin was extracted from pig pancreas. Synthetic secretin was not yet available.) Since the initial Horvath *et al.* paper there has been a massive amount of media coverage and research on the possible use of secretin in the treatment of autism, the final 'headline result' being that secretin is *ineffective* as a treatment for children with ASD (Esch and Carr 2004). Systematic randomized controlled studies could not replicate the initial findings reported by Horvath's group in their three initial cases. (For a review see Sturmey 2005.) Is this the correct conclusion to draw?

A crucial premise for the conclusion that 'secretin does not help those with ASD' would be that the later trials had been carried out on children the same as those studied by Horvath's team – that they were comparing like with like. It may, however, have been the case that some biological factor common to all the responders in the initial paper established a crucial difference in their biological makeup.

A small pharmaceutical company, the Repligen Corporation, had started to investigate the possible use of synthetic secretin as a treatment for ASD. Although their Phase II trial results were disappointing overall, as few of their treatment cases showed benefit, they did highlight that there could be specific biological differences in the few children they found to be secretin responders. They had carefully selected individuals with ASD, co-morbid learning disability and gastrointestinal problems, matching the descriptions of the children in the Horvath *et al.* paper. From their clinical presentation, these cases looked, on the face of it, to be the same as the original cases reported by Horvath *et al.* Despite this matching, only a small subgroup in the trial was secretin responsive. These individuals differed from most of the Repligen ASD trial group in having low levels of two biomarkers – called 'fecal calprotectin' and 'chymotrypsin' – when compared to secretin non-responders. This finding suggests that only a small subgroup of a small subgroup, i.e. a minority within a small subgroup of those with ASD, may benefit. It also suggests that this small subgroup could possibly be identified and treated, apparently to good effect. Other research groups are now also reporting possible benefits from secretin, again in subgroups of those with ASD and not in the whole population (Pallanti *et al.* 2005).

It has also been found that a subgroup of people with ASDs have heterozygous sequence variants of the gene coding for secretin, which is found at 11p15.5 (Yamagata *et al.* 2002). To date, however, the two findings have not been put together – so that we don't know if those who show these secretin gene variants also have low calprotectin and chymotrypsin, and may respond to secretin treatment. If that turned out to be the case, we would have a genetic test that identified those children who could benefit from being given secretin therapeutically.

At the time when the research studies on secretin were attempting to replicate the initial findings by Horvath *et al.*, it was assumed that gastrointestinal problems were no more common in ASD populations than in the general population. More recent research has found that such problems are significantly more common in ASD.

The view that treatments can only be effective if they produce benefits across most or all of those with ASD has the potential drawback of discounting valuable treatments that help subgroups of the population with ASDs. Such reasoning can be compared to giving the same strength of reading glasses to everyone with reading problems (those with differing degrees of poor vision, those with dyslexia and those with learning difficulties), and concluding that glasses do not help *anyone* read better, because for some the glasses blurred their vision, or had no impact on their reading difficulty, while only a small subgroup – i.e. those whose eyesight happened to be corrected by the strength of glasses being trialled – could read better as a result of using them.

Mainstream medical and psychiatric approaches to ASD have been a quest for the 'Holy Grail' of a single effective treatment for ASD. Putting to one side the fact that many with an ASD do not want or need to be treated, this quest is based on a fundamental misconception of the nature of the ASDs.

There is a strong incentive for the pharmaceutical industry to find a 'one size fits all' treatment approach for ASD. There are now more 'patient years' of ASD than of Alzheimer's disease (Gerlai and Gerlai 2003). With a condition that is now thought to affect almost one per cent of the population, a 'single problem – single treatment' view becomes tremendously appealing for the industry, with a large, 'cradle to grave' client population – always assuming, of course, that such a treatment could be found.

Let's assume a scale on which we can plot models of autism from monolithic views that see it as a single entity to views of autism that propose a number of independently sufficient causes. At the monolithic end of the spectrum is the *laissez faire* view that, whatever is learnt about their causes, the ASDs are unchanging and unchangeable. This gains some credence from reviews of therapeutic approaches that show scant evidence of benefit (see Howlin 1997; Scottish Intercollegiate Guideline Network 2007). At this same end of the spectrum we also see views of autism as a consequence of some single factor (key genes/organophosphate exposure/vitamin B12 deficiency/excess TV, or whatever). Clinicians who adopt such a view see autism as a single, treatable condition, working from the assumption that the neurobiological underpinnings of all ASDs are the same, so that a similar approach to treatment should help all people with ASDs.

These views are naive and based on conjecture and overgeneralization, and have the potential drawback of either convincing people that nothing will be of benefit, or of giving the false hope that a particular treatment will help one person with ASD because it has helped another.

As is now abundantly clear, the biological basis, and the likely response to treatment, often differ from one person to the next. Whether someone has a myosin defect like Duchenne, a cholesterol defect like SLOS, a B12 defect like methylmalonic acidaemia or a glutamate abnormality like fragile-X can have major implications for how that person could be helped – if indeed help were needed.

Figure A2 represents the continuum from the view of ASD as a single condition (with varying opinions on how changeable it is), to a view of the ASDs as having multiple sufficient causes with different potential treatment strategies.

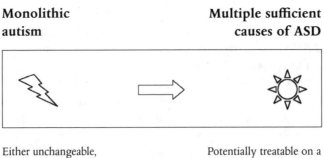

Monolithic autism	**Multiple sufficient causes of ASD**
Either unchangeable, or one treatment should work for all.	Potentially treatable on a case-by-case basis when a modifiable specific basis can be identified.

Figure A2: ASD resulting from single versus multiple sufficient causes

Some 'alternative' medical practitioners (Jepson and Johnson 2007; McCandless 2007) use a variety of metabolic assessments as a basis for their interventions and are looking at 'biochemical individuality' (Williams R.J. 1956). Where this type of approach can be married to a knowledge of specific biological mechanisms underpinning such differences, it holds much promise.

At the present time, however, for many of the approaches that are being advocated, there is a weak evidence base linking demonstrated biological difference either to a biologically plausible causal mechanism, or to evidence of benefit from intervention.

From a range of sources, it is now apparent that the 'monolithic' view of autism as due to a single, core genetic mechanism is untenable – since, despite exhaustive research, no common gene or group of genes has emerged which accounts for a large proportion of those with an ASD. Instead, there are clearly a number of independently sufficient factors that increase the likelihood of developing an ASD.

ASD and 'inborn errors of metabolism'

A number of the conditions we will go on to consider are known as 'inborn errors of metabolism'. A British paediatrician, Sir Archibald E. Garrod, pioneered work in this area with his early studies of a condition known as alcaptonuria (Garrod 1902) and in his book *Inborn Errors of Metabolism* (1909). Garrod is acknowledged as the first to establish a link between enzymes and behaviour. (For an excellent overview of Garrod's contributions, see Scriver 2001.)

Alcaptonuria is *not* known to be associated with ASD; it is a rare, easily recognized disorder. It results in urine that quickly turns black through contact with the air, and in the production of red or black earwax. The nappies of affected infants usually horrify unsuspecting parents, who assume that their baby is bleeding internally.

Before Garrod's work, alcaptonuria was thought to result from a bacterial infection. He demonstrated that it was an inherited disorder, more frequently seen in first cousin marriages. It resulted from the build-up of a chemical (alkaptonuric acid, aka homogentisic acid) and was due to lack of a specific enzyme (homogentisic acid oxidase).

One of Garrod's lasting contributions was his recognition of individual differences in metabolism and susceptibility to disease:

> Owing, as I believe, to their chemical individuality different human beings differ widely in their liability to individual maladies, and to some extent in the signs and symptoms which they exhibit. (Quoted in Prasad and Galbraith 2005).

Table A1 outlines a number of inborn errors of metabolism now known to be associated with ASDs.

Table A1: Inborn errors of metabolism associated with ASD

• Adenylosuccinate lyase (ADSL) deficiency	[9]
• Dihydropyrimidine dehydrogenase (DPYS) deficiency	[30]
• Guanidinoacetate methyltransferase (GAMT) deficiency	[37]
• Phenylketonuria (PKU)	[57]
• Smith-Lemli-Opitz syndrome (SLOS)	[66]
• Succinic semialdehyde dehydrogenase (SSADH) deficiency	[69]

As the biology underpinning these conditions is becoming better understood, clinical approaches to management are becoming more sophisticated and outcomes are improving.

In addition, several organic acidurias (also known as acidaemias) have been described in association with ASDs. These are conditions in which there is a buildup of compounds resulting from fatty acid and deaminated amino acid degradation. Those described in association with ASD are detailed in Table A2.

Table A2: Organic acidurias associated with ASD

• L-2-hydroxyglutaric aciduria	[40]
• 2-methylbutyryl-CoA dehydrogenase deficiency	[47]
• methylmalonic acidaemia	(genetics not clear)

Biochemical individuality: are we all the same?

The idea that individual biological differences affect susceptibility to disorders is a key concept that underpins this book. Roger Williams coined the term in his 1956 book of the same name, where he introduces the notion of individual biological vulnerabilities.

One of the most important aspects to refining this general approach lies in linking our knowledge of several apparently disparate areas:

- behavioural phenotyping (clear description of the behaviours which can typify someone with an ASD)

- metabolic medicine (the differences in biological processes which can be identified on biological testing)

- molecular genetics (the study of the genetic and epigenetic mechanisms and individual differences which can result in metabolic abnormalities, and ultimately in the behaviours that give rise to the diagnosis, and suggest how we might be able to correct them).

Aymé (2000) discusses a range of online resources that allow phenotypic, genetic and metabolic information to be integrated (mainly detailed in the appendices to this volume).

As the science develops, it is becoming more and more apparent that advances in this area will come out of multidisciplinary collaboration across clinical and academic areas which have previously had little common ground – something which requires a lot of new learning for people from any traditional discipline (see discussions in Plomin and Davis 2009; Reiss 2009).

Unless we can understand the processes involved, we will always be one step behind in helping, as otherwise we need to wait on the behaviour of the person being sufficiently different to establish diagnosis before we can do anything. *A biological level of understanding allows **prediction** of likely behaviour on the basis of knowledge of the processes involved, and can lead to preventive rather than remediative intervention.*

A good example of this is phenylketonuria (PKU) [57]. PKU is discussed in more detail in Section B. This condition was at one time commonly associated with ASD, and still is in some parts of the world (Vanli *et al.* 2006). It is diagnosed in infancy by a heelstick blood test – the 'Guthrie test'. Today we would never say, 'The Guthrie test indicates that this child has phenylketonuria, let's wait *until* we see if there are any developmental problems and then consider whether to use dietary intervention,' because we understand, in part at least, the processes involved, and we are confident that developmental problems *will* arise *unless* we intervene. Equally, a phenylalanine-restricted diet will only help those with PKU, and will not help those who may have a similar behavioural phenotype but without this physiological difference. In this instance we have an understanding of the biology and the effect that this will have on development and behaviour if it is not addressed.

If an early attempt had been made to treat ASD with a phenylalanine-free diet, it would have been shown to be ineffective, as only a small proportion of those with ASD would have shown any treatment response. Identifying the small group who would respond, based on their disorder, has made their detection and treatment both clinically useful and highly cost-effective.

Many similar examples now exist where we can link genetic differences to outcome – Smith-Lemli-Opitz syndrome (SLOS) [66] is a condition where the body fails to make adequate amounts of cholesterol. If we screened for SLOS and intervened with early cholesterol supplementation, the evidence suggests that we could markedly improve outcome and quality of life for those with this genetic basis to their developmental problems (Aneja and Tierney 2008). As SLOS may be the most common genetic factor in ASD, with a previously unrecognized high population prevalence (Ciara *et al.* 2006), the implications for the individual and family could be substantial, and at the level of the national economy the financial impact could be enormous (Knapp, Romeo and Beecham 2009). The exciting developments in our understanding of fragile-X syndrome [35] suggest that it may also soon present similar opportunities for early intervention.

The study of 'behavioural phenotypes' is a relatively new field (Aitken 1998; Goodey 2006; O'Brien and Yule 1996), and is still not well known to many clinicians working in the ASD field. There are slightly different definitions in the clinical literature, but in essence the study of behavioural phenotypes is the study of syndrome-specific patterns of behaviour that characterize and help to differentiate between particular clinical conditions.

To quote from a review of the complexities of understanding the genetics of ASDs:

> …the field of complex genetics is replete with many researchers and reviewers who want to promote their overly focused interest in one method at the exclusion of others. However, it is essential that the restricted interests of patients with autism not be reflected in overly restrictive genetic approaches if we are to better understand the genetics of autism… (Veenstra-Vanderweele, Christian and Cook 2004)

I hope that a careful reading of this book will help put paid to the view that any single treatment approach could be found which would help everyone with ASD. ASD is not a single condition, and the wide range of sufficient mechanisms that can lead to ASD behaviour will not respond to a common approach to treatment. The take-home message is not that there is no treatment for ASD but that the idea that there could ever be *one* treatment is wrong. There are many appropriate treatments for many of the conditions that result in ASD behaviour. It is also true to say that at the time of writing there are also many sufficient causes for which we do not as yet have any specific treatments. The issues here are complex and so, for many of those affected, will be the solutions.

Environmental influences have major effects on human cognition, on development and on the likelihood of psychopathology (McGue and Bouchard 1998; Shonkoff and Phillips 2000). Environmental stressors may be important in predicting ASD symptomology.

ASD behaviours are more commonly reported in studies of children exposed to extreme environmental stresses – in adopted Romanian children, from extremely stressed residential facilities, both ASD symptomology and autistic disorder were found to be more common (Hoksbergen *et al.* 2005; Rutter *et al.* 1999). It is always possible, however, that the initial placement of these children was due, at least in part, to their own constitutional difficulties, and that expectations played a part in subsequent records of their behaviour.

Supporting the relevance of environmental factors, even where genetic aspects are known, there is emerging evidence for changes in DNA methylation and for changes in brain development resulting from differences in maternal behaviour. Maternal licking and grooming in rats markedly affects gene expression and suggests a far more direct influence of social environment on genetics than had previously been suspected (Kaffman and Meaney 2007; Weaver, Meaney and Szyf 2006). Similarly, dietary factors can also have marked effects on gene expression (Dolinoy, Weidman and Jirtle 2007).

A 'single cause' view of autism led to the idea of a single mechanism and the idea that there could possibly be a single treatment. It also led to studies of interventions with groups on the basis that those treated were the same by virtue of having an ASD diagnosis. For some approaches, such as the use of structured, predictable, non-distracting environments, there is little doubt that they are helpful, but the effect of such factors is hardly autism-specific.

In a prescient paper, Michael Rutter provided a useful overview of eleven *misconceptions* about disorders that have a genetic component (Rutter 1991). Given how little the picture has changed since then these misconceptions are worth reiterating here.

1. Strong genetic effects mean that environmental influences must be unimportant.

2. Genes provide a limit to potential.

3. Genetic strategies are of no value in studying environmental influences.

4. Nature and nurture are separate.

5. Genes for serious diseases are necessarily bad.

6. Diseases have nothing to do with normal variation.

7. Genetic findings won't help identify diseases.

8. Genetic influences diminish with age.

9. Disorders that run in families must be genetic.

10. Disorders that seem not to run in families cannot be genetic.

11. Single major genes lead only to specific rare diseases that follow a Mendelian pattern.

The essence of Rutter's arguments, as I understand them, is that genes are always relevant but not always prescriptive, and that many of the models used to assess genetic effects do not necessarily lead to the conclusion that what is being looked at is a genetic phenomenon.

Our understanding of how genetic mechanisms operate is constantly growing and changing. Identifying a genetic cause does not condemn someone's condition to be unchangeable. Genetic factors can, as we will see, influence nutritional requirements (Stover 2006; Stover and Garza 2002). The same genetic difference can have hugely different effects on two individuals, in some cases due to an interaction with other, often also genetically driven, metabolic differences – something which has been called 'synergistic heterozygosity' (Vockley *et al.* 2000).

As we broaden our assessments of individuals with a range of developmental disorders, we are finding that the variation in outcome is often far greater than reading about typical or classic cases would lead anyone to believe. This is partly because the most obvious, most similar and sometimes the most impaired cases are likely to be discovered first and found to have some common underlying features before less obvious and less severe cases come to light.

Here is a brief example of the same problem from a slightly different area. Aicardi syndrome is a complex developmental disorder (*not* said to be associated with ASD, so far at least). In this syndrome, there is a range of reported abnormalities in the structure of the brain and visual system, with early onset epilepsy and typically, in the published literature, with severe developmental delay. Despite this typical reported pattern of associations, there are now a number of case reports of Aicardi syndrome with normal cognitive development in the presence of all of the other features (see Grosso *et al.* 2007b for a case report and literature review).

In contrast to the polarized (autism is genetic, therefore unchangeable, *vs* autism is biological but environmental, and therefore changeable) camps which view ASD as a singular phenomenon, but with different emphases on what this implies, here we make a different initial assumption, that *there is no single entity which we can call autistic spectrum disorder*, and so, at our current level of knowledge, for most situations we need to try to understand the causes in the individual case. This approach draws inspiration from various clinicians and researchers who have consistently argued that the ASDs are *not* caused by a single, but as yet still nebulous, mechanism, but can be caused by a range of independently sufficient processes. It is better understanding of these processes that should lead to better understanding of, and in some cases to specific treatments for, those underlying conditions (Coleman 2005; Gillberg and Coleman 1996).

One important aspect of this viewpoint, which many of those who adopt the more polarized views of autism often fail to grasp, is that, for some of the genetic factors at least, later intervention can be beneficial (Ehninger *et al.* 2008). We are not merely talking about ways of reclassifying people who cannot be helped, but about ways of classifying which can enable help to be focused more effectively.

This view also suggests that individualized approaches only become relevant after appropriate investigations have identified the specific nature of the difficulties in any given case.

This book provides information on a range of differences that can result in, or increase the likelihood of, ASDs. We will go on to discuss a wide range of conditions and a number of advances in genetic understanding. We will examine how many of these conditions are currently thought to differ from each other, and whether knowledge of these differences has, or may have, implications for provision of more individualized treatment, and a new agenda for and perspective on ASD research.

Some of these conditions (such as Timothy syndrome [70]) are rare and, although they may have implications for treatment of the affected individual, are unlikely causes within the broader scheme of things. Others (like fragile-X syndrome[35]) are common genetic causes with practical implications for a significant ASD subgroup. Some differences, such as Potocki-Lupski syndrome [60], are of unknown prevalence – they may be common factors in ASD but we do not currently have information on how common they are. Finally, there are other conditions still (such as Smith-Lemli-Opitz syndrome (SLOS) [66]), which are much more common than had previously been appreciated, which may account for a significant proportion of individuals with ASD, and which have specific treatment implications.

We need to develop ways of assessing the bases for the differences in clinical pattern and variation in clinical treatment response seen across those with a diagnosis of ASD. A critical component of this process is to learn how to understand individual differences in terms of their genetic bases, how this leads to specific clinical and behavioural phenotypes, and the consequences this may have for health and development. (For a general discussion of these ideas, see Valle 2004.)

In the area of work with autistic spectrum disorders, there is a general rule: *one size does not fit all.* Anyone who attempts to argue that ASDs can all be viewed as resulting from some common genetic defect or some common reaction to an environmental exposure is clearly wrong. The evidence, whatever way we look at it, no longer supports either of these views. With the level of research and clinical evidence now available, it is simply not good enough to adopt the *laissez faire* view that is too often promulgated, namely:

a) ASD is a single entity/condition/disorder/difference, but

b) we don't know what that entity/condition/disorder/difference is, and therefore

c) there is little we can do, so

d) we will do very little.

As we shall see:

a) ASD can result from a wide range of factors, and

b) we do know what many of these factors are, and

c) with some we can intervene to markedly improve quality of life and outcome, so

d) often we can do a lot.

Genetic factors are being implicated in a huge range of human faculties. There is a general assumption that differences from 'normal' will be problematic, but this turns out to be far from the case. We have many examples where genetic differences from the 'typical' convey an advantage; for example:

- over the history of the Olympic games, Kalenjin runners have been by far the most successful in long-distance running events. Part of the reason for the pre-eminence of the Kalenjin tribal groups from Kenya in Olympic long-distance running comes from a genetic enzyme difference in metabolizing lactate (Moran *et al.* 2004; Vollind *et al.* 2004). This allows Kalenjin runners to carry out more exercise before lactate builds up in muscle and impairs performance

- differences in creative dance performance ability seem to be linked to differences in a serotonin transporter and an arginine vasopressin receptor polymorphism (Bachner-Melman *et al.* 2005)

- in humans and in many other species (Lee, S.-J. 2007), the myostatin gene controls muscle development, with a homozygous mutation resulting in a marked increase in muscle bulk. This type of mutation has been shown to significantly enhance the race performance of 'bully' whippets which have larger, stronger muscles than their genetically normal competitors (Mosher *et al.* 2007). The same phenomenon is seen in Texel sheep and Belgian blue cattle (Lee, S.-J. 2007). In one German boy, homozygous mutation resulted in increased muscle bulk and strength with him being dubbed 'the Strongest Boy in the World' (Reilley 2006; Schuelke *et al.* 2004).

To take a more extreme example, primates were, until recently, unique on earth in having the ability to discriminate red and green, due to the presence of two types of cone cells in the retina. The development of 'knock-in' mice with equivalent receptors has produced, for the first time, mice with a colour sense equivalent to that of primates (Onishi *et al.* 2005; Smallwood *et al.* 2003). Such mice are reliably able to make red–green choice distinctions (Conway 2007).

These findings do not mean that it is *necessarily* pointless entering a long-distance competition against a Kenyan running team; that you will *necessarily* be a hopeless dancer without the right genetic makeup; that you can never develop bigger muscles by working out in a gym; or even that the methods that can produce colour-blindness *de novo* in mice will in future be capable of correcting colour-blindness in humans. In the same way, many of the conditions we go on to discuss do not mean that someone will *necessarily* develop an ASD. These biological differences change the likelihood – they load the dice, and better understanding of the mechanisms may, and in some cases does, provide the potential to bring about change.

Many times in the history of clinical genetics, conclusions have been drawn based on studies of clinical groups before comparative data has been available from the rest of the population. With XYY, for example, initial conclusions linking it with aggressive behaviour and criminality were drawn from looking at prison populations and finding higher than expected rates, *before* the general population prevalence of having an additional Y chromosome was known (Jacobs P.A. *et al.* 1965). Subsequent research revealed that there was no such link, and that the slightly increased rate of XYY in prison populations was largely due to the increased chance of being caught for those with a mild learning disability in general (Witkin *et al.* 1976). It may prove to be the case that some of the associations suggested in this book will also turn out to be less clear-cut, as larger groups are studied.

In this volume, you will find a number of conditions that were once thought to be distinct, but which have the same genetic basis. You will find others that were thought to be the same, but which have proved to be caused by independent mechanisms. For many of these we have not yet screened the general population. This stage is important, as the difference might be benign in some, and without this information we may be assuming that the presence of a given deletion, inversion, transposition or difference will *necessarily* lead to a given outcome, when it is just as likely not to – the mistake that was made in interpreting the prevalence of XYY within the prison population.

For most of the conditions we go on to discuss, the likelihood of ASD appears, on current evidence, to be higher than it is in the rest of the population, but it is not a one-to-one link. Equally, there is a proportion of individuals who do not have any of the conditions discussed here, but who are autistic in any event. It may also turn out that some of the biological factors discussed here are biological *vulnerabilities* which increase risk only when they are combined with some type of environmental exposure. An example of this type of mechanism seems to be the link between differences in the PON1 gene and the effects seen in people exposed to organophosphates and certain pesticides (D'Amelio *et al.* 2005). The genetic difference in PON1 is more common in American than in Italian autistic children, as is their level of exposure to organophosphates. It is the combination of genetic risk and environmental exposure that seems to be the critical factor.

Is ASD getting more common?

This has been a subject of much heated debate. Are there really more people than there used to be with ASD, or is this just a combination of changing criteria, better public and professional awareness, and better recognition? After much research and argument we still do not know the answer to this critical question, despite strident arguments for (Blaxill 2004) and against (Fombonne 2005) a real risk. Prevalence (the number of people identified as having ASD within any given community) is definitely up, but incidence (the numbers of new cases per head of population, using the same criteria) may or may not be.

There will continue to be debate over the reasons behind the rise in *prevalence* of the ASDs – far more children are being identified and diagnosed with ASD today than was the case a decade ago, even when using the same criteria (Hertz-Picciotto and Delwiche 2009). Whether this reflects a true increase in incidence ultimately transpires, or simply a concatenation of factors such as better public and clinician awareness, an increase in numbers of appropriately trained clinicians, earlier diagnosis and better access to services, remains to be definitively addressed, although all these factors clearly play some role. Recognizing the numbers and adequately addressing the needs of those with ASD who are now agreed to exist, whatever the reasons for this, implies a huge strain on available resources.

Current figures suggest that ASD is as common as schizophrenia (Honda, Shimizu and Rutter 2006; MacDermott *et al.* 2007; Reading 2006) and that it has outstripped Alzheimer's disease in terms of number of client years (Gerlai and Gerlai 2003). ASD is identified far earlier than either of these other conditions, and also carries a normal life expectancy (Shavelle, Strauss and Pickett 2001). When the needs of those with ASDs are adequately resourced, it is also highly expensive for affected families, clinical and support services, and the community at large (Jarbrink and Knapp 2001; Knapp, Romeo and Beecham 2009).

A brief history of ASD research

Dr Leo Kanner, a Viennese-born psychiatrist who lived in the USA and worked in New York, is credited with penning, in 1943, the first accepted and clear description of autism (Kanner 1943). In his early writing we learnt of a condition that he described as '*a biologically provided defect in affective contact*'. This description captures the essence of the autism – it is a biological difference in the individual that interferes with their ability to function socially.

In Kanner's time, genetics was virtually unknown as a clinical discipline; the 'double helix' structure of DNA was yet to be discovered, and although heritability was accepted (certain characteristics, like eye colour, skin colour and male pattern baldness, were known to be inherited as were certain illness propensities – haemophilia, for example) we had no understanding of the mechanisms by which developmental disorders came into being. It was no accident that, when biological factors in psychiatry began to be studied in earnest, schizophrenia came to be viewed as 'the graveyard of the clinical geneticist'. The frequent contradictions and failures of replication in the psychiatric genetic literature continue to perplex many working in this field (Persaud 2007). There are many reasons why genetic investigation of 'psychiatric' conditions is fraught with difficulty (Bearden, Reus and Freimer 2004), not least the difficulty in reaching agreement over the endophenotypes (key biological features) for many such disorders (Bearden and Freimer 2006). Recent developments, many due to the requirements of the Human Genome Project, have broadened the range of methods for addressing such issues through the use of powerful high-throughput low-cost techniques (Ropers 2007).

Psychiatry and biomedical sciences have never been easy bedfellows. (I would accept that this is far more the case in Europe, including the UK, than in the USA, where biomedical assessment has assumed a much more prominent position within mainstream psychiatry.)

There has only ever been one Nobel Prize awarded to someone practising in psychiatry – the Austrian, Julius Wagner-Jauregg, in 1927. Wagner-Jauregg discovered, by chance, that, after contracting malaria, individuals with the then common condition known as generalized paralysis of the insane (GPI) often improved dramatically. By deliberately infecting patients with malaria he found that he could effect clinical improvement in those with GPI who were under his care. GPI was caused, although this was not known at the time, by contracting syphilis. The mechanism by which these problems were related, and the way in which the cure worked, were unknown. The Nobel Prize, in this instance, was awarded for the inspired application of a chance observation. It subsequently transpired that Wagner-Jauregg's treatment, which predated the sulphonamide drugs that replaced it, worked by causing a spike in body temperature. The change in body temperature made it too hot for the spirochetes that caused the syphilis to survive, thus bringing about the improvement. (For an excellent review of the history of syphilis, its apparent association with giftedness and its sequelae, see Hayden 2003.)

Unfortunately, the last half-century has been largely devoid of such serendipitous psychiatric observations, and the psychiatric trophy room has been devoid of any further serendipitous Nobels.

The intervening years have seen huge changes in factors like the diagnostic classifications in use and the waxing and waning of enthusiasm in psychiatry for a huge range of treatments – from insulin coma to electroconvulsive therapy to psychosurgery to various forms of pharmacotherapy – without major strides being made in understanding of mechanism or in treatment effectiveness.

As an interesting aside, it has been found that both the onset of autism (Mankoski *et al.* 2006), and of an acquired form of semantic-pragmatic communication disorder (Carter J.A. *et al.* 2006) are sometimes seen after high fever and convulsions brought on by severe malaria. One paper has speculated on differences in fever suppression being linked to autism aetiology (Torres 2003).

How far things have progressed in some respects and how little in others can be seen from an early systematic review by Edward Ornitz of the state of play in the field of autism some 30 years ago (Ornitz 1973; an historical account of the development of ideas on autism can be found in Wolff 2004).

It is only with the focusing of biomedical sciences on conditions such as ASD, in the first decade of this century, that significant advances are being made in our understanding of the biology of the ASDs. Reading the autobiography of Nobel laureate Eric Kandel (Kandel 2006) (who grew up in the Vienna of Freudian psychoanalysis, and trained in psychiatry early in his career, but went on to excel in the experimental understanding of the neurobiology of memory in aplysia – a type of marine mollusc that has been used a lot in researching memory) you begin to grasp some of the massive changes in biological understanding which have taken place in the past half-century in the biological sciences. Kandel's classic paper 'Psychotherapy and the single synapse: the impact of psychiatric thought on neurobiological research' (Kandel 1979) stands out as an early call for biological and psychological fields of understanding to inform each other.

In the early post-war years, autism was described in the framework of psychiatric disorders as a condition in what at the time was the fledgling area of child psychiatry. Once its status as a learning difficulty was accepted, it became a precious 'jewel in the crown' of this emerging specialism, apparently validating the notion of a psychiatric disorder resulting from extreme stress and/or deprivation. Coupling the characterization of the condition with an increasing belief that it was 'psychogenic' in origin (i.e. due solely to psychological factors such as a cold, emotionless style of parenting), this led to several other incorrect notions:

1. that autism was a single condition, which would, in the fullness of time, have a single treatment

2. that autism was a psychogenic condition

3. that it was outside the areas of interest, knowledge and expertise of medical specialities other than psychiatry

4. that biological factors did not contribute either to its genesis or to its development

5. that autism was largely an interest of child psychiatry, and of limited interest to adult psychiatric services.

Let's look at each idea in turn.

False Premise 1: 'Autism is one thing'

> Autism is a common and heterogeneous childhood neurodevelopmental disorder. Analogous to broad syndromes such as mental retardation, autism has many etiologies and should be considered not as a single disorder but, rather, as 'the autisms'. (Geschwind and Levitt 2007)

Scarcely a week goes by without a claim to have discovered *the* cause of autism. A huge range of possibilities has been proposed, from 'refrigerator parenting' (Bettelheim 1955, 1967) to excessive TV watching (Waldman, Nicholson and Adilov 2006), and we are still seeing attempts to provide general models that account for the similarities across disparate aetiologies in ASD, for example the disconnection syndromes model (Geschwind and Levitt 2007) and the foetal testosterone model (Knickmeyer and Baron-Cohen 2006).

Working from the idea that autism is a single condition, considerable effort has been expended in trying to ensure that subjects in research studies are 'phenotypically comparable'. To this end methods for selecting homogeneous ASD populations for research are being developed (Gotham, Pickles and Lord 2009; Kolevzon *et al.* 2004).

Age, IQ and autism severity are important variables which affect other aspects of autistic presentation while restricted, repetitive behaviours and resistance to change seem to vary independently (Hus *et al.* 2007).

Much excellent and important work has been carried out based on the notion of homogeneity within the ASD population – that a common diagnosis means a common basis. For many things such as schooling and social care, the similarities across ASD may be more important by far than the differences within this population. A large amount of useful research has also been generated using this paradigm. To take one brief example, there appear to be differences in auditory processing, particularly of human speech, which are characteristic of the autistic population (Boddaert *et al.* 2003, 2004; Ceponiene *et al.* 2003; Kuhl *et al.* 2005). It is important to recognize that such common differences do not necessarily indicate a common *genetic* difference, but could reflect something else, such as an effect of selective attention and exposure. The results found differ from those found in normal controls but no systematic research has tried to compare those with an ASD diagnosis to other relevant clinical groups or to non-affected sibling controls.

When we examine how the human brain processes birdsong, we find that experts on birds are different from other people in the way their brains process birdsong (Chartrand,

Filon-Bilodeau and Belin 2007). Such differences can as easily be a cause as an effect – practice in birdsong discrimination may hone certain brain networks and prune others, as is thought to happen when infants learn to discriminate their own language from others (for an introduction to this literature, see Condon and Sander 1974; Feldman 2007; Kuhl 2000; Trevarthen and Aitken 2001), or maybe people whose brains have an innate facility for birdsong recognition are more likely to specialize in this area. The same may be true of the differences in auditory processing seen in ASD.

The issue of diagnostic validity – that the condition being studied is a 'real' phenomenon and not just an arbitrary set of signs and symptoms – has plagued psychiatric assessments of ASD. Improvements in diagnostic *reliability* have not been paralleled by improved diagnostic validity:

> Diagnosis has confounded psychiatry for the past century, with the *DSM* approach enhancing diagnostic reliability but not validity. (Insel and Fenton 2005)

A huge amount of research funding has been poured into the search for genes that cause autism. The first biological 'hunch', based on the high likelihood of identical twins both being affected, compared with non-identical twins, coupled with a steady rate in the population (reported as around 4.5 in every 10,000 live births), was that autism would turn out to be a single disorder caused by a small number of necessary and sufficient genes. This idea, although consistent with the literature at the time it was first put forward, seems less and less tenable. A paper published in the journal *Nature Neuroscience* (Happé, Ronald and Plomin 2006) concludes that the various behavioural components which make up the 'autistic triad of impairments' (social interaction, verbal and non-verbal language impairment and repetitive/stereotyped activities), if indeed they are coherent entities, at the very least vary independently and cannot be viewed as resulting from any common genetic basis. As these researchers have come from a background that historically emphasized the discrete and singular nature of autism, it is interesting to note that their scholarly review comes to very different conclusions:

> …if different features of autism are caused by different genes, associated with different brain regions and related to different core cognitive impairments, it seems likely they will respond to different types of treatment. Abandoning the search for a single cause for a single entity of autism may also mean abandoning the search for a single 'cure' or intervention. (Happé, Ronald and Plomin 2006)

It seems that, at best, people who argue for a common mechanism are now looking for three groups of partially co-occurring genes affecting systems which are sometimes all affected in the same individual, rather than looking for a single genetic mechanism which is applicable to all. Even this watered-down, single genetic mechanism view is poorly supported by the large number of screening studies that have attempted to find common genetic differences across people with a clinical diagnosis of autism.

In some respects it is worrying, given the variability within the clinical population, that attempts are being made to find methods by which more homogeneous research populations can be selected within the range of ASD (Kolevzon *et al.* 2004). It is also worrying if this is the basis on which treatment trials are carried out and evaluated. If a subgroup responds to a given treatment and is differentiable from others with an ASD diagnosis, while the rest of the treatment group does not respond, this should not be grounds for dismissing a treatment as ineffective. On the contrary, it provides grounds to criticize the study as flawed in its design, by dealing with a heterogeneous population but analysing it as if it were a homogeneous one.

We now have strong evidence of a large number of genetic differences that occur in subgroups of those who fulfil the behavioural criteria for an ASD diagnosis (Autism Genome Project Consortium 2007; Freitag 2007; Sebat *et al.* 2007; Yang and Gill 2007). There is a steadily expanding group of identified genetic conditions that show different clinical phenotypes, but which all, to a greater or lesser extent, overlap with, or fit, current criteria for ASD.

In some areas, we are finding evidence suggesting an underlying genetic aetiology for a particular pattern of presentation, but as yet only in small numbers of reported cases. The possible link between 13q12–q13 abnormalities, autistic diagnosis, language deficits and auditory processing problems provides such an example (Bradford *et al.* 2001; Smith, M. *et al.* 2002).

ASD often presents as part of a complex picture along with other physical and behavioural features. Where other factors lead to closer monitoring, this can make diagnosis more likely in some circumstances (ascertainment bias), while in others it lowers likelihood of diagnosis, with ASD features being attributed to something else (such as developmental delay or epilepsy) – this is known as 'diagnostic overshadowing' (see Skuse 2007 for further discussion).

All of this notwithstanding, much progress has been made in identifying biological mechanisms sufficient to cause ASD, and in line with the conclusions reached by Happé, Ronald and Plomin (2006) we are now seeing the emergence of a number of discrete treatments that target the specific biological differences stemming from different genetic aetiologies.

False Premise 2: 'Autism is psychogenic in origin'

The view that autism was a psychogenic disorder can be traced to early post-World War II developments in American psychotherapy. It was most heavily influenced by the writings and clinical work of Bruno Bettelheim, whose own experiences in a German concentration camp had strongly coloured his views of the extent to which behaviour and development could be affected by early emotional experience (Bettelheim 1955, 1967). Many were convinced that the evidence, such as it was, was strongly against a genetic basis:

> Though claims have been made for genetic determinants in the causation of autism, it is unlikely that any are involved, for we have quite a number of records of identical twins, one of whom was autistic and the other was not. (Montagu 1986)

A useful early discussion of the psychogenic model of ASD can be found in Rutter (1968).

As we discover more sophisticated research methods, many autistic conditions are being shown to have genetic bases, both at the level of resolution, with subtelomeric deletions being shown to have effects (Barbosa-Gonçalves *et al.* 2008), and by using techniques which increase the probability of finding associated genes (such as 'homozygosity mapping' – looking at families where shared ancestry increases the likelihood of finding autosomal recessive genes, as is the case in certain cultural groups; Morrow *et al.* 2008).

False Premise 3: 'Autism is outside the area of interest, knowledge and expertise of specialities other than psychiatry'

> Although genetic influences predominate in autism, it is clear that it is a multifactorial disorder, and it must be expected that some environmental factors will be implicated in the causal pathways. (Rutter 2006)

Historically it was clearly the case, during the period when autism was viewed as a psychogenic condition, that few clinical specialities other than psychiatry were interested in the ASDs, and while the ASDs were viewed as a single genetic condition of unknown aetiology, this view continued to hold true. A seminal book by Dr Bernard Rimland (Rimland 1964) led to a change of perspective on ASDs, from psychogenic to biologically based, but did not fundamentally change clinical practice at the time.

The second historical phase in our understanding of autism saw the condition being viewed as genetic in origin, as predetermined (not 'experience dependent') and, consequently, unaffected by environmental factors. This view led logically to emphasis on finding the genes involved, since only by achieving this were we likely to unravel the process and the specific approach to treatment that this level of understanding would bring about. This has led to the current situation, where we have a plethora of independently sufficient, predisposing genetic factors which increase the risk of developing autism (Veenstra-Vanderweele, Christian and Cook 2004).

False Premise 4: 'Biological factors do not contribute to the genesis of autism, nor to its development'

The past 20 years have seen a gradual realization that the earlier view of autism (as psychiatric, psychogenic, non-genetic and untreatable) is incorrect. The first decade of this millenium has seen the neurobiological understanding of ASDs move on at the same rapid pace as biological understanding in many other areas of neuroscience.

At the time of writing, the MRC Research Review published in 2001 has identified from the published literature, and submissions to the review panel which were recommended for further investigation, a number of biomedical areas of potential clinical significance. These include assessing the importance of:

- casein- and gluten-free diets
- sulphation problems (Alberti *et al.* 1999; McFadden 1996)
- immune abnormalities
- gastrointestinal problems.

Although not reflected in MRC funding since 2001, further investigation has yielded information in all of these areas, some of which will be further discussed later in this book.

It is clear that many intrinsic and extrinsic biological factors contribute to the nature and severity of ASD, and that understanding gene–environment interactions is likely to be one of the crucial areas in future work on ASD.

False Premise 5: 'Autism is largely an interest of child psychiatry, and of limited interest to adult psychiatric services'

It is clearly the case that at the time of writing there is little adult research; there are few well-developed adult clinical services and few other adult resources. The epidemiological work to date suggests that the prevalence of *diagnosed* ASD in adults is low compared to children and adolescents. This in probably because Asperger and Rett syndromes did not officially exist until 1994, and re-diagnosis of people who already have an established clinical diagnosis is uncommon. The heavy reliance on early developmental history in establishing diagnosis is another factor that can make late diagnosis more complex.

Clinicians, researchers and politicians are starting to appreciate the economic impact of ASD persisting into adult life (Jarbrink *et al.* 2007).

Current understanding suggests that the following should be reflected in our knowledge of ASD.

1. A large number of conditions are sufficient to result in ASD behaviour.

2. Appropriate assessment should involve a range of medical and non-medical specialities.

3. Biological factors are important, and in many instances knowledge of these factors is critical to providing appropriate help to those with ASD.

4. Problems such as sleep difficulties, epilepsy, digestive problems and poor immune function are common in those with ASDs. Whether they are part of the cause of the ASD or not, they should not be ignored, and should in many cases be part of the routine assessment process.

The most recent phase has been the recognition that a single-cause view of ASD was becoming progressively less tenable, and that subgroups of people with a diagnosis of ASD had discrete and often treatable disorders. Various factors have contributed to this change of view, including the following:

1. Recognition that aspects of the social environment can act as mediating variables

In more stressful situations it may be more likely that an ASD will manifest in a manner which brings it to clinical attention – as in the Romanian adoptee studies. Here, removing the psychological stressors can bring about improvement.

2. Understanding the role of epigenetic factors

A whole range of mechanisms may allow or prevent a genetic difference from having an effect. Here I am using the term 'epigenetic' in the more restricted sense used in current cell biology (see Bird A. 2007; Jaenisch and Bird 2003) rather than the broader sense popularized earlier by Conrad Waddington (see Slack 2002 for discussion). A brief historical discussion of epigenetics can be found in Holliday (Holliday 2006).

The principal epigenetic mechanisms currently known are telomere modification (Blasco 2007); chromatin remodelling through histone modification (Ausio *et al.* 2003); RNA associated gene silencing (an important defect in fragile-X syndrome [35, 36]); and genomic imprinting (as seen in Angelman syndrome [11] and Prader-Willi syndrome [61]). Hendrich and Bickmore (2001) usefully review chromatin defects and chromatin remodelling as involved in Coffin-Lowry syndrome [21], Rett syndrome [63a, 63b] and Rubinstein-Taybi syndrome [64]. (For a simple introduction to these mechanisms as applied to psychiatric disorders, including Rett syndrome, see Tsankova *et al.* 2007. For a discussion of how diets, nutrient differences and medication can affect epigenetic processes, see Junien 2006. For more general overviews of how these epigenetic factors influence the expression of DNA and can alter the course of brain development see Dolinoy, Weidman and Jirtle 2007; Jiang, Bresler and Beaudet 2004 and McClung and Nestler 2007.)

There is considerable interest in the ways in which epigenetic mechanisms can affect disease susceptibility (Jirtle and Skinner 2007; Jirtle, Sander and Barrett 2000), and early environmental stress can affect gene expression and subsequent behaviour (Murgatroyd *et al.* 2009).

The conditions we go on to discuss in this book in which such epigenetic processes are known to be particularly important include Angelman syndrome [11], Coffin-Lowry syndrome [21], Prader-Willi syndrome [61], Rett syndrome [63a, 63b] and Rubinstein-Taybi syndrome [64]. Many of these are conditions that arise from defects in chromatin structure and modification (see Hendrich and Bickmore 2001).

The importance of epigenetic factors for the development of clinical conditions is becoming far better understood and appreciated (Falls *et al.* 1999; Gosden and Feinberg 2007; Jiang, Bresler and Beaudet 2004; Jirtle and Skinner 2007; Rodenhiser and Mann 2006; Waggoner 2007). The concept of imbalanced genomic imprinting as a specific risk factor for ASD has been advanced (Badcock and Crespi 2006).

There are now significant improvements in the technologies available to enable rapid profiling of epigenetic mechanisms in the individual case, such as DNA methylation profiling (Schumacher *et al.* 2006). These are not yet commonly available as clinical tools, but should become so as their utility and validity become better known and established.

Inheritance of epigenetic factors has become an important area for both research and clinical understanding, and the complexities of what is inherited over and above nuclear DNA are only now becoming apparent.

In the nuclei of sperm, protamines are found in place of histones. These protamines are displaced, after the egg is fertilized, by histones derived from the egg. Some epigenetic factors are therefore inherited almost entirely from the mother, as are mitochondria in most cases. This gives a whole new Darwinian spin to sociobiology – female preference for a mate may be 'warts and all', partly on the basis that, for her offspring, the 'warts' are probably not part of the procreational deal, since a range of epigenetic factors is far less likely to be passed on from the father than from the mother, and so need not affect her choice of partner.

3. Recognizing the role of genetic modifiers

The wide phenotypic variability often seen in conditions where a core genetic mechanism (a 'target gene') has been identified is also increasing interest in the role of 'genetic modifiers' (Nadeau 2001; Slavotinek and Biesecker 2003). These are other genes that are neither necessary nor sufficient for the occurrence of a condition, but which, when present, affect the expressed phenotype.

We will go on to discuss conditions such as Biedl-Bardet syndrome [17] where such effects are known, and other possible modifier effects such as the role of GRIK2 (which has been established as playing a role in the expression of Huntington's disease; Rubinsztein et al. 1997): GRIK2 is a gene involved in glutamate metabolism, and has been linked to autism in screening studies (Jamain et al. 2002; Shuang et al. 2004).

4. The importance of copy number variations (CNVs)

This relates to understanding the variation in heritability across the human population in general (for discussion, see Feuk, Carson and Scherer 2006) and the variations seen across different ethnic populations (Redon et al. 2006). CNVs (deletions, duplications and large copy number variants) are common, introduce a variety of mechanisms by which genetic differences arise, and were, until recently, relatively unknown. They are not readily detected by single nucleotide polymorphism (SNP) technology (where a single nucleotide/base is altered, creating a unique genotype), and as a result many of the genetic screening studies that have been carried out using SNP-only methods are likely to have missed many cases where such genetic differences may have been important.

5. Understanding the interplay of biologically determined factors and the effects of social environment

For a simple introduction to many of these issues, see Jablonka and Lamb (2005). There is increasing data which suggests that gene expression can be affected by factors such as early parental care and attention (Kaffman and Meaney 2007; Weaver, Meaney and Szyf 2006).

6. The roles of translated non-coding RNA

In contrast to the widely expressed view that much DNA is accumulated 'junk', it now appears that a high proportion of human DNA is expressed, despite the fact that only around 1.5 per cent of human DNA codes for proteins (Wong and Nielsen 2004). The rest is translated into non-coding RNA (RNA) which is thought to be involved in processes such as epigenetic imprinting (Cavaille *et al.* 2000, 2002) and within-cell transactions (Mattick 2004). Epigenetic imprinting is involved in a range of mechanisms which are relevant to factors such as disease susceptibility (Jirtle, Sander and Barrett 2000), and the effects of exposure to toxins (Murphy and Jirtle 2000).

7. Understanding the biological products of genetic differences expressed in ASD

Proteomics – the study of differences in protein expression associated with a given condition – is beginning to demonstrate differences in the ASD population (Corbett *et al.* 2007).

8. The potential role of toxicologic substances in disrupting epigenetic processes

It is known that inhibition of histone deacetylation and DNA methylation disrupt imprinting (Hu, Vu and Hoffman 1996; Hu *et al.* 1998; Svensson *et al.* 1998). A number of environmental toxins can be involved in this process, potentially leading to increased prevalence of a partuicular genetic cause as a result of gene–environment interaction.

The factors discussed above, in varying combinations, account for many of the variations typically seen across those with a given genetic predisposing factor, and also account for the apparent absence of a genetic contribution in many of the cohort screening studies.

It is not rare for two ASD members of the same family, with the same genetic condition (even for identical twins), to vary markedly in how severely they are affected, and to differ in the presence or absence of associate features such as epilepsy or cardiac problems.

As the sufficient independent causes of ASDs have become more apparent, there has been increasing interest in, and work on, many speciality areas related to differentiation within, and better understanding of, the ASDs, including specialities such as:

- **bacteriology** (Finegold *et al.* 2002)

- **gastroenterology** (Afzal *et al.* 2003; Galli-Carminati, Chauvet and Deriaz 2006; Horvath and Perman 2002b; Sullivan 2008a; White 2003)

- **genetics** (Autism entry OMIM No 209850, accessed at www.ncbi.nlm.nih.gov; Autism Genome Project Consortium 2007; Folstein and Rosen-Sheidley 2001; Freitag 2007; Lauritsen and Ewald 2001; Muhle, Trentacoste and Rapin 2004; Schaefer and Lutz 2006; Sykes and Lamb 2007)

- **immunology** (Ashwood, Wills and Van de Water 2006; Burger and Warren 1998; Cabanlit *et al.* 2007; Stern *et al.* 2005; Zimmerman *et al.* 2007)

- **neurology** (Bauman 2005; Ito 2004; Tuchman and Rapin 2002b)
- **neurovirology** (Hornig and Lipkin 2001; Hornig, Chian and Lipkin 2004; Pletnikov, Moran and Carbone 2002)
- **studies of metabolic differences** (James, Culver and Golabi 2006; MacFabe *et al.* 2007; Page 2000; Zimmerman *et al.* 2005).

There is considerable debate over the 'diagnostic yield' from such lines of investigation and whether any or all of the above should constitute part of a standard biological assessment for those with ASD (Hahn and Neubauer 2005; Stern *et al.* 2005; Tomas Vila 2004).

It has been claimed that, while conventional genetic analysis gives a diagnostic yield of some ten per cent (Battaglia and Carey 2006; Herman *et al.* 2007), a far greater yield of between 40 and 65 per cent of cases shows genetic differences which can be identified using available techniques when a more detailed protocol is adopted (Aitken 2008; Cass, Sekaran and Baird 2006; Schaefer and Lutz 2006; Schaefer and Mendelsohn 2008; for further discussion, see Martin C.L. and Ledbeter 2007). Many of the investigations required to test for rarer genetic disorders are currently difficult to access in many areas, for a variety of practical reasons (for discussion see Willems 2008), so it would be unfair to suggest that a significant improvement in routine genetic screening for many of the disorders discussed is likely to become commonplace for some time to come.

As these other assessments are not currently components of the diagnostic process, and as, irrespective of their results, there will be no difference in diagnosis – a particular constellation of behaviours fulfils criteria for an ASD diagnosis, irrespective of results of lymphocyte profiling, serum glutamate levels, abnormalities of melatonin release, EEG abnormalities, etc. – their relevance has been marginalized, based on the hypothesis that there will be one common mechanism which underpins ASDs. The same is true of more widely accepted components of assessment, such as neuropsychological profiling: knowledge of executive function, working memory and NVLD (nonverbal learning difficulties) difficulties can be important in informing appropriate interventions, but do not contribute to knowledge that affects diagnosis.

In one study of 182 patients seen over the period 1995–1998 by the Mayo clinic (Challman *et al.* 2003), 'aetiologically relevant' conditions were identified in around four per cent of cases; however, only a proportion of cases underwent testing, and a far higher percentage showed evidence of epilepsy, EEG and structural brain abnormalities, and abnormalities of uncertain significance.

In practice, the range of assessments which are available and used in routine clinical practice is expanding all the time, and changing as newer techniques replace older ones. (For example, the wide availability of functional magnetic resonance imaging, and its relative safety compared to older brain imaging techniques which relied on radioactivity, has made studies of how the brain is working during many activities far easier to study and in far greater numbers of subjects.) Clinical developments in this area are both driven and constrained by their utility and cost-effectiveness, with the most rapid progress being made in the North American private healthcare systems. (For discussion see Williams M.S. 2003.)

Clinical practice in many areas has failed to keep pace with the exponential increase in biological understanding. The massive injection of research funding in this area, particularly in the USA since 2006, will only see this avalanche of research information accelerate.

In what I hope is a simple, user-friendly fashion, I will take readers through some of the known links between ASD, genetics and neurobiology, and their implications for management and intervention.

I will discuss a range of tests that may be helpful in establishing differences in the individual. I would stress at the outset that not all tests are implicated for or relevant to everyone, and that investigations change over time as better, less invasive or more helpful techniques are evolved.

Early presenting features of ASDs

One of the few factors over which there has been reasonable consensus in the area of ASD is that, using appropriate methods, earlier intervention results in better outcome. Early identification of individuals with ASD has therefore become the 'Holy Grail' of autism research: Identify Early > Intervene Early > Improve Outcome.

The past decade has seen steady improvement in age at first concern over development, and a shortening of the period from referral to diagnosis, in many Western countries.

There is information to suggest that obstetric risk factors increase the likelihood of a child with ASD. However, none of these factors, as yet, is sufficiently well established to be useful in screening (Kolevzon, Gross and Reichenberg 2007).

A range of standardized early screening tools is now available to aid the clinician in early identification, such as the Checklist for Autism in Toddlers (CHAT). (For overviews, see Levy S.E., Mandell and Schultz 2009; Scambler, Hepburn and Rogers 2006.) The substantial and sustained rise in reported cases (see, for example: MMWR 2007a, 2007b, 2007c) is, however, placing a steadily increasing burden on the clinicians involved in this process. Improvements in detection need to be backed up with clarification of the basis for the condition, and optimized intervention to achieve the best quality of life for the individual.

There is still much confusion over the concept of regression in ASD. Many parents perceive their child's development to have been normal in the first year to 18 months – the point at which parents begin to develop concerns over the development of their child (De Giacomo and Fombonne 1998). Various factors may be relevant to regressive phenomena in the ASD population.

- There is now some evidence to suggest that boys with autism and a MeCP2 gene defect, more typically seen in Rett syndrome [63a, 63b], may be more likely to show developmental regression (Xi *et al.* 2007).

- A subset of autistic children has been reported where developmental regression is linked to gene differences at 21q and 7q (Molloy, Keddache and Martin 2005).

- The effects of having co-morbid epilepsy are often complex, but it is common for children with epilepsy and ASD to show loss of language skills, autistic regression, or both. (For review and discussion, see Tuchman 2006.) The regressive factors specific to epilepsy, such as language loss in Landau-Kleffner syndrome, are additional to the ASD-specific problems often seen in the same individuals.

- Unrecognized metabolic factors can result in regression, as with B12 depletion due to vegan diet (Casella *et al.* 2005).

Table A3 shows conditions in which a regressive pattern of onset of ASD symptomology is reported or expected.

Table A3: Conditions associated with regressive onset of ASD

• Adenylosuccinate lyase (ADSL) deficiency	[9]
• B12 depletion	(see Casella *et al.* 2005)
• Bannayan-Riley-Ruvalcaba syndrome	[15]
• Basal cell naevus syndrome	[16]
• Cortical dysplasia–focal epilepsy (CDFE) syndrome	[19]
• Cowden syndrome	[26]
• Duchenne muscular dystrophy	[33]
• L-2-hydroxyglutaric aciduria	[40]
• Landau-Kleffner syndrome	(see Tuchman 2006)
• Male autistics with a MeCP2 defect	(see Xi *et al.* 2007)
• Mitochondrial gene defects	(see Poling *et al.* 2006)
• Proteus syndrome	[62]
• Rett syndrome	[63a]
• Rett syndrome (Hanefeld variant)	[63b]
• Schindler disease	[65]

What sorts of things should give rise to early concerns?

Parental age

A link between increasing parental age and risk of ASD has been found in a number of studies (for example, Hultman, Sparen and Cnattingius 2002; Mouridsen, Rich and Isager 1993; Reichenberg *et al.* 2006). This finding has been corroborated in a study of families contributing to the Autism Genetic Resource Exchange (AGRE) (Cantor *et al.* 2007). Two further studies to address the issue of parental age (Croen *et al.* 2007; Durkin *et al.* 2008) have both found that increasing maternal and paternal age seem to be independently associated with an increased risk of ASD.

It seems likely that parental age may be associated with a number of the genetic conditions discussed here in systematic ways.

• The likelihood of Down syndrome [31], for example, has long been known to increase with increasing maternal age (Penrose 1933).

• The increasing prevalence, with ageing, of defects in mitochondrial DNA would also provide a possible risk process linking autism to parental age. Many conditions linked with epilepsy have a mitochondrial component. Most mitochondrial inheritance is matrilineal (from the mother) and this suggests that the likelihood of co-morbid epilepsy will become much greater particularly as maternal reproductive age increases than it will as paternal age increases.

• The prevalence of sperm containing both an X and a Y chromosome (instead of the more normal single X or single Y sex chromosome) makes it appear more likely that as paternal reproductive age increases so does the risk of Klinefelter's syndrome (XXY syndrome [3]) in boys (Lowe *et al.* 2001).

An overview of Californian birth cohort data from almost five million birth records from 1992 to 2000 has suggested that having an older mother represents a higher risk of autism than having a older father (King, M.E *et al.* 2009).

Parental health

Mothers of autistic children are significantly more likely to have autoimmune problems such as type 1 diabetes, adult rheumatoid arthritis, hypothyroidism, systemic lupus erythematosus (Comi *et al.* 1999) and epilepsy (Leonard *et al.* 2006) when compared to controls. Whether this is in some way causally related to the subsequent development of the affected child, or whether both are linked to some further factor, has not yet been established.

A long-term follow-up of Danish parents of children diagnosed with infantile autism has suggested associations with paternal type 1 diabetes and maternal ulcerative colitis (Mouridsen *et al.* 2007).

The at-risk pregnancy

Studies of perinatal risk show little evidence of association between specific birth/ perinatal difficulties and ASD. There is a slight increase in perinatal difficulties overall, but no specific difficulty appears to convey a significant increase in risk (Stein *et al.* 2006).

Although the idea may appear biologically plausible, the evidence to date does not seem to support the notion that ASD arises as a consequence of factors such as increased head circumference (making birthing more difficult, or increasing the chances of problems such as perinatal anoxia) or congenital malformations (Maimburg and Vaeth 2006). One study has found no evidence of accelerated brain growth *in utero* (Hobbs *et al.* 2007). A number of studies have demonstrated a higher rate of pre- and perinatal risk factors (such as abnormal growth rate both *in utero* and after birth; enlarged head at birth; bleeding in pregnancy; and low Apgar scores) in infants who go on to receive a subsequent diagnosis of autism (Dementieva *et al.* 2005; Glasson *et al.* 2004; Hultman, Sparen and Cnattingius 2002; Redcay and Courchesne 2005; Torrey *et al.* 2004).

Studies of umbilical cord blood samples have suggested that differences in levels of various neuropeptides and neurotrophins can, in some cases, differentiate those infants who go on to receive diagnoses of autism from other groups. The variations in findings across studies by the same research group suggest, however, that this cannot be used at the present time to differentiate reliably (Nelson K.B. *et al.* 2001; Nelson P.G. *et al.* 2006).

Anderson, G.M. *et al.* (2007) found significantly higher rates of trophoblast inclusions in a small group of archived placental samples from autistic births (6/27 or 22.2 per cent) compared to an anonymous control series (12/154 or 7.8 per cent). Inclusions were found in a proportion of both groups, so were not ASD-specific. However, as no attempt was made to look for other biological factors in the ASD group, and the positive controls could not be further investigated, the most that can be said at this point is that, if replicated, the finding could form part of an early high-risk screening process.

Approximately five per cent of the variance in head circumference can be explained on the basis of the HOXA1 A218G G allele (Conciatori *et al.* 2004). So a genetic basis underpins a small proportion of the general group differences in somatic growth.

The at-risk infant

Prematurity with very low birthweight is associated with increased ASD risk. A screening study using the Modified Checklist for Autism in Toddlers (M-CHAT) with 91 two-year-olds who had weighed less than 1.5kg at birth found 26 per cent to have ASD (Limperopoulos *et al.* 2008). Whether this was a consequence of the increased learning, motor and behavioural and social difficulties experienced by this population, or is due to factors that also predispose to premature birth, is uncertain. A further study has reviewed the Atlanta records for three-year-old children born between 1981 and 1993, and found a birthweight of less than 2.5kg doubled the likelihood of ASD diagnosis, but this was particularly for autism with associated learning problems, and there was a major gender effect, with a much stronger risk in girls (Schendel and Bhasin 2008).

There is a range of markers in infancy that can also indicate increased likelihood of developing ASD (Gray and Tonge 2001), particularly pre-verbal and nonverbal communication skills (which we have elsewhere called aspects of 'intersubjectivity') (Trevarthen and Aitken 2001; Trevarthen *et al.* 2006), and pre-verbal play.

A high-risk cohort followed from 14 to 36 months of age could be clearly differentiated into an early-diagnosed group who exhibited differences in play, social functioning and communication by 14 months, and a second, later diagnosed group who, although not distinguishable from controls at 14 months, were clearly exhibiting similar difficulties by 24 months (Landa, Holman and Garrett-Mayer 2007).

There is an increased risk of ASD in the children of women with diabetes, who are almost three times as likely to have a child with ASD, and of women with epilepsy, whose risk is more than quadrupled (Leonard *et al.* 2006). These findings should help identify at-risk pregnancies and children who should receive more intensive early follow-up.

Sodium valproate is an anti-epileptic medication that is a safe treatment for epilepsy but a teratogen to the developing foetus that increases the risk of autism (Alsdorf and Wyszynski 2005). Risks from antenatal valproate exposure in epileptic women, who require treatment through pregnancy, can be minimized through various strategies (Genton, Semah and Trinka 2006).

Some markers should be high on the public health agenda, such as the significantly increased risk to infants who are given non-supplemented formula feeds (those feeds not supplemented with docosahexaenoic and arachidonic acid) (Schultz *et al.* 2006), or are fed vegan breast milk or bottle milk (Casella *et al.* 2005), and those placed on early vegan diets (Cundiff and Harris 2006).

The beneficial effects of breastfeeding in organic acidaemias and the possible links between ASD and methylmalonic acidaemia also lend support to the benefits of breastfeeding in ASD, in most cases (Gokcay *et al.* 2006).

As long-chain polyunsaturated fatty acids are principally incorporated into the grey matter of the developing brain and their presence is highly dependent on dietary sources (Wainwright 2002), the above findings are unsurprising. Here, changes in public awareness and a change in policy concerning formula preparation could both have a marked impact on prevalence of ASD. This factor is most likely to have an effect in the USA, where formula supplementation is optional and parental decision-making is often based on relative cost.

Cord blood samples may be able to predict ASD diagnosis from the levels of several biochemical compounds: substance P (SP), vasoactive intestinal peptide (VIP), pituitary adenylate cyclase-activating polypeptide (PACAP), calcitonin gene-related peptide (CGRP) and the neurotrophins nerve growth factor (NGF), brain-derived neurotrophic factor (BDNF), neurotrophin 3 (NT3) and neurotrophin 4/5 (NT4/5). BDNF differences look to be the most promising predictor (Nelson *et al.* 2001, 2006); however, one study has failed to corroborate its usefulness as an early biomarker (Croen *et al.* 2008). Material which makes such studies possible is available in some areas – in California, umbilical cord blood samples are stored from every birth – where the retrospective studies to date have been carried out, but collection of such samples is not yet a routine part of health surveillance in most places.

Although not currently identifying large numbers of cases (see, for example, Sempere *et al.* 2010), newborn metabolic and endocrine screening can be used to identify and intervene with a range of conditions (Braun *et al.* 2003).

As antenatal diagnosis using techniques such as serum sampling, amniocentesis and chorionic villous sampling of a range of genetic conditions becomes more widely used, coupled with the high potential demand for such screening as clear preventative treatment implications become apparent (Caughey *et al.* 2004), early interventions should become more feasible.

A range of early behavioural features is seen in infants and pre-schoolers, particularly in early reciprocal social interaction and pre-verbal play (Gray and Tonge 2001). CHAT studies have shown that several early behaviours can predict a proportion of cases based on three specific behaviours (Baron-Cohen *et al.* 2000b):

1. lack of protodeclarative pointing (pointing to draw joint attention to something – 'Look at this, Mummy!') as opposed to protoimperative pointing (pointing to obtain something – 'Get me that!')

2. lack of/poor eye contact

3. lack of fantasy/pretend play.

There have been various refinements of the CHAT, such as the M-CHAT (Robins *et al.* 2001) and perhaps most successfully the as yet unreplicated CHAT-23 (Wong *et al.* 2004). There are various other early screening tools available. The First Year Inventory

(FYI) (Watson *et al.* 2007) may prove useful, but has so far had limited validation and seems to have a significant false negative rate. The Early Screening for Autistic Traits Questionnaire (ESAT) (Dietz *et al.* 2006) appears to have comparable sensitivity and specificity. This would not require clinician administration and would thus prove simpler to administer for early screening (Groen *et al.* 2007).

There is now a rich body of early family videotape material (see Palomo, Belinchon and Ozonoff 2006 for an overview). In summary, this provides evidence for early differences which can identify a subgroup of cases; however, for a high proportion of currently diagnosed children where earlier videotape evidence is available, this shows no obvious sign of early differences. Video evidence can, on current evidence, be used to 'rule-in' or confirm cases, but not to 'rule-out' or exclude a diagnosis of ASD.

It seems almost a truism, but age at recognition of differences correlates with factors such as the severity of the disorder, the degree of associated learning difficulty and the extent of associated medical problems (Baghdadi *et al.* 2003). That said, a US study using the Autism Diagnostic Interview–Revised (ADI-R) (Chawarska *et al.* 2007) found that age at initial concerns in autism was 14.7 months (N=51), while in Pervasive Developmental Disorder – Not Otherwise Specified (PDD-NOS – a less severe diagnosis on the American DSM system) it was 14.9 months (N=24). There was, however, an association between severity of early social disability and subsequent diagnosis: greater early social disability increased the likelihood that someone would later receive a diagnosis of autism.

There is some work to suggest that discrete subgroups of infants can be identified based on tools such as the Infant Behavioral Summarized Evaluation (IBSE), which predict distinct clinical subtypes of autistic disorder from early behaviour (Malvy *et al.* 2004).

There is also some evidence to suggest that early diagnosis may be possible on the basis of early patterns of movement and facial expressions, such as mouth shape (Teitelbaum *et al.* 1998). This is exciting and potentially related to some of the conditions discussed here – the 'Mobius mouth' reported as a common feature in this study of early videotapes is a typical feature of those with a cranial nerve VI and VII palsy, and is seen in classically in Mobius syndrome [48]. However, not all cases of Mobius syndrome have an ASD. Further validation of the technique on unselected cases, and ascertainment of false positive and false negative rates – the number of misdiagnosed and missed cases – would need to be clarified before this could be used as a screening test in isolation.

Without specific interventions or therapies, there is clear evidence that some children diagnosed as having ASD in infancy improve. One paper compares a group of 13 children who 'lost' their ASD diagnosis by age four to a group of 60 who maintained their diagnosis over time, and a group of 17 normal controls. The only factor that appeared to discriminate the children who outgrew their ASD was that they had significantly better motor skills on the Vineland adaptive behaviour scales than those who did not (Sutera *et al.* 2007).

In conclusion

At present, a significant proportion of those with ASD can be identified in the first two years of life if appropriate screening assessments are used by adequately trained clinicians. The limited numbers of such trained clinicians in many areas is a barrier to such screening. A number of methods can be used to identify high-risk groups based on risk factors such as maternal epilepsy and diabetes, and certain lifestyle factors such as vegan diet. Some screening tests may be able to pick up 'at-risk' cases with birth screening of blood biochemistry, but much further work is required before such techniques are likely to become reliable and sensitive enough to use in routine clinical practice.

Physical checklist of features that can be seen on physical examination and which may have clinical relevance

A large number of clinical conditions are known to be associated with autism (Gillberg and Coleman 1996; Zafeiriou, Ververi and Vargiami 2006; Section B of this volume), particularly when genetic effects or exposure are at a similar time post-conception. For an early discussion of this idea, see Aitken (1991).

A number of physical differences are seen more commonly in people with ASDs, and minor physical anomalies, particularly of the head, ears, mouth and hands, are prevalent in this group (Tripi *et al.* 2007).

This section briefly discusses some of the main physical anomalies that can give rise to concerns.

Cardiac abnormalities

A number of conditions linked to ASD have associated cardiac abnormalities. Some problems are complex, such as tetralogy of Fallot, and, although uncommon, require early attention, while others may require careful monitoring.

Table A4: ASD conditions associated with cardiac abnormalities

• CATCH 22	[18]
• CHARGE syndrome	[20]
• Coffin-Lowry syndrome	[21]
• De Lange syndrome	[27]
• DiGeorge syndrome I	[29a]
• Down syndrome	[31]
• Noonan syndrome	[52]
• Timothy syndrome	[70]
• Velocardiofacial syndrome	[76]
• Williams syndrome	[77]

Connective tissue disorders

Several conditions that result in defects of connective tissue have been linked to ASD. Connective tissue, made from collagen, provides the strength and rigidity in many tissues including cartilage, blood vessels and bone.

Table A5: Connective tissue conditions associated with ASD

• Ehlers-Danlos syndrome (EDS)	[34]
• Marfan's syndrome	
• Williams syndrome	[77]

'Cupid's bow' upper lip (aka 'Mobius mouth')

This feature is typically associated with a cranial nerve VI and VII palsy. It is seen in Mobius syndrome [48]; in Smith-Magenis syndrome [67]; and in non-Mobius cases from ratings of early autism videos by Philip Teitelbaum's group in Florida (Teitelbaum *et al.* 1998). Mobius syndrome is also associated with abnormal ear rotation (see below).

Enlarged head circumference

Many of those with ASDs have larger than average heads, and a range of 'overgrowth syndromes', such as Sotos syndrome [68], are reported. There are also reports that in some cases this can be related to a genetic difference in a specific homeobox gene (the HOXA1 A218G polymorphism) (Conciatori *et al.* 2004), or part of a general picture of increased somatic growth (Torrey *et al.* 2004). The pattern is typically one of accelerated head growth during the first year, followed by a marked deceleration during the second year, which coincides with worsening of autistic behavioural symptomology (Dawson *et al.* 2007). There is marked variation, however, with some studies reporting accelerated growth through the pre-school period (see Redcay and Courchesne 2005 for a review). There is also a suggestion that the accelerated brain growth is regionally specific, being more obvious in frontal association areas (Carper and Courchesne 2005), something that would be consistent with the results seen on functional neuroimaging studies.

Some preliminary data (based on 45 autistic and 222 normal control subjects) suggests that overall foetal head growth in ASD is not outside of normal limits (Hobbs *et al.* 2007).

One, albeit small, study found that within a fragile-X [35, 36] population in the first year of life there was no difference in head growth between those who fulfilled criteria for autism and those who did not, but that by 30 and 60 months those with autism showed evidence of increased head circumference, whereas those with fragile-X alone were no different from the general population norms (Chiu *et al.* 2007).

Having an abnormally enlarged head can be benign, but can also be associated with immune problems in the absence of any features consistent with ASD (Cogulu *et al.* 2007). One study of a large sample (N=241) of nonsyndromic autistic subjects found that there was a significant association between larger head size and the prevalence of allergic/immune disorders (Sacco *et al.* 2007). This finding fits with the early speculations of Norman Geschwind and Albert Galaburda (Geschwind and Galaburda 1985a, 1985b, 1985c) who related this general association (of increased head circumference with immune problems) to increased levels of *in utero* testosterone exposure. When this is artificially manipulated in other species there is increased head growth, coupled with retarded development of immune structures such as the thymus gland (Geschwind and Galaburda 1985a, 1985b, 1985c).

Facial asymmetries (hemifacial microsomia)

Differences in the rate of growth of the two sides of the jaw and associated facial musculature, often with partial development of the lower ear, are seen in Goldenhar syndrome [38], while hemiovergrowth is also seen in neurofibromatosis [51] and Proteus syndrome [62].

General physical overgrowth

There is a general tendency towards increased physical stature in those with an ASD.

Are there specific ASD conditions that might make someone larger than normal? Yes. A number of overgrowth syndromes are associated with ASD. The classic, but fairly technical, overview of overgrowth syndromes, which deals with most of those we discuss here, is Cohen, Neri and Weksberg (2002).

Table A6: Overgrowth syndromes associated with ASD

• Bannayan-Riley-Ruvalcaba syndrome (BRRS)	[15]
• Basal cell naevus syndrome	[16]
• Cortical dysplasia–focal epilepsy (CDFE) syndrome	[19]
• Cole-Hughes macrocephaly syndrome (macrocephaly/autism syndrome)	[24]
• Cowden disease (aka Cowden syndrome)	[26]
• Orstavik 1997 syndrome	[56]
• Proteus syndrome	[62]
• Sotos syndrome	[68]

The above conditions are all associated with being significantly larger than would be predicted from family size (excluding other family members who also have the gene in question).

In general terms, larger parents will have larger children, with the stronger influence on the size of the child being maternal build. (A smaller mother and a larger-sized father will tend to have a smaller child, while a larger mother with a smaller father will tend to have a larger child.)

Although a number of overgrowth syndromes are more commonly seen in ASD, the association in these conditions is far from 100 per cent (not everyone with, say, Sotos syndrome has an ASD), and there are many other overgrowth syndromes that have not been found in association with ASD.

Table A7 lists the more common overgrowth syndromes with no known link to ASD at the time of writing.

Table A7: Overgrowth syndromes which have not to date been linked to ASD

- Beckwith-Wiedemann syndrome
- Hemihyperplasia
- Klippel-Trelaunay syndrome
- Maffucci syndrome
- Parkes Weber syndrome
- PEHO syndrome
- Perlman syndrome
- Simpson-Golabi-Behmel syndrome type 1
- Sturge-Weber syndrome
- Weaver syndrome

Muscular involvement

A range of conditions has been reported where ASD is linked to a neuromuscular problem. Whether one or other aspect is causal, or both are linked due to associations with other mechanisms, has yet to be ascertained. Management and treatment of several of these conditions have undergone major developments that will be discussed later. In particular, the treatment of Duchenne muscular dystrophy with tamoxifen, and reversal of the Rett phenotype in animal models of the disease, seem particularly promising. Clinically, where there is a consistent developmental history of slower motor development (late walking, poor functional hand use, skill regression) and atypical development (such as 'Gower's sign' – using the hands to push up the body when first standing in Duchenne), evaluation is important.

The following neuromuscular conditions have been reported in association with ASD and should be part of the differential diagnosis in cases where development of motor skills has been abnormal.

Table A8: Neuromuscular conditions linked with ASD

• Adenylosuccinate lyase (ADSL) deficiency	[9]
• Becker muscular dystrophy	[33]
• Duchenne muscular dystrophy	[33]
• GAMT deficiency	[37]
• Myotonic dystrophy type 1/Steinert's myotonic dystrophy	[50]
• Rett syndrome	[63a]
• Rett syndrome (Hanefeld variant)	[63b]
• Schindler disease	[65]
• Sotos syndrome	[68]

Obesity

Although not an essential feature, excessive body fat is a common characteristic of a number of the genetic syndromes associated with ASD.

Table A9: ASD conditions in which obesity tends to be reported

• Biedl-Bardet syndrome	[17]
• Cohen syndrome	[23]
• Fragile-X syndrome	[35]
• Prader-Willi syndrome	[61]
• Rubinstein-Taybi syndrome	[64]

A useful review of genetic obesity syndromes can be found in Goldstone and Beales (2008).

Palatal abnormalities

Several conditions are associated with abnormalities of the palate, a number of which may require surgical correction. Amongst the most common are the following.

Table A10: ASD conditions linked with palatal abnormalities

• Apert syndrome	[12]
• Basal cell naevus syndrome	[16]
• Biedl-Bardet syndrome	[17]
• CATCH 22	[18]

- CHARGE syndrome [20]
- De Lange syndrome [27]
- DiGeorge syndrome I [29a]
- Hypomelanosis of Ito [42]
- Smith-Lemli-Opitz syndrome [66]
- Smith-Magenis syndrome [67]
- Velocardiofacial syndrome [76]

Skin pigmentation differences
Café-au-lait spots (skin hyperpigmentation)

These are 'coffee-coloured' patches of skin. The most common genetic cause is neurofibromatosis (NF1) [51].

There are case reports of unusual pigmentation abnormalities. One report documents a case which appears to combine the typical skin lesions seen in both tuberous sclerosis [73] and neurofibromatosis [51], while testing negative for both conditions, with developmental delay and ASD (Buoni *et al.* 2006).

A number of conditions can result in 'depigmentation', a loss or reduction of melanophores from the skin. These are the cells that contain melanin and produce tanning in response to sunlight.

'Mongolian' spots

These are dense collections of melanophores. The skin in these areas is a deep bluish-brown in colour. The lesions tend to be most pronounced at birth, and to fade with age. They are the most common birthmark, and are typically benign, but can be associated with inborn errors of metabolism such as lysosomal storage disease and the mucopolysaccharidoses (Ashrafi *et al.* 2006).

Table A11: Conditions with skin pigmentation differences associated with ASD

- Adrenomyeloneuropathy (AMN) [10]
- Bannayan-Riley-Ruvalcaba syndrome [15]
- Hypomelanosis of Ito [42]
- Neurofibromatosis type 1 [51]
- Oculocutaneous albinism [55]
- Proteus syndrome [62]
- Tuberous sclerosis [73]
- Xeroderma pigmentosum (Complementation group C) [79]

'Chicken skin'

This term is used to describe areas of bumpy skin, found usually on the upper arms and thighs of people with phospholipid deficiencies. This appearance typically indicates problems with lipid metabolism and may be an indication for phospholipid (Meguid *et al.* 2008) or, in some cases, cholesterol (Aneja and Tierney 2008) supplementation.

The apparent benefits from cholesterol supplementation in conditions such as Smith-Lemli-Opitz syndrome [66] contrast with the hypercholesterolaemia that has been reported in some ASD populations (Dziobek *et al.* 2007). As elevated cholesterol levels appear linked to raised levels of anxiety and obsessive-compulsive behaviour, normalization of short-chain fatty acid metabolism seems the best aim from current evidence.

Other skin differences

A number of the specific genetic ASD conditions we go on to discuss have been linked to skin problems of various sorts. Those where dermatological differences are commonly reported are principally the following.

Table A12: ASD conditions associated with dermatological abnormalities

• Bannayan-Riley-Ruvalcaba syndrome	[15]
• Basal cell naevus syndrome	[16]
• Cowden syndrome	[26]
• DiGeorge syndrome I	[29a]
• Hyper IgE syndrome with autism	[41]
• Hypomelanosis of Ito	[42]
• Neurofibromatosis type 1	[51]
• Noonan syndrome	[52]
• Prader-Willi syndrome	[61]
• Proteus syndrome	[62]
• Tuberous sclerosis	[73]
• X-linked ichthyosis	[80]

Several of these conditions are known as 'phacomatoses' (Nowak 2007) that have combined differences in the skin with an increased possibility of neurological involvement. The conditions typically classified as phacomatoses that are associated with ASD are Bannayan-Riley-Ruvalcaba syndrome [15]; neurofibromatosis type 1 [51]; Proteus syndrome [62]; and tuberous sclerosis [73].

Thumb adduction, external ear rotation, upper limb malformation and cranial nerve VI and VII abnormalities

The combination of thumb, ear, upper limb and cranial nerve anomalies seems to be associated with a group of autistic conditions that result from interference with embryonic development at the same stage during pregnancy. They are well documented in cases of ASD resulting from various teratogens (thalidomide, valproic acid and misoprostal having been most carefully studied), while for certain other causes clear genetic origins have been identified (for example fragile-X [35, 36] and Mobius [48] syndromes). (For discussion see Miller *et al.* 2005.)

Further clinical aspects that may require investigation

Abnormal glutamate metabolism

The amino-acid neurotransmitters glutamate and gamma-amino butyric acid (GABA) have received limited attention in the study of ASDs. Researchers have begun to investigate the role of these factors in the pathogenesis and development of ASD and the potential implications for treatment.

Glutamate is the principal excitatory amino-acid neurotransmitter found in all vertebrate nervous systems. An imbalance between excitatory and inhibitory transmitter systems provides a reasonable theoretical model for certain presentations of ASD (Rubenstein and Merzenich 2003).

GABA receptor subunit gene differences have been found to occur frequently in particular patterns in the ASD population (Ma *et al.* 2005).

The Affymetrix 'Genchip' study (also referred to as the NAAR Autism Genome Project) is an international collaborative project that has screened large numbers of multiplex ASD families using a SNP high-density microarray that enables genotypes and copy number variations to be screened across large samples and a clinical database of ASD susceptibility genes to be developed (for recent findings from this project, see Weiss et al. 2009). The Affymetrix study of autism risk loci (Autism Genome Project Consortium 2007), although not identifying glutamate-specific genes within its own dataset, makes much in its discussion of the large number of reported ASD susceptibility genes affecting glutamatergic neurotransmission (such as 2q13; 4q28.3; 7q21.3; 9p24.2; 9q34.11; 11q12-13; and 15q25.2) which are being implicated as promising candidate genes for ASD. They note that in both fragile-X [35, 36] and tuberous sclerosis [73] there is dysregulation of glutamate signalling.

The physiological effects of glutamate are ubiquitous (Carlson 2001; Kandel, Schwartz and Jessell 1995). GABA is converted from glutamate by the enzyme glutamic acid decarboxylase (GAD). Pyridoxal phosphate (vitamin B6) is an essential co-enzyme in this process. GAD is the rate-limiting step in the synthesis of GABA, and reduction in GAD activity would thus lead to excess levels of glutamate. There are some preliminary results suggesting that ASD may be associated with abnormal GABA A receptor genes on chromosome 4 (Vincent *et al.* 2004), and with a defect in the metabotropic glutamate receptor 8 at chromosome 7q13 (Serajee *et al.* 2003).

Abnormalities in neuroligin 3 and neuroligin 4 have both been reported in association with ASD (Blasi *et al.* 2006; Chocholska *et al.* 2006; Jamain *et al.* 2003; Laumonnier *et al.* 2004). As with many such associations, the findings are not common in larger population samples (Vincent *et al.* 2004).

Examination of brain levels of GAD in five autistic and eight control subjects at post-mortem found that this enzyme was reduced by 48–61 per cent in parietal and cerebellar areas of the brain in individuals with autism, compared to controls (Fatemi *et al.* 2002). As the 'excitotoxic' effects of glutamate interfere with neuronal development, and have their maximal effect during the second year of human life (Kornhuber *et al.* 1989), it seems plausible that such a difference in glutamate metabolism may be implicated in the brain differences reported in the ASDs. A further study of adult autistic serum levels of glutamate also provides support for the involvement of abnormal glutamergic neurotransmission in autism (Shinohe *et al.* 2006).

In addition to being the period of maximal effects of glutamate on neural maturation, the middle of the second year is the time when parents typically first note concerns over development in those children who go on to receive a diagnosis of autism (De Giacomo and Fombonne 1998).

A further post-mortem study of ten autistic and 23 group-matched control brains found a range of neurogenetic differences. Of particular interest here is that mRNA levels of excitatory amino acid transporter 1 and glutamate receptor AMPA 1 were elevated, specifically in cerebellum, while AMPA-type glutamate receptor density was significantly reduced, also selectively in cerebellum (Purcell *et al.* 2001).

The interactions between glutamate, GABA and the other neurotransmitter systems involved in brain development, such as serotonin and dopamine, are complex (Sodhi and Sanders-Bush 2004) and not yet fully understood (see Attwell 2000 and Lam, Aman and Arnold 2005 for reviews of the neurochemistry).

Various environmental factors such as chronic stress increase circulating glutamate levels (Abraham *et al.* 1998), activating N-methyl D-aspartate (NMDA) receptors and increasing likelihood of cell death (Kandel, Schwartz and Jessell 1991).

There is also increasing interest in a possible link between glutamate receptor differences and a heightened risk of various conditions, including ADHD (Turic *et al.* 2004), epilepsy (Smith 2005) and hepatic encephalopathy (Platt 2007).

Anti-glutamergic agents are receiving increasing attention for their potential role in the management of ASDs (see, for review, King and Bostic 2006). Glutamatergic overactivity is also known to be associated with an increased risk of seizures (Hussman 2001). It is well recognized that seizure problems are more common in the autistic population (Tuchman and Rapin 2002b), with more severely impaired individuals having a greater likelihood of also having seizures (Gabis, Pomeroy and Andriola 2005). However, the potential link between these various aspects has yet to be systematically explored.

Researchers have found abnormalities of cellular development in the limbic system and cerebellum at post-mortem (Raymond, Bauman and Kemper 1996; Schumann and Amaral 2006) consistent with abnormal antenatal development of these structures.

We now have evidence for differences in the GABA receptor pathways (as indicated by the abnormal GAD levels reported above), in the ionotrophic glutamate receptor system (as indicated by the AMPA 1 differences above) and metabotropic glutamate receptors (as we will see in the sections on fragile-X [35, 36]).

In summary: Glutamate abnormalities appear to occur in ASDs at a higher than expected rate. These may be primary and genetic in origin, driven by secondary factors such as anxiety, or a compound of such effects. As we will go on to discuss, in some conditions such as fragile-X [35, 36], response to certain receptor-blocking agents in animal knockout models provides strong evidence for reversibility, and human clinical trials are underway. Whether the more extensive abnormalities of glutamate metabolism that have been reported in ASD respond similarly to manipulation of glutamate pathways remains to be tested.

Abnormal sterol metabolism

Sterols, such as cholesterol, are complex hydrocarbons that are key elements in cell membranes. Abnormalities could have effects on the permeability of structures like the lining of the intestine and the blood–brain barrier.

The complex role played by sterols in conditions as disparate as heart attacks, obesity and Alzheimer's disease is fascinating, and we are constantly being bombarded by health messages concerning sterols, in the media and in the supermarket. Everything from bread to eggs and ice-cream seems to have labels claiming 'added omega 3' or 'low cholesterol'. The history of the science in this area is intriguing and is well reviewed in a popular book by American science journalist Susan Allport (Allport 2006).

The issues are complex. To take some brief examples, battery-farmed, grain-fed chickens produce eggs with around ten per cent of the omega 3 content of eggs from chickens reared on a diet rich in omega 3 (Simopoulos and Salem 1989), while the omega 3 content of farmed fish is lowered by a higher grain content in their feed than would be the case for equivalent wild fish. Although there are reports of individuals with coeliac disease reacting to the gluten content in farmed fish – a phenomenon previously unheard of – by and large, the effects of this are moderated by the fact that fish tend not to tolerate such dietary adulteration readily (Ruyter *et al.* 2000).

The potential role of abnormal cholesterol metabolism in ASD is highlighted by a number of disparate findings in the clinical literature.

A variety of abnormalities in short chain fatty acid metabolism have been hypothesized as being involved in some forms of ASD (see Porter 2002 for discussion of a number of inborn errors of cholesterol metabolism). Abnormal long chain acyl-CoA dehydrogenase (LCAD), for example, has been found in an autistic patient, with consequent defects in the beta-oxidation of branched and unsaturated fatty acids, with reduced synthesis of omega 3 DHA and abnormal cholesterol metabolism (Clark-Taylor and Clark-Taylor 2004). A small French series showed marked plasma omega 3 deficiencies but no reduction in omega 6 in ASD cases (N=15), compared to learning disabled controls (N=18) (Vancassel *et al.* 2001).

Reporting on a chance finding, Bell *et al.* (2000) described abnormal erythrocyte cell membrane phospholipids – in particular, reduced levels of highly unsaturated fatty acids (HUFAs), which were most obvious after cold storage. This suggested the possibility of more rapid breakdown of these compounds in people with ASDs. In a later paper by the same group (Bell *et al.* 2004), their initial finding was replicated. In addition, physical symptoms of fatty acid deficiency were found to be over-represented in the ASD population, and these features were more commonly seen in those who presented with a regressive autistic presentation than in those with 'classical' autism.

A small study from the Institute for Basic Research in Developmental Disabilities (Chauhan *et al.* 2004b) has shown an increased level of amino-glycerophospholipids in the plasma of 14 autistic children compared to their non-autistic sibling controls. This confirms the earlier finding by Bell and colleagues that there is abnormal erythrocyte membrane composition in those with autistic disorder, and presumably differences in the membranes of many or all body tissues. This raises the possibility of differences in membrane integrity both in the intestine – a possible basis for 'leaky gut syndrome' – and at the blood–brain barrier (currently a hotly debated topic, both in terms of infiltration (Shusta 2005) and of development of more effective pharmacotherapies (Egelton and Davis 2005)).

A study carried out by Elaine Tierney's group at the Kennedy Krieger Institute at Johns Hopkins in Baltimore has found that a significantly larger than expected group of people with ASD had abnormal lipid levels, with 19 of the 100 samples analysed showing cholesterol levels below the fifth centile, compared to expected values (Tierney *et al.* 2006).

A further study of 22 adults with Asperger's syndrome found significantly elevated whole cholesterol and LDL (low density lipoprotein) levels, compared to closely matched controls (Dziobek *et al.* 2007).

A considerable amount of research has now been carried out on the biology of Smith-Lemli-Opitz syndrome (SLOS) [66] (Tierney, Nwokoro and Kelley 2000). This is a condition that results from a defect in the final stage of cholesterol biosynthesis, due to an inborn error of the gene for 3 beta-hydroxysteroid Delta7-reductase (DHCR7), and commonly results in ASD if not treated by early cholesterol supplementation.

Epidemiological and clinical studies have suggested that DHCR7 may be the most prevalent genetic deficit which can be linked to ASD, and that early dietary intervention can have a beneficial effects.

Dietary deficiencies in essential fatty acid intake appear to be relatively common in children with neurological disabilities (Hals *et al.* 2000).

In 57 per cent of people with Smith-Magenis syndrome [67], their cholesterol levels were above the 95th centile (i.e. were at levels seen in only five per cent of the general population) (Smith A.C.M. *et al.* 2002), suggesting a possible genetic basis to abnormal cholesterol metabolism linked to 17p11.2 deletion.

A small, double-blinded, group-matched, randomized, placebo-controlled pilot study of omega 3 fatty acid supplementation in autistic children provides evidence for a significant effect on hyperactivity and stereotypy in an unselected autistic population (Amminger *et al.* 2006; for comment, see Gilbert 2007). A further open trial of PUFA (polyunsaturated fatty acid) supplementation found significant improvements in ASD symptomology in 20 of 30 cases as rated on the CARS (Childhood Autism Rating Scale), and normalization of blood PUFA levels assessed using thumbprick blood testing (Meguid *et al.* 2008).

In summary: Abnormalities of sterol metabolism are common in the ASD population. Some of the biological bases have clear, well-understood mechanisms and effective intervention approaches.

Anxiety, overarousal, self-injury, aggression and sleep and behaviour problems

A range of behavioural and emotional problems is common in the ASDs. Anxiety, overarousal (excessive excitability and excitement), self-injuring behaviours, aggressive behaviours, sleep problems and stereotypies (repetitive movements and/or noises) are typically reported among the most common and the most distressing.

In some clinical conditions, there is a predictable pattern of co-morbidities. In fragile-X syndrome [35, 36], for example, the constellation of ASD, anxiety disorder, specific learning problems and learning disability is commonly seen.

The effects of stress and anxiety on behaviour and development begin before birth. In animal models, antenatal psychological stress results in a significant reduction in cell proliferation in particular midbrain structures (the nucleus accumbens and hippocampus (Kawamura *et al.* 2006)).

Stress and anxiety are among the commonest problems seen in clinical practice, and are modulated by glutamate. There is now a considerable body of research on differences in glutamate receptor function (Chen, Tracy and Nam 2007) and glutamate metabolism linked to differences in levels of anxiety and stress, and on clinical response to modulation of metabotropic glutamate receptors (Bergink, van Megen and Westenberg 2004; Swanson *et al.* 2005). There is also work suggesting a role for secretin both in the central nervous system and in the gastrointestinal system, as a stress-regulating neuropeptide (Welch M.G. *et al.* 2006).

In a study of normal healthy humans there was a correlation between the level of stress (rated on the Derogatis Stress Profile) and the size of the anterior portion of the hippocampus (Szeszko *et al.* 2006). A study of children with ASD found that there was an association between the size of the amygdala and assessed level of anxiety on a standardized scale, with the size of the right side of the amygdala varying in proportion to the level of anxiety (Juranek *et al.* 2006).

In a detailed animal study, it has been shown that a large number of gene effects (upwards of 500) are mediated by the pattern of maternal care. Effects on the development of hippocampal structure and of glutamate mGluR5 receptors was down-regulated in mothers who showed lower levels of licking, grooming and arched-back nursing compared to others (Weaver, Meaney and Szyf 2006). It also appears that such effects of early experience are potentially reversible. Glutamate mGluR5 receptors are implicated in fragile-X syndrome [35, 36].

Self-injuring behaviour is a well-recognized problem that is overrepresented in many forms of ASD, such as Smith-Lemli-Opitz syndrome [66] (Tierney *et al.* 2001) and fragile-X syndrome [35, 36] (Symons *et al.* 2003).

In one interesting study with ASD adults (McDougle *et al.* 1996), tryptophan depletion led to a significant increase in behaviours such as whirling, flapping, pacing, banging and hitting self, rocking and toe walking. Abnormal tryptophan levels have been a well-recognized feature in ASD for many years (Jorgensen, Mellerup and Rafelsen 1970).

There are a number of mechanisms involved in anxiety that may contribute to difficulties in those with ASDs. Neuroendocrine mechanisms such as oxytocin (a neuropeptide) reduce the responses of the hypothalamic–pituitary–adrenal (HPA) axis to stress (Heinrichs and Gaab 2007). The oxytocin receptor gene, located at 3p24.1, has been identified as being associated with ASD (Ylisaukko-oja *et al.* 2004, 2006).

Aggression is another type of challenging behaviour that is frequently reported in ASD (Dunlap, Robbins and Darrow 1994).

Anxiety, aggressive behaviour and psychosis can all be presenting features of epilepsy (Kanner 2004), and this should be considered as a possible basis where these features occur.

In adults with Asperger syndrome, there is a correlation between obsessive-compulsive difficulties, anxiety and a number of markers of abnormal phospholipid metabolism, with elevation of cholesterol and low-density lipoprotein levels correlating with increased ratings of both anxiety and obsessive-compulsive symptoms (Dziobek *et al.* 2007). This suggests that modifying what are normally thought of as cardiac risk markers may reduce both anxiety and obsessive compulsive symptomology.

Consistently, despite the rising prevalence of reported cases of ASD, a strong excess of males seems to be a robust characteristic of the ASD population, i.e. significantly more boys than girls are diagnosed. Given the sex bias, an 'extreme male brain theory' of autism has been proposed (Baron-Cohen 2002). This theory provides support for the possible role of neuroendocrine mechanisms that operate differently in males and females and may be implicated in the different prevalence and presentation of ASD across the sexes.. Although it receives only cursory acknowledgement in Baron-Cohen's (2002) work, the idea seems strongly reminiscent of the earlier work of Geschwind and Galaburda on the effects of testosterone on brain development and developmental psychopathology (Geschwind and Galaburda 1985a, 1985b, 1985c).

The possible role of *in utero* testosterone exposure has been much emphasized. As we will see, although much has been made of a link between 'male behaviour' and conditions such as congenital adrenal hyperplasia [25], the evidence is far from clear or convincing. Two other potentially relevant neurohormonal sex differences are in arginine vasopressin (an androgen-dependent neuropeptide which strongly influences male behaviour) and oxytocin (an analogous neuropeptide with many similar behavioural functions in females) (Carter 2007).

An interesting finding is that, in a double-blind placebo-controlled within-subjects study with healthy male volunteers, inhalation of 24 IU of oxytocin significantly improved their performance on a 'mind-reading' task (Domes *et al.* 2007), which suggests that such neuropeptide mechanisms may be important in social perception and relevant to the deficits seen in ASD. For an overview of the effects of oxytocin and vasopressin, see Caldwell and Young (2006).

Sleep problems are commonly reported in those with ASD (Liu *et al.* 2006; Richdale and Schreck 2009). There is evidence that both central factors, such as abnormalities of melatonin production (Tordjman *et al.* 2005), and associated problems, such as gastro-oesophageal reflux (Horvath *et al.* 1999), may be involved in individual cases.

One study shows that in some cases reduced levels of melatonin synthesis are associated with polymorphisms in the ASMT gene that encodes the final enzyme (acetylserotonin methyltransferase (aka hydroxyindole-O-methyltransferase)) that is involved in melatonin biosynthesis (Melke *et al.* 2007). In some individuals with ASD, the section of the X or Y chromosome involving the ASMT gene (Xpter-p22.32/Ypter-p11.2 respectively) is deleted.

Certain conditions associated with ASD appear to result in elevated rates of sleep problems. From the literature, the following are the most likely to result in significant sleep difficulties.

Table A13: Conditions in which sleeping problems and ASD co-occur

• XXY syndrome	[3]
• Angelman syndrome	[11]
• Cortical dysplasia–focal epilepsy (CDFE) syndrome	[19]
• Down syndrome	[31]
• Dravet's syndrome	[32]
• Hypothyroidism	[43]
• Joubert syndrome	[44]
• Neurofibromatosis type 1	[51]
• Potocki-Lupski syndrome	[60]
• Prader-Willi syndrome	[61]
• Rett syndrome	[63a]
• Rubinstein-Taybi syndrome	[64]
• Smith-Lemli-Opitz syndrome	[66]
• Smith-Magenis syndrome	[67]
• Succinic semialdehyde dehydrogenase (SSADH) deficiency	[69]
• Tourette syndrome	[71]

The use of melatonin supplementation appears successful in a high percentage of published cases (Phillips and Appleton 2004), and in the first, albeit small, randomized controlled trial (Garstang and Wallis 2006). Melatonin has also proved beneficial in certain specific subgroups, as in those with Angelman syndrome (Braam *et al.* 2008).

An oddity of the US licensing system has made prescription licensing of melatonin difficult because it is already available as an over-the-counter supplement. As a consequence, synthetic analogue melatonin agonists such as Ramelteon (Rozerem

[Takeda Pharmaceutical Company Ltd, Osaka, Japan], aka TAK-375) are being explored as patentable alternatives (Pandi-Perumal *et al.* 2007).

A further factor shown to be associated with sleep difficulties in some ASD cases is low serum ferritin secondary to dietary insufficiency (Dosman *et al.* 2007). It is of interest that, in this study of 33 children, 77 per cent had restless sleep, all of whom responded with significant improvement to treatment with 6mg/kg of elemental iron per day. Levels of serum transferrin, an antioxidant iron-binding protein, have been found to be significantly reduced in ASD, and to correlate (along with abnormally low levels of ceruloplasmin, a copper-binding protein) with loss of language skills (Chauhan *et al.* 2004a).

In summary: Anxiety, over arousal, self-injuring behaviour, aggression and sleep and behaviour problems are all more common in the ASD population. Some, such as anxiety and sleep difficulties, are particularly associated with certain specific conditions, and can have direct management implications.

Cancer risk

A number of conditions have been reported in association with specific cancers. Conditions have been noted where such associations have been described.

Table A14: ASD conditions associated with an increased risk of cancer

• XXY syndrome	[3]
• Bannayan-Riley-Ruvalcaba syndrome	[15]
• Basal cell naevus syndrome	[16]
• CATCH 22	[18]
• Cowden syndrome	[26]
• Down syndrome	[31]
• Neurofibromatosis type 1	[51]
• Noonan syndrome	[52]
• Sotos syndrome	[68]
• Xeroderma pigmentosum	[79]
• X-linked ichthyosis	[80]

In summary: A range of physical features is found in association with certain presentations of ASD. A number of these associations are linked with specific clinical syndromes and conditions which are discussed in this volume.

Gastrointestinal disturbance

Gastrointestinal (GI) problems have been reported in ASD in a significant proportion of cases. Although the majority of the literature has looked at GI problems in all autistic spectrum disorders, some studies have also found such problems in several of the genetic conditions linked to ASD. In a systematic review published in 2002 (Horvath and Perman 2002a), Karoly Horvath documents the high prevalence of GI symptomology in the ASD population.

Table A15: ASD conditions linked with gastrointestinal problems

• Angelman syndrome	[11]
• Autism secondary to autoimmune lymphoproliferative syndrome (ALPS)	[14]
• Bannayan-Riley-Ruvalcaba syndrome (BRRS)	[15]
• Down syndrome	[31]
• Williams syndrome	[77]

In addition, the MET (mesenchymal epithelial transition) receptor tyrosine kinase variant at 7q31 (Campbell *et al.* 2006, 2008), which is a pleiotropic gene involved in both brain development and gastrointestinal repair, has been shown from a screening of 918 individuals on the Autism Genetic Resource Exchange (AGRE) database to be associated with the co-morbid presentation of gastrointestinal problems and ASD (Campbell *et al.* 2009).

The issue of gastrointestinal involvement in ASD has been hotly debated, in large part due to the controversies surrounding the issue of a putative link between mumps, measles, rubella (MMR) vaccine and autism. The initial theory advanced for a possible link between MMR vaccine exposure and a novel form of bowel disorder called 'ileal-lymphoid-nodular hyperplasia' (ILNH) or 'autistic enterocolitis' suggested that there may be a causal link between MMR vaccine exposure and the subsequent development of ASD. This was based on research suggesting that persistent viral infection was detectable in intestinal biopsy samples (Uhlmann et al. 2002). Subsequent research using rigorous methods and involving the laboratories which had made the original claims failed to replicate the suggestion of a persistent vaccine strain virus (Hornig et al. 2008). ILNH is an unusual bowel pathology that has been reported in a recently reported case of Bannayan-Riley-Ruvalcaba syndrome [15] linked to ASD (see Boccone et al. 2006).

Often, GI disturbance has been attributed to faddy eating, and it is true that extreme self-imposed food restriction does occur in some cases and can have major developmental consequences (Uyanik *et al.* 2006).

A number of systematic reviews of the literature on GI problems in ASD are now available (Erickson *et al.* 2005; Horvath and Perman 2002a, 2002b; White 2003). All of these reviews suggest that there is a significantly elevated prevalence of GI symptomology in ASD.

Various reasons for possible GI disturbance being linked to ASD have been advanced. One of them is abnormal intestinal permeability (often called the 'leaky gut hypothesis'). This view has been strongly advocated by several groups who claim to have found evidence of high levels of diet-derived peptides in the urine of a high percentage of those with ASDs. These peptides, often called casomorphins and gluteomorphins, are thought to derive from casein and gluten in the diet (Anderson *et al.* 2002; Reichelt and Knivsberg 2003). The early history of interest in casein- and gluten-derived neuropeptides has been reviewed comprehensively elsewhere (Klavdieva 1996).

Critics of this view have made highly contrasting claims. A group based in York in the UK has claimed that the presence of indolyl-3-acryloyglycine (IAG) (one of the gluten-derived opioids said to be involved in ASD) in the urine of those with ASD was not important because, although they could detect IAG at significant levels in ASD urines, they could also find similar levels of IAG in all of the other children tested, including non-autistic age-, sex- and school-matched controls (Wright *et al.* 2005). A second group, from Edinburgh in Scotland, could not isolate opioid peptides from the urine of 11 autistic children, from their non-autistic sibling controls, or from adult controls (Hunter L.C. *et al.* 2003).

There are, of course, conditions which we will go on to discuss, such as Down syndrome [31] and Williams syndrome [77], where coeliac disease can often result in a clear clinical indication of gluten intolerance (Giannotti *et al.* 2001). In such cases, antibody testing and appropriate intervention should be a routine part of clinical assessment and management.

The potential clinical utility of casein and gluten restriction diets was identified as a research priority in the Medical Research Council's MRC research review (MRC 2001), but, at the time of writing, no such research has been funded.

In spite of the controversy over mechanism, the data, albeit limited, on effects of intervention with restriction diet are positive (Knivsberg *et al.* 2002; Reichelt and Knivsberg 2003). Some further limited support comes from the finding of reduced autistic symptomology in response to long-term naltrexone treatment (Cazzullo *et al.* 1999). Naltrexone is a selective opioid receptor blocking agent that would also attenuate the effects of diet-derived opioid substances. It could, of course, prove to be the case that casein and gluten restriction are beneficial, but for different reasons to those which have been proposed, such as ketogenesis (where, as in the Atkins diet, the body breaks down fats as its primary energy source when carbohydrate is restricted, resulting in the production of Ketones as a by-product; see Aitken 2009), or GI problems caused by a phophatase and Tensin Homologue (PTEN) defect such as Bannayan-Riley-Ruvalcaba syndrome [15] (Boccone *et al.* 2006).

The current situation therefore, with respect to the usefulness of casein-free/gluten-free diets, is that they appear to be helpful for a proportion of those with ASD, but no large-scale, systematic studies have been carried out, and there continues to be controversy over why such diets can be effective.

In a 2003 case series of 103 autistic and 29 normal controls who were suffering from abdominal pain (Afzal *et al.* 2003), a significantly higher proportion of the autistic group were reported as having megacolon (a larger lower intestine) on rectosigmoid loading (a physical test of the capacity of the lower intestine). This was seen in 54 per cent of the autistic group, compared to 24 per cent of the controls. The ASD cases were also more likely to suffer with severe constipation (seen in 36 per cent, compared to ten per cent of the controls).

Gastrointestinal problems are common in the ASD population. This association is now generally well accepted by clinicians so that, despite continuing debate over what causes such problems, their presence and the need to adequately investigate and treat them should be well accepted.

A survey of 500 families with children with ASD (Lightdale, Siegel and Heyman 2001) found that approximately 50 per cent of family members with ASD had loose stools/diarrhoea; one in three suffered from abdominal pain and one in five had frequent bowel motions (three or more per day). There were no controls, however, and it is unclear how subjects were asked to take part.

A further study (Melmed et al. 2000) reported on 385 children attending the local ASD centre in Phoenix, Arizona, 102 unrelated controls and 48 sibling controls. They found in their ASD group that 19 per cent had diarrhoea, 19 per cent had constipation, and seven per cent alternated between the two. The combined rate for these problems was under ten per cent in both of the control groups. How the problems were defined is not clear from the paper, but we can assume that it was the same for all three groups, indicating that such problems were four-and-a-half times more common in this ASD group than in the controls.

Karoly Horvath et al. at Johns Hopkins University Medical School in Baltimore reported on a questionnaire survey of 412 children with ASD and 43 normal controls, and later on interview validation with a subset (112 of the children with ASD and 44 siblings now of age to take part) (Horvath and Perman 2002a, 2002b; Horvath, Medeiros and Rabszlyn, 2000). Their data show clear differences between their ASD cases and controls in the prevalence of GI symptomology. In an earlier case series they had shown that in ASD cases with gastro-oesophageal reflux there was a high prevalence of sleep disorders which responded to appropriate management of the reflux (Horvath et al. 1999).

One study has found clear differences in the level of GI symptomology in ASD compared both to those with other developmental problems and to those with no such difficulties (Valicenti-McDermott et al. 2006). In this study the group differences were also strongly associated with self-restricted diet and rejection of novel foods in the ASD group compared to the others. No link between GI symptomology and a family history of autoimmune problems was found in this series.

A further paper by this group (Valicenti-McDermott et al. 2008) looked for possible overlap between ASD, language regression, GI symptomology and a family history of autoimmune problems in a series of 100 families. Within this group, language regression and abnormal GI function were associated with a family history of autoimmune problems (specifically history of coeliac or irritable bowel disease or of rheumatoid arthritis).

In the ASD population, there does not seem to be a relationship between the extent, or severity, of GI symptomology and dietary intake of calories, carbohydrates, fats or protein (Levy S.E. *et al.* 2007). This absence of an association suggests that the problems seen are more likely to be constitutional in origin than due purely to dietary factors.

It is interesting to note that, in a study of congenital anomalies, defects are, on the whole more common in a subsequently diagnosed ASD population than in an age-, sex- and hospital of birth-matched cohort. However, when broken down into congenital anomaly by organ system, only GI anomalies were significantly more common in the ASD group (Wier *et al.* 2006).

In a review of the evidence concerning GI problems in ASD (Erickson *et al.* 2005), their general conclusion was that the data was difficult to interpret if looking for ASD-specific gastroenterological symptoms. It is clear, however, from the studies they review, that the rate of such symptoms in those with ASD is significantly higher than in the general population.

In a letter to *The Lancet* in 2003, Dr Simon Murch of the Royal Free Hospital stated his opinion as a gastroenterologist treating children with ASD, as follows:

> This department has continued to assess children with autism on straightforward clinical grounds, since large numbers show improvement in abdominal pain and sleep disturbance if constipation, gastritis, or colonic inflammation are recognized and treated. However, not all children with autism show such response, a finding that needs further study. (Murch 2003)

There is now general acceptance of the prevalence of GI problems in the ASD population and of the need, where these are present, for appropriate treatment and management.

In one Swiss survey of a sample of 118 learning-disabled adults, 43 with and 75 without co-morbid pervasive developmental disorder (PDD can be taken as synonymous with ASD – Galli-Carminati, Chauvet and Deriaz 2006), clinical reports of GI disorders were found in 48.8 per cent of the clinical notes of the ASD group, and in eight per cent of cases of those with learning disability alone. The authors conclude that 'gastrointestinal disorders may be considered as a feature of PDD' (p.711).

There is ongoing debate over the extent to which such problems are due to some process or difference that can be said to be ASD-specific, and to their cause (MacDonald and Domizio 2007), but emerging consensus on the need for appropriate investigation as required (Buie *et al.* 2010a, 2010b).

One study of 24 consecutive autistic children of unknown aetiology found no clear evidence of a link between autism and the presence of intestinal inflammatory markers (nitric oxide and calprotectin), except in two of the children – one who had recently had severe *clostridium difficile* GI problems, and one with extreme constipation (Fernell *et al.* 2007).

In summary: Gastrointestinal problems are significantly more common in those with ASD than in others, but the nature and severity of such problems based on presenting clinical symptoms is not specific. They should be investigated on clinical merit in the individual case, and there is no reason to support the view that the co-morbidity of ASD and GI disturbance should lead to the GI problems not being investigated. If anything, the presence of an ASD should indicate to the clinician the need to collect a clear history of this aspect of the person's development and functioning and to give treatment for these aspects as indicated.

Immune dysfunction

The immune system consists of cells and antibodies throughout the body that are primarily involved in recognizing and combating infections, identifying foreign materials and recognizing foodstuffs likely to provoke reactions.

Autoimmune problems occur where, rather than warding off infection, the immune system reacts to factors within the individual. This can result from processes such as 'molecular mimicry', where antibodies that typically react to an infection react to structures within the individual instead. A good example of this is 'PANDAS' (paediatric autoimmune neurodevelopmental disorder secondary to group A streptococcal infection). This is a type of movement disorder seen in children. It often starts shortly after a throat infection, where the antibodies raised by the immune system to fight the throat infection go on to affect parts of the central nervous system motor system, reacting to them as if they were the same as the infection. (See Pavone *et al.* 2006 for discussion.)

What is the evidence of immune dysfunction in ASDs?

One study compared serum antibodies to brain endothelial cells and to cell nuclei in two children with Landau-Kleffner syndrome, 11 children with Landau-Kleffner syndrome variant, 11 with ASD, 20 with other neurological conditions, and 22 with non-neurological conditions (Connolly *et al.* 1999). IgG autoantibodies to brain tissue were found in 27 per cent of the ASD cases and in 45 per cent of the Landau-Kleffner syndrome variant cases, but in only two per cent of controls. IgM autoantibodies were found in 36 per cent of ASD and nine per cent of Landau-Kleffner syndrome variant cases, but were not present in controls. This suggests an autoimmune component of some cases of ASD. A further paper from the same group highlighted an interaction between immune differences and elevated brain-derived neurotrophic factor (BDNF) in both ASD and childhood disintegrative disorder (Connolly *et al.* 2006).

In a review, Paul Ashwood and colleagues from the MIND institute (Ashwood, Wills and Van de Water 2006) emphasize the discovery of defects in a number of genes in ASD that are known to be involved in immune function (human leukocyte antigen-DRB1 and complement C4 alleles), and a range of factors which indicate abnormal immune function:

- abnormal, or skewed, T helper cell type 1 TH1/TH2 cytokine profiles
- decreased lymphocyte numbers
- decreased T cell mitogen response
- imbalance of serum immunoglobulin levels.

A single family pedigree with three children, the first normal, the second with ASD and the third with severe specific language impairment, was reported in 2003, in which maternal neuronal antibodies were identified. The same antibodies were shown to have effects on coordination and cerebellar function in mice, and were speculated to be associated with the children's developmental problems (Dalton *et al.* 2003). A further small study of 11 mothers of children with ASD looked at antibodies from the mothers which reacted to foetal brain tissue, and found that the mothers did have specific serum antibodies which reacted to foetal but not to postnatal tissue, and which were not found in controls, suggesting that such autoantibodies could have crossed the placenta and affected foetal brain development (Zimmerman *et al.* 2007).

Pioglitazone is a medication that has been noted to reduce glial-mediated inflammatory responses through its action on tyrosine kinsase in animal inflammatory models. It is marketed as Actos® in the USA and Glustin® in Europe, respectively, by the pharmaceutical companies Takeda and Eli Lilly. It is a thiazolidinedione which acts as an agonist of the peroxisome proliferator activated receptor gamma (PPARγ), a nuclear hormone receptor that modulates insulin sensitivity and has been used in treating type 2 diabetes. It has been suggested as a novel treatment approach in ASD in cases where such inflammatory Th2 type immune differences are seen (Emanuele *et al.* 2007).

There has been only one clinical trial of pioglitazone to date (Boris *et al.* 2007). This was an open trial with 25 children, for the duration of 3–54 months of treatment. Significant beneficial effects were noted on irritability, lethargy, stereotypy and hyperactivity as rated on the Autism Behavior Checklist, with no medical side effects. Proper double-blinded trials in individuals with ASD matched for such inflammatory markers would be required before pioglitazone treatment could be advocated in management of ASD cases with immune dysfunction.

A further immune modulating medication called spironolactone (marketed variously as Aldactone®, Novo-Spiroton®, Spiractin®, Spirotone® or Berlactone®) is an aldosterone antagonist and potassium-sparing diuretic with anti-inflammatory and immune-modifying actions. It lowers androgen levels and has been used extensively in the management of acne, hirsutism and precocious puberty on this account. It reduces the levels of inflammatory markers such as TNFα and MCP-1 in cell culture. It has been proposed as a treatment for appropriately profiled ASD cases (Bradstreet *et al.* 2007). This paper also details the positive response seen in a single ASD case. As with pioglitazone, proper double-blinded trials in individuals with ASD matched for inflammatory markers would be required before spironolactone treatment could be advocated in management of ASD cases with immune dysfunction.

Animal research now clearly demonstrates that antibody subsets to systemic lupus erythematosus (one of several autoimmune conditions overrepresented in the families of those with ASD) (Comi *et al.* 1999) can affect both cognitive functions, such as associative memory, and emotional behaviours, such as fear-conditioning, together with damage to hippocampal neurons when given to mice whose blood–brain barrier function has been weakened by administration of lipopolysaccharide (Huerta *et al.* 2006).

In summary: There is clear evidence of immune dysfunction in a significant proportion of ASD cases, and in close family members. However, in clinical practice it is not typical at the present time for immune status to be assessed. A family history of autoimmune conditions may be relevant to pathogenesis. The clinical interventions mentioned above are currently speculative and could not be advocated on the basis of the existing level of evidence without further supportive clinical research.

MMA (methylmalonic acidaemia), vitamin B12 (methylcobalamin) and cobalt levels

The structure of vitamin B12 was first described in 1956 (Hodgkin *et al.* 1956). Methylmalonic acidaemia (MMA) was first described in children in 1967 (Oberholzer *et al.* 1967; Stokke *et al.* 1967), and had previously been described in adults with pernicious anaemia. It presents early in infancy with encephalopathy. MMA is a progressive disorder with a number of sufficient genetic causes that results from a deficiency of either methylmalonyl-CoA mutase (the principal enzyme involved in converting methylmalonyl-CoA to succinyl-CoA) or of adenosine cobalamin, an essential co-factor that is derived from vitamin B12 (cobalamin). It is a branched-chain organic aciduria like maple syrup urine disease (MSUD), isovaleric acidaemia (IVA) and propionic aciduria (PA) (Cox and White 1962).

Cobalamin deficiency is a well-recognized problem in infants (de Baulny and Saudubray 2002) and in the elderly (Andres *et al.* 2004), where it is often a problem of malabsorption rather than dietary deficiency.

There are well-recognized neurological–psychiatric sequelae of impaired intracellular synthesis of adenosylcobalamin and methylcobalamin (cobalamin C disease) that is an inborn error of metabolism (Roze *et al.* 2003).

Vitamin B12 deficiency can arise for a variety of reasons, including mother adhering to a vegan diet during pregnancy and while breastfeeding (Casella *et al.* 2005; Ciani *et al.* 2000), or through strict adherence to a vegan diet taken by the subjects themselves (Cundiff and Harris 2006). Such restriction on B12 intake can result in developmental regression with hypotonia and cerebral atrophy (Casella *et al.* 2005), and in West syndrome with hypotonia and developmental delay (Erol, Alehan and Gümüs 2007). The few cases reported to date suggest that improvements in response to intramuscular vitamin B12 injections can be rapid and dramatic.

A genetic basis to some forms of vitamin B12-dependent methylmalonic acidaemia has now been identified (Dobson *et al.* 2002). Imerslund-Gräsbeck disease is an autosomal recessive problem with B12 absorption, coupled with proteinurea (Gräsbeck 2006).

There are, then, as outlined above, a number of possible causes of tissue B12 deficiency, such as:

1. inadequate B12 intake (typically seen in vegans)

2. malabsorption of B12 (seen in pernicious anaemia)

3. defective cell delivery due to a defect in transcobalamin II

4. failure of cellular adenosylcobalamin synthesis

5. failure of cellular methylcobalamin synthesis

6. Imerslund-Gräsbeck disease (14q32, 10p12.1)

7. Biermer's disease (Zittoun 2001)

8. a primary cobalt deficiency.

The above are usually associated with megaloblastic anaemia and methylmalonic acidaemia.

Some research indicates little association between improved biochemical indicators of response to B12 and the lack of apparent clinical benefit as measured by measures of anaemia, gastrointestinal or neurologic changes in randomized controlled trials with a community sample of adults with elevated plasma MMA levels (Hvas, Ellegaard and Nexø 2001).

In general, the prognosis for MMA has been steadily improving over recent decades (de Baulny *et al.* 2005). Improved newborn screening techniques may make early detéction and intervention a much more standardized aspect of early screening programmes (Dionisi-Vici *et al.* 2006).

The neuropathlogy of non-B12 responsive MMA, though scant, is consistent with that reported in general in the ASD literature (Kanaumi *et al.* 2006), with a reduction in granule cell density, hypomyelination, and abnormalities of the cerebral cortex, limbic system and cerebellum.

There is some evidence for abnormalities in methylation in ASD, and for amelioration of the identified biochemical defects by the use of a combination of folinic acid, betaine and methylcobalamin (James S.J. *et al.* 2004).

From the literature to date, there are clinical cases that appear to show beneficial effects of vitamin B12 supplementation. However, as the prevalence of such cases is uncertain, no clear general recommendations can be given at this time.

One paper (James S.J. *et al.* 2006) introduces the concept of metabolic endophenotypes in ASD associated with differences in the transmethylation and transsulphuration of methionine. On a series of 360 autistic children and 205 controls, they have shown abnormal rates of allele frequency or gene–gene interactions in the following:

- reduced folate carrier (RFC 80G > A)
- transcobalamin II (TCN2 776G > C)
- catechol-O-methyltransferase (COMT 472G > A)
- methylenetetrahydrofolate reductase (MTHFR 677C > T and 1298A > C)
- glutathione-S-transferase (GST M1).

Another paper documented a slight increase in the prevalence of glutathione-S-transferase M1 (GST M1) differences in parents of children with autism (Buyske *et al.* 2006). (GST M1 is a condition where it is difficult to ascertain the prevalence of heterozygous carriers, making conventional heritability estimates difficult.) This study examined 137 family members from 49 ASD families. Where mothers carried a specific glutathione-S-transferase P1 haplotype this increased the likelihood of ASD in their children, suggesting that the effect was due to differences in the foetal environment resulting from this difference (Williams T.A. *et al.* 2007).

A screening study looking for folate abnormalities in a group of 138 children with ASD found that MTHFR C677T is a significant risk factor, being found in 16.3 per cent of those with ASD compared to 6.5 per cent of non-ASD controls (Mohammad *et al.* 2009).

In one Chinese series of 77 cases of MMA, two cases were reported as showing autistic symptoms, but no further detail is given (Yang *et al.* 2006b).

Much has been made in the literature on comparative and alternative medicine of the benefits of cobalamin and the need to use alternative routes for administration due to the high level of vitamin breakdown when it is taken orally. B12 is absorbed in the small intestine (aka the ileum), so is not affected by gut dysbiosis. Various preparations have been employed, including transdermal creams, transdermal patches, subcutaneous injections and nasal sprays. A synthetic form of B12 and compounded methylcobalamin sprays are also available.

Although it is true that there is a high level of breakdown with oral administration, there is an extensive literature on the effective use of high-dose oral B12 (Conley *et al.* 1951; Kuzminski *et al.* 1998; Unglaub and Goldsmith 1955).

Although one subcutaneous methylcobalamin study is nearing completion (see http://clinicaltrials.gov/ct) no comparative studies of B12 response are currently available. At the time of writing, only the James *et al.* small-N open dose study of combined folinic acid, betaine and subcutaneous methylcobalamin (James S.J. *et al.* 2004) is available in the peer-reviewed published literature.

The progressive visual condition Leber's hereditary optic neuropathy (LHON) is associated with B12 deficiency (Pott and Wong 2006). However, B12 supplementation, particularly with cyanocobalamin, has been reported to accelerate the condition, perhaps due to the reduced activity of thiosulfate sulfur transferase activity in the liver, seen in such cases. Thiosulphate sulphur transferase rids the body of cyanide (Cagianut *et al.* 1984). Cyanide is a compound that is part of the synthetic cyanocobalamin form of B12. It is important, therefore, that this approach be used with caution in cases of ASD with optic neuropathy. Note that LHON is different from Leber's amaurosis, a condition that has been reported in association with autism (Rogers and Newhart-Larson 1989). As the diagnostic validity of Leber's amaurosis is currently uncertain (Traboulsi *et al.* 2006), it has not been given specific treatment in this volume. It is interesting to note, however, that clinical research on intra-ocular gene therapy appears to be producing beneficial effects in such cases (see Cideciyan *et al.* 2008).

In summary: A range of factors affecting vitamin B12 metabolism have been described, which impact on development. These seem to be more common in ASD than was previously appreciated, and in the preliminary studies to date show promising responses to treatment interventions. Adequate trials in selected ASD groups are required before we can be clear about possible clinical benefits from this approach.

Evidence for the selective benefits from different methods of B12 administration is not available. Assessment for optic neuropathy may be advisable.

Seizures, fits and epilepsy

There is continuing debate amongst epileptologists over the increasing clinical benefits of being able to apply genetic information to diagnosis and treatment for seizures (Delgado-Escueta and Bourgeois 2008).

In general, seizure problems are significantly more common in those with ASD than in comparable non-ASD populations. ASD symptomology is also more common within the epileptic population (Clarke *et al.* 2005). Some case series, however, have reported lower rates of epilepsy in autistic subjects (Pavone *et al.* 2004). On balance the rate is higher, but variations may reflect factors such as the nature of the clinical populations reported on – tertiary neurological clinics will see a higher proportion of neurogenetic disorders, compared with what might be seen in general paediatric clinics, and are likely to have a higher proportion of epileptic cases referred to them.

A review of the literature on epilepsy and ASD can be found in Spence and Schneider (2009).

In a review of all Icelandic cases of epilepsy for the period 1982–2000, a higher prevalence of autism was found in those who had presented with unprovoked seizures in the first year of life (Saemundsen *et al.* 2007). All children whose parents had concerns over their development were studied (N=84), of whom six (7.1 per cent) (four girls and two boys – a similar sex ratio to the overall group) had an ASD, while all six had an associated learning disability.

A useful overview of the management of epilepsy in those with autism can be found in Peake, Notghi and Philip (2006). Investigation of seizures should be on a clinical basis for each case.

There is currently insufficient evidence to recommend either for or against the use of routine EEG screening in ASDs (Kagan-Kushnir, Roberts and Snead 2005). However, in one clinical series of 889 patients with ASDs collected by a Chicago clinic over a nine-year period (Chez *et al.* 2004), none of whom had epilepsy or a known genetic condition or clinical malformation, over 60 per cent showed evidence of epileptiform activity on ambulatory EEG recording. In the majority, the clinical activity was over the right temporal lobe. Of 176 who were treated prophylactically with sodium valproate, a widely used antiepileptic medication (i.e. where it was prescribed on the basis of the EEG recording alone, and not, as would be typical, on a clinical diagnosis of epilepsy), 80 showed normalization of the EEG and, of those, 30 showed clinical improvements.

One retrospective case series (Park 2003) found that, of 59 autistic patients with previously poorly controlled seizures who had then been treated with an implanted vagal nerve stimulator (a technique where embedded electrodes are used to stimulate the vagal nerve in the neck – a technique that has proven effective for some types of seizures that are unresponsive to other approaches), 58 per cent showed at least a 50 per cent reduction in seizure frequency, and 76 per cent showed improvements in 'quality of life', particularly in alertness, by one year after the device was implanted. The study discriminated between types of seizure activity, but not between types or causes of ASD. In a single adult case of Asperger syndrome with temporal lobe epilepsy, both seizure severity and behavioural components of his Asperger symptomology (judged on the Yale-Brown Obsessions and Compulsions scale and a physician rating of quality of life) were significantly improved through use of an implanted vagal nerve stimulator (Warwick *et al.* 2007).

Within the ASD population epilepsy is more prevalent, with three factors being associated: there is increasing prevalence with age, with a second peak for seizure onset at adolescence, in addition to the more typical onset peak in the preschool years (Volkmar and Nelson 1990); there is also an association with lower level of cognitive functioning; and with poorer receptive language skills (Tuchman and Rapin 2002a). These may also provide an index of the extent of organic involvement – in tuberous sclerosis [73], for example, the numbers of tubers seen on brain scanning increase with age, suggesting a progressive condition (Wong and Khong 2006).

Cases have been reported where epilepsy has been linked to a neurometabolic disorder, as with creatine defects due to either guanidinoacetate methyltransferase (GAMT) deficiency [37] or arginine:glycine amidinotransferase deficiency. These disorders are reported to respond clinically to treatment with creatinine monohydrate (Leuzzi 2002).

It is possible that in some cases ASD behaviour is actually caused by anti-epileptic medication (often referred to as an iatrogenic effect), and cases are recorded where paradoxical normalization has occurred in response to change in such medications (Amir and Gross-Tzur 1994).

It has also been argued that in some conditions, such as Landau-Kleffner syndrome, tuberous sclerosis [73] and CSWS (continuous spike and wave in slow wave sleep), epilepsy is a causal factor in the pathogenesis of ASD (Deonna and Roulet 2006).

Often parents get confused because so many different words and sets of terms are used in describing epilepsy. Below is a brief list of terms used to classify the various types of seizure.

Types of seizure

- *Tonic seizures* consist of stiffening of all or part of the body, without any associated jerking movements.

- *Generalized tonic-clonic seizures (GTCS)* are the classic 'grand mal' seizures most people tend to think of when epilepsy is discussed. They consist of a stiffening phase at the start, which then progresses to rhythmic jerking of the body that is often most prominent in the arms and face.

- *Drop attacks* (aka atonic seizures) consist of a very sudden head drop or complete loss of postural control.

- *Myoclonic seizures* are sudden, brief, shock-like jerks that may involve the entire body, or any part of the body.

- *Typical absence seizures* are staring spells that usually occur in isolation.

- *Atypical absence seizures* are staring spells that are slower in onset than typical absence seizures and can occur alongside other types of fit.

- *Partial simple seizures with motor symptoms* consist of stiffness and rhythmic jerking of part of the body, without alteration of consciousness.

- *Partial complex seizures* are prolonged staring spells that may be associated with jerking of parts of the body.

Types of structural difference seen in the epileptic brain

In addition to the type of seizure, differences in the brain structures involved and in how the seizures arise can be important. The neurological differences apparent in ASD are now becoming quite well documented (see, for a review, Stanfield *et al.* 2007). A number of types of structural differences in the brain underpin the neuropathology of epilepsy.

- *Focal cortical dysplasia (FCD)*: this term, introduced in 1971 (Taylor *et al.* 1971), covers a group of disorders (Palmini and Luders 2002), some of which are thought to be a mild variant of tuberous sclerosis. Because they are associated with poorly controlled epilepsy, surgery is often considered as a treatment of last resort. At present, there is no agreed classification within this group of conditions.

- *Periventricular heterotopia*: this term means clustering of nerve cells around the ventricles (the fluid-filled spaces in the centre of the brain). Seizure onset in such cases is not usually until late adolescence, but reading difficulties are common (Chang *et al.* 2005). It is an abnormality of the way in which the brain cells have developed that has been reported in fragile-X syndrome [35] (Moro *et al.* 2006).

- *Polymicrogyria*: the normal brain surface is covered with small folds called gyri. Polymicrogyria is the term for an excessive number of smaller than normal gyri. A variety of polymicrogyric presentations have been described (Barkovich *et al.* 2001). The distribution can be on one or both sides of the brain, the most common form being bilateral perisylvian polymicrogyria (BSP), affecting both sides of the cortex and predominantly around the sylvian fissure (Barkovich, Hevner and Guerrini 1999). BSP presents with epilepsy, pseudobulbar palsy, spastic quadriplegia and learning disability. Unilateral polymicrogyria can be associated with mutations to the PAX6 homeobox gene at 11p13 (Mitchell *et al.* 2003). 11p13 is a gene position which has been linked to ASD (Yonan *et al.* 2003).

- *Lissencephaly*: in lissencephaly the surface of the brain appears smooth rather than gyrated. *Gene loci:* 17p13.3 (LIS1); Xq22.3–q23 This term relates to a condition associated in most cases with the microtubule binding gene LIS1 (Reiner and Coquelle 2005), and in a proportion of the remaining cases with the expanding group of doublecortin (DCX) mutations (Reiner *et al.* 2006). Developmental problems are typically of early onset, with muscle hypotonia, profound learning disability and severe epilepsy. A mild form of lissencephaly, associated with cerebellar hypoplasia, has been reported in association with a Reelin mutation (Boycott *et al.* 2005; Hong *et al.* 2000). The a Reelin gene, at 7q21–q36, is a susceptibility locus for ASD (Serajee, Zhong and Mahbubul Huq 2006).

- *Subcortical band heterotopias*: these are disorders which affect females with DCX mutations (which in males result in lissencephaly). A separate band of cells forms between the cortical mantle and the ventricular zone, clearly visible on magnetic resonance imaging (MRI), and the extent of developmental problems and severity of epilepsy appear to correlate inversely with the thickness of the subcortical band (Lian and Sheen 2006).

- *Dysembryoplastic neuroepithelial tumours (DNETs)*: are small areas of abnormal nerve cell proliferation within cortical tissue, which are associated with focal epilepsy. The tumours are not malignant and can respond well to stereotactic surgical removal (Daumas-Duport *et al.* 1988).

The clinical pathology underpinning seizure activity based on the above classifications has been systematically reviewed (Lian and Sheen 2006; Sisodiya 2004).

Table A16: Conditions in which ASD and epilepsy are more common

• 15q11–q13 duplication	[1]
• 22q13 deletion syndrome	[7]
• Adenylosuccinate lyase (ADSL) deficiency	[9]
• Angelman syndrome	[11]
• ARX gene mutations	[13]
• CATCH 22	[18]
• Cortical dysplasia-focal epilepsy (CDFE) Syndrome	[19]
• Juvenile dentatorubral-pallidoluysian atrophy	[28]
• Down syndrome	[31]
• Dravet's syndrome	[32]
• Fragile-X syndrome	[35]
• GAMT deficiency	[37]
• HEADD syndrome	[39]
• Neurofibromatosis type 1	[51]
• NAPDD	[53]
• Orstavik 1997 syndrome	[56]
• Phenylketonuria	[57]
• Rett syndrome	[63a]
• Rett syndrome (Hanefeld variant)	[63b]
• Schindler disease	[65]
• Sotos syndrome	[68]
• Tuberous sclerosis	[73]

A further important point to note is that treatment with many anti-epileptic medications increases excretion of D-glucaric acid (Park and Kitteringham 1988; Tutor-Crespo, Hermida and Tutor 2005). Urinary porphyrin levels are also elevated in treated epileptic patients; however, coproporphyrin levels do not correlate with either D-glucaric acid levels or enzymatic effects of medication, so may originate in a renal problem common to those with epilepsy with or without an ASD (for discussion, see Tutor-Crespo, Hermida and Tutor 2005). As no study has so far been conducted looking at porphyrin levels in drug-naive epileptic subjects, it is also possible that porphyrin levels are elevated by the presence of epilepsy *per se*. Given the high rates of epileptic activity in those with ASD, this is an important factor to address in any systematic clinical overview of such issues (Chez *et al.* 2006).

There is current interest in elevated porphyrins as a possible marker variable in ASD (Austin and Shandley 2008; Nataf *et al.* 2006). This is being used by some to identify individuals who might benefit from chelation. It is important to be aware that elevated porphyrin levels will occur with anti-epileptic medication, whether or not a person is autistic, so the results of testing taken in isolation have the potential to be misleading if the person is epileptic or taking medication for epilepsy, and could result in the use of inappropriate and potentially dangerous treatment.

With some forms of epilepsy, the association with ASD seems to be related to the site and type of seizure activity. In West syndrome (often referred to as 'infantile spasms'), for example, the presence of hypsarrhythmia (an unusual pattern of electrical seizure activity in the brain), particularly when detected from the frontal lobes of the brain, is strongly associated with the later onset of ASD (Kayaalp *et al.* 2007). One early onset West syndrome case was secondary to the infant breastfeeding from a mother with mild methylmalonic aciduria. The infant presented with seizures, hypotonia and developmental delay (Erol, Alehan and Gümüs 2007). In this case, intramuscular vitamin B12 injections resulted in rapid and dramatic normalization of development and the cessation of epilepsy.

A rare but well-recognized subgroup of epilepsies is caused by defects in the autosomal recessive gene responsible for production of glutamic acid decarboxylase (for review see Rajesh and Girija 2003). These cases are responsive to treatment with pyrodoxine (vitamin B6).

Certain findings suggest that there is an association between low selenium levels and epilepsy (Ashrafi *et al.* 2007a) with the selenium-dependent antioxidant glutathione peroxidase (Ashrafi *et al.* 2007b).

A further issue of interest is that abnormal glutamate metabolism is involved in some forms of epilepsy which are seen in ASD. In such cases, it seems likely from the research to date that anti-epileptic medications such as topiramate (which has a selective effect on glutamatergic systems) may prove beneficial. Here, the problem lies in the mGluR5 receptor pathway, especially in the kainate systems of the amygdala (Gryder and Rogawski 2003; Kaminski, Banerjee and Rogawski 2004; Rogawski *et al.* 2003), and medications that affect this pathway are likely to be selectively beneficial. As fragile-X selectively affects the mGluR5 pathway and is associated with both ASD and epilepsy, it is thought that this group in particular may benefit from topiramate.

There is a direct association between leptin levels and seizure control. Leptin is a peripheral hormone, the levels of which are directly proportional to body fat stores, and appears to be linked to seizure control (for discussion, see Diano and Horvath 2008).

There is increasing evidence for beneficial effects of ketogenic diets (i.e. diets in which fat is the principal energy source rather than carbohydrate) in the control of seizure activity (Neal *et al.* 2008) and in the management of ASD (Evangeliou *et al.* 2003). (This literature is summarized in Aitken 2009.) These findings strengthen the clinical importance of evaluating phospholipid function in individuals with ASD and co-morbid epilepsy.

In summary: Epilepsy is a common problem seen in the ASD population. There are many conditions that will be discussed later in this volume where epilepsy is seen in most cases. Epilepsy treatments may complicate the interpretation of other biomedical parameters, and as 'subclinical' EEG abnormalities, which are common in the ASD population. Screening for such difficulties should be an important component of baseline assessment, depending on the basis of the epilepsy.

In addition to medication and surgical interventions a number of factors may be relevant to seizure control, including dietary factors such as level of glutamate intake and cobalamin (vitamin B12).

Vitamin B6 and magnesium

One of the earliest alternative biological treatments for autism was the use of high-dose vitamin B6 and magnesium supplementation. The finding came about through analysis of the first thousand E2 questionnaires completed and returned to the Autism Research Institute in San Diego. After behavioural management advice, the next most likely thing to be reported as having produced a significant clinical benefit was a multivitamin supplement, and the sole factor common to the vitamin supplements used was vitamin B6. In initial studies with high dose B6 supplements, many verbal children with ASD reported tingling in their fingers and toes, a sign of peripheral nerve dysfunction that is a well-recognized and reversible side effect of excess vitamin B6 (Parry and Bredesen 1985; Schaumburg *et al.* 1983). The problem was due to magnesium depletion, and the addition of magnesium was found to be necessary to ensure that there were no peripheral nerve problems.

There are a range of conditions and disorders that can result in a need for additional vitamin B6 (typically given as pyridoxal 5 phosphate (P5P), the most readily absorbed form). (See Clayton 2006 for a more detailed discussion than can be given here.)

A defect in the PNPO (pyridox(am)ine 5'-phosphate oxidase) gene that converts B6 from the diet into intracellular pyridoxal 5 phosphate results in a severe condition called neonatal epileptic encephalopathy (Mills *et al.* 2005). The gene for PNPO is at 17q21.2, a site which has been found to be linked to ASD (with a MLS of 2.26) and is also the site of HOXB1, a homeobox gene involved in the development of the nervous system (McCauley *et al.* 2005). It has long been known that treatment with intravenous B6 can be highly effective in management of otherwise intractable neonatal or early infant seizures (Kroll 1985). However, worsening of seizures is also sometimes seen (Hammen *et al.* 1998).

Levels of P5P have been found generally to be lower in unsupplemented autistic children than in controls (Adams and Holloway 2004). The enzyme pyridoxal phosphate, which converts B6 to P5P, has been reported as showing lower binding affinity in people with autism. One study has found high plasma levels of B6 in a series of 35 unsupplemented autistic children, compared to controls (Adams *et al.* 2007). Taken together, these three, albeit small, studies suggest difficulties in the conversion of B6 to P5P in many individuals with ASD and provide support to a rational biological basis for P5P supplementation being beneficial in a proportion of ASD cases.

Two French publications provide some further information that bears on this issue – a first study (Mousain-Bosc *et al.* 2006a) looked at 40 children with attention deficit hyperactivity disorder (ADHD) and 36 non-intervention controls. This showed deficiencies in erythrocyte magnesium in the ADHD group pre-supplementation, which improved with Mg-B6 supplementation. This was paralleled by improvements in ratings of hyperactivity, hyperemotivity/aggressiveness and school attention. Deterioration occurred after cessation of supplementation.

In a second study by the same group (Mousain-Bosc *et al.* 2006b), an open trial of Mg-B6 in 33 autistic children was reported and compared with 36 non-treatment normal controls. The study demonstrated significant group differences in pre-supplementation levels of erythrocyte magnesium, which improved with magnesium supplementation, and coincided with clinical improvement in pervasive developmental disorder symptomology in 23 of the 33 children. As in the ADHD study, deterioration occurred after cessation of supplementation, suggesting an ongoing need for the substrate.

As noted at many points in this volume, there are a number of conditions in which ADHD and ASD symptomology co-occur.

In summary: Vitamin B6 supplementation has a long history of anecdotal support in the literature, but of equivocal results in controlled supplementation trials with unselected ASD cases. As the problem in some cases may lie with the PNPO gene involved in the conversion of B6 to P5P, which shows a significant link to ASD, and studies have not been set up to intervene specifically with this subgroup, the results are unsurprising. The literature to date suggests that a more systematic evaluation of this treatment approach should be undertaken, and that P5P has a higher likelihood of showing successful treatment response than vitamin B6.

Genetic clinical conditions linked with autism

Section B of this book provides a summary of many of the biological conditions that have been reported in those with ASDs: what they look like, how they present, and factors which can be important in their assessment and treatment. At the end of the volume, some of this material is presented in table form for ease of comparison across these conditions.

Some of these conditions, like fragile-X and SLOS, are common causes of ASD; many of the others are not frequently considered and may easily be missed.

As the science progresses, we are discovering that there is sometimes considerable overlap between identified genetic conditions with different genotypes, and equally (and giving rise to equal confusion) there is in some cases wide variation between individuals with the same genetic difference – to give two brief examples:

1. Angelman syndrome

Angelman syndrome is a condition that typically results from deletions, paternal isodisomy (getting both copies of the affected 15q11–q13 gene from father), or imprinting defects in the 15q11–q13 gene (Bolton *et al.* 2004; Shao *et al.* 2003; Thomas J.A. *et al.* 2003). The process of gene expression is turning out to be more complex than originally anticipated (Hogart *et al.* 2008a).

Angelman syndrome has also been reported without 15q11–q13 defects but in association with the MeCP2 gene defect typically seen in Rett syndrome and found on the X chromosome at Xq28 (Kishino, Lalande and Wagstaff 1997) – at a gross level at least, the same genotype gives rise to a different phenotype.

2. 22q11.2

22q11 is a chromosome region that is closely involved in programming the embryonic development of the forebrain, the heart and the limbs (Maynard *et al.* 2003).

Several phenotypes can be found with the same genetic difference. A number of clinical conditions that were first thought to be separable have turned out to have deletions on chromosome 22 at 22q11.2 (Scambler 2000 and Table A17 below). Most of these were described and grouped clinically on the physical and behavioural phenotype (on physical differences and differences in behaviour), well before genetic testing became available, and this was the basis, for example, for discriminating between DiGeorge syndrome and velocardiofacial syndrome (for discussion see Hall 1993; Shprintzen 1994). It now seems clear that both of these conditions as previously defined are extremely variable and overlapping (for further discussion of 22q11DS, see Ousley *et al.* 2007).

Takao velocardiofacial syndrome, described in Japanese groups, is reported as having a much more obvious cardiac component but the same genetic anomaly (Shimizu *et al.* 1984); it seems similar in clinical description to another 22q11.2 syndrome called Cayler cardiofacial syndrome (Giannotti *et al.* 1994).

Sedlackova syndrome was described in 1955 in a series of 26 Czech children with hypernasal speech, shortening of the soft palate and facial dysmorphism (Sedlackova 1955). Subsequent cases were detailed with associated cleft palate and heart defects. It has been described as a variant of velocardiofacial syndrome (Fokstuen *et al.* 2001).

Now that we can screen relatives of people identified with such 22q11.2 deletions and pick up other family members who also have the deletion, it has come as a surprise to some that only around half of the children and a third of the adults who carry the deletion have any problems which would have brought them to clinical attention (McDonald-McGinn *et al.* 2001).

The clinical presentation in monozygotic twins can also vary, and it is relatively common, for example, for one twin to have a serious heart problem while their brother or sister with the same genetic condition has none (Vincent *et al.* 1999).

So a genetic screen showing up a deletion or problem at 22q11.2 may be benign or could be associated with any of a broad range of clinical conditions:

Table A17: 22q11.2 conditions associated with ASD

Condition	Gene locus	Key references
CATCH 22	22q11.2	Niklasson *et al.* 2002 Roubertie *et al.* 2001
Cayler cardiofacial syndrome	22q11.2	Giannotti *et al.* 1994
DiGeorge syndrome I	22q11.2	Lajiness-O'Neill *et al.* 2005
Shprintzen's syndrome/ velocardiofacial syndrome	22q11.2	Shprintzen *et al.* 1981
Sedlackova syndrome	22q11.2	Fokstuen *et al.* 2001; Sedlackova 1955
Takao velocardiofacial syndrome (conotruncal anomaly face syndrome)	22q11.2	Shimizu *et al.* 1984
22q11.2 deletion syndrome	22q11.2	Fernández *et al.* 2005
Unselected relative findings (lack of clear genotype– phenotype correlation)	22q11.2	McDonald-McGinn *et al.* 2001
Opitz G/BBB syndrome	22q11.2	Fryburg, Lin and Golden 1996; LaCassie and Arriaza 1996; McDonald-McGinn *et al.* 1995

The variations seen both within and between the various 22q11.2 conditions above may be due to differences in the epigenetic mechanisms highlighted earlier, to different subsets of 22q11.2 genes being involved, to environmental exposures at critical times in early development, to a combination of such factors, or to other factors affecting variation in phenotypic expression.

A similar cluster of conditions is seen at 22p11.2, with ARX [13], Coffin-Lowry syndrome [21], oculocutaneous albinism [55], Rett syndrome [63a, 63b] and X-linked ichthyosis [80] all being linked to defects in the same small area of DNA.

In summary: For many of the conditions discussed in this volume, at our current level of understanding the link between genotype and phenotype is, as yet, poorly understood, and in many cases involves mechanisms such as mitochondrial function and epigenetic factors which are not yet part of routine clinical investigation. One important consequence of this is that an atypical phenotype should not rule out a role for genetic investigation.

'Alternative' approaches

It is important for clinicians to be aware of the extent to which complementary and alternative medicine approaches (CAMs) are currently employed by families with members who have ASD, and equally for such families to be aware that CAMs may interact with conventional treatments.

In one US survey of 284 children with ASDs, approximately 30 per cent were using CAMs (Levy S.E. *et al.* 2003). A further survey of 479 families found a wide range of treatments being employed, including dietary interventions by approximately 27 per cent (129), chelation by 32 families (6.7 per cent) and multiple conventional medications used by many (Goin-Kochel, Myers and Mackintosh 2007). The types of CAMs used by parents predict the types of CAMs they are likely to use with their own children (Yussman *et al.* 2004).

Many of the dietary approaches which are advocated (for example, casein-free/gluten-free, simple carbohydrate and Atkins diets) result in marked carbohydrate restriction and, although markedly beneficial to some, can lead to a variety of problems such as osteoporosis, copper imbalance, kidney and visual problems, if not properly implemented and monitored (for discussion see Aitken 2009).

Alternative treatments such as chelation (treatment for heavy metal toxicity, which can take a variety of forms) could conceivably be beneficial in some cases if used appropriately and where clinically warranted. However, chelation can also be harmful if used in cases where not clinically indicated (Stangle *et al.* 2007) and can even prove fatal if used inadvisedly (MMWR 2006). There is only limited evidence on clinical benefits from mercury chelation where there are elevated mercury or lead levels from known exposure (Chisolm 2001; Liu *et al.* 2002; McFee and Caraccio 2001). Chelation will also bind biologically essential minerals (Guldager *et al.* 1996), and ensuring that essential minerals are not unduly depleted is an important component of such approaches. The evidence on efficacy is limited at best (Rush, Hjelmhaug and Lobner 2008), and typical methods of challenge testing to justify treatment maintenance appear difficult to justify (Charlton and Wallace 2009). Based on the current evidence, the approach should only be adopted with caution, where there is clear evidence of toxic exposure and accumulation, and under competent medical supervision.

The issue of potential benefit from chelation has become confounded with the issue of mercury exposure and the mercury-based thiomersal/thimerosal preservative which has been used in certain 'killed' vaccines (for contrasting opinions on this area see Bradstreet *et al.* 2003; Fombonne *et al.* 2006; Holmes, Blaxill and Hayley 2003). This has politicized rather than clarified the issue, with many now viewing the issues more from the standpoint of litigation and possible cover-up rather than from that of biology. It is possible that some children with ASD may have problems with the clearance of heavy metals, making them more vulnerable to the effects of toxic metal exposure. I fear that objectivity on this issue is likely only to come with 20/20 hindsight, as with the effects of tobacco smoke on lung cancer, where decades of research were effectively ignored due to the power of the tobacco lobby. Similarly, in relation to the developmental effects of lead exposure from petrol fumes, it is instructive to look at the tentative conclusions in reviews of this area shortly *after* the withdrawal of lead from petrol (Rutter 1983).

A further word of caution is needed with respect to some of the tests that are argued to indicate the presence of problems requiring chelation (Austin and Shandley 2008; Nataf *et al.* 2006) It is true that urinary porphyrins can be elevated with acute and excessive heavy metal exposure. Urinary porphyrins are also elevated in treated epileptic patients, and coproporphyrin elevation may be due to a renal problem common to those with epilepsy, rather than to heavy metal retention. (For further discussion see Tutor-Crespo, Hermida and Tutor 2005.) As epilepsy is common in those with ASD, with epileptiform EEGs being reported in over 60 per cent of one large series of over 800 routinely screened ASD cases, this may be a highly important and relevant factor (Chez, Memon and Hung 2006). Although only two subjects in the Nataf *et al.* series were diagnosed as epileptic, it is unclear how many had received EEGs. Elevated porphyrin levels occur in epileptics on active anti-epileptic medication, whether or not the person is autistic, and the results of such testing taken in isolation, without screening for seizure activity, have the potential to be misleading, potentially resulting in inappropriate and dangerous treatment.

As there is emerging evidence from animal research that chelation of animals which are not heavy-metal toxic can result in lasting cognitive deficits, such approaches should on current evidence be treated with caution (Stangle *et al.* 2007). A second reason for caution is the evidence from primates that there is little correlation between blood and brain levels of heavy metals, or of reduction in brain levels in response to chelation (Cremin *et al.* 1999).

In general in the ASD area, there is an urgent need for well-conducted clinical assessments of the various biologically plausible and clinically justifiable treatments and approaches that are being used (Bodfish 2004; Chez, Memon and Hung 2004; Levy S.E. and Hyman 2005). It is critical to recognize that some treatments may be highly effective for some who have ASD but ineffective, harmful or even fatal for others.

Increasingly, calls are being made for new approaches to evaluating treatments and interventions across the biomedical area. These calls are coming from both conventional and CAM clinicians. There is concern over the extent to which the 'evidence-based' approach to management has been skewed by the role of funding agencies and political pressures (Angell 2004; Smith R. 2006) and from the tight regulatory restrictions that discourage innovation in pharmaceutical development (Epstein 2006).

For matters to progress, it is important for us to understand the biological basis of ASD in the individual, and there is an urgent need to develop a research base on which people can be assessed and clinical interventions can be based.

What is unrealistic, but far too often the case, is to expect families to accept the view that lack of peer-reviewed published evidence is a sufficient reason to recommend not doing anything. The literature, and clinical experience, suggest that most families will 'vote with their feet', and, in the face of clinicians saying things like 'There are no randomized controlled trials of CF-GF diet/B12/secretin…let's wait and see what the research shows before proceeding', will go ahead anyway. This is understandable for two main reasons.

1. There has been a surprising lack of research funded to look into the effects of many of the available treatments, so that even where systematic research has been started, we are likely to be several years away from clear answers.

2. What we do know is that with effective treatments, whatever they may be, the later they are started the less successful they seem to be.

As a parent, I would not want to be told 'OK, we now have the evidence that this seems to work' five years too late to help my child. Unfortunately, this situation places vulnerable families in a position where they can far too easily be exploited by private clinics offering false hope without adequate knowledge or expertise.

We also need to move away from a view of ASD where clinicians say something like 'I have found that this sometimes works, so why don't we try it?' to one where we are able to say:

• 'Treatment 1 is likely to help because he/she has A/B/C.'

• 'Treatment 2 is unlikely to work for them because…'

• 'Treatment 3 could cause problems because…'

I would not disagree that many people with ASDs show clinical benefit from approaches which are purely symptom-focused – helping with sleep/gastric discomfort/anxiety, for example. These sorts of problems are often present, and symptom-based management is the basis for most current conventional and CAM approaches. I would suggest, however, that a better biological understanding of why a given set of problems occurs in a particular individual is far more likely to generate a successful outcome. To develop an understanding of the causes of ASD at this level, we need a better understanding of the metabolic and, in many cases, the genetic factors involved.

SECTION B

Clinical disorders seen in the autistic spectrum disorders

Genetic conditions and ASD

But words are things, and a small drop of ink, falling, like dew, upon a thought produces that which makes thousands, perhaps millions think. (Lord Byron, *Don Juan* (Canto III, st. 88))

1

15q11–q13 duplication

Gene locus: 15q11–q13

Key ASD references: Bolton *et al.* 2004; Christian *et al.* 2008; Hogart, Wu *et al.* 2008b; Ouldim *et al.* 2007; Thomas, Roberts and Browne 2003

How common is 15q11–q13 duplication? Only a small number of (non-Angelman or Prader-Willi) cases have so far been described, so no clear idea of prevalence can be given at present. Angelman and Prader-Willi are both deletion syndromes. The other conditions reported are low copy repeat duplication syndromes.

Main clinical features: Epilepsy; learning problems; hypotonia; motor delay; lactic acidosis.

Clinically and genetically, there is an overlap with both Angelman [11] and Prader-Willi [61] syndromes, both of which are caused by a 15q11–q13 deletion abnormality.

Is there a link between 15q11–q13 duplication and ASD? 15q abnormalities are amongst the most common genetic disorders (Smalley 1997), and have been found in between 0.5 and three per cent of individuals with ASD so far reported (Browne *et al.* 1997; Cook E.H. *et al.* 1997; Schroer *et al.* 1998; Sebat *et al.* 2007; Weiss *et al.* 2008).

- A link with autism was first suggested in a paper on two patients (Baker *et al.* 1994). A subsequent paper (Flejter *et al.* 1996) reported on a further two cases where autism was seen in association with epilepsy, learning problems and mild hypotonia. In all four cases, the affected chromosome appeared to have been inherited from the mother. A further study to suggest a link between 15q11–q13 stressed the parent of origin effect is where the phenotype resulting for a given genetic difference is different depending on whether this is inherited from the mother or from the father. In this case the condition typically results from a 15q11–q13 abnormality which is maternal in orgin – of three affected children, two inherited the duplication from their mothers, while the third had an apparently *de novo* mutation (Cook E.H. *et al.* 1997).

- In 1997, 15q11–q13 was identified as a candidate gene region for autism susceptibility (Pericak-Vance *et al.* 1997).

- In a further study of a group of 100 ASD cases, four were shown to have proximal 15q abnormalities, all inherited from their mothers (Schroer *et al.* 1998).

- One study (Wolpert *et al.* 2000) reported on three unrelated autistic patients with maternally inherited isodicentric chromosomes, in all of which the proximal region of 15q11.2 was affected. Their review of earlier case reports had suggested a number of possibly associated features – delayed milestones, learning disability, hypotonia and seizures.

- In 2003, two autistic children were described, with moderate motor delay, lactic acidosis, severe hypotonia, normal EEG and MRI, both of whom had a 15q11–q13 inverted duplication (Filipek *et al.* 2003). Both boys had muscle enzyme results on biopsy that showed evidence of excessive mitochondrial activity and a respiratory chain block, suggesting that 15q11-13 may be critical in affecting mitochondrial function.

- One study of 221 autistic individuals, using autism as a covariate, yielded evidence for linkage to 15q11–q13 with a Lod score of 4.71 (Shao *et al.* 2003).

- In one series of three families with an interstitial duplication (15q11–q13) (Thomas, Roberts and Browne 2003), two families demonstrated multigenerational matrilineal inheritance. The affected cases had minor anomalies with learning disability. Four of the five children examined meeting criteria for an autistic diagnosis or stated as being in the 'autistic range'.

Treatment and management: No specific treatment approaches have so far been developed. The link to defective mitochondrial function may lead to specific treatments focused on correcting respiratory chain activity.

Differential diagnosis: The principal conditions that can present with this phenotype are Angelman syndrome [11] and Prader-Willi syndrome [61] both of which more typically result from deletion of genetic material from 15q11–q13.

Further information and support:
In the USA:
IDEAS (Isodicentric 15 Exchange Advocacy and Support)
18 Kings Road
Canton
MA 02021
Tel.: 503-253-2872
Fax: 503-253-2872
Website: www.idic15.org

2

Chromosome 2q37 deletion

Gene locus: 2q37

Key ASD reference: Lukusa *et al.* 2004

How common is 2q37 deletion? This is not known, but the condition is assumed to be rare.

Main clinical features: Hypotonia (muscle weakness), large forehead, broad nose, small hands and feet, mild developmental delay, poor eye contact, overactive, anxious.

Is there a link between 2q37 deletion and ASD?

- In 2004, Lukusa and colleagues reported the case of a 12-year-old girl with a terminal 2q37.3 cryptic deletion. She had presented with hypotonia and feeding difficulties during infancy. She had coarse facial features, with a notably prominent forehead and large eyebrow ridges, a broad, flat bridge to her nose, and round cheeks. She had small hands and feet with bilateral brachymetaphalangism, proximal implantation of the thumbs, and short toenails. She had a mild degree of learning disability and she presented with autistic behaviour. The specific behaviours which were reported as autistic included early lack of eye contact and limited social interaction, propensity to be stereotypically busy and to get easily and excessively anxious. She had two older siblings with a similar but less extensive 2q37 gene deletion who did not have ASD.

- One study, on three cases of autism where a 2q37.3 terminal deletion was found, identified deletions that involved the centaurin gamma-2 gene (CENTG2) (Wassink *et al.* 2005). CENTG2 is involved in membrane trafficking and seems an attractive candidate gene for ASD.

The association of 2q37 deletions with learning disability and dysmorphic features has been reported for some time (Wilson L.C. *et al.* 1995). Reports have also appeared suggesting an association with partial callosal agenesis (failure of development of part of the major fibre tract that connects between the two hemispheres of the brain (Sherr *et al.* 2005), and with osteodystrophy (Smith M. *et al.* 2001).

Differential diagnosis: The main conditions that can be confused with 2q37 deletion syndrome are Albright hereditary osteodystrophy (Falk and Casas 2007) and Turner's syndrome [74].

Treatment and management: No specific treatment approaches have so far been developed.

Further information and support: No specific support group at present. Chromo-Zone is a website currently under construction for a USA-based group for families with 2q abnormalities. A link should be accessible through www.chromosomehelpstation.com

3

XXY syndrome

aka • Klinefelter's syndrome

Gene locus: Those with Klinefelter's syndrome possess an additional copy of the X chromosome. In addition, mitochondrial DNA (mtDNA) haplotypes in Klinefelter individuals seem to be unique and appear different from their mother (typically MtDNA is inherited from the mother), suggesting an unusual pattern of mitochondrial involvement and inheritance in this condition (Oikawa *et al.* 2002).

Key ASD references: Jha, Sheth and Ghaziuddin 2007; Merhar and Manning-Courtney 2007; Stuart, King and Pai 2007.

Klinefelter's syndrome is an eponymous condition – named after Dr Henry Klinefelter, who first described a group of symptoms found in some men with an additional X chromosome. Even though all men with Klinefelter's syndrome have an extra X chromosome, not every XXY male has all of the symptoms he first described, and the term 'XXY male' is typically used to describe such people.

How common is XXY syndrome? XXY syndrome is the most common sex chromosome copy number difference, and one of the most common genetic anomalies seen in humans overall. It is seen in approximately one in 500 liveborn males (Nielsen and Wohlert 1991).

Main clinical features: Many males with an additional X chromosome are asymptomatic and do not come to clinical attention. There is a wide variability in clinical presentation.

Early physical development tends to be slow, with later achievement of early motor milestones and poor muscle tone and power. Children with XXY syndrome are often late in talking and have problems with processing both spoken and written language. For around 25 per cent of those with XXY, language difficulties continue to have a significant effect into adult life. This is typically associated with an IQ that is 15–16 points lower than in the general population. (See, for review, Visootsak and Graham 2006.)

Is there a link between XXY syndrome and ASD? Three publications to date point to a possible association.

- Jha, Sheth and Ghaziuddin (2007) described two cases of autism in association with supernumary sex chromosomes – one with an XXY genotype and the other with an XXYY genotype.

- Merhar and Manning-Courtney (2007) presented two cases where, in a single individual (a boy in both instances), severe communication disorders and abnormal EEGs were seen, one of the boys also had clinical seizures.

- Stuart, King and Pai (2007) presented the case of a seven-year-old boy with autism and an XXY genotype, who also had a 3p21.31 duplication.

In addition to the reported cases of ASD, there is clear evidence of impaired social perception in individuals with Klinefelter's syndrome (van Rijn *et al.* 2006) and of higher self-ratings on autism screening tools (van Rijn *et al.* 2008).

In line with the more general evidence of differences in the structure and function of the amygdala in ASD (Schulkin 2007), there is now structural imaging data that demonstrates that the amygdala is significantly reduced in size in individuals with XXY (Patwardhan *et al.* 2002).

XXY syndrome is a genetically defined disorder characterized by the presence of an additional X chromosome. It can reveal insights into genotype–phenotype associations. Increased vulnerability to psychiatric disorders characterized by difficulties in social interactions, such as schizophrenia and autism, has been reported in people with XXY.

The normal increase in testicular volume that occurs at around 11–12 years of age in boys fails to occur in Klinefelter's, and their testicular volume falls away from normal centile levels, having been normal pre-pubertally. This is typically coupled with lack of, or severe reduction in, spermatogenesis and most individuals with Klinefelter's are sterile.

Motor function, muscle development, vocal tone and the appearance of facial and body hair can be changed considerably by testosterone treatment at puberty (typically at 11–12 years). This can be achieved using oral preparations that do not affect liver function, such as testosterone undecanoate – an ester of testosterone which converts into testosterone in the body, or through injections of testosterone preparations. Excessive sleepiness is another common problem reported by people with XXY that often improves with testosterone supplementation.

Most boys with Klinefelter's are of broadly normal intelligence, but with a slight skewing down of the overall distribution. In addition, on neuropsychological assessment they show evidence of executive function problems relative to their overall ability level (Temple and Sanfilippo 2003). There is often a delay in speech development, typically involving auditory memory and receptive and expressive language skills (Bender *et al.* 1983), that should be addressed by appropriate speech and language therapy.

A number of health concerns are more common in adulthood, including autoimmune conditions such as systemic lupus erythematosus and autoimmune hepatitis (Sasaki *et al.* 2006), breast cancer (Aguirre *et al.* 2006), veinous diseases, osteoporosis and tooth decay.

XXY males can have normal sex lives, but typically produce little or no sperm – as a result, between 95 and 99 percent are infertile.

Often those with XXY are shy, quiet and less active than others. They tend to do less well at sport, as they tend to tire easily and have motor difficulties.

Differential diagnosis: Although easily diagnosed on genetic testing XXY can be confused phenotypically with Kallman syndrome. In Kallman syndrome, in addition to underdeveloped genitalia, affected individuals also lack a sense of smell (anosmia) (Rugarli 1999). The prevalence of Kallman syndrome, which is more common in males, is thought to be one in 10,000.

Treatments and management: Testosterone replacement therapy (TRT) can greatly help XXY males get their testosterone levels into normal range. Having a more normal testosterone level can help in a range of areas – it can result in larger muscles, improve endurance, deepen the voice, and help with the growth of facial and body hair. TRT is often started when a boy reaches puberty. It also thought to reduce the later risk of osteoporosis, immune disorders and breast cancer (Nielsen, Pelsen and Sorensen 1988).

One paper (Swarts *et al.* 2007) describes an ornithine transcarbamylase deficiency in a 20-month-old boy with XXY syndrome who showed clinical improvement on a low-protein diet with accompanying treatment with benzoate and phenylbutyrate. (Ornithine transcarbamylase deficiency is a genetic disorder that interferes with the ability to metabolize the amino acid alanine.)

Further information and support:

In the UK:
Klinefelter Organization
PO Box 223
Bolton
BL1 8PS
E-mail: ko.info@talk21.com
Website: www.klinefelter.org.uk

A useful introduction to the condition and its effects has been produced by the Turner Center at Risskov in Denmark, and can be found at www.aaa.dk.

4

XYY syndrome

Gene locus: Supernumary Y chromosome

Key ASD references: Geerts, Steyaert and Fryns 2003; Gillberg, Winnergard and Wahlstrom 1984; Nicolson, Bhalerao and Sloman 1998

47,XYY is a sex chromosome aneuploidy caused by the presence of an additional Y chromosome.

How common is XYY syndrome? It is a relatively common genetic anomaly, being found in between one in 1,200 and one in 1,800 live births (Hansteen *et al.* 1982; Jacobs *et al.* 1974; Nielsen and Wohlert 1991). Birthweight typically does not differ from controls (Ratcliffe, Butler and Jones 1990; Robinson A. *et al.* 1990).

Mosaicism, where some cells are 47,XYY and some are 46,XY, is found in approximately 10–20 per cent of all cases (Jacobs *et al.* 1974; Nielsen and Wohlert 1991). The cause is always nondisjunction of the Y chromosome at either the second meiotic division or after mitosis of the zygote.

Main clinical features: Obvious physical abnormalities are not seen in infancy (Buyse 1990; Jacobs *et al.* 1974), there is no increased risk of learning difficulties, and overt behaviour problems are not common. Early year postnatal diagnosis is therefore uncommon (Abramsky and Chapple 1997; Nielsen and Videbech 1984), and the condition is more likely to be found by chance than deliberate clinical intent.

Is there a link between XYY and ASD? Three papers to date have pointed to a possible association:

- Gillberg, Winnergard and Wahlstrom (1984) note previous cases of childhood psychosis in association with XYY, and present a case of infantile autism with XYY.

- Nicolson, Bhalerao and Sloman (1998) described two boys, both with an XYY genotype. One fulfilled criteria for autistic disorder, the other for the DSM-III diagnosis of Pervasive Developmental Disorder – Not Otherwise Specified.

- Geerts, Steyaert and Fryns (2003) presented perhaps the most useful dataset to date, describing a series of 38 children with XYY, which indicated that, although many children with XYY are of normal ability, psychosocial problems are noted in around half of all cases, and the likelihood of ASD diagnosis seems to rise with age, perhaps suggesting a presentation more consistent with Asperger's syndrome than autism.

Various screening methods could pick up an affected baby before birth. The methods include amniocentesis and chorionic villous sampling. Other findings can be suggestive, such as increased 'nuchal translucency' (here there is a fluid-filled space behind the base of the baby's neck that can be seen on ultrasound). This is more commonly seen in association with Down syndrome [31]. These methods would not form part of routine screening, and it is not typically the case that XYY is identified antenatally (Sebire et al. 1998; Spencer, Tul and Nicolaides 2000). The exception is where screening is carried out for other reasons such as increased maternal age (Abramsky and Chapple 1997), or when screening for Down syndrome (Ryall et al. 2001). It is thus likely that an age bias in clinical but not in epidemiological samples will reflect the correlation of increased likelihood of screening with increasing maternal age.

It does appear that there is a heightened incidence of speech delay, hyperactivity and educational difficulties, particularly in the postnatally diagnosed XYY population (Buyse 1990; Linden, Bender and Robinson 1996; Walzer, Bashir and Sibert 1990). The lower rates of developmental difficulties reported in the prenatally diagnosed population (Linden and Bender 2002) could, however, represent an ascertainment bias, as routine genetic screening would be considered more often in those presenting clinically with issues such as speech delay, hyperactivity and educational problems. In general, psychosocial problems are common but tend to be mild in the XYY population, and are not typically severe enough to result in psychiatric diagnosis (Fryns *et al.* 1995).

Physically, those with XYY tend to be taller and leaner than average (Buyse 1990; Linden, Bender and Robinson 1996).

Those with 47,XYY are typically fertile (Linden, Bender and Robinson 1996). However, they are more likely to have a number of genital anomalies, including hypospadias, and small or undescended testes (Buyse 1990).

One case of 47,XYY in an individual who was phenotypically female has been reported in the clinical literature (Benasayag *et al.* 2001).

There is no increased risk of 47,XYY linked to later maternal age at conception (Ferguson-Smith and Yates 1984), which is perhaps unsurprising, given that the origin of the additional chromosome will be paternal. Neither does there appear to be increased risk with increasing age of fathers producing aneuploid sperm (over the age range from 22 to 80 years of age) (Wyrobek *et al.* 2006). This suggests that there is something about spermatogenesis in the fathers of those with XYY that predisposes to this process.

47,XYY has been reported as more common in infants conceived by intracytoplasmic sperm injection (ICSI) (Aboulghar *et al.* 2001), but not to date through any other means of assisted conception.

Differential diagnosis: XYY is easily diagnosed on genetic testing. Phenotypically it could be confused with other conditions resulting in taller thinner stature such as Marfan syndrome (De Paepe *et al.* 1996).

Treatment and management: XYY, although associated with ASD, appears remarkably benign. There are no major difficulties reported for which specific treatments appear warranted. The biological effects of having an additional Y chromosome are not currently well known.

47,XYY is a sex chromosome aneuploidy that often goes undetected in early life. It is not associated with learning disability. It is associated with being taller, leaner, and having a proneness to speech delay, hyperactive behaviour and educational problems. To date, there is a paucity of information on any central nervous system sequelae. There have been a number of case reports of XYY in association with ASD; however, no systematic assessments of this association have been carried out.

Further information and support:

In the USA:
KS&A
11 Keats Court
Coto de Caza
CA 92679
Tel. (toll-free): 888 999-9428;
888 XYY-WHAT – 47,XYY Syndrome Support
Line
Website: www.genetic.org

5

10p terminal deletion

Gene locus: 10p

Key ASD reference: Verri *et al.* 2004

10p teminal deletion is a rare condition, and has only been reported to date in one ASD case, that of a 33-year-old man who was reported in addition as having hypoparathyroidism, severe mental retardation, and calcification of the basal ganglia.

How common is 10p terminal deletion? There have been no population studies of the prevalence of this condition but it is thought to be very rare. As cases have been reported in conditions that are themselves linked to ASD, the association, though uncommon, may indicate a specific pathogenic mechanism that is involved in a subgroup of those with an ASD diagnosis.

Main clinical features: Large forehead; small teeth; congenital heart defect; kidney problems; dilated cerebral ventricles; developmental delay.

Is there a link between 10p terminal deletion and ASD? The 10p region is not identified from the various gene marker studies as being associated with ASD.

* There is one clinical report of an association (Verri *et al.* 2004). It may prove relevant, as 10p deletions have been reported in association with both the DiGeorge II [29b] (Yatsenko *et al.* 2004) and velocardiofacial [76] syndromes (Gottlieb *et al.* 1998). Both of these conditions are overrepresented in the ASD population, and typically the case reports of 10p terminal deletion to date have not looked in any detail for possible ASD behaviour.

In a review of 36 patients with a 10p deletion (van Esch *et al.* 1999), affected individuals showed a phenotype similar to a partial DiGeorge syndrome I [29a]. In addition, however, a consistent feature of those with 10p deletion was that they also had a sensorineural hearing loss.

In one paper (Sunada, Rash and Tam 1998), with a partial 10p monosomy, seizures and cortical atrophy are well documented, as well as the previously reported phenotypic characteristics – bossing of the frontal bones of the skull; small teeth; congenital heart defect; kidney problems; dilated cerebral ventricles; and developmental delay.

Differential diagnosis: This is a rare disorder with varied clinical presentation. No specific differential diagnoses have so far been proposed.

Treatment and management: The biological basis to this association is not known at the present time and no specific approach has been developed to date.

Further information and support: There are no support groups specifically dedicated to 10p terminal deletion.

In the UK:
Unique
PO Box 2189
Caterham
Surrey
CR3 5GN
Tel.: 01883 330766
E-mail: info@rarechromo.org

6

45,X/46,XY mosaicism

Gene locus: 45X/46XY

Key ASD reference: Telvi *et al.* 1999

How common is 45,X/46,XY mosaicism? Mosaicism is seen in fewer than two per cent of Turner's syndrome cases (Van Dyke and Wiktor 2006). Turner's syndrome affects some 32/100,000 (Gravholt *et al.* 1996) and gives a suggested prevalence of 6.4/1,000,000, so we would expect to find 6.4 people with a Turner's mosaic genotype in every million people and 324.6 with the full 45, X Turner's syndrome.

Main clinical features: This condition, as a mosaic, shows a wide range of phenotypic presentation, from normal male to Turner's syndrome female. Some 90 per cent of antenatally diagnosed cases are male, while a broader range of post-natally diagnosed phenotypes are seen. This pattern may change with greater use of antenatal diagnostics. The most common features currently reported are 'Ulrich-Turner stigmata' (drooping of the upper eyelid, coupled with 'webbing' on the neck).

Is there a link between 45,X/46,XY mosaicism and ASD?

- Only one study to date has examined this issue. Telvi *et al.* (1999) reported on a series of 27 45,X/46,XY mosaic cases, four of whom were learning disabled and two of whom had a diagnosis of autism. If this rate were reflected in larger samples, it would indicate a strong association between the two presentations.

In typical Turner's syndrome cases [74], all cells are 45,XO, the individual is missing a sex chromosome, and the person is phenotypically female. A person who is genotypically 46,XY has a full chromosome complement and is phenotypically male. In 45,X/46,XY mosaicism, some cells are 45,X and some are 46,XY. The proportion of cells of each type is currently not possible to predict. Most individuals with this karyotype are phenotypically normal males with unexplained short stature, but tend not to be routinely screened for 45,X/46,XY mosaicism. This should be done, and, where found, checks should be done for possible problems associated more typically with Turner's syndrome:

- an echocardiogram to check for possible heart defects

- a renal ultrasound to check kidney function

- a cognitive assessment to check for a nonverbal learning disability profile.

Short stature in children with an apparently normal male phenotype can result from 45,X/46,XY mosaicism and can respond successfully to growth hormone treatment. In one study (Richter-Unruh *et al.* 2004), 5/6 cases, all treated before puberty, responded favourably to growth hormone replacement, while the non-responsive case was not commenced on treatment until after he was 14.

Differential diagnosis: The phenotype shows wide variations from normal male to a classic Turner's syndrome presentation. Differential diagnosis based on phenotype would be dependent on the presentation in the individual case.

Treatment and management: Ongoing care and management should be dependent on clinical findings, not on genotype.

Further information and support:

In Australia:
PO Box 112
Frenchs Forest
NSW 1640
Tel.: (02) 9452 4196
Fax: (02) 9975 4037
E-mail: turnersyn@netpro.net.au
Website: www.turnersyndrome.org.au

In Canada:
Turner's Syndrome Society of Canada
323 Chapel Street
Ottawa, Ontario
K1N 7Z2
Toll-free: 800-465-6744
Tel.: 613-321-2267
Fax: 613-321-2268
E-mail: tssincan@web.net
Website: www.turnersyndrome.ca

In France:
Association des Groupes Amitié Turner
AGAT C/O A.A.A.F.A
2 rue André Messager
B.P. 5
75860 Paris Cedex 18
Tel.: 01 53 28 14 86
E-mail: association_agatts@yahoo.fr
Website: www.agat-turner.org

In Germany:
Ringstraße 18
D-53809 Ruppichteroth
Tel.: 02247 759750
Fax: 02247 759756
E-mail: geschaeftsstelle@turner-syndrom.de
Website: www.turner-syndrom.de

In the UK:
Turner Syndrome Support Society (TSSS)
13 Simpson Court, 11 South Avenue
Clydebank Business Park
Clydebank
G81 2NR
Tel.: 0141 952 8006
Fax: 0141 952 8025
Helpline: 0845 230 7520
E-mail: Turner.Syndrome@tss.org.uk
Website: www.tss.org.uk

In the USA:
Turner Syndrome Society of the United States
14450 TC Jester
Suite 260
Houston
Texas
TX 77014
Toll-free: 800-365-9944
Tel.: 832-249-9988
Fax: 832-249-9987
E-mail: tssus@turner-syndrome-us.org
Website: www.turnersyndrome.org/

7

22q13 deletion syndrome

aka • Phelan-McDermid syndrome

Gene locus: 22q13.3

Key ASD references: Cusmano-Ozog *et al.* 2007; Goizet *et al.* 2000; Manning M.A. *et al.* 2004; Moessner *et al.* 2007; Phelan 2008; Prasad *et al.* 2000

How common is 22q13 deletion syndrome? 22q13 deletion syndrome is relatively rare, with fewer than 150 cases reported in the world literature. To date there is no clear indication of the prevalence of this condition, as the phenotype is not well recognized and the deletion does not form a routine part of clinical chromosome studies. From one subtelomeric chromosome deletion survey it was the second most common deletion seen after deletions of 1p36.3 (Heilstedt *et al.* 2003).

Main clinical features: Typical features in 22q13 deletion are developmental delay, failure of speech development and hypotonia. Features seen in a significant minority of cases are epileptic seizures, and a number of craniofacial features including the presence of epicanthic folds, large prominent ears, long eyelashes, a prominent brow, pointed chin and irregular dentition. Many of those affected have large hands and in-growing toenails. Slower breathing, chewing on non-food objects (pica) and reduced sensitivity to pain are also reported to be more common. Many cases show lack of perspiration, so have difficulty regulating their temperature – extra care should be taken with exposure to sunlight and during periods of illness. Minor ear infections are common and could in part account for delayed language development. Gastro-oesophageal reflux is not uncommon (seen in around 30 per cent of cases), with cyclical vomiting reported in 25 per cent. Lymphoedema is seen in around ten per cent of cases (Phelan 2008). Taking smaller, more frequent meals, coupled with avoidance of spicy foods, can prove helpful. Most reported cases have been born at term, appropriately sized for their gestational age. Most cases have grown normally but experienced global developmental delay with slower acquisition of motor milestones and either slowed or absent development of communication skills. Acquisition of bowel and bladder control also tends to be slow, due in part to more global motor problems and in part due to communication difficulties. Speech is often acquired to a limited extent and then regresses, but with greater preservation of receptive language skills. Occasional neurological abnormalities have been reported – arachnoid cysts being the most common; reduced size of the frontal lobes, agenesis of the corpus callosum and dilated ventricles have also been reported. There are no characteristic findings on EEG or structural neuroimaging.

In some cases, hyperactivity, anxiety and self-stimulatory behaviours are sufficiently extreme to warrant treatment. Sleep problems are quite common and may be linked to reduced production of melatonin.

No individuals with 22q13.3 have reproduced, but puberty and menstruation occur normally in girls, and conception would appear possible.

Is there a link between 22q13 deletion syndrome and ASD? Several papers have reported a possible association. Individuals with 22q13 deletion typically have poor eye contact, motor stereotypies and severe communication difficulties in association with learning disability. These features are consistent with ASD in many cases, but could also reflect overall level of learning disability.

- Goizet *et al.* (2000) described a case of autism, developmental delay and communication difficulties associated with a *de novo* cryptic 22q13 deletion detected by FISH (fluorescence in-situ hybridization).

- Prasad *et al.* (2000) documented three clinical cases with 22q13 deletions. One of the three cases met criteria on the Childhood Autism Rating Scale for an autism diagnosis with co-morbid learning disbility. Her initial diagnosis had been thought to be 22q11 and she had been included in an earlier case series and reported as such (Chudley *et al.* 1998).

- Manning M.A. *et al.* (2004) described 11 cases of ASD with severe speech and language delay and hypotonia in association with a microdeletion at 22q13.3.

- Cusmano-Ozog *et al.* (2007) review the evidence for a consistent phenotype associated with 22q13 deletion syndrome, suggesting that the constellation of developmental delay, hypotonia, delayed or absent speech and receptive language difficulties, autistic behaviour, with normal growth and head circumference, form a consistent 22q13 phenotype.

- In one cohort of 400 screened ASD cases, three defects in SHANK 3 (see below) were found (Moessner *et al.* 2007), indicating that, assuming this sample is representative, possibly 0.75 per cent of people with ASD may present with such problems. Estimates of the prevalence of ASD within those with 22q13 deletion range from under five per cent to 54 per cent of cases. This variability reflects a range of factors such as changing diagnostic criteria and diagnostic overshadowing.

- Phelan (2008) provides a detailed overview of 22q13 deletion.

Dysfunction of a 100kb segment of DNA at 22q13 appears to be the critical factor in this condition (Anderlid *et al.* 2002). Clinically, the use of two gene probes – the arylsulphatase A probe and a specific subtelomere probe (D22S1726) – should identify 100 per cent of cases.

The deletion can be inherited from either parent, but in 80–85 per cent of cases is a *de novo* deletion in the affected individual. Where a deletion has been inherited, in most cases it is from the paternal chromosome (Luciani *et al.* 2003; Wilson H.L. *et al.* 2003). The gene locus lies close to the gene defect that causes adenylosuccinate lyase deficiency [9] that is at 22q13.1. No gene markers with Lod scores above 2.2 have been identified at any location on chromosome 22.

In around 75 per cent of cases, the defect is a simple deletion, while in the others it arises from an unbalanced translocation or other chromosomal rearrangement.

What causes it? The gene involvement in this condition is deletion of the gene known as SHANK 3 or PROSAP2 (proline-rich synapse associated protein 2). This gene produces a scaffolding protein for the postsynaptic density complex where it binds with neuroligins (Meyer *et al.* 2004), which are important in combination with neurexins, particularly at glutamatergic synapses. Both neuroligin defects (Laumonnier *et al.* 2004) and abnormalities of glutamatergic transmission (see fragile-X syndrome [35]) have been described in ASD, so defective production of a protein involved in the function of these substances is not surprising. SHANK 3 also has a role in the development of the dendritic spines of nerve cells (Boeckers *et al.* 2002).

A study of 56 individuals examined the size of the 22q13 deletion and the parental origin of the deletion (Wilson H.L. *et al.* 2003). They also studied the gene SHANK 3. Approximately two-thirds of the deletions found were in the paternally inherited chromosome, and one third in the maternally inherited one. Deletions varied in size between 130 kilobases and nine megabases, with no association between the size of the deletion and the physical or behavioural phenotype. A degree of both developmental and speech delay occurred in all of these cases.

A number of other conditions can present with phenotypic and behavioural similarities to 22q13 deletion syndrome, amongst the more commonly suggested being the ones listed in Table A18.

Table A18: Conditions with similar presentation to 22q13 deletion syndrome (Phelan-McDermid Syndrome)

Angelman syndrome	[11]
Cerebral palsy	Cans (2009)
FG syndrome	Ozonoff, Williams, Rauch & Opitz (2000)
Fragile-X syndrome	[35]
Prader-Willi syndrome	[61]
Smith-Magenis syndrome (SMS)	[67]
Sotos syndrome	[68]
Trichorhinophalangeal syndrome	Vaccaro, Guarneri & Blandino (2005)
Velocardiofacial syndrome (VCF)	[76]
Williams syndrome	[77]

Ring chromosome 22 has been reported in association with autism (MacLean *et al.* 2000). It appears that, where the association is seen, the expression of SHANK 3 has been affected (Jeffries *et al.* 2005), with a larger deletion from the distal portion of what would normally have been the long arm of the chromosome.

Ring chromosome 22 cases are more likely to show short stature (seen in a quarter of cases) and microcephaly (seen in one third), both of which are uncommon in 22q13.3 cases (Ishmael *et al.* 2003; Luciani *et al.* 2003).

Differential diagnosis: As 22q13 deletion presents with hypotonia and developmental delay, the early presentation can be confused with a number of other syndromes that have also been linked to ASD: Angelman syndrome [11]; fragile-X syndrome [35]; Prader-Willi syndrome [61]; Smith-Magenis syndrome [67]; Sotos syndrome [68]; velocardiofacial syndrome [76]; Williams syndrome [77]; and ring chromosome 22. Ring chromosome 22 is more likely than 22q13 deletion to present with short stature and microcephaly. Both cerebral palsy and trichorhinophalangeal syndrome can present with similar physical phenotypes.

Treatment and management: There is only one study to date which has investigated treatment for Phelan-McDermid syndrome. This was an exploratory trial of intranasal insulin. The results of this small trial are encouraging, but clinical use of this approach is not yet warranted in improving intellectual functioning (Schmidt *et al.* 2008).

Further information and support:

In Canada:
Chromosome 22 Central
237 Kent Avenue
Timmins, ON
P4N 3C2
Tel.: 705-268-3099
E-mail: a815@c22c.org
Website: www.c22c.org

In the USA:
22q13 Deletion Syndrome Foundation
Greenwood Genetic Center
2 Doctors Drive
Greenville
South Carolina
SC 29605
E-mail: info@22q13.org
Website: www.22q13.org/contacts.html

The 22q13 Deletion Syndrome/Phelan-McDermid
Syndrome Support Group
250 East Broadway
Maryville,
TN 37804
USA
Tel.: 800-932-2943
Fax: 865-380-9191
E-mail: kphelan@mplnet.com
Website: www.22q13.org

Chromosome Deletion Outreach, Inc
PO Box 724
Boca Raton
FL 33429-0724
Tel.: 888-CDO-6880 (888-236-6680); 561-395-4252 (family helpline)
E-mail: info@chromodisorder.org
Website: www.chromodisorder.org

8

Aarskog syndrome

aka • Aarskog-Scott syndrome

Gene locus: At present the gene locus has not been definitively located, but mutations in the FGD1 gene (Xp11.21) have been described in some cases (Orrico, Hayek and Burroni 1999).

Key ASD reference: Assumpcao *et al.* 1999

How common is Aarskog syndrome? Aarskog syndrome, first described in 1970 (Aarskog 1970), is a rare connective tissue condition that has been reported in less than 200 cases in total worldwide (Grier *et al.* 1983; Teebi, Rucquoi and Meyn 1993; Welch 1974).

Main clinical features: Aarskog syndrome is typically reported as being associated with short stature, hypertelorism and 'shawl scrotum' (see Grier *et al.* 1983 for a review). In addition, learning difficulties, behavioural problems and hyperactivity have been reported (Fryns 1992).

In one family, males in three successive generations were affected (Welch 1974).

Is there a link between Aarskog syndrome and ASD?

• There is a brief report on an association between this condition and autism (Assumpcao *et al.* 1999) which gives three case descriptions of boys, all of whom had significant learning difficulties, hyperactivity and the physical phenotype characteristic of Aarskog syndrome. All three fulfilled DSM criteria for autistic disorder.

Differential diagnosis: The main differential diagnoses are Noonan syndrome [52] and Robinow syndrome (Paton and Afzal 2002).

Treatment and management: Two specific areas of treatment have been studied. The use of growth hormone supplementation has been shown to be useful in correction of short stature (Darendeliler *et al.* 2003; Petryk *et al.* 1999), and restorative dental care is both feasible and potentially useful (Batra *et al.* 2003).

No treatments specific to the behavioural aspects of ASD in Aarskog syndrome have been reported.

Further information and support: The Aarskog Syndrome Family Support Group International Network was founded in 1993. Its aims are mutual support, networking, and sharing of ideas for families of children and adults affected with Aarskog syndrome. It offers phone support, a pen pal club, e-mails, addresses and contact pages with mailing addresses for support via correspondence.

In the USA:
Aarskog Syndrome Family Support Group
62 Robin Hill Lane
Levittown
PA 19055
Tel.: 215-943-7131
E-mail: shannonfaith49@msn.com

9

Adenylosuccinate lyase (ADSL) deficiency

Gene locus: 22q13.1

Key ASD references: Edery *et al.* 2003; Jaeken and van den Berghe 1984; Jaeken *et al.* 1988

How common is ADSL? There are no screening studies as yet, so prevalence is unknown. Fewer than 100 cases have been reported to date in the clinical literature. Five cases were identified in 2,000 children screened with neurodevelopmental disorders in one Czech series, suggesting a very low prevalence in the learning disabled population (Sebesta *et al.* 1997). Unique single cases have been reported from Poland (Jurkiewicz, Mierzewska and Kusmierska 2007) and the UK (Marinaki *et al.* 2004).

In the Czech study (Sebesta *et al.* 1997) urine samples from more than 2,000 children with unexplained neurologic disease were screened. Two boys and three girls in four kindreds were identified with ADSL. Two of the four kindreds were of Romany origin.

Most cases of adenylosuccinase deficiency are detected through metabolic testing of infants with severe psychomotor retardation. However, the initial presentation can be of infantile seizures (Maaswinkel-Mooij *et al.* 1997; Marinaki *et al.* 2004).

Main clinical features: Psychomotor retardation; hypotonia-ataxia; seizures; poor eye contact; stereotypies. Approximately 50 per cent of reported cases fulfil criteria for a diagnosis of autism.

Two forms of the disorder are recognized (Jaeken *et al.* 1988). The first presents with early onset epilepsy and severe psychomotor retardation; the second with psychomotor retardation and autistic symptomology. A variety of additional features have been reported in some but not all cases, such as microcephaly, brain atrophy, lissencephaly and delayed myelin formation (Edery *et al.* 2003; Holder-Espinasse *et al.* 2002; Nassogne *et al.* 2000).

Is there a link between ADSL and ASD?

- In 1984, Jaeken and van den Berghe described three children with severe psychomotor delay and autism. They identified two specific compounds – succinyladenosine (S-Ado) and succinylaminoimidazole carboxamide (SAICA) riboside – in the cerebro-spinal fluid, plasma and urine at well above normal levels (normally not detectable in CSF or plasma and only at trace levels in urine). These authors concluded that ADSL is a clinically specific cause of autism.

- In a subsequent paper on eight children with ADSL (Jaeken *et al.* 1988), seven showed significant developmental delay, epilepsy was noted in five, autistic features were seen in three, and growth retardation associated with muscular wasting in two siblings. One girl was only mildly delayed (and was strikingly less developmentally delayed than the others). She also showed lesser biochemical differences.

- In 1989, Maddocks and Reed published results of a urinary test for succinyladenosine, which could discriminate between urine from ADSL autistic cases and urine from normal control samples in a blinded assay (Maddocks and Reed 1989).

- One paper (Edery *et al.* 2003) described three siblings, all of whom had the same homozygous ADSL mutation. Two had presented with autism and the third with psychomotor regression coupled with atrophy of the cerebellar vermis.

- A screen carried out with 119 Canadian autistic patients found no subjects to have a point mutation on the ADSL gene, and on the subset tested there was no evidence of novel mutations on any of the four ADSL exons (Fon *et al.* 2005), suggesting that, although ADSL is a specific cause of autism, it is also a rare one.

What causes ADSL? ADSL is an autosomal recessive clinical disorder of purine synthesis (the production of compounds called purines which are some of the essential building blocks of DNA and key elements in all chromosomes) that has been reported in association with mental retardation and autism (Jaeken and van den Berghe 1984). It was the first known defect of human purine synthesis to be found. The purine synthesis pathway is complex, involving 10 discrete steps in converting 5-phosphoribosylpyrophosphate (PRPP) to inosine monophosphate (IMP). The adenine and guanine nucleotides of DNA are formed from IMP.

ADSL is associated with the build-up of two enzyme substrates in body fluids – succinylaminoimidazole carboxamide (SAICA) riboside and succinyladenosine (S-Ado) (Race *et al.* 2000). The ratio of these two compounds predicts the severity of the condition (Kmoch *et al.* 2000) and is likely to be the key to effective treatment. From the available information to date, it is inferred that levels of SAICA are critical in predicting level of disability, and that higher relative levels of S-Ado are protective (Jaeken *et al.* 1992). Succinyladenosine (S-Ado) is reduced in ADSL and can be tested for reliably (Maddocks and Reed 1989).

A review by Spiegel, Colman and Patterson (2006) addresses many of the issues. At the present time there is a wide variability in the gene mutations, the biochemistry and the behaviour that are taken to characterize ADSL.

What do we know of the genetics? Despite its rarity, a wide variety of both missense and point mutations have been reported in ADSL (Kmoch *et al.* 2000; Marie *et al.* 1999; Stone *et al.* 1992).

Differential diagnosis: ADSL deficiency is one of a number of inborn errors of purine and pyrimidine metabolism (Jurecka 2009), which have been associated with ASD: dihydropyrimidine dehydrogenase deficiency [30], NAPDD [53] and hereditary xanthinuria type II [78].

Treatment and management: Treatment approaches to date have met with limited success. Only one published study, using D-ribose supplementation, has shown positive effects on both purine synthesis and behaviour (Salerno *et al.* 1999). In this single case, improved purine metabolism was paralleled by decreased ataxia, stereotypies and seizure activity, and increased eye contact. A further series of four cases has failed to show similar treatment response (Jurecka *et al.* 2008).

One area that gives some promise for the development of genetic interventions is the identification of Exon skipping as at least one of the mechanisms that can result in ADSL (Hide *et al.* 2001). This type of mechanism has been found to be important in various other conditions discussed here, such as Duchenne muscular dystrophy [33] and velocardiofacial syndrome [76]. In Duchenne, in particular, results to date are extremely promising. (See, for review, Muntoni and Wells 2007.)

Further information and support: There are no specific support groups at present; further information can be obtained from below.

In the USA:
National Organization for Rare Disorders (NORD)
55 Kenosia Avenue
PO Box 1968
Danbury,
CT 06813-1968
Tel.: 203 744-0100
Website: www.rarediseases.org

10

Adrenomyeloneuropathy (AMN)

Gene locus: Xq28

Key ASD reference: Swillen *et al.* 1996

Adrenomyeloneuropathy (AMN) is a mild form of adrenoleukodystrophy (ALD). ALD can take seven primary forms (Moser *et al.* 2000). In AMN, as in the other forms, the problem is an inability to metabolize very long chain fatty acids (VLCFAs), resulting in a build-up in both plasma and body tissues. The essential biochemistry appears the same in AMN and ALD (Lazo *et al.* 1988).

They are peroxisomal disorders, affecting the membranes of peroxisomes – small, subcellular organelles that have been known since the 1950s to be involved, alongside mitochondria, in α- and β-oxidation of fatty acids. (For an overview, see Tabak, Braakman and Distel 1999.) Peroxisomes differ in their role in fatty acid oxidation as they lack a Krebs cycle (the biochemical process that takes place in mitochondria producing adenosime triphosphate – ATP, and can only shorten the chain length of fatty acids where mitochondria can completely oxidize them (Hashimoto 1999).

The gene defect identified is in the gene for a peroxisome membrane transporter protein, not for the enzyme very long chain fatty acyl-CoA synthetase (VLCS). This structural defect, in turn, interferes with the function of VLCS (Smith K.D. *et al.* 1999).

How common is AMN? AMN is a rare condition. It affects approximately one in 50,000 liveborn boys.

It was first reported almost a century ago (von Neusser and Wiesel 1910), but late and incomplete recognition has resulted in less research being carried out than on the more severe or rapidly progressing forms of ALD.

A large number of deletions and point mutations have been reported, with no apparent correlation between these and the nature of the resulting phenotype. Phenotypic variations between identical twins with the same Xq28 gene defect suggest that other factors also affect expression (Rzeski *et al.* 1999).

Most of those affected with AMN are the brothers or other close relatives of patients with classic adrenoleukodystrophy.

Main clinical features: Impaired β-oxidation and build-up of VLCFAs. (See, for reviews, Wanders 1999; Wanders *et al.* 2001.) There is no apparent change in tissue levels of VLCFAs with age.

VLCFAs accumulate in the adrenal glands and the testes, interfering with the function of these tissues (Spurek *et al.* 2004). Primary adrenocortical insufficiency is seen in approximately 70 per cent of cases, and testicular atrophy is common.

There is progressive muscle weakness and weight loss. Problems with bladder function are common, with urgency, frequency or incontinence. Many people with ALD are wheelchair bound by between the ages of five and 15 years. Muscle weakness is greatest in the lower limbs. There is progressive pansensory loss and loss of proprioceptive abilities, affecting balance and coordination. The skin is typically hyperpigmented, so would tend, in fair-skinned families, to be darker than in other family members.

Physical and cognitive prognosis is better without gross MRI evidence of neurological involvement (seen in approximately 50 per cent of those affected). As neuroimaging improves, it may be possible to discriminate more subtle central nervous system changes which help to classify cases and aid in monitoring change (Teriitehau *et al.* 2007).

Brain auditory evoked responses are abnormal in all affected males and approximately 50 per cent of females carrying the condition.

VLCFAs are elevated in approximately 85 per cent of female carriers, who typically have a late onset myelopathy (with onset between the ages of 20 and 55).

This is a non-inflammatory myelopathy that mainly affects the glial cells that support axonal function (Powers *et al.* 2000).

Affective disorders are common in this condition (Walterfang *et al.* 2007), but the extent to which anxious and depressive symptomology is seen does not affect how well the adrenal glands function.

Is there a link between AMN and ASD?

- To date there has been only a single paper that has suggested a possible link between AMN and ASD (Swillen *et al.* 1996). In this paper, a single autistic case in a Dutch residential home was diagnosed with AMN as well as ASD.

Differential diagnosis: Principal differential diagnoses are with amyotrophic lateral sclerosis, and with other peroxisomal disorders which result in VLCFA (very long chain fatty acid) abnormalities, such as infantile Refsum's disease and Zellweger syndrome. AMN is not easily confused with other conditions that have been associated with an ASD diagnosis.

Treatment and management: A variety of strategies have been used or advocated for use with AMD:

1. gene therapy (Unterrainer *et al.* 2000)

2. bone marrow transplantation (Krivit *et al.* 1995; Moser *et al.* 1992)

3. cholesterol-lowering medication (Singh *et al.* 1998)

4. 'Lorenzo's oil' (Moser *et al.* 1992, 2005, 2007)

5. antioxidants (Deon *et al.* 2007; Perlman 2002)

6. steroid replacement – this has been used successfully to address the adrenal problems

7. gene therapy (Cartier and Aubourg 2008; Cartier *et al.* 2009).

Large studies have now been carried out to evaluate the efficacy of, in particular, 'Lorenzo's oil'. At present the results suggest that, once symptomatic, outcome is not improved in the majority (van Geel *et al.* 1999), but that outcome is more likely to be improved where the treatment is started early, while the person is asymptomatic (Moser *et al.* 2005).

The use of allogeneic haemopoetic cell transplants from matched donor cells has been available for some time (Cartier and Aubourg 2008). A paper has described the use of gene therapy in boys whom matched donors could not be found (Cartier *et al.* 2009). This was achieved by modifying the subjects' own CD34+ cells with a lentiviral vector coding for the unaffected gene. This arrested deterioration in two seven-year-old boys with ALD with success equivalent to allogeneic haemopoetic cell transplants. Further research is needed to confirm the safety of this technique, especially as earlier apparent gene therapy successes have had initially unrecognized side effects (Nienhuis, Dunbar and Sorrentino 2006).

Further information and support:

In the UK:
The following (a general group which deals with adrenoleukodystrophy, of which adrenomyeloneuropathy is a subtype) has information on treatments which may be of benefit.

ALD Life
PO Box 43642
London
SE22 0XR
Tel.: 020 8473 7493
E-mail: info@aldlife.org
Website: www.aldlife.org

In the USA:
United Leukodystrophy Foundation
2304 Highland Drive
Sycamore,
Illinois

60178
Tel.: 800-728-5483
Fax: 815-895-2432
E-mail: office@ulf.org
Website: www.ulf.org

The Stop ALD Foundation
500 Jefferson Street, Suite 2000
Houston,
Texas
77002-7371
Tel.: 713-756-3232
Fax: 713-654-8704
E-mail (Chief Science Officer, Dr Rachel Salzman):
rachel@stopald.org
Website: www.stopald.org

11

Angelman syndrome (AS)

aka • 'happy puppet syndrome'/'marionette joyeuse'/'pantin hilare'

Gene loci: Xq28; 15q11–q13

Key ASD references: Bonati *et al.* 2007; Bundey *et al.* 1994; Pelc, Cheron and Dan 2008; Peters *et al.* 2004; Trillingsgaard and Østergaard 2004

Angelman syndrome (AS) is named after Harry Angelman, a British paediatrician from Warrington who first described the condition in 1965 (Angelman 1965). He claimed that his term 'puppet children' came from associating his patients with Giovanni Francesco Caroto's sixteenth-century painting 'Boy with a Puppet'.

AS is a complex disorder that can be caused by four main genetic factors, each with different methods of action and different patterns of presentation. Most people with AS have delayed developmental milestones, severe learning and communication difficulties, epilepsy, motor difficulties and gastrointestinal problems. They often have obsessions with foods and can be prone to becoming overweight.

How common is AS? There is no indication of a skewed sex ratio, or any difference in ethnic distribution. No prevalence studies have been published to date, but the estimated prevalence is thought to be approximately one in 10,000–40,000 (Buckley, Dinno and Weber 1998; Kyllerman 1995; O'Brien and Yule 1996). It could be higher, as milder cases may often go undetected.

Detailed reviews of AS can be found in Dan (2008) and Pelc, Cheron and Dan (2008).

Main clinical features: AS is associated with severe learning disabilities, and concentration difficulties and hyperactive behaviour are common. Most children are nonverbal but some develop a small vocabulary of up to 50 words. Some 80–96 per cent of people with AS develop epilepsy, most commonly with myoclonic, atonic, generalized tonic-clonic or atypical absence seizures (Valente, Koiffmann *et al.* 2006). Epilepsy is often seen before AS diagnosis is made, and seizure control often improves with age. However, those who inherit a maternal deletion of 15q11–q13 are more likely to develop severe myoclonic epilepsy (Minassian *et al.* 1998). UBE3A cases are less likely to be epileptic.

The EEG pattern seen appears to be characteristic of the condition (Viani *et al.* 1995). Valproic acid and clonazepam appear well tolerated and the most effective reported anti-epileptic medications. An EEG is sometimes helpful in clarifying early diagnosis (Galván-Manso *et al.* 2005).

People with AS typically walk stiffly, with their legs wider apart than normal. They normally have fine peripheral muscle tremors, hand flapping and arm jerks.

Delayed early motor and communication milestones are also typical. Feeding problems are also common. In three-quarters of cases early problems are seen in sucking, and consequently there is often poor early weight gain.

Individuals with AS are typically sociable and laugh frequently during social exchanges.

Their head circumference is below average, and they typically have a brachycephalic (broader than normal) head shape. The rear of the skull often appears 'flattened'. Fair hair and blue eyes are more common (being seen in approximately 60 per cent of Caucasian cases). The pale blue irises are a result of abnormal choroidal pigmentation, as noted in several studies (see, for example, Fryburg, Breg and Lindgren 1991). Pale skin is also commonly reported (in 40–75 per cent of cases) (King *et al.* 1993), typically in combination with pale blue eyes (Smith A. *et al.* 1996). A similar hypopigmentation pattern is also seen in Hypomelanosis of Ito [42] and Potocki-Lupski syndrome [60]. Hypopigmentation is the only feature that appears to be restricted to non-deletion cases (Saitoh *et al.* 1994).

A number of minor facial features are also reported – a large protruding jaw (prognathism); widely spaced teeth; a thin upper lip; a wide mouth; tongue protrusion (the proportion of cases in which this is reported lessens markedly with age); and deep-set eyes. Only limited data is available on how commonly these features are found. In one study, tongue protrusion was found in all cases (Buntinx *et al.* 1995). A squint is reported in 40 per cent of cases, and curvature of the spine (scoliosis) in ten per cent.

As in many other ASD syndromes, sleep problems are common, as are fascination with running water and tactile materials such as crinkly paper or plastic, and increased heat sensitivity. Food-related and gastrointestinal problems are commonly reported – particularly obsessions with certain foodstuffs, diet-related obesity and constipation.

A consensus paper on diagnostic criteria for AS has been produced (Williams C.A. *et al.* 2006).

The clinical features of AS persist into adulthood, though some, such as seizures, when present, typically lessen with age (Sandanam *et al.* 1997).

Is there a link between AS and ASD? Two overviews have suggested that there is a low prevalence of ASD in the AS population (Cohen D. *et al.* 2005; Veltman, Craig and Bolton 2005). However, a number of co-morbid cases have been described in the literature, and two studies outlined below do suggest a high prevalence of ASD in people with AS. A number of papers are suggestive of a link:

- The first publication to suggest that AS and ASD could co-occur was by Bundey and colleagues in 1994. They described a single male case with a maternally inherited 15q11-13 duplication, autism, epilepsy and ataxia.

- Williams, Lossie and Driscoll (2001) suggest that AS can mimic other conditions such as ASD.

- Peters *et al.* (2004) used the ADOS-G and ADI-R (Autism Diagnostic Interview – Revised) to characterize autistic symptomology in a sample of 19 children with AS. The found that those with dysregulation of UBE3A were most likely to fulfil criteria for ASD. Forty-two per cent (8/19) fulfilled ADOS-G criteria for ASD.

- Trillingsgaard and Østergaard (2004) assessed 16 children with AS on the ADOS-G (Autism Diagnostic Observation Scale – Generic). Ten fulfilled criteria for ASD and three for PDD-NOS. The authors felt that there was possible overdiagnosis of ASD due to the severity of co-morbid learning disability.

- Bonati *et al.* (2007) also found ASD diagnosis in AS cases to be associated with UBE3A mutation. They reviewed 23 AS cases and found 14 (61 per cent) to meet criteria for co-morbid ASD diagnosis on the ADOS algorithm. ASD diagnosis in this group tends to be associated with lower developmental level, and this is in turn linked to a higher rate of repetitive sensory and motor behaviour and poorer communication skills.

- Pelc, Cheron and Dan (2008) reviewed the studies on autistic behaviour in AS, and concluded that there was a risk of overdiagnosis due to the nature of the social and communication impairments seen in AS.

Differential diagnosis: Several conditions can present with a similar phenotype to Angelman syndrome (Williams, Lossie and Driscoll 2001). Some have been linked to ASD: 22q13 deletion syndrome [7]; mitochondrial conditions such as HEADD syndrome [39]; and in girls, Rett syndrome [63a] can sometimes be confused with Angelman syndrome. In addition, several other conditions present with similar features: cerebral palsy and Mowat-Wilson syndrome (Zweier *et al.* 2005).

What do we know about the genetic mechanisms? The first detailed clinical description of the type of children that Angelman had originally identified appeared in 1967 (Bower and Jeavons 1967). Bower and Jeavons used the term 'happy puppet syndrome' in an attempt to capture the happy disposition and frequent bouts of laughter that seemed typical of many people with AS. The term 'Angelman syndrome' was suggested by Williams and Frias (1982) as a more acceptable alternative.

Several genetic mechanisms can result in AS:

Genetic basis:	*typically reported in:*
• maternal *de novo* deletions at 15q11–q13	about 70 per cent of cases
• paternal isodisomy of 15q11–q13	about 2 per cent of cases
• imprinting defects at 15q11–q13	about 3 per cent of cases
• mutations in the ubiquitin-protein ligase gene (UBE3A) at Xq28	about 8–25 per cent of cases

These mechanisms are complex and involve a number of discrete epigenetic factors (Lalande and Calciano 2007).

The association with 15q11–q13 found in three-quarters of all cases has been well described in a number of studies (for example Thomas, Roberts and Browne 2003; for discussion of the link with UBE3A, see Kishino, Lalande and Wagstaff 1997).

The majority of AS cases result from *de novo* deletions at 15q11–q13 and these cases are expected to have a low risk of recurrence. A low recurrence risk is also seen in paternal isodisomy cases. In contrast, the recurrence risk arising from both imprinting defects and mutations of UBE3A can be as high as 50 per cent.

An interesting fact is that a gene deletion at 15q11–q13 that results in AS when inherited from the mother can cause a different condition, Prader-Willi syndrome (PWS) [61], when inherited from the father (Knoll *et al.* 1989). This is typically called a 'parent-of-origin' effect, known as genomic imprinting. It seems, however, that the specific genes sufficient for the two conditions are slightly different but lie side-by-side, and both genes are often affected in either condition (Jiang *et al.* 1998).

A number of patients with a diagnosis of AS based on their clinical and behavioural phenotype have been shown to have a MeCP2 deletion on subsequent genetic testing. This seems to be rare (Hitchins *et al.* 2004). Where it does occur, this may be because the MeCP2 difference found in Rett syndrome interferes with UBE3A expression, a phenomenon known as an imprinting defect (Makedonski *et al.* 2005).

More detailed genetic information: A number of genetic anomalies, single gene deletions and symptom complexes can present as similar to AS, especially in the early stages, including several covered elsewhere in this volume:

Table B11: Conditions that can have similar early presentations to Angelman syndrome

•	Atypical Angelman syndrome	[11]
•	CATCH 22	[18]
•	CHARGE syndrome	[20]
•	DiGeorge syndrome I	[29a]
•	DiGeorge syndrome II	[29b]
•	Fragile-X syndrome	[35]
•	Prader-Willi syndrome	[61]
•	Ring chromosome 22	
•	Smith-Magenis syndrome	[67]
•	Velocardiofacial syndrome	[76]
•	Williams syndrome	[77]

Several case reports have described families with several affected children, suggesting a genetic basis to AS (Baraitser *et al.* 1987; Robb *et al.* 1989).

One review (Jedele 2007) has pointed to the clinical overlap between the features of AS and Rett syndrome resulting from the effects of MeCP2 on the UBE3A expression.

Maternal 15q deletions and genomic imprinting: Magenis *et al.* (1988) proposed that patients with AS and PWS share an identical deletion on chromosome 15q11. They did suggest that the more severe learning and communication difficulties typically seen in AS were likely to be due to larger deletions. More recent work has shown that most of the genes responsible for AS and PWS are overlapping in the same region of 15q11–q13, but are different both in position and mode of action (Jiang *et al.* 1998; Saitoh *et al.* 1997).

A high-resolution cytogenetic study of ten AS children and of their parents in nine of the cases, and of seven children with PWS (Magenis *et al.* 1990), found that the same proximal band, 15q11.2, was deleted in both disorders. In AS, the deletion tended to be larger, though of variable size, including q12 and part of q13.

Defects in the imprinting centre: Two reported families have provided clear evidence of genomic imprinting. In the first family (Greenstein 1990), both PWS and AS were present, with maternal transmission of AS and paternal transmission of PWS. In the second family (Hulten *et al.* 1991), with two cases of PWS and one of AS, again females passed on AS while males passed on PWS.

Defects in a small (6kb) area of chromosome 15 are capable of causing AS, but are insufficient to cause PWS (Saitoh *et al.* 1997).

Methylation abnormalities consistent with imprinting defects have been reported in several studies (for example, Beuten *et al.* 1996; Reis *et al.* 1994)

In an interesting pair of papers (Wagstaff *et al.* 1992; Wagstaff, Shugart and Lalande 1993), the gene for AS was transmitted from a grandfather through his son to three sisters who in turn had four children with AS, indicating that maternal transmission was necessary for expression. A sister of the grandfather had transmitted the same genotype to four children, all of whom were phenotypically normal. This finding is consistent with the view that the effects of the imprinting centre involved in AS and PWS depend for their expression on the sex of the grandparent transmitting the difference (Buiting *et al.* 1995). This suggestion was borne out by further work suggesting a grandparent-of-origin effect in a further series of cases where an imprinting basis to AS was found (Buiting *et al.* 1998).

Possible imprinting defects associated with male infertility treatment: A number of AS cases have been linked to a particular form of treatment for infertility called intracytoplasmic sperm injection (ICSI) (Sanchez-Albisua *et al.* 2007). This was thought to be a specific risk factor when originally reported, but there now appears to be a more general link to conception in subfertility (Ludwig *et al.* 2005).

Paternal uniparental disomy: In approximately two per cent of cases of AS, both copies of 15q11–q13 come from the father (Malcolm *et al.* 1991). The ways in which such paternal uniparental isodisomy can arise are reviewed in Engel (1993). Males who carry the 15q11–q13 gene do not normally father children with ASD.

Mutations in the UBE3A gene: Mutations of UBE3A were first noted as a cause of AS in 1997 (Matsuura *et al.* 1997).

In one series (Lossie *et al.* 2001), seven out of 104 with AS had UBE3A mutations. They tended to be less severely affected, were taller and heavier than others with AS, and were less likely to require anti-epileptic medication.

Two first cousins have been reported with the same UBE3A frameshift mutations but with discordant phenotypes – one with AS, the other with severe asymmetric motor problems (Molfetta *et al.* 2004), suggesting possible cell mosaicism.

Genotype–phenotype associations: Those with 15q11–q13 deletions appear to be more severely affected than non-deletion forms (AS due to parental isodisomy; imprinting defects and UBE3A mutations; Moncla *et al.* 1999).

A series of seven patients has been reported (Gillessen-Kaesbach *et al.* 1999) with mild learning disability, obesity and hypotonia but none of the other typical characteristics of AS. Methylation studies of two AS-specific sites – SNRPN and D15S63 – were consistent with AS, but chromosome analyses were routinely normal, suggesting that they had a possible mosaicism or partial imprinting defect.

In a small study comparing 21 deletion with four uniparental isodisomy cases, those with uniparental isodisomy were diagnosed later and developed epilepsy later, also tending to walk earlier and have better language development (Fridman *et al.* 2000).

A further study compared presentation in 58 AS patients of whom nine had a uniparental isodisomy (Varela *et al.* 2004). Again uniparental isodisomy was associated with lower severity of associated difficulties – swallowing problems, hypotonia seizures and microcephaly were all less common; speech was more common; on average they were more able; and they were typically diagnosed several years later than other cases.

At the present time, there is some merit in subclassifying AS dependent on the genetic basis. However, the numbers analysed are small and the findings need to be treated as preliminary.

Treatment and management: At the time of writing, there is no specific treatment for Angelman syndrome. The specific GABA receptor abnormalities reported may lead to development of specific targeted medications for the seizure problems in Angelman syndrome (Meldrum and Rogawski 2007).

As there is a specific deletion in the GABA-A receptor region linked to the presence of seizure activity in Angelman syndrome (Saitoh *et al.* 1992), and this has been implicated in the excitatory–inhibitory balance in epilepsy (Fritschy 2008), it seems possible that medications which have a specific effect on GABA-A function, such as stiripentol, could be of potential benefit. Stiripentol has not been licensed in Europe or the USA for this purpose but is used with a much wider range of seizure conditions in Asia (see discussion of zonizamide in Shorvon 2005).

Many people with Angelman syndrome have epilepsy that is poorly controlled on existing medications. In one series of 45 AS cases, Valente *et al.* (2006a) reported four who had been poorly controlled on drug therapies, but whose epilepsy responded well to ketogenic diet. (Information on a study of ketogenic diet sponsored by the Angelman Syndrome Foundation can be found at www.angelman.org. For further discussion of ketogenic diets, see Aitken 2009. For one family's account of their child with AS who responded to ketogenic diet, see www.ourangeltyler.com.) A survey of 150 UK families found only one using ketogenic diet, but in this case there was said to be a good response with improved seizure control (Ruggieri and McShane 1998). Currently the Massachusetts General Hospital Pediatric Epilepsy Program is conducting a study of low glycaemic index (GI) diets in AS and their effect on seizure control (see 'Further information and support' below).

There is some evidence of beneficial effects of melatonin for the sleep problems seen in AS (Braam *et al.* 2008). Melatonin supplements can reduce the time taken getting to sleep, lengthen time slept, and reduce night wakening. To date there has been no work to investigate whether there is an abnormal pattern of melatonin production in AS (as has been reported in a number of other conditions linked to ASD).

Early work to maximize communication skills is important, given the progressive nature of the communication difficulties in many cases. Simple forms of communication using alternative and augmentative systems should be emphasized, given that the likely level of adult communication will be limited.

Other aspects of care and management should be dealt with on a case-by-case basis depending on clinical presentation.

Further information and support: A useful summary and resource listing can be found in Randi Hagerman's excellent if slightly dated little book, *Neurodevelopmental Disorders: Diagnosis and Treatment* (Oxford University Press, 1999).

International Angelman Syndrome Organization
Website: www.asclepius.com

In Australia:
Angelman Syndrome Association
PO Box 554
Sutherland
NSW 2232
Website: www.angelmansyndrome.org/home.html

In Canada:
Canadian Angelman Syndrome Society
PO Box 37
Priddis,
Alberta,
T0L 1W0
Tel.: 403-931-2415
Fax: 403-931-4237
E-mail: info@AngelmanCanada.org
Website: www.angelmancanada.org

In France:
Association Francophone du Syndrome d'Angelman
Website: www.angelman-afsa.org

In Germany:
Angelman e.V.
Am Gänsrain 6
97892 Kreuzwertheim
Tel.: 09342 858 841
Fax: 09342 914 534
E-mail: as-info@angelman.de
Website: www.angelman.de/

In Italy:
Organizzazione Sindrome di Angelman
via Bressa n° 8–31100
Treviso
Tel.: 0422 421643
Fax: 0422 422444
E-mail: orsa@sindromediangelman.org
Website: www.sindromediangelman.org/it/contatti.htm

In the UK:
Angelman Syndrome Support Education and Research Trust
ASSERT
PO Box 4962
Nuneaton
CV11 9FD
Tel.: 0300 999 01 02
Website: www.angelmanuk.org

In the USA:
Angelman Syndrome Foundation
4255 Westbrook Drive
Suite 219
Aurora,
IL 60504
Tel.: 800-432-6435 or 630-978-4245
Fax: 630-978-7408
Website: www.angelman.org/

12

Apert syndrome

Gene locus: 10q26

Key ASD reference: Morey-Canellas, Sivagamasundari and Barton 2003

Apert syndrome is a rare condition characterized by an unusual skull shape and dental abnormalities that increase the complexity of dental management (Hohoff *et al.* 2007).

The first clinical description of the skull shape together with abnormal development of the hands and feet was published in France in 1906 (Apert 1906).

It is one of a group of syndromes known as 'craniosynostoses' (for a review, see Cohen 1977). There is a clinical overlap, in terms of the skull abnormalities seen, with several other conditions. To date Apert syndrome is the only craniosynostosis that has been linked to ASD.

Based on a large series of cases, cardiovascular and genitourinary abnormalities are common and should be screened for, while gastrointestinal anomalies are less common (Cohen and Kreiborg 1993).

Cases are typically sporadic (there is no family association). However, familial inheritance has been reported in two families where there was an affected mother and daughter (Roberts and Hall 1971; Weech 1927); in one with an affected mother and son (Van den Bosch, cited in Blank 1960); one with an affected father and daughter (Rollnick 1988); and one with two affected sisters (Allanson 1987).

How common is Apert syndrome? The reported prevalence is around one in 65,000–100,000. It appears to be as common in boys as in girls, to be most prevalent in Asiatic families, and to be associated with advanced paternal age: in one study, almost 50 per cent of fathers were over 35 at the time of the affected child's birth (Tolarova *et al.* 1997). The likelihood of FGFR2 mutations at 10q26 in sperm increases with age (Glaser *et al.* 2003), and *de novo* mutations appear to be entirely paternal in origin (Moloney *et al.* 1996).

The literature is varied on the developmental level in Apert syndrome. In one early series of cases, 14/29 cases were of normal or borderline normal IQ, while the others had IQs of 70 or below (Patton *et al.* 1988). Better psychosocial and cognitive outcome seems to be associated with early cranial surgery to decompress the skull (Reiner *et al.* 1996).

Main clinical features: Physically Apert syndrome is a congenital disorder of growth characterized primarily by early closure of skull sutures and abnormal development of the skull that increases with age (Schauerte and St-Aubin 1966). This is coupled with differences in the development of the face, the hands and the feet. In typical cases, a single fingernail joins across the second, third and fourth fingers. Additional fingers and toes have been reported in a small number of cases (Mantilla-Capacho *et al.* 2005). All of these features vary widely in their presentation.

Cases are typically *de novo* and sporadic. However, autosomal dominant inheritance has also been reported (Mantilla-Capacho *et al.* 2005).

The skin is typically moist, and becomes oily at adolescence with a tendency to acne (Cohen and Kreiborg 1993, 1995).

A variety of differences have been reported on brain imaging (Quintero-Rivera *et al.* 2006), and raised cerebro-spinal fluid pressure is common (Rich, Cox and Hayward 2003).

Mutations in the FGFR2 gene at 10q26 have been reported in over 98 per cent of cases with the Apert phenotype, with two exon 7 mutations accounting for virtually all cases. A small proportion of individuals with the FGFR2 genotype do not show an Apert's physical phenotype (Lajeunie *et al.* 1999).

Is there a link between Apert syndrome and ASD?

- There is only a single case reported to date with both Apert syndrome and ASD. Morey-Canellas, Sivagamasundari and Barton (2003) have described a seven-year-old boy with Apert syndrome, developmental delay and ASD.

Differential diagnosis: Several other conditions characterized by craniosynostosis, midface hypoplasia and syndactyly need to be considered: Crouzon syndrome (Glaser *et al.* 2000); Jackson-Weiss syndrome (Jackson *et al.* 1976); and Pfeiffer syndrome (Cohen 1973, 1977).

Treatment and management: To date, no Apert-specific treatment strategies are known. Early surgery to decompress the skull is associated with better cognitive and psychosocial outcomes, and specialist dental care is usually required. Cosmetic surgery can also be of benefit in altering facial features. The high rate of ventricular enlargement could also provide a focus for earlier identification and treatment.

Summary: Apert syndrome is a genetic disorder caused by defects in the FGFR2 gene at 10q26. It results in abnormal skull growth and fusion of the fingers and toes.

The reported link to autistic spectrum disorder is consistent with the evidence of increased head growth in ASD (Maimburg and Vaeth 2006). The structural brain studies report abnormalities of the cerebellum and limbic system, both areas implicated in ASD pathogenesis (Raymond, Bauman and Kemper 1996; Schumann and Amaral 2006).

Further information and support:

Specific support group in Sweden:
Apertföreningen
c/o Barnhabiliteringen Näckrosen
631 88 Eskilstuna

See also http://members.tripod.com for a range of useful web links.
Parental account: McDermott, J. (2000) *Babyface: A Story of Heart and Bones.* Bethesda: Woodbine House.

13

ARX gene mutations

Gene locus: Xp22.3–p22.1.1

Key ASD references: Kato *et al.* 2004; Sherr 2003; Strømme *et al.* 2002c; Turner *et al.* 2002

How common is ARX? ARX is a well-documented but rare cause of autism in learning-disabled populations. ARX stands for the Aristaless-related homeobox gene, important in the development of the brain. Chaste *et al.* (2007) found no cases of ARX mutation in a group of 226 male patients with autism and learning disability. ARX screening is warranted, however, in autistic individuals with severe learning disability on the basis of the range of disorders that have now been documented in such individuals with Xp22.3–p22.1.1 mutations.

A Danish study screened 682 males with learning difficulties, and found only seven with ARX mutations (Grønskov *et al.* 2004), concluding that it was a rare cause of learning disability. A small number of autistic individuals were also examined; none were found to have ARX mutations. ARX mutation was also found in 1/188 normal male controls.

How ARX mutations affect development, through transcription repression, is just beginning to be understood (McKenzie *et al.* 2007). This is through the binding of the ARX protein to a molecule called TLE.

Main clinical features: The clinical spectrum seen with ARX mutations is broad. This isn't too surprising, given the large number of reported mutations. ARX mutations have been implicated in a range of disorders with severe mental retardation, including West syndrome, with variable phenotypes that can include lissencephaly, hand dystonia, epilepsy, autism and abnormalities of the genitals.

An X-linked condition with the combination of mild to moderate learning disability and dystonic hand movements has been reported in association with ARX mutation. This has sometimes been called Partington syndrome after the principal author of the first paper to describe it (Partington *et al.* 1988). Subsequent studies have indicated a wide variation in clinical presentation with the same mutation (Partington *et al.* 2004). In one study of 18 individuals with the same ARX defect, all had learning disability but only two-thirds had hand dystonia and one third epileptiform EEGs, so that the majority could be said to have Partington syndrome but a third could not (Szczaluba *et al.* 2006).

The combined prevalence of ARX mutations warrants systematic screening in non-syndromic X-linked learning disability syndromes (Poirier *et al.* 2006). To date, some 59 ARX mutations have been reported in seven different X-linked clinical disorders associated with learning disability (for an overview, see Gecz, Cloosterman and Partington 2006).

ARX mutations have been reported in a subgroup of West syndrome (a condition with infantile spasms, an unusual EEG pattern – hypsarrythmia – and progressive learning disability; Scheffer *et al.* 2002), in Ohtahara syndrome (another early onset seizure disorder with an unusual EEG pattern of 'burst-suppression'; Kato *et al.* 2007) and in a syndrome of infantile spasms, subclinical seizures and complex movements (Poirier *et al.* 2008).

As cases accumulate, clear associations between specific ARX defects and specific clinical and endophenotypes are being found (see Kato *et al.* 2004). Clearly interference with the ARX homeobox can have wide effects across a range of characteristics. (The term for this is 'pleiotropy'.)

Generally, larger deletions, frameshifts, nonsense mutations and splice site mutations in exons 1–4 caused X-linked lissencephaly, together with anomalous genitalia (XLAG; Kitamura *et al.* 2002; Uyanik *et al.* 2003), or hydranencephaly (a rare condition with normal development of the skull but where the skull is largely filled with cerebrospinal fluid), also with abnormal genitalia (Kato *et al.* 2004). Nonconservative missense mutations within the homeobox caused less severe XLAG, whereas conservative substitution in the homeodomain caused agenesis of the corpus callosum with abnormal genitalia (Proud, Levine and Carpenter 1992).

Both syndromic and non-syndromic mental retardation can result from defects in the same ARX gene (Frints *et al.* 2002).

One XLAG case has been reported with significant gastrointestinal involvement with severe watery diarrhoea which responded to a medication – octreotide – that reduces intestinal secretion (Nanba, Oka and Ohno 2007). There is no evidence at present on the prevalence of such symptoms in other types of ARX presentation.

Is there a link between ARX and ASD?

- The first paper to suggest a link between ARX mutations and ASD was Strømme *et al.* (2002c). This paper presented data on ARX screening in 50 learning-disabled cases. Four of those screened had co-morbid autism, all with the 428–451 duplication mutation.

- Kato *et al.* (2004) also note the association between ASD and a mild ARX mutation phenotype, but in their paper do not go into any detail concerning this association.

Two studies have explicitly looked for but failed to find ARX autistic cases:

- Grønskov *et al.* (2004) established a general population rate of 1/188 for ARX mutations, but failed to find evidence of ARX defects in a small number of autistic cases examined.

- Chaste *et al.* (2007) screened 226 people with ASD and failed to find evidence of ARX mutations across this group.

Strømme *et al.* (2002b) identified the ARX gene, and its association with X-linked mental retardation and epilepsy. Using Northern blotting and expressed sequence tag (EST) analyses, their work indicates that ARX is expressed predominantly in foetal and adult brain and skeletal muscle. In animals, the same group identified ARX protein as important in various types of nerve cells in the cortex and in axonal guidance (Strømme *et al.* 2002b).

ARX is transmitted as an X-linked recessive condition, so female carriers are clinically unaffected.

Differential diagnosis: There is wide variation within the ARX mutation group with a number of clinical disorders being defined, but the genotype–phenotype variation is wide, and as screening studies are being conducted, unaffected ARX carrier males are being identified (Grønskov *et al.* 2004). The presence of lissencephaly with ambiguous development of the genitalia coupled with hand dystonia is fairly unambiguously related to ARX mutation. However, the range of more mildly presenting phenotypes – typically with learning disability but occasionally without, often with seizure activity or abnormalities on EEG – would suggest that this is a potential diagnosis in a wider range of ASD cases. Dysarthria in a quarter of cases, and long, triangular facial features, have been remarked upon (Szczaluba *et al.* 2006).

Treatment and management: There are few specific treatments that have been investigated for the management of ARX. In some single case reports, patients have proved responsive to symptomatic treatments such as treatment of gastrointestinal symptoms with octreotide (Nanba, Oka and Ohno 2007).

Treatment at present needs to be focused on the presenting clinical features – appropriate physiotherapy and occupational therapy for motor control issues if present;

treatment for seizures depending on nature and extent; and assessment and treatment of gastrointestinal features.

At the present time there is no specific approach to treatment and management.

The characterization of the condition as affecting primarily GABAergic neuronal systems suggests that treatments targeting glutamate pathways may hold some promise, as has been the case in fragile-X where the mGluR5 receptor is affected.

Further information and support: There is no specific ARX support group at the time of writing.

In the UK:
Unique
Rare Chromosome Disorder Support Group
PO Box 2189
Surrey
CR3 5GN
E-mail: info@rarechromo.org
Telephone helpline: 01883 330766
Website: www.rarechromo.org

In the USA:
Chromosome Deletion Outreach, Inc.
PO Box 724
Boca Raton,
FL 33429-0724
Family helpline 561-395-4252
E-mail: info@chromodisorder.org
Website: www.chromodisorder.org

14

Autism secondary to autoimmune lymphoproliferative syndrome (ALPS)

aka
- Canale-Smith syndrome
- Evans syndrome
- autoimmune haemolytic anaemia
- idiopathic thrombocytopenia
- Coombs-positive haemolytic anaemia
- immune thrombocytopenia

Gene locus: 10q24.1

Key ASD reference: Shenoy, Arnold and Chatila 2000

ALPS is a condition in which cells produced by the immune system accumulate in the body, with resulting enlargement of the lymph nodes and the spleen. These are secondary problems with autoimmune damage to other organ systems, including anaemia due to the destruction of red blood cells.

How common is ALPS? The prevalence of ALPS is currently not established. The condition is found in both sexes and appears equally common across racial and ethnic groups.

The limited data available indicate that the condition is compatible with survival well into adult life (Drappa *et al.* 1996).

Main clinical features: ALPS is a pleiotropic condition, whose clinical presentation can vary (Straus, Lenardo and Puck 1997). The earliest clinical description of ALPS (Canale and Smith 1967) suggested a common clinical presentation in childhood with enlargement of the lymph glands and the spleen, autoimmune haemolytic anaemia and thrombocytopenia. Later series (for example Straus, Lenardo and Puck 1997) have suggested greater clinical variability.

Two reviews summarize the features and genetics of the condition (Bleesing, Johnson and Zhang 2007; Le Deist 2004).

The most common presenting features, which are usually apparent by the age of five, are:

- an enlarged spleen and liver (often referred to as 'hepatospenomegaly')
- enlarged lymph nodes, especially in the neck and under the arms
- urticarial skin rashes
- frequent nosebleeds and bruising, with lengthened clotting time for cuts and abrasions
- slow wound healing
- haemolytic anaemia.

ALPS interferes with the production of a specific lymphoid protein called Fas. Fas is involved in programmed cell death (also called apoptosis), the main process by which embryonic development takes place, and in this case leads specifically to a build-up of immune system T-cells.

Is there a link between ALPS and ASD?

- To date a single case has been reported. In the *Journal of Pediatrics* in 2000, Shenoy and colleagues reported on a child who had been developmentally normal but who regressed, losing speech, gestures and eye contact at around 18 months, coincident with development of lymphoproliferative symptoms and haemolytic anaemia (Shenoy, Arnold and Chatila 2000).

He had regular speech and occupational therapy over the following 15 months but continued to deteriorate.

At 33 months, oral treatment with prednisone dramatically improved physical symptoms: both chronic diarrhoea and a skin rash improved. The size of his enlarged spleen and lymph nodes also reduced. There was also a gradual improvement in autistic symptomology, and he had built up a vocabulary of over 200 spoken words after one year of steroid therapy.

Differential diagnosis: The differential diagnosis of ALPS from other ASDs is based on the presence of lymphatic, spleen and haematologic abnormalities. As regressive onset ASD symptomology coupled with gastrointestinal problems is being reported more frequently, gastrointestinal function should be explored in ALPS cases (Werner and Dawson 2006).

Differential diagnosis of ALPS from other immunodeficiency disorders would be from the following:

Table B14: ALPS phenocopies

- Common variable immunodeficiency disease (CVID) (Piqueras *et al.* 2003) – although features of both the Goldenhar and cri du chat syndromes can be seen in the same individuals with caspase-8 mutations (Chun *et al.* 2002)
- Hyper IgM (HIGM) syndrome
- X-linked lymphoproliferative syndrome (XLP)
- Wiskott-Aldrich syndrome (WAS)
- B-cell or T-cell lymphoma

Treatment and management: At present there is no treatment that can cure ALPS, except for bone-marrow transplantation (Kahwash *et al.* 2007). Other aspects of treatment are complex, primarily involving management of the immune and haematologic features. There are some helpful reviews of treatment and prognosis (see Bleesing 2003; Bleesing, Johnson and Zhang 2007).

Further information and support:

In the UK:
The PISCES (People in Search of a Cure for Evans Syndrome) Trust
11 Burrough Close
Oakwood
Warrington
Cheshire
WA3 6QF

Tel./fax: 01925 488825
E-mail: piscestrust@hotmail.com

15

Bannayan-Riley-Ruvalcaba syndrome (BRRS)

aka • Bannayan-Zonana syndrome (BZS)

- macrocephaly, with multiple lipomas and haemangiomata
- macrocephaly with pseudopapilloedema and multiple haemangiomata
- Riley-Smith syndrome
- Ruvalcaba-Myhre-Smith syndrome (RMSS)
- PTEN MATCHS (phosphatase and tensin homologue – Macrocephaly, Autosomal dominant, Thyroid disease, Cancer, Hamartomata and Skin abnormalities)
- PTEN hamartoma tumour syndrome (PHTS)

Gene locus: 10q23.31

Key ASD references: Boccone *et al.* 2006; Butler *et al.* 2005; Lynch N.E. *et al.* 2009

The term 'Bannayan-Riley-Ruvalcaba syndrome' was suggested by Michael Cohen (1990). BRRS is a PTEN-related form of macrocephaly. Differences in PTEN are common in those who have an ASD and a large head (Vaccarino and Smith 2009).

PTEN is known as a tumour-suppressor gene, and defects in this gene are associated with vascular malformations and an increased risk of tumour formation. Useful discussions of the functions of PTEN can be found in Waite and Eng (2002), and Eng (2003).

The earliest clear descriptions of cases with the triad of impairments (macrocephaly, lipomatosis and vascular malformations) now classified as BRRS were made at autopsy in a single paediatric case by George Bannayan at Johns Hopkins Hospital in Baltimore in 1971. Shortly after, Zonana, Davis and Rimoin (1975) and Zonana, Rimoin and Davis (1976) described the same triad of features in a father and two sons.

How common is BRRS? Over 50 cases have been described in the clinical literature, but no true prevalence studies have been carried out. Prevalence has been estimated at one in 200,000 (Nelen *et al.* 1999).

A number of other conditions have overlapping clinical features. These include Proteus syndrome, Klippel-Trenaunay syndrome (Jacob *et al.* 1998), Cowden syndrome (Lachlan *et al.* 2007) and macrocephaly/autism syndrome. Some of the research to date suggests that Cowden syndrome and BRRS may, essentially, be slightly different manifestations of the same genotype (Marsh *et al.* 1999).

Main clinical features: BRRS is an overgrowth syndrome with associated macrocephaly, lipomas and vascular malformations. The typical presentation is early in life with macrocephaly, developmental delay, hypotonia and slower early milestones. Growths such as intestinal polyps and subcutaneous and visceral lipomas are common, as are vascular malformations. The skin is often affected with pigmented macules, often referred to as café-au-lait spots, particularly on the penis.

More complex clinical presentations in association with PTEN mutations are reported in the clinical literature. For example, one of the cases reported by Zigman *et al.* (1997) had a complex heart defect in addition to the characteristic BRRS phenotype and bilateral clubfoot.

Cases have been reported where the phenotype has no apparent genetic basis (Carethers *et al.* 1998), or a different anomaly such as 19q translocation has been found (Israel *et al.* 1991).

Is there a link between BRRS and ASD?

• Butler and colleagues looked at a group of 18 autistic subjects aged 3–18 (15 males and three females), all with macrocephaly. Three of the males were found to have the PTEN mutations seen in BRRS.

• A Sardinian case has been reported (Boccone *et al.* 2006) with the classic physical features of BRRS together with autism and reactive ileo-colonic nodular lymphoid nodular hyperplasia.

• In a series of six BRRS cases (Lynch N.E. *et al.* 2009), two were reported to have autistic features and one had a diagnosis of Asperger's syndrome. In all three cases, the mother also carried the PTEN mutation.

So, although further information is required, the limited studies to date suggest that BRRS is important to investigate in ASD cases with macrocephaly.

Differential diagnosis: The constellation of features overlaps with a number of other disorders, and cases have been reported variously. PTEN mutations are seen in a number of conditions that have been linked to ASD, including BRRS [15], BCNS [16], Cowden syndrome [26] and Proteus syndrome [62]. Sotos syndrome was reported in two cases with macrocephaly, intestinal polyps, and pigmented macules on the penis (Ruvalcaba, Myhre and Smith 1980).

Treatment and management: Regular monitoring of both vascular abnormalities and growth formation is advisable (Tan *et al.* 2007). In addition, annual screening has been recommended from infancy for intestinal hamartomas (Hendriks *et al.* 2003).

Low muscle carnitine levels are common and appear to respond to supplementation in many cases. In one study 27 cases from 17 families showed increased muscle lipid content and typical clinical features were seen in all of the clinical cases studied (11) and in the affected relatives (4) tested (Powell, Budden and Buist 1993); they also had significantly lowered muscle carnitine levels. An L-carnitine supplement was given to all 27 cases and clinical benefit was noted in 17 (63 per cent).

Further information and support:

In the USA:
Cowden's Syndrome and Bannayan-Riley-Ruvalcaba Syndrome Foundation
1394 Wedgewood Drive
Salne
MI 48176
Tel.: 734-944-8313

National Organization for Rare Disorders (NORD)
55 Kenosia Avenue
PO Box 1968

Danbury,
CT 06813-1968
Tel.: 203-744-0100
Tollfree: 800-999-6673 (voicemail only)
TDD Number: 203-797-9590
Fax: 203-798-2291
E-mail: orphan@rarediseases.org
Website: www.rarediseases.org/info/contact.html

16

Basal cell naevus syndrome (BCNS)

aka
- naevoid basal cell carcinoma syndrome
- Gorlin syndrome
- Gorlin-Goltz syndrome
- *epithéliomatose multiple généralisée*
- fifth phakomatosis
- hereditary cutaneomandibular polyoncosis
- multiple basalioma syndrome

Gene locus: 9q22.3

Key ASD reference: Swillen *et al.* 1996

Naevoid basal cell carcinoma syndrome is an autosomal dominant condition. It is known as a phacomatosis (Nowak 2007) – this is a condition with abnormal tissue growth, particularly in the nervous system, together with characteristically pigmented birthmarks.

In basal cell naevus syndrome (BCNS), multiple jaw keratocysts develop typically between ages 10 and 20, and/or basal cell carcinomas between 20 and 30 years of age. In approximately two-thirds of cases, there is a recognizable physical phenotype with macrocephaly, bossing of the forehead, facial milia and coarse facial features.

How common is basal cell naevus syndrome? Prevalence estimates vary. A screening study in the UK gave a figure of one in 57,000 (Evans, Birch and Orton 1991). However, the rate is likely to be higher still, as milder cases are likely to have been missed.

Main clinical features: Wide-set eyes, a broad nasal bridge, a prominent forehead and a protruding chin are common features, together with the basal cell naevi that give the condition its name.

Diagnosis is currently based on having two major diagnostic criteria or one major and three minor criteria (Evans *et al.* 1993). Genetic screening is highlighting a broader phenotype than is identified on these features alone.

Major criteria: unusual skull calcification; jaw keratocysts; small pits on the palms or soles of the feet showing up as small white/pink areas; multiple basal cell carcinomas (small areas of pink, orange or brownish skin); having an affected first-degree relative (parent, brother or sister).

Minor criteria: childhood primitive neuroectodermal tumour (PNET) (aka medulloblastoma); cysts of the lymphatic system, the mesentery or the pleura; having a large head (head circumference above the 97th centile); cleft lip or palate; abnormal spinal vertebrae; having extra fingers; fibromas of the ovary or heart; eye abnormalities (including abnormal retinal pigmentation and cataract).

Diagnosis of BCNS is typically made at around two years of age.

The large head size seen in most cases is often noted first, and many babies with BCNS are born by caesarean section because of pelvic disparity.

PNETs are usually detected at around two years of age, and to respond favourably to surgical excision (Amlashi *et al.* 2003).

Jaw keratocysts usually present in adolescence as painless swellings, but can lead to abnormal dentition if left unattended.

Although basal cell naevi provide the label for this condition, one in ten BCNS cases does not have any such lesions. Their occurrence is partly dependent on skin type. Pale skin which burns easily in sunlight seems particularly susceptible.

There is normal life expectency in most cases.

Children who present with medulloblastoma (a type of malignant brain tumour which originates in the cerebellum or posterior fossa), particularly in the preschool years, need to be investigated for BCNS, as radiotherapy used in the management of the tumour can cause the additional problem of accelerating the growth of basal cell carcinomas.

The mean age for presentation of medulloblastoma in the population is around seven years, but in BCNS it is much earlier, typically around three years. This suggests that the intact PTCH gene acts as a tumour suppressor (Cowan *et al.* 1997). A PTCH gene defect at 9q22.3 can be identified in about 70 per cent of BCNS cases that conform to current clinical criteria.

Typically, a series of X-rays are key to diagnosis (due to the abnormalities often seen in the skull, jaw, vertebrae and ribs). Repeat X-rays are not advisable, as people with BCNS seem particularly susceptible to effects from radiation, with possible development of multiple basal cell carcinomas (Evans, Birch and Orton 1991).

Is there a link between BCNS and ASD? To date few cases of BCNS in association with ASD have been reported and none has been described in detail (see Swillen 1996). The overlap with other conditions which are more strongly linked to ASD (see Differential Diagnosis below), and the clinical reports of cases, together with the specific problems associated with this condition, make it an important consideration in cases which have BCNS clinical features.

Differential diagnosis: In a child presenting with autistic behaviour and a large head, the principal differential diagnoses will be Bannayan-Riley-Ruvalcaba syndrome [15], Cole-Hughes macrocephaly syndrome [24], Cowden syndrome [26], Proteus syndrome [62] and Sotos syndrome [68]. A rarer possibility would be Orstavik 1997 syndrome [56].

Arsenic toxicity is a separate factor that can result in basal cell carcinoma through exposure.

Where the differential diagnosis is based on the skin anomalies, BCNS needs to be discriminated from various dermal conditions, primarily from Bazex syndrome, in which there is also basal cell carcinoma, and where the backs of the hands tend to be particularly badly affected.

As BCNS is a disorder with significant risk of complications, and only arises *de novo* in 20–30 per cent of cases, screening of at-risk relatives is important. Where a parent is also affected, there will be a 50 per cent risk that siblings and offspring of the affected individual will also be affected.

Treatment and management: Many of the most important considerations are preventative, such as minimizing exposure to X-rays and protecting against excessive exposure to sunlight.

BCNS affects multiple organ systems and requires ongoing monitoring and care by specialists in several areas, such as orthopaedics, ophthalmology, cardiology, dentistry and plastic surgery, depending on the nature and extent of the clinical presentation. Head growth and heart function should be closely monitored from early in life.

Both keratocysts and basal cell carcinomas should be treated promptly when present. Current best practice is that ovarian fibromas that require surgical excision should be treated leaving as much ovarian tissue *in situ* as possible (Seracchioli *et al.* 2001).

Photodynamic therapy appears to be safe and effective for treatment of basal cell carcinomas (Rhodes *et al.* 2007). Various topical treatments are under investigation (Stockfleth *et al.* 2002).

Treatment of basal cell carcinoma can be carried out in various ways and with good success. Treatments range from surgical excision to topical treatment with methyl aminolevulinate.

Further information and support:

In the UK:
Gorlin Syndrome Support Group
Telephone helpline: 01772 517624
E-mail: info@gorlingroup.co.uk
Website: www.gorlingroup.co.uk/index.htm

In the USA:
BCCNS Life Support Network
PO Box 321
14606 West Park Street #201
Burton,
OH 44021
Tel.: 440-834-1895
Toll-free: 866-834-1895
Fax: 440-834-1894
E-mail: info@bccns.org
Website: www.bccns.org

17

Biedl-Bardet syndrome (BBS)

aka • Bardet-Biedl syndrome

• Laurence-Moon-Bardet-Biedl syndrome

Gene loci: 20p12; 16q21; 15q22.3-q23; 14q32.1; 12q21.2; 11q13; 9q31–q34.1; 7p14; 4q27; 3p12-q13; 2q31

Key ASD references: Barnett *et al.* 2002; Gillberg and Wahlstrom 1985

This condition is characterized by progressive obesity and visual loss. It was first described in 1866 by J.Z. Laurence and R.C. Moon in a London family. George Bardet described two French girls with BBS in his thesis submitted in 1920. Arthur Biedl described two Austrian children in a research report published in 1922.

How common is BBS? The typically reported prevalence is one in 160,000 in Europe (Klein and Ammann 1969) and one in 100,000 in North America (Croft and Swift 1990). Higher rates have been reported in some areas such as Newfoundland (one in 17,500) and in the Bedouin population of Kuwait (one in 13,500).

Biedl-Bardet syndrome is an autosomal recessive condition. Diagnosis is currently on the combination of four primary or three primary and two secondary clinical features (Beales 2005). In terms of genetics, 12 genes have been identified that are associated with BBS. These are detailed in Table B17. They are identified as BB1–BBS12. Only BBS1, which it is thought may account for around 35 per cent of cases, is tested for clinically as the others only account for a very small percentage of cases.

Diagnosis is often only after some years as a result of the onset of obvious visual impairment, the other early features, unless the child has additional fingers or toes, being quite non-specific.

A useful review of BBS can be found in Ross and Beales (2007).

Main clinical features: The main presenting features in a person with BBS are: obesity (this is typically progressive), retinal dystrophy (the visual problems are slow to develop but progressive, with night blindness present typically by 7–8 years, and most children being diagnosed as functionally blind by their mid teens), additional fingers and toes in some cases, small genitals, moderate learning disability and kidney dysfunction. (Kidney problems are chronic and can be fatal.) A number of secondary problems are also seen. Elevated cholesterol levels and diabetes are characteristics that require ongoing monitoring and management. Speech acquisition is often delayed with single word speech typically beginning around age four.

Primary features: cone–rod dystrophy – this is progressive and not usually apparent before five, but by 17 there is rarely more than a small central visual field; macular degeneration is clear by some time in the teenage years, but occasionally earlier; truncal obesity; postaxial polydactyly – additional fingers and/or toes – is seen in two-thirds of cases; learning disability; males show hypogonadotrophic hypogonadism (small penis/small testes); affected females show various complex female genitourinary malformations; and kidney dysfunction.

Secondary features: speech delay/disorder; strabismus/cataracts/astigmatism; brachydactyly and syndactyly are common; developmental delay; excessive thirst and urination; ataxia/poor coordination/imbalance; mild hypertonia (especially lower limbs); diabetes mellitus (typically type 2) diabetes, often linked to obesity; dental crowding/hypodontia/small dental roots/high-arched palate; cardiovascular anomalies (in about seven per cent of cases); liver problems; high blood pressure (in two-thirds of cases); and subclinical hearing loss is apparent on testing in almost half of all cases.

There is a characteristic facial appearance, with a narrow forehead, large ears, narrow eyelids, a long, shallow nasal philtrum, a thin upper lip and small, downturned mouth, and most affected males have a receding hairline (Moore *et al.* 2005).

Table B17: Principal BBS genes

Gene	Gene locus	Percentage of BBS cases reported with the anomaly	Key references
BBS1	11q13	~23.2%	Katsanis 2004
BBS2	16q21	~8.1%	Katsanis 2004
ARL6/BBS3	3p12–q13	~0.4%	Katsanis 2004
BBS4	15q22.3–q23	Not yet known	Chiang *et al.* 2004
BBS5	2q31	~0.4%	Katsanis 2004
MKK5/BBS6	20p12	~5.8%	Katsanis 2004
BBS7	4q27	~1.5%	Katsanis 2004
TTC8/BBS8	14q32.1	~1.2%	Katsanis 2004
B1/BBS9	7p14	Not yet known	
BBS10	12q21.2	~20%	Stoetzel *et al.* 2006
BBS11/TRIM32	9q31–q34.1	<0.4%	Chiang *et al.* 2006 Katsanis 2004
BBS12	4q27	~5%	Stoetzel *et al.* 2007

In some families it appears that three of the BBS genes are required for the condition to manifest – triallelic inheritance (Katsanis *et al.* 2001), a mechanism which may be seen in some ten per cent of cases.

Is there a link between BBS and ASD?

- BBS was identified in one of 66 ASD cases screened for genetic conditions in a Swedish case series (Gillberg and Wahlstrom 1985).

- In a series of 21 BBS cases (Barnett *et al.* 2002), aged from three years seven months to 18 years, 12 families consented to screening for ASD symptomology using the Childhood Autism Rating Scale (CARS) (Schopler *et al.* 1980). Two cases scored as severely autistic and two as mild–moderate on the CARS; however, no more detailed assessments were carried out. Parental interviews established that a number of behaviours were common to this BBS group as a whole, including social and emotional immaturity (90.5 per cent); obsessions (80.9 per cent); routines (57.1 per cent); and repetitive play (42.9 per cent).

At the present time it is not clear whether the link between BBS and ASD is specific to any of the dozen susceptibility loci for BBS that have been identified.

Differential diagnosis:

1. *McKusick-Kaufman syndrome (MKKS)* results from a 20p defect in a region that is also a BBS susceptibility gene. These individuals have abnormal genital development, polydactyly and congenital heart problems, but seem to lack the other features of BBS. They may be part of the same phenotypic continuum.

2. *Alström syndrome* results from a defect in the ALMS1 gene at 2p13. This condition also causes a cone–rod dystrophy, obesity, a dilated cardiomyopathy, type 2 diabetes and developmental delay. There is, in addition, a progressive sensorineural hearing impairment.

3. In *Biemond 2 syndrome* no gene has so far been identified. The key features are learning disability, obesity, iris coloboma, additional digits (postaxial polydactyly); smaller genitalia (hypogonadism), hydrocephalus and facial synostosis.

Treatment and management: A significant area of help where individuals with BBS require specialist care and advice is in the selection and use of visual aids and communication systems that takes account of their progressive loss of vision. At present, there is no treatment that prevents or slows the visual deterioration.

Dietary approaches can help with management of obesity, elevated cholesterol, elevated blood pressure and type 2 diabetes. As these are later onset aspects of the condition, regular monitoring is important to identify difficulties at an early stage and institute secondary preventative measures.

Additional fingers and toes often require surgical removal to minimize problems with hand function and walking.

Early educational interventions and speech and language input also need to make allowance for progressive visual loss and greater reliance on auditory and tactile processing with age. Here the differential diagnosis of Alström syndrome is important, given the additional problems of progressive hearing loss.

Further information and support:

In Switzerland:
Retina International
Ausstellungsstrasse 36
CH-8005 Zurich
Tel.: 011-41-1-444-10-7
Fax: 011-41-1-444-10-7
E-mail: info@rpinternational.org
Website: www.retina-international.org

In the UK:
Laurence-Moon-Bardet-Biedl Society
10 High Cross Road
Rogerstone
Newport
NP10 9AD
Tel.: 01633 718415

E-mail: chris.humphreys4@ntlworld.com
Website: www.lmbbs.org.uk

In the USA:
Foundation Fighting Blindness
11435 Cronhill Drive
Owings Mill
MD 21117-2220
Tel.: 888-394-3937 (toll-free); 800-683-5555 (toll-free TDD); 410-568-0150 (local)
E-mail: info@blindness.org
Website: www.blindness.org

Web chatroom:
Laurence-Moon-Bardet-Biedl Syndrome Association
Website (chatroom): http://mlmorris.com/lmbbs

18

CATCH 22

---

aka • Cayler cardiofacial syndrome

• DiGeorge syndrome

• Takao velocardiofacial syndrome

• conotruncal anomaly face syndrome

• 22q11.2 deletion syndrome

• Sedlackova syndrome

• Shprintzen syndrome

• velocardiofacial syndrome

• Opitz G/BBB syndrome

Gene locus: 22q11.2

Key ASD references: Fine *et al.* 2005; Kozma 1998; Niklasson *et al.* 2001, 2002; Roubertie *et al.* 2001

CATCH 22 is an acronym, coined by John Burn. The term stands for **C**ardiac anomaly, **A**nomalous face, **T**hymus hypoplasia/aplasia, **C**left palate and **H**ypocalcaemia caused by a deletion of part of chromosome 22. It is caused in almost all cases by a deletion of genetic material at 22q11.2.

How common is CATCH 22? It is estimated that 22q11.2 deletions occur in one in every 4,000 live births (Tézenas Du Montcel *et al.* 1996). This is felt to be an underestimate as it is based on cases identified by phenotype, and milder and somatic mosaic cases have also been reported. Prevalence reports vary from one in 3,800 in US Hispanic populations to one in every 7,090 live births in a large Swedish study.

It typically occurs as a *de novo* mutation in the affected individual, but can be inherited (in approximately seven per cent of cases), and is transmitted as an autosomal dominant condition. Parents of an affected child should also be tested, as mildly affected parents and parents with somatic mosaic status have both been reported.

Where a parent is also affected the risk to siblings will be 50 per cent, but in *de novo* cases the risk appears low. Children of an affected individual will have a 50 per cent risk of also being affected.

Main clinical features: Most people with CATCH 22 have a learning disability (Moss *et al.* 1995). Immune problems are also seen in a high proportion (around 70 per cent). Complex heart problems are found in around three-quarters of cases, tetralogy of Fallot being most common and affecting more than one in five cases. Over 90 per cent of fatalities result from complications of such cardiac difficulties. Renal problems are seen in around one in three cases.

Overviews of the physical and behavioural phenotype can be found in Antshel *et al.* 2005) and Arriola-Pereda, Verdú-Pérez and de Castro-De Castro (2009).

A 22q11.2 deletion is the gene defect most commonly associated with a cleft palate, and is found in around seven per cent of cases, with over two-thirds having some form of palatal problem. Around half of all cases have hypocalcaemia, but the effect lessens with age. Seizure problems, when seen, are usually associated with hypocalcaemia. One in three have significant problems with feeding, which can be severe and may require nasogastric tube feeding and/or a gastrostomy.

Typically both motor and communication milestones are delayed (mean age at walking 18 months; first speech at 2–3 years). Around 80 per cent of cases show severe motor delay, with the same proportion showing some degree of learning difficulty.

A nonverbal learning disability profile on IQ is the most commonly reported cognitive profile (a significant gap between verbal and nonverbal skills). (See Wang P.P. *et al.* 1998.) However, the results are variable, both within and across studies (Sobin *et al.* 2005; Stiers *et al.* 2005). Problems with numeracy skills are common (Simon *et al.* 2002).

A range of behavioural features is seen in CATCH 22 – both 'disinhibition and impulsiveness' and 'shyness and withdrawal' are more common (Swillen *et al.* 1999). Inattention, anxiety and executive deficits such as perseveration are seen, as are difficulties with social interaction (Niklasson *et al.* 2001; Swillen *et al.* 1999).

Abnormalities of immune function are also common. Juvenile rheumatoid arthritis is around 20 times as common as it is in the general population, and a variety of other immune conditions, including coeliac disease, are also seen (Keenan *et al.* 1997; Sullivan *et al.* 1997). Immune problems such as haemolytic anaemia and juvenile arthritis are more common because of abnormal development of the thymus gland and a reduction in T-cell production (Sullivan 2004); however, this problem tends to lessen with age. Kidney and genitourinary problems are reported in approximately one third of cases (Wu *et al.* 2002).

Hearing can be affected, and chronic ear and nasal infections are common due to the poorer ability to fight off infection. Typically, it is advised that, where immune abnormalities are present, live vaccinations are delayed in this group unless there is a high background rate of disease, as their compromised immune status could increase the risk of atypical reactions.

There are a number of reports of hepatoblastoma, a form of liver cancer that is rare in the general population, suggesting a possible association with 22q11.2 (Scattone *et al.* 2003).

Characteristic facial features are seen in Caucasian populations. These include abnormalities of the ear and nose; 'hooded eyelids'; ocular hypertelorism; cleft lip and palate; facial asymmetry when crying; craniosynostosis; an elongated face; and flat cheeks. These features do not seem to be characteristics in the facial features of affected individuals from African-American populations.

Although adult stature is within normal limits, often children are growth retarded, and in some cases benefit from consideration for growth hormone treatment (Weinzimer *et al.* 1998).

Seizures are less common, being reported in seven per cent in one series. Ataxia and cerebellar atrophy have been reported, but to date only in a single case (Lynch *et al.* 1995).

Skeletal abnormalities of the ribs and vertebrae are fairly common.

Enlargement of the sylvian fissures of the brain has been reported in one study and was detectable in infancy. Functional MRI scans indicate reduced growth of the rear half of the dominant hemisphere compared to controls.

A detailed description of 250 22q11.2 deletion cases can be found in McDonald-McGinn *et al.* (1999). Despite the complex nature of the phenotype and the relatively large numbers who have been studied, no clear association between the extent of the genetic lesion and the phenotype has yet emerged (McDonald-McGinn *et al.* 2001).

A number of psychiatric disorders have been reported in association with 22q11.2 – in particular, schizophrenia, which is seen in around 25 per cent of adult cases. Bipolar disorder, anxiety, ADHD and depression have also been reported.

Is there a link between CATCH 22 and ASD? Several papers have commented on the level of ASD symptomology in people with CATCH 22.

- Lena Niklasson and her colleagues from Goteborg in southern Sweden have published two papers describing the neuropsychological/neuropsychiatric phenotype in 22q11.2 and raised the idea of an association with ASD symptomology (Niklasson 2001 *et al.* 2002).

- Agatha Roubertie and colleagues from Montpellier published detailed neurological descriptions of three cases, one of whom was autistic and the others affected by epilepsy (Roubertie *et al.* 2001).

- A separate group from Philadelphia published neuropsychological data on 80 22q11.2 microdeletion cases and described a consistent profile of nonverbal learning disability, with additional language and social deficits (Woodlin *et al.* 2001).

- Fine and colleagues (Fine *et al.* 2005) systematically examined the prevalence of ASD symptomology in 98 children who had a confirmed 22q11.2 deletion. Twenty-two children showed significant levels of autistic symptomology, and 14 had an autistic spectrum diagnosis, of whom 11 had autism. Significant autistic symptoms were thus seen in around 20 per cent of cases, and an ASD in around 15 per cent.

Differential diagnosis: The conditions which present with the most similar physical symptomology in conjunction with ASD are Goldenhar syndrome [38], a 14q32 deletion which results in complex symptomology but typically also involving reduced growth of one side of the face; and Smith-Lemli-Opitz syndrome [66], an overgrowth condition which can be identified genetically and results in a defect in cholesterol metabolism.

The central nervous system and phenotypic characteristics also overlap with those reported in Ovitz G/BBB syndrome (MacDonald M.R. *et al.* 1993), a condition linked to Xp22. Although similarities are seen in the physical phenotype, there have been no reports of Ovitz G/BBB in association with ASD. Xp22 is, however, the area on the X chromosome which is affected in a number of other ASD conditions: CHARGE syndrome [20]; DiGeorge syndrome I [29a] and velocardiofacial syndrome (VCFS) [76].

A large number of conditions have been named and described in association with a 22q11.2 gene deletion. Given the variability in presenting phenotype, there is ongoing debate concerning differentiation within this population. Much emphasis has been placed on a specific gene, TBX1, that is sufficient but not necessary for the presentation of the 22q11.2 phenotype. The discovery of a number of candidate genes that interfere with mitochondrial function on the same section of chromosome 22q11.2 (Maynard *et al.* 2008) suggests that these may be involved in the phenotypic variability observed.

Sedlackova syndrome/velofacial hypoplasia was thought to be a distinct entity, until a study (Fokstuen *et al.* 2001) indicated that 80 per cent of those tested with a DiGeorge/VCFS region-specific probe showed evidence of a 22q11.2 deletion in the same region.

One study has described elevated proline levels in a subset of cases (Raux *et al.* 2007).

Treatment and management: Regular follow-up of most 22q11.2 cases is required by a range of specialisms. Screening for heart problems should be undertaken at an early stage, and is often how the condition is first identified. Treatment is no different than it would be for others with the same cardiac problem.

Palatal abnormalities may require surgical correction and, where present, need to be evaluated by a craniofacial surgical team.

Feeding problems may require the use of modified cutlery, antacids for gastro-oesophageal reflux, medication to improve gastric motility and modified seating to improve posture to aid digestion.

Bleeding problems are more common in this group and should be treated as in others where they are found, so should be assessed and, where required, treated by a haematologist.

Growth retardation is also more common and growth hormone supplementation may be beneficial in some cases.

Hypocalcaemia is common, and low serum calcium concentration can be corrected with calcium supplementation. An increased risk of kidney stones from long-term use of calcium supplements needs to be borne in mind, keeping oxalate levels to a minimum (Aitken 2009).

Where there are immune problems, as are seen in the majority of cases, assessment by a clinical immunologist is advisable, as in some cases prophylactic antibiotics, intravenous immunoglobulin or a thymus transplant may be required.

Early intensive intervention to improve interaction and communication skills are as for other ASD conditions, and should ideally involve an appropriate team of psychologists, speech and language therapists and early education specialists. Ideally, baseline speech and language assessments should be carried out as early as possible. These can also aid in recognition of more subtle palatal defects. Given the profile of learning problems that characterizes this group, where present, strategies to aid with nonverbal learning disabilities should be put in place.

Where psychiatric symptomology is seen – especially ADHD, anxiety, bipolar or psychotic features – these should be evaluated, and where necessary treated by appropriate mental health professionals.

Further information and support:

In Canada:
Chromosome 22 Central
237 Kent Avenue
Timmins
Ontario
P4N 3C2
Tel.: 705-268-3099
E-mail: a815@c22c.org
Website: www.c22c.org

In the UK:
The 22q11 Group
PO Box 1302
Milton Keynes
MK13 0LZ
Tel.: 01908 320 852
E-mail: 22q11@melcom.cix.co.uk
Website: www.vcfs.net

Max Appeal
Landsdowne House
Wollaston
Stourbridge
West Midlands
DY8 4QN
Tel.: 01384 821227
E-mail: info@maxappeal.org.uk
Website: www.maxappeal.org.uk

In the USA:
The International 22q11.2 Deletion Syndrome Foundation, Inc.
1874 E. Route 70 Suite 3
Cherry Hill
NJ 08003
Tel.: 877-739-1849
E-mail: mabissi@22q.org
Website: www.22q.org

International DiGeorge/VCF Support Network
c/o Family Voices of New York
46 1/2 Clinton Avenue
Cortland
NY 13045
Tel.: 607-753-1621 (day); 607-753-1250 (eve)
Fax: 607-758-7420

Velo-cardio-facial Syndrome Educational Foundation, Inc. (VCFSEF, Inc.)
PO Box 874
Milltown,
NJ 08850
E-mail: kgkushner@vcfsef.org
Website: www.vcfsef.org/index.html

Chromosome Deletion Outreach, Inc
PO Box 724
Boca Raton
FL 33429-0724
Tel.: 888-CDO-6880 (888-236-6680); 561-395-4252 (family helpline)
E-mail: info@chromodisorder.org
Website: www.chromodisorder.org

Velo-cardio-facial Syndrome Education Foundation
PO Box 874
Milltown
NJ 08850
Tel.: 866-VCFSEF5 (866-823-7335); 732-238-8803
E-mail: info@vcfsed.org
Website: www.vcfsef.org

19

Cortical dysplasia–focal epilepsy (CDFE) syndrome

Gene locus: 7q36

Key ASD references: Alarcón *et al.* 2008; Arking *et al.* 2008; Bakkaloglu *et al.* 2008; Fisher and Scharff 2009; Jackman *et al.* 2009; Poot *et al.* 2009; Rossi *et al.* 2008; Strauss *et al.* 2006

CDFE is caused by an abnormality in contactin associated protein-like 2 (CASPR2) encoded by the CNTNAP2 gene at 7q35–q36. Having previously been identified as a risk factor for early language delay, this has now been confirmed as a risk factor for ASD in four independent studies. Clinically it usually presents with early onset seizures overactive behaviour and poor concentration.

How common is CDFE? This condition has only recently been identified. The multiple independent replications of a link between CNTNAP2 and ASD in different populations suggest that prevalence may be high. It has been identified as a cause of developmental disability in Old Order Amish, a population in which ASD has historically been reported to be infrequent.

Main clinical features: The key diagnostic features are, unsurprisingly, cortical dysplasia and focal epilepsy. The head is larger than predicted from familial head size, but growth is within normal parameters in other respects. Diminished deep-tendon reflexes are usually seen. Epileptic seizures are seen in most cases from early childhood, and are often difficult to control. Seizures, typically simple, partial or complex partial types, usually begin between 14 and 20 months. The seizures tend to resolve spontaneously, but only after a number of years. Slow early language development or language regression is typical of cases so far described. Hyperactivity, impulsive and aggressive behaviour and learning disability were reported in all of the Old Amish series originally described (Strauss *et al.* 2006).

Is there a link between CDFE and ASD?

- In a clinical series of nine CDFE cases (Strauss *et al.* 2006), six fulfilled criteria for ASD. All had learning disabilities, and seven fulfilled criteria for ADHD. Hyperactivity, inattention and aggression were the most common behavioural difficulties reported in this series between seizure episodes. All cases had complex partial seizures, and in addition four had secondary generalized seizures, three *status epilepticus* and three simple partial seizures. All of the cases in this series came from Old Amish families of Lancaster, Pennsylvania, in the USA. This is a population in which autism has been infrequently reported.

- Alarcón et al. (2008) published a screening study of DNA material from the AGRE (Autism Genetic Resource Exchange) database of established autistic cases. A strong association was found between autistic diagnosis and CNTNAP2 variants; this was preferentially found in males. By screening 304 independent parent–child trios an association between CNTNAP2 and age at first word in ASD was demonstrated. This followed on from an earlier study which had linked 7q35 defects to language learning problems in ASD (Alarcón et al. 2005b).

- Arking et al. (2008) also used data from the AGRE database. An analysis based on 78 sibling pairs and 145 parent–child trios also found CNTNAP2 to be an autism susceptibility gene, with a gender effect more commonly associated with male gender, and a parent-of-origin effect which seems to be inherited through the female line.

- Bakkaloglu et al. (2008) sequenced the CNTNAP2 gene in 635 ASD and 942 control cases. In the ASD cases 13 nonsynonymous changes in CNTNAP2 were found, while in the controls there were 11. This is a small absolute difference, suggesting an association, but this is a relatively rare factor in the overall ASD population.

- Rossi et al. (2008) have reported a case of an adult female with a deletion spanning 7q33–q35. This has deleted two genes, CNTNAP2 (the gene linked to ASD in the above studies) and NOBOX, which has been associated with primary amenorrhoea. This lady's case is well described, and she is diagnosed with both ASD and amenorrhoea. She had shown delayed early speech, with first words only by around the age of four years. She had had frequent nocturnal wakening in infancy and had two isolated seizures at age 16. Her IQ could not be formally assessed, but appeared likely to be in the moderately learning disabled range from her vocabulary and her scoring on other materials reported – Ravens coloured matrices and the Token test.

- A further case of an Amish girl with a single base pair deletion in the CNTNAP2 gene has a number of clinical features – severe learning disability, bilateral frontal slowing on EEG, cystic lesions on MRI consistent with periventricular leukomalacia, hepatomegaly and behaviour ratings on the ADOS-G and the Gilliam Autism Rating Scale, consistent with an autistic disorder (Jackman et el. 2009).

- A boy with speech delay and an ASD diagnosis has been reported, who had a disruption both to CNTNAP2 and to FOXP2. The latter has been independently reported in association with impaired speech development (Fisher and Scharff 2009).

- A further study has identified contactin-4 abnormalities that have a different genetic basis but some functional similarities in some individuals with ASD (Roohi et al. 2008). This is a 3p deletion syndrome with a distinct neurocognitive phenotype.

How does CDFE cause problems? The CNTNAP2 gene is involved in the regulation of axonal membrane proteins and controlling potassium channels at the nodes of Ranvier in axonal cells in the nervous system (Traka et al. 2003). It is thus important for saltatory conduction (the way in which electrical signals transmit more rapidly by jumping from node to node) (Poliak and Peles 2003).

Differential diagnosis: CNTNAP2 deletions have also been reported in association with Tourette syndrome [71] in two affected children whose father had a diagnosis of obsessive compulsive disorder (Verkerk *et al.* 2003). As Tourette syndrome is also associated with ASD and ASD was not screened for in this pedigree, this could indicate an alternative clinical phenotype or a basis to co-morbidity.

Treatment and management: To date there are no specific treatments which have been implemented or evaluated, as CDFE has only been characterized in the past four years. From the phenotype described to date, early identification of cases and provision of early intervention to improve communication may help to minimize language delays and improve cognitive outcome. Monitoring for early seizure activity and prophylactic treatment may also be of benefit. The reported overlaps with speech disorders and Tourette syndrome may prove to be important in identifying mechanisms and treatment approaches. At present, no studies have been carried out looking at early communication in this group. Established approaches to promoting early communicative development such as Hanen and Intensive Interaction (see contact information below) would seem the most likely to be beneficial.

The extent to which other problems such as sleep difficulties are characteristic of, or overrepresented in, CDFE is yet to be established.

Further information and support: At the time of writing there are no specific information or support groups for CDFE.

General support sites on epilepsy, ASD, Tourette syndrome, speech and rare biomedical conditions are likely to prove helpful.

For epilepsy

In the UK:
Epilepsy Action
New Anstey House
Gate Way Drive
Yeadon
Leeds
LS19 7XY
Tel.: 0113 210 8800
Fax: 0113 391 0300
E-mail: epilepsy@epilepsy.org.uk
Website: www.epilepsy.org.uk

In the USA:
Epilepsy Foundation
8301 Professional Place
Landover
MD 20785
Tel.: 800-332-1000
Website: www.epilepsyfoundation.org

For early communication

In Canada:
The Hanen Centre
Suite 515–1075 Bay Street
Toronto
Ontario
M5S 2B1
Tel.: 416-921-1073
Toll-free: 877-HANEN 55
Fax: 416-921-1225
E-mail: info@hanen.org
Website: www.hanen.org

Intensive Interaction
Website: www.intensiveinteraction.co.uk

See the sections on autism support groups and rare biomedical conditions in the appendices.

20

CHARGE syndrome

aka • Hall-Hittner syndrome

Gene loci: 8q12.1; 7q21.1

Key ASD references: Davenport, Hefner and Mitchell 1986; Fernell *et al.* 1999; Graham *et al.* 2005; Hartshorne, Grialou and Parker 2005; Hartshorne *et al.* 2007; Johansson *et al.* 2006; Johansson, Gillberg and Råstam 2009; Jure, Rapin and Tuchman 1991; Rapin and Ruben 1976; Sanlaville and Verloes 2007; Simon Harvey, Leaper and Bankier 1991; Smith I.M. *et al.* 2005; Vervloed *et al.* 2006; Wiznitzer, Rapin and Van de Water 1987

What is CHARGE? The name CHARGE is an acronym which stands for **C**oloboma of the eye, **H**eart defects, **A**tresia of the choanae, **R**etardation of growth and/or development, **G**enital and/or urinary abnormalities, and **E**ar abnormalities and deafness. This set of physical and sensory features is used in making a clinical diagnosis.

The first descriptions of CHARGE were provided by Hall (1979) and Hittner *et al.* (1979).

Genetic basis: Two specific genes appear linked to CHARGE association: CHD7, seen in the majority of cases, and SEMA3E, so far reported in only two cases (Lalani *et al.* 2004).

The CHD7 gene at 8q12 has been found to be mutated in around 60 per cent of cases (Jongmans *et al.* 2006; Lalani *et al.* 2006).

The SEMA3E translocation (Martin D.M., Sheldon and Gorski 2001) resulted from a balanced *de novo* chromosome 2–7 translocation in one well-described CHARGE association case, and in one further case identified in screening a group of other CHARGE cases.

How common is CHARGE syndrome? The best current estimate is that CHARGE syndrome affects between one in 8,500 live births (Issekutz *et al.* 2005) and one in 12,000 live births (Kallen *et al.* 1999).

Main clinical features: In individuals diagnosed with CHARGE syndrome, there is a wide variation in their behavioural profile on instruments that screen for autism. Based on the published studies to date, perhaps one in 42,500 live births will have CHARGE syndrome and go on to receive a diagnosis of ASD.

Typical features are as follows: choanal atresia (blockage of the nasal passages due to an overgrowth of bone or tissue); ocular coloboma (a developmental eye defect that can result in retinal detachment or glaucoma and requires regular assessment); nerve abnormalities (causing problems with olfaction, swallowing, facial palsy and deafness alone or in combination); ear malformation – cup shape to the outer ear, often with inner ear abnormalities and deafness; heart anomalies; learning disability, with delayed motor and cognitive milestones; growth retardation; underdeveloped genitals; cleft lip/palate.

The number and severity of features is highly variable, but at least three of the above features, excluding growth retardation, would need to be present to conclude that the CHARGE association was present.

Sleep disturbance is seen in approximately 60 per cent of cases, more commonly in those who are deaf–blind and who also tend to present with frequent middle-ear infections and with delayed walking.

Is there a link between CHARGE and ASD?

- Sandra Davenport *et al.* (Davenport, Hefner and Mitchell 1986) described 15 CHARGE cases, concluding that the constellation of features constituted a real clinical disorder. The ear malformations and audiogram results were felt to be key diagnostic features, and facial paralysis was viewed as very common, as were feeding difficulties. They also commented on one child as seemingly autistic with a profound level of learning disability. They have described this individual in further publications (for example, Hartshorne, Hefner and Davenport 2005).

- Wiznitzer, Rapin and Van de Water (1987) reported on neurological findings in 100 children with ear malformations; 65 had central nervous system involvement. Of these 65, 44 had learning disabilities, seven with autism, and one with the CHARGE association.

- Jure, Rapin and Tuchman (1991) carried out a review of 46 children, including a number with the CHARGE association, who had both hearing problems and ASD. In 11 the autism was diagnosed only several years after the hearing loss, while in ten the opposite delay was seen. The importance of assessment of both areas in parallel was stressed for appropriate early education.

- Elisabeth Fernell and colleagues from Sweden (1999) described three cases of CHARGE syndrome who were all reported to be autistic. In two this was in combination with significant learning difficulties.

- Graham *et al.* (2005) compared a series of 14 boys with CHARGE to 20 with Down syndrome [31], 17 with Prader-Willi syndrome [61] and 16 with Williams syndrome [77]. The view of the authors was that the autistic-like behaviours seen in the CHARGE cases, in contrast to the other groups, were secondary to sensory impairments – all 14 were deaf, and ten were classified as blind.

- In one survey of 160 ABC checklists returned from 204 families with CHARGE children (78 per cent return rate), 27.5 per cent would be classified as autistic (Hartshorne, Grialou and Parker 2005). This suggests that at a minimum around one in five people with CHARGE syndrome might be classified as autistic.

- Smith I.M. *et al.* (2005), in a preliminary paper from a Canadian epidemiological study that included 78 CHARGE cases, described the ten cases aged above four to five years on whom screening data had been completed. From telephone interview data, six of the ten were judged to present moderate to strong evidence of ASD diagnosis.

- Maria Johansson and colleagues (2006) described 31 individuals aged from one month to 31 years of age with CHARGE. ASD ascertainment proved impossible in three infants and three other deaf–blind cases. Of the remaining 25, five were classified as autistic, five as autistic-like, and seven as having autistic traits, suggesting autistic symptomology in some two-thirds of cases. Visual problems were seen in all of the autistic children. Hearing problems appeared to be independently associated with severity of ASD. Learning disabilities did not appear to correlate with ASD symptomology, but all of those with ASD diagnosis had a learning disability.

- In a study by Vervloed *et al.* (2006), which attempts to correlate medical difficulties with presenting problems, deaf–blindness was associated with delayed communication, while cardiac problems were associated with a lower level of behavioural difficulties. No association between medical presentation and ASD was found.

- Hartshorne *et al.* (2007) published a study on executive function (EF) in CHARGE syndrome and the association between EF and ASD symptomology. This large study of 98 children, using the Behavior Rating Inventory of Executive Function (BRIEF) and the Autism Behavior Checklist (ABC), demonstrated ABC scores higher than in other deaf–blind groups but lower than in typical ASD populations. There was a correlation between EF deficits and ABC scores.

- Sanlaville and Verloes (2007), in a useful update review, conclude that there is still no consensus on whether the ASD symptomology reported is true ASD, or ASD behaviour secondary to sensory impairment.

- In a survey of several genetic disorders that included a group of 31 CHARGE cases, Johansson, Gillberg and Råstam (2009) found that 68 per cent fitted criteria for an ASD diagnosis using the Autism Diagnostic Interview – Revised (ADI-R), Childhood Autism Rating Scale (CARS) and ABC scales and two independent clinical diagnoses. The authors caution about the use of diagnostic scales alone in assessing deaf–blind cases.

Differential diagnosis: A range of mental health conditions are diagnosed in CHARGE, the most common being ASD, obsessive-compulsive disorder, attention deficit disorder and Tourette syndrome. The likelihood of tics is linked to the presence and severity of cardiac problems.

Van Meter and Weaver (1996) described two cases who both showed features of the CHARGE association and Goldenhar syndrome [38].

The symptomology overlaps significantly with Kallman syndrome, in which the combination of underdeveloped genitals and a poor sense of smell is typical. A number of Kallman syndrome cases are also being found to have CHD7 mutations at 8q12 (Jongmans *et al.* 2009).

Tetralogy of Fallot is the most frequent type of heart defect reported in the CHARGE association (Cyran *et al.* 1987), being seen in approximately one in three cases with cardiac lesions (Wyse *et al.* 1993).

Choanal atresia is strongly associated with central nervous system anomalies. Lin, Siebert and Graham (1990) noted malformations in some 55 per cent, predominantly of the frontal structures.

In a report in 1996, Tellier *et al.* reviewed 41 CHARGE cases and noted a correlation with increased paternal but not maternal age.

Genital hypoplasia is most obvious in boys, but affects both sexes (Wheeler *et al.* 2000). Hormonal measurements in infancy can aid in diagnosis and enable treatment to minimize secondary difficulties.

Treatment and management: This is a very complex disorder that is likely to require at least close monitoring and follow-up of cardiac and airway function and swallowing. Surgical correction of choanal atresia, cardiac problems and palatal abnormalities may be required. There are to date no studies to suggest that any aspects of ASD presentation are specifically related to the CHARGE association, other than the increased severity of communication difficulties that can arise from palatal abnormalities, and the increased likelihood of motor tics related to severity of cardiac problems.

A single-case study from Taiwan has reported beneficial effects of a casein- and gluten-free diet in a boy with CHARGE syndrome, reporting significant improvements in growth, eye contact and language use over an 11-month period after commencing the diet at 42 months (Hsu *et al.* 2009).

Further information and support:

Chromosome 22 Central
www.c22c.org

In the USA:
CHARGE Syndrome Foundation, Inc.
409 Vandiver Dr.
Suite 5-104
Columbia,
MO 65202
Tel.: 573-499-4694

Toll-free: 800-442-7604
Fax: 573-499-4694
E-mail: marion@chargesyndrome.org
Website: www.chargesyndrome.org
A review of CHARGE syndrome can be found at www.ojrd.com:
Blake, K.D. and Prasad, C. (2006) 'CHARGE syndrome.' *Orphanet Journal of Rare Diseases 1*, 34 doi:10.1186/1750-1172-1-34.

21

Coffin-Lowry syndrome (CLS)

Gene locus: Xp22.2

Key ASD reference: Manouvrier-Hanu *et al.* 1999

CLS is a clinical disorder caused by a defect in the RPS6KA3 gene at Xp22.2 (Jacquot *et al.* 2002). Those affected tend to be short and overweight, with short tapering fingers and a small head. There is little apparent correlation between the genotype and the clinical phenotype. Most cases are caused by *de novo* Xp22.2 defects – 44/45 cases are reported in one series (Delaunoy *et al.* 2006).

CLS was first described by Coffin, Siris and Wegienka (1966). Credit for recognizing that there was a common underlying condition to the presenting phenotype goes to Temtamy, Miller and Hussels-Maumenee (1975) who recognized that all of the reported cases had a similar pattern of facial features, abnormalities of the fingers and toes, and learning disability.

How common is Coffin-Lowry syndrome? There are no accurate data available. One author has given an estimate of between one in 50,000 and one in 100,000 (Hanauer 2001).

Main clinical features: Affected males have severe to profound levels of learning disability. They are typically of short stature, and commonly microcephalic. They have fleshy hands with short tapering fingers. There are characteristic facial features, with large ears, large mouth with full lips, and broad, flattened nose. Scoliosis (curvature of the spine) is a common feature that is progressive and seen in almost half of all males with this syndrome (Hunter 2002). Obesity is a common problem, but may be secondary to the fact that many individuals need to be in wheelchairs due to frequent stimulus-induced drop attacks (SIDEs).

In the only small systematic study of cognitive function to date, Simensen et al. (2002) reported on two African-American families with three normal male and three normal female family members, six affected males and seven carrier females. A clear association between genetic status and IQ was found, with the following average scores on standardized testing: unaffected 90.8; carrier 65; affected 43.2.

SIDEs, a form of epileptic attack brought on by suddenly being startled, resulting in the person dropping down without loss of consciousness, are seen in approximately one in five cases (Stephenson et al. 2005). Epilepsy is seen in some five per cent, usually as a progression from SIDEs to myoclonic epilepsy and tonic spasms.

Cardiac problems are common and can take a variety of forms (Hunter 2002).

Problems with intestinal function, teeth, vision and hearing (Hartsfield et al. 1993; Sivagamasundari et al. 1994) have all been reported, but on current evidence are not typical of CLS.

Behavioural difficulties such as self-injury and destructive behaviour have been reported, but whether they are common is unknown (Hunter, Schwartz and Abidi 2007).

Clinical presentation can vary widely. For example, Facher et al. (2004) described a boy with developmental and physical features of CLS, who presented at 14 years of age with sudden onset of symptoms of congestive heart failure.

Heterozygous females have developmental levels ranging from normal to profound learning disability. They also show the characteristic hand differences and are prone to develop scoliosis in around one third of cases. Depression has been reported in several papers (for example, Sivagamasundari et al. 1994) but it is unclear whether this is biologically driven or a reactive process, and no systematic research has been undertaken.

In one small study Harum, Alemi and Johnston (2001) found in a sample of five boys and two girls with CLS that there was a correlation between their level of cognitive functioning and levels of CREB (factor cAMP response element-binding protein).

CREB production is affected by RPS6KA3 (a gene involved in ribosome function). It was suggested that genes responsive to CREB could be implicated in other phenotypic characteristics such as the facial and skeletal differences seen in CLS.

A brain imaging report compared individuals from two families with CLS to matched controls. The study found the brains of those with CLS to be consistently smaller, particularly the cerebellum and hippocampus, with a suggestion that the extent of difference in hippocampal size is associated with cognitive level (Kesler *et al.* 2007).

A useful summary of CLS can be found in Hunter, Schwartz and Abidi (2007).

Is there a link between Coffin-Lowry syndrome and ASD?

• In 1999 Manouvrier-Hanu *et al.* reported on two brothers with a mild CLS phenotype, and a previously unreported RSK2 missense mutation genotype. Both boys had transient but severe hypotonia, large heads and delayed closure of the fontanelles, and both had mild learning disability. In the first sibling, a diagnosis of autism was based on psychomotor regression and slow language acquisition, with progressive social isolation and development of motor stereotypies. Intensive early psychotherapy led to an improvement in social engagement. Motor and communication development remained slow and continence was delayed.

No systematic screening of CLS cases for the presence of ASD symptomology has yet been carried out.

Differential diagnosis: Several other conditions share some characteristics with CLS, but none have the characteristic hand features seen in CLS. Williams syndrome [77] is the most relevant to consider in a person with an ASD.

Treatment and management: SIDEs can be distressing but can be managed effectively with medication (O'Riordan, Patton and Schon 2006).

Self-injurious and destructive behaviours can occur, and there is some evidence that medications such as risperidone may also be helpful in reducing these (Valdovinos *et al.* 2002).

The major clinical features which are important to monitor regularly and to treat as required are the cardiac features and scoliosis, where present. Management of both would be no different to their care in others and both can have a major impact on both quality of life and longevity.

Further information and support:

In the USA:
The Coffin-Lowry Syndrome Foundation
National Association Area Agencies on Aging
3045 255th Avenue S.E.
Sammamish,
WA 98075
Tel.: 425-427-0939 after 5:30pm PST
E-mail: clsfoundation@yahoo.com
Website: http://clsf.info
Group discussion: http://groups.yahoo.com/
group/clsfoundation

22

Coffin-Siris syndrome (CSS)

aka • fifth digit syndrome

Gene locus: Not established. There is a suggestion from two cases (McGhee *et al.* 2000; McPherson *et al.* 1997) that the gene may be on 7q32–q34.

Key ASD references: Hersh, Bloom and Weisskopf 1982; Swillen *et al.* 1995.

CSS is a syndrome with learning disability, abnormalities to the little fingers and toes, coarsening of facial features and excessive hair growth, associated with multiple congenital anomalies. Feeding problems and frequent infections are also common (Fleck *et al.* 2001).

How common is Coffin-Siris syndrome? This is an uncommon disorder. To date only around 40 cases have been reported in the world literature. No estimate of the prevalence of CSS is possible on current information.

Main clinical features: The condition was first described in a paper by Coffin and Siris (1970). They gave details of three unrelated girls, all with learning disability and an absent nail and last section of the fifth finger. The equivalent portion of the little toe was also absent or reduced in size on each foot. These finger and toe abnormalities gave rise to the alternative term 'fifth digit syndrome'. There was no family history in any of the original cases; however, two cases have now been reported where there is partial expression in one parent (Haspeslagh, Fryns and van den Berghe 1984; Tunnessen, McMillan and Levin 1978).

Several pieces of information have been taken to suggest an autosomal recessive pattern of inheritance, in particular the occurrence of affected siblings (Franceschini *et al.* 1986), and a child born to consanguineous parents (Richieri-Costa, Monteleone-Neto and Gonzales 1986). There is still some debate over the inheritance pattern.

Several cases have been reported with a 'Dandy-Walker malformation' (for example, Imai *et al.* 2001), a condition with abnormal development of the outer layers of the cerebellar vermis and dilation of the fourth cerebral ventricle, but without enlargement of the other cerebral ventricles. This pattern is well described in the autism literature by Courchesne (1997) and others.

Is there a link between Coffin-Siris syndrome and ASD?

- Hersh, Bloom and Weisskopf (1982) described a six-year-old girl with growth retardation, dysmorphic facial features and abnormal little fingers and toes, consistent with CSS. She had learning disability and a 'severe behavioral relating disorder was observed which was consistent with a diagnosis of childhood autism'.

- In a series of 12 cases documented by Swillen *et al.* (1995), aged between two-and-a-half and 19 years, all exhibited learning difficulties (three mild and nine moderate).

All showed significant expressive language delay, while those old enough to be systematically assessed showed language comprehension commensurate with their mental age. Gross motor skills were also developmentally appropriate. Five showed pervasive developmental disorder, a DSM-IIIR diagnosis consistent with ASD. Obsessional routines and rituals and unusual fears characterized the older children, while difficult, aggressive and disruptive behaviour was more typical of the younger children.

Differential diagnosis: The condition that can present with similar features to CSS and is also reported in association with ASD is Cornelia de Lange syndrome [27] (Fryns 1986; Musio *et al.* 2006).

Choanal atresia, a typical feature of CHARGE association [20], has also been reported in CSS, which could cause confusion between the two conditions (DeJong and Nelson 1992).

Treatment and management: To date, there are no specific treatment or management approaches that have been shown to be helpful specifically based on the diagnosis of CSS.

Further information and support:
In the USA:
Coffin-Siris Syndrome Support
1524 Marshall Street
Antioch
CA 94509
Tel.: 925-754-6568
E-mail: jxgarris@aol.com

23

Cohen syndrome

---

aka • Pepper syndrome

Gene locus: 8q22–q23

Key ASD references: Howlin 2001; Howlin, Karpf and Turk 2005; Karpf, Turk and Howlin 2004.

Cohen syndrome is an autosomal recessive condition resulting from a defect in the COH1 gene. The wide variation in clinical features seems to result from the varied mutations that are sufficient for the condition to express. In one study of 20 cases from 12 family pedigrees from Brazil, Germany, Lebanon, Oman, Poland and Turkey, 17 separate novel mutations of COH1 were found (Hennies *et al.* 2004). Seifert *et al.* (2006) identified 25 different COH1 mutations in 24 patients from a variety of ethnic backgrounds.

How common is Cohen syndrome? Cohen syndrome is a rare condition. The prevalence has been estimated as one in 105,000; however, the small numbers of cases reported suggest that if the estimated prevalene is correct many cases go undetected (Falk, Wang and Traboulski 2006; Kivitie-Kallie *et al.* 1999)

The original paper by Cohen *et al.* appeared in 1973. It described a brother and sister and a further unrelated patient with poor muscle tone, obesity, high nasal bridge and prominent incisor teeth. All the cases had a learning disability.

Main clinical features: Cohen syndrome is an autosomal recessive condition that is more common in families of Finnish descent (Norio 2003). In this population, the phenotype is characteristic – mild to moderate motor delay; clumsiness; microcephaly; joint hyperlaxity; childhood hypotonia; a progressive retinochoroid dystrophy; myopia; intermittent neutropaenia; and a happy disposition (Kolehmainen *et al.* 2003). Progressive myopia seems to be a characteristic seen in the majority of cases (Seifert *et al.* 2006).

This phenotype has been described in non-Finnish populations (Chandler *et al.* 2003).

In addition, there are characteristic facial features that seem more specific to Finnish individuals with Cohen syndrome: high-arched or wave-shaped eyelids, short broad nostrils, thick hair and a low hairline. Retinal mottling appears a feature specific to Finnish cases (Kondo, Nagataki and Miyagi 1990). Facial measurements on Finnish cases show the upper face to be normally proportioned and the lower face to be narrower, making the face seem more pointed (Hurmerinta *et al.* 2002).

An MRI study of 18 people with Cohen syndrome (Kivitie-Kallio *et al.* 1998) and 26 volunteer controls found that there was an enlarged corpus callosum in the context of an overall microcephaly. This is an unusual finding in learning disability. Grey and white matter intensities appeared normal, with an overall reduction in central nervous system volume. Further research may confirm this as a clear diagnostic marker of Cohen syndrome diagnosis.

Is there a link between Cohen syndrome and ASD?

- The first paper to suggest a possible link between Cohen syndrome and ASD was published in 2001 (Howlin 2001). It presented information from a postal survey of families of 31 affected individuals (18 male, 13 female), aged two to 45 years. From 19 of these, the results obtained were consistent with criteria for autism. If substantiated this would suggest that approximately 57 per cent of those with Cohen syndrome could have an ASD.

- Karpf, Turk and Howlin (2004) reported results from cognitive, linguistic and adaptive assessments of 45 individuals diagnosed with Cohen syndrome. Twenty (10 male and 10 female) were classed as 'definite', based on clinical features. In the 'definite' group there was wide variation in performance IQ: from 20 to 104 (average 48.1). Scores on all areas on the Vineland Adaptive Behavior Scales were low, in general falling in line with performance IQ. The sociable temperament characteristic of individuals with Cohen syndrome helps explain the high scores. Howlin, Karpf and Turk (2005) reported on behaviour and autistic features in the same cohort described by Karpf, Turk and Howlin (2004). On the ADOS (Autism Diagnostic Obeservation Scale), 23/43 (53 per cent) fitted criteria for autism and 34 (79 per cent) criteria for an ASD.

Differential diagnosis: Similarities have been noted between Cohen syndrome and Prader-Willi syndrome [61] (Fuhrmann-Rieger, Kohler and Fuhrmann 1984).

Kolehmainen *et al.* (2004) assessed 76 people thought to have possible Cohen syndrome on the basis of clinical phenotype. They were scored on the presence or absence of eight features: developmental delay; microcephaly; typical Cohen syndrome facial features; truncal obesity with slender extremities; overly sociable behaviour; joint hypermobility; high myopia and/or retinal dystrophy; and neutropaenia. Roughly half of the group met six or more criteria, of whom 60 per cent had COH1 mutations at 8q22–q23. None of those who met five or fewer criteria were found to have COH1 mutations.

Eight individuals from two large Amish kindreds have been described (Falk *et al.* 2004) who had early-onset pigmentary retinopathy and myopia, global learning disability, microcephaly, short stature, low muscle tone, joint hyperlaxity, small hands and feet and a friendly disposition, and the genetic basis was mapped to COH1 at 8q22–q23. This provides evidence of a second genetic condition linked to ASD within the Amish (the other being cortical dysplasia–focal epilepsy syndrome [19]).

Treatment and management: To date no specific treatments have been developed for Cohen syndrome that differ from those for others with ASD. The fairly specific retinal problems require careful monitoring and treatment as required.

Further information and support:
In the UK:
Cohen Syndrome Support Group
45 Compton Way
Middleton Junction
Middleton
Manchester
M24 2BU
Tel.: 0161 653 0867

24

Cole-Hughes macrocephaly syndrome (CHMS)

aka • macrocephaly/autism syndrome

Gene locus: Not clearly established – some cases have mutations of the PTEN tumour suppressor gene (Butler *et al.* 2005). There may be an overlap with Bannayan-Riley-Ruvalcaba syndrome [15].

Key ASD references: Butler *et al.* 2005; Naqvi, Cole and Graham 2000

How common is CHMS? There is no information available on the prevalence of CHMS. If it is genetically contiguous with Bannayan-Riley-Ruvalcaba syndrome [15], the two conditions may turn out to have the same basis, despite the apparent lack of BRRS features in the cases described by Butler *et al.* (2005).

Main clinical features: CHMS was first recognized in a larger cohort study investigating Sotos syndrome [68] by Cole and Hughes (1991). Six of the cases they described had a characteristic physical and behavioural phenotype. In these six, out of 79 individuals evaluated, the same craniofacial characteristics were seen – a square outline to the face with a pronounced narrow forehead, and long narrow nostrils. Birthweight and body proportion were normal at birth, but there was rapid weight gain, and all were obese on follow-up. In addition, language and social skills were significantly poorer than motor function.

In a review of 100 ASD cases, Stevenson *et al.* (1997) found progressive postnatal macrocephaly in 24, of whom 15 (62 per cent) had one or both parents with macrocephaly.

Is there a link between CHMS and ASD?

- Naqvi, Cole and Graham (2000) described two patients with the features reported in CHMS who also showed Characteristics consistent with co-morbid diagnoses of both ASD and ADHD.

- Butler *et al.* (2005) studied a group of 18 subjects aged from three to 18 with ASD and a significant degree of macrocephaly. There were no features suggestive of Bannayan-Riley-Ruvalcaba syndrome [15], except for pigmented macules on the glans penis of one boy, nor of Cowden syndrome [26]. As a number of other cerebral overgrowth syndromes have now been characterized in association with ASD, Butler *et al.*'s conclusion of CHMS by exclusion is not adequate to characterize their group. In three of the 18 cases, there was a PTEN mutation consistent with Bannayan-Riley-Ruvalcaba syndrome (BRRS) and one of the three had pigmented macules on his genitalia consistent with the typical BRRS phenotype.

Differential diagnosis: This condition presents with a pronounced macrocephaly and the other conditions listed in Table A6 should be considered along with benign familiar megalencephaly/macrocephaly (Day and Schutt 1979).

Treatment and management: No specific treatment or management implications can be drawn from our current level of understanding of this condition.

Further information and support: There is no specific Cole-Hughes macrocephaly syndrome support group at the time of writing, but the organizations below can be approached.

In the UK:
Unique
Rare Chromosome Disorder Support Group
PO Box 2189
Surrey
CR3 5GN
Telephone helpline: 01883 330766
E-mail: info@rarechromo.org
Website: www.rarechromo.org

In the USA:
Chromosome Deletion Outreach, Inc.
PO Box 724
Boca Raton,
FL 33429-0724
Family helpline: 561-395-4252
E-mail: info@chromodisorder.org
Website: www.chromodisorder.org

25

Congenital adrenal hyperplasia (CAH)

aka   • 21-hydroxylase-deficient congenital adrenal hyperplasia

   • adrenogenital syndrome (AG syndrome)

   • C-21-hydroxylase deficiency

   • congenital adrenocortical hyperplasia

Gene locus: 6p21.3

Key ASD references: Falter, Plaisted and Davis 2008; Knickmeyer *et al.* 2006; Sieg 2009

CAH is a group of autosomal recessive disorders that interfere with the ability of the adrenal cortex to manufacture cortisol from cholesterol. It most commonly results from a gene defect in CYP21A2, the gene responsible for the production of the enzyme 21-hydroxylase (21-OHD).

How common is CAH? There are so-called 'classic' and 'non-classic' forms of CAH. Current estimates for the overall prevalence of 'classic' CAH, based on over 6.5 million screened infants, suggest an overall rate of one in every 10,000 live births (Orphanet Reports Series 2008). Reported rates vary from one in 300 in the Yupik Eskimos to one in 23,000 in New Zealand.

There is less information on the prevalence of 'non-classic' CAH, mostly from New York where prevalence in the general population has been estimated at one in 100, with the highest rates (one in 27) in the Ashkenazi Jewish population (Speiser *et al.* 1985).

Main clinical features: In all classic cases, cortisol production is low. The classic form of CAH, if not treated neonatally, presents in both sexes with virilization and genital enlargement, and smaller testes in males. There is accelerated appearance of pubic and underarm hair, bone age and rapid physical growth. Severe acne is common. Premature bone fusion results in shorter adult stature compared to unaffected family members, and is not subsequently corrected by cortisol treatment. Untreated girls have a high incidence of menstrual problems, hirsutism, male pattern baldness and reduced fertility.

The non-classic form does not typically result in lowered cortisol production and is a later onset problem, but in many other respects presents similar issues when compared to the classic form. Premature bone fusion can cause short stature, and hirsutism, acne and other virilizing aspects of excessive androgen exposure are also seen. Females with the non-classic form can have reduced fertility (seen in 50 per cent) and severe menstrual problems (seen in ten per cent). Polycystic ovaries are common.

Is there a link between CAH and ASD? This putative association has received much attention and is discussed here solely for this reason. There is no substantive evidence for a link.

In 2006, Knickmeyer and colleagues published a paper on the Autism Spectrum Quotient (ASQ) scores of individuals with CAH (34 females, 26 males) and their unaffected relatives (24 females, 25 males). Based on the 'extreme male brain theory' of ASD, their prediction was that androgenized CAH females would have elevated ASQ scores, while CAH males would not show differences (Baron-Cohen 2002). Their results bore out this prediction; however, the size of the effect was small and placed the CAH female scores well below the cutoff for any clinical suspicion of ASD.

- One single-case report (Sieg 2009) presented a 12-year-old Caucasian boy with CAH who fulfilled criteria for autism, with an overall score of 126 on the Autism Behavior Checklist.

The 'extreme male brain' theory of ASD (Baron-Cohen 2002) developed from a more general theory concerning neurodevelopmental disorders proposed by Norman Geschwind and Albert Galaburda (Geschwind and Galaburda 1985a, 1985b, 1985c). The basic theory suggested that an increased rate of neurodevelopmental disorders could be related to increased pre-birth exposure to male sex hormones. Geschwind and Galaburda claimed that this could result in megalencephaly, with greater cerebral symmetry, an increased rate of anomalous handedness, immune disorders and epilepsy, and would be overrepresented in males. One test of this general model has been to evaluate the effects of conditions that result in increased male sex hormone exposure, such as 'classic' CAH in girls. Would such conditions through producing higher *pre-birth* exposure to testosterone result in more masculinized behaviour? The results to date appear to support this general hypothesis (see, for example, Pasterski *et al.* 2007).

A further questionnaire survey using the testosterone-related medical questionnaire, based on the predictions of the 'extreme male brain' theory, investigated the presence of medical features consistent with elevated testosterone in a sample of 54 women with ASD, 74 mothers of children with ASD and 183 controls. The theory would have predicted that some of the women with ASD and possibly the mothers of children with ASD would have elevated levels compared to the controls. Some conditions related to increased testosterone were more common in the ASD cases and mothers, but contrary to prediction CAH was seen in two affected controls but in none of the mothers or ASD cases (Ingudomnukul et al. 2007).

Okten, Kalyoncu and Yaris (2002) concluded based on a review of 26 clinical CAH cases that *in utero* androgen exposure significantly affects the physical development of the foetus.

Falter, Plaisted and Davis (2008) argue that increased androgen exposure alone cannot account for all of the findings in CAH. They review the evidence from growth studies – largely, to date, the relative length of the second and fourth fingers, coupled with the level of testosterone exposure – and discuss genetic conditions that alter *in utero* androgen exposures. They conclude that *in utero* androgen exposure is not sufficient to account for the cognitive aspects of CAH and challenge the view that this is sufficient to result in ASD.

Clinical diagnosis: The diagnosis is usually made or suspected in four situations:

- in children born to CAH cases
- in girls with precocious or accelerated virilization
- in boys who show virilization in childhood (i.e. pseudoprecocious puberty)
- in any infant with a salt-losing crisis in the first four weeks of life (typically between one and four weeks of age).

Differential diagnosis: CAH has been reported in association with a sex chromosome aneuploidy (XYY syndrome) [4], which would of itself have accelerated *in utero* virilization by increasing circulating testosterone levels (Mallin and Walker 1972). This has only been reported in a single case and is unlikely to be a common factor, but rather the reason for this particular boy to have come to clinical attention.

Phenotypic cases have also been reported in association with muscular dystrophy [33] with glycerol kinase deficiency (Francke *et al.* 1987), and with Ehlers-Danlos syndrome [34], hypermobility type. The association with Ehlers-Danlos is due to contiguity of the CYP21A2 gene involved in CAH and the TNX gene involved in this variant of Ehler-Danlos (Schalkwijk *et al.* 2001). The cases reported do not appear to have an ASD.

Treatment and management: In classic cases the disorder requires treatment and monitoring throughout life; however, in non-classic cases, treatment is not always required.

Treatment for classic 21-OHD CAH includes glucocorticoid replacement therapy, which needs to be increased during periods of stress. Individuals with the salt-wasting form of 21-OHD CAH require treatment with 9alpha-fludrohydrocortisone, and often active salt replacement. Bilateral adrenalectomy may be indicated for individuals with severe homozygous 21-OHD CAH.

Surgical removal of the adrenal glands has been reported as being helpful in some homozygous cases not responsive to hormone replacement (Meyers and Grua 2000).

As the biology is complex and appropriate intervention multidisciplinary, and the topic is not central to the focus of this volume, the reader is referred to the reviews cited below for further information.

Overviews of CAH biology, genetics, treatment and management: There are several excellent reviews of CAH and its clinical implications (Forest 2004; New 2004; Ogilvie *et al.* 2006; Speiser and White 2003). Any link between CAH and ASD is theoretical rather than substantial at this time. Despite screening of large groups in whom one might have expected to find cases had the link been substantive and significant, only a single case has been reported (Sieg 2009). The reader is referred to the above reviews for more specific information on CAH, and to the papers noted above for current speculation.

Further information and support:

There is a useful link website at
http://congenitaladrenalhyperplasia.org

In Australia:

Congenital Adrenal Hyperplasia Support Group
Australia Incorporated
CAHSGA Inc
PO Box 100
Mitcham
Victoria 3132
Answering service tel.: 61 03 95139255

In the UK:

Climb: Congenital Adrenal Hyperplasia UK
Support Group
2 Windrush Close
Flitwick
Bedfordshire
MK45 1PX
Tel.: 01525 717536
E-mail: sue@cah.org.uk
Website: www.cah.org.uk

In the USA:

Congenital Adrenal Hyperplasia Research
Education and Support
CARES Foundation, Inc.
2414 Morris Avenue
Suite 110
Union
NJ 07083
Tel.: 973-912-3895 (in New Jersey);
866-227-3737 (toll-free out-of-state)
Fax: 973-912-8990
Website: www.caresfoundation.org

The Rare Genetic Steroid Disorders Consortium
Registry
The Mount Sinai School of Medicine
One Gustave L. Levy Place,
Box 1198
New York
NY 10029-6574
E-mail: maria.new@mssm.edu
http://rarediseasesnetwork.org maintains a contact
registry

A downloadable guide to CAH caused by
21-hydroxylase deficiency for patients and families
can be found at www.hopkinschildrens.org

26

Cowden syndrome (CS)

aka
- PTEN hamartoma tumour syndrome (PHTS)
- Bannayan-Ruvalcaba-Riley syndrome (BRRS)
- Bannayan-Riley-Ruvalcaba syndrome (BRRS)
- Bannayan-Zonana syndrome
- Riley-Smith syndrome
- Ruvalcaba-Myhre-Smith syndrome
- Proteus syndrome

Gene loci: 10q23.31, 10q22.3

Key ASD references: Butler *et al.* 2005; Goffin *et al.* 2001

The difficulty in presenting separate sections in this volume dealing with the various hamartoma disorders that have been reported in association with ASD concerns the current uncertainty over the extent to which these are discrete conditions, the extent to which they overlap with one another, or are actually synonymous. Butler *et al.* (2005) for example, talk about 'Cowden syndrome (a cancer syndrome) *and other* **related** *hamartoma disorders* such as Bannayan-Riley-Ruvalcaba syndrome, Proteus syndrome, and Proteus-like conditions' (my emphases). Butler *et al.*, then, assume that the conditions are discrete. Marsh *et al.* (1998), by contrast, drawing on PTEN mutation genotype–phenotype data from 43 BRRS [15] and 37 Cowden syndrome cases, conclude that they may be overlapping phenotypic presentations of the same genetic condition. Others (see, for example, Gustafson *et al.* 2007) subsume these various conditions under the umbrella term of 'PTEN hamartoma tumour syndrome' (PHTS). PTEN mutations are seen in 85 per cent of individuals who meet the diagnostic criteria for CS (Marsh *et al.* 1998; Zhou *et al.* 2003).

Nuclear PTEN appears to mediate cell cycle arrest, while cytoplasmic PTEN is required for apoptosis (Chung and Eng 2005). Abnormalities of apoptosis can result in brain overgrowth, as the major factor that produces normal brain differentiation is selective cell death. PTEN appears to remove phosphate groups from three amino acids – tyrosine, serine and threonine. It plays an important role in the inhibition of cell migration, a factor that is important in keeping cancer growth in check.

How common is Cowden syndrome? Due to the diagnostic uncertainties mentioned above, 10q22–q23 defects tend to be estimated on joint prevalence. The true prevalence is unknown but has been estimated at one in 200,000 (Nelen *et al.* 1999); if we assume CS to be a discrete condition, this figure is likely to be an underestimate. In some of the 20 per cent of cases with a Cowden phenotype but without a polymerase chain reaction (PCR) detectable 10q22–q23 PTEN defect, germline promoter mutations and deletions have been reported (Zhou *et al.* 2003). The variable and sometimes mild or absent phenotypic features (Haibach *et al.* 1992; Schrager *et al.* 1998) mean that many individuals go undiagnosed and may in effect have the genotype without phenotypic manifestations. This factor may also lead to a misleading indication of likely severity.

Main clinical features: CS is a multiple hamartoma syndrome with a high risk of both benign and malignant thyroid, breast and endometrial cancers. Affected individuals usually have macrocephaly, trichilemmomas (tumours which form around the hair follicles) and papilloma (small benign skin tumours), and all are typically present by the time the person is in their late twenties. The lifetime risk of developing breast cancer is 25–50 per cent, with an average age of diagnosis between 38 and 46 years (Starink *et al.* 1986). Breast cancer has been noted in both male and female cases (Fackenthal *et al.* 2001), and is strongly associated with the presence of PTEN mutations (Marsh *et al.* 1998). Thyroid nodules, adenoma and goitre occur in up to 75 per cent of cases of CS (Harach *et al.* 1999), while the lifetime risk for thyroid cancer is around ten per cent. The risk of endometrial cancer is not well documented.

Most cases have clear clinical features indicative of the disorder by their third decade of life.

Is there a link between CS and ASD?

- Goffin *et al.* (2001) reported a mother and son with a diagnosis of Cowden syndrome and a PTEN mutation. The boy presented with autistic behavior and learning disability. His mother had normal intelligence and social skills. The authors stressed the association between progressive head growth and pervasive developmental disorder, and that the combination was associated with PTEN mutations.

- Butler *et al.* (2005) presented information on a series of 18 cases of ASD who had associated extreme macrocephaly (head circumference 2.5 to 8.0 standard deviations above the population mean).

Differential diagnosis: The main differential diagnoses, assuming that the conditions are separable, are BRRS [15] and Proteus syndrome [62]. Other possible but less likely differential diagnoses associated with ASD are basal cell naevus syndrome [16] and neurofibromatosis type 1 [51].

The clinical presentation in BRRS is argued to be somewhat different. The cancer risks are equivalent, which may be related to the PTEN gene defect in both conditions (Marsh *et al.* 1998). There is clear symptom overlap between the two diagnoses (Marsh *et al.* 1998). Similarly, there is a demonstrated genetic overlap with Proteus syndrome, cases having been described with mutations identified as causing both BRRS and CS (see, for example, Zhou *et al.* 2001).

Relatives can be tested, and if they do not have the PTEN mutation they are not at increased cancer risk. If parents carry the mutation, then siblings have a 50 per cent risk of having the mutation. Where parents do not carry the gene, the risk to siblings is low.

All children of someone carrying a PTEN mutation have a 50 per cent risk of being affected. Where one parent carries the mutation, their blood relatives are also at increased risk of being affected.

Treatment and management: The most serious consequences of CS relate to the increased risk of breast, thyroid, endometrial and renal cancers, and so the most important aspect of management, as for other PTEN defects, is increased cancer surveillance and appropriate management of identified cancers. Information on an appropriate surveillance regime can be found in Zbuk, Stein and Eng (2006). There is no evidence to date for beneficial effects of prophylactic treatment to reduce cancer risk.

mTOR inhibitors are showing promise in the treatment of malignancies in individuals who have a germline PTEN mutation. These are not yet available for clinical use. No clinical trials have yet been carried out specifically with individuals with a PTEN hamartoma tumour syndrome.

Further information and support:

In the USA:
Cowden's Syndrome Foundation
1394 Wedgewood Drive
Salne
MI 48176
Tel.: 734-944-8313
E-mail: Rosalita@msn.com

27

De Lange syndrome (CdLS)

aka • Cornelia de Lange syndrome

• Brachmann-de Lange syndrome (BDLS)

includes • NIPBL-related Cornelia de Lange syndrome

• SMC1L1-related Cornelia de Lange syndrome

Gene loci: 5p13.1 (NIPBL); Xp11.22–p11.21 (SMC1L1); 10q25 (SMC3 and SMC1A)

Key ASD references: Basile *et al.* 2007; Bhuiyan *et al.* 2006; Moss *et al.* 2008

CdLS is one of a group of disorders known as cohesinopathies. The primary defect is in one of the mechanisms involved in chromosome segregation (McNairn and Gerton 2008a, 2008b). A probable case of CdLS was first described by Willem Vrolik in 1849 (Vrolik 1849). The condition is named after a Dutch paediatrician, Cornelia de Lange, who documented cases in 1933, originally using the term 'degeneration (typus Amstelodamensis)', which first became known in English as 'Amsterdam dwarfism' (de Knecht-van Eekelen and Hennekam 1994).

How common is de Lange syndrome? De Lange syndrome is equally common in males and females. It is thought to have a prevalence of 1.24 in 100,000 births (Barisic *et al.* 2008). As milder phenotypes are often not recognized this may be an underestimate and figures as high as one in 10,000 have been suggested by some (Opitz 1985).

Main clinical features: From the European Surveillance of Congenital Anomalies (Barisic *et al.* 2008), the most common associated physical features are limb defects (73.1 per cent); heart defects (45.6 per cent); central nervous system malformations (40.2 per cent); and cleft palate (21.7 per cent).

Low birthweight is seen in around two-thirds of cases and is associated with more severe complications. Boys are significantly more likely to have limb malformations.

The main diagnostic features of CdLS include: dysmorphic facial features (a low frontal hairline; a small, upturned nose with a triangular tip; a crescent-shaped mouth; arched eyebrows, often with synophrys (a single eyebrow across both eyes); small, widely spaced teeth; hirsutism in general; slow antenatal and postnatal growth; microcephaly). Reduced upper limb growth is the most common feature, with relative preservation of the lower limbs. Cardiac defects are seen in around a quarter of all cases (Tsukahara *et al.* 1998), and can be complex, but ventricular septal and atrial-septal defects are the most common; cleft palate is seen in 20 per cent (Sataloff *et al.* 1990). Other problems which are reported include gastrointestinal dysfunctions; seizures, in around 25 per cent of cases; hearing loss (in 80 per cent) (Sataloff *et al.* 1990); and visual problems (Levin *et al.*

1990). A significant proportion engage in eye pressing and eye poking, related to having dry eyes (blepharitis).

An unusual, low-pitched cry is described in three-quarters of cases in infancy (Jackson *et al.* 1993), but to date has not been specifically studied or recorded.

Milder physical phenotypes with the same gene mutation are reported more commonly than the classic presentation described above (Allanson, Hennekam and Ireland 1997).

Self-injurious behaviour is seen in around 55 per cent of cases (Oliver *et al.* 2003).

Slower growth is typical of those with CdLS, most having noticeable intrauterine growth retardation (Boog *et al.* 1999), being born at lower birthweight (Barisic *et al.* 2008) and remaining below the fifth centile throughout their lives (Kline, Barr and Jackson 1993; Kousseff *et al.* 1993).

Intellectual functioning varies widely. Most individuals are of limited ability, with the mean reported IQ being 53 (Kline *et al.* 1993). A number of cases have been reported of normal IQ, typically seen in those of higher birthweight (>2.5 kilos) without associated limb malformations (Saal *et al.* 1993 and see discussion in Basile *et al.* 2007).

A wide range of NIPBL gene mutations has been reported in CdLS (truncating, splice-site, missense, in-frame deletion and regulatory) (Selicorni *et al.* 2007). Gene deletions have been reported but do not appear to be viable (Hulinsky *et al.* 2005).

One unusual feature which has been reported is that the chromatids separate earlier than normal during cell division – something called 'precocious sister chromatid separation' (PSCS) – presumably due to the cohesin defect (Kaur *et al.* 2005).

CdLS is inherited either as an X-linked or as an autosomal dominant condition. To date, four genes have been identified as causing the de Lange phenotype. The first, NIPBL, accounts for around 50 per cent of cases tested. NIPBL was identified in 2004 (Krantz *et al.* 2004). Three other genes have also been identified as linked (SMC1L1, SMC1A and SMC3). Of these others, SMC1L1 has been reported in one family and one sporadic case (Musio *et al.* 2006) and SMC3-SMC1A in a single case (Deardorff *et al.* 2007). An early suggestion of a link to 3q has not been borne out (Krantz *et al.* 2004) and mutations in this area are now a differential diagnosis. To date a genetic basis is identifiable in around 70 per cent of cases diagnosed by phenotype, suggesting that other sites or sub-threshold defects may be involved (Borck *et al.* 2004).

The severity of the phenotype is linked to the genotype, and the extent to which the cohesin system is impaired. Cohesinopathies are multisystem developmental disorders that result from defects in the system that maintains chromosome cohesion between replicating sister chromatids. Typically CdLS arises as a *de novo* mutation, and fewer than one per cent of people affected have the gene difference identified in either of their parents. Therefore, on this basis and in view of the lowered likelihood of someone who is affected having children, it is unlikely that others in the family will be affected. If a parent carries the mutation, then the likelihood of a sister being affected will be 50 per cent, but for a brother, 50 per cent only when the mother carries the mutation. Affected men could only pass on a CdLS gene to their daughters but not to their sons.

A number of abnormalities overlap phenotypically with those seen in CdLS, including certain 3p deletion and 12q duplication abnormalities (DeScipio *et al.* 2005).

Cutaneous differences: mottling of the skin ('cutis marmorata') is seen in around 60 per cent of cases. Single palmar creases and abnormal finger whorls are also commonly reported (Smith G.F. 1966). Incomplete development of the nipples and the umbilicus are also seen in around 50 per cent of cases.

Gastro-oesophageal reflux (GER) is seen in almost all classic cases (Bull *et al.* 1993), and can require surgical correction (Jackson *et al.* 1993). A variety of other gastrointestinal problems are reported, including pyloric stenosis, which causes persistent vomiting in around 25 per cent, diaphragmatic hernia and intestinal malrotation. The presence of reflux is often associated with unusual body postures and with body banging.

Undescended testes (73 per cent) and *small genitalia* (57 per cent) are seen in a high percentage of males, and *kidney problems* are seen in around 12 per cent (Jackson *et al.* 1993).

A range of orthopaedic problems has been reported, but none are characteristic and few require surgical intervention. Of 34 patients referred for orthopaedic evaluation in Toronto, only two required surgery, both for bilateral equinovarus (clubfoot) (Roposch *et al.* 2004).

A low platelet count has been reported in some cases (Froster and Gortner 1993; Fryns and Vinken 1994), but no further papers have appeared and the diagnostic and clinical significance is not known.

Is there a link between CdLS and ASD?

- A number of earlier clinical and review papers have described autistic-like behaviours in de Lange syndrome (Bay *et al.* 1993; Bryson *et al.* 1971; Johnson *et al.* 1976; Opitz 1985; Sarimski 1997; Shear *et al.* 1971).

- The first paper to suggest that there may be an association between ASD and de Lange syndrome was much more recent (Bhuiyan *et al.* 2006). This study, of 39 cases, used two standardized assessment scales: the Developmental Behaviour Checklist (DBC) and the Diagnostic Interview for Social and Communication Disorders (DISCO). Both scales identified seven cases as fulfilling criteria for autism, albeit slightly different but overlapping subsets of this population. The authors speculate that the autistic behaviours may have been a reflection of a level of global learning disability – the more severely disabled cases were more likely to be autistic, but more research would be needed to clarify the issue.

- Basile *et al.* (2007) carried out a questionnaire survey of 56 Italian children with de Lange syndrome. They also employed standardized rating scales of autistic symptomology – the Childhood Autism Rating Scale (CARS) and Autism Behavior Checklist (ABC) scales. Fifteen of the children presented behaviour consistent with an autistic pattern. As in the Bhuiyan *et al.* study, ASD symptomology was correlated with learning disability.

- The most recent study (Moss *et al.* 2008) again used standardized screening measures – the Autism Diagnostic Observation Scale (ADOS), which uses direct observation, and the Social Communication Questionnaire (SCQ), screening 34 de Lange cases, of which 21 (62 per cent) were found to be above the autism cut-off. In a comparison group of children with *cri du chat* syndrome (a rare condition resulting in learning disability), a condition not to date linked to ASD, 39.2 per cent were also above the clinical cut-off.

Differential diagnosis: Four conditions have clinical presentation similarities to CdLS:

1. *Partial 3q trisomy* translocation and duplication (Ireland *et al.* 1995) can present with the facial features, cardiac and palate abnormalities.

2. *2q31 deletion* (Del Campo *et al.* 1999) presents with the upper limb abnormalities, but not the facial characteristics.

3. *Fryns syndrome* (Fryns *et al.* 1979) has many similar characteristics – poor development of the forearms and lower leg is seen in 75 per cent; cleft palate in 30 per cent; cardiac, kidney and genital abnormalities are also common.

4. *Foetal alcohol syndrome* (Miles *et al.* 2003; Nash *et al.* 2008) can result in intrauterine growth problems and early failure to thrive, sinophrys, a small nose and cardiac defects. Increased nuchal translucency (a collection of fluid behind the nape of the foetal neck, which can be seen on ultrasound) has been described in the first trimester (Huang and Porto 2002). This is a finding more typically reported in association with Down syndrome.

The facial features consistent with CdLS can be recognized from ultrasound scanning *in utero* (Boog *et al.* 1999; Urban and Hartung 2001).

There is a suggestion of genotype–phenotype association, with truncating mutations resulting in more severely affected cases and missense mutations in a milder phenotype (Gillis *et al.* 2004); however, as over 50 genetic NIPBL variants have so far been reported (Tonkin *et al.* 2004), and numbers of clinical cases remain small, the strength of this association is unclear.

Treatment and management: This is a complex disorder with a variable phenotype, so initial assessment must be multidisciplinary. The extent of follow-up assessments depends on the findings at this stage.

The high rate of gastrointestinal problems warrants evaluation for management and possible surgery. A similar approach is needed with cardiac function. Kidney function should also be evaluated, and a neurological screening, including an EEG, should be carried out. Audiology and ophthalmology (vision and hearing) assessments should be undertaken once these are feasible. Regular assessment of growth against CdLS centiles would be sensible. Platelet and white blood cell levels should be measured, although their significance has not yet been established. Orthopaedic assessment is sensible as scoliosis can occur, and equinovarus can impair motor development.

Speech and language, physiotherapy, occupational therapy and cognitive/developmental assessments should be carried out to guide self-help and communicative development. An assessment of ASD symptomology using a standardized scale, such as the Autism Diagnostic Observation Schedule (ADOS), should also be carried out as a baseline.

A number of possible complications of CdLS may require surgical intervention – for example, for gastro-oesophageal reflux; intestinal malrotation; gastrostomy tube placement in severe failure to thrive; correction of cardiac defects; interventions to improve manipulation of hands, or correct clubfoot; and orchiopexy to correct undescended testes.

Medication may be required for seizure control, and antibiotics may be required in the management of kidney problems. Problems with the regulation of body temperature may be seen, and this can be an important factor during any type of surgical procedure (Papadimos and Marco 2003).

Further information and support:

The following is a useful book on self-injury: Oliver, C., Moss, J., Petty, J., Arron, K., Sloneem, J. and Hall, S. (2003) *Self-injurious Behaviour in Cornelia de Lange Syndrome: A Guide for Parents and Carers.* Coventry: Trident Communications Ltd. It can be downloaded from www.cdlsusa.org.

Websites and support groups

International:

CdLS-World is an international 'hub' for worldwide organizations and communities united by Cornelia de Lange Syndrome. Country-specific contact information is available on the CdLS website, www. cdlsworld.org.

In Australasia (Australia, Malaysia, New Zealand, Philippines, Singapore and SE Asia):

CdLS Association (Australasia), Inc.
159 Boddington Crescent
Australian Capital Territory
Kambah 2902
Australia
Tel.: 02 62 31 6866
E-mail: pcrawfor@dynamite.com.au
Website: www.cdlsaus.org/

In Canada:

1258 Pettit Road
Fort Erie,
Ontario
L2A 5A3
Tel.: 905-994-0499
E-mail: cdls@iaw.on.ca

In Denmark:

Storringvej 7b Lillering
8462 Harlev J.
Tel.: (45) 86 94 10 20
Fax: (45) 86 94 10 55
E-mail: cdlbot@post6.tele.dk

In France (also Belgium and parts of Switzerland):

Association Française du Syndrome de Cornelia de Lange
6 Ter Rue Pasteur
78330 Fontenanay Le Fleury
Tel.: (33) 1 34 60 06 22
Fax: (33) 1 34 60 10 39
E-mail: afscdl-fr@wanadoo.fr

In Germany:

Ober-Liebersbach 27
69509 Morlenbach
Tel.: (49) 06 209 6650 or (49) 821 451826
Fax: (49) 713 193
E-mail: Kegel-moerlenbach@t-online.de
or brigitte.metken@newsfactory.net

In Italy:

Associazione Nazionale di Volontariato Cornelia de Lange
Strada Delle March, 49
61100 Pesaro
Tel.: (39) 07 21 34238
Fax: (39) 07 21 850897
E-mail: famigliecdl@abanet.it
Website: www.corneliadelange.org

In Japan:

CdLS Japan
E-mail: kmihoko@tg7.so-net.ne.jp

In Norway:

Bergsto 58
4790 Lillesand
Tel.: (47) 37 27 32 34
Fax: (47) 38 04 11 56
E-mail: anne.aune@gjensidige.no (work)

In Portugal:

Rua Major Rosa
Santos Bastos
No. 39 Loures
Tel.: (351) 1 980 50 53

In Spain:

Tel.: (973) 377-6021 (United States)
E-mail: coughlan@montblanc.com

In Sweden:

Magnebergsvagen 8
Enskededalen
12133 Stockholm
Sweden
Tel.: (46) 8 649 95 47
Fax: (46) 8 678 81 33
E-mail: Snorre.hermansson@swipnet.se

In Switzerland:
Croisettes 7,
1066 Epalinges
Tel.: (011-41) 21 652 93 42
E-mail: lpesse@freesurf.ch

In the UK and Ireland:
CdLS UK and Ireland
Tall Trees
106 Lodge Road
Grays,
Essex
RM16 2UL
Tel.: 01373 756439
Fax: 01712 364740
E-mail: cdls@barkers.co.uk
Website: www.cdls.org.uk

In the USA:
Cornelia de Lange Syndrome Foundation Inc.
302 West Main St.
Suite 100
Avon
CT 06001
Tel.: 800-223-8355 or 860-676-8166
Fax: 860-676-8337
E-mail: info@cdlsusa.org
Website: www.cdlsusa.org
The Foundation has useful charts for early physical growth and early milestones in CdLS, which can be freely downloaded from the 'Be Informed' section of their website. This also contains useful information on nutrition, management and treatment.

28

Juvenile dentatorubral-pallidoluysian atrophy (JDPLA)

aka   •   Naito-Oyanagi disease

Gene locus: 12p13.31

Key ASD references: Licht and Lynch 2002; Wada *et al.* 1998

JDPLA is inherited as an autosomal dominant condition. It was first described by Smith, Conda and Malamud (1958), and the term dentatorubral-pallidoluysian atrophy first appears in Smith's chapter in the classic Vinken and Bruyn *Handbook of Clinical Neurology* (1975). A useful review can be found in Kanazawa (1998).

The neurological features seen at autopsy give the condition its rather cumbersome name: the combined degeneration of the dentatorubral system (a nerve fibre system beginning in the dentate nucleus in the cerebellum and projecting to the red nucleus in the midbrain) and the pallidoluysian system (which projects from the globus pallidus – part of the lentiform nucleus in the midbrain – to subthalamic nuclei).

JDPLA is a cytosine–adenosine–guanine (CAG) triplet expansion condition – a small section of DNA has been copied significantly more often than normal, resulting in abnormal production of mRNA, and interfering with normal protein production. Triplet repeats are seen in a number of ASD-related conditions. There is mounting consensus that triplet repeat disorders are underpinned by the same general mechanism (Kaplan, Itzkovitz and Shapiro 2007), notwithstanding their differences in clinical presentation.

JDPLA is most commonly reported in Japanese populations, in whom it was first clearly described (Naito and Oyanagi 1982). Several Japanese series have been reported (for example, Iizuka, Hirayama and Maehara 1984). It may also be more common in other Asiatic groups; however, so far such cases have only been reported from Hong Kong (Yam *et al.* 2004). There are reports of Portuguese families of Asiatic origin who have a high prevalence of JDPLA (Martins *et al.* 2003), and there is a higher than expected prevalence in the UK, in South Wales (Wardle *et al.* 2007). Otherwise only sporadic cases have been reported.

How common is JDPLA? JDPLA is a disorder that appears rare in European Caucasian populations (prevalence estimated at <1 per 1,000,000). It is significantly more common in Japan. The prevalence estimate from one combined review of Japanese and Caucasian cases estimates overall prevalence at 0.2–0.7 per 100,000 (Takano *et al.* 1998).

Main clinical features: The juvenile or early onset form of dentatorubral-pallidoluysian atrophy typically presents with progressive myoclonic epilepsy and dementia. The clinical features and progression of JDPLA are highly variable, even within the same family (Saitoh *et al.* 1998); however, most of those affected are completely physically dependent by between five and 20 years of age.

There seems to be a link between the size of the expansion and the pattern of progression, with larger expansions resulting in an earlier onset and more severe presentation (Ikeuchi *et al.* 1995; Koide *et al.* 1994), although care needs to be taken in interpreting this information, as so few cases have been reported (Potter 1996). From the work of Koide *et al.* it appears that maternal transmission leads to a shortening of the repeated DNA sequence, while paternal transmission leads to lengthening. Longer triplet sequences are associated with greater severity and earlier onset, so where the condition is inherited rather than a *de novo* mutation, establishing the parent of origin is an important aspect of assessment.

Hirayama *et al.* (1981) tried to characterize three distinct forms of dentatorubro-pallidoluysian atrophy (DRPLA): an ataxic-choreoathetoid form; a pseudo-Huntington form; and a myoclonic epilepsy form.

It seems likely that there is a link between expansion size, age of onset and phenotype, with the largest expansion being seen in the myoclonic type, intermediate expansion in the pseudo-Huntington type, and smallest expansion in the ataxic-choreoathetoid type. Childhood-onset presentation normally includes myoclonic epilepsy, while later onset cases are seldom epileptic (Tomoda *et al.* 1991). For example, Shimojo *et al.* (2001) report two unrelated cases with very early onset, cortical atrophy, severe motor and seizure difficulties, and particularly large CAG expansions.

It may be that the pseudo-Huntington form results from the effects of a secondary gene such as GRIK2 (Rubinsztein *et al.* 1997). This gene is involved in glutamate metabolism, and has been linked to autism in screening studies (Jamain *et al.* 2002; Shuang *et al.* 2004). DRPLA has been reported in cases diagnosed with Huntington's chorea (Connarty *et al.* 1996).

Anticipation has been shown in some families – increasing severity in successive generations. A family reported by Aoki *et al.* (1994) was documented over three generations. In the first, there were late onset symptoms (aged 52–60 years) with mild cerebellar ataxia; the mother in the second generation showed severe cerebellar ataxia with onset in her thirties; the child in the third generation had learning difficulties and myoclonic epilepsy beginning at age 8. In 71 affected individuals from 12 Japanese families, Komure *et al.* (1995) found between 7 and 23 CAG repeats in unaffected family members, and between 53 and 88 in those affected. Longer repeat lengths were associated with earlier age of onset. Vinton *et al.* (2005) describe similar differences dependent on age at presentation and expansion size in a three-generation Caucasian family of Balkan origin.

From studies of sperm in affected men, and those from several other expansion disorders, CAG expansion in DRPLA produces the strongest anticipation effect seen to date in a triplet expansion disorder (Takiyama *et al.* 1999).

In contrast, however, cases are reported from the same families where the same level of expansion results in very different phenotypes (Saitoh *et al.* 1998), which suggests that other factors are involved.

Is there a link between JDPLA and ASD?

- The first suggestion of a link with ASD appears in a paper by Wada *et al.* in 1998. They reported on an 11-year-old boy with ASD who had had psychomotor difficulties from infancy with cerebellar ataxia; at six years he began having myoclonic seizures. Genetic testing had identified a 12p13.31 expansion.

- Licht and Lynch (2002) report on six North American cases, two of whom, cousins and the youngest in the family pedigree, had JDPLA and autism. The basis for autistic diagnosis is unclear.

Differential diagnosis: There is a complex differential diagnosis within the ataxias (Manto 2005; Poretti, Wolf and Boltshauser 2008), but JDPLA is the only such condition so far reported in association with ASD.

'Haw River syndrome' in the USA is caused by the same triplet repeat polyalanine expansion, but it presents with a different clinical phenotype – without the myoclonic seizures seen in the JDPLA, but with calcification to the basal ganglia and subcortical demyelinization that are not reported in JDPLA. To date only a small number of Haw River syndrome cases have been reported, and all have been from African-American families (Burke *et al.* 1996).

JDPLA has a highly variable early presentation. The differential diagnosis in ASD would most probably be with other conditions, resulting in certain early motor problems and/or seizure involvement. The principal conditions that would need to be considered are: adenylosuccinate lyase deficiency [9]; Angelman syndrome [11]; ARX mutations [13]; CATCH 22 [18]; Down syndrome [31]; Dravet's syndrome [32]; Duchenne and Becker muscular dystrophy [33]; fragile-X syndrome [35]; GAMT deficiency [37]; myotonic dystrophy type 1 [50]; Schindler disease [65]; and (in girls) Rett syndrome [63a] and Rett syndrome (Hanefeld variant) [63b].

A further consideration in the early stages, particularly in Nordic populations, would be infantile neural ceroid lipofudcinosis; however, the lack of JDPLA cases in this population would appear to make diagnostic confusion unlikely.

Some cases present with the appearance of Huntington's chorea (Hirayama *et al.* 1981; Norremolle *et al.* 1995); however, these cases have later onset.

Treatment and management: At the present time there is no specific treatment for JDPLA. Clinical management is focused on physiotherapy for the motor problems, together with medical management of the epilepsy that is typically seen in the juvenile form. One paper describes a 16-year-old girl whose seizure control had shown a positive response to ketogenic diet (Matsuura *et al.* 2009).

If there is a common basis to triplet expansion, as has been suggested (Kaplan, Itzkovitz and Shapiro 2007), successful therapeutic strategies, as appear likely in fragile-X syndrome [35], hold out some promise for the possibility of targeted clinical intervention in JDPLA.

Further information and support:

In Germany:
DHAG: Deutsche Heredo-Ataxie-Gesellschaft. e.V.
Hofener Str. 76
70372 Stuttgart
Tel.: 49 (0)711 5504644
Fax: 49 (0)711 8496628

In Italy:
AISA: Associazione Nazionale Lotta alle Sindromi Atassiche – ONLUS
Via Cina 91
00144 Roma
Tel.: 39 06 5201490
Fax: 39 06 5201490

In the UK:
CLIMB: Children Living with Inherited Metabolic Diseases
Climb Building
176 Nantwich Road
Crewe
CW2 6BG
Tel.: 0870 770 0326
Fax: 0870 770 0327

Pan-European:
euro-ATAXIA (European Federation of Hereditary Ataxias)
Ataxia UK
9 Winchester House
Kennington Park
Cranmer Road
London
SW9 6EJ
United Kingdom
Tel.: 020 7582 1444
E-mail: marco.meinders@euro-ataxia.eu
www.euro-ataxia.eu

A simple description of the neurology of DRPLA can be found on the HOPES (Huntington's Outreach Project for Education at Stanford) website, accessible at http://images.google.co.uk.

29a

DiGeorge syndrome I (phenotypic overlap)

Gene locus: 22q11.2

Key ASD references: Antshel *et al.* 2007; Evers *et al.* 2006; Fine *et al.* 2005; Lajiness-O'Neill *et al.* 2005; Mukaddes and Herguner 2007; Niklasson *et al.* 2001; Paylor *et al.* 2006

See also CATCH 22 [18]; velocardiofacial syndrome [76].

DiGeorge syndrome I is a condition that affects the migration of nerve cells and has effects on a number of organ systems, including the development of the thymus gland and cardiovascular system. It was first described in a 1965 discussion paper by paediatrician Dr Angelo DiGeorge, who described the constellation of hypoplasia of the thymus gland, T-lymphocyte deficiency, congenital hypoparathyroidism, hypocalcaemia and moderate facial dysmorphism (DiGeorge 1965).

It was first linked to a genetic condition by de la Chapelle *et al.* (1981). These French authors reported on a 20;22 translocation, suggesting that DiGeorge syndrome might be due to a deletion within chromosome 22 or to a partial duplication of 20p. They also suggested that DiGeorge syndrome might result from 22q11 monosomy. This speculation was confirmed the following year by a report on three DiGeorge patients with 22q11 translocation (Kelley *et al.* 1982). The T-Box 1 or TBX1 gene which maps to this area was identified and cloned in 1997 (Chieffo *et al.* 1997).

DiGeorge syndrome is inherited as an autosomal dominant condition. Most cases (93 per cent) occur as spontaneous mutations.

The typical person with a DiGeorge syndrome diagnosis has a large deletion at 22q11.2 involving some 30 genes. Few of these have been well characterized, and the variation across these gene combinations is likely to account for much of the wide phenotypic variation seen.

How common is DiGeorge syndrome? The combined prevalence of DiGeorge syndromes I + II has been estimated as between 13.2 and 23.3 per 100,000. Overall, 22q11 defects are reported as being present in around one in 4,000 live births (Burn *et al.* 1995).

Interesting to note is that in a large study by Goodship *et al.* (1998) of 207 infants with congenital heart disease, drawn from a birth cohort of 69,129 five had 22q11 deletions consistent with DiGeorge syndrome. This gives a birth prevalence of approximately 13 per 100,000. As the rate of cardiac problems in DiGeorge syndrome is reported as being around 75 per cent, this suggests either that there may be under-ascertainment, or that the prevalence of DiGeorge syndrome in those with cardiac anomalies is the same as in those without. The data demonstrate that 22q11 deletions are the second most likely genetic factor associated with congenital cardiac problems after Down syndrome [31].

Main clinical features: DiGeorge syndrome is one of a number of conditions affecting T-box genes (Packham and Brook 2003). Individuals with a 22q11.2 deletion are typically of short stature and have mild to moderate learning disability. Campbell, Daly *et al.* (2006) found that 39 children with 22q11.2 deletion (mean age 11 years) had an IQ of 67+/-10, while 26 sibling controls (mean age 11 years) had an IQ of 102+/-12. Individuals with a 22q11.2 deletion typically exhibit deficits in executive functions (normally viewed as problems with anticipating consequences, mental flexibility and in interpreting the actions of others) (Bearden, Reus and Freimer 2004).

The facial features are low-set ears, a bulbous nose, small mouth and jaw, cleft palate (with resultant hypernasal speech) and occasionally cleft lip.

The early presenting features are typically: cardiac problems; immune abnormalities (low T-cells resulting in increased susceptibility to infections due to poor development of the thymus gland); and/or hypocalcaemia due to hypoparathyroidism (often presenting as neonatal seizures, due to poor development of the parathyroid gland).

Stewart et al. (1999) found that 5/13 cases with 22q11.2 microdeletion had kidney problems. Kujat et al. (2006) found that 5/6 cases studied had kidney problems. This has not been investigated in larger studies to date, but suggests that these renal problems may be common.

The amygdala is enlarged (Kates et al. 2006), the cerebellum is smaller than normal (van Amelsvoort et al. 2004), and there are differences in the development of the prefrontal cortex (Kates et al. 2005). All are differences reported in autism. The amygdala is significantly larger in those with both 22q11.2 deletions and ASD than in those with 22q11.2 alone, and in most this is also in the context of further psychiatric co-morbidity. On brain imaging, polymicrogyria is commonly reported (Robin et al. 2006), particularly on the right.

In adult cases psychiatric presentations, particularly schizophrenia and depressive disorder, are more common than expected. In one series of 78 adult cases (Bassett et al. 2005) over 22 per cent were found to be schizophrenic, while over 92 per cent had learning difficulties. Some adult cases also present with late-onset hypocalcaemia (Kar et al. 2005).

A proportion of people with 22q11.2 deletions have virtually no symptomology. This may be true of 10–25 per cent of cases (Levy et al. 1997). As 'benign' cases are unlikely to be screened in the general population, prevalence estimates based on clinical presentation may underestimate rates.

In a study of 13 DiGeorge phenotype cases with no apparent 22q11 deletion, Yagi et al. (2003) identified several TBX1 mutations as sufficient to cause the five major phenotypic features – typical facial features; conotruncal cardiac defects; cleft palate; hypoplasia of the thymus gland; and parathyroid dysfunction with hypocalcaemia. Unlike deletion cases, mutations did not appear to result in any associated learning difficulties.

Discordant clinical phenotypes in monozygotic twins suggest that factors other than the 22q11.2 deletion are required to produce the clinical phenotype (Vincent et al. 1999).

Is there a link between DiGeorge syndrome I and ASD?

- In the first systematic study, Fine et al. (2005) reported on 98 people with a 22q11.2 deletion screened for ASD. Fourteen qualified for a diagnosis of ASD, and 22 displayed significant levels of ASD symptomology.

- In a neuropsychiatric review, Lajiness-O'Neill et al. (2005) compared the memory function of a group of 39 children with 22q11.2 deletion syndrome and their siblings to that of a group of children diagnosed with autism and their siblings. On most measures both groups showed similar deficits in verbal memory and memory for faces, compared to siblings, demonstrating differences in the functioning of the dorsolateral prefrontal cortex. ADHD was seen in 44 per cent and an ASD in 31 per cent, while only six per cent were of normal overall IQ.

- Evers *et al.* (2006) document a 52-year-old adult case with a 22q11.2 deletion, a diagnosis of velocardiofacial syndrome with dementia, and 'autistic features'. He had shown progressive cognitive decline since the age of 36. He was reported as having an autistic sister who also carried the deletion.

- In a paper describing Tbx1 haploinsufficiency, Paylor *et al.* (2006) describe one family with an affected mother and two sons, where the mother had a major depressive illness and one of the sons had a diagnosis of Asperger's syndrome.

- Antshel *et al.* (2007) found that 17/41 (41 per cent) of a series of 22q11.2 children aged from 6.5 to 15.8 years fulfilled diagnostic criteria for an ASD. This was a significantly higher proportion of individuals than reported in the general population, and in the earlier study by Fine *et al.* The latter could be because of the differences in ADI-R (Autism Diagnostic Interview – Revised) scoring used in the two studies.

- In 2007, Mukaddes and Herguner reported on a nine-year-old girl with a 22q11.2 duplication, who was diagnosed with autistic disorder, language delay and behavioural problems.

Immune differences: Poor or absent function of the thymus gland results in reduced or absent T-cells, which can be measured by assessing levels of CD4 cells (Wilson *et al.* 1993). Parathyroid abnormality can be assessed by measuring any reduction of thyrocalcitonin immunoreactive cells (C-cells) (Burke *et al.* 1987; Palacios *et al.* 1993). Jawad *et al.* (2001) studied 195 patients with chromosome 22q11 deletion syndrome and found that diminished T-cell counts in the peripheral blood are common. Four presented with juvenile rheumatoid arthritis and eight with idiopathic thrombocytopenic purpura (a bleeding disorder caused by low platelet levels). A variety of autoimmune conditions were seen in individual cases.

A general overview of immunological aspects of DiGeorge syndrome can be found in McLean-Tooke *et al.* (2008) who also reported on T-cell abnormalities in a further series of 27 child cases.

Differential diagnosis: A variety of other clinical diagnoses are given to individuals with 22q11.2 deletion anomalies. Amongst the most common are: CATCH 22 [18]; CATCH phenotype; Cayler cardiofacial syndrome; Shprintzen's syndrome/velocardiofacial syndrome [76]; Takao velocardiofacial syndrome (conotruncal anomaly face syndrome); 22q11.2 deletion syndrome; and Opitz G/BBB syndrome, or, more rarely, Kousseff syndrome (Maclean *et al.* 2004). As several of these conditions have been reported specifically in association with ASD and there is still debate over their differentiation, separate discussion is given to those that have been reported as being linked with ASD. Shprintzen (1994), for example, believed velocardiofacial syndrome to be a specific condition, and viewed DiGeorge syndrome as heterogeneous. Burn (1999) suggests that the primary presentation in the individual case should dictate the diagnostic label used: *Takao syndrome* where the major problem is cardiac defect; *DiGeorge syndrome* where there is neonatal presentation with hypocalcaemia and hypoplasia of the thymus gland;

velocardiofacial syndrome where there is abnormality of the palate with speech problems; replacing *CATCH phenotype* instead of CATCH 22 for people with the combination of a cardiac abnormality, T-cell deficit, cleft palate and hypocalcaemia. He also thought the term '22q11 deletion syndrome' was an acceptable diagnostic term. De Decker and Lawrenson (2001) suggest a common gene defect with a diverse phenotype.

A distal deletion of 22q11.2 shows some phenoptypic overlap, but the presentation seems sufficiently different to be treated as a separate condition (Ben-Shachar *et al.* 2008). Mosaic microdeletion cases are also now being reported with cardiac anomalies, learning disability and dysmorphic facial features (Halder *et al.* 2008).

Several other genetic differences have been reported in association with the DiGeorge phenotype. Greenberg *et al.* (1988) reported one case in association with del10p13 (now known as DiGeorge II [29b]) and a further case with a 18q21.33 deletion, and Fukushima *et al.* (1992) reported on a female infant with a deletion at 4q21.3–q25. It is possible that these early cases would also be found to have 22q11.2 microdeletions on present-day testing.

A DiGeorge-like phenotype can also be produced by the teratogenic effects of foetal exposure to alcohol or to low levels of retinoic acid (from vitamin A) during pregnancy (see Vermot *et al.* 2003 for discussion).

Several reports have now documented hyperthyroidism (Graves disease) in DiGeorge syndrome. Kawame *et al.* (2001) described five patients with chromosome 22q11.2 deletion (four girls and 12 boys) who manifested Graves disease between the ages of 27 months and 16 years, in one case with seizure disorder, and suggested that Graves disease may be part of the clinical spectrum of this disorder. Gosselin *et al.* (2004) documented three further cases of Graves disease in association with 22q11.2.

It is more common in the inherited cases of DiGeorge syndrome for the gene anomaly to be inherited from the mother (Demczuk *et al.* 1995).

Treatment and management: Calcium supplementation can be helpful, as most cases have marked hypocalcaemia. The poor immune status of many can present complications for surgical intervention, which may be required for thymus transplant or corrective heart surgery.

In the small proportion of patients who do not have a thymus gland (about one per cent), thymus transplantation is generally well tolerated and can in some cases restore normal immune function (Markert *et al.* 1999, 2007). There have been steady improvements in the techniques involved (Hudson *et al.* 2007). Markert *et al.* (1999) suggest that early transplantation may hold out the greatest hope for correction of immune problems.

There are a range of conotruncal cardiac defects seen in association with 22q11.2 (Carotti *et al.* 2008; Marino *et al.* 2001). Treatment for cardiac abnormalities should be as for any other people with similar defects, bearing in mind the complications secondary to compromised immune status.

Speech and language therapy may be required, particularly where articulatory problems are present. Therapies aimed at improving executive functioning and working memory may be helpful, once assessment to establish a baseline level of functioning has been carried out.

Further information and support:

In Australia:
Australian 22q Group
19 Eleanor Crescente/Rooty Hill
Sydney
NSW 2766
Tel.: 61 2 625 3710
E-mail: vcfsfa@pnc.com.au

In Canada:
Canadian 22q Group
320 Cote Street Antoine
West Montreal
Quebec
H3Y 2J4
E-mail: hsugarmill@aol.com

Chromosome 22 Central
232 Kent Avenue
Timmins
Ontario
P4N 3C3
Tel.: 705-268-3099
E-mail: c22c@hotmail.com

In the UK:
Max Appeal!
Lansdowne House
13 Meriden Avenue
Wollaston
Stourbridge
West Midlands
DY8 4QN
Website: www.maxappeal.org.uk

The 22q11 Group
PO Box 1302
MK13 0LZ
Tel.: 01908 320852
E-mail: 22q11@melcom.cix.co.uk
Website: www.vcfs.net

In the USA:
International DiGeorge/VCF Support Network
c/o Family Voices of New York
46 1/2 Clinton Avenue
Cortland
NY 13045
Tel.: 607-753-1621 (day); 607-753-1250 (eve)
Fax: 607-758-7420

29b

DiGeorge syndrome II (DGS II)

aka • velocardiofacial syndrome II

• 10p13–p14 deletion syndrome

• HDR syndrome

Gene locus: 10p13–14

Key ASD reference: No specific papers to date (see discussion below).

Cases with an apparent DiGeorge phenotype who have a deletion at 10p but no 22q11.2 deletion were first reported by Greenberg *et al.* (1988) in a series of DiGeorge phenotype cases who were screened for genetic anomalies.

The critical gene region for DGS II has been identified by mapping the deletion in 12 patients with 10p deletions, nine of whom showed a DiGeorge phenotype (Schuffenhauer *et al.* 1998).

How common is DGS II? 10p13–14 has not shown up as having significant linkage to ASD. Investigation of DGS II is typically considered where there is a DiGeorge phenotype with a negative finding on deletion testing of 22q11.2, the gene implicated in DiGeorge syndrome I. The prevalence of DGS II is uncertain at this time. Bartsch *et al.* (2003) studied a series of 295 patients with a DiGeorge phenotype and did not identify any with a 10p14 defect – they recommend that screening for 10p anomalies is not warranted on the basis of clinical phenotype. That said, no studies in other groups have been carried out, and prevalence could have been lower in the central European population studied by this group

Main clinical features: The main clinical features reported are as for DiGeorge syndrome I, including hypoparathyroidism, conotruncal cardiac defects, immune deficiency, deafness and kidney abnormalities (see above under [29a]). As an example, Yatsenko *et al.* (2004) described a boy with an interstitial 10p deletion, craniofacial dysmorphology, developmental delay and an atrial-septal heart defect.

These findings suggest that the key genetic features in both DiGeorge syndromes impact on the same neurodevelopmental and somatic processes.

Is there a link between DGS II and ASD? DGS II is included here for discussion as the phenotype is highly similar to that described in DiGeorge syndrome I; many people given a DiGeorge syndrome diagnosis are 22q11.2 deletion negative and no systematic screening has yet been carried out. It seems likely that there will be ASD cases with DGS II; however, as the prevalence is small compared to 22q11.2, identifying such cases has been slower.

Differential diagnosis: Based on phenotype, the differential diagnosis is as for DiGeorge syndrome I.

Treatment and management: Although uncommon, the severe hypocalcaemia in such cases (as reported in a paternally inherited balanced translocation of 10p13 and 3q29) can lead to cardiac failure, unless the hypocalcaemia is aggressively managed (Chao *et al.* 2009).

Further information and support: See above under DiGeorge syndrome I [29a].

30

Dihydropyrimidine dehydrogenase (DPYS) deficiency

---

aka • uraciluria thyminuria

Gene locus: 1p22

Key ASD references: Berger *et al.* 1984; Marshall *et al.* 2008; van Gennip *et al.* 1997; van Kuilenburg *et al.* 1999

DPYS deficiency is an inborn error of metabolism. It is an autosomal recessive disorder of pyrimidine catabolism. Lack of the enzyme dihydropyrimidine dehydrogenase (DPYD) interrupts the first stage in the catabolism of uracil and thymine by the liver, with a consequent excess of uracil, thymine and 5-hydroxymethyluracil, which can all be detected at high levels in the urine of those affected. A Dutch group first described it in 1984 (Berger *et al.* 1984). There is no obvious clinical or behavioural phenotype.

DPYS has two major metabolic consequences – it alters the metabolism of the amino acids thymine and valine – which results in a build-up of beta-aminoisobutyric acid. These may provide a direct focus for treatment as they have effects on the levels of alanine-containing peptides (van Kuilenburg *et al.* 2004, 2006).

How common is DPYS deficiency? There is no general epidemiological data on prevalence of DPYS deficiency. From studies in cancer, rates in Caucasian populations are around three to five per cent (Lu, Zhang and Diasio 1993; Lu *et al.* 1998; Relling *et al.* 1992). There is limited information on other ethnic groups, with reports of Indian (Saif *et al.* 2006), Pakistani (Yau *et al.* 2004) and Japanese (Ogura 2006) cases; however, the only systematic data is on African-American populations which have higher rates, particularly in females, in whom over 12 per cent are reportedly affected (Mattison *et al.* 2006). Limited screening to date has shown G>A splice site mutations to be fairly common in Finnish and Taiwanese populations (Wei *et al.* 1996).

Screening for DPYS is not routine, even in individuals requiring 5-fluorouracil cancer chemotherapy (van Kuilenburg 2006).

Main clinical features: As the general population prevalence figures reported are high, it would appear that for most situations the effects of DPYS deficiency are benign and that there is no obvious physical or behavioural phenotype. In children presenting with problems the presentation is variable, including craniofacial abnormalities, ocular problems, seizures, microcephaly, developmental delay, hypotonia, brisk reflexes and autistic features (van Gennip *et al.* 1997; van Kuilenburg *et al.* 1999; Yau *et al.* 2004).

The catabolism of pyrimidine is the only source of alanine in humans (Gonzalez and Fernandez-Salguero 1995; Wasternack 1980). As dihydropyrimidines do not accumulate in DPYS deficiency, urine needs to be tested for metabolites (van Gennip *et al.* 1994). Clinical findings that suggest screening for disorders of purine and pyrimidine metabolism have been discussed by Duran *et al.* (1997).

Is there a link between DPYS deficiency and ASD?

- In the initial paper (Berger *et al.* 1984), three cases were described, two boys and one girl. The first boy (aged eight) had slow speech development and solitary behaviour with autistic features, but was described as of normal intelligence; the second boy (aged three) had severe growth retardation, microcephaly and learning difficulties; the girl (aged 13) had absence seizures, dry skin and learning difficulties.

- Van Gennip *et al.* (1997) first reported autistic features in a series of DPYS cases, and in a systematic review van Kuilenburg *et al.* (1999) reported autism as affecting five of their 22 cases (23 per cent).

The various linkage studies to date have not reported a significant association between 1p22 and ASD. One genome-wide copy-number variation study (Marshall *et al.* 2008) did identify this as a novel, previously unreported, ASD susceptibility locus.

At the present time this appears to be a rare but important association with a condition that has a high population prevalence.

Differential diagnosis: The constellation of features reported in DPYS deficiency could be confused phenotypically with other conditions such as INCL (infantile neural ceroid lipofuscinosis) (Wisniewski *et al.* 2000), Rett syndrome [63a] and Rett syndrome (Hanefeld variant) [63b], in which there is also hypotonia, microcephaly and autistic symptomology. As all have a specific genotype and DPYS has a clear metabolic profile, clinical differentiation should not be problematic.

A number of ASD conditions are linked to increased cancer risks. Differentiation from these conditions is important. The ASD conditions reported in association with cancer are: XXY [3]; Bannayan-Riley-Ruvalcaba syndrome [15]; basal cell naevus syndrome [16]; CATCH 22 [18]; Cowden syndrome [26]; Down syndrome [31]; neurofibromatosis type 1 [51]; Noonan syndrome [52]; Sotos syndrome [68]; xeroderma pigmentosum [79]; and X-linked ichthyosis [80]. Differentiating may be important where treatment using chemotherapies metabolized by dihydropyrimidine dehydrogenase is being considered, as a failure to recognize DPYS could prove dangerous or even fatal.

Genetics: The principal interest to date has been in the effect of DPYS deficiency in causing severe adverse reactions to 5-fluoracil-based cancer chemotherapy (Morrison *et al.* 1997). 5-fluoracil is used extensively in the treatment of various cancers, including HIV-associated malignancies. Wide variations in DPYD activity are seen in the general population (Ridge *et al.* 1998). As DPYD breaks down 5-fluoracil in normal circumstances, an unrecognized lack of the enzyme can lead to severe toxicity or fatality due to toxic build-up (Ezzeldin and Diasio 2004; van Kuilenburg *et al.* 2001). This is potentially a problem for up to one in 20 people going for cancer chemotherapy. Effects on the action of a range of medications used in cancer therapy, as well as muscle problems and viral and fungal infections, are now known (Schmidt *et al.* 2005).

Treatment and management: Assessment for DPYS may be advisable where there are neurological symptoms such as epileptic seizures, with or without learning disability (Schmidt *et al.* 2005).

In addition to a build-up of uracil, thymine and 5-hydroxymethyluracil, a direct consequence of DPYS deficiency is a lack of alanine. Alanine is usually a non-essential amino acid, as it is derived through this pathway. Deficits are therefore likely only in DPYS in combination with a diet low in alanine-containing foods – principally meat, seafood and dairy but also (at lower levels) cereals, nuts, some legumes and yeast.

Alanine is produced alongside lactate during anaerobic exercise – the alanine is converted to glucose in the liver, with urea as a byproduct.

Although no trials have yet been carried out, it seems possible that alanine supplementation may be beneficial in DPYS. Clinical trials of alanine supplementation have been carried out on insulin-dependent diabetes, where it stabilizes night-time glucose levels, and in benign enlarged prostate, where it reduces symptoms. Alanine is required for the metabolism of tryptophan, and is important in maintaining glucose levels.

Further information and support: There is no specific support or advocacy group for DPYS. Further information and general support can be found through the organizations cited below.

The National Organization for Rare Disorders
(NORD)
Website: www.rarediseases.org

The Genetic Alliance
Website: www.geneticalliance.org

31

Down syndrome (DS)

---

aka   •   mongolism (historical)

Gene locus: Trisomy of chromosome 21 (critical region 21q22.2)

Key ASD references: Bregman and Volkmar 1988; Buckley 2005; Carter J.C. *et al.* 2007; Cohen *et al.* 2005; Ghaziuddin 1997, 2000; Ghaziuddin, Tsai and Ghaziuddin 1992; Howlin, Wing and Gould 1995; Kent, Perry and Evans 1998; Prasher and Clarke 1996; Rasmussen P. *et al.* 2001; Starr *et al.* 2005; Wakabayashi 1979

DS was first described in an essay printed in 1866 (Down 1867). It was the first clearly described and differentiated form of learning disability. There is now a huge clinical literature, with over 23,000 clinical and research papers published.

Down syndrome is the most frequent genetic cause of learning disability. It typically results from trisomy of chromosome 21. In 95 per cent of cases, there are three copies of chromosome 21, which are clearly visible on karyotyping. In most of the other five per cent of cases, one copy is translocated to another chromosome, typically 14 or 21.

How common is Down syndrome? Down syndrome is currently reported in around 50 per 100,000 live births (Orphanet Report Series No1 2009). Various factors affect this figure such as sociodemographic and ethnic differences and differences in antenatal screening (see, e.g. Khoshnood *et al.* 2004). Maternal age at conception is also important with increased maternal age being associated with increased risk (Morris and Alberman 2009).

Main clinical features: Down syndrome was first documented, based on the clinical phenotype, almost a century and a half ago (Down 1867). It is typically caused by the presence of an additional copy of chromosome 21 (Lejeune, Gautier and Turpin 1959). Down syndrome remains one of the most common chromosome anomalies seen in clinical practice in learning disability.

The risk of having a child with trisomy 21 increases with maternal age, from one in 1,000 at age 30 to one in 110 at age 40 (Hook, Cross and Schreinemachers 1983; Lamson and Hook 1980). There is a strong independent effect of age of maternal grandmother on likelihood of Down syndrome (Malini and Ramachandra 2006).

The effect of maternal age is confounded with sociodemographic/ethnic factors (Khoshnood *et al.* 2000), which suggests that these findings need to be replicated across different cultural groups.

No equivalent paternal age effect has so far been reported. Roecker and Huethner (1983) found no such effect in a US Caucasian population. However, no large studies or studies in different ethnic groups are available. To date, no study has attempted to link maternal age either to the likelihood of co-morbid autism, or to the possibility of an interaction between the paternal age effect in autism and maternal age effect in DS.

Prevalence at birth does not seem to vary markedly across ethnic groups; however, research is sparse (Carothers, Hecht and Hook 1999; Sherman *et al.* 2007).

Median life expectancy has steadily improved; however, there are major disparities within populations, in the USA at least (MMWR 2001). For the most recent year on which data has been published (1997), the median life expectancy for white individuals with DS was 50, for African-americans 25, and for other ethnic groups about 11 years of age.

A number of malformations and disorders are significantly more common in DS.

Cardiac problems are seen in up to 40 per cent of cases. A small proportion are atrioventricular septal defects and tetralogy of Fallot, which are significantly more common in DS and carry greater operative risks (Stos *et al.* 2004).

A specific gene mutation in the CRELD1 gene found at 3p25.3 has been linked to atrioventricular septal heart defects and found to be present in 2/39 of one DS series (Maslen *et al.* 2006).

Gastrointestinal malformations are more common (Cleves *et al.* 2007). Coeliac disease is also significantly more common (Wallace 2007).

A review of GI concerns in 57 adults attending a general clinic for DS (Wallace 2007) found 56/57 had GI problems. Of these, 6/51 tested positive for (likely) coeliac disease; 29/43 who were tested had helicobacter pylori; 13/53 tested had hepatitis B; and 17/47 tested had hepatitis A. Only 12 had a history of institutional care, the factor to which such infections have typically been attributed.

Coeliac disease is a common concomitant of DS which is now well recognized in the literature (Shamaly *et al.* 2007). There are dietary implications of coeliac disease and there appears to be a strong link between coeliac and the presence of more generalized autoimmune disorders (over 30 per cent compared to 15 per cent in the DS population in general). One large study screened 1,202 DS cases and found 55 with coeliac disease

(4.6 per cent) (Bonamico *et al.* 2001). In addition to their antibody profiles, those with coeliac disease had low serum calcium and iron.

Gallbladder problems are seen in about 25 per cent of cases – some five times more common than in matched general population adult controls (Tyler, Zyzanski and Runser 2004).

Leukaemia is some 10 to 20 times more common in DS than in the general population (Robinson 1992), with an increased risk of acute lymphoblastic leukaemia (ALL) and a marked increase in acute megakaryoblastic leukaemia (AML) (Puumala *et al.* 2007). Megakaryocytic leukaemia (MKL) is 200 to 400 times more common (Zipursky, Peeters and Poon 1987). One study indicates that the increased risk of leukaemia is associated with mutations in the GATA1 gene (Wechsler *et al.* 2002), a transcription factor which affects myeloid lineage commitment (Look 2002). The link with GATA1 is strengthened by the results of other studies which link GATA1 to transient myeloproliferative disorder in DS, a condition which precedes AML in some 30 per cent of cases (Hitzler *et al.* 2003).

There is *accelerated onset and increased prevalence of dementia*, and particularly of Alzheimer's disease (Margallo-Lana *et al.* 2007).

Individuals with DS develop features of Alzheimer's disease more commonly and much earlier than those without a trisomy 21 (Wisniewski, Wisniewski and Wen 1985). From the neuropathology to date, the typical plaques and tangles of Alzheimer's neuropathology are seen earlier than is usual, possibly accelerated by triplication of the gene on Ch21 for amyloid precursor protein. It appears that genetic risk factors such as APOE epsilon 4 increase Alzheimer's risk in DS (Deb *et al.* 2000). An APOE 4 carrier individual has a 2.7-fold increased risk of developing Alzheimer's disease (Rubinsztein *et al.* 1999).

The premature onset of Alzheimer's may be related to higher amyloid precursor protein and/or elevated levels of the inflammatory marker neopterin in children and adolescents with DS, both of which are now being reported in some cases (Mehta *et al.* 2007). No follow-up studies have yet been carried out to indicate the extent and clinical significance of this association. It is interesting to note that, in adults with DS and Alzheimer's type neuropathology, the neurochemistry is different from other AS cases and does not show the same degree of cortical and cerebellar GABA depletion (Seidl *et al.* 2001).

Epilepsy is seen in some eight per cent of DS cases (Goldberg-Stern *et al.* 2001; Prasher, 1994).

Thyroid problems are common, with a wide variation in reported rates, some series reporting as many as 35 per cent of DS cases with thyroid dysfunction (see Prasher 1999 for an extensive review).

Significant hearing loss is seen in about 90 per cent of people with Down syndrome, the most common form being conductive hearing loss. (Mazzoni, Ackley and Nash 1994).

Early cataract formation is a further sensory difficulty experienced by some 1.4 per cent of DS children (Haargaard and Fledelius 2006).

The facial and oral differences seen in DS may contribute to a variety of difficulties – poorer articulation; lower self-esteem; poorer peer relationships. There is some evidence that the use of palatal plates (Bäckman *et al.* 2007), if started early in life, can lead to improved oromotor function, facial expression and speech. Whether there are benefits to cosmetic facial surgery is hotly debated (see Roizen 2005 for discussion), and currently purely cosmetic operations are not actively encouraged. That said, there is an extensive literature in this area, and it may be that some surgery has functional benefits – for example, the shape of the ear can be corrected successfully (O'Malley *et al.* 2007), and the effect of this may be both cosmetic and beneficial to hearing.

High-altitude pulmonary oedema is common in DS (Durmowicz 2001), typically related to a pre-existing cardiac condition. This suggests that people with DS, particularly with a history of cardiac problems, should exercise caution when considering air travel or high-altitude activities like mountaineering.

In giving the above list of medical conditions, the aim is to provide a brief but reasonably thorough overview of factors which are important to rule in or rule out in someone with DS. Many of these conditions have direct implications for help – for example, coeliac individuals require good dietary advice and help, and may benefit from calcium and iron supplementation.

Is there a link between DS and ASD?

- The typical description of the DS child as sociable, affectionate and outgoing was the antithesis of the ASD stereotype (see, for example, Gibbs and Thorpe 1983), and the co-morbidity has been said to be uncommon (for example, Rutter and Schopler 1988). Although occasional single cases have been described (for example, Bregman and Volkmar 1988; Prasher and Clarke 1996; Wakabayashi 1979), these are typically thought of as unusual.

- The first paper to suggest an association between ASD and DS (Howlin, Wing and Gould 1995) described four boys with DS and co-morbid autism, and noted the difficulties in getting clinical recognition of ASD in this group.

- A series of case reports from Michigan reported by Ghaziuddin (Ghaziuddin 1997, 2000; Ghaziuddin, Tsai and Ghaziuddin 1992) provided further case material and illustrated autistic features in the parents of co-morbid cases.

- A 2001 paper documented a case series of 25 co-morbid DS–ASD cases that had presented to the Queen Sylvia Hospital in Goteborg over a 15-year period (Rasmussen *et al.* 2001). This series illustrated a number of factors – the relatively late age at ASD diagnosis (mean: 14.4 years); prevalence of severe infections, principally recurrent otitis media (72 per cent); prevalence of ASD in first or second degree relatives (20 per cent); and prevalence of epilepsy (20 per cent). This is a clinical, not a population, series, with no indication of the overall numbers of DS cases seen over this period, but does suggest this is a significant clinical issue.

- In a small screening study of a self-selected group of 13 DS families (Starr *et al.* 2005) using standardized scales, five were considered to have an ASD. This study again provides evidence for the possibility of co-morbidity, but does not allow any conclusions concerning the prevalence of such a link to be drawn.

- One study, again of a selected sample, provides evidence concerning the behavioural profile of 127 DS subjects on two standardized scales, 64 with co-morbid ASD, 19 with stereotypic movement disorder, 18 with disruptive behaviours, and 26 with no behavioural co-morbidities. The principal conclusion in the current context is that those with ASD showed a distinctive pattern of behaviours (anxiety, social withdrawal and odd/bizarre stereotyped behaviours) which differentiated them from the other groups (Carter J.C. *et al.* 2007).

No studies to date have attempted to differentiate ASD–DS cases from non-ASD–DS cases on the basis of factors such as genetic differences or neurobiology. Two reviews (Cohen *et al.* 2005; Reilly 2009) could not come to clear conclusions over the extent of the association.

The limited epidemiological research that has looked for a possible link antedates the higher currently reported ASD prevalence rates. This will have reduced the apparent prevalence of DS within the broader ASD population. On earlier studies, co-morbidity is seen in between 1.7 per cent and 2.5 per cent of the ASD population (see Fombonne *et al.* 1997; Ritvo *et al.* 1990).

It may be that there is no *biological* basis to the association between DS and ASD. Both conditions are seen more frequently in association with learning disability. Their co-occurrence may merely reflect the heightened occurrence of both in this group. Whatever transpires to be the case, there are significant numbers of people who have both ASD and DS. The complexity of their presentation requires knowledge of the biological factors common to each.

Genetic mechanisms in Down syndrome: Three principal genetic mechanisms result in Down syndrome:

1. Most affected individuals (about 95 per cent) have trisomy 21 with three separate copies of chromosome 21.

2. In about three per cent of patients, one copy of the critical region is translocated to another acrocentric chromosome, most often either to chromosome 14, or to an additional section of chromosome 21 incorporated through expansion of chromosome 21 (Petersen *et al.* 1991).

3. In a further two to four per cent of cases there is a mosaicism, combining a trisomic and a normal cell line – here only a proportion of cells have an extra copy of chromosome 21. Depending on the stem lines involved, these cases tend to be less severe.

Down syndrome is also occasionally associated with a ring chromosome 21.

A range of physical features are commonly seen in DS. These include:

- 'epicanthic folds' – small folds of skin at the side of the nose that obscure the inner edge of the eye, giving the appearance of more widely spaced eyes. These are seen in most infants, but typically disappear as the nasal bridge develops

- a flattened nasal bridge

- slightly protruding (sometimes called 'cockleshell') ears

- 'hypoglossia' – an enlarged tongue
- a hypotonic lower lip
- a receding chin
- small hands
- short stature.

The origins of an additional copy of chromosome 21: Where there is an additional copy, this is typically of maternal origin, and an error in meiosis I (in about 70 per cent of cases), with some 20 per cent resulting from errors in meiosis II. In these cases there is a correlation with maternal age. In the further five per cent that arise from errors in mitosis, and the five per cent where the error is in spermatogenesis, there is no link to maternal age.

The origins of the translocation forms of trisomy 21: All of the *de novo* t(14;21) trisomies studied to date are of maternal origin (Shaffer *et al.* 1992). In *de novo* t(21;21) Down syndrome the situation is different (Shaffer *et al.* 1992). In most cases (14 out of 17) the t(21;21) is an isochromosome (dup21q) (formed by transverse as opposed to the normal longitudinal division of the chromosome). Maternal and paternal inheritance of isochromosome (dup21q) appears equally likely. In a small number of cases, the *de novo* t(21;21) is a maternal Robertsonian translocation – here both long arms of chromosome 21 are inherited rather than the long and short arms.

The region of chromosome 21 critical for the development of DS: The area of chromosome 21 which appears critical to the development of DS is part of 21q22.1–q22.3 that includes DS2S55 and MX1. Differences in MX1 have been associated with many of the physical characteristics and developmental problems in DS (Delabar *et al.* 1993) including learning difficulties; epicanthic folds; flat nasal bridge; short stature; and unusual fingerprints.

Four separate DS critical regions have been identified (DSCR1 at 21q22.1–q22.2; DSCR2 at 21q22.3; DSCR3 at 21q22.2; and DSCR4 at 21q22.2).

MTHFR polymorphisms and DS: MTHFR (Methionine Tetrahydrofolate Reductase) polymorphisms in mothers significantly increase their risk of having a child with DS (Rai *et al.* 2006) and have also been linked to ASD (Boris *et al.* 2004). In those with DS, the presence of the MTHFR 677T allele has also been linked to lower IQ, as has a specific transcobalamin 776G allele (Gueant *et al.* 2005). This suggests the possibility that altered methylation and abnormal B12 metabolism may be implicated in the severity of certain aspects of the DS phenotype.

There are wide ethnic variations in the prevalence of the 677T allele in the general population (Botto and Yang 2000), however, there has been no research to date attempting to link the prevalence of this allele to the prevalence of DS or of ASD.

Oxidative stress and DS: Oxidative stress is linked to DS, ASD (James *et al.* 2004) and Alzheimer's disease (Zana, Janka and Kalman 2007). As the therapeutic implications are of potential significance, further research on this issue is important.

Much of the theoretical interest in the possible role of oxidative stress in DS comes from the fact that a key enzyme in the oxidation of free radicals to hydrogen peroxide (superoxide dismutase/SOD 1) is encoded on chromosome 21 (at 21q22.1). There is evidence from multiple studies for increased SOD 1 activity in trisomy 21 DS, but of normal SOD 1 activity in translocation and mosaic DS (see, for example, De-la-Torre *et al.* 1996).

There is thus evidence of increased oxidative stress in certain individuals with DS (Jovanovic, Clements and MacLeod 1998), and of the presence of biological factors that may account for this, such as elevation of thiobarbituric acid reactive substances (TBARS), uric acid, seric superoxide dismutase and catalase (Garces, Perez and Salvador 2005).

Problems such as coeliac disease, leukaemia, abnormal melatonin production and oxidative stress, coupled with the unusual physiology of those with DS, are important to explore, and may have implications for more individualized management approaches.

Differential diagnosis: Genetic diagnosis is definitive; however, in early life several other diagnoses may give a similar phenotype: trisomy 18, aka Edward syndrome (Kitanovski, Ovcak and Jazbec 2009); multiple X chromosomes; Zellweger syndrome; and other peroxisomal problems (Yik *et al.* 2009).

Treatment and management: Treatments for the cardiac, haematologic, seizure and other biological co-morbidities seen in DS have been remarkably successful in improving mortality and resulted in marked improvements in life expectancy, from a median age of survival of one year in 1968 to 49 years in 1997 for those with DS in the USA (MMWR 2001).

At present, despite the best efforts over the past 140 years, there is no medical approach to the treatment of the developmental and psychosocial aspects of DS that has shown any robust and appreciable benefits for the condition. As a consequence, many families have turned to complementary and alternative therapies in response; however, many of the claims of benefit have proved difficult to justify.

Biologically distinct subgroups can be identified at the *genetic* level; ring 21, mosaic and translocation cases may all differ in severity, co-morbidity, outcome and response to intervention from supernumary 21 cases. At the *behavioural* level it is currently unclear whether specific behavioural phenotypes such as DS–ASD have differences in their response to treatment. At the *biomedical* level, presence of hearing loss, cardiac differences, coeliac diseases, gallbladder disease, leukaemia, epilepsy and differences in oxidative stress, may all have critical effects on development and outcome.

A range of medications has been used in improving the management of individuals with DS (see Prasher 2004).

There has been long-standing and extensive debate and argument over the role of dietary factors in the care of those with DS (Ani, Grantham-McGregor and Muller 2000; Ciaccio *et al.* 2003; Golden 1984; Roizen 2005; Sacks and Buckley 1998; Salman 2002).

Systematic reviews of prenatal multivitamin supplementation does not suggest that this conveys a reduced risk of DS (Goh *et al.* 2006), although it does appear that periconceptional use by women who go on to have a DS child does reduce leukaemia in those children. There is some evidence that periconceptional vitamin supplementation by mothers of those with DS significantly lowers the subsequent likelihood of ALL but not of AML (Ross J.A. *et al.* 2005). AML in DS appears to respond well to treatment with ultra low-dose cytarabine (Al-Ahmari *et al.* 2006).

Early approaches to multiple supplementation in DS: Complex but empirically unsupported multiple supplement approaches were developed in the USA in the 1940s by Dr Henry Turkel (Turkel and Nusbaum 1985).

In the 1980s, Dr Ruth Harrell and colleagues proposed a similar multimineral (N=11), multivitamin (N=8) and (variable) thyroid hormone supplement as improving IQ in a learning-disabled group (including DS) based on earlier work (Harrell *et al.* 1981). The outcome of this study was difficult to interpret.

A wide range of supplements have been used, individually and in combination. A useful overview can be found in Thiel and Fowkes (2004), summarized in the following.

Vitamin A: There is only one paper that has attempted to systematically address the effects of vitamin A supplementation in DS (Palmer 1978). Over a six-month period reduced infection rates were seen compared with controls, but other findings were difficult to interpret.

There has been some speculation that ASD may in some cases have a basis in abnormal vitamin A processing (Megson 2000); however, caution has been urged in its use. Close monitoring should be undertaken, as inappropriate supplementation can lead to liver damage with both chronic low-dose (Geubel *et al.* 1991) and acute high-dose use (Castaño, Etchart and Sookoian 2006).

Vitamin B6: Two randomized controlled trials of vitamin B6 in DS have been published (Coleman *et al.* 1985; Pueschel *et al.* 1980). Outcome in both studies showed no effect of supplementation on development.

Some studies have claimed benefits from B6 in ASD (see, for discussion, Aitken 2009); however, it appears that in general plasma B6 levels are elevated in unsupplemented children with autism when compared to controls (James, George and Audhya 2006).

5HTP and tryptophan: There was only one controlled clinical trial of tryptophan use with DS infants (Airaksinen 1974). This found improved muscle tone with supplementation.

Tryptophan was banned from use by the FDA (United States Federal Drug Administration) due to the appearance of a condition – eosinophilia myalgia syndrome – that killed 37 and permanently disabled 1,500 taking a tryptophan supplement produced by Showa Denko (as far as I am aware, this was the first vitamin supplement to be produced by genetically engineered bacteria). The problem was due to a toxin from the GM production process and not due to tryptophan itself. (For a detailed discussion of the case, see Smith J.M. 2003.) Tryptophan has since been re-approved for use as a supplement.

5HTP is the intermediate between tryptophan (a dietary amino acid) and the neurotransmitter serotonin. Serotonin in turn is metabolized to produce melatonin, the chronobiotic compound which controls the sleep–wake cycle.

Three studies have looked at behavioural effects of 5HTP supplementation in DS (Partington and MacDonald 1971; Pueschel *et al.* 1980; Weise *et al.* 1974). Although there were some differences in favour of the supplemented children, results are difficult to interpret.

There is little evidence that 5HTP affects the sleep pattern in DS (Petre-Quadens and de Lee 1975).

Melatonin: There is some, albeit limited, evidence of a wide variation in melatonin production by individuals with DS (Reiter *et al.* 1996). Some have normal circadian release, whilst others show no fluctuation through the day. The normal pattern is high levels at night and low levels through the day.

Recent evidence in learning-disabled children in general suggests that melatonin supplementation is well tolerated and largely effective in the long-term treatment of otherwise treatment-resistant circadian rhythm sleep disorders. In a long-term randomized, placebo-controlled follow-up study of 50 individuals with such problems, including a subgroup with DS, results were highly positive (Carr *et al.* 2007; Wasdell *et al.* 2008).

There is also evidence of effects of melatonin on SOD 1 levels and antioxidant function in general, which may be important in DS (Rodriguez *et al.* 2004).

Folate: Folate levels are reduced in epileptics on active medication (Botez *et al.* 1993). Folate levels are low in those with DS (David *et al.* 1996). They have an eight per cent likelihood of having co-morbid epilepsy (Goldberg-Stern *et al.* 2001; Prasher 1994), and some 60 per cent of those with ASD show EEG evidence of epileptiform activity (Chez *et al.* 2006). In epilepsy, folate supplementation can reduce the levels of anticonvulsant required to achieve seizure control (Mattson *et al.* 1973). On this basis folate supplementation in DS may prove to be clinically useful.

A randomized placebo-controlled trial of folinic acid (an active form of folate) and antioxidants, alone or in combination, in 156 infants with Down syndrome, begun at around four months and continued through to 22 months, failed to demonstrate any significant effects on development (Ellis *et al.* 2008).

Low folate levels are associated with leukaemia (Zittoun 1995), DNA damage and increased risk of cancer (Blount and Ames 1995).

Vitamin B12: In one early paper, a three-year-old girl with DS was found to have a problem with B12 metabolism without proteinuria (Cartlidge and Curnock 1986). In contrast, in 1990, a large series of 83 DS children was assessed on various biochemical parameters, including B12 (Ibarra *et al.* 1990), and all were shown to have normal B12 levels.

As B12 supplementation can cause problems in some metabolic liver conditions (see, for example, Linnell and Matthews 1984), and there is evidence of liver dysfunction in at least some cases of DS (Shaposhnikov, Khal'chitskii and Shvarts 1979), with no information on the prevalence of such differences, use of B12 supplementation in DS should be considered carefully before use.

Calcium: Serum calcium levels are lower in those with DS and coeliac disease (Bonamico *et al.* 2001). No studies of specific calcium supplementation (except in older cases to prevent bone demineralization) have been undertaken to date.

Iron: No supplementation studies have been carried out. Again, those individuals with DS and coeliac appear to have lowered serum iron levels (Bonamico *et al.* 2001).

Selenium: Serum selenium levels appear to be low in DS (Kadrabová *et al.* 1996). A reasonable case has been made for the biological rationale supporting selenium supplementation (Antila and Westermarck 1989). These authors argue for the importance of selenium as an antioxidant in limiting the effects of overexpression of SOD 1.

In the only reasonably well-controlled study of selenium supplementation in DS (Antila *et al.* 1990), there was a predicted improvement in immune function.

Zinc: The findings of low serum, plasma and whole blood zinc are amongst the more robust in the DS literature (for a review, see Sacks and Buckley 1998). Supplementation has been shown to normalize the pattern and strengthen immune function (Björkstén *et al.* 1980).

Zinc sulphate as been shown to be beneficial in reducing thyroid stimulating hormone levels in hypothyroid DS cases (Bucci *et al.* 1999); however, there are some reservations (Bucci *et al.* 2001).

Carnitine: There is some evidence that carnitine levels are lower in younger children with DS, normalizing, compared to control values, at around five years of age (Seven *et al.* 2001). As carnitine has been found to be helpful in some cases of dementia, it was proposed that supplementation might be beneficial in DS. The only controlled study to date found no beneficial effects of supplementation (Pueschel 2006). No baseline assessment of carnitine levels was made in this study, and it may be that positive effects would result from supplementation at an earlier stage, or specifically in those with low levels.

Phenylalanine: A small, unreplicated Russian study of four DS patients subjected to phenylalanine loading compared to ten normal controls (Shaposhnikov, Khal'chitskii and Shvarts 1979) found biochemical changes in the DS cases consistent with impaired liver phenylalanine hydroxylase activity. This finding suggested that the DS subjects they studied would have had problems in metabolizing normal dietary levels of phenylalanine.

A single case study has reported marked improvements in an individual with DS treated through adherence to a low phenylalanine diet (Marsh and Cabaret 1972).

In summary: the wide range of studies to date have shown limited evidence of efficacy, with the exception of selenium and zinc. This may be because limited research has been done rather than because there is evidence that they are ineffective.

Combined supplement effects: As with many other conditions, interventions in DS to date have relied on the view that there will be no differences within the population that would be likely to affect response to treatment.

Our increased knowledge of the underpinning biology of DS now gives a situation where, for the first time, treatment interventions can be based on knowledge of many of the biological factors involved. The increasing evidence of specific problems with oxidative stress, and the role of factors such as selenium, zinc and SOD 1 in these processes, are leading to more biologically grounded and testable treatment hypotheses (Garcez, Perez and Salvador 2005).

Further information and support:

In Canada:
Down Syndrome Research Foundation and
Resource Centre
3580 Slocan Street
Vancouver
British Columbia
V5M 3E8
Tel.: 604-431-9694
Fax: 604-431-9248
Website: www.dsrf.org

In Japan:
Japanese Down Syndrome Network
E-mail: momotani@affrc.go.jp (Tsukuba, Eastern
Office)
Website: http://jdsn.ac.affrc.go.jp/dowj1-e.html

In the UK:
Down's Syndrome Association
Langdon Down Centre
2a Langdon Park
Teddington
TW11 9PS
Tel.: 0845 230 0372
Fax: 0845 230 0373
E-mail: info@downs-syndrome.org.uk
Website: www.downs-syndrome.org.uk

The Down's Syndrome Research Foundation
Limited
18 Daws Hill Lane
High Wycombe
Bucks
HP11 1PW
Tel.: 01494 521826
E-mail: dsrf@dsrf.co.uk
Website: www.dsrf.co.uk

In the USA:
National Down Syndrome Society
666 Broadway
New York
NY 10012
Tel.: 800-221-4602
Fax: 212-979-2873
E-mail: info@ndss.org
Website: www.ndss.org

National Down Syndrome Congress
1370 Center Drive,
Suite 102
Atlanta,
GA 30338
Toll free: 800-232-NDSC (6372)
Local: 770-604-9500
Fax: 770-604-9898
E-mail: info@ndsccenter.org
Website: www.ndsccenter.org/index.php

International Mosaic Down Syndrome Association
PO Box 1052
Franklin
TX 77856
Toll-free: 888-MDS-LINK
Tel.: 979-828-4177
Fax: 775-295-9373
By E-mail President: imdsapresident@imdsa.com
Website: www.imdsa.com

Information on a large number of internet sites
for international Down syndrome groups can be
accessed at www.ds-health.com/ds_sites.htm#natl.
This is part of an excellent US website maintained
by the MD father of a boy with Down syndrome.

There is also an e-mail list for families and others
who want to support those with a dual ASD Down
syndrome diagnosis. This list can be accessed at
http://groups.yahoo.com/community/ds-autism.

Useful books:
Pueschel, S.M. (2001) *A Parent's Guide to Down
Syndrome: Towards a Brighter Future* (revised and
updated) Baltimore: Paul Brookes.

Sears, M. and Soper, K.L. (eds.) (2007) *Gifts:
Mothers Reflect on How Children with Down Syndrome
Enrich Their Lives.* Bethesda: Woodbine House.

32

Dravet's syndrome

aka • severe myoclonic epilepsy in infancy (SMEI)

• SCN1A-related seizure disorders

Includes • intractable childhood epilepsy with generalized tonic-clonic seizures

• SCN1A-related generalized epilepsy with febrile seizures

• severe myoclonic epilepsy in infancy

• simple febrile seizures

Gene loci: 5q31.1–q33.1; 2q24

Key ASD references: Caraballo and Fejerman 2006; Weiss *et al.* 2003; Wolff, Casse-Perrot and Dravet 2006

Dravet's syndrome is a form of epilepsy resulting from a mutation in the SCN1A gene at 2q24. It is named after Charlotte Dravet, a French psychiatrist and epileptologist who worked at the Centre St Paul in Marseille from 1965 to 2000. Also known as 'severe myoclonic epilepsy in infancy' (SMEI), it was first described by Dravet (1978). Upwards of 500 clinical cases have been reported in the literature to date.

Formal international recognition came in 1989 when the revised classification of the International League Against Epilepsy (ILAE) recognized the validity of this syndrome (Commission on Classification and Terminology of the International League Against Epilepsy 1989).

A number of general books on epilepsy and epilepsy management have useful sections on Dravet's syndrome (see, for example, Roger *et al.* 2005; Shorvon 2005).

How common is Dravet's syndrome? A precise estimate is currently not known (Hurst 1990; Yakoub *et al.* 1992). Prevalence is thought to be between one in 20,000 and one in 40,000.

Main clinical features: Before seizures start, development is recorded as normal. Severe myoclonic epilepsy always begins in the first year. Over time, seizure activity usually starts with unilateral clonic or generalized seizures, often alternating from one side of the body to the other without any warning signs, and, as they progress, myoclonic jerks and partial seizures normally appear. Progressive developmental delay from time of seizure onset is typical, becoming more apparent through the second year, with ataxia and corticospinal signs appearing later.

The initial seizures can vary in duration. In most cases, they appear in association with a raised body temperature, typically from fever, but sometimes even triggered by a hot bath (Awaya *et al.* 1990).

The same types of seizures often recur, sometimes without a rise in temperature, and can be difficult to classify. A variety of other types of seizure also occur in this condition, with the pattern changing as the condition evolves. Myoclonic seizures, absence seizures, complex partial seizures and status epilepticus are all seen (Dravet *et al.* 1992).

The initial EEGs after febrile episodes may not show any epileptiform activity. Later, the EEG between seizure events shows varied features, with a strong response to photic stimulation being seen in a large proportion of cases. EEGs carried out between seizures show a complex picture characterized by generalized, focal and multifocal anomalies (Dravet *et al.* 2005). There is a light-strength-dependent photosensitive response in many cases (Takahashi *et al.* 1999), and often a sleep EEG will show more evidence of abnormality than an awake EEG (Dravet *et al.* 2005).

In one autopsied case, neuropathology demonstrated cerebellar and cerebrocortical microdysgenesis (Renier and Renkawek 1990), suggesting a problem with apoptosis; however, for most, no significant pathology has been reported. Structural neuroimaging may show mild diffuse atrophy, but is not usually helpful (Dravet *et al.* 2005).

In the majority of cases (around 80 per cent), there is no family history of Dravet's or of other types of epilepsy. The finding of a number of concordant identical twin pairs (Fujiwara *et al.* 1990; Ohki *et al.* 1997) and one concordant non-identical twin pair (Ohtsuka *et al.* 1991), and of families with more than one affected sibling (Ogino *et al.* 1989; Dravet *et al.* 2005), strongly suggested a genetic aetiology. Long-term follow-up of one identical twin pair shows a strong similarity in clinical progression (Fujiwara 2006).

A genetic basis to Dravet's syndrome was first reported in 2001, when Claes *et al.* reported a defect in the SCN1A gene in all seven of a series of cases. SCN1A is involved in sodium channel function in the central nervous system. Lower rates of SCN1A gene defects in association with the Dravet's phenotype have been reported in a number of other studies (for example, Wallace *et al.* 2003 (33.3 per cent); Fukuma *et al.* 2004 (44.8 per cent)); however, the range of SCN1A mutations is huge (Ceulemans, Claes and Lagae 2004), with 338 separate mutations being reported at the last count, 309 of which are associated with Dravet's syndrome and three of which have been reported in association with autism (Weiss *et al.* 2003).

Defects in SCN1A are examples of one class of ion channelopathies, now known to be involved in a range of epilepsy syndromes (for a review, see Hirose 2006).

Is there a link between Dravet's syndrome and ASD? To date, three studies have suggested a possible link between Dravet's syndrome and ASD.

- The first paper was a screening study looking for SCN1A, SCN2A and SCN3A channelopathies in 117 multiplex ASD families involved with the AGRE (Autism Genetic Resource Exchange) project. Six affected families were identified, five with defects on SCN1A and one on SCN2A, with possible effects on sodium channel function.

- Caraballo and Fejerman (2006) reviewed casenotes on 55 cases that fitted the ILAE's criteria for Dravet's syndrome. The cases had been seen at their clinic in Argentina over a 14-year period (1990–2004). The authors found two cases (3.5 per cent) that fitted criteria for autism. Eighty-five per cent of cases fitted criteria for hyperactivity. It is not possible from the report to draw any conclusions concerning co-morbidity.

- Wolff, Casse-Perrot and Dravet (2006) discuss the natural history of Dravet's syndrome, drawing on their analysis of a series of 20 cases. 'Autistic traits' and hyperactivity are both described as being 'frequent', but no further information is given, other than that this is describing behaviour over the period between two and four years of age, during which there is typically a developmental deterioration, followed by a severe level of learning difficulty, after initial normal development.

Differential diagnosis: As Dravet's syndrome often begins with febrile convulsions, differentiation in the early stages from more benign febrile fits is important. In Dravet's syndrome onset is usually earlier and the convulsions are often clonic and one-sided, rather than bilateral and tonic-clonic.

A further, much milder epileptic condition – generalized epilepsy with febrile seizures plus (GEFS+) – which also has onset with febrile convulsions is also linked to defects in SCN1A (Escayg et al. 2001).

Various studies have commented on individuals with the same clinical course and outcome but without the polyclonias and characteristic EEG described by Dravet (see, for example, Doose et al. 1998). These are transpiring to have genetic profiles somewhat different to Dravet's syndrome.

At the current level of understanding, a diagnosis can be neither ruled in nor ruled out by testing for an SCN1A defect. Diagnosis is currently based on the pattern of evolution of clinical symptoms.

Treatment and management: Although the research evidence to date is unreplicated and on small numbers, it appears that a ketogenic diet can reduce seizure frequency in a significant proportion of the cases where it has been tried (Caraballo et al. 1998, 2005).

Two medications – stiripentol (Chiron et al. 2000; Kassaï et al. 2008; Landmark and Johannessen 2008) and topiramate (Coppola et al. 2002; Kröll-Seger et al. 2006) – have been shown to be effective, both individually and in combination, in controlling seizure activity, though again in fairly small numbers of cases and centres. There is one randomized controlled trial of stiripentol that in 15/21 patients produced a 50 per cent drop in clonic and tonic-clonic seizures (Kanazawa and Shirane 1999). Stiripentol appears to work through a direct influence on the GABA A receptor (Fisher 2008). Stiripentol (zonizamide) interacts with a number of other anti-epileptic medications and has a number of possible side effects, such as renal stones and rash (see discussion in Shorvon 2005).

Other medications have also shown efficacy, sodium valproate, clonazepam and lorazepam being found the most useful, while other medications have been helpful in certain types of seizures, as with phenobarbital and potassium bromide in convulsive seizures, and ethosuximide in myoclonic and absence seizures. Carbamazepine and lamotrigine have been reported to exacerbate seizure activity (Guerrini et al. 1998; Wallace 1998).

As raised temperature and infection appear to be strong triggers for seizure activity in Dravet's syndrome, avoidance and prompt treatment of these are important for achieving the best level of fit control.

Although the outcome in Dravet's syndrome has historically been of significantly reduced life expectancy and deteriorating seizure control coupled with significant learning disability, improvements in medical management of cases may improve outcome. In particular the positive results with use of stiripentol, topiramate and ketogenic diet, coupled with the possibilities of earlier identification through genetic screening, may significantly improve outcome.

Further information and support:
IDEAL (International Dravet syndrome Epilepsy
Action League) is a part of the American Epilepsy
Outreach Foundation.
Weblink: www.idea-league.org
This is a useful site with links to further
information and to other more general epilepsy
support groups. One useful resource on IDEAL is
the family network.

33

Duchenne (DMD) and Becker (BMD) muscular dystrophy

aka • Duchenne disease

• muscular dystrophy – Duchenne type (aka benign pseudohypertrophic muscular dystrophy)

Gene loci: Xp21.2; 12q21

Key ASD references: Hendriksen and Vles 2008; Komoto *et al.* 1984; Kumagai *et al.* 2001; Wu J.Y. *et al.* 2005; Zwaigenbaum and Tarnopolsky 2003

The first case of Duchenne muscular dystrophy was described by Conte and Gioia (1836). Duchenne muscular dystrophy is named after Guillaume-Benjamin Duchenne (1806–1875), the French neurologist. Becker muscular dystrophy is named after the German neurologist Peter Emil Becker (1908–2000).

Duchenne and Becker muscular dystrophies are X-linked dominant genetic conditions that result in production of defective dystrophin protein, a key constituent of skeletal muscle. Dystrophin is a cytoplasmic protein that is over 3,500 amino acids in length and coded for by the longest human gene so far detected. The immediate consequences of these defects are inability to form normal muscle, with muscle wasting and loss of functional mobility.

In DMD virtually no functional dystrophin is produced, while in BMD a truncated (shortened) form of the dystrophin protein is produced with some functionality. There are four shortened forms, and the biology is more complex than it is possible to explain here (but see Muntoni, Torelli and Ferlini 2003). There is variability depending on the specific gene defect, and the clinical phenotype is largely dependent on the amount of functional dystrophin produced (Monaco *et al.* 1988).

How common is DMD? Estimates vary between one in 5,618 live male births (Bushby, Thambyayah and Gardner-Medwin 1991) to one in 50,000 live male births (estimated, Orphanet 2008).

How common is BMD? For BMD, the prevalence is estimated at one in 18,450 live male births (Bushby, Thambyayah and Gardner-Medwin 1991).

Main clinical features: DMD presents in early childhood with slow achievement of early motor milestones. Proximal weakness causes a waddling gait and difficulty with climbing, and the classic 'Gower's sign' with the child pulling him/herself to standing using the arms. It progresses rapidly, with most children being in a wheelchair by about 12 years. Heart muscle weakness is usually by age 18. Parents are typically first concerned over motor development, with generally slow motor development causing concern in over 40 per cent. Gait problems, including persistent toe-walking and flat-footedness, are cause for concern in almost a third, and delayed walking in 20 per cent. Parents often do not notice 'Gower's sign' as being abnormal (Marshall and Galasko 1995). Clinical diagnosis is often given at about four years ten months (range: 16 months–eight years) (Bushby 1999).

Few of those affected survive through their thirties, with complications of respiratory infection or cardiac problems being the main causes of death. The typical presentation of cardiomyopathy is of left ventricular dilation and congestive heart failure. Female carriers of DMD mutations are more likely to develop dilated cardiomyopathy. In addition, other aspects of development, such as acquisition of language milestones, are slowed (Cyrulnik *et al.* 2007).

A diagnosis is arrived at if there is a positive family history suggesting X-linked recessive inheritance that is supportive, and in addition the following clinical findings are present: there is progressive bilateral muscular weakness, greater for the upper arms and legs, sometimes with enlargement of the calf muscles, and sometimes of the muscles of the tongue. The enlarged muscle is gradually replaced by fat and connective tissue, hence the use of the term 'pseudohypertrophic'. Symptoms are almost invariably present before the child is five years old. Almost all individuals with DMD will be unable to walk by the age of 13. DMD and BMD can usually be distinguished by the age at which those affected become wheelchair-dependent: those with DMD typically before age 13 years, and those with BMD after age 16 years. In practice, there is an overlap between the groups.

Death is typically from cardiac failure or secondary to weakness of the chest muscles, leading to difficulties in coping with lung infections.

In DMD, enlargement of the heart muscles, with congestive heart failure, typically presents between 20 and 40 years of age in men, and somewhat later in women. Death typically results a few years after onset of congestive heart failure in males, with slower progression in females (Beggs 1997).

Serum creatine phosphokinase (CPK) levels are elevated in DMD (typically to more than ten times normal levels), and in BMD to over five times normal levels in all cases. In female carriers, varyingly elevated levels are seen in around half of all cases.

As people get older, there is a gradual drop in serum creatine kinase, with the loss of dystrophic muscle fibres (Zatz *et al.* 1991). Normal concentrations of serum CPK have been reported in some cases of DMD-related dilated cardiomyopathy (Mestroni *et al.* 1999).

Some *boys* with DMD have been reported who in addition have other X-linked disorders such as retinitis pigmentosa (seen in Biedl-Bardet syndrome [17]) chronic granulomatous disease, McLeod red cell phenotype, glycerol kinase deficiency and congenital adrenal hyperplasia [25] (Darras and Francke 1988; Francke *et al.* 1985, 1987). The conditions that have been reported are due to contiguous gene deletion syndromes.

Girls who are affected can have DMD through four major mechanisms:

- an X chromosome rearrangement involving Xp21.2

- an X chromosome deletion involving Xp21.2

- complete absence of one X chromosome (as seen in Turner syndrome)

- a uniparental maternally inherited X chromosome isodisomy (where both copies of the X chromosome are inherited from the mother).

A number of genetic techniques can detect the deletions that account for the majority of mutations in both DMD and BMD. Southern blotting and quantitative PCR can also detect duplications that account for the mutations in some six to ten per cent of DMD and BMD (Den Dunnen *et al.* 1989 Galvagni *et al.* 1994). For the remainder of the mutations so far found, mutation scanning and sequence analysis detect the small deletions or insertions, single-base changes and splicing mutations seen (Bennett *et al.* 2001; Dolinsky, de Moura-Neto and Falcao-Conceicao 2002).

Ethnic variations in the prevalence of different types of DMD mutation have been reported, with high rates of *de novo* mutation in northern Indian (Sinha *et al.* 1996) and Mexican (Alcántara *et al.* 1999) populations, and a high frequency of duplications in the Japanese (Hiriashi *et al.* 1992).

A variety of testing methods like SCAIP (single condition amplification internal primer sequencing) (Flanigan *et al.* 2003), DGGE (denaturing gradient gel electrophoresis-based whole-gene mutation scanning) (Hofstra *et al.* 2004) and MLPA (multiplex ligation-dependent probe amplification) (Hwa *et al.* 2007) are being developed to attempt to identify the one third or so of cases where the genetic basis cannot currently be identified using conventional techniques.

Quantitative real-time PCR can successfully identify mutations caused by deletion or duplication in all cases (Joncourt *et al.* 2004).

Clinical testing should first establish that there is an elevated level of CPK, and, in the context of associated clinical findings, this should lead on to genetic testing, which, if negative, as it would be in one third of cases, would lead on to muscle biopsy.

There are two genetic 'hotspots', one at exons 2–20 (seen in 30 per cent of cases with identified gene deletions) and one at exons 44–53 (seen in 70 per cent), which are implicated in both DMD and BMD (Den Dunnen *et al.* 1989).

Most DMD and BMD cases (around 90 per cent) have some degree of cardiac involvement. It is the cause of death in one in five DMD and one in two BMD cases.

In dilated cardiomyopathy (DCM), the ventricles of the heart are typically enlarged but do not function normally. Boys with DCM will present in their twenties and thirties, and will typically survive for up to two years after the diagnosis has been made (Finsterer and Stollberger 2003). In carrier girls, onset is later, typically in their forties to fifties, and progression is slower. DCM is seen in both BMD and DMD (Palmucci *et al.* 2000). Isolated DCM is also seen, with a failure to produce dystrophin in cardiac muscle (Ferlini *et al.* 1999), and elevated CPK (Towbin *et al.* 1993).

Cardiomyopathy becomes increasingly frequent with age – in boys, 95 per cent have evidence of cardiomyopathy by age 16, and 100 per cent by age 18. In contrast, for carrier females, the incidence is lower, with around 55 per cent being affected by their early twenties, and 80 per cent by their mid-fifties (Nigro *et al.* 1990). ECG abnormalities, due to dystrophin deficiency, are found in over 90 per cent of DMD cases (Takami *et al.* 2008).

Overall, studies of intellectual function in DMD have shown a lower IQ, predominantly with a lower verbal than performance IQ (Bresolin *et al.* 1994; Leibowitz and Dubowitz 1981; Moizard *et al.* 1998). Approximately one in three DMD cases have associated learning difficulties (IQ <70) (Mochizuki *et al.* 2008). This has been linked to a short-term memory impairment that has greater impact on verbal than nonverbal IQ test results (Hinton *et al.* 2000, 2001; Wicksell *et al.* 2004).

DMD is associated with a progressive reduction in mobility. As a result, boys with DMD have decreasing bone density due to postural decalcification, and an increased risk of bone fractures (Soderpalm *et al.* 2007).

In BMD, development of muscle weakness is slower, and affected individuals are often independently mobile into their twenties. Heart problems can be more pronounced, and heart problems secondary to DCM are the most common cause of death (Cox and Kunkel 1997). Life expectancy in BMD is typically into the mid-forties (Bushby and Gardner-Medwin 1993). With clear delineation of the genotype, mildly affected BMD cases are now being identified, including some with very late onset of symptoms (Quinlivan *et al.* 1995; Yazaki *et al.* 1999).

Female DMD carriers can show features of DMD and BMD where there are X-chromosome rearrangements involving the DMD locus, a single X chromosome, or non-random X-inactivation (Bodrug *et al.* 1987; Richards *et al.* 1990). It is not uncommon for DMD and BMD carriers to show symptoms of mild muscular weakness and cardiac involvement, which are seen in around one in five (Hoogerwaard *et al.* 1999). As onset of cardiac problems is delayed in females compared to males, monitoring can usually begin in the teenage years (Nolan *et al.* 2003).

A particular isoform of dystrophin (Dp140) appears to be specifically associated with learning difficulties in DMD (Felisari *et al.* 2000). It may also prove to be the case that the Dp140 isoform is important for intellectual development in others.

In DMD-related DCM the mutations in the DMD gene affect two gene areas that specifically transcribe dystrophin used in cardiac muscle. Two other dystrophin-producing genes prevent effects in skeletal muscles (Beggs 1997). Only 30 per cent of normal dystrophin levels are required to prevent muscular dystrophy (Neri *et al.* 2007).

Treatment of DCM with ACE-inhibitors and beta-blockers as needed can, in most cases, result in normalization of the size of the left ventricle and normal systolic function early on (Towbin J.A. 2003).

A heart transplant may be required in the most severe and intractable cases.

Care should be taken to minimize risk of respiratory infection.

Supplementation with vitamin D and calcium should be used, particularly once the person is non-ambulant, to reduce the risks of osteoporosis and bone fracture.

Physical and occupational therapy should be used to maintain functional mobility and prevent flexion contractures of the ligaments.

As activity level reduces, care should be taken to ensure there is no excess weight gain.

Survival in BMD is longer, with affected individuals typically living into their forties (Bushby and Gardner-Medwin 1993).

Parents of children with DMD experience high levels of stress, primarily as a consequence of their child's problem behaviours, particularly in social interaction, as opposed to the physical aspects of their disease (Nereo, Fee and Hinton 2003).

Is there a link between DMD/BMD and ASD?

- The initial report of DMD in association with what at the time was known as 'infantile autism' was a single case study of an 11-year-old boy (Komoto *et al.* 1984).

- Kumagai and colleagues subsequently reported on a series of DMD (N=94) and BMD (N=43) cases (Kumagai *et al.* 2001). Eight patients in their DMD series and two of those with BMD were diagnosed as autistic. The reported prevalence of ASD in this clinic series was well above what would be predicted from population prevalence; however, there is a possibility of ascertainment bias. The variation in ASD phenotype in 3/8 sibling pairs with the same genetic dystrophin defect in this series suggests that the association may be due to other mechanisms, or to other genetic factors.

- Two further reported cases of autism associated with muscular dystrophy from North America (Zwaigenbaum and Tarnopolsky 2003) transpired in one instance to be BMD type and, in the other, congenital autosomal recessive muscular dystrophy.

- In a series reported by Wu and colleagues (Wu J.Y. *et al.* 2005), eight boys were identified with both autism and DMD, from a total population of 158 boys with DMD, in the state of Massachusetts. Within the population with DMD in the state of Massachusetts this gives an autism rate of of one in 26, which is significantly above the rate of concordance that would be predicted by chance. Again, however, there is a problem of ascertainment bias – virtually all muscular dystrophy cases will be identified, and they will be closely monitored for any developmental concerns, thereby inflating recognized co-morbidity levels.

- In 2008, Hendriksen and Vles reported on a questionnaire survey of parents of 351 DMD cases. The specific topics of interest were ADHD, obsessive-compulsive disorder and ASD. Based on the questionnaire data, 11.7 per cent were co-morbid for ADHD, 4.8 per cent for OCD and 3.1 per cent for ASD, the general conclusion being that DMD affects brain function as well as the peripheral nervous system, increasing the likelihood of 'neuropsychiatric' conditions.

Reports on ASD behavioural phenotypes can also be found in various other sources (Hinton V.J. *et al.* 2006; Poysky 2007).

DMD and BMD are two of the nine primary muscular dystrophies, the other seven being: congenital; distal; Emery-Dreifuss; facioscapulohumeral; limb-girdle; myotonic; and oculopharyngeal. To date the only reported associations with ASD (other than the single case of congenital muscular dystrophy reported by Zwaigenbaum and Tarnopolsky) are cases of DMD and BMD. As no screening across the other types has yet been carried out, it is not possible to say at this point whether the association may be specific to the DMD and BMD types, or is a more general association with the muscular distrophies.

Duchenne and Becker are the same yet different – modern developments have effectively enabled Duchenne to be turned into a Becker-type muscular dystrophy. The difference between them is that in Duchenne no functional dystophin is produced and progressive muscle weakness leads to death. By 'exon skipping', a truncated but working form of dystropin can be produced, resulting in a non-fatal form of muscular dystrophy that looks and functions like Becker. The single case of congenital autosomal recessive muscular dystrophy with ASD is the only other primary muscular dystrophy that has been reported (Zwaigenbaum and Tarnopolsky 2003).

Differential diagnosis: Several other conditions are possible differential diagnoses for the motor component, but have not as yet been reported in association with ASD: limb-girdle muscular dystrophy; Emery-Dreifuss muscular dystrophy; spinal muscular atrophy; and dilated cardiomyopathy.

Treatment and management: At the time of writing, no treatments prevent the primary features of either DMD or BMD.

Surveillance and monitoring: There should be routine monitoring of cardiac and lung function, particularly from the stage at which a person becomes wheelchair-dependent. Regular monitoring of possible orthopaedic complications from osteoporosis and scoliosis in particular need to be monitored and treated as appropriate.

Medications: A number of medications are used with good effect in controlling some of the symptoms of both DMD and BMD. In particular, prednisolone has been shown to improve muscular strength and physical abilities (Backman and Henriksson 1995; Fenichel *et al.* 1991; Mendell *et al.* 1989) and to prolong walking (DeSilva *et al.* 1987). Various side effects are reported, including significant weight gain (40 per cent) with a 'cushingoid' appearance, elevated blood pressure, behavioural deterioration, slowing of physical growth and cataracts (Griggs *et al.* 1993; Mendell *et al.* 1989). It has been shown to slow the muscular deterioration in DMD without marked negative effects on quality of life (Beenakker *et al.* 2005; Manzur *et al.* 2008).

The optimal age for prednisolone treatment has yet to be established and the appropriate duration of treatment has not been established, but current recommendations suggest beginning as soon as a diagnosis has been made (Merlini *et al.* 2003). No long-term or large-group controlled trials have so far been conducted.

Prednisolone is a steroid that is converted in the liver from prednisone, a corticosteroid medication. Prednisolone is also the name of a synthetic corticosteroid with the same mode of action.

Deflazacort, which is an artificial prednisolone derivative, is available in Europe but not currently in the USA. It appears to produce less weight gain (Mesa *et al.* 1991), but has a significantly increased risk of causing asymptomatic cataracts (30 per cent) (Biggar *et al.* 2004). A systematic review and meta-analysis of 15 studies found improved muscle strength and motor function compared to placebo (Campbell C. and Jacob 2003). To date there are no direct trials of deflazacort against prednisolone.

Oxandrolone is an anabolic steroid that has been shown in a pilot study to have effects similar to prednisolone, but has fewer reported side effects (Fenichel *et al.* 1997). In one RCT, oxandrolone was shown to produce minor improvements in muscle strength (Fenichel *et al.* 2001).

Therapies under investigation for the prevention of secondary complications: A number of experimental gene therapies are currently under investigation (Gregorevic and Chamberlain 2003; Nowak and Davies 2004; Tidball and Spencer 2003; van Deutekom and van Ommen 2003).

Gentamycin is an aminoglycoside that can override premature stop codon defects in DMD. One preliminary open study gave two weeks of gentamycin (7.5 mg/kg/day) to four people with DMD. No full-length dystrophin was produced by their muscles (Wagner *et al.* 2001).

Stem cell therapy is under investigation, but at this time remains an experimental rather than a clinical treatment (Blau 2008; Gussoni *et al.* 1997, 1999, 2002; Skuk *et al.* 2004;).

Creatine monohydrate has been studied as a potential treatment in muscular dystrophies and neuromuscular disorders (Louis *et al.* 2003), with slightly improved bone density. In a randomized, controlled, crossover treatment study, 30 boys with DMD were given creatine (~0.1 g/kg/day) over an eight-month period (Tarnopolsky *et al.* 2004). Modest benefits were found in muscle mass and grip strength, but with no improvement in function. For an overview of creatine supplementation see Evangeliou *et al.* (2009).

In some 13 per cent of cases, DMD is due to a nonsense mutation that results in premature insertion of a stop codon. This means that a functional version of the essential muscle protein, dystrophin, is not produced. Administering a particular antibiotic, gentamycin, enables the gene to 'skip' over the stop codon and produce the dystrophin protein by ignoring the stop codon and reading the full genetic sequence. The side effects of gentamycin with long-term use – deafness and kidney damage – make this problematic as a treatment approach. Other aminoglycoside antibiotics have similar effects, but similar though less severe side effect profiles. A further antibiotic negamycin has shown some promise in animal models (Arakawa *et al.* 2003). For a useful discussion of this topic, and of the phase III trials of genetic approaches under way at the time of writing, see Muntoni and Wells (2007).

Another novel treatment showing promise is an experimental 1,2,4-oxadiazole nonaminoglycoside medication, PTC124 (Hamed 2006). It has similar effects on the production of dystrophin in nonsense cases, but without the side effects reported with gentamycin (Hirawat *et al.* 2007; Welch *et al.* 2007). PTC124 is showing promise in phase II clinical trials that began in May 2007 (for further information see www.ptcbio. com). This type of approach may prove helpful where the DNA sequence for dystrophin is present but disrupted, but would not work in other DMD cases where the gene is deleted or rearranged.

Some work on the long-term use of perindopril, an 'ACE-inhibitor' (angiotensin-converting enzyme inhibitor), has shown a significant reduction in mortality over a ten-year period through its protective effects on cardiac and respiratory muscle function (Duboc *et al.* 2007). This study randomly assigned patients (aged 9 to 13.5 years at the start of the trial) blindly to two groups, 28 receiving perindopril, 29 placebo. Over a ten-year follow-up period, 26 of the 28 receiving active medication survived, compared to only 19 of 29 in the control group.

Dietary approaches to managing problems secondary to treatments such as steroids are important, but as yet poorly researched (see, for a review, Davidson and Truby 2009).

Mechanical devices to prolong mobility: Orthotic devices to maintain physical movement in muscular dystrophy as physical power diminishes are being developed. Dr Tariq Rahman at the University of Delaware has one of the more advanced programmes, involving a device called WREX (the Wilmington Robotic Exoskeleton). (See Rahman *et al.* 2001, and the Nemours website cited at the end of this section).

Gene therapies: The most exciting developments in potential treatment for DMD involve gene therapies (Cossu and Sampaolesi 2007). There are a number of limitations to gene therapies as currently developed, particularly in their ability to improve cardiac function. A number of novel approaches to gene delivery are in active developments that hope to circumvent current limitations (Goncalves *et al.* 2008; Nelson S.F. *et al.* 2009).

Genetic counselling: Males with DMD do not have children, although this may be possible with increasing life expectancy.

As BMD is an X-linked condition, affected fathers would not pass it on to their sons (who will inherit their X chromosome from their mother), but all of their daughters will be carriers, as they must inherit an affected X chromosome. One family has been described with five affected family members over two generations, and apparent patrilineal inheritance (Purushottam *et al.* 2008).

Mothers who carry a defective BMD or DMD gene must pass this on to their sons, and have a 50 per cent chance of passing the gene on to their daughters.

Males with BMD or with DMD-related dilated cardiomyopathy (DCM) can usually father children. As with DMD, when this happens, they will have affected daughters (all of whom would inherit their father's DMD X chromosome), while sons would be unaffected.

Mothers of DMD and BMD cases have an increased risk of DCM and should be monitored.

Where a mother has more than one affected son and there is no other family history, there are various genetic possibilities (see van Essen *et al.* 1992, 1997, 2003). Genetic investigation is required to clarify whether there is somatic or germline mosaic inheritance or a maternal *de novo* mutation.

If the affected person has a *de novo* gene mutation, there is no increased risk to siblings. If the mother has a germline mosaic, there is a 15–20 per cent risk of siblings being affected (van Essen *et al.* 2003).

Further information and support:

http://dystrophy.com/ is a website which provides information on muscular dystrophies.

In Australia:
Muscular Dystrophy Association Inc
36–38 Henley Beach Road,
Mile End SA 5031
GPO Box 414,
Adelaide SA 5001
Tel.: (08) 8234 5266
Fax: (08) 8234 5866
E-mail: info@mdasa.org.au
Web: www.mdasa.org.au

In Canada:
Muscular Dystrophy Association of Canada
2345 Yonge Street
Suite 900
Toronto
Ontario
M4P 2E5
Tel.: 866-MUSCLE-8
Fax: 416-488-7523
E-mail: info@muscle.ca
Website: www.mdac.ca

In France:
Association Francaise contre les Myopathies
A.F.M.
1, rue de l'Internationale
BP 59 – 91 002
Evry
Tél.: (33) 169472828
Website: www.afm-france.org

In Germany:
Germany – Deutsche Gesellschaft fur Muskelkranke
e V (DGM)
Im Moos 4
79112 Freiburg
Tel.: (49) 7665 94 47 – 0
Fax: (49) 7665 94 47 – 20
E-mail: info@dgm.org
Website: www.dgm.org

In Greece:
E-mail: info@mdahellas.gr
Tel.: 210 3616980-1
Fax: 210 3616982
MDA Hellas, Ομηρου 51, Αθηνα 10672
E-mail: info@mdahellas.gr
Website: www.mdahellas.gr/

In New Zealand:
New Zealand Muscular Dystrophy
PO Box 16-238
Sandringham
Auckland
Tel.: (64) 9 815 0247
Fax: (64) 9 815 7260
E-mail: director@mda.org.nz
Website: www.mda.org.nz

In Poland:
Towarzystwo Zwalczania Chorob Miesni
ul. Sw. Bonifacego 10
02-914 Warsaw
Tel.: (48) 22 642 7507
Fax: (48) 22 642 7507
E-mail: mrupar@kki.net.pl
Website: www.idn.org.pl/tzchm

In the UK:
Duchenne Family Support Group
78 York Street
London
W1H 1DP
Tel.: 0870 241 1857
helpline: 0870 606 1604
E-mail: info@dfsg.org.uk
Website: www.dfsg.org.uk

Muscular Dystrophy Campaign
61 Southwark Street
London
SW1 0HL
England
Tel.: 0207 803 4800
E-mail: info@muscular-dystrophy.org
Website: www.muscular-dystrophy.org

Action Duchenne
Epicentre
41 West Street
Leytonstone
London
E11 4JL
National Office Tel.: 020 8556 9955
Website: http://actionduchenne.org

In the USA:
Muscular Dystrophy Association – USA
3300 E. Sunrise Drive
Tucson
AZ 87718-3208
Tel.: 520-529-2000
Fax: 520-529-5000
E-mail: mda@mdausa.org
Website: www.mdausa.org

Parent Project Muscular Dystrophy
1012 North University Boulevard
Middletown
OH 45042
Tel.: 800-714-5437; 513-424-0696
Fax: 513-425-9907
E-mail: pat@parentprojectmd.org
Website: www.parentprojectmd.org

A helpful 2008 paper for parents, 'Research Approaches for a Therapy of Duchenne Muscular Dystrophy', by Dr Guenter Scheuerbrandt, can be downloaded from www.endduchenne.org.

Biomechanical Research
Nemours
Dr Tariq Rahman
Department of Biomedical Research
University of Delaware
A.I. duPont Hospital for Children
1600 Rockland Road
Wilmington,
DE 19899
USA
Tel.: 302-651-6831
Fax: 302-651-6895
E-mail: trahman@nemours.org
Website: www.udel.edu/bio/nemours/people/trahman.html

34

Ehlers-Danlos syndrome (EDS)

aka
- Chernogubov's syndrome
- Danlos' syndrome
- Meekeren-Ehlers-Danlos syndrome
- Sack's syndrome
- Sack-Barabas syndrome
- Van Meekeren's syndrome I

Gene loci:

Type I	17q21.31–q22; 9q34.2–q34.3; 2q31
Type II	9q34.2–q34.3
Type III	6p21.3; 2q31
Type IV	2q31
Type V	Not known
Type VI	1p36.3–p36.2; 16q2
Type VII	17q21.31–q22
Type VII	5q23
Type VIII	12p13
Cardiac valvular form	7q22.1
Progeroid form	5q35.2-q35.3
Type	X2q34--q36
Periventricular heterotopia variant	Xq28

Key ASD references: Fehlow *et al.* 1993; Lumley *et al.* 1994; Sieg 1992

The first clinical description of EDS was given by a Dutch surgeon, Job Janszoon Van Meekeren. It was published two years after his death in 1668. Edvard Ehlers, a Danish dermatologist, described the first clinical cases in 1901, and Henri-Alexandre Danlos, a Parisian physician, published further descriptions in 1908.

EDS is the term now used to describe a group of disorders of collagen, the main protein found in connective tissues in the body. All of the EDS gene defects produce abnormalities of collagen with a variety of physical features: most result in hyperextensible joints, some in skin fragility, some in easy bruising, and some in scoliosis. To date, there are 14 distinct genetic sites that have been linked to EDS, and over ten distinct subtypes are recognized. (For an overview, see Mao and Bristow 2001.)

The Villefranche classification, which is commonly used (Beighton *et al.* 1998), classifies six distinct subtypes:

Table B34: Ehlers-Danlos subtypes

• classical	Type I/II
• hypermobility	Type III
• vascular	Type IV
• kyphoscoliosis	Type VI
• arthrochalasia	Type VIIa, b
• dermatosparaxis	Type VIIc

Most forms are inherited in an autosomal dominant fashion; however, two – kyphoscoliosis (EDS type VI), which results from a defect in lysyl-hydroxylase, and dermatosparaxis (EDS type VIIc), which results from a defect in procollagen N-peptidase – are autosomal recessive conditions. Exon skipping appears to be the mechanism which results in a number of the specific forms of EDS identified in type I, type II, type IV, type VIIa and type VIIb (Nicholls *et al.* 1996).

How common is Ehlers-Danlos syndrome? The best current estimate for the Ehlers-Danlos group of conditions is 3.5 per 100,000 (Orphanet 2008); however, some estimates are as high as one in 5,000 (Steinmann, Royce and Superti-Furga 1993).

Main clinical features: All of the EDS gene defects produce abnormalities of collagen with a variety of physical features: most result in hyperextensible joints, some in skin fragility, some in easy bruising, and some in scoliosis (particularly in type VI). Gastrointestinal involvement is seen and can sometimes present with severe complications (Saucy, Eidus and Keeley 1980; Shaikh and Turner 1988).

Cardiac problems are reported in a small proportion of cases but appear to be a rare concomitant of EDS (Beighton 1969; D'Aloia *et al.* 2008).

Central nervous system involvement is reported, with an association between EDS and the periventricular heterotopia variant (Sheen *et al.* 2005; Thomas *et al.* 1996). This association has been linked to a common defect in the filamin A gene that has not been reported in other forms of EDS. Filamin A is at Xq28 (Fox *et al.* 1998; Sheen *et al.* 2005; see also Sheen and Walsh 2006). In the vascular (type IV) form, intracerebral aneurysms have been reported (Kato *et al.* 2001).

Is there a link between EDS and ASD?

- Several reports of cases in which individuals with Ehlers-Danlos syndrome also have ASD have been published; however, to date no systematic studies of this issue have appeared. It is unclear, therefore, whether this is a chance association or there is some causal linkage involved, and as the association has not been with a specific type of EDS, the genetic basis, if any, is still unclear.

- Sieg (1992) published the first report as a letter in the *American Journal of Child and Adolescent Psychiatry*.

- Fehlow *et al.* (1993) described a 19-year-old patient with early infantile autism and learning disability who died after extreme distension of the stomach induced by aerophagy (air-swallowing).

- Lumley and colleagues, from Wayne State University in Detroit, interviewed and tested 48 individuals with EDS – 41 adults and seven children (Lumley *et al.* 1994). More than two-thirds of those examined had a history of mental health problems. The authors suggest that these problems are linked to chronic pain and dissatisfaction with the medical system. Many of the difficulties they report – interpersonal concerns and avoidance of relationships and social activities – could easily reflect an ASD.

In much of the literature EDS has been linked with 'alexithymia' (a term which is not in the DSM or ICD systems but is used to describe a personality disorder in which there are problems in understanding, processing and describing emotions).

- In a separate paper Lumley and colleagues (1996) included a sample of 40 EDS subjects along with normal controls in a study of alexithymia, health problems and perceived social support. Using a number of scales of alexithymia and the PILL (Pennebaker Inventory of Limbic Languidness) (Pennebaker 1982), they were able to demonstrate an association between physical symptomology, poor social support and poorly perceived social skills (suggesting that a difficulty in understanding, processing and describing emotions characterizes the EDS behavioural phenotype).

Differential diagnosis: The features of EDS are not typically confused with other conditions; however, Williams syndrome [77], which results in a defect in connective tissue due to defective production of elastin, and Marfan's syndrome, which presents with similar features due to a defect in the production of both elastin and fibrillin-1 (a further protein important in connective tissue formation – see discussion in Dietz 2007), have both been linked wth ASD (see Tantam, Evered and Hersov 1990 for a paper on the co-occurrence of Marfan's syndrome and ASD).

Treatment and management: As the features of EDS are highly variable, the treatment approach cannot be prescriptive. At the present time, there is insufficient information to give separable behavioural phenotypes for the different forms of EDS; however, there are emerging suggestions of different behavioural phenotypes associated with the different types of EDS (Lumley *et al.* 1994). It seems most plausible that a link between EDS and ASD would involve type IV and/or the periventricular heterotopia variant.

The increased risks of vascular damage, bruising and damage to the skin are important aspects of ongoing care, but in other respects there are no specific features relevant to ASD apparent at this time.

Further information and support:

In Australia:
Australian EDS Support Group
PO Box 106
Marulan
NSW 2579
Tel./Fax: 0011 61-2-4841 1111
E-mail: prairie@goulburn.net.au or EDSAussie@altavista.net

In Canada:
The Canadian Ehlers-Danlos Association
88 De Rose Avenue
Bolton,
Ontario
L7E 1A8
E-mail: ceda@rogers.com
Website: www.ehlersdanlos.ca

In France:
L'Association Française des Syndromes d'Ehlers-Danlos
AFSED 38 avenue Pompidou 69 003
Lyon
Tel.: (33) 803 00 11 33
Fax: (33) 04 78 53 92 49
E-mail: m.h.boucand@wanadoo.fr
Website: http://perso.wanadoo.fr/ehlers.danlos/

In New Zealand:
New Zealand Ehlers-Danlos Syndrome Support Group
Maraetuna Farm
Craggy Range Road,
R.D.12.
Havelock North
Hawkes Bay
Tel.: 06 874 7799 or 021 2153 471
E-mail: flopsy@ihug.co.nz
Website: www.edfnz.org.nz

In the UK:
Ehlers-Danlos Support Group
PO Box 337
Aldershot
GU12 6WZ
Tel.: 01252 690940
Website: www.ehlers-danlos.org/

United Kingdom Ehlers Danlos Syndrome Association
1 Chandler Close
Richmond
North Yorkshire
Tel./Fax: 01748 823867
E-mail: EDSUK@compuserve.com

In the USA:
Ehlers-Danlos National Foundation
EDNF National Office
3200 Wilshire Blvd
Suite 1601, South Tower
Los Angeles
CA 90010
Tel.: 213-368 –3800
Fax: 213-427-0057
E-mail (President and CEO): clauren@ednf.org
Website: www.ednf.org

EDS Today Newsletter
PO Box 88814
Seattle,
WA 98138-2814
E-mail: edstoday@uggen.net
Website: www.edstoday.org

35

Fragile-X syndrome (FRAX)

aka • Martin–Bell syndrome

• marker-X syndrome

Gene locus: Xq27.3 (FMR1 – Fragile-X Mental Retardation 1)

Key ASD references: August and Lockhart 1984; Blomquist *et al.* 1985; Brown *et al.* 1982b; Cohen *et al.* 1991; Gillberg 1983; Hatton *et al.* 2006; Hernandez *et al.* 2009; Kaufmann *et al.* 2004; Klauck *et al.* 1997; Loesch *et al.* 2007; Meryash, Szymanski and Gerald 1982

There are a large number of genes (over 130 currently known) that can result in X-linked mental retardation (XLMR), a significant proportion of which result in clinically indistinguishable non-syndromic forms (NS-XLMR), where the genetics is inferred from the familial inheritance pattern (Ropers 2006). The most common X-linked condition that causes neurodevelopmental problems is known as fragile-X syndrome. This is also the condition most commonly linked to autism in the clinical literature. Fragile-X syndrome is thought to be the second most prevalent genetic cause of learning disability after Down syndrome [31] (Rousseau *et al.* 1995). The phenotype associated with fragile-X syndrome is significantly more common in boys.

Fragile-X syndrome results from a triplet repeat expansion of the FMR1 locus. It is inherited as an X-linked dominant condition. A normal FMR1 gene is some 38 kilobases of DNA, with 17 exons (Eichler *et al.* 1993). The triplet expansion was first described in fragile-X syndrome by Verkerk *et al.* (1991). Although triplet repeat expansions were originally thought to be unusual, over 40 neuromuscular, neurodegenerative and neurological disorders have now been described resulting from such expansions (Pearson, Edamura and Cleary 2005). Structurally, fragile-X results in morphologically distinct spinal neurons (Bagni and Greenough 2005).

The FRM1 gene ceases to function in about 99 per cent of cases, due to a triplet expansion with direct effects on methylation. The FMR1 region codes for the RNA-binding protein known as fragile-X mental retardation protein (FMRP) (Kooy, Willemsen and Oostra 2000). In the other approximately one per cent of cases, the condition arises from deletions (Hammond *et al.* 1997) or point mutations (Wang Y.C. *et al.* 1997) within the FMR1 locus. Fragile-X syndrome is thus caused by inactivation of the gene and the reduction or absence of FMRP. The transcription process is partly controlled by two other genes, Nrf-1 and Sp1, and is not regulated by DNA methylation alone (Garber *et al.* 2006).

The CGG (cytosine–guanine–guanine) nucleic acid sequence involved in the production of FMRP repeats some 6–55 times in the general population. In mothers of affected individuals the same CGG sequence repeats some 55–230 times – this used to be called a 'pre-mutational' expansion (but see FXTAS below), while in diagnosed individuals some 230–1000 copies are typically seen (Fryns *et al.* 2000). The condition usually affects the X chromosome in boys, who will have inherited their Y chromosome from their father and their X chromosome from their mother. Although *de novo* mutation and uniparental isodisomy with patrilineal inheritance are theoretically possible neither has been reported to date.

FMR1 expansions are not invariably associated with developmental problems. One paper documents a woman with a full mutation who is of above average IQ, but has an anxiety disorder and specific learning disabilities (Angkustsiri *et al.* 2008). Unmethylated FMR1 expansions with normal development have been reported (Hagerman, Ono and Hagerman 2005), as have cases of normal development with partial methylation (Rousseau *et al.* 1994).

The first clinical account of the fragile-X syndrome phenotype was a paper written by two clinicians working at Queen Square in London, Martin and Bell (1943), and so it was referred to as Martin–Bell syndrome (see, for example, Opitz, Westphal and Daniel 1984). Many of the cases in this initial report were children of the daughters of two unaffected brothers. The first identification of an X-chromosome defect in such cases was reported in 1969, when this was identified in chromosomes cultured in a folate-reduced medium (Lubs 1969). It was in 1977 that Sutherland demonstrated the importance of folate reduction for FMR1 expansion to be visible.

Fragile-X syndrome was the first condition in which our understanding of the neurobiology grew rapidly through the development of mouse and fruit-fly models of the condition (Zarnescu *et al.* 2005a, 2005b).

How common is fragile-X syndrome? The full mutation form is found in some one in 3,717 to one in 8,918 of the male Caucasian population, with a higher prevalence rate of some one in 1,289 to one in 2,545 in the Afro-American male population. Infant screening suggests a far lower rate of some one in 10,046 in the Taiwan Chinese.

From the studies to date, the prevalence of expansions in women is far higher than expected. A French-Canadian screening study of 10,624 women found that one in 259 were pre-mutational carriers. An Israeli study of 14,334 women found 127 carriers, three with full mutations, giving a prevalence of one in 113, with one in 69 carriers having more than 50 repeats.

Founder effects, where the presence of fragile-X can be traced back to a particular individual or family, have been demonstrated in populations in the USA, Australia, Finland and Israel and in several circumpolar groups (Norwegian, Kola Saami and Siberian Nenet). The length of CGG repeats seen in fragile-X within given populations appears to correlate with the time that fragile-X has been found within that population, suggesting increasing expansion over historical time. Some populations, such as Nova Scotia, appear not to have FRAX expansions or mutations at the present time.

Main clinical features: There is no obvious early physical phenotype, and without genetic testing diagnostic confusion is common (Stoll 2001). Ideally DNA testing should be routine for children presenting with delayed milestones, autistic behaviour, learning disability without obvious cause, or where there is a positive family history.

The most obvious early signs of the condition are marked gaze avoidance and hand flapping. An enlarged forehead with an occipito-frontal head circumference above the 50th centile is common. The physical features that are typically quoted – long face, protruding ears and large testes – become markedly more prominent after puberty, and are often unremarkable earlier.

In affected males with an FMR1 expansion, a range of behavioural features are commonly seen:

- learning disability (IQ typically 30–50), often in the context of a family history of learning disability

- hyperactivity

- short attention span

- tactile defensiveness

- hand flapping

- hand biting

- poor eye contact

- perseverative speech.

Poor fine-motor control appears to differentiate fragile-X + ASD from fragile-X without ASD (Zingerevich *et al.* 2009).

With a full mutation, boys typically show delayed milestones for both motor development and communication, walking and talking, with clear words at about 20 months.

The key physical features are:

- hyperextensible metacarpophalangeal joints

- large or prominent ears

- large testes

- Simian/single palmar crease. (A single palmar crease is seen in a range of ASD conditions including Aarskog syndrome [8]; de Lange syndrome [27]; Down syndrome [31]; and Smith-Lemli-Opitz syndrome [66].)

Physical features usually become more obvious after puberty.

Table B35.1: Physical and behavioural features in boys with fragile-X syndrome

Feature	Percentage of boys with feature
Perseveration	95
Hyperactivity	89
Poor eye contact	88
Hand flapping	85
Flat feet	82
Hyperextensible metacarpophalangeal joints	81
Prominent ears	78
Tactile defensiveness	76
Long face	64
Hand biting	64
Double-jointed thumbs	58
High-arched palate	51
Hand calluses	18

Adapted from Hagerman and Hagerman 2002a.

Macro-orchidism (large testes) is commonly reported in males with FMR1. The evidence to date suggests that there is an association, as some 44 per cent of those with FMR1 and learning disability have macro-orchidism, which can be more marked than in the general learning-disabled male population. However, this may be associated more with the degree of learning disability than with FMR1 *per se* (Vatta *et al.* 1998).

Table B35.2: Common physical problems in males with FMR1

Feature	Percentage of males with feature
Recurrent otitis media	85
Strabismus	36
Recurrent emesis	31
Sinusitis	23
Seizures	22
Motor tics	19
Failure to thrive	15

Hernia	15
Apnoea	10
Joint dislocation	3

Adapted from Hagerman and Hagerman 2002a

The physical phenotype reported in women with a full FMR1 expansion, the poor eye contact and the increased rate of stereotyped behaviours are similar to the features reported in full mutation FMR1 males.

Table B35.3: Physical and behavioural features in women with the full fragile-X mutation

Feature	Percentage of women with feature
Poor eye contact	73
Long face	66
High-arched palate	59
Double-jointed thumbs	42
Prominent ears	42
Hyperextensible metacarpophalangeal joints	24
Flat feet	24
Scoliosis	22
Strabismus	20
Hand flapping	17
Hand biting	7

Adapted from Hagerman and Hagerman 2002a

The prevalence and range of features, in both affected males and females clearly identify differences from the normal population; however, none is either necessary or specifically associated with a diagnosis of fragile-X.

The clinical diagnosis relies on the identification of an FMR1 expansion on genetic testing (or, more rarely, point mutation; deletion; or missense mutation interfering with FMR1 function), coupled with abnormal methylation.

Certain other features, such as sleep difficulties, appear to be common in fragile-X syndrome (Weiskop, Richdale and Matthews 2005) and might be related to biological differences. From the work to date, aspects such as melatonin secretion seem extremely variable (Gould et al. 2000).

There have been reports of cardiac abnormalities, such as mitral valve prolapse (Hagerman and Synhorst 1984; Pyeritz *et al.* 1982) and mild dilatation of the aorta (Hagerman and Synhorst 1984). No formal studies of cardiac function have been published.

Ligamentous laxity has also been reported in two early papers (Hagerman *et al.* 1984; Opitz, Westphal and Daniel 1984). However, again, no studies have been published on this issue.

A small-scale study of early videotapes of development in children with fragile-X (N=11) compared this group to other children with autism (N=11), children with other developmental disorders (N=10) and normal controls (N=11) (Baranek *et al.* 2005). The results suggested that those with fragile-X showed early differences in their sensori-motor development, differentiating them from those with autism *without* fragile-X. The findings in the fragile-X group were most similar to those seen in the other developmental disorders *not* including ASD. This suggests a possible difference between fragile-X autism and others with autism. One limitation is that the study did not discriminate within the fragile-X group between those who would have qualified for an ASD diagnosis (normally around 20–30 per cent in reported samples to date) (Feinstein and Reiss 1998; Rogers, Wehner and Hagerman 2001), and those who would not.

A further study compared a group of 24 21–48-month-old FRAX cases to 27 with autism and 23 with developmental delay on various instruments (Rogers, Wehner and hagerman 2001). They found that one third of the FRAX cases clearly met criteria for an ASD while the rest did not, suggesting additional genetic influences on the behavioural phenotype in FRAX.

When we look at the proportion of those with an ASD diagnosis who have a fragile-X expansion on genetic testing, the results vary widely, with somewhere between 0 and 16 per cent of cases typically being reported (see Dykens and Volkmar 1997 for a review). The proportion of fragile-X positive cases is likely to have fallen with the broadening of diagnostic criteria in the ICD-10 and DSM-IV criteria introduced in 1994. One systematic study in particular which reviewed a large ASD sample (Klauck *et al.* 1997) concludes that, although cases where fragile-X and ASD co-occur can be found, the level of the association is minimal. In this study, the authors concluded that a link between autism and fragile-X at Xq27.3 was non-existent. A screening study found that the rate of FMR1 in the ASD population was similar to that in the learning-disabled population in general (Hagerman *et al.* 1994b).

Within the fragile-X population, receptive language skills appear to be an area of relative strength, except in those who also fulfil criteria for autism. Those with fragile-X autism, in common with most other autistics, show relative deficits in receptive language (Philofsky *et al.* 2004). Where early population screening is available, this may prove to be a way of identifying those who are at risk of ASD within the fragile-X population, and of targeting early interventions.

An early study established that FMR1 expression in the foetal brain is most pronounced in the nucleus basalis magnocellularis and the hippocampus (Abitbol *et al.* 1993). FMRP is localized in dendrites and reduced in synapses by activation of the specific metabotropic glutamate receptor mGluR5 (Antar *et al.* 2004). In rats, at least, mGluR5 can be detected during embryonic development (Lopez-Bendito *et al.* 2002), and is most prominent in zones of active neurogenesis (Gerevini *et al.* 2004). Its expression rises through the first two postnatal weeks, then falls to adult levels (Romano *et al.* 2002).

Neuroanatomically FRAX results in an excess of long, thin dendritic spines seen in both human central nervous system autopsy tissue from affected individuals (Irwin, Galvez and Greenough 2000) and in brain tissue from genetically engineered knockout mice (Comery *et al.* 1997). Dendritic anomalies are common to a number of disorders associated with learning problems; however, the nature, location and extent of these defects seem to be disorder-specific (Kaufmann and Moser 2000; Ramackers 2002). In fragile-X, the effect of the FMRP defect is to produce a syndrome-specific abnormality of dendritic spine morphology (Vanderklish and Edelman 2005).

Studies of the brain in fragile-X have shown *structural differences*, with enlargement of the hippocampus and reduction in the size of the cerebellum and the superior temporal gyrus (Reiss *et al.* 1991; Reiss, Lee and Freund 1994), *functional differences* (Rivera *et al.* 2002) and *differences in neuroendocrine function*, particularly affecting the hypothalamo-gonadal-pituitary axis (Hessl, Rivera and Reiss 2004). The presence of periventricular heterotopias in unrelated cases (Moro *et al.* 2006) suggests that one aspect of fragile-X is a neural migration defect.

In certain brain areas, expression of FMRP mRNA is regulated by a brain-derived neurotrophic factor (Castre *et al.* 2002). A complex range of mRNAs binds to fragile-X gene products, partly accounting for the wide variation in phenotype (Gantois and Kooy 2002; Jin *et al.* 2004). Studies are beginning to elucidate the metabolic chain that culminates in fragile-X syndrome (Pietrobono *et al.* 2005).

In FRAX there is a well-recognized physical and behavioural phenotype (Hagerman and Cronister 1996). Seizure problems affect some 10–20 per cent of cases, with complex partial seizures being most common (Sutherland, Gecz and Mulley 2002).

That the association of FRAX with autism is at well above chance levels is now well accepted (Goodlin-Jones *et al.* 2004). The reporting of cases where autism has been found in children with pre-mutational expansions (Miller 2006) strengthens the idea of a common underlying pathophysiology to both the fragile-X-specific physical and behavioural phenotype and the behavioural phenotype of autism. This may lead on to a clearer understanding of sufficient neurobiological mechanisms in the pathogenesis and maintenance of autistic symptomology.

In a German study, Backes *et al.* (2000) assessed 49 boys with fragile-X syndrome and 16 controls in a group comparison study. The FRAX group had mild to moderate learning disability assessed on the Kaufman Assessment Battery for Children. ADHD, oppositional defiant disorder, enuresis and encopresis were the most common mental health difficulties. There was no clear association between the phenotype and genotype.

A systematic review (Cornish *et al.* 2004) has suggested that a neuroconstructivist systems view, rather than a purely genetic view of development in fragile-X best captures the subtle and complex interplay of genetic, brain and environmental factors.

The considerable interest in the neurobiology of fragile-X syndrome (Belmonte and Bourgeron 2006; Hagerman 2006; Miller 2006) has been stimulated by several major developments.

First the recognition that the grandfathers of those affected by fragile-X syndrome often presented in later life with a condition now known as fragile-X-associated tremor/ataxia syndrome (FXTAS) (Amiri, Hagerman and Hagerman 2008). The condition has also been reported in carrier sisters who have preferential activation of the pre-mutational X allele (Berry-Kravis *et al.* 2005). It appears that FXTAS in carrier women does not convey the same increased risk of dementia as it does in males, although it does present with tremor and ataxia (Hagerman *et al.* 2004).

Approximately one in 25 adult onset cerebellar ataxias in men is thought to result from a pre-mutational FMR1 expansion (Brussino *et al.* 2005).

There is also a possible link between pre-mutational expansion and risk of autism, with several cases and one systematic study reporting this (Farzin *et al.* 2006; Goodlin-Jones *et al.* 2004) – this suggests that pre-mutational expansions may not be benign, but may convey risk in pre-mutational males.

Studies have shown that it is the inclusion of untranslated FMR1 messenger RNA which results in the inclusion bodies seen in the glial cells and neurons in the hippocampus and cerebral cortex of pre-mutational males (Chiurazzi, Tabolacci and Neri 2004; Welt, Smith and Taylor 2004).

Second, there is strong evidence for premature ovarian failure in approximately 20 per cent of female carriers of a pre-mutational expansion (typically classified as ceasing menstruation before age 40) (Bretherick, Fluker and Robinson 2005; Sherman 2000), but not of other potentially associated difficulties (Hundscheid *et al.* 2003). A large international collaborative study of some 790 women from fragile-X families clearly established the link between female FMR1 carrier status and premature ovarian failure (Allingham-Hawkins *et al.* 1999).

There is a particular neuropsychological profile in some female carriers who have problems with selective attention (Steyaert *et al.* 2003). There is, in addition, a small effect of carrier status and of the size of pre-mutational expansion on verbal IQ in female carriers (Allen *et al.* 2005).

Third, following on from the previous point, the main effect of the fragile-X expansion is to interfere with metabotropic glutamate receptor-coupled pathways (specifically of those involving mGluR5) (Bear 2005). This possibility was first proposed in 2004 (Bear, Huber and Warren 2004) and has quickly established empirical support from both animal and human studies. An interesting finding is that mGluR5 receptors respond to glutamate preferentially, but also to cysteine, aspartate and asparagine (Frauli *et al.* 2006).

From the variety of phenotypes associated with differences in FMR1, and the increasing evidence of benefits from therapeutic intervention, there is increasing interest in population screening (Hagerman and Hagerman 2008; Tassone *et al.* 2008).

Various brain areas, including the cerebellum and limbic system, have high numbers of glutamate receptors. Researchers have theorized that overactivity of glutamate could result in 'excitotoxicity', and could cause aberrant neuronal development (Bittigau and Ikonomidou 1997). In mice, FMR1 deletion affects the development of a wide range of neural structures, with abnormal mGluR1-dependent long-term depression in hippocampus and in cerebellum (Huber *et al.* 2002). If the glutamergic system is hyperfunctional, it is likely that neuronal growth and connectivity would be damaged during critical periods of early development.

The potential role of glutamate in a number of conditions as disparate as post-traumatic stress disorder, Alzheimer's disease, anxiety disorders and schizophrenia has been well recognized (Bergink, van Megen and Westenberg 2004; Javitt 2004).

The role of mGluR5 in learning and memory has been extensively studied (Simonyi, Schachtman and Christoffersen 2005). From the animal research to date, there are two splice variants – mGluR5a and mGluR5b – with the b variant predominating in the adult brain, and mGluR5 mRNA being found predominantly in the hippocampus, amygdala, caudate-putamen and cortex.

There has been a steadily growing interest in metabotropic glutamate receptors as a potential target for pharmacotherapy (Nicoletti *et al.* 1996). A number of specific pre- and post-synaptic mGluR5 antagonists have now become available (Gasparini *et al.* 1999; O'Leary *et al.* 2000; Schoepp, Jane and Monn 1999). See Berry-Kravis and Potanos (2004) for a more broad-ranging review of pharmacotherapy in FRAX.

Testing FMRP levels: Levels of FMR protein have been shown to correlate inversely with level of ASD symptomology (Hatton *et al.* 2006; Loesch *et al.* 2007). Testing of levels is not routine, but can be performed (Willemsen *et al.* 1997), and may be helpful in population screening and in profiling individuals for biological markers of severity (Tassone *et al.* 1999).

Genotype–phenotype correlations: Most research has been carried out on the triplet repeat forms of FMR1, as this is the most prevalent presentation. This does not necessarily match what is typical in other types of FMR1 condition, such as deletion and point mutation cases.

Pre-mutational expansions (59–200 CGG repeats): These can result in symptoms more typically seen with a full mutation (Hagerman and Hagerman 2002b). Some 'transmitting' males who have pre-mutational expansions are of normal ability and are fertile. There is some evidence of neuropsychological difficulties in pre-mutational males, with deficits in executive functions and working memory (Moore *et al.* 2004).

Transmitting males and carrier females are at risk of developing tremor-ataxia syndrome in later life.

With maternal pre-mutational expansions of over 90 repeats, the majority of offspring are likely to be born with full mutations, while with less than 70 repeats, fewer than six per cent of children will have full mutations (Nolin *et al.* 2003).

Full mutation (200 repeats or more): Individuals with a full FMR1 mutation are said to have fragile-X syndrome. Males typically have moderate to severe learning disability. Gaze avoidance, distractibility and hand-flapping are usual in childhood, but all may improve with age. The physical features, although common, are not always found, and overlap considerably with a number of other conditions. Around 50 per cent of females with a full FMR1 expansion are similarly affected, but tend to be slightly more able than males. The extent of developmental problems in women appears to be inversely associated with the level of FMRP that they produce.

Mosaic presentations: FMR1 mosaics account for 15–20 per cent of cases. Mosaics can present with either a combination of pre-mutational and full mutational expansions or with methylation mosaicism where only a proportion of the expansions are methylated (Smeets *et al.* 1995). As the effect of mosaicism on levels of FMRP are typically less than in the full mutation (Tassone *et al.* 1999), the phenotype is less severe, with higher cognitive functioning (Coffee *et al.* 2008); however, the more severe fragile-X phenotype has also been reported (MacKenzie, Sumargo and Taylor 2006).

Prenatal diagnosis: FRAX can be diagnosed antenatally by analysis of a sample taken from the lining of the womb (chorionic villus sampling) (Sutherland *et al.* 1991).

Is there a link between fragile-X and ASD? Within those who have a full fragile-X mutation, 21 per cent of all cases, and some 25.9 per cent of males, exhibit behaviour consistent with an autistic diagnosis (Hatton *et al.* 2006). They report an inverse correlation between severity of autistic symptomology and level of FMRP, suggesting a quantitative relationship between the two factors. This was also a finding in earlier research (Tassone *et al.* 1999). FMRP is primarily expressed in neurons (Devys *et al.* 1993), with a role in the maturation and apoptosis of synapses (Weiler and Greenough 1999).

- The first papers to suggest an association between ASD and fragile-X were a couple of publications by Brown *et al.* (1982a, 1982b) describing four male cases of autism in association with an FMR1 expansion.

- Another paper published in the same year also suggested an association (Meryash, Szymanski and Gerald 1982).

- In 1983, Christopher Gillberg reported on a set of triplets who were moderately learning-disabled, all showing physical characteristics consistent with fragile-X syndrome. The triplets were all diagnosed with infantile autism on Rutter's criteria. Each showed between 8 and 12 per cent fragile-X positive cells. Their mother and singleton sister also had high numbers of fragile-X positive cells.

- In 1983, G.J. August suggested that fragile-X was a gene marker associated with autism, and the following year August and Lockhart (1984) presented two brothers with autism, learning disability and fragile-X mutations, who had also had twin brothers with autism and learning disability, but the twins had died in a fire before any genetic assessment was carried out.

- In 1985 a Swedish multicentre study (Blomquist *et al.* 1985) investigated 212 children with diagnoses of infantile autism. Fragile-X was found in 13 of 83 boys, but in none of the 129 girls tested.

- Demonstration of a fragile-X mutation in 18 out of a series of 144 male autistic cases provided strong evidence of an association between the two conditions, rather than reporting of cases where the two co-occur by chance (Fisch *et al.* 1986).

- In 1991, Ira Cohen and colleagues reviewed the literature, noting inconsistent findings to that time, but concluding overall that autism and fragile-X are associated and that a clearer understanding of X-chromosome abnormalities may be important in understanding the aetiology of autism.

- Kaufmann *et al.* (2004) examined the profiles of 56 boys with fragile-X on a battery of measures of cognition, autistic behaviour, behaviour problems, adaptive behaviours and language. This was an attempt to look for fragile-X-specific ASD profiles and found a strong association between impaired social interaction and ASD diagnosis. It clearly indicated that there is a subgroup of fragile-X individuals who fulfil criteria for ASD diagnosis.

- A further paper from the same group (Kau *et al.* 2004) compared and contrasted various groups, including fragile-X, with autism, developmental language delay with autism and idiopathic autism (without either language delay or fragile-X). This study reported that there was a specific profile seen in those with fragile-X autism. They were less impaired, both on the Achenbach Child Behavior Checklist withdrawn subscale and on the ADI-R assessment of reciprocal social interaction, but scored more highly on measures of behavioural stereotypy and communication difficulty.

- Hatton *et al.* (2006) from the University of North Carolina at Chapel Hill documented autistic behaviour in a large sample of children with fragile-X syndrome. Twenty-seven out of 129 cases (21 per cent) were above the clinical cutoff for diagnosis on the CARS. They also reported on a longitudinal subset of 116 children. CARS scores increased over time and there was an inverse correlation between levels of fragile-X mental retardation protein (FMRP) and severity of autistic behaviour.

- An Australian–US collaborative study (Loesch *et al.* 2007) found that both in full mutation (N=147) and pre-mutational cases (N=59) scores on the ADOS-G were significantly elevated, compared with non-fragile-X relatives (N=59). Full-scale IQ and executive functioning skills were the major predictors of ASD diagnosis, with social interaction and communication difficulties correlating strongly and inversely with levels of FMRP, but contributing to a lesser extent to ASD diagnosis.

- A longitudinal follow-up of the 56 fragile-X cases from the Kennedy Krieger group (Hernandez *et al.* 2009) established that the fragile-X + autism group is a remarkably stable and distinctive subphenotype of fragile-X.

- A German group (Klauck *et al.* 1997) presented data on 141 autistic patients from 105 simplex and 18 multiplex families. Bloods were collected from all cases and tested for FMR1 expansion. In only two males, both from the same multiplex family, was there an FMR1 expansion. Both had a mosaic expansion with a partly functional gene. One met ASD criteria, the other had mild learning difficulties. The authors concluded that there was no basis to conclude that there was an association between FMR1 and ASD. In the context of the other research reviewed above, this suggests that there may, in addition to the ethnic differences in prevalence noted above, be marked differences in geographic/population prevalence.

Differential diagnosis: As the physical phenotype only becomes obvious postpubertally, and prepubertal physical and cognitive features are variable, a range of alternative diagnoses needs to be explored in someone presenting with a fragile-X phenotype. Testing for FMR1 is now a routine part of initial screening in many centres. These alternative diagnoses are most likely to be explored if the person has screened as FMR1 negative.

Learning disability is seen in most FMR1 cases, but only one in 20 learning-disabled cases will have an FMR1 expansion, it is important that other possible causes are investigated in children with slow development, persevertive behaviours, overticity, poor eye contact and hand-flapping (Curry *et al.* 1997; Shevell *et al.* 2003).

A number of other overgrowth conditions should be considered, such as Bannayan-Riley-Ruvalcaba syndrome (BRRS) [15]; basal cell naevus syndrome [16]; cortical dysplasia–focal epilepsy (CDFE) syndrome [19]; Cole-Hughes macrocephaly syndrome (macrocephaly/autism syndrome) [24]; Cowden syndrome [26]; fragile-XE syndrome (Hamel *et al.* 1994, Mulley *et al.* 1995); Orstavik 1997 syndrome [56]; Prader-Willi syndrome [61]; Proteus syndrome [62] and Sotos syndrome [68].

There is some evidence for a Prader-Willi syndrome like FMR1 phenotype (de Vries *et al.* 1995).

De novo FMR1 expansion has never been reported. The most likely way in which a fragile-X mutation is inherited is from a mother with either a pre-mutational or a full expansion. Pre-mutational expansions will typically result in larger expansions in offspring who inherit the mutation; however, reduction in CGG repeats have been reported from both a mother-to-daughter transmission (Vits *et al.* 1994) and a mother-to-son transmission (Tabolacci *et al.* 2008).

In very rare cases, both parents have FMR1 expansions (Linden *et al.* 1999; Mila *et al.* 1996; Russo *et al.* 1998).

Treatment and management: A range of ameliorative strategies is available to address patterns of presentation as appropriate to the specific individual. Seizures, cardiac problems and ophthalmic and cosmetic issues should be treated as in other cases (Hagerman 1997, 1999; Hagerman and Cronister 1996).

Until very recently, there were no treatment approaches that were thought to improve function substantively in fragile-X syndrome. Based on the exciting findings in animal models, several approaches are now being actively pursued, and promising intervention studies have appeared.

A number of treatment approaches are being actively explored in attempts to correct the biological differences found. Four simple summaries of this work can be found in Berry-Kravis (2008), Hagerman *et al.* (2009), Reiss and Hall (2007) and Rueda, Ballesteros and Tejada (2009).

Some treatments, such as memantine, have only preliminary findings (Erickson, Mullett and McDougle 2009). A number of approaches have a more robust evidence base namely:

Folic acid: Folic acid has been shown to be of some benefit (Hagerman *et al.* 1986); however, not all studies have yielded positive results (Rosenblatt *et al.* 1985), and it is thought that it might exacerbate seizure activity in some cases. Folic acid deficiency is implicated in a range of conditions including epilepsy, vascular disease and neurodevelopmental defects (Moore 2005).

Certain antibiotics containing trimethoprim or other antagonists to folate production have been suggested as potentially hazardous to children with FRAX (Lejeune *et al.* 1982), and it has been suggested that they should be avoided during pregnancies where there is a risk of FRAX (Hecht and Glover 1983). There has been no recent research on this issue.

MGluR5 antagonists: The biology of glutamatergic differences in fragile-X syndrome is now becoming well understood (Dolen and Bear 2005). The results of treatment studies in animal models are highly encouraging.

Lithium has been shown to reverse the memory problems seen in fragile-X drosophila (McBride *et al.* 2005) and audiogenic seizures seen in fragile-X mice (Chen and Toth 2001), and there are reports that these are also reduced in response to lithium (Berry-Kravis *et al.* 2008).

Various medications that block the mGluR5 pathway have been undergoing evaluation, such as fenobam (Hagerman *et al.* 2008) and 2 methyl-6 (phenylethynyl) pyridine (MPEP).

Human trials of an mGluR5 antagonist (STX107) are under way in the USA at the time of writing (see Seaside Therapeutics www.seasidetherapeutics.com/ who are actively researching the clinical benefits of STX107).

Various other treatment approaches are currently being evaluated at present.

Mifepristone, which is being researched by Dr Alan Reiss's group at Stanford University, blocks the effects of cortisol. In one preliminary study, cortisol has been shown to be elevated at rest in children with fragile-X, and to increase in response to social stress (Wisbeck *et al.* 2000). No results of this work are available at the current time.

GABA agonists: Drugs that increase GABA (gamma-aminobutyric acid) pathway activity are known to reduce glutamatergic receptor activity by competition. On this basis, a number of GABA agonists are being investigated for their potential use in the treatment of FRAX – in particular, baclofen, which is known to reduce aggressive and self-injurious behaviour, and ganaloxone (Kerrigan *et al.* 2000), which is showing some success in seizure control, are being investigated.

P21 activated kinase (PAK) inhibitors: PAK is involved in the activation of protein synthesis by mGluRs. There has been promising animal research (Hayashi *et al.* 2007), and some of the medications in development for the treatment of neurofibromatosis type 1 [51] are PAK inhibitors that could also prove beneficial in the treatment of FRAX.

Ampakines: Ampakine (AMPA) receptor activity is reduced with FXMRP deficiency (Nakamoto *et al.* 2007). AMPA increases the activation of brain-derived neurotrophic factor (BDNF). BDNF activity is reduced in FRAX. This suggests that increased AMPA activation could be beneficial. One medication that upregulates AMPA activity, piracetam, has been shown to have positive effects in autism in combination with risperidone (Akhondzadeh *et al.* 2008). Ampakine (CX516), an AMPA receptor activator, is being evaluated, based on findings in knockout mice in which memory is impaired and cortical AMPA receptors are reduced in number. Preliminary results of a randomized placebo controlled trial (N=49) suggest that, while well tolerated for the most part, ampakine produced no effects on memory, language, executive functions or behaviour overall. Benefits were observed, but only in those subjects who were already receiving antipsychotic medication, and it is possible that the dosage of ampakine used was sub-therapeutic. The ampakine 'CX515' has been the subject of a randomized, double-blind, placebo-controlled trial in adults with fragile-X, and was well tolerated; however, effects on cognition and behaviour were minimal, except when used in conjunction with risperidone (Reiss and Hall 2007).

Minocyclidine: Minocyclidine is a medication that has been used in the treatment of acne. Its mode of action is reduction of one of the proteins regulated by FMRP. An NIH (National Institute Health) approved and funded study will provide evidence on possible efficacy in FRAX (July 2008, NIH Trial Number: NCT00409747, web ref: www.clinicaltrials.gov/ct).

Further information and support:

In Australia:
Fragile-X Association of Australia
10 Geddes St
Balgowlah Heights 2093
Tel.: 0409 987 012
E-mail: fragilexassociation@optusnet.com.au
Website: www.fragilex.org.au

In Canada:
The Fragile-X Research Foundation of Canada
167 Queen St. W.
Brampton
Ontario
L6Y 1M5
Tel.: 905-453-9366
E-mail: fxrfc@on.aibn.com
Website: www.fragile-x.ca/

In Germany:
Interessengemeinschaft Fragiles-X e.V.
24576 Bad Bramstedt
Goethering 42
Tel.: 04192/4053
Fax: 07944/411
E-mail: verein@frax.de
Website: www.frax.de

In the UK:
The Fragile-X Society
Rood End House
6 Stortford Road
Great Dunmow
Essex
CM6 1DA
Tel.: 01371 875100
Fax: 01371 859915
E-mail: info@fragilex.org.uk
Website: www.fragilex.org.uk

In the USA:
FRAXA Research Foundation
45 Pleasant St.
Newburyport,
MA 01950
Tel.: 978-462-1866
Fax: 978-463-9985
E-mail: fraxa@seacoast.com or kclapp@fraxa.org
Website: www.fraxa.org

National Fragile-X Foundation
PO Box 190488
San Francisco,
CA 94119
Tel.: 800-688-8765 or 510-763-6030
Fax: 510-763-6223
E-mail: natlfx@sprintmail.com
Website: www.nfxf.org or http://fragilex.org

National Ataxia Foundation
2600 Fernbrook Lane Suite 119
Minneapolis
MN 55447
Tel.: 763-553-0020
Fax: 763-553-0167
E-mail: naf@ataxia.org
Website: www.ataxia.org

WE MOVE (Worldwide Education and Awareness for Movement Disorders)
204 West 84th Street
New York
NY 10024
Tel.: 800-437-MOV2 (800-437-6683)
Fax: 212-875-8389
E-mail: wemove@wemove.org
Website: www.wemove.org

Fragile-X Research and Treatment Center
UC Davis MIND Institute
2825 50th Street
Sacramento
CA 95817
Tel.: 916-703-0280
Website: www.ucdmc.ucdavis.edu/mindinstitute/
research/fxrtc.html

36

Fragile-X permutation (partial methylation defects)

Gene locus: Xq27.3

Key ASD reference: Nolin *et al.* 1994; Reddy 2005

Permutation defects have been covered to some extent under fragile-X syndrome [35] . Permutations are partial methylation defects due to mosaicism.

How common is fragile-X permutation? The overall literature on fragile-X permutation suggests that some 15–20 per cent of cases show some degree of mosaicism (see, for example, Petek *et al.* 1999).

As no studies of the tissue distribution of mosaicism have yet been undertaken, the significance of this finding is currently uncertain, and it could reflect differences in technique or sampling.

Matching permutation against levels of FMRP activity may provide some insight into the apparent level of association and how this may be linked to central nervous system factors.

Main clinical features: These are variable, based on the limited literature to date, these are as for fragile-X syndrome but less pronounced.

Is there a link between fragile-X permutation and ASD?

- FRAX permutation appears to be more common in ASD than might be expected, with Reddy reporting 43 per cent of the fragile-X ASD males in her study to be mosaics, and Nolin *et al.* (1994) reporting a rate of 41 per cent in affected males.

Differential diagnosis: As for fragile-X syndrome[35].

Treatment and management: Largely as for fragile-X syndrome[35].

Further information and support: As for fragile-X syndrome [35].

37

GAMT deficiency (guanidinoacetate methyltransferase deficiency)

Gene locus: 19p13.3

Key ASD references: Mercimek-Mahmutoglu *et al.* 2006; Sykut-Cegielska *et al.* 2004 (See also Lion-François *et al.* 2006.)

GAMT deficiency is an autosomal recessive condition. It is an inborn error of creatine metabolism. Creatine is a compound derived from animal protein in the diet and also through metabolic processes in the body (see Figure B37). It is likely, therefore, that the condition would have a more pronounced effect on those adhering to a vegan or vegetarian diet as they do not have alternative sources of creatine. GAMT deficiency interferes with the body's ability to produce the compound guanidinoacetate, which is the metabolic precursor of creatine.

Most of the small numbers of cases described to date are Portuguese, or of Portuguese origin (Almeida *et al.* 2007), suggesting a possible founder effect in this population, however, a number of Turkish cases have also been reported, and systematic screening of other populations does not yet appear to have been carried out. One US series of eight GAMT cases is from a wide variety of ethnic backgrounds (Dhar *et al.* 2009).

The first paper to describe the condition appeared in 1994 (Stöckler *et al.* 1994).

The GAMT gene was mapped to chromosome 19p13.3 in 1998 (Chae *et al.* 1998). It is one of three genetic factors which have an effect on creatine metabolism, the others being defects in the X-linked creatine transporter gene SLC6A8 (AKA CT1) (Salomons *et al.* 2001) and AGAT (arginine:glycine amidinotransferase deficiency) (Item *et al.* 2001).

The key clinical features seen with these metabolic defects are learning difficulties, communication problems and epilepsy. They are present in those with GAMT, AGAT and CT1 (creatine transporter 1) defects. Autistic behaviour and hyperactivity are commonly reported in more mildly affected GAMT cases. They may be present in AGAT and CT1 cases; however, this has yet to be investigated. This may be important, as all of these conditions appear equally responsive to treatment intervention. (For AGAT, see Battini *et al.* 2006; for CT1 see Chilosi *et al.* 2008.)

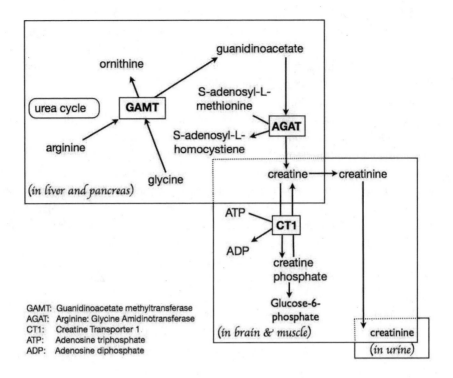

Figure B37: The metabolic pathway for creatine and creatinine production

How common is GAMT deficiency? At present, there is no epidemiological data on the incidence or prevalence of GAMT. Given the positive response to treatment and the potential benefits from antenatal identification, neonatal screening and early intervention, it is important that this is established.

Cerebral creatine deficiency syndromes overall appear to be fairly common in males with unexplained learning difficulties. In a survey of 188 children (114 boys, 74 girls) referred to a paediatric neurology department for investigation of unexplained learning problems with a normal karyotype and no fragile-X expansion, GAMT deficiency was established in one and a creatine transporter defect in four (Lion-François *et al.* 2006). All of those affected were boys. The boy with GAMT deficiency and two of those with transporter defects were reported as showing autistic behaviour. All were reported to have language impairments. The boy with GAMT deficiency and one of those with a transporter defect had seizure problems.

From work to date, urinary creatinine levels appear to be lower in the ASD population (Whiteley *et al.* 2006), and this correlates with reduced creatine levels (Sykut-Cegielska *et al.* 2004). It thus seems possible that GAMT/AGAT/CT1 abnormalities may account for a significant subgroup of those with ASD.

Main clinical features: The disease usually presents with concerns over delayed development in the first months after birth. Various neurological symptoms to be reported include muscle weakness, poor head control, movement problems and seizures. Seizures, hyperactive and autistic behaviour and self-injury have all been reported in a significant proportion of the older cases that have been described in the literature.

Learning difficulties, seizures and speech delay characterize the presentation of all of the genetic disorders of creatine metabolism.

As might be expected, given that more extreme cases are typically the first to be characterized, the earlier cases reported fall into the 'severe' category (Sykut-Cegielska *et al.* 2004). Stöckler *et al.* (1994), for example, reported a 22-month-old boy with hypotonia and a progressive extrapyramidal movement problem. He showed extremely low urinary excretion of creatinine, and low creatine and creatine phosphate, with accumulation of guanidinoacetate in the central nervous system detected by magnetic resonance spectroscopy (MRS). Stöckler, Hanefeld and Frahm (1996) described their original case and another four-year-old female patient with severe learning difficulties, hypotonia, ataxia, uncontrolled epilepsy and a similar biochemical profile.

Schulze *et al.* (1997) described a Kurdish girl who presented at two-and-a-half and was clearly regressing at age three. She had had *grand mal* seizures from 14 months. She was the child of a consanguineous marriage. MRS established creatine depletion and guanidinoacetate build-up in the central nervous system. Urinary creatinine was reduced in her case, but there was no clinical response to creatine supplementation.

Is there a link between GAMT deficiency and ASD? Two papers are of particular note concerning a GAMT link with ASD. In the first of these.

- Sykut-Cegielska *et al.* (2004), based on a systematic review of creatine deficiency syndromes, suggest that there are three 'types' of GAMT phenotypic presentation, graded by severity:

  o *severe*: intractable epilepsy; early global developmental delay; extrapyramidal movement disorder; abnormalities of the basal ganglia

  o *intermediate*: moderate/severe learning disability; speech delay; autistic and hyperkinetic behaviour; epilepsy

  o *mild*: learning disability; autistic behaviour; speech delay.

The second paper, by Mercimek-Mahmutoglu *et al.* (2006), looked at a large international series of individuals who all had a GAMT defect: 21 (78 per cent) of the 27 patients reported on were 'hyperactive, autistic and self-injurious'.

In one further paper, three boys with autistic behaviour, one with a GAMT deficiency and two with a CT1 defect have been described (Lion-François *et al.* 2006).

Differential diagnosis: As diagnosis is typically based on biochemical features coupled with the behaviours that are seen in all of the creatine disorders, differentiation is based on biochemistry coupled with brain MRS. At the present time, no reports on the behavioural phenotype associated with either AGAT or CT1 abnormalities apart from Lion-François *et al.* (2006) have been published, and a possible link to ASD based on a common pathophysiology cannot be excluded.

A screening study of 180 residential patients with severe learning disabilities identified four with GAMT deficiency, of whom three were related, and all of whom had absent or limited language development (Caldeira Araujo *et al.* 2005).

From the screening study by Lion-François *et al.* (2006) detailed above, it may be that CT1 abnormalities are more common, and they may also be linked to ASD.

Treatment and management: Clinical reports to date indicate that GAMT deficiency can respond successfully to creatine supplementation (Ganesan *et al.* 1997; Schulze *et al.* 1997; Stöckler, Hanefield and Frahm 1996). It has also been shown that creatine supplementation can have more general effects – for example, to have the ability to improve performance in endurance sports (Engelhardt *et al.* 1998). In a double-blind, placebo-controlled crossover trial, oral creatine monohydrate supplementation was found to significantly improve memory and cognitive performance of vegan and vegetarian subjects aged 18–40 (Rae *et al.* 2003).

In an early case study, Stöckler *et al.* (1994) were able to show that oral supplementation with creatine monohydrate and arginine, but not with arginine alone, improved cerebral creatine and normalized urinary and serum creatinine, as well as improving neurological symptoms and motor development, in a 22-month-old boy.

A separate factor which appears to link to the often intractable seizures seen in GAMT is the accumulation of central nervous system guanidinoacetate. This appears to be the result of a creatine-dependent negative-feedback mechanism, and also appears to respond to the combination of arginine restriction and ornithine supplementation with improved seizure control and better developmental outcome (Schulze, Mayatepek and Rating 2000; Schulze *et al.* 2001).

The combined use of creatine monohydrate, arginine restriction and ornithine supplementation, when used from an early stage, appears able to reverse the neurochemical, structural, epileptic and behavioural abnormalities seen in the GAMT and AGAT creatine deficiency syndromes (Schulze 2003). To date, there has been no successful treatment strategy that has ameliorated the creatine deficiency cases that are caused by creatine transporter abnormalities (Stöckler, Schutz and Salomons 2007).

With population screening, pre-symptomatic identification and treatment is likely to provide the best clinical outcome (Schulze and Battini 2007).

Further information and support: There is no specific support group for families affected by defects in creatine metabolism. A summary of GAMT deficiency by Sylvia Stöckler-Ipsiroglu can be found at www.orpha.net. There is a further review in Arias-Dimas *et al.* (2006). General support and information can be accessed from the following

In the UK:

CLIMB: Children Living with Inherited Metabolic Diseases
Climb Building
176 Nantwich Road
Crewe
CW2 6BG
Tel.: 0870 770 0326
Fax: 0870 770 0327
Website: www.climb.org.uk

Research Trust for Metabolic Diseases in Children (RTMDC)
Golden Gates Lodge
Weston Road
Crewe
CW2 5XN
Tel.: 01270 250221

In the USA:

Association for Neuro-Metabolic Disorders
5223 Brookfield Lane
Sylvania
Ohio
OH 43560-1809
Tel.: 419-885-1497
E-mail: volk4olks@aol.com

Metabolic Information Network
PO Box 670847
Dallas
Texas
TX 75367-0847
214-696-2188
E-mail: mizesg@ix.netcom.com (or lx.netcom.com)

Chat groups:

The Inborn Errors of Metabolism Family Support List (IEM): www.familyvillage.wisc.edu/lib_meta.htm
This is a Yahoo chatgroup for families with children with different inborn metabolic errors.

38

Goldenhar syndrome

aka • Goldenhar-Gorlin syndrome

  • Franceschetti-Goldenhar syndrome

  • hemifacial microsomia (HFM)

  • oculoauriculovertebral dysplasia (OAV dysplasia)

  • facioauriculovertebral sequence (FAV sequence)

  • oculoauriculovertebral spectrum (OAVS)

Gene locus: 14q32

Key ASD references: Johansson *et al.* 2007; Landgren, Gillberg and Stromland 1992; Miller *et al.* 2004, 2005; Stromland *et al.* 2007

Goldenhar syndrome is named after the Belgian-American ophthalmologist and general practitioner Maurice Goldenhar, who published a review of cases in 1952. The first clinical description consistent with the condition was in a work on eye conditions by the German physician Carl Ferdinand von Arlt (1881).

How common is Goldenhar syndrome? Goldenhar syndrome is thought to affect approximately one in 20,000 live births (Araneta *et al.* 2002). Lower rates have been reported – one Northern Irish study estimated a minimum prevalence of one in 45,000 (Morrison *et al.* 1992). There are also reports of higher prevalence. Gorlin (1990) reported a general population rate of one in 5,800. A study of the offspring of US Gulf War veterans (Araneta *et al.* 2002) reported a rate of one in 6,800. There are anecdotal reports of links to exposure to toxins such as dioxin; ingestion of some known teratogenic agents (cocaine, thalidomide, retinoic acid, tamoxifen); various environmental exposures (insecticides, herbicides); and effects of maternal diabetes.

Rollnick *et al.* (1987) found male cases to be roughly twice as common as female cases (191 to 103).

Rollnick and Kaye (1983) found that, in the 433 first-degree relatives of 97 Goldenhar cases, eight per cent had the same or a similar anomaly, while six per cent of 176 siblings were similarly affected.

Possible anticipation has been reported in one affected mother with two affected pregnancies (Stoll *et al.* 1998).

Main clinical features: *The physical features are:*

- unilateral or bilateral underdevelopment of the lower jaw (mandible)

- unilateral or bilateral microtia (reduced size or absence of the outer ear)

- unilateral or bilateral reduction in size, and flattening, of the maxilla (upper jaw)

- narrowing of the opening of the eye

- coloboma of the upper eyelid

- epibulbar dermoids that can impair vision (small benign tumours that typically form over the lateral aspect of one eye).

Tracheo-oesophageal fistulas have been reported in five per cent of cases in one clinical series (Sutphen *et al.* 1995).

There are reports of abnormal caruncles at the medial angle of the eye. Nijhawan *et al.* (2002) reported seven such cases.

The main classifications in use for hemifacial microsomia are the 'OMENS' (Vento, LaBrie and Mulliken 1991) and subsequently 'OMENS Plus' (Horgan *et al.* 1995) systems. The acronym stands for **O**rbital asymmetry; **M**andibular hypoplasia; **E**ar deformity; **N**erve involvement; and **S**oft tissue deficiency. OMENS plus includes further non-craniofacial anomalies that can affect any organ system (see Kapoor, Mukherjee, Paul and Dhingra 2006). The system seems both simple and clinically useful (see Poon, Meara and Heggie 2003).

A review of a series of 87 cases has identified cardiac abnormalities in 28 (32 per cent) (Digilio *et al.* 2008), with conotruncal, atrial and ventriculoseptal defects accounting for the greatest proportion (71 per cent of cardiac anomalies).

Frank neurological defects are seen, typically in association with more severe physical features, such as anophthalmia or cleft lip and palate (Schrander-Stumpel *et al.* 1992).

Wang *et al.* (2002) reported on a series of 30 Spanish cases and found a significantly increased risk of Goldenhar syndrome associated with maternal diabetes, suggesting that maternal diabetes can interfere with neural crest migration. Maternal diabetes has not been found to be a risk factor for the development of autism (Hultman, Sparén and Cnattingius 2002).

Prenatal diagnosis: A review was carried out of ultrasound analyses of 21 foetal cases with multiple congenital anomalies scanned between 14 and 35 weeks post conception (Castori *et al.* 2006). A wide range of physical anomalies was evident and demonstrable in around half of all cases.

Is there a link between Goldenhar syndrome and ASD?

- The initial report on co-ocurrence of Goldenhar syndrome and autism was a report on two girls (Landgren, Gillberg and Stromland 1992). In the first of these cases, Goldenhar syndrome was diagnosed in the early weeks of life, and autism was diagnosed at age five years. In the second case, both diagnoses were made at age seven, when the child was referred for ASD assessment.

- Between 1998 and 2007 a series of 20 cases of Goldenhar syndrome was studied and reported in three papers (Johansson *et al.* 2007; Miller *et al.* 2004, 2005). Johansson's group reported various multisystem malformations and functional problems:

Table B38.1: Common problems in Goldenhar syndrome

Problem	Numbers (%)
Systemic/ocular malformations	
• microsomia	15/20 (75)
• ear tags	14/20 (70)
• ocular dermoids	13/20 (65)
• lipodermoid	13/20 (65)
• gastrointestinal	11/20 (55)
• epibulbar dermoids	10/20 (50)
• microtia	10/20 (50)
• vertebral anomaly	10/20 (50)
• genitourinary	7/20 (35)
• cardiovascular	6/20 (30)
• fistula	4/20 (20)
Cranial nerve involvement	
• facial nerve palsy	8/20 (40)
• neurosensory deafness	3/20 (15)
Functional problems	
• hearing	14/20 (70)
• all developmental delay	7/20 (35)
• severe developmental delay	4/19 (21)
All ASD	11/20 (55)
• autistic traits	5/20 (25)
• possible autistic spectrum disorder	3/20 (15)
• autistic disorder	2/20 (10)
• autistic-like condition	1/20 (5)

Table based on Johansson *et al.* (2007) and Miller *et al.* (2004, 2005).

Three individuals were diagnosed with an ASD. All three had associated gastrointestinal problems.

- The most recent paper (Johansson *et al.* 2007) on this series presented data on the ADI-R assessments of this group, and also evidence from structural neuroimaging.

- Rates of hyperactivity are also reported to be elevated in this population.

- A review of 18 patients produced by the same group (Stromland *et al.* 2007) also reported high rates of functional impairment, but provided less detail on milder ASD symptoms:

Table B38.2: Functional impairment in Goldenhar syndrome

• Hearing impairment	15	(83%)
• Visual impairment	5	(28%)
• Combined visual and hearing impairment	5	(28%)
• Feeding difficulties	9	(50%)
• Articulation problems	10	(56%)
• Mental retardation	7	(39%)
• Severe autistic symptoms	2	(11%)

There are few reports of other mental health problems associated with Goldenhar syndrome, with one case reported as 'schizophreniform disorder' in a 27-year-old male (Brieger *et al.* 1998).

Goldenhar syndrome, along with Mobius syndrome [48] and thalidomide embryopathy, has helped to provide a model which gives a temporal window when disruption to neural development gives rise to the ASD behavioural phenotype. This suggests that, for one group of ASD disorders at least, genetic and/or environmental factors can result in ASD *provided* they act on neural development at certain crucial times in embryogenesis (for further discussion see Aitken 1991; Miller *et al.* 2005; see Rodier *et al.* 1996). More detailed knowledge of the associated timing in Goldenhar cases may help to specify this association, as the patterns of microtia and associated abnormalities appear to cluster into distinct groupings which may indicate a time window during which development is affected. (For discussion, see Kaye *et al.* 1989; Miller *et al.* 2005.)

Causal mechanisms: One study (Wieczorek *et al.* 2007) found an excess of monozygotic twins in a cohort of normally conceived individuals with Goldenhar syndrome, and an excess of Goldenhar cases in a series of assisted conceptions. The study was conducted by comparing a sample of 72 Goldenhar cases and a series of 3,372 assisted conceptions (by intracytoplasmic sperm injection) to normal population data. The excess of twin cases may go some way in explaining the research reports of higher rates of twinning in autism in some series (Betancur, Leboyer and Gillberg 2002; Ho, Todd and Constantino 2005).

Over 20 discordant identical twins, where one has hemifacial microsomia and one does not, have now been reported (Balci *et al.* 2006; Boles, Bodurtha and Nance 1987;

Burck 1983; Connor and Fernandez 1984; Ebbesen and Petersen 1982; Setzer *et al.* 1981; Wieczorek *et al.* 2007), and three separate cases in sets of triplets where only one was affected (Jongbloet 1987; Roesch *et al.* 2001; Yovich *et al.* 1985) have now been reported.

Most cases of Goldenhar syndrome arise sporadically; however, some familial cases have been reported that show autosomal dominant inheritance.

Goldenhar syndrome is typically described as being characterized by the triad of hemifacial microsomia (a common birth defect involving the first and second branchial arch derivatives), epibulbar dermoid cysts and abnormal development of the vertebrae and ribs. Ocular anomalies are seen in over half of all cases, lipodermoid being the most common. Lipodermoids are usually localized in the inferotemporal epibulbar area, and can often be missed. Abnormal ear development is found in over 70 per cent of cases. Various abnormalities of the vertebrae and ribs are found, including absent vertebrae, hemivertebrae, fused ribs, kyphosis and scoliosis. Cleft lip and palate are reported in approximately two per cent of cases.

Differential diagnosis: In classical Goldenhar cases where there is hemimicrosomia, differential diagnosis is not usually problematic. Where there is a bilateral growth defect, the issue is more complex. Unilateral cases are roughly twice as common as bilateral ones (193 vs 98 in the series reported by Rollnick *et al.* 1987).

Several factors point to a link between Goldenhar and CHARGE syndrome [20]. An early paper (Van Meter and Weaver 1996) described two infants (a male and a female) with significant symptoms of both conditions. Kallen *et al.* (2004) studied the relationships between different malformations, identifying individuals with Goldenhar, CHARGE [20], VATER (**V**ertebral anomalies/dysgenesis and vascular anomalies; **A**nal atresia; **T**racheo-oesophageal fistula; **E**sophageal atresia; and **R**enal anomalies) and OEIS (**O**mphalocele; **E**xstrophy; **I**mperforate anus; and **S**pinal defects) from data held on 5,260 infants on four large congenital malformation registers. Goldenhar symptomology, then, seems to overlap with other conditions with known gene loci at 8q12.1 and 7q21.1. An overlap between the clinical features of Goldenhar syndrome, VATER and sirenomelia (a condition in which there is fusion of the legs and partial or total fusion of the feet) has also been noted (Duncan and Shapiro 1993).

There has also been a case report of a male infant who presents with the clinical features of both the Goldenhar and *cri du chat* syndromes (*cri du chat* is a chromosome 5p deletion syndrome in which slow physical growth, learning disability, hypotonia and heart defects are associated with an unusual high-pitched cry in infancy) (Choong *et al.* 2003). This suggests that the genetic bases to the two conditions in this case may be contiguous, and a possible further gene locus for Goldenhar syndrome near to the 5p14 locus for *cri du chat* syndrome identified in this case. The genetics of *cri du chat* are not fully clarified at the time of writing; the 5p region produces a variety of clinical presentations of *cri du chat* (Mainardi 2006).

A case with a Goldenhar-like phenotype has been reported in a boy with a 22q11 deletion and a conotruncal heart defect (Derbent *et al.* 2003). 22q11 deletions are strongly associated with ASD.

In series of eight cases with a Goldenhar phenotype and anal anomalies consistent with Townes-Brocks syndrome, one proved to have a nonsense mutation of the SALL1 gene at 16q12.1 (Keegan *et al.* 2001).

Most reported cases are sporadic, and routine genetic analysis has been unrewarding. Autosomal dominant transmission has been shown in three families with multiple affected members and father-to-son transmission (Godel *et al.* 1982; Regenbogen *et al.* 1982; Summitt 1969).

A study by Kaye *et al.* (1992) looked at physical malformations in the families of 74 Goldenhar individuals. Their analysis demonstrated patterns consistent with an autosomal dominant pattern of inheritance.

The genotype is currently speculative. Linkage to a site at 14q32 has been reported based on one family pedigree (Kelberman *et al.* 2001) but could not be found either in a further family pedigree or from analysis of a large series of 120 sporadic cases.

A separate site on chromosome 14 (14q11.2–q12) has been found to be associated with an autosomal dominant ear defect (accessory auricular anomaly) (Yang *et al.* 2006a).

A number of cases are described where Goldenhar syndrome is associated with chromosome 22 defects – terminal 22q deletion (Herman, Greenberg and Ledbetter 1988) and complete (Kobrynski *et al.* 1993), partial (Balci *et al.* 2006) or mosaic (Pridjian, Gill and Shapira 1995) trisomy 22.

In one Goldenhar case with a t (4;8) translocation, the chromosome 4 breakpoint was found to be close to the BAPX1 gene (Fischer *et al.* 2006), a homeobox gene involved in craniofacial development and inner ear formation (Tucker *et al.* 2004).

A further case report describes a case of Goldenhar syndrome in a girl with a pericentric (p11:q13) inversion of chromosome 9 (Stanojevic *et al.* 2000).

Treatment and management: Various aspects of Goldenhar syndrome may need to be addressed (see Cousley and Calvert 1997).

Surgical treatment may be indicated to correct the size and shape of the mandible and maxilla on the affected side (Lima *et al.* 2007), to rebuild the structure of outer ear (Romo, Fozo and Sclafani 2000; Romo, Presti and Yalamanchili 2006), and to build up the structure of the cheeks. Where present, surgery may be required to correct cleft lip and palate. Orthodontic supervision is essential, and dental management can be complex (Moulin-Romsee *et al.* 2004). Surgical correction of scoliosis may be required for those cases where vertebral problems are significant (Anderson and David 2005).

Further information and support:

In Canada:
Goldenhar Syndrome Support Network Society
9325 163 Street
Edmonton
Alberta
T5R 2P4
E-mail: support@goldenharsyndrome.org
Website: www.goldenharsyndrome.org

In the UK:
Goldenhar Family Support Group (UK)
Durrington
Ridgeway Close
Horsell
Woking
GU21 4RD
Website: www.goldenhar.org.uk/index.html

Changing Faces
The Squire Centre
33–37 University Street
London
WC1E 6JN
E-mail: info@changingfaces.org.uk
Website: www.changingfaces.org.uk
Website for young people: www.iface.org.uk

In the USA:
Children's Craniofacial Association
13140 Coit Road Suite 307
Dallas
TX 75240
Tel.: 800-535-3643; 214-570-9099
Fax: 214-570-8811
E-mail: contactCCA@ccakids.com
Website: www.ccakids.com

Little Baby Face Foundation
135 East 74th Street
New York
NY 10021
Tel.: 212-333-5233
E-mail: info@littlebabyface.org
Website: www.littlebabyface.org/index.html

FACES: The National Craniofacial Association
PO Box 11082
Chattanooga
TN 37401
Tel.: 800-332-2373
Website: www.faces-cranio.org/Disord/Golden.htm

39

HEADD syndrome

Gene locus: Mitochondrial DNA defect

HEADD syndrome is a clinical phenotype associated with a defect in mitochondrial function. The term is an acronym that stands for **H**ypotonia, **E**pilepsy, **A**utism and **D**evelopmental **D**elay.

Key ASD reference: Fillano *et al.* 2002

How common is HEADD syndrome? There are few reports of ASD series in which an assessment of mitochondrial function has been performed. Consequently it is difficult to estimate the likely prevalence of mitochondrial dysfunction in this population.

A useful overview is provided in Smith, Spence and Flodman (2009).

In one Portuguese series of 120 ASD cases (Oliveira *et al.* 2005), 69 had plasma lactate levels checked to screen for possible mitochondrial dysfunction. In fourteen, their levels were found to be abnormally elevated, and five of these results were due to a mitochondrial disorder. All five mitochondrial cases had severe autism (rated on the CARS), were positive on the ADI-R, and had moderate to severe learning disability. None, however, were epileptic.

Is HEADD linked to ASD? In a way, this is a circular question – as autism is a key feature required to arrive at the diagnosis, the two 'conditions' must be linked, assuming that HEADD is a valid diagnostic entity.

Main clinical features: Fillano *et al.* (2002) described a group of 12 children who presented with hypotonia, epilepsy, autism and developmental delay. The results obtained indicated that defects in mitochondrial DNA, enzyme activity and/or ultrastructure could be identified in most of the cases. The variation I results suggest that the common factor is interferences with mitochondrial energy metabolism, rather than a precise gene defect.

A systematic review of 25 patients with ASD and a mitochondrial disorder (Weissman *et al.* 2008) found that, compared to others with ASD, the group was characterized by excessive fatigueability (76 per cent), unusual patterns of developmental regression (40 per cent), and marked delay in early milestones (32 per cent).

Defects in beta-oxidation indicate mitochondriopathy, and are commonly reported in ASD, often due to specific mitochondrial defects such as LCAD (Clark-Taylor and Clark-Taylor 2004).

Mitochondrial defects are well recognized as being associated with childhood epilepsy (Kang *et al.* 2007).

Differential diagnosis: The primary differential diagnosis is from other mitochondrio-pathies affecting energy metabolism (Finsterer 2004).

Treatment and management: A Cochrane review (Chinnery *et al.* 2006) found six randomized controlled trials of treatments for mitochondrial disorders with varying results. From this review there is some evidence for supplementation with co-enzyme Q10, some for the use of creatine, and some for the use of dichloroacetate. The heterogeneous nature of the population is likely to be the key factor in outcome variability. To date, no interventions have been specifically implemented with HEADD syndrome.

Further information and support:

In the UK:
The Children's Mitochondrial Disease Network
EMDN
MAYFIELD HOUSE
30 Heber Walk
Chester Way
Northwich
CW9 5JB
Mito Help and Information Line: 01606 43946
E-mail: info@cmdn.org.uk
Website: www.emdn-mitonet.co.uk

In the USA:
The United Mitochondrial Disease Foundation
8085 Saltsburg Road,
Suite 201
Pittsburgh,
PA 15239
Tel.: 412-793-8077
Toll-free: 1-888-317-UMDF (8633)
Fax: 412-793-6477
E-mail: info@umdf.org
Website: www.umdf.org/site/c.
dnJEKLNqFoG/b.3793037

40

L-2-hydroxyglutaric aciduria (L-2 HGAA)

Gene locus: 14q22.1

Key ASD reference: Zafeiriou *et al.* 2007

L-2 HGAA is a rare autosomal recessive condition. It results in a disorder of glycosylation – the process that adds sugars to proteins and fats on cell surfaces of the endoplasmic reticulum of the cell.

How common is L-2-hydroxyglutaric aciduria? The prevalence is currently not known, but reports are more common in areas with higher rates of consanguineous marriage (Shafeghati, Vakili and Entezari 2006). It has been described worldwide in around 75 cases to date.

Main clinical features: The condition is progressive in nature, with gradual intellectual decline, deterioration in motor skills with cerebellar ataxic gait, intention tremor, macrocephaly and seizures being the most characteristic features (see, for example, Topçu *et al.* 2005). These changes are accompanied by metabolic differences – elevated L-2-hydroxyglutaric acid (L-2 HG) and elevated levels of lysine in plasma, urine and CSF (Barth *et al.* 1992).

L-2-hydroxyglutaric aciduria has been linked to a number of developmental problems, including infantile spasms and psychomotor regression with subcortical abnormalities (Mahfoud *et al.* 2004; Seijo-Martínez *et al.* 2005).

There is as yet no robust evidence on the mechanisms involved. There is preliminary evidence for the presence of a central nervous system toxic FAD-dependent L-2-hydroxyglutarate dehydrogenase mutation, initially in rat tissue and subsequently in two affected families with L-2-hydroxyglutaric aciduria (Rzem *et al.* 2004).

Is there a link between L-2-hydroxyglutaric aciduria and ASD?

- A study detailing the development of a single three-year-old boy with L-2 HGAA has suggested an association between L-2-hydroxyglutaric aciduria and ASD (Zafeiriou *et al.* 2007). The boy presented with mild motor delay, profound difficulties with communication, and a score on the CARS (44/60) consistent with severe autism.

This inborn error of metabolism results from a difficulty in metabolizing certain sugars, including galactose, a sugar uniquely derived from lactose (found only in milk in the Western diet). An overview of the biochemistry of L-2 HGAA can be found in Van Schaftingen, Rzem and Veiga-da-Cunha (2009).

Differential diagnosis: As for a number of the other conditions we discuss, diagnosis is clear after genetic and metabolic testing, but in the initial stages, differential diagnosis should consider other conditions that are associated with macrocephaly (Shafeghati, Vakili and Entezari 2006) (see Table A6).

Treatment and management: Knowledge of the biochemistry involved has led to reports of beneficial treatment. Samuraki *et al.* (2008) report on an adult female case who had developed normally through elementary school and graduated from high school, but who showed a gradual deterioration in gait and increase in hand tremor, coupled with a decline in intellectual function to an assessed IQ of 47 at age 43. She was treated with flavin adenine dinucleotide sodium (a metabolic derivative of riboflavin) and levocarnitine chloride (involved in fatty acid transport across mitochondrial cell membranes). This combined treatment reversed the problems in her gait and tremor, and further cognitive decline was arrested.

A further report of treatment of an adolescent boy with L-2 HGAA reports beneficial effects from treatment with riboflavin (vitamin B2) (Yilmaz 2009).

Many families claim to see clinical benefit from casein- and gluten-free diets or casein-, gluten-, soy- and egg-free diets, and from the 'specific carbohydrate diet'. Such approaches are time-consuming and require considerable commitment to undertake and to persevere with. There is a clinical literature that is supportive of such dietary interventions in some cases (see, for example, Reichelt and Knivsberg 2003); however, the mechanisms that underlie such apparent improvement are far from clear.

As one of the other genes involved in lactose digestion corresponds to the highest Lod score locus for ASD so far reported – 3q26.1–q26.3 – it seems likely that, for some cases at least, where removal of milk products has proven beneficial, the difference may result from removal of lactose rather than from removal of casein.

The prevalent theory for why this type of approach may be of benefit concerns deficient gut enzymes involved in casein digestion, coupled with increased intestinal permeability, resulting in the entry of opioid-like compounds into the bloodstream and ultimately into the brain. (For discussion of this model, see information on the Autism Research Unit Website: http://osiris.sunderland.ac.uk.) There are various possible reasons for such differences, one being the presence of heterozygous sequence variants of the secretin gene at 11p15.5 (Yamagata *et al.* 2002). Such a difference could increase intestinal permeability by increasing intestinal acidity and altering gut flora.

Another possible reason for beneficial effects from this approach may be the removal of galactose from the diet. Galactose is one of the two sugars produced by the degradation of lactose (milk sugar), the other being glucose. One of the key genes involved in galactose metabolism is found at 3q26.1–q26.3. To date, from the gene marker studies, this site on chromosome 3 has the highest reported Lod score for ASD of any gene association so far reported – 4.81 (Auranen *et al.* 2002).

Further information and support:

In the UK:
CLIMB: Children Living with Inherited Metabolic Diseases
Climb Building
176 Nantwich Road
Crewe
CW2 6BG
Tel.: 0870 770 0326
Fax: 0870 770 0327

Research Trust for Metabolic Diseases in Children (RTMDC)
Golden Gates Lodge
Weston Road
Crewe
CW2 5XN
Tel.: 01270 250221

In the USA:
Association for Neuro-Metabolic Disorders
5223 Brookfield Lane
Sylvania
Ohio
OH 43560-1809
Tel.: 419-885-1497
E-mail: volk4olks@aol.com

Metabolic Information Network
PO Box 670847
Dallas
Texas
TX 75367-0847
Tel.: 214-696-2188
E-mail: mizesg@ix.netcom.com (or lx.netcom.com)

Chat groups:
The Inborn Errors of Metabolism Family Support List (IEM): www.familyvillage.wisc.edu/lib_meta.htm
This is a Yahoo chatgroup for families with children with different inborn metabolic errors.

41

Hyper IgE syndrome with autism (HiES)

aka • Buckley syndrome

• Job syndrome

Gene loci: 4q21 (precise location not yet known); 17q21

Key ASD reference: Grimbacher *et al.* 1999a

Hyperimmunoglobulin E syndrome (HiES) was first described in 1966 in two red-haired girls (Davis, Schaller and Wedgwood 1966). It was originally called 'Job's syndrome', as a feature of the condition was recurrent staphylococcal abscesses – in the Bible, Job's body was covered in boils by Satan. The patients reported on by Davis *et al.* presented with boils, eczema, hyperextensible joints, and distinctive coarse facial features. Those affected show a weakened inflammatory response to infection.

In addition to the immune component, Hyper IgE is known to be a multisystem disorder, affecting all organ systems in the body (Grimbacher *et al.* 1999b). A genetic basis to the condition has been linked to chromosome 4 (Grimbacher *et al.* 1999c). A second group of genetic factors – defects in the interleukin-6 mediator STAT3 (17q21) – have been reported in a further series of HiES cases (Holland *et al.* 2007) and appear to provide a second sufficient genetic mechanism.

How common is HiES? There are no studies to date which indicate the prevalence of HiES. It is a rare disorder that appears to affect both sexes equally and has been found in all racial groups so far examined.

Main clinical features: Elevated serum IgE levels were first reported by Buckley *et al.* in 1972 (Buckley, Wray and Belmaker 1972), and are associated with recurrent lung and skin infections, principally staphylococcus aureus and candida. A number of immune problems are reported – TH1:TH2 lymphocyte skewing and elevated interleukin-4 (Borges, Augustine and Hill 2000), with reductions in chemokine (Chehimi *et al.* 2001), and cell adhesion molecule production (Vargas *et al.* 1999).

The early features are, most commonly severe eczema (typically with infection), and recurrent otitis media and sinusitis, which persist into adult life.

A paper documents the MRI findings in a series of 50 patients with HiES (Freeman *et al.* 2007). Central nervous system abnormalities, particularly hyperintensities apparent on T2 imaging, were common, being seen in 70 per cent of cases.

There appear to be both autosomal dominant (Grimbacher *et al.* 1999c) and autosomal recessive (Renner *et al.* 2004) forms of HiES. Neurological complications appear more common in the recessive form. Sporadic cases typically resemble the dominant form

(Grimbacher, Holland and Puck 2005). It seems likely that the co-morbid case reported by Grimbacher *et al.* (1999a) has the dominant phenotype.

The autosomal dominant form (but not the recessive form) has a distinctive facial appearance (Borges *et al.* 1998) that is seen by mid-childhood. Typically, those affected have a prominent forehead, and a bulbous nose with a broad nasal bridge. A cleft lip and palatal abnormalities have been reported. A few cases have been documented with craniosynostosis.

A variety of joint and skeletal abnormalities are also seen – some 70 per cent are reported to have hyperextensible joints (and those affected are prone to fractures), have osteoporosis and typically develop scoliosis over time. Those affected are typically late in losing their milk teeth.

Neither the facial nor the skeletal characteristics can be explained on the basis of the immune differences so far described.

Is there a link between HiES and ASD?

- Only one paper has appeared to date that has documented ASD in an individual with HiES (Grimbacher *et al.* 1999a). This describes a 17-year-old boy who has mild learning disability, autism and a sporadic HiES. His genetic basis is an analphoid ring marker chromosome derived from an interstitial deletion of 4q21 on the maternally inherited chromosome.

Differential diagnosis:

- atopic dermatitis – the most likely alternative (but does not have the typical facial and skeletal appearance found in HiES)

- other primary immunodeficiencies with eczematous dermatitis, including Wiskott-Aldrich syndrome (WAS) and chronic granulomatous disease (CGD) (which also lack the typical facial and skeletal appearance found in HiES)

- Omenn syndrome (an 11p13 condition) – a severe combined immunity disease (SCID) variant that has elevated IgE as part of a more complex symptomology that is fatal if untreated. It can be successfully treated by bone marrow transplantation (Gomez *et al.* 1995), in contrast to HiES (Gennery *et al.* 2000)

- common variable immunodeficiency disease (CVID), which has similar immunological features but without the skeletal or facial differences seen in HiES

- IPEX (**I**mmune dysregulation, **P**olyendocrinopathy, **E**nteropathy, **X**-linked inheritance syndrome), which has early-onset diabetes as part of the clinical presentation (Bennett *et al.* 2001)

- elevation of IgE can be a (rare) manifestation of HIV infection (Seroogy *et al.* 1999).

Treatment and management: HiES is treated prophylactically with chronic antibiotics to help protect against staphylococcal infection and candidiasis (DeWitt *et al.* 2006). Medium and high-dose intravenous gamma-globulin have been used successfully in some cases with severe eczema (Bilora *et al.* 2000; Kimata 1995). Skeletal abnormalities should be treated as required, with monitoring for possible scoliosis, and adequate calcium intake should be ensured to protect against osteoporosis.

Further information and support:

In the UK:
International Patient Organization for Primary
Immunodeficiencies
Firside
Main Road
Downderry
Cornwall
PL11 3LE
Tel.: 01503 250668
Fax: 01503 250668
E-mail: info@ipopi.org
Website: www.ipopi.org

In the USA:
Immune Deficiency Foundation
40 West Chesapeake Avenue
Suite 308
Towson,
MD 21230
Tel.: 410-321-6647
Fax: 410-321-9165
Tel.: 800-296-4433
E-mail: idf@primaryimmune.org
Website: www.primaryimmune.org

42

Hypomelanosis of Ito (HI)

aka • *incontinentia pigmenti achromians*

Gene loci: Various genes have been reported – 9q33–qter, 15q11–q13, and Xp11

Key ASD references: Akefeldt and Gillberg 1991; Davalos, Merikangas and Bender 2001; Gomez-Lado *et al.* 2004; Hermida-Prieto *et al.* 1997; Pascual-Castroviejo *et al.* 1988, 1998; von Aster *et al.* 1997; Zapella 1993

HI was first described, purely as a cutaneous phenomenon, by Ito (1952) in a 22-year-old Japanese woman with a curious pattern of depigmentation, but who was otherwise normal. She had depigmented areas on her trunk and spine and linear depigmentation on her arms. The clinical presentation of HI is very varied but around three-quarters of cases have abnormalities of other organ systems, particularly of the central nervous system.

It is thought to be the third most common neurocutaneous condition after neurofibromatosis type 1 [51] and tuberous sclerosis [73].

How common is HI? The incidence in live births and the population prevalence are reported as being one in 7,540 and one in 82,000 respectively (Ruggieri and Pavone 2000). HI appears to be around twice as common in girls as in boys.

Main clinical features: HI, previously called *incontinentia pigmenti achromians*, results in hypopigmented skin, particularly the formation of asymmetric but typically bilateral de-pigmented macules across the chest along the 'Blaschko lines' (Nehal, PeBenito and Orlow 1996), in zigzag patterns on the spine, and in vertical lines on the arms (Donnai *et al.* 1988). A range of other congenital organ system defects are also reported, with multiple congenital defects, particularly of the central nervous system, but with additional skeletal, hair and dental findings. The cutaneous features are visible from birth.

HI also presents with ocular abnormalities (Amon, Menapace and Kirnbauer 1990; Weaver, Martin and Zanolli 1991).

Most cases appear to arise *de novo*, with no previous family history.

The most commonly associated problems are congenital anomalies, learning disability and epileptic seizures, all of which should be kept under review.

Pascual-Castroviejo *et al.* (1998) reviewed 76 cases of HI. They reported that 57 per cent of patients had an IQ score of less than 70, of whom 40 per cent had an IQ less than 50. A high proportion of cases have mild to moderate learning disabilities.

Is there a link between HI and ASD? A number of papers have suggested a link between Hypomelanosis of Ito and ASD.

- In a review of neurological complications in 34 cases of HI, Pascual-Castroviejo *et al.* (1988) noted that four of their cases had a diagnosis of autism.

- Akefeldt and Gillberg (1991) described three cases – two girls and one boy, all with typical features of HI and all with ASD. One was autistic, one had Asperger's syndrome and one was atypical autistic. The authors recommended that skin examination should be part of the clinical workup for those with an ASD.

- Zapella (1993) presented two twin pairs – one monozygotic and one dizygotic pair. Both pairs were concordant for HI and autism.

- Hermida-Prieto *et al.* (1997) described two further female HI cases, one with learning disability in addition to her autism.

- Von Aster *et al.* (1997) described a 13-year-old boy who had presented neonatally with failure to thrive and on follow-up had a diagnosis of atypical autism.

- Pascual-Castroviejo *et al.* (1998) presented the first large case series of HI. They described the presentation of 76 cases seen over a 30-year period. Fifty-six per cent had significant learning disability and ten per cent of those were co-morbidly autistic. Twenty-two per cent were of normal overall IQ (>85). Forty-nine per cent were epileptic. Twelve were macrocephalic and six were microcephalic. Fourteen were significantly hypotonic. (It is not clear whether this series extends the series reported by this group in 1988, but this seems likely to be the case.)

- Davalos, Merikangas and Bender (2001) describe a 35-year-old female case of HI whose clinical presentation was consistent with an autistic disorder.

- In 2004, Gomez-Lado and colleagues retrospectively reviewed 14 cases of HI. Learning disability was noted in 11, with co-morbid autism in two. Abnormal dentition was noted in six, hyperacusis in five and seizures in two.

As HI is a rare condition, the number of reported cases with ASD, typically associated with central nervous system involvement and learning disability, suggests that there is an association that has a common biological basis.

Differential diagnosis: The range of genes which appear to interfere with melanin metabolism and the reports of mosaicism (Donnai *et al.* 1988; Fritz *et al.* 1998) are thought to account for the high degree of phenotypic variability (Glover, Brett and Atherton 1989). There have been cases reported with 15q11–13 (Pellegrino *et al.* 1995), an area of chromosome 15 implicated in Angelman [11], oculocutaneous albinism [55] and Prader-Willi syndromes [61] – all three of which can present with hypopigmentation, and can be found with ASD.

Several rare cutaneous conditions can present with similar features to HI: the fourth stage of *incontinentia pigmenti*; linear and whorled naevoid hypermelanosis; and *naevus depigmentus*.

Treatment and management: The cutaneous aspects of HI do not require any specific management approach; however, there are a number of approaches to treating hypopigmentation, which may be used where the cosmetic aspects cause distress (Brenner and Hearing 2008; Schaffer and Bolognia 2003). In other respects, the biology is not yet understood to a level where there are any specific treatment implications.

A number of specific problems have been reported in association with HI that may require additional treatment on a case-by-case basis:

Table B42: Problems in Hypomelanosis of Ito

• seizures	(Pascual-Castroviejo *et al.* 1988)
• palatal abnormalities	(Fryns *et al.* 1993)
• dental malformations	(Fryns *et al.* 1993; Happle and Vakilzadeh 1982)
• hearing loss	(Griebel, Krageloh-Mann and Michaelis 1989)
• visual problems	(Scott *et al.* 2008)
• renal problems	(Coward *et al.* 2001; Vergine *et al.* 2008)
• orthopaedic problems	(Pascual-Castroviejo *et al.* 1988)

Further information and support:

In the UK:
HITS
33 Fernworthy Close
Torquay
Devon
TQ2 7JQ
E-mail: info@hitsuk.org.uk
Tel.: 01803 401018
Website: www.e-fervour.com/hits

The Ectodermal Dysplasia Society
108 Charlton Lane,
Cheltenham
Gloucestershire
GL53 9EA
E-mail: diana@ectodermaldysplasia.org
Tel.: 01242 261332
Website: www.ectodermaldysplasia.org

43

Hypothyroidism

Gene loci: 8q23–q24; 2q33

Key ASD references: Comi *et al.* 1999; Gillberg, Gillberg and Kopp 1992; Molloy *et al.* 2006; Raja and Azzoni 2008; Sweeten *et al.* 2003

Hypothyroidism typically results from abnormal structural development of the thyroid gland (seen in 75 per cent of cases), but can also result from abnormal production of the compounds which metabolize iodine or of other enzymes involved in the production of thyroxine (ten per cent), abnormal pituitary function (five per cent), or can be secondary to maternal hypothyroidism/transplacental exposure to maternal antibodies (ten per cent). Hypothyroidism is one of the most common metabolic disorders. It is estimated that around ten per cent of women of childbearing age have some degree of thyroid dysfunction.

Hypothyroidism can also arise due to a chronic iodine deficiency in the diet. Iodine is added to table salt and dietary deficiency is virtually unknown today. Iodine deficiency is extremely unlikely, except in some isolated, land-locked, mountainous regions such as parts of the Himalayas; however, other maternal dietary factors such as flavonoid ingestion could cause transient foetal hypothyroidism and affect brain development (Román 2007).

How common is congenital hypothyroidism? On US figures, congenital hypothyroidism is reported to affect one in 3,500 of the general population. Rates vary markedly, however, depending on the population studied and criteria used, with one epidemiological study giving a rate of 46/1,000, or about one in 22 (Hollowell, *et al.* 2002).

Main clinical features: A number of early features are characteristic: babies tend to be born after their due date, and are heavy for their gestational age. They tend to be slow in developing a bowel pattern, have prolonged jaundice, are hypoactive and feed poorly, are prone to hypothermia, and have laboured breathing and a hoarse cry.

If left untreated, there is markedly delayed physical growth and progressive cognitive decline (previously called cretinism).

There are differences in racial prevalence, with Hispanics being most likely to be affected, followed by Caucasians, with Afro-Caribbeans being least likely to be affected. Girls are twice as likely as boys to be affected.

Neonatal screening detects the vast majority of cases, and early treatment (typically by giving thyroxine replacement) prevents emergence of the later features of the condition.

Is there a link between hypothyroidism and ASD? Several studies point to a possible link between thyroiditis and ASD:

- Gillberg, Gillberg and Kopp (1992) described three boys and two girls, two with ASD, whose mothers were likely to have been hypothyroid during their pregnancies, and three who had hypothyroidism themselves. They suggest that there is a possible link between the conditions, due either to effects of low thyroid hormone exposure on early central nervous system development, or to autoimmune factors involved in both conditions. These cases, therefore, are associated with abnormal foetal thyroid exposure or congenital hypothyroidism.

- Comi *et al.* (1999) surveyed families to look for links between family autoimmune problems and ASD, comparing questionnaire responses from families of 61 autistic patients to responses from families of 46 healthy controls. Mothers were eight times as likely to report autoimmune disorders, compared to mothers of controls (16 per cent vs. 2 per cent), with type 1 diabetes, adult rheumatoid arthritis, hypothyroidism and systemic lupus erythematosus being the most commonly reported conditions.

- Sweeten *et al.* (2003) carried out a large questionnaire study of 101 families with a child with ASD, 101 families with a child presenting with an autoimmune disorder, and families of 101 healthy controls. The frequency of autoimmune problems was significantly higher in the families of children with ASD than in the other two groups, particularly the prevalence of Hashimoto's thyroiditis and rheumatic fever. Hashimoto's thyroiditis is a later-onset autoimmune condition where the thyroid becomes damaged.

- Molloy *et al.* (2006) carried out telephone interviews about family history of autoimmune problems with the families of 308 children with ASD who were part of the Collaborative Programs of Excellence in Autism network. They specifically compared those who had a history of regression (N=155) to those with no regressive history (N=153). The only significant difference between the groups was that families whose children had regressed were significantly more likely to report a family history of autoimmune thyroid disease (64 vs 38).

- In a paper on co-morbidity of Asperger's syndrome and bipolar disorder, one of the cases presented was a 30-year-old man with adrenal insufficiency and hypothyroidism as part of his clinical presentation (Raja and Azzoni 2008).

Clearly there is a need for further systematic research on this issue; however, the published literature to date suggests that lower than normal levels of thyroid hormone exposure may be a risk factor for the development of ASD, and particularly for regressive onset ASD. Since, in many of these cases, the reported link is with maternal hypothyroidism during pregnancy, or in families with a history of autoimmune problems, thyroid levels should be closely monitored antenatally.

The lack of any systematic screening of thyroid function in ASD to date makes it impossible to speculate on the strength of any possible link.

Differential diagnosis: One other deficiency syndrome that results in autistic behaviour and has a similar clinical presentation as part of a complex and severe neurodevelopmental disorder is 5-oxoprolinase deficiency (Cohen *et al.* 1997).

Treatment and management: In most cases, underactivity of the thyroid gland can be corrected by supplementation with thyroxine or levothyroxine. Response to treatment is monitored by checking levels of TSH (thyroid stimulating hormone), a compound produced by the pituitary gland that normally controls thyroid function, and levels of which are controlled by negative feedback of circulating thyroxine levels.

Further information and support:

In the UK:

The British Thyroid Foundation
PO Box 97
Clifford
Wetherby
West Yorkshire
LS23 6XD
Tel/Fax: 01423 709707
or 01423 709448
Website: www.btf-thyroid.org/index.htm

In the USA:

American Foundation of Thyroid Patients
PO Box 820195
Houston,
TX 77282

Tel.: 281-496-4460 (Houston, TX)
888-996-4460 (toll-free)
E-mail: thyroid@flash.net

American Thyroid Association
6066 Leesburg Pike, Suite 550
Falls Church,
VA 22041
For clinicians
Tel.: 703 998-8890
Fax: 703 998-8893
E-mail: thyroid@thyroid.org

For patients
1-800-THYROID
Website: www.thyroid.org

44

Joubert syndrome

Gene loci: 2q13; 3q11.2; 6q23.3; 8q21.1–q22.1; 9q34.3; 11p12–13.3; 12q21.32; 16q11.2

Key ASD references: Alvarez Retuerto *et al.* 2008; Holroyd, Reiss and Bryan 1991; Ozonoff *et al.* 1999; Takahashi *et al.* 2005

Joubert syndrome was first described by Joubert *et al.* (1969) in a paper which presented cases with an inherited pattern with poor development of the cerebellar vermis, in association with periodic rapid breathing, motor ataxia, abnormal eye movements and learning difficulties. The clinical picture is complex, with variable features and a range of severity and possible complications.

It is a cerebello-oculo-renal syndrome, affecting motor control, vision and kidney function. A number of helpful clinical summaries are available (see, for example, Parisi and Glass 2007; Parisi *et al.* 2007). It has an autosomal recessive pattern of inheritance.

To date, no attempt has been made to examine the prevalence of ASD symptomology in specific genetic forms of Joubert syndrome apart from AHI1, and it could transpire that the link is only with particular genetic types of Joubert syndrome and not with the diagnosis *per se*.

How common is Joubert syndrome? No good epidemiological studies have been carried out. The best estimate that is currently available is 0.85 per 100,000 (Orphanet 2008).

Main clinical features: Diagnosis is currently on the basis of the phenotype, combined with the classic 'molar tooth' appearance (the image of this area on the brain scan looks like an extracted molar tooth) on axial brain imaging of the area where the pons and midbrain join (Quisling, Barkovich and Maria 1999). The molar tooth sign is seen as a necessary feature for a diagnosis of Joubert syndrome to be given.

The key behavioural features are infantile hypotonia, delayed acquisition of developmental milestones, and abnormal breathing (either hyperventilation or apnoea) all of which typically improve with age. In addition there are often abnormal eye movements. Truncal ataxia is typical, as would be expected with central vermal hypoplasia. There is a broad range of cognitive ability, from severe learning disability to normal IQ.

Behaviourally and phenotypically discordant identical girl twins have been reported (Raynes *et al.* 1999). Both show the molar tooth sign on MRI. At the time of the report, the girls were 7.5 years of age and had a 21-month-old affected sister with ocular abnormalities, motor delay, the molar tooth sign and cerebellar vermal hypoplasia. The twins had very different physical and behavioural phenotypes, one being ambulant, verbal and not reported as autistic, the other wheelchair-bound, nonverbal and reportedly autistic. The genotype in these three cases was not reported.

Intellectual function is variable, from normal ability to severe learning disability. Some can go on to attend college independently. In a study that followed a group over time, 11/15 had intelligible speech and six had begun mainstream education at five years of age (Hodgkins *et al.* 2004). A further study (Braddock *et al.* 2006) found that communication level was in line with IQ, but that there is a specific type of apraxia that makes non-verbal communication more difficult. As motor impairment is variable.

A variety of behavioural difficulties are reported in some, but not all, cases. Behavioural problems, including impulsivity, inattention, overactivity and temper tantrums, are present in perhaps 20 per cent of those with Joubert syndrome (Deonna and Ziegler 1993; Hodgkins *et al.* 2004). These problem behaviours are associated with high levels of parental stress (Farmer *et al.* 2006).

The typical facial features are a long, narrow face with low-set ears, high-arched eyebrows, a protruding jaw, prominent bridge to the nose, and small, triangular mouth. To date, however, these features have not been characterized well or consistently enough in the literature, or linked to the specific genotypic markers, to tell how consistently they are present.

A range of physical features are sometimes seen, including the following:

Ophthalmologic findings: The retinal problems reported in Joubert syndrome resemble those seen in Leber's congenital amaurosis. Interestingly, Leber's amaurosis has been reported in association with a number of the genetic ciliary defects implicated in Joubert syndrome, such as CEP290 and RPGRIP1 (den Hollander *et al.* 2008). A variety of visual apractic defects are reported, and incomplete retinal development is not uncommon (Saraiva and Baraitser 1992).

Kidney findings:

- A variety of renal problems can occur, normally progressively with age (Saraiva and Baraitser 1992; Steinlin *et al.* 1997).

- Polydactyly of the fingers and/or toes is frequently documented (Saraiva and Baraitser 1992).

- Abnormalities of the tongue are common and can often lead to problems with chewing, swallowing and breathing.

- Epilepsy has been reported in individual cases, but the prevalence is not known (Saraiva and Baraitser 1992).

Is there a link between Joubert syndrome and ASD?

- Holroyd, Reiss and Bryan (1991) described two cases of Joubert syndrome, one of whom met DSM-III-R criteria for autism, while the other showed autistic features. The genetic basis to the cases was not described.

- Ozonoff *et al.* (1999) assessed 11 children with Joubert syndrome using the Autism Diagnostic Interview – Revised and the Autism Diagnostic Observation Scale – Generic. Three met criteria for autistic disorder, and one for pervasive developmental disorder – not otherwise specified, while all of the other seven exhibited some features of autistic spectrum disorders. The genetic basis to these cases was not described.

- Alvarez Retuerto *et al.* (2008) have looked at a possible association between variants in the AHI1 gene at chromosome 6q23.3, which is seen in a significant proportion of Joubert syndrome cases, and autism, using the Autism Genetic Resource Exchange (AGRE) database. A significant association between AHI1 variants and autistic diagnosis was found (some 40 per cent of AHI1 cases also had ASD).

- Takahashi *et al.* (2005), however, compared 31 Joubert syndrome families to families with autism and to Down syndrome controls. None of the Joubert syndrome children met ASD criteria on the Autism Behavior Checklist, and family histories were not similar to the other groups, suggesting that Joubert syndrome was aetiologically distinct. The Autism Behavior Checklist is a less robust tool for ASD diagnosis than the ADI-R; however, the finding is on a large sample and the contrasting prevalence is surprising.

To date, no attempt has been made to examine the prevalence of ASD symptomology in specific genetic forms of Joubert syndrome apart from AH11, and it could transpire that the link is only to particular genetic types of Joubert syndrome and not with the diagnosis per se.

Heritability: Joubert syndrome is an autosomal recessive condition.

Tracing the ancestry of the French–Canadian family first described with the condition, Joubert *et al.* (1969) revealed a 'founder effect', identifying that the condition began with an individual who emigrated from France to Quebec in the 1600s (Badhwar *et al.* 2000).

Eight gene loci have to date been linked to Joubert syndrome, and a number of the genes involved – NPHP1, AHI1, CEP290, TMEM67, ARL13B and RPGRIP1L – are involved in ciliary function.

Table B44.1: Joubert syndrome gene loci

Gene locus	Gene product	Key reference/s
2q13	NPHP1	Castori *et al.* 2005; Parisi *et al.* 2004
3q11.2	ARL13B	Cantagrel *et al.* 2008
6q23.3	AHI1	Dixon-Salazar *et al.* 2004 Ferland *et al.* 2004 Parisi *et al.* 2006 Utsch *et al.* 2006
8q21.1–q22.1	MKS3 (TMEM67)	Baala *et al.* 2007
9q34.3	JBTS1/CORS1	Saar *et al.* 1999 Valente *et al.* 2005
11p12–13.3	JBTS2/CORS2	Keeler *et al.* 2003 Valente *et al.* 2005
12q21.32	CEP290 (NPHP6)	Sayer *et al.* 2006 Valente *et al.* 2006b
16q11.2	RPGRIP1L	Arts *et al.* 2007 Brancati *et al.* 2008 Delous *et al.* 2007

As both parents must be recessive carriers and asymptomatic, and each child has a 50 per cent chance of inheriting an affected gene from each parent, one in four children will inherit two affected genes and have Joubert syndrome, two in four will be carriers and one in four will inherit two unaffected genes. The aunts and uncles of an affected person will also have a 50 per cent risk of carrying the recessive gene involved.

It is possible that someone with Joubert syndrome could reproduce, although to date no such cases have been reported. Affected males are likely to have lowered fertility due to their ciliary defect.

Serial prenatal ultrasound can be successful in identifying phenotypically obvious at-risk cases (Doherty *et al.* 2005); however, the variability in phenotype means that this can be used to rule in, but cannot be used to exclude, possible cases.

In the original cases reported (Joubert *et al.* 1969), one case had an occipital meningoencephalocoele and agenesis of the cerebellar vermis, and one only agenesis of the cerebellar vermis, while two had agenesis only of the posterior occipital cerebellar vermis.

Differential diagnosis: The 'molar tooth' sign has also been described in other clinical syndromes (Gleeson *et al.* 2004; Satran, Pierpont and Dobyns 1999), so is not truly diagnostic of Joubert syndrome:

Table B44.2: Diagnoses reported to show the 'molar tooth' sign

• COACH syndrome	(Gentile *et al.* 1996)
• Cogan oculomtor apraxia syndrome	(Betz *et al.* 2000)
• Dekaban-Arima syndrome	(Dekaban 1969)
• Leber congential amaurosis - like	(Steinlin *et al.* 1997)
• Nephronophthisis	(Otto *et al.* 2003, 2005)
• Oculomotor apraxia	(Steinlin *et al.* 1997)
• Senior-Løken syndrome	(Løken *et al.* 1961; Senior, Freidmann and Braudo 1961)
• Varadi-Papp syndrome	(Munke *et al.* 1990)

There is ongoing debate over whether these are varying presentations of the same condition, or separable conditions with discrete aetiologies. To date, the lack of a consistent protocol for investigation has not allowed this issue to be successfully addressed. The finding of the molar tooth sign in all of the above (Chance *et al.* 1999; Gleeson *et al.* 2004; Pellegrino *et al.* 1996; Satran, Pierpoint and Dobyns 1999) has been used to argue for a common aetiology.

In those people with CEP290 mutations where neuroimaging has been carried out, the molar tooth sign and/or cerebellar vermal hypoplasia have been shown, usually in combination with retinal dystrophy or congenital blindness (Sayer *et al.* 2006; Valente, Silhavy *et al.* 2006b). Nephronophthisis is also a common feature (Sayer *et al.* 2006). The combination of nephronophthisis, retinal dystrophy and molar tooth sign are the key features of Senior-Løken syndrome.

COACH – **C**olobomas, **O**ligophrenia (learning disability), **A**taxia, **C**erebellar vermis hypoplasia and **H**epatic fibrosis – syndrome (Gentile *et al.* 1996) also presents with the molar tooth sign.

A number of other conditions present with clinical features overlapping with Joubert syndrome and need to be considered during diagnosis. These are:

- the eight other cerebello-oculo-renal syndromes (Valente, Silhavy *et al.* 2006b)
- Biedl-Bardet syndrome (BBS) [17] (Baskin *et al.* 2002)
- Cogan syndrome (Betz *et al.* 2000)
- Dandy-Walker malformation (Patel and Barkovich 2002)
- X-linked cerebellar hypoplasia (Bergmann *et al.* 2003)
- ataxia and oculomotor apraxia types 1 and 2 (Le Ber, Brice and Durr 2005)
- congenital disorders of glycosylation (CDG) (Jaeken and Hagberg 1991; Morava *et al.* 2004)
- 3-C syndrome (cranio-cerebello-cardiac syndrome or Ritscher-Schinzel syndrome) (Leonardi *et al.* 2001)
- the pontocerebellar hypoplasias/atrophies (Barth 1993)

- oral-facial-digital (OFD) syndrome type II (Mohr syndrome) (Reardon *et al.* 1989)
- Meckel-Gruber syndrome (Kyttala *et al.* 2006; but see Baala *et al.* 2007).

Treatment and management: Animal models are beginning to show some potential for early treatment of renal impairment caused by lack of a specific compound 'nephrocystin-6' as a result of CEP290 knockdown (Tobin and Beales 2008), but at the present time there are no treatment approaches that are specific to Joubert syndrome. As the presentation is complex and variable, assessment, therapy and follow-up needs to be on a case-by-case basis.

This is a rare and complex disorder that requires coordinated management of a range of possible contributory factors potentially affecting the central nervous, visual and renal systems, and in more complex cases also affecting motor function and digestion. Assessment and follow-up should be focused on detailed evaluation of the various systems that may be involved and with the appropriate involvement of a variety of specialists:

- neurological assessment and management as appropriate – for example, of encephalocoele, hypotonia and oculomotor and oromotor function (mastication, swallowing and articulation)
- gastrostomy feeding may be required in severely dysphagic cases, and appropriate management of seizures and of ventricular dilatation where these are present
- assessment of respiratory function with treatment as required
- assessment and correction, as appropriate, of physical abnormalities such as palatal clefting, polydactyly and tongue restrictions. Physical growth can be restricted and should be monitored
- ophthalmologic assessment, particularly of retinal function, with treatment as required
- assessment of renal and hepatic function and endocrine screening are important. Dialysis or transplantation can be required for renal problems.

Once it is developmentally appropriate, assessment of cognitive and language development and of activities of daily living skills should be carried out, and difficulties and delays addressed when identified.

Parenting stress should be assessed and support provided as appropriate, including management help in those cases where this is related to behavioural difficulties such as poor impulse control or anger control issues.

Further information and support:

In the UK:
There is no specific support group but it may be possible to contact other families through:
Contact a Family
209–211
City Road
London
EC1V 4JN
Tel.: 020 7608 8700
E-mail: info@cafamily.org.uk
Website: www.cafamily.org.uk

In the USA:
The Joubert Syndrome Foundation and Related Cerebellar Disorders
6931 South Carlinda Avenue
Columbia
MD 21046
E-mail: jjgund@aol.com
Website: www.joubertsyndrome.org

45

Kleine-Levin syndrome

aka   • Kleine-Levin hibernation syndrome

Gene locus: 6p21.3 in some but not all reported cases

Key ASD references: Berthier *et al.* 1992; Mukaddes, Fateh and Kilincasian 2008

First reported in 1862 by Brierre de Boismont, Kleine-Levin syndrome is named after two early twentieth-century clinicians, Willi Kleine, who described various cases of episodic hypersomnia (Kleine 1925), and Max Levin, who noted the association between hypersomnia and hyperphagia (Levin 1929, 1936).

How common is Kleine-Levin syndrome? At the present time, the prevalence of Kleine-Levin syndrome is not known. Around 300 cases are reported in the clinical literature to date (Arnulf *et al.* 2005; Schenck, Arnulf and Mahowald 2007).

There is increasing evidence that Kleine-Levin syndrome results from factors interfering with the functioning of the major histocompatability complex at DQB1 on chromosome 6p (BaHammam *et al.* 2007; Dauvilliers *et al.* 2002), perhaps providing a mechanism for increased susceptibility to infection.

Main clinical features:

Table B45: Clinical features of Kleine-Levin syndrome

• hypersomnia	100%
• cognitive changes (including a specific feeling of derealization	96%
• eating disturbances	80%
• depressed mood	48%
• hypersexuality	43%
• compulsions	29%

Adapted from Arnulf *et al.* 2005

The behavioural aspects reported appear to be episodic, with normal behaviour in these respects between attacks (Popper *et al.* 1980).

An infectious aetiology was first proposed by Critchley and Hoffman (1942), and subsequently a number of cases have been reported with onset shortly after infection (Dauvilliers *et al.* 2002; Katz and Ropper 2002). A useful overview can be found in Lisk (2009).

Is there a link between Kleine-Levin syndrome and ASD? Two papers have reported co-morbid cases:

- Berthier *et al.* (1992) described two adolescent males with Asperger's syndrome who also had recurrent bouts of hypersomnia. The report preceded the adoption of ICD or DSM criteria for Asperger's syndrome, but has been quoted in the literature as an association between ASD and Kleine-Levin syndrome (Zafeiriou, Ververi and Vargiami 2006).

- Mukaddes, Fateh and Kilincasian (2008) have presented a further two cases of Kleine-Levin syndrome with associated autistic disorder.

A number of papers have highlighted neuropsychiatric symptomology in Kleine-Levin syndrome (Masi, Favilla and Millepiedi 2000; Mukaddes *et al.* 1999). A systematic review has detailed 186 cases reported between 1962 and 2004 (Arnulf *et al.* 2005). This review indicated a mean age of onset in the mid-teens, and, as with many neuropsychiatric disorders, a higher prevalence in males but greater severity in presenting females.

Differential diagnosis: The presentation is unusual, episodic and distinctive. It is unlikely that Kleine-Levin syndrome would be confused with other types of presentation.

Treatment and management: There is a lack of evidence concerning pharmacological treatments for Kleine-Levin syndrome (Oliveira *et al.* 2009).

The most successful reported treatment to date for the recurrent hypersomnia is lithium (Arnulf *et al.* 2005). In some cases at least, there appears to be a close association between lithium level achieved and clinical improvement (Muratori, Bertini and Masi 2002).

A case has been described who went into complete remission on carbamazepine (El Hajj *et al.* 2009).

Further information and support:

In the USA:
KLS Foundation
PO Box 5382
San Jose
CA 95150-5382
Tel.: 408-265-1099
Fax: 408-269-2131
E-mail: facts@klsfoundation.org

46

Lujan-Fryns syndrome

---

aka   • mental retardation, X-linked, with Marfanoid habitus

Gene locus: Xq13, and a reported additional link to terminal 5p deletion

Key ASD references: Gurrieri and Neri 1991; Lerma-Carrillo *et al.* 2006; Purandare and Markar 2005; Spaepen, Hellemans and Fryns 1994; Stathopulu, Ogilvie and Flinter 2003; Swillen *et al.* 1996

This syndrome was first described in 1984 by J. Enrique Lujan (Lujan, Carlin and Lubs 1984).

Those affected are tall and slim with long, slender fingers and toes, and narrow faces with small jaws and prominent foreheads. They typically have mild to moderate learning difficulties, obsessive-compulsive disorder, attentional and overactivity problems and conduct disorder, together with extreme shyness.

A useful review of Lujan-Fryns syndrome can be found in Van Buggenhout and Fryns (2006).

How common is Lujan-Fryns syndrome? There have been no prevalence studies to date, as the genes implicated in this condition have only recently been identified, making the possibility of screening studies possible for the first time.

Main clinical features: Mild to moderate learning disability is seen in most cases, but normal levels of cognitive function are reported (Williams M.S. 2006). The individual in the case described by Williams, despite his normal IQ, had major problems with learning and memory and a complex behavioural presentation that included elements of Oppositional Disorder, ADHD and conduct disorder, together with extreme shyness.

The phenotype is described as 'Marfanoid', and both hyperextensible joints and cardiac defects are reported (Wittine, Josephson and Williams 1999), as seen in Marfan's syndrome (Le Parc 2005). The majority of reported cases are male.

A tall, slender physique with long fingers and toes, and limited subcutaneous fat, an aqualine nose, thin upper lip, prominent forehead, maxillary hypoplasia and small jaw are typical, as is macro-orchidism.

Behaviourally, in addition to the ASD features, shyness (Lacombe *et al.* 1993) and hyperactivity (De Hert *et al.* 1996; Wittine, Josephson and Williams 1999) are frequently reported.

Epilepsy is reported in some cases, but how common and how consistent a feature is uncertain.

There is progressive scoliosis in many cases that may require surgical correction in some.

Research with some of the originally reported families has identified a missense mutation in the MED12 gene at Xq13 (Schwartz *et al.* 2007), while terminal 5p deletion has also been reported in association with the condition (Stathopulu, Ogilvie and Flinter 2003).

Is there a link between Lujan-Fryns and ASD? Despite the limited literature on Lujan-Fryns, a number of papers have suggested an association with ASD:

- Gurrieri and Neri (1991) reported on a brother and sister with Lujan-Fryns and co-morbid ASD.

- Spaepen, Hellemans and Fryns (1994) reported on a series of 14 Lujan-Fryns cases and found that 12 of the 14 exhibited autistic or autistic-like behaviour.

- Swillen *et al.* (1996) reported that four of the 21 residential learning-disabled ASD cases they reported had the Lujan-Fryns phenotype.

- Stathopulu, Ogilvie and Flinter (2003) described a 16-year-old man with a Lujan-Fryns phenotype and a small 5p terminal deletion. This may prove to be a phenocopy disorder with a separate aetiology.

- Purandare and Markar (2005) provided a systematic review of the psychiatric symptomology, including ASD, reported in association with Lujan-Fryns.

- Lerma-Carrillo *et al.* (2006) documented a 23-year-old male with borderline IQ, who had been admitted to psychiatric hospital because of behavioural disturbance and firesetting. He had the classic Lujan-Fryns phenotype and a history of ADHD and disturbed behaviour. His presenting behaviour was consistent with an ASD. On MRI he was found to have callosal agenesis. A maternal uncle had a similar presentation, abnormal dentition and a heart defect. Both men had autistic behaviour. They authors suggest from their review of the literature and their own cases that around 90 per cent of cases have ASD symptomology.

Differential diagnosis: The differential diagnosis should include assessment to exclude XXY [3] and XYY [4] aneuploidies; 22q11 deletion syndromes [18, 20, 29, 76]; fragile-X syndrome [35, 36]; Marfan syndrome; and homocystinuria, all of which can present with a similar physical and behavioural phenotype.

Lalatta *et al.* (1991) were the first to suggest that psychotic presentations may be common in this condition. A number of cases have been described with visual and auditory hallucinations, and schizophrenia has been diagnosed in some cases (De Hert *et al.* 1996; Purandare and Markar 2005).

Treatment and management: At the present time there is no specific treatment for Lujan-Fryns syndrome. The likelihood of scoliosis and joint problems, cardiac abnormalities and the risk of seizures should all be monitored.

The ASD, ADHD and social shyness that are characteristics of the condition should respond to approaches used with others. As there is an increased likelihood of hallucinations these should be monitored and treated where present.

Further information and support: There is no specific support group for individuals or families with this condition. Umbrella groups for rare conditions are likely to provide the best supports.

In the UK:
Unique
Rare Chromosome Disorder Support Group
PO Box 2189
Surrey
CR3 5GN
E-mail: info@rarechromo.org
Telephone helpline: 01883 330766
Website: www.rarechromo.org

Genetic Interest Group
Unit 4D
Leroy House
436 Essex Road
London
N1 3QP
Tel.: 020 7704 3141
Fax: 020 7359 1447
E-mail: mail@gig.org.uk
Website: www.gig.org.uk/index.html

Contact a Family
209–211 City Road
London
EC1V 1JN
Tel.: 020 7608 8700
Fax: 020 7608 8701
Helpline: 0808 808 3555
Textphone: 0808 808 3556
Freephone for parents and families (10am–4pm,
Mon–Fri)
E-mail: info@cafamily.org.uk
Website: www.cafamily.org.uk

Linking site for families with the same condition:
www.makingcontact.org

In the USA:
National Organization for Rare Disorders (NORD)
55 Kenosia Avenue
PO Box 1968

Danbury,
CT 06813-1968
Tel.: 203-744-0100
Toll-free: 800-999-6673 (voicemail only)
TDD Number: 203-797-9590
Fax: 203-798-2291
E-mail: orphan@rarediseases.org
Website: www.rarediseases.org/info/contact.html

Genetic Alliance
4301 Connecticut Ave, NW
Suite 404
Washington,
WA 20008-2304
Tel.: 800-336-GENE;
202-966-5557
Fax: 202-966-8553
E-mail: info@geneticalliance.org
Website: www.geneticalliance.org

47

2-methylbutyryl-CoA dehydrogenase deficiency

aka • short/branched-chain acyl-CoA dehydrogenase deficiency (SBCADD/ 2-MBADD)

Gene locus: 10q25–q26

Key ASD reference: Kanavin *et al.* 2007

This inborn error of metabolism was first reported by Gibson *et al.* in 1999. It typically presents with severe developmental delay, epilepsy, motor and social problems.

How common is 2-methylbutyryl-CoA dehydrogenase deficiency? 2-methylbutyryl-CoA dehydrogenase deficiency is thought to be rare (<one in 100,000) but there are no population prevalence figures. There is an exception in the Hmong population of both southeastern Asia (the Hmong are originally thought to be from Laos, Cambodia and southern China) and in Hmong American families, of whom between one in 250 and one in 500 people are affected (van Calcar *et al.* 2007). Several cases have been reported in the clinical literature from Eritrea and Somalia, suggesting that the condition may also have a significant prevalence in these populations.

This is an autosomal recessive inborn error of metabolism, specifically concerned with the metabolism of the amino acids isoleucine and valine (Andresen *et al.* 2000). It is typically detected by the presence of the compounds 2-methylbutyryl glycine and 2-methylbutyryl carnitine in urine.

Main clinical features: Typically, SBCADD cases present with severe developmental delay, seizures, poor social responsiveness and motor problems, diagnosed variously as hypotonia, muscle wastage and cerebral palsy (Akaboshi *et al.* 2001; Andresen *et al.* 2000; Gibson *et al.* 2000; Madsen *et al.* 2006).

A number of gene differences are sufficient to result in SBCADD. These produce a range of levels of deficiency and some, particularly missense variants, are common in the general population (Pedersen *et al.* 2008). As a number of the reported cases appear to have one parent with 2-methylbutyryl glycinuria, but without any clinical symptomology, SBCADD may be a condition that requires an additional factor to manifest. The possibility of changes in diet coinciding with a critical phase in foetal development may be one possibility, given the reported cases in Eritrean, Somali and Hmong now domiciled in Europe or North America.

A Swedish paper (Barnevik-Olsson, Gillberg and Fernell 2008) suggests that the rate of autism in the Somali population of Stockholm is three to four times higher than the indigenous rate amongst Swedes.

Is there a link between 2-methylbutyryl-CoA dehydrogenase deficiency and ASD?

- To date, only a single case of ASD with SBCADD and autism has been reported. The case is a four-year-old Somali boy born to healthy parents. The child had presented in Somalia with seizures, but the details were lost to follow-up when the family moved to Norway when he was 18 months old (Kanavin *et al.* 2007).

Differential diagnosis: 2-methylbutyryl-CoA dehydrogenase deficiency should be differentiated from other inborn errors of isoleucine metabolism (Korman 2006).

Treatment and management: Current clinical management typically involves the use of protein restriction together with l-carnitine supplementation. In one girl whose mother had started this routine antenatally after having a first affected child, development of her second affected child to age four years eight months was reported as asymptomatic, with normal behaviour (Madsen *et al.* 2006). Postnatal dietary management has not so far been found to be beneficial.

Further information and support: There is no specific support group for SBCADD at present. More general help concerning inborn metabolic errors that may be useful can be found through the following organizations.

In the UK:
CLIMB (Children Living with Inherited Metabolic Diseases)
Climb Building
176 Nantwich Road
Crewe
CW2 6BG
Tel.: 0800 652 3181 or 0845 241 2172 Mon-Fri 10.00am–4.00pm GMT
E-mail: info.svcs@climb.org.uk
Website: www.climb.org.uk/
Provides an excellent information resource covering a wide range of inherited metabolic disorders. Also provides disease-specific information and family support.

In the USA:
The Genetic and Rare Diseases Information Center
P.O. Box 8126
Gaithersburg
Maryland
MD 20898-8126
Tel.: 888-205-2311 (Phone)
888-205-3223 (TTY)
301-519-3194 (International Telephone Access Number)
Fax: 240-632-9164
E-mail: GARDinfo@nih.gov

48

Mobius/Möbius/ Moebius syndrome

Gene locus: 13q12.2–q13

Key ASD references: Bandim *et al.* 2003; Briegel 2006; Gillberg 1992; Gillberg and Steffenburg 1989; Gillberg and Winnergard 1984; Johansson *et al.* 2001; Verzijl *et al.* 2003

Mobius syndrome is a condition which affects cranial nerves VI and VII and limits the range of facial expression. It is usually genetic, but a number of environmental factors have been shown to produce the phenotype, in particular misoprostol and thalidomide (neither of which is in widespread use).

A probable case of Mobius syndrome was first described by Alfred von Graefe in 1880; however, the description by the German neurologist Paul Julius Möbius in 1888 is usually taken as the first clinical account (for a brief biography of Möbius, see Steinberg 2005).

How common is Mobius syndrome? There is only one epidemiological study to date on Mobius syndrome (Verzijl *et al.* 2003). Based on a Dutch population survey, this paper estimated the incidence of Mobius syndrome in the Dutch population in 1996 to be 0.002 per cent (four cases were found in 189,000 births).

Main clinical features: The condition typically involves abnormal function of cranial nerves VI and VII, resulting in flattened facial affect. In addition, a number of other cranial nerves can also be affected. In around 125 per cent of cases, there is nerve involvement resulting in difficulties with tongue protrusion and articulation.

The condition is typically noted in infancy due to poor sucking, drooling, lack of eyelid closure during sleep, and flattened facial affect. The persistence of flattened facial affect makes it difficult for the person to convey emotion through facial expression, compounding difficulties with social interaction. Because of the lack of facial innervation there is an absence of skin wrinkling and the appearance of the face is exceptionally smooth. External ocular nerve palsies are seen in around 80 per cent of cases.

Intelligence is typically within the normal range (Verzijl *et al.* 2003); however, a subgroup have mild learning disabilities.

One small (N=13) study has reported behavioural difficulties, particularly aggressive behaviour, oppositional defiance and anxiety in boys, to be reasonably common in a sample of prechool children with Mobius syndrome (Briegel, Hofmann and Schwab 2007). Caregivers also reported a high level of perceived stress in themselves.

It is common for those affected to have a small mouth with large lips, and to be unable to fully close their mouth, which adds to their swallowing difficulties. Sucking and swallowing problems can be severe in infancy and can contribute, along with respiratory problems, to increased early mortality.

Inability to close the mouth also makes it difficult to produce certain sounds, and speech is often indistinct as a result. Similarly, inability to fully close the eyelids during sleep leads to an increased risk of recurrent conjunctivitis.

There is a high incidence of other congenital abnormalities. *Talipes equinovarus*, or clubfoot, is a commonly associated abnormality, seen in around one third of cases. Abnormalities of the jaw and hand (syndactyly, brachydactyly and finger webbing) are also common. Abnormal formation of the microtia/inner ear is common, as is the presence of a hypoplastic thumb.

There is no indication of a higher prevalence in either sex or in particular racial groups.

No systematic study of sleep problems in Mobius syndrome has been carried out. There have been four separate cases of cataplexy (a rare condition where the person collapses without warning while laughing): one was a single case report (Tyagi and Harrington 2003) and three were from a series of 19 attending a sleep clinic (Parkes 1999).

In a study of 37 Mobius patients aged from six months to 53 years (Verzijl *et al.* 2003), 86 per cent were noted to have had feeding difficulties from birth due to abnormalities of the palate and pharynx; 90 per cent had craniofacial abnormalities; 86 per cent had abnormalities of the hands and/or feet and 88 per cent were noted to have motor clumsiness.

Is there a link between Mobius syndrome and ASD?

- Gillberg and Winnergard (1984) described a five-year-old boy with Mobius syndrome, a mild to moderate level of learning difficulty and a childhood psychosis described as 'possibly infantile autism'. This was the first such case described in the clinical literature.

- Gillberg and Steffenburg (1989) presented data from a screening study of 17 children and young adults with Mobius syndrome. Using the Checklist for Autism developed by Mildred Creak (Creak 1963) 5/17 were said to fulfil criteria for a DSM-III-R diagnosis of autism.

- Gillberg (1992) reviewed 59 autism cases with a variety of co-morbid medical conditions, including Mobius syndrome. He concluded that there were clear differences in the behavioural phenotype that depended on the associated medical condition.

- Johansson *et al.* (2001) published a detailed assessment of 22 Mobius cases, using several ASD assessments. Six cases fulfilled diagnostic criteria for autism, all with co-morbid learning disability.

- A study in northeastern Brazil (Bandim *et al.* 2003) screened 23 Mobius syndrome cases for possible autism. Of those aged under two years, 2/5 showed autistic features, while of those over two years, 5/18 met diagnostic criteria for autism. All had co-morbid learning disability. One of the cases under two and three of the older cases had been exposed to misoprostol during the first trimester. Misoprostol is used in the treatment of stomach ulcers, and is also an abortifacient that can produce teratogenic effects consistent with those seen in the genetic form of Mobius syndrome (Miller *et al.* 2005).

- Verzijl *et al.* (2003) carried out a screening study of 37 Mobius cases. No specific assessments were used, but it was noted that two cases had a diagnosis of autism. The paper implies that both had co-morbid learning disability.

- A review of the neuropsychiatric sequelae of Mobius syndrome can be found in Briegel (2006), who suggests that the rate of ASD in Mobius syndrome is 5–29 per cent compared to a general population prevalence of 0.63 per cent.

Overall (with the exception of the lower rate found by Verzijl *et al.* 2003), this suggests that perhaps 28 per cent of those with Mobius syndrome fulfil criteria for ASD, so co-morbid cases may occur in perhaps one in 140,000 of the population if the limited epidemiology is broadly correct.

Genetics: Two early papers suggested a link to genetic defects at 13q12.2–q13. Various patterns of inheritance have been reported consistent with autosomal dominant and recessive and with X-linked recessive patterns of inheritance, or with several sufficient genetic mechanisms. Overall the risk of inheritance from someone affected by the condition is said to be approximately two per cent (Baraitser 1977, 1982); however, there have been no recent studies of this issue.

One family presented with a Mobius phenotype across three generations, where all of those affected had reciprocal translocations between 1p34 and 13q13, but unaffected family members did not (Ziter, Wiser and Robinson 1977). In the second case, Mobius syndrome was associated with a 13q12.2 deletion in a two-and-a-half-year-old girl (Slee, Smart and Viljoen 1991).

A gene defect at 13q12.2–q13 has been reported as sufficient to cause Mobius syndrome. A number of environmental causes have also been reported to be independently sufficient causes. In particular, thalidomide, which was used for a number of years in the management of morning sickness in early pregnancy (in Europe but not in North America), has been shown to have teratogenic effects which can cause both Mobius syndrome and ASD (Miller *et al.* 2005). Misoprostol (Bandim *et al.* 2003), an abortifacient, has also been found capable of producing the combination of Mobius syndrome and ASD. Cases have also been reported in association with ergotamine exposure (Smets, Zecic and Willems 2004) and cocaine use during pregnancy (Puvabanditsin, Garrow and Augustin 2005). It is important, therefore, in exploring the pathogenesis, to identify any possible exposures to relevant teratogenic agents.

The common factor appears to be *when* neural development has been affected, rather than by what. A useful discussion of the embryology underpinning Mobius syndrome and linking the constellation of features to timing of disruption to early growth, can be found in Miller *et al.* (2005).

The pattern of inheritance is still unclear, with family pedigrees reported which are consistent with X-linked recessive inheritance (Journel, Roussey and Le Marec 1989), and with both autosomal dominant and autosomal recessive inheritance (Legum, Godel and Nemet 1981).

Differential diagnosis: The principal differential diagnoses are the neuromuscular conditions, and initial differentiation can be difficult (Imamura *et al.* 2007). Alternative possible diagnoses include hereditary congenital facial paresis (Verzijl *et al.* 2003, 2005), which affects only the facial nerves and has no central or brainstem component, facioscapulohumoral muscular dystrophy (Tawil 2008), infantile myotonic dystrophy (Yoshimura *et al.* 1989) and Charcot-Marie-Tooth disease (Herrmann 2008).

A paper has detailed a Mobius-like syndrome that presents with similar muscular impairment but very distinct neuroimaging (Dumars *et al.* 2008).

There have been rare cases of Mobius syndrome in combination with other anomalies such as Goldenhar syndrome [38] and hypoglossia-hypodactyly (having a small tongue and fewer fingers and/or toes than normal) (Preis *et al.* 1996).

A study has evaluated the use of various ASD scales with this population, questioning the applicability of current diagnostic tools such as the Autism Diagnostic Interview–Revised (ADI-R), the Childhood Autism Rating Scale (CARS) and the Autism Behavior Checklist (ABC) in this population if the subject is deaf-blind (Johansson, Gillberg and Råstam 2009).

Treatment and management: This is a static and not a progressive condition. Treatment is dependent on the clinical profile in the individual case.

Surgical treatment can be required to correct deformities of the hand foot or jaw. Surgery may be considered to correct strabismus (crossed eyes) and to address flattened facial affect through transfer of innervation and musculature to animate the corners of the mouth. A tracheostomy may sometimes be required to help those with severe breathing difficulties.

Some will require some form of assisted feeding, such as nasogastric tube feeding.

Further information and support:

In the UK:
Moebius Syndrome Support Network (UK)
41 Westley Ave
Whitley Bay
Tyne and Wear
NE26 4NW
Tel.: 0191 253 2090
Fax: 0191 253 2090
E-mail: moebius@alex-b.net

In the USA:
Mobius Syndrome Foundation
PO Box 147
Pilot Grove
MO 65276
Tel.: 660-834-3406
Fax: 660-834-3407
E-mail: vicki@Mobiussyndrome.com
Website: www.Mobiussyndrome.com/

FACES: The National Craniofacial Association
PO Box 11082
Chattanooga
TN 37401
Tel.: 800-332-2373
Website: www.faces-cranio.org/

49

Myhre syndrome

aka • growth–mental deficiency syndrome of Myhre

Gene locus: not yet identified

Key ASD references: Burglen *et al.* 2003; Titomanlio *et al.* 2001

In 1981 Myhre and colleagues described two unrelated learning-disabled young men with similar physical phenotypes (Myhre, Ruvalcaba and Graham 1981). Both were short and heavily built, with small mouths, jaws and noses, limited joint movement, undescended testes and hearing loss. Older paternal age was noted in both cases. A number of case reports followed this initial description (see for example, Garcia-Cruz *et al.* 1993; Soljak, Aftimos and Gluckman 1983).

Reviews of Myhre syndrome can be found in Becerra-Solano *et al.* (2008) and Burglen *et al.* (2003).

How common is Myhre syndrome? The prevalence and incidence are not currently known. Only 20 cases have so far been reported.

Main clinical features: Short stature, heavy, muscular build, hearing loss, decreased joint mobility, thickened, hard skin, underdeveloped upper jaw and prominent lower jaw and narrow eyelids are typically reported. These features are usually associated with learning disability; however, there is a report of Myhre syndrome phenotype with normal intelligence (Rulli *et al.* 2005).

A 2001 paper from Scotland (Whiteford *et al.* 2001) described a single case – a 13-year-old male with short stature, learning disability, hearing difficulty, heavy muscular build and limited joint mobility.

Is there a link between Myhre syndrome and ASD?

- One paper (Titomanlio *et al.* 2001) describes a 14-year-old boy with the clinical features of Myhre syndrome, including impaired growth and a co-morbid ASD diagnosis.

- Burglen *et al.* (2003) reported on four cases of Myhre, one of whom was reported to have an 'autistic-like' condition.

- A further case of an eleven-year-old boy, with autism and similar neurocutaneous findings but with physical overgrowth, has been reported (Buoni *et al.* 2006).

There is no genetic marker for Myhre syndrome and the extent of phenotypic variability in this condition is unknown. Variation can be marked in many of the conditions we have considered. The above may be presentations of the same underlying mechanism, but could conceivably represent similar phenotypes with differing underlying bases.

Whether two cases from a world literature of around 20 in total constitutes a meaningful association between these conditions will await the reporting of a larger clinical population.

Differential diagnosis: In those with the physical phenotype, hearing problems and learning disability, the most likely differential dignosis is LAPS (**L**aryngotracheal stenosis, **A**rthropathy, **P**rognathism and **S**hort stature) (Lindor *et al.* 2002).

Treatment and management: No specific treatment approaches have been developed to date.

Further information and support: There are no specific support groups for Myhre syndrome at the time of writing. Several organizations will be able to provide help and information, including the following:

In the UK:
Unique
Rare Chromosome Disorder Support Group
PO Box 2189
Surrey
CR3 5GN
E-mail: info@rarechromo.org
Telephone helpline: 01883 330766
Website: www.rarechromo.org

In the USA:
Little People of America, Inc.
250 El Camino Real
Suite 201
Tustin,
CA 92780

Tel.: 714-368-3689;
888-572-2001
E-mail: info@lpaonline.org
Website: www.lpaonline.org
This is non-profit organization that provides support for families of people of short stature, which would include those with Myhre syndrome.

National Organization for Rare Disorders (NORD)
55 Kenosia Avenue
PO Box 1968
Danbury,
CT 06813-1968
Tel.: 203-744-0100
Website: www.rarediseases.org/info/contact.html

50

Myotonic dystrophy (MD1)

---

aka • dystrophia myotonica 1;

• Steinert's muscular dystrophy

Gene Locus: 19q13.2–q13.3

Key ASD references: Blondis *et al.* 1996; Ekström *et al.* 2008; Paul and Allington-Smith 1997; Yoshimura *et al.* 1989

Myotonic dystrophy type 1 is the second most common type of muscular dystrophy after Duchenne [33]. It is an autosomal dominant CTG triplet repeat expansion disorder affecting the production of DMPK (dystrophia myotonica-protein kinase). In the general population, CTG repeats of up to 37 copies are seen. Anticipation is seen in MD1, so one or other parent typically has a pre-mutational expansion of 37 to 50 copies. Larger mutations are usually associated with maternal transmission. Affected individuals have between 50 and 4,000 copies. With shorter expansions (50–400 copies) there is a correlation between repeat length and age of onset. Above 400 copies earlier onset is consistently seen.

MD1 was originally called Steinert's muscular dystrophy after the German nineteenth-century neurologist Hans Gustav Wilhelm Steinert, who described the condition in an early paper published in 1910.

There are a number of useful reviews of MD1, such as Bird T.D. (2007) and Schara, Benedikt and Schoser (2006).

How common is myotonic dystrophy type 1? Estimates of prevalence vary for myotonic dystrophy type 1. The current best overall estimate is a rate of between one in 20,000 and one in 100,000 (Bird T. D. 2007). Reported rates vary from one in 100,000 in Japan to one in 10,000 in Iceland.

Main clinical features: MD1 is a multisystem disorder that affects all major body systems except the skeleton. It is an autosomal dominant condition caused by a mutation at 19q13.2–q13.3. This is a region transcribed into RNA but not into protein. The principal effects appear to be on the chloride channel CIC-1, resulting in myotonia, and affecting the insulin receptor INSR, causing insulin resistance (Cho and Tapscott 2007).

There are effects on both skeletal and smooth muscle, as well as on the eye, heart, endocrine system and central nervous system.

MD1 cases are typically divided into three groups by severity:

1. *mild,* in which the typical presentation is of a sustained but slight myotonia combined with cataract and normal life expectancy

2. *classic,* in which gradual onset hypotonia, myotonia and muscle wasting, combined with cataract, are typical, cardiac problems are common, and life expectancy is shortened

3. *congenital,* characterized by congenital hypotonia and severe weakness, breathing difficulties, learning disability in most cases, and short life expectancy.

A study of cognitive and adaptive abilities in a sample of 31 male and 24 female DM1 cases (mean age 12 years one month; range between two years seven months and 21 years five months) found a negative association between severity of dystrophy and both IQ and adaptive level (Ekström *et al.* 2009).

Is there a link between MD1 and ASD?

• In the earliest case report, Yoshimura *et al.* (1989) described an 11-year-old girl with congenital myotonic dystrophy and infantile autism.

• Blondis *et al.* (1996) described one ten-year-old girl with MD1 and co-morbid Asperger's syndrome.

• Paul and Allington-Smith (1997) described two boys with MD1 and diagnoses of Asperger's syndrome, one aged 16, one 14.

• Despite its being a well-recognized and physically quite obvious condition, the first paper to systematically investigate an association between myotonic dystrophy and ASD did not appear until 2008 (Ekström *et al.* 2008). This paper examined 57 children and adolescents with MD1 (26 girls and 31 boys). Forty-six per cent of the MD1 cases they examined fulfilled criteria for an ASD diagnosis, suggesting a strong but previously largely unrecognized association between the two conditions.

Differential diagnosis: There are no other causes of multi-system myotonic dystrophy which have been identified. Diagnosis is based on identifying the presence of a cytorine–thymine–guanine expansion of the DMPK (dystrophia myotonica protein kinase) gene at 19q13.2–q13.3. As in most triplet repeat expansion conditions, there is anticipation – the carrier parent will have a shorter expansion than the affected person – and there is an association between the severity of the condition and the size of the expansion. In the normal population, the number of CTG copy repeats is between 5 and 30. A typical person with MD1 will have 50–80 copies, but expansions of up to 2,000 repeats have been reported.

Treatment and management: The wide range of presentation leads to a range of appropriate treatment interventions depending on the main areas of difficulty.

A review of medication for the management of myotonia has appeared in the Cochrane Library (Trip *et al.* 2009). The review identified ten small randomized trials; however, the quality of the published studies was poor. One small study demonstrated a significant beneficial effect of taurine (Durelli, Mutani and Fassio 1983), but despite its finding of significant benefits and absence of apparent side effects, it remains unreplicated over 25 years later.

As gradual muscle wastage is a common feature, systematic approaches to exercise are being evaluated. One study (Omgreen, Olsen and Vissing 2005) has shown improvements in oxygen uptake and muscle function through the use of graded aerobic exercise on static exercise bikes. As respiratory problems are one of the most important predictors of life expectancy, such programmes may prove particularly beneficial.

As a consequence of MD1, a number of specialist services may be involved in assessment and ongoing management – the muscular abnormalities can lead to problems with motor control, respiration, cardiac function and digestion. There are associated problems with vision – cataract is a common finding that may require surgical correction.

In the congenital form, significant breathing problems can be present from birth and result in a need for ventilator support (Keller *et al.* 1998).

Males with MD1 often have low testosterone levels (Griggs *et al.* 1985), but are typically not infertile. Obstetric difficulties are common; however, only women with multisystem involvement appear at significantly increased risk of having affected offspring (Koch *et al.* 1991).

As the basis for the association between ASD and MD1 is unclear, and interest in the association is very recent, specific implications for treatment or management (if any), are unclear.

Further information and support:

In the UK:
Myotonic Dystrophy Support Group
35A Carlton Hill
Carlton
Nottingham
NG4 1BG
Tel.: (helpline): 0115 987 0080
Tel.: (office): 0115 987 5869
Website: www.mdsguk.org

In the USA:
Myotonic Dystrophy Foundation
3031 Stanford Ranch Road,
Suite 2332
Rocklin,
CA 95765
Tel./Fax: 86-MYOTONIC (866-968-6642)
E-mail: info@myotonic.com
Website: www.myotonic.com/go/mdf
Tel./Fax: 86-MYOTONIC (866-968-6642)

51

Neurofibromatosis type 1 (NF1)

---

aka • von Recklinghausen disease

Gene loci: 17q11.2; 2p22–p21

Key ASD references: Folstein and Rutter 1988; Gillberg 1992; Havlovicova *et al.* 2007; Marui *et al.* 2004a; Mbarek *et al.* 2000; Mouridsen *et al.* 1992; Williams and Hersh 1998

NF1 was described in 1768 by Mark Akenside, a London medical practitioner. It was for many years known as von Recklinghausen's syndrome, after the German pathologist Friedrich Daniel von Recklinghausen, who published detailed autopsy reports on two cases in 1882. Multiple café-au-lait/coffee-coloured spots, under the arm and most commonly across the abdomen, are the most prominent physical features.

NF1 is complex, with over 240 separate mutations recorded to date. When inherited, it is passed on in an autosomal dominant fashion. Over half of all cases appear to arise as *de novo* mutations, making it one of the most common forms of spontaneous mutation known. The condition results in loss or production of truncated forms of neurofibromin. At the present time the function of neurofibromin is not fully understood.

NF1 is characterized by the growth of non-cancerous tumours called neurofibromas. It is classified as a phacomatosis (Nowak 2007) – a condition that is dysplastic (results in abnormal tissue growth), tending to form tumours in the skin, nervous system and viscera.

The process of tumour growth in NF1 is complex and determined by multiple genetic loci (Upadhyaya *et al.* 2004).

Systematic reviews of clinical and genetic issues in NF1 can be found in Ferner (2007); Friedman (2007) and Lee and Stephenson (2007).

How common is neurofibromatosis type 1? Most prevalence estimates for NF1 mutations vary between one in 2,000 and one in 5,000 of the general population (Friedman 1999; Lammert *et al.* 2005; Rasmussen and Friedman 2000). Prevalence of the condition is typically quoted as being one in 4,000 and one in 5,000 (Ferner 2007; Huson *et al.* 1989), but reports vary from one in 960 (Garty, Laor and Danon 1994) to one in 7,800 (Sergeyev 1975). The wide differences in reported rates may reflect differences in their genetic makeup, and account for the considerable differences in reported co-morbidity with ASD in different populations.

Main clinical features: The clinical features of NF1 vary in presentation and severity (Friedman and Birch 1997). The typical picture in neurofibromatosis, as noted above, is of multiple café-au-lait/coffee-coloured spots, under the arm and most commonly across the abdomen.

Multiple discrete dermal neurofibromas, and iris Lisch nodules (small benign tumours on the iris), are seen in most, except for certain mosaic cases.

Affected individuals tend to be of short stature and to have low levels of pituitary growth hormone and liver insulin-like growth factor-1. The brain is typically larger than normal, but there is no correlation between grey matter volume and cognitive function (Greenwood *et al.* 2005). Head circumference is typically above average (Virdis *et al.* 2003). Puberty is often delayed (Virdis *et al.* 2003).

Hypertension is seen, but age of onset varies (Friedman 1999; Lama *et al.* 2004). In one series of 75 cases under 16 (McKeever *et al.* 2008) only one case of hypertension was reported. It can be essential hypertension but can also arise from specific NF1-related lesions, and a specific abnormality affecting both cardiovascular and renal function is often found (Fossali *et al.* 2000; Han and Criado 2005).

Learning difficulties are noted in around half of all cases (North 1999; North *et al.* 1997); however, the effect is a small one and not found in all studies (see review in Levine *et al.* 2006).

A range of difficulties are reported, the most common being visual–spatial deficits on performance tasks and problems with sustained attention and concentration (Levine *et al.* 2006). Learning difficulties continue to be reported through adulthood (Pavol *et al.* 2006; Zoller, Rembeck and Backman 1997).

Children with NF1 often show difficulties in their social skills (Barton and North 2004). Quality of life has been reported to be poor in children and adolescents (Graf *et al.* 2006; Wolkenstein *et al.* 2008) and in adults (Page P.Z. *et al.* 2006). Sleep problems are reported as being more common (Johnson H. *et al.* 2005).

Skeletal problems are common – scoliosis, which is seen in some ten per cent of cases (Akbarnia *et al.* 1992), developing usually between six and ten years of age, abnormal skeletal growth and pseudoarthrosis being the most common and problematic (Alwan, Tredwell and Friedman 2005) – with a significant impact on quality of life (Wolkenstein *et al.* 2008). Scoliosis often requires complex surgical correction (Shen *et al.* 2005).

Cardiovascular problems are more common in individuals with NF1 (Lin *et al.* 2000), and specific recommendations have been made concerning management (Friedman *et al.* 2002).

Headaches are frequently reported. Seizures (Vivarelli *et al.* 2003) and hydrocephalus (see, for example, Creange *et al.* 1999) have been occasionally reported.

Children without a positive family history are often not recognized as having the condition in their early years. Through childhood, the features of NF1 tend to become more noticeable with age, and most *de novo* cases meet diagnostic criteria by around age eight (DeBella, Poskitt, Szudek and Friedman 2000). Many features of NF1 increase in frequency with age (DeBella, Szudek and Friedman 2000).

The average life expectancy of individuals with NF1 appears to be shorter than normal. One US study suggests that it is reduced by about 15 years (Rasmussen S.A. *et al.* 2001) – a mean life expectancy of 54.4 compared to 70.1 for the same geographic population. Malignant tumours were the most likely cause of death.

In those with a positive family history, recognition tends to be earlier, in most cases through the presence of café-au-lait spots (DeBella, Szudek and Friedman 2000).

Is there a link between NF1 and ASD?

- A link between neurofibromatosis type 1 and ASD was first suggested in 1988 when, in a prescient paper, Susan Folstein and Michael Rutter suggested that it was likely that more than one genetic factor may be implicated in the pathogenesis of autism and that neurofibromatosis type 1 and fragile-X were amongst such factors.

- Christopher Gillberg (1992) reviewed 59 cases of infantile autism and noted the occurrence of a number of known genetic conditions including NF1 in this group.

- Mouridsen et al. (1992) reviewed 341 children with ASD seen in two Danish clinics over a 25-year period, but could only identify a single case of NF1 in their series. Their conclusion was that at 0.3 per cent, although the two conditions could co-occur, they did not do so in a way suggesting any aetiological relationship.

- Williams and Hersh (1998) provide a brief report on three cases co-morbid for NF1 and autism.

- Mbarek et al. (2000) suggest that, although NF1 is a rare factor in ASD, it is still some 150 times more common than it is in the general population. This estimate needs to be revised down considerably on current ASD prevalence figures, but a ten-fold increased likelihood of co-occurrence seems realistic. From screening a French series of 85 ASD cases and 213 controls, Mbarek et al. identify one specific allele (allele 5 of the GXAlu marker) which appears to be specific to ASD–NF1 cases associated with a severe clinical picture with poorer motor development and muscle tone in 4.3 per cent of their ASD cases. An attempt to replicate this finding in a South Carolina series of 204 cases (Plank et al. 2001) failed to find any GXAlu cases in a group of 204 ASD patients or in 200 controls. Similarly, Marui et al. (2004a) failed to find evidence of this six-allele repeat polymorphism in a Japanese ASD cohort.

- Lauritsen et al. (2002), in their review of medical co-morbidities, suggest that the literature states that anywhere between 0.2 per cent and 14 per cent of ASD cases are found to have NF1, and note that Mouridsen et al. (1992) had suggested a weighted probability of 1.8 per cent.

- Marui et al. (2004a), although failing to confirm the link found by Mbarek et al. (2000), did identify differences in NF1 allele distribution in 74 autistic subjects compared to 122 controls, suggesting a pattern that could be consistent with increased susceptibility.

- A paper from the Czech Republic (Havlovicova et al. 2007) describes a young girl with atypical autism, hyperactivity, distractibility, learning disability (IQ 45), mild dysmorphic features, growth retardation and epilepsy. Genetic testing showed her to have a mosaic ring chromosome 17.

Genetic testing: Large or complete NF1 gene deletions are seen in 1–4 per cent of cases (Kluwe et al. 2004) and can be assessed using various techniques (Wimmet et al. 2006). These are tested for when suspected clinically from maternal transmission, the early appearance of numbers of cutaneous neurofibromas, and associated learning disability (Mensink *et al.* 2006).

There is a positive family history in around half of all cases. Where a parent is positive for an NF1 defect, the risk to siblings is one in two, but where neither parent is affected, the risk is low. Half of the children of someone with NF1 are also likely to be affected.

NF1 is an unusually large gene that has introns coding for several other genes within it.

A large number of genetic variants and types of defect have been described that interfere with the production of neurofibromin, but none has been found in more than a small percentage of families studied (Ars *et al.* 2003). The majority interfere with mRNA splicing (Ars *et al.* 2003).

Differential diagnosis: In someone presenting with a physical phenotype consistent with NF1, and a behavioural phenotype consistent with ASD, several alternative possibilities should be investigated if an NF1 defect is excluded. The conditions most likely to present in this way are the following:

Other ASD-linked phacomatoses:

- Bannayan-Riley-Ruvalcaba syndrome [15]

- Hypomelanosis of Ito [42]

- Noonan syndrome [52]

- Proteus syndrome [62]

- tuberous sclerosis [73]

- LEOPARD syndrome (a condition genetically related to Noonan syndrome but with skin pigment changes)

- Klippel-Trenaunay-Weber syndrome (an overgrowth condition genetically related to Proteus syndrome).

A number of conditions can also present with an NF1 physical phenotype, in particular the following:

Phacomatoses with no known link to ASD:

- Sturge-Weber syndrome (Rodríguez-Bujaldón *et al.* 2008)

- neurofibromatosis type II (Nowak 2007)

- homozygosity for one of the genes for hereditary non-polyposis colon cancer (Lynch syndrome) caused by a defect in MSH2 (Ostergaard, Sunde and Okkels 2005)

- Schwannomatosis (MacCollin *et al.* 2003)

- multiple café-au-lait spots (Hoo and Shrimpton 2005)

- McCune-Albright syndrome (Zacharin 2007)

- multiple endocrine neoplasia type 2B

- multiple lipomatosis

- juvenile hyaline fibromatosis

- congenital generalized fibromatosis
- Weaver syndrome
- multiple intradermal naevi.

A number of cases have been reported with an NF1 genotype but without an NF1 or NF1-like phenotype:

- a two-year-old boy has been reported with encephalocraniocutaneous lipomatosis (Fishman syndrome) (Legius *et al*. 1995)
- there have been reports of three families with multiple spinal neurofibromas, but without café-au-lait spots (Kaufmann *et al*. 2001; Kluwe *et al*. 2003)
- there has been a report of a man with an isolated optic glioma but no other NF1 diagnostic features (Buske *et al*. 1999).

Around one in 19 cases that present with an NF1 genotype have a phenotype which is similar to Noonan syndrome [52] (De Luca *et al*. 2005; Huffmeier *et al*. 2006). The genetic bases for this association are not fully understood, and more than one possible mechanism has been identified (Bertola *et al*. 2005; Carey 1998).

Treatment and management: The wide variation in presenting phenotype and clinical progression seen in NF1 does not lead to a simple approach to assessment, monitoring or management.

Routine initial evaluation should include a standard medical history, paying particular attention to family history and clinical features of NF1; a detailed physical examination with particular attention to the skin; and assessment of vision and optic nerve function, skeleton, cardiovascular system, and central nervous system. A neurodevelopmental assessment is also recommended. Some authorities also recommend EEG, brain MRI, body X-rays, brainstem auditory evoked potentials and audiography (Riccardi 1999). Aspects that show abnormality should be subject to regular review.

The cosmetic aspects of NF1 are often the most distressing to those who are affected (Wolkenstein *et al*. 2000). However, response to surgical removal of plexiform neurofibromas can be poor, with a tendency for these to recur (Gottfried *et al*. 2006).

The development of several of the associated lesions seen in NF1 is often slower than would otherwise be expected. This is true of optic gliomas and of brainstem and cerebellar gliomas, and complicates the approach to management. A static picture or slower progression of optic gliomas is well documented in several series (Czyzyk *et al*. 2003), and spontaneous regression has been noted in a number of papers (Parsa *et al*. 2001; Perilongo *et al*. 1999; Rosser and Packer 2002; Zizka, Elias and Jakubec 2001). This complicates decisions concerning best management (Sylvester, Drohan and Sergott 2006). Similarly, brainstem and cerebellar astrocytomas develop less rapidly than normal (Rosser and Packer 2002). There are also reports of spontaneous improvement (Leisti, Pyhtinen and Poyhonen 1996; Rosser and Packer 2002; Schmandt *et al*. 2000).

The number and size of neuofibromas may increase during pregnancy (Dugoff and Sujansky 1996). This is thought to be due to increased production of lysophosphatidic acid through the pregnancy, a factor that increases the migration and survival of

Schwann cells (Nebesio *et al.* 2007). Hypertension may begin during, or be exacerbated by, pregnancy.

The use of radiation therapy has been found to accelerate the development of malignant peripheral nerve sheath tumours (Evans *et al.* 2002; Sharif *et al.* 2006) so should be considered with caution.

Therapies under investigation: A number of medical treatments for plexiform and spinal neurofibromas are under investigation (Liebermann and Korf 1999; Packer and Rosser 2002; Packer *et al.* 2002). These include pirfenidone, medication that inhibits collagen synthesis and blocks fibroblast proliferation (Babovic-Vuksanovic *et al.* 2006); tifiparnib, which interferes with RAS protein function (Widemann *et al.* 2006); and surgical intervention (Gottfried *et al.* 2006).

The diffuse plexiform neurofibromas that can be found on the face in some cases have been shown to respond to treatment with radiofrequency therapy (Baujat *et al.* 2006).

There has been considerable interest in the possible use of statins in treating the cognitive difficulties seen in NF1, however, preliminary published results show no evidence of benefit (Krab *et al.* 2008).

Preliminary evidence suggests that interfering with the suppression of neurofibromin (using imatinib mesylate (Gleevec)) may limit the development of neurofibromas through enabling the functioning of rasGTPase (see, for example, Trovo-Marqui and Tajara 2006).

A useful listing of ongoing clinical therapeutic trials can be found on the Children's Tumor Foundation website at www.ctf.org.

Further information and support:

In Australia:
Neurofibromatosis Association of Australia
PO Box 603
Lindfield
New South Wales
NSW 2070
Tel. 61 2 94166244
E-mail: info@nfaa.org.au
Website: www.nfaa.org.au

In the UK:
The Neurofibromatosis Association
Quayside House
38 High Street
Kingston on Thames
Surrey
KT1 1HL
Tel.: 020 8439 1234
Fax: 020 8439 1200
Helpline: 0845 602 4173
Minicom: 020 8481 0492
E-mail: nfa@zetnet.co.uk
Website: www.nfauk.org

In the USA:
The Children's Tumor Foundation
95 Pine Street,
16th Floor
New York
NY 10005
Tel: 212-344-6633
Toll free at 1-800-323-7938
E-mail: info@ctf.org
Website: www.ctf.org

Neurofibromatosis, Inc.
PO Box 18246
Minneapolis
MN 55418
Tel.: 301-918-4600/800-942-6825
E-mail: link through website
Website: www.nfinc.org/index.shtml
Understanding NF1, a resource about neurofibromatosis 1 for parents, patients and carers, can be accessed at www.understandingnf1.org/index.html.

52

Noonan syndrome (NS)

Gene loci: SOS1 at 2p22–p21; PTPN11 at 12q24.1; KRAS at 12p12.1

Key ASD references: Ghaziuddin, Bolyard and Alessi 1994; Paul, Cohen and Volkmar 1983

The first described case of NS may have been a 20-year-old German male described in the late nineteenth century (Kobylinski 1883).

NS is named after Jacqueline Anne Noonan, an American paediatric cardiologist who, together with Dorothy Ehmke, described the condition in six boys and three girls in a conference abstract in 1963. All cases were of short stature, with pulmonary stenosis, hypertelorism and abnormal skeletal development. In 1968 she described 19 cases with this clinical phenotype. They were reported as resembling Turner syndrome but without the obvious karyotype. The term 'Noonan syndrome' was first used in a conference abstract published in 1965 (Opitz *et al.* 1965).

For a historical overview of our understanding of the condition, see Noonan (2002).

How common is NS? The best current estimates of prevalence are one in 1,000–2,500 (Sharland *et al.* 1992; Tartaglia and Gelb 2005).

NS appears to be equally common in males and females.

Main clinical features:

Feeding difficulties are common in early life

- low-normal short stature is typically reported, but growth is slower than normal

- ocular abnormalities

- congenital heart defects (typically pulmonary stenosis, but more complex problems are reported) and ECG abnormalities are common, even without apparent structural defects

- broad or webbed neck (*pterygium colli*)

- unusual chest shape with protrusion of the upper part and intrusion of the lower portion – sometimes called a 'shield-shaped' chest

- apparently low-set nipples

- cryptorchidism in males

- characteristic facies, which become less obvious with age, include a low hairline, epicanthic folds, low-set, backward-turned ears, wide-spaced, blue/blue-green eyes and small lower jaw

- blood clotting problems, easy bruising and lymphatic dysplasias are common features

- renal problems are seen in around ten per cent of cases

- café-au-lait spots are noted in some cases.

A study of 48 children with NS found a mean IQ of 84, with 25 per cent have learning difficulties (Lee D.A. *et al.* 2005). Approximately 50 per cent show evidence of motor clumsiness (Henderson 1987). Between 10 and 15 per cent are placed in special education (Sharland *et al.* 1992; van der Burgt *et al.* 1999).

Speech difficulties are seen in around two-thirds of cases, and typically respond well to speech therapy (Allanson 1987).

Lee D.A. *et al.* (2005) were unable to identify any consistent behavioural phenotype associated with NS.

Effects on male sexual development are varied. In girls, onset of menstruation tends to be late, but fertility appears to be normal (Sharland *et al.* 1992).

Inheritance is autosomal dominant. An affected parent is identified in 35–40 per cent of cases, and the rest arise *de novo*. There is a 50 per cent risk that a child of someone with NS will be similarly affected. In all cases reported to date where the condition has been inherited, it has been inherited from the father (Tartaglia *et al.* 2004), predominantly to male offspring, and correlated with older paternal age than in other Noonan cases.

Where a mutation in the presenting case has been found, parents should be screened, and if a parent tests positive, siblings should also be screened, as they will be at 50 per cent risk. Children of the individual will also be at 50 per cent risk of being similarly affected.

Is there a link between NS and ASD?

- Paul, Cohen and Volkmar (1983) reported on a boy with NS who had a severe learning disability, communication disorder, limited social interest and motor stereotypies, and who was described as having autistic features.

- Ghaziuddin, Bolyard and Alessi (1994) describe NS co-morbidity with mild learning disability and ASD.

As few cases have been described with both the NS phenotype and ASD, and these predate genetic screening, it is unclear whether there is an association with any of the three NS susceptibility sites. At the present time, there are no clear phenotypic features that discriminate between the three genotypes found in NS.

Although Noonan syndrome appears in many review papers on genetic syndromes associated with ASD, it is difficult to tell from the cases reported to date whether the association is greater than chance.

Standard karyotyping gives normal results. On molecular genetic testing, 50 per cent of cases test positive for PTPN11 abnormalities at 12q24.1, ten per cent for abnormalities of SOS1 at 2p22–p21, and five per cent for abnormalities of KRAS at 12p12.1 (Schubbert *et al.* 2006). Tests for all three sites are available on a clinical basis, and would be screened for based on the clinical phenotype – so currently some 65 per cent of phenotypic cases carry one of the three gene markers so far identified.

Differential diagnosis: The principal differential diagnoses are Aarskog syndrome [8]; neurofibromatosis type 1 [51]; Turner syndrome [74]; and Williams syndrome [77].

LEOPARD syndrome overlaps clinically with NS, and has also been shown to result from a PTPN11 mutation (Legius *et al.* 2002).

Three other rare conditions show phenotypic overlap: cardiofaciocutaneous (CFC) syndrome (Rodriguez-Viciana *et al.* 2006); Watson syndrome (Allanson *et al.* 1991); and Costello syndrome (Troger *et al.* 2003).

Treatment and management: Multiple organ systems that can be involved should be assessed. After initial diagnosis, baseline assessments of growth, cardiac and renal function, vision, hearing and central nervous system are required.

The cardiovascular abnormalities in NS can be managed as for others with the same heart problems. Summaries of the surgical cardiac issues in NS are reviewed in Formigari *et al.* (2008).

Results of growth hormone supplementation studies show that this is an effective approach to increasing adult height in NS (Noordam *et al.* 2008; Ogawa *et al.* 2004).

In view of the blood and liver problems that are often seen, medications that affect blood clotting should only be used under medical advice.

Speech therapy is required in around two-thirds of cases, and is of established benefit (Allanson 1987) and up to one in four people with NS will require special educational placement.

Further information and support:

In the UK:
Noonan Syndrome Society
Unit 5
Brindly Business Park
Chase Side Drive
Cannock
Staffordshire
WS11 1GD
Tel.: 08700 70 70 20 (helpline);
01543 468888 (admin);
01543 468999

In the USA:
The Noonan Syndrome Support Group
PO Box 145
Upperco
MD 21155
Tel.: 888-686-2224; 410-374-5245
E-mail: info@noonansyndrome.org
Website: www.noonansyndrome.org

Human Growth Foundation
997 Glen Cove Avenue
Suite 5
Glen Head
NY 11545
Tel.: 800-451-6434
Fax: 516-671-4055
E-mail: hgf1@hgfound.org
Website: www.hgfound.org

The MAGIC Foundation
6645 West North Avenue
Oak Park
IL 60302
Tel.: 800-362-4423; 708-383-0808
Fax: 708-383-0899
E-mail: info@magicfoundation.org
Website: www.magicfoundation.org

53

NAPDD

Gene locus: Not known

Key ASD references: Page 2000; Page *et al.* 1997

The acronym NAPDD stands for **N**ucleotidase-**A**ssociated **P**ervasive **D**evelopmental **D**isorder. The first use of the term appears in a paper in 1997 (Page *et al.* 1997).

A nucleotidase is an enzyme that catalyses the hydrolysis of a nucleotide into a nucleoside and a phosphate. In this case, the affected nucleotidase catalyses purines and pyrimidines. In addition, nucleotidases are key components in a range of cellular functions such as cell–cell communication, DNA repair, purine salvage, signal transduction, and membrane transport.

NAPDD may constitute the basis for a hypouricosuric form of 'purine autism'. Hyperuricosuric forms (with elevated rather than lowered uric acid and urate levels) have also been documented (Page and Coleman 2000).

How common is NAPDD? At the time of writing, the frequency of this condition is unknown. To date it has only been reported by one clinical group working in Southern California.

Main clinical features: A variety of behavioural and physical features have been reported to characterize those with NAPDD: extreme hyperactivity, impulsiveness, absent or greatly delayed speech, abnormal social interaction, seizures, ataxia and frequent infections.

Is there a link between NAPDD and ASD? By definition, all NAPDD cases fulfil criteria for ASD; however, the prevalence of NAPDD within the ASD population is not established.

- Page *et al.* (1997) described four cases, and the review of metabolic factors in autism (Page 2000) documents a number of further cases, but without detailed case information. No independent reports of cases have so far been published in the literature.

Metabolic differences in cytosolic 5' nucleotidase activity have been reported in this group (Trifilio and Page 2000).

Differential diagnosis: The principal differential diagnoses are other ASD conditions that result in hyperactivity, ataxia, seizures and infection. At the present time, other than on metabolic assessment, NAPDD is not sufficiently well characterized to provide clear criteria for different diagnosis.

Treatment and management: NAPDD is potentially important in view of the apparent response to treatment. In a small, double-blinded, placebo-controlled trial of uridine in four cases, remarkable improvement in speech and behaviour were reported, with a decrease in both seizure activity and frequency of infection. There was rapid regression on all parameters when on placebo (Page *et al.* 1997). In a review of treatment approaches, Page (2000) notes a further eight clinical cases with varying degrees of benefit from uridine. A single case report of treatment over a two-year period with reversals resulting in behavioural deterioration was also published (Page and Moseley 2002). The way in which uridine operates is currently unclear. It could be through its effects on dopamine receptor function.

In his review, Page (2000) notes other treatments to have been of some benefit, including intravenous immunoglobulin and a combined treatment with ribose, uridine-5 monophosphate and cetyl myristoeate. These are commented on *passim* with no referencing.

As the 5-nucleotidases act to regulate nucleotide and drug metabolism, the implications for various aspects of management may be fairly broad-ranging (Hunsucker, Mitchell and Spychala 2005).

Further information and support:

There is a support group for 'purine autism' that provides information and support:
The Purine Research Society
E-mail: purine@erols.com
Website: www.purineresearchsociety.org

In the UK:
Purine Metabolic Patients' Association (PUMPA)
Purine Research Laboratories
3rd Floor Block
7 South Wing
St Thomas' Hospital
Lambeth Palace Road
London
SE1 7EH
E-mail: info@pumpa.org.uk
Website: www.pumpa.org.uk/index.php

More general support should be available through the following:

In the UK:
Unique
Rare Chromosome Disorder Support Group
P.O. Box 2189
Surrey
CR3 5GN
Telephone helpline: 01883 330766
E-mail: info@rarechromo.org
Website: www.rarechromo.org/

In the USA:
National Organization for Rare Disorders (NORD)
55 Kenosia Avenue
PO Box 1968
Danbury,
CT 06813-1968
Tel.: 203-744-0100
Website: www.rarediseases.org/info/contact.html

54

Oculocutaneous albinism (OCA)

Gene loci: Type 1 (TYR): 11q14.3

Type 2 (OCA2): 15q11.2–q12; 16q24.3

Type 3 (TYRP1): 9p23

Type 4 (MAT P): 5p13.3

Key ASD references: Bakare and Ikegwuonu 2008; Ornitz, Guthrie and Farley 1977; Rogawski, Funderburk and Cederbaum 1978

OCA is one of a number of 'inborn errors of metabolism' first described in 1908 by Sir Archibald Garrod (see Garrod 1909). It is an error in the production and/or distribution of melanin, primarily in the skin, hair and visual system of the affected individual. Melanin is produced from the essential amino acid tyrosine.

A review of OCA can be found in Grønskov, Ek and Brondum-Nielsen (2007), and more specifically of OCA2 in King and Oetting (2007).

How common is OCA? There are four main forms of OCA. In total, the best estimate is that the various forms of OCA have a cumulative population prevalence of 7.15 per 100,000 (Orphanet 2008). OCA2 specifically is reported to occur in one in 38,000 to one in 40,000 of the population worldwide. There is a markedly higher prevalence in African and African-American populations, being found in between one in 1,500 and one in 8,000 (Lund *et al.* 1997; Spritz *et al.* 1995; Stevens *et al.* 1995; Stevens, Ramsay and Jenkins 1997).

Main clinical features: OCA is characterized by reduced skin, iris and hair pigmentation, and a number of specific ocular changes. The iris is light coloured – typically blue or grey, but can be brown. Nystagmus and increased translucency of the iris are seen. The fovea is hypoplastic, resulting in reduced visual acuity (Creel, O'Donnell and Witkop 1978). A number of features are due to the misrouting of the optic nerves through the optic chiasma, with alternating strabismus, a consequent reduction in stereoscopic vision, and altered visual evoked potentials (Bouzas *et al.* 1994).

In OCA2, there is some degree of pigmentation that develops with age, while in the type 1 (TYR) form there is a complete lack of pigmentation.

Those with OCA have normal levels of intelligence, normal life expectancy and fertility.

Is there a link between OCA and ASD?

- The first mention of OCA in ASD is in a paper by Ornitz, Guthrie and Farley in 1977. They noted OCA in one four-year-old boy in a retrospective analysis of the early development in a series of 74 young autistic children.

- Rogawski, Funderburk and Cederbaum (1978) published a paper detailing the association in two further autistic boys.

- In 2007, Robert DeLong reported a link between GABA A receptor differences, parent-of-origin effects and OCA in some cases of ASD.

- Bakare and Ikegwuonu (2008) reported on a 13-year-old Nigerian boy with ASD, who clearly presents with the OCA2 form.

It seems likely that the cases of OCA reported in association with ASD are type 2. This form results from a lack of a tyrosine transporter referred to as polypeptide P, and does not lack tyrosinase, the enzyme that converts tyrosine to melanin and which is missing in the type 1 form.

This suggests a possible common mechanism for the development of ASD in OCA, Angelman [11] and Prader-Willi [61] syndromes and Hypomelanosis of Ito, due to a common genetic mechanism in the 15q11 region. It is possible that the common mechanism involves dysfunction of the GABA A receptor alpha-5 polypeptide that has been mapped to 15q11.2–q12 and implicated in Angelman and Prader-Willi syndromes (Wagstaff *et al.* 1991) and in OCA2 (DeLong 2007). We will not provide any detail here on types 1, 3 and 4 of OCA, which are reviewed in Grønskov, Ek and Brondum-Nielsen (2007).

Differential diagnosis: Angelman syndrome [11], Hypomelanosis of Ito [42] and Prader-Willi syndrome [61] can all present with hypopigmentation. Each, like OCA2, can result from a 15q11 defect, and all can be found with ASD.

The other conditions which present with hypopigmentation (Hermansky-Pudlak syndrome, Chediak-Higashi syndrome, Griscelli syndrome, and Waardenburg syndrome type II) have not been reported in ASD.

Treatment and management: The principal issues in treatment and ongoing management of OCA2 are twofold (see Grønskov, Ek and Brondum-Nielsen 2007).

1. *The skin:* low levels of pigmentation make those affected more prone to sunburn and could increase the risk of skin cancers without adequate precautions such as hats, adequate sunscreen, and clothing that blocks ultraviolet light.

2. *Eye problems:*

- lack of iris pigmentation results in difficulties in coping with bright light, which can be helped with the use of dark glasses or tinted contact lenses

- poor visual acuity – because of the poor development of the fovea, visual acuity is typically poor and corrective glasses are usually required

- nystagmus (oscillating rhythmic eye movements) may improve with contact lenses, or may require surgery to the eye muscles

- strabismus (where the eyes are not focused on the same point) can respond to eye patching to encourage better use of the non-dominant eye

It is possible that specific GABA receptor-based treatment strategies will be developed that target the biological defect resulting in autism. Such a treatment would be likely to be of benefit in Angelman syndrome, Prader-Willi syndrome and Hypomelanosis of Ito, in addition to being of benefit in OCA2 cases.

Further information and support:

NOAH
The National Organization for Albinism and Hypopigmentation
PO Box 959
East Hampstead
USA

NH 03826-0959
Tel.: 800-473-2310 (USA and Canada)
Tel.: 603-887-2310 (International)
Fax: 800-648-2310
Website: www.albinism.org

55

Ornithine carbamyltransferase deficiency (OCTD)

aka • ornithine transcarbamylase deficiency

Gene locus: Xp21.1

Key ASD reference: Gorker and Tuzun 2005

Ornithine carbamyltransferase is a nuclear-encoded mitochondrial matrix enzyme on the short arm of the X chromosome that codes for the second enzyme of the urea cycle. OCTD is the most common X-linked disorder of the urea cycle. The principal consequence of this condition is an inability to metabolize the amino acid alanine from protein in the diet.

The molecular basis to the clinical variation observed in the presentation of OCTD is beginning to be unravelled, and shows the likely operation of multi-factorial causes rather than the operation of a single gene abnormality (Tuchman, McCullough and Yudkoff 2000).

How common is OCTD? The best current estimate of prevalence is that OCTD occurs in one in 40,000 of the general population (Wraith 2001).

Main clinical features: The clinical presentation of OCTD is varied. Boys with a full mutation can present with anything from neonatal failure to thrive, encephalopathy and severe hyperammonaemia to chance asymptomatic cases detected in adulthood (Matsuda *et al.* 1996). Boys with later presentation typically present with disturbed behaviour, vomiting and drowsiness (Drogari and Leonard 1988).

In female carriers, the severity of the phenotype is dependent on the extent of inactivation of the affected X chromosome in liver cells, but appears to be independent of peripheral X chromosome status (Yorifuji *et al.* 1998). The extent of hyperammonaemia is correlated with the level of X inactivation of the affected chromosome, in liver but not in peripheral cells.

Well over 300 mutations to the OCT gene have now been reported (Yamaguchi *et al.* 2006).

OCT mosaicism in males has been reported (Maddalena *et al.* 1988). It has been known for a number of years that this can present with 'psychotic' behaviour in response to elevated protein intake (DiMagno *et al.* 1986); however, the prevalence of this is at present not known.

Is there a link between OCTD and ASD?

- A single report to date details the case of a girl with PDD-NOS (pervasive developmental disorder – not otherwise specified) together with aggression and hyperactivity (Gorker and Tuzun 2005). The girl was found to have an ornithine carbamyltransferase deficiency, together with an arginase deficiency.

Differential diagnosis: A number of other inborn errors affect urea cycle metabolism, but to date only one, argininosuccinic acid synthetase, has been reported in association with psychiatric sequelae, in which postpartum psychotic features have been reported (Enns *et al.* 2005).

Other possible factors that can have similar presentation are vascular liver damage and viral liver infection (Summar and Tuchman 2003).

Treatment and management: Useful reviews of treatment can be found in Grompe, Jones and Caskey (1990) and Wraith (2001). Treatment response (typically to protein restriction and citrulline supplementation) in males presenting neonatally are uniformly poor to date. In girls and in later presenting boys, results are more optimistic. Accurate diagnosis and rapid treatment can lead to good recovery from acute encephalopathy (Mak *et al.* 2007).

One paper (Swarts *et al.* 2007) describes an ornithine transcarbamylase deficiency in a 20-month-old boy with Klinefelter's (XYY) syndrome [3]. He showed clinical improvement on a low-protein diet together with benzoate and phenylbutyrate.

In the ASD case reported by Gorker and Tuzun (2005), the girl was treated with a combination of protein restriction, coupled with sodium benzoate and arginine supplementation. After one year of treatment, her hyperactivity and autistic symptoms had resolved.

Further information and support:

In the UK:
Organic Acidaemias UK
5 Saxon Road
Middlesex
TW15 1QL
Tel.: 01784 245989
E-mail: davidpriddy@bigfoot.com

In the USA:
National Urea Cycle Disorders Foundation
4841 Hill Street
La Canada
CA 91011
Tel. 818-790-2460;
800-386-8233
E-mail: info@nucdf.org
Website: www.nucdf.org

National Organization for Rare Disorders (NORD)
55 Kenosia Avenue
PO Box 1968
Danbury,
CT 06813-1968
Toll-free: 800-999-6673 (voicemail only)
Tel.: 203-744-0100
TTY: 203-797-9590
Fax: 203-798-2291
E-mail: orphan@rarediseases.org
Website: www.rarediseases.org

56

Orstavik 1997 syndrome

Gene locus: Not known at the time of writing

Key ASD reference: Orstavik *et al.* 1997; Steiner *et al.* (2003)

The constellation of features reported makes this presentation a candidate for a genetic condition, and it has been discussed as such in a number of reviews on the genetics of ASD. The lack of more detailed biological information and genetic testing makes it impossible to draw any more specific conclusions.

How common is Orstavik 1997 syndrome? As to date only one family pedigree has been reported; the prevalence is unknown.

This condition has been reported to date in a single family pedigree from Norway, with two affected sisters. There was no associated genotype, but the phenotype was felt to constitute a previously unrecognized clinical syndrome.

Main clinical features: Given the small number of reported cases no key criteria can be given. The features in the original reported cases are given below.

Table B56: Features reported in Orstavik 1997 syndrome

	Sister 1	Sister 2
• OFC[1] at birth (cm)	36	34
• birthweight (g)	3,600	2,600
• macrocephaly	From birth and progressive	Small at birth but progressive
• psychomotor delay	Yes	Yes
• epilepsy	Yes	Yes
• autistic features	Yes	Yes
• large forehead	Yes	Yes
• short philtrum	Yes	Yes
• bush eyebrows	Yes	Yes
• additional feature		Coeliac disease

1. Orbito-frontal circumference/head circumference

Sister 2 died at the age of five years, probably from an epileptic seizure. Three similar cases – a pair of eight year old female twins and their four year old brother have been noted in one Brazilian clinic series (Steiner, Guerreiro and Marques-de-Faria 2003), the girls both fulfilled criteria for autism and all had learning disabilities. None was noted to have a seizure problem.

Is there a link between Orstavik 1997 syndrome and ASD?
To date, only five possible cases have been described.

- In the original paper (Orstavik et al 1997), both sisters were described as having psychomotor delay, epilepsy and autistic features in the context of a distinct physical phenotype.

- In the second possible case series documented, three similar cases – a pair of eight year old female twins with ASD and learning disability were described (Steiner, Guerreiro and Marques-de-Faria 2003). Neither girl was noted to have a seizure problem.

Differential diagnosis: Given the paucity of information, differential diagnosis is difficult. The reported phenotype with macrocephaly and epilepsy suggests that Sotos syndrome [68] should be considered as a potential differential diagnosis.

Treatment and management: No specific treatment approaches have been developed.

Further information and support: There is no specific support group, as no further cases have emerged. Should anyone accessing this resource recognize the phenotype in someone they know, the best sources of support would be likely to be the following.

In the UK:
Unique
PO Box 2189
Caterham
Surrey
CR3 5GN
Tel.: 01883 330766
E-mail: info@rarechromo.org

In the USA:
National Organization for Rare Disorders (NORD)
55 Kenosia Avenue
PO Box 1968
Danbury,
CT 06813-1968
Tel.: 203-744-0100
Toll-free: 800-999-6673 (voicemail only)
TDD Number: 203-797-9590
Fax: 203-798-2291
E-mail: orphan@rarediseases.org
Website: www.rarediseases.org/info/contact.html

57

Phenylketonuria (PKU)

aka • Folling disease

  • *imbecillitas phenylpyruvica* (historical)

  • *oligophrenica phenylpyruvica* (historical)

Gene locus: 12q24.1

Key ASD references: Baieli *et al.* 2003; Chen and Hsiao 1989; Lowe *et al.* 1980; Miladi *et al.* 1992

Although in Europe and North America PKU autism is now largely of historical interest, the general mechanisms involved still appear to be implicated in some cases, and in countries where screening is not routine, new cases continue to be reported. The Guthrie heelstick blood test is administered to all neonates, in most of Western Europe and North America, usually within the first three days after birth, allowing the early introduction of a special 'phenylalanine-free' diet thus avoiding any major developmental problems.

The classic form of PKU is an autosomal recessive condition, with most variation being due to the individual being heterozygous for a mutant allele. It is an inborn error of metabolism first identified in Norway by the paediatrician Asbjörn Folling in 1934 (Folling 1934; see Centerwall and Centerwall 2000). He used a ferric chloride urine test (this normally turns reddish-brown in response to the presence of ketones) on two children with unexplained developmental problems. The test unexpectedly, and repeatedly, turned green – a previously unrecorded reaction. Subsequent analysis of urine, collected faithfully over several months from the two children, Liv and Dag Egeland, led to identification of the compound causing the effect: phenylpyruvic acid. Folling used the terms *imbecillitas phenylpyruvica* and *oligophrenica phenylpyruvica* for the condition.

Penrose and Questel suggested the term phenylketonuria in 1937. Several years later, Jervis (1947) identified the metabolic problem as an inability to oxidize phenylalanine in order to convert it to tyrosine.

PKU is typically caused by a defect in the gene at 12q24.1 involved in the production of the liver-specific enzyme phenylalanine hydroxylase (PAH). Failure to produce phenylalanine hydroxylase results in a problem in metabolizing the amino acid phenylalanine, with a build-up of circulating levels and a condition known as hyperphenylalaninaemia if below a clinical cut-off level for PKU, or phenylketonuria if above this level. Phenylalanine hydroxylase requires a further compound, 6(R)-erythro-5,6,7,8-tetrahydrobiopterin (BH4), to function.

Guthrie (1996) discusses the introduction of newborn screening for PKU. The test had been developed in the early 1960s (Guthrie and Susi 1963). The first recorded case of a phenylalanine-restricted diet being used to improve the condition of a child with PKU and learning disability is well described in three papers by Bickel and colleagues (Bickel 1996). Use of a phenylalanine-restricted casein hydrolysate feed resulted in dramatic improvement in the status of a girl patient at the University Children's Hospital in Zurich in 1949. Low phenylalanine diets have proved highly successful, but are also unpalatable.

The first PKU mutation identified was a single base change in the PAH gene, and over 400 PAH mutation variants have now been reported.

How common is PKU? PKU has major variations in ethnic and geographical distribution. It is reportedly rare in Ashkenazi Jewish populations. It occurs in one in 100,000 of the Finnish population. In Switzerland it is seen in one in 16,000. In the USA incidence is around one in 8,000 and in Scotland one in 5,550. The rate in Western Poland is one in 5,000 and in Ireland the rate is quoted as one in 4,500, with similar rates reported in Lithuania. In Turkey, which has the highest reported rate, one in 2,600 are affected.

From ten years of newborn-screening data collected in Maryland, PKU affects some one in 50,000 US Black nationals. This is one third of the rate seen in Caucasians.

In a Kuwaiti series, seven cases of PKU were identified in a residential population of 451 learning-disabled people (1.9 per cent of that population).

The gene abnormalities that cause PKU also vary – 80 per cent of Chinese and Japanese cases are caused by the same haplotype 4 defects, while in Europe a wider variety of mechanisms are seen. The range of PAH mutant alleles also varies markedly in Turkish families compared to those from northern European countries. The major haplotypes associated with severe PKU in Caucasian populations are not seen in the Polynesian population.

In the UK, a large proportion of those with PKU are from families originating from Ireland and the West of Scotland. There is a great diversity of PAH-causing mutations in the UK populations. Some of the mutations seen in these Celtic populations are also found in Norwegian families. Whether this indicates an influence of Celtic mutations on the Norwegian population, or of Viking mutations on the Celts, has been the subject of much debate.

Main clinical features: In addition to possible ASD, a number of other features characterize untreated or later-treated PKU cases (Paine 1957; Vanli *et al.* 2006) – learning disability; the presence of a 'mousey' odour (caused by the excretion of phenylacetic acid); hypopigmentation; unusual gait, stance and sitting posture; eczema; and epilepsy (Paine 1957).

It is well known that the cognitive profiles of those with PKU reflect their level of dietary control, with control at age two being a reasonable predictor of later IQ (Griffiths *et al.* 2000).

Cases of PKU that are unresponsive to low phenylalanine diet and developed neurological problems have been reported for several decades (Danks 1978). The mechanisms, typically involving BH4 deficiency, have slowly been unravelled (Dhond *et al.* 1981).

BH4 acts as a co-factor in the conversion of phenylalanine into tyrosine. It is also essential in the regulation of tyrosine and tryptophan hydroxylase, and involved in the rate-limiting steps in the production of the neurotransmitters dopamine, norepinephrine, epinephrine and serotonin (Pearl *et al.* 2005).

BH4 deficiency causes severe developmental problems, and responds to supplementation. It should be screened for in all neonates with persistent levels of phenylalanine elevation unresponsive to diet (Smith M. 2006).

A study of BH4 in the treatment of PKU (Matalon *et al.* 2004) produced positive responses to oral supplementation in 21 of 36 (58.3 per cent) cases. A single daily dose of 10 mg/kg resulted in a reduction of over 30 per cent in blood phenylalanine levels.

BH4 is able to prevent the rapid breakdown of the PAH variants produced by a number of the milder PKU and phenylalaninaemic variants (Pey *et al.* 2004).

Pterin levels are also reported as elevated in the ASD population (Harrison and Pheasant 1995; Messahel *et al.* 1998), and there is a literature on the use of BH4 in the treatment of individuals with ASD.

An open clinical study found marked-to-moderate clinical improvement in 52/97 ASD cases on dosages of 1–3mg/kg/per day, significantly improving social, language and cognitive functioning with follow-up over a period up to two years (Takesada *et al.* 1992).

A further study has reported improvements in social functioning and eye contact in a (N=6) group of 3–5-year-olds treated over a three-month period and monitored with standardized measures (Fernell *et al.* 1997).

There is some preliminary evidence from one small, double-blind, randomized controlled trial (N=12) for significant benefits in social interaction from BH4 supplementation in children who had lowered pre-treatment CSF levels of BH4 (Danfors *et al.* 2005).

There is a clear association between tyrosine levels and phenylalanine metabolism, with low tyrosine levels in PKU that may impact on neurotransmitter levels. This is well illustrated in one study of PKU plasma tyrosine levels (Hanley *et al.* 2000):

Table B57.1: Plasma tyrosine levels in phenylketonuria (PKU)

	Non-fasting plasma tyrosine level	N
• classical PKU	41.1 micromol/litre	99
• mild PKU	53.3 micromol/litre	26
• mild hyperphenylalaninaemia	66.6 micromol/litre	35
• non-PKU controls (hospital data)	64.0 micromol/litre	102
• private practice volunteers	69.1 micromol/litre	58
• literature values for infants, children and adolescents[1]	64–78.8 micromol/litre	

1 Literaure values are the range of reported values in the published literature for normal subjects.

Disturbances to tyrosine levels are reported in ASD; however, both elevated (Aldred *et al.* 2003) and lowered (Arnold *et al.* 2003) plasma levels have been reported, and no attempt has been made to date to link these findings to genetic factors, or to the severity of ASD. It would be interesting to know if the BH4-responsive cases had abnormal tyrosine levels.

BH4 responsiveness seems to characterize a high proportion of those approximately 50 per cent of patients with mild hyperphenylalaninaemia (elevated levels of phenylalanine that are below the clinical cut-off for PKU) or with mild phenylketonuria (above the clinical cut-off level but at the low end of the clinical distribution). Some 87 per cent of cases in one series (N=31) showed lowered blood phenylalanine levels, while none of seven classical PKU cases reported derived benefit (Muntau *et al.* 2002). Erlandsen and

Stevens (2001) suggested that BH4-responsive patients might have missense mutations of the phenylalanine hydroxylase gene.

With current screening methods, few PKU cases are missed and those cases typically show evidence of learning disability. In one large 'post-Guthrie test introduction' screening study of 280,919 adults (Levy *et al.* 1970), only three previously unknown cases with PKU were identified, all with a learning disability.

In addition to a 12q24.1 gene defect, a number of other factors can cause a build-up of phenylalanine (Scriver *et al.* 1994). For example, GTP cyclohydrolase deficiency; 6-pyruvoyl-tetrahydropterin synthase deficiency; dihydropteridine reductase deficiency and pterin-4α carbinolamine dehydratase deficiency all typically result in PKU levels of serum phenylalanine, but are unresponsive to a PKU diet.

More detail on specific conditions and tetrahydrobiopterin deficiencies can be obtained from the commercially sponsored site www.bh4.org/BH4_Start.asp.

Hyperphenylalaninaemia, a milder problem than classical PKU, breeds true in families, with phenylalanine hydroxylase levels around five per cent of normal being found on liver biopsy (Kaufman, Max and Kang 1975).

Is there a link between PKU and ASD?

* An early paper suggested a link between PKU and autism: Lowe *et al.* (1980) screened 65 children with ASDs and found three with untreated PKU. The three children with PKU showed symptomatic and developmental improvement when placed on phenylalanine-free diets. With screening, such cases have become far less common. Occasional single case reports have been published. In 1989, a case report of a 12-year-old Chinese boy with autism who was discovered to have PKU on clinical investigation was published (Chen and Hsiao 1989). In 1992, a three-and-a-half-year-old Tunisian girl with autism was also found to have PKU on clinical investigation (Miladi *et al.* 1992).

Two studies have suggested that the ASD link is with poor dietary control, rather than being an obligatory link with having a gene defect in phenylalanine hydroxylase:

* First, a paper published in 2003 (Baieli *et al.* 2003) screened 243 patients with various levels of PKU and milder forms of hyperphenylalaninaemia for possible ASD. Only two cases who met criteria for ASD were identified; both were male, and both were late-diagnosed.

* Second, in one case series from Turkey (Vanli *et al.* 2006), 15 out of 146 PKU cases (10.27 per cent) were found to be autistic. All of the autistic children from this group were late-diagnosed and late-treated. Only 47 of the children in this series received treatment before two months of age, 70 per cent of whom were of normal cognitive ability, while only three of those who received later treatment (three per cent) were functioning normally. As the authors point out, their cases appear to have more severe problems than some other reported groups, and this may reflect a severity bias in their population that led to paediatric neurology referral.

PKU no longer causes autism or learning disability where universal neonatal screening and appropriate dietary management supports are in place and adhered to.

In a study comparing well and poorly controlled PKU cases to those with high functioning ASD and a further group with closed head injuries (Dennis *et al.* 1999), the closest similarity was between those with poorly controlled PKU and those with ASD. Both groups showed relatively good performance on block design (a visuo-spatial constructional task) compared to comprehension. This profile has been well documented in the ASD population (Shah and Frith 1993). No attempt has so far been made to match this finding to phenylalanine hydroxylase levels in ASD.

Maternal phenylketonuria: Poor dietary control during the pregnancy of women with PKU can result in developmental problems in their offspring. As more women with PKU and lesser variant PAH defects are now developing normally and having children, this has become a significant clinical issue. (For an early discussion, see Komrower *et al.* 1979.) One study has shown a clear association between poorer dietary control during pregnancy and poorer developmental outcome in the children of mothers with PKU (Maillot *et al.* 2008), an effect which was found even when maternal phenylalanine levels were within the target range for good control.

Huntley and Stevenson (1969) described two sisters with PKU who had a total of 28 pregnancies. Of these, 16 ended in spontaneous foetal loss within the first trimester. All of the babies they carried to term were growth retarded with microcephaly, and 75 per cent had associated cardiac malformations.

In one study of five children born to mothers who had PKU and who were poorly controlled through pregnancy, compared to two siblings of a mother with well-controlled PKU (Levy *et al.* 1996), there was evidence of underdevelopment of the corpus callosum in the poorly controlled cases, but there was evidence, in all cases, of behavioural effects such as hyperactivity, irrespective of pregnancy control.

The Maternal Phenylketonuria Collaborative Study (MPKUCS) reported in 1997 on a collaborative study of children born to mothers with PKU (Rouse *et al.* 1997). The frequency of malformations such as congenital heart defects, small head size and facial anomalies rose with maternal phenylalanine levels in the earlier stages, and of neurological involvement with higher levels through the pregnancy.

A further report from the MPKUCS (Guttler *et al.* 1999) reported findings concerning genetic makeup, biochemical phenotype, and IQ in females with phenylalanine hydroxylase deficiency. In a series of 222 hyperphenylalaninaemic mothers, a total of 84 different PAH mutations were identified, with an association between the mutation type and severity of their clinical presentation.

A further report from the MPKUCS (Levy *et al.* 2001) reported on 416 babies born to PKU pregnancies, with 14 per cent of the 235 cases with poor metabolic control through the first two months having congenital heart disease, compared to one in 100 non-PKU controls, and one of 50 hyperphenylalaninaemic cases.

Phenylalanine control through pregnancy, genotype and developmental outcome were studied in a large group of 354 pregnant women with PKU (Rouse *et al.* 2000). Thirty-one of the resulting infants had congenital heart disease and 17 had microcephaly. Both problems were strongly associated with poor control of phenylalanine levels through pregnancy, and all of those affected had been the result of poor control over the first two months.

In a large study of 149 children with PKU and 33 with hyperphenylalaninaemia (Waisbren *et al.* 2000), using a standardized IQ scale at four years, children were compared on the basis of stage of pregnancy when metabolic control was gained: later control correlated with poorer performance. Where maternal control was achieved before conception, IQ was normal for age (IQ 99, normal range 85–115). Where control had not been achieved by five months post-conception, IQ averaged 70 or below, with 30 per cent showing social and behavioural problems. The link here may be due to poorer dietary control being exercised by more stressed families (Olsson, Montgomery and Alm 2007; Walter *et al.* 2002), emphasizing the need for good medical and family supports in such circumstances.

In a study of 15 adolescent patients with good dietary control, abnormalities on structural MRI brain scanning were either absent (10) or slight (5) (Ullrich *et al.* 1994). There was no association between blood phenylalanine levels, age or sex and MRI findings.

Alterations in brain white matter were seen in ten individuals with PKU (15–30 years of age) not adhering to a phenylalanine-free diet, and clinical phenotype was found to correlate with brain concentration of phenylalanine measured by *in vivo* proton magnetic resonance spectroscopy (Leuzzi *et al.* 2000).

In one study of MRI scans of patients with PKU (34 cases, aged 8–33), severity of MRI changes were related both to concurrent plasma phenylalanine levels and, in those not currently on a diet, to time since diet cessation (Thompson *et al.* 1993). Adults who have received effective dietary treatment through childhood continue to show evidence of impaired cerebral metabolism in response to phenylalanine loading (Pietz *et al.* 2003). A study of 27 cases (mean age 27 ± 7 years) and matched controls found an association between grey matter volume and dietary control, with reduced volume correlating with lower IQ and later age at diagnosis. All of these findings are consistent with the fact that in animal studies increased levels of phenylalanine have been shown to increase the turnover of myelin.

Even in those cases with good early dietary control, a variety of brain structures are demonstrably smaller in PKU cases than in controls – in particular, the cerebral cortex, corpus callosum, hippocampus and the pons (Pfaendner *et al.* 2005). These findings are presumably a result of the effects of *in utero* exposure to phenylalanine.

As many as one in ten infants who have a positive Guthrie test result are hyperphenylalaninaemic, as opposed to having classic PKU, and are not currently considered to require dietary treatment. In the Northern Irish population this is typically (in 70 per cent of cases) associated with one particular mutation (T380M) (Zschocke *et al.* 1994).

The phenylalanine hydroxylase locus was identified as 12q22–q24.1 by *in situ* hybridization (Woo *et al.* 1984), allowing for reliable prenatal diagnosis.

A major European collaborative study (Guldberg *et al.* 1998) examined 686 phenylalanine hydroxylase patients from seven centres and looked in more detail at the phenotypic characteristics of 297 functionally hemizygous patients. They were able to demonstrate a close association between the genetic deficit identified and the severity of the resulting clinical phenotype.

Differential diagnosis: The wide use of screening means that most cases are identified in the early neonatal period. The metabolism of phenylalanine is well documented (Williams, Mamotte and Burnett 2008). Differential diagnosis is from other genetic anomalies that interfere with the metabolism of tetrahydrobiopterin (Thöny, Auerbach and Blau 2000).

Treatment and management: Current evidence suggests that it is only when phenylalanine intake is limited prior to conception that foetal damage can be prevented (Drogari *et al.* 1987); however, dietary restriction through pregnancy does limit the extent of damage and developmental problems (Hanley *et al.* 1996). In one UK series, 3/6 babies born to mothers with PKU who exercised dietary control only post-conception had congenital heart disease, with two infants dying from this, while 34/34 babies born to mothers with PKU with good pre-conceptional dietary control had no evidence of heart disease (Brenton and Lilburn 1996).

A range of dietary factors can affect plasma phenylalanine levels. Aspartame, an artificial sweetener, is 50 per cent phenylalanine, 30 per cent aspartic acid and 20 per cent ethanol. Digestion of aspartame frees a significant amount of phenylalanine into the bloodstream. One study (Stegink *et al.* 1989) examined whether aspartame intake from artificially sweetened drinks would affect levels in persons heterozygous for PKU. Moderate and clinically insignificant elevations were seen when measured 30–45 minutes after drinking. A further study (Trefz *et al.* 1994) has shown no effects on cognitive function but significantly increased plasma levels in a double-blinded, placebo-controlled crossover trial. These results suggest that, notwithstanding the minimal effects on the individual, aspartame intake should be minimized through pregnancy to limit the potential effects on the foetus.

In individuals homozygous for PKU; however, the effects of aspartame will be markedly more pronounced (Janssen and van der Heijden 1988).

To date, there have been few studies on the effects on foetal development of dietary factors in hyperphenylalaninaemia. The results to date suggest that, with similar pre-conceptional and antenatal care, the effects are less than with PKU; however, they can still be significant. One survey of 86 affected mothers (all of normal IQ, 47 per cent college graduates) identified PKU in 22 children (13 per cent of the sample), congenital heart disease in four, and other severe anomalies in a further five. For mothers who had phenylalanine levels above 400 micromol/litre, there was a negative association between level and the child's IQ (based on 81 tested children), but all were functioning within the normal IQ range (Levy *et al.* 1995).

No phenylalanine hydroxylase activity or immunoreactive protein was detected in the liver of one foetal case of PKU (Ledley *et al.* 1988). Both compounds could be measured in control specimens of similar gestational age.

One extreme treatment for PKU is liver transplant. This would not normally be considered, given the good response to other treatments and the lack of concomitant liver problems. In one ten-year-old boy with PKU and unrelated cirrhosis, PKU was cured when he underwent a liver transplant to address the cirrhosis (Vajro *et al.* 1993).

In a study comparing ten boys and ten girls who were off-diet but early-treated PKU patients, at age 11 and later at 14, compared to 20 controls matched for age, sex and IQ

(Weglage *et al.* 1999), initial results showed a correlation between neuropsychological performance and blood phenylalanine levels. Follow-up testing, albeit showing continued elevated levels, found that the initial deficits found in the PKU cases were reduced, indicating that central nervous system vulnerability to elevated PKU seems to lessen over time.

In a study of 125 Northern Irish children with either classical PKU or hyperphenylalaninaemia, there was an association between likely reduction of IQ after dietary relaxation and level of residual enzyme activity – the lower the residual activity, the higher the likelihood of cognitive decline on dietary relaxation between ages eight, 14 and 18 (Greeves *et al.* 2000).

A low phenylalanine diet is also typically low in long-chain polyunsaturated fatty acids (LCPUFAs). LCPUFAs are essential for the formation of cell membranes and myelination of the brain and peripheral nervous system. A study of 12-month supplementation with LCPUFAs found enhanced levels of docosahexaenoic acid (DHA), an increase in lipid levels in blood cell membranes, and enhanced visual function on electrophysiological assessment (Agostoni *et al.* 2000). A further study by the same group, published in 2003 (Agostoni *et al.* 2003), found that group differences seen in the first study had disappeared three years after ceasing supplementation.

Another factor that is deficient unless supplemented in those on a PKU diet is carnitine. Carnitine production requires precursors derived from phenylalanine. This seems to be correctable by appropriate oral supplementation (Vilaseca *et al.* 1993). Mild carnitine deficiency has been noted as a general feature in ASD and thought to indicate mitochondrial dysfunction (Filipek *et al.* 2004). Carnitine supplementation has also proven to be beneficial in small-scale trials with Rett syndrome [63a] (Ellaway *et al.* 2001).

An early paper speculated that the reason for developmental problems in PKU, rather than hepatic damage, is that phenylpyruvic acid inhibits the action of pyruvate decarboxylase in the brain, thus interfering with myelin formation and nerve cell development (Bowden and McArthur 1972). This model would be consistent with the beneficial effects of LCPUFA supplementation.

A study by Koch *et al.* (2000) suggests that blood and brain phenylalanine levels can diverge, with low brain and high blood levels being seen in some individuals with normal IQ – the implication being that magnetic resonance spectroscopy may be of use in recommending sensible dietary levels of phenylalanine. In general; however, small fluctuations in phenylalanine level have marked effects on cognitive function, with particular effects being seen on tasks requiring sustained attention and working memory (Huijbregts *et al.* 2002).

Based on a 32-year follow-up study of 68 from an original cohort of 125 children, the long-term maintenance of dietary restriction into adulthood is associated with a lower prevalence of mental health problems (Koch *et al.* 2002). At follow-up, 61 were off-diet and nine were continuing to exercise dietary restriction, so numbers are small – nevertheless, approximately twice the proportion of those off-diet experienced mental health difficulties such as depression and phobias (24/59 vs 2/9).

Table B57.2: Recent developments in treatment for PKU

Mode of action	Therapeutic approach
More palatable phenylalanine-free formulae	New phenylalanine-free formulae (see Macdonald *et al.* 2004)
Reduced intestinal uptake of phenylalanine	Purified phenylalanine ammonia-lyase (for original basis, see Hoskins *et al.* 1980; Kim *et al.* 2004)
Alternative degradation pathways	Recombinant phenylalanine ammonia-lyase (mouse model – Sarkissian *et al.* 1999) Pegylated phenylalanine ammonia-lyase (under development – see Gámez *et al.* 2005; Ikeda *et al.* 2005; Sarkissian and Gámez 2005)
Increasing PAH enzymatic activity	Tetrahydrobiopterin (BH4) supplementation (Matalon *et al.* 2004)
Competitions for blood–brain barrier carriers	Large neutral amino acid supplementation (mouse model – Matalon *et al.* 2003; Koch *et al.* 2003b)
Gene therapy	Low immunogenic vector PAH expression in tissues other than liver (see, for reviews, Ding, Harding and Thöny 2004; dos Santos *et al.* 2006)
Improved cell membrane integrity	Long-chain polyunsaturated fatty acid supplementation (adjunctive) (Agostoni *et al.* 2000)

Expanded and adapted from dos Santos *et al.* 2006.

Giving large, neutral amino acid supplements (supplementing with tyrosine, tryptophan, threonine, isoleucine, leucine, valine, methionine and histidine) could theoretically be of benefit, and is effective in the mouse model, by virtue of the fact that these other amino acids compete for the same transporter mechanism as phenylalanine to cross the blood–brain barrier (Oldendorf and Szabo 1976).

Some supplement regimes can prove problematic in those with phenylalanine-processing difficulties. A 16-year-old with mild hyperphenylalalinaemia developed a range of problems (headache, deteriorating school performance and mild depression) while taking a high-protein bodybuilding supplement. The problems reversed when the supplement was stopped, and further clinical improvement was found with BH4 supplementation (Koch *et al.* 2003a).

It seems likely that high-protein diets in general will be problematic for many with clinical and subclinical phenylalanine difficulties. This could be important for foetal development even in mild hyperphenylalalinaemia, as many factors circulating in the maternal bloodstream are concentrated in foetal blood.

In the UK, the National Society for PKU provides excellent dietary information that can be used by members, in conjunction with a dietician, and information on what is available on prescription. This can all be downloaded from their website at: www.nspku.org.

Summary: PKU is the first example of a treatable inborn error of metabolism. 'Classic' PKU is now a rare cause of ASD, but should be considered where neonatal screening may have been missed. ASD is virtually unknown in early-detected and early-treated PKU. PKU autism provides a clear demonstration of a genetic factor leading to a correctable imbalance which, if not addressed, can lead to ASD. Dietary intervention can produce improvement even after late diagnosis.

There have been a large number of developments in treatment, as outlined above.

Whether lesser variants, such as hyperphenylalaninaemia unmanaged in pregnancy, increase ASD risk has yet to be addressed. From the studies on the effects of poor dietary control coupled with the increased intake of refined foods high in phenylalanine, and the rise in numbers of fertile women with metabolic defects in phenylalanine metabolism, this issue is important to address.

The beneficial effect of BH4 in a range of individuals with both PKU and in ASD suggests that this approach warrants further systematic clinical research.

Further information and support:

In the UK:
The National Society for PKU (NSPKU)
PO Box 26642
London
N14 4ZF
Tel.: 020 8364 3010
Fax: 0845 004 8341
E-mail: info@nspku.org
Website: www.nspku.org

In the USA:
Children's PKU Network
3790 Via De La Valle,
Suite 120
Del Mar
California
CA 92014
Tel.: 858.509.0767
Toll-free: 800.377.6677
Fax: 858.509.0768
E-mail: pkunetwork@aol.com
Website: www.pkunetwork.org

58

Pituitary deficiency

Gene loci: 3p11; 3p21.2–p21.1; 5q; 9q34.3

Key ASD references: Gingell, Parmar and Sungum-Paliwal 1996; Hoshino *et al.* 1984; Polizzi *et al.* 2006; Ritvo *et al.* 1990

How common is pituitary deficiency? Overall growth hormone deficiencies related to pituitary dysfunction are fairly common, affecting one in 4,000 to one in 10,000 live births (Procter, Phillips and Cooper 1998).

The type of combined pituitary hormone deficiency linked to SOD (Septo-Optic Dysplasia) and ASD that has been reported with defects in the homobox gene HESX1 is far rarer, only accounting for a small percentage of such cases (Vieria, Boldarine and Abucham 2007).

Main clinical features: Homozygous inactivating mutations of HESX1 mutations result in a specific physical phenotype with hypopituitarism, SOD and structural agenesis of various midline structures in the nervous system.

To date, some 13 separate mutations have been identified that are associated with SOD and hypopituitarism (see discussion in Sajedi *et al.* 2008). In addition, a number of heterozygous missense the homobox gene HESX1 mutations have now been identified in individuals with a range of mild pituitary abnormalities (Thomas *et al.* 2001).

Is there a link between pituitary deficiency and ASD? Only four papers have so far appeared which bear on this issue.

- Hoshino *et al.* (1984) were the first to suggest that there were abnormalities of pituitary function associated with some cases of ASD, after demonstrating abnormal plasma growth hormone levels in response to L-5HTP loading.

- Ritvo *et al.* (1990) documented 12 rare diseases in their epidemiological survey of 233 cases of ASD in Utah. One of these was a boy with pituitary deficiency diagnosed shortly after birth. He also had a SOD, so was blind from birth. As blindness is an independent factor associated with ASD, interpretation of the role of pituitary dysfunction in contributing to his ASD was problematic.

- Gingell, Parmar and Sungum-Paliwal (1996) described a nine-year-old boy with ASD who also had multiple pituitary deficiency. This is the only case reported to date without additional complications.

- Polizzi *et al.* (2006) described a series of eight cases of ASD associated with SOD, similar to the original case described by Ritvo *et al.* (1990). They point out that midline hypothalamic-pituitary structural malformations are commonly seen in addition to the optic nerve dysplasia, and that autistic behaviour is a frequent concomitant.

Most of the cases of ASD in association with pituitary deficiency are also reported to have SOD. The association of SOD and pituitary dysfunction has been found to be linked to a mutation/deletion of the HESX1 gene at 3p21.2–p21.1.

The phenotype associated with HESX1 is broad and usually, but not always, includes SOD: 9/10 of the ASD cases associated with pituitary dysfunction include SOD. Based on this, discussion this section is confined to multiple pituitary deficiency resulting from HESX1.

Differential diagnosis: Mutations in a number of separate genes can result in pituitary deficiency.

Treatment and management: Optimal management of pituitary deficiencies depends on the basis to the disorder, the range of hormone imbalances, and the age and sex of the affected individual. This is ideally managed and monitored through a specialist endocrinology service.

As there is a wide range of phenotypic presentation in HESX1 cases, good baseline assessment and monitoring of response to appropriate treatment as required is important.

Further information and support:

In the UK:

The Pituitary Foundation
PO Box 1944
Bristol
BS99 2UB
Tel.: 0845 450 0376 (Administration Line);
0845 450 0375 (Support and Information Helpline);
0845 450 0377 (Endocrine Nurse Helpline)
(available Monday evenings from 5.30 to 9.30
and Thursday mornings from 9.00 to 1.00 in the
afternoon)
Fax: 0117 933 0910

In the USA:

Los Angeles
PO Box 1958
Thousand Oaks, CA 91358
Tel.: 805-499-9973
Fax: 805-480-0633
E-mail: info@pituitary.org
Website: www.pituitary.org/home.aspx

59

Port-wine facial staining and autism

Genetic basis: A gene, RASA1, at 5q13.3, has been implicated in some cases of Sturge-Weber syndrome (Eerola *et al.* 2003), but has not been tested for in the reported ASD cases (Eerola *et al.* 2003).

Key ASD reference: Chugani *et al.* 2007

This is a previously unreported condition that appears phenotypically to resemble Sturge-Weber syndrome. A key feature of Sturge-Weber syndrome not seen in these cases is the occurence of leptomeningeal angiomas – the dilated blood vessels on the surface of the affected areas of the brain thought to result in seizures and brain injury. These can be subtle, and can sometimes be overlooked or are too small to be detected at the resolution of the imaging systems currently being used.

How common is port-wine facial staining in association with autism? As the aetiology is uncertain at the present time, the prevalence of this condition is not known. It may turn out to be a variant of one of the neurocutaneous conditions, such as Sturge-Weber syndrome, that have not previously been reported in which case prevalence should be ascertainable from the clinical literature.

Main clinical features: This condition is characterized by deep purple-red coloured patches on the skin of the face or scalp caused by the growth of a net of abnormal blood vessels in the affected areas. Of the four cases reported by Chugani *et al.* (2007), all fulfilled criteria for an ASD, three had a history of seizures and two were ongoing and maintained on medication at the time of the report. Two had eye problems that would be consistent with Sturge-Weber syndrome.

Is there a link between port-wine facial staining and ASD? As the aetiology is currently uncertain, it is difficult to say whether these are cases from a known clinical group in whom ASD has previously not been reported, or represent a novel aetiology that is more strongly associated with ASD.

Differential diagnosis: Whether there is a clear differentiation between these cases and more phenotypically normal Sturge-Weber syndrome remains to be established.

Treatment and management: As only four cases have so far been reported, and the aetiology remains uncertain, no specific treatments are known. It seems probable that there is a high likelihood of seizures in this group, and monitoring and treatment of seizure activity would seem sensible. Assuming Sturge-Weber syndrome is the underlying aetiology, there have been developments in best practice, including the possible role of ketogenic diet, that may be relevant (see Comi 2006, 2007).

Further information and support:

In Germany:
Die Interessengemeinschaft Sturge-Weber-Syndrom e.V.
E-mail: contact details available through website
Website: www.sturge-weber.de

In the UK:
Sturge Weber Foundation UK
Burleigh
348 Pinhoe Road
Exeter
Devon
EX4 8AF
Tel.: 01392 464675
Fax: 01392 464675
E-mail: support@sturgeweber.org.uk
Website: www.sturgeweber.org.uk

In the USA:
Sturge Weber Syndrome Community
SWSC
PO Box 24890
Lexington
KY 40524-4890
Tel.: (859) 272-3857
E-mail: swsc@swscommunity.org
Website: www.swscommunity.org

The Sturge-Weber Foundation
PO Box 418
Mt. Freedom
NJ 07970-0418
Tel.: 800-627-5482/973-895-4445
Fax: 973-895-4846
E-mail: swf@sturge-weber.com
Website: www.sturge-weber.org

60

Potocki-Lupski syndrome (PTLS)

aka • (dup)17(11.2p.11.2)

Gene locus: 17p11.2

Key ASD references: Moog *et al.* 2004; Potocki *et al.* 2000a, 2007

Potocki-Lupski syndrome is a reciprocal microduplication syndrome which is the homologous recombination reciprocal of Smith-Magenis syndrome [67] (Potocki *et al.* 2000a). It was the first such reciprocal microduplication syndrome to be predicted. The first paper to describe 17p11.2 duplication described two unrelated males with developmental delay and mild dysmorphic features (Brown *et al.* 1996). These are the typical features, combined with learning disability, language problems, and features of ADHD and ASD.

How common is PTLS? There is no data on the prevalence of PTLS at the time of writing.

Main clinical features: The first description of the clinical presentation of (dup)17(11.2p.11.2) (Brown *et al.* 1996) was of two unrelated male cases with learning disability and slightly dysmorphic facial features.

The consistent clinical features are: delayed early development; language impairment; learning disability; hypotonia; failure to thrive. In addition, poor feeding in infancy; oral-pharyngeal dysphasia; autism; obstructive and central sleep apnoea; structural cardiovascular abnormalities; epileptiform electroencephalogram (EEG) abnormalities; scoliosis; and hypermetropia are all reported to be common features.

The small number of cases reported to date, and the likelihood that milder cases are largely untested, should lead to caution in interpreting genetic results as a strong indication of the above as a likely or typical phenotype.

Is there a link between PTLS and ASD?

- A link between PTLS and ASD was first suggested in a paper by Potocki *et al.* (2000a), which described seven unrelated learning-disabled cases with *de novo* 17(11.2p.11.2) duplications. The clinical features described included mild facial dysmorphic features, dental malformations, short stature, mild learning disabilities and various behavioural features, including ADHD and autism.

- A further case, a six-year-old boy, was reported in 2004 (Moog *et al.* 2004). He had moderate learning disability, a gait disturbance, an 'autism related disorder', and mild facial dysmorphic features, with a broad forehead, thin upper lip, and ear anomalies. Genetic testing had identified duplication consistent with hereditary motor and sensory neuropathy type 1a (Charcot-Marie-Tooth disease). It is now known that the abnormalities in this region can result in four disorders: Charcot-Marie-Tooth disease type 1A; hereditary neuropathies with liabilities to pressure palsies; Smith-Magenis syndrome; and what is now known as Potocki-Lupski syndrome.

- In one case series Potocki and colleagues (2007) reported on ten subjects. Delayed early development (10/10), language impairment (10/10), learning disability (10/10) and hypotonia (10/10) were the most characteristic clinical features. In addition, poor feeding (8/10) and failure to thrive (10/10) in infancy, oral-pharyngeal dysphasia (8/9), autism (9/10), obstructive and central sleep apnoea (8/9), structural cardiovascular abnormalities (5/9), epileptiform electroencephalogram (EEG) abnormalities (5/9) and hypermetropia (8/10) were common features. The majority of cases (9/10) were reported as exhibiting autism.

- A paper using well-standardized tools found no evidence of ASD in three cases, but replicated the other reported features: all showed hypotonia, failure to thrive, and language delay, while two-thirds showed early developmental delay and all exhibited learning disability (Greco *et al.* 2008).

- The most recent case described was found to be autistic with a co-morbid severe expressive language delay (Nakamine *et al.* 2008).

From the cases of PTLS reported to date, there is clearly a significant group who exhibit autistic behaviour, typically in the context of learning disability, communication disorder, early feeding difficulties and sleep problems.

Differential diagnosis: Based on the genetic result, there is a clinical overlap between PTLS and Smith-Magenis syndrome [67], which also results from a deletion at 17p11.2, and with two of the hereditary neuropathies (Charcot-Marie-Tooth disease type 1A and hereditary neuropathies with liabilities to pressure palsies). Only PTLS and Smith-Magenis have to date been reported in association with ASD.

Treatment and management: Currently there is insufficient understanding of this condition to provide any specific guidance on treatment. As for a number of the other conditions discussed, management needs to be on a case-by-case basis. No cases are reported with epilepsy, but a number have been reported with generalized and focal epileptiform EEG abnormalities, while non-epileptic abnormalities were fairly consistently associated with obstructive sleep apnoea (7/8 cases) (Potocki *et al.* 2007).

Further information and support:
There is an active Yahoo discussion group for families at http://health.groups.yahoo.com/group/Dup-17p11-2.

In the UK:
Unique
PO Box 2189
Caterham
Surrey
CR3 5GN
Tel.: 01883 330766
E-mail: info@rarechromo.org

61

Prader-Willi syndrome (PWS)

aka • Prader-Labhart-Willi syndrome

Gene locis: 15q12; 15q11–q13

Key ASD references: Bolton *et al.* 2001; Descheemaeker *et al.* 2006; Dimitropoulos and Schultz 2007; Milner *et al.* 2005; Veltman, Craig and Bolton 2005

The English physician John Langdon Haydon Down first described in 1887 a patient who would today be given a diagnosis of PWS. His description was of a 25-year-old woman with learning disability, short stature, small hands and feet, hypogonadism, and marked obesity. She was also reported as having a voracious appetite.

The Swiss clinicians Andrea Prader, Alexis Labhart and Heinrich Willi reported a series of similar patients in 1956 and this led to the characterization of the condition we now know as Prader-Willi syndrome (PWS).

In 1981, Ledbetter *et al.* identified chromosome 15 deletions, specifically of 15q11-13, as the cause of PWS. PWS typically results from inheriting a paternal mutation of 15q11–q13, while inheritance of the same mutation from the mother results in Angelman syndrome [11].

PWS was the first clinical disorder to be attributed to genomic imprinting (where the condition differs depending on which parent passes on the affected gene).

How common is PWS? A variety of prevalence rates have been reported in the literature, from one in 8,000 to one in 52,000 (Akefeldt, Gillberg and Larsson 1991; Burd *et al.* 1990; Whittington *et al.* 2001).

Main clinical features: Consensus diagnostic criteria for PWS were published in 1993 (Holm *et al.* 1993) with separate cut-off levels given for those aged under three (5 points with at least 3 from major criteria) and over three years (8 points with at least 5 from major criteria):

Major criteria (1 point for each):

1. infantile central hypotonia

2. infantile feeding problems and/or failure to thrive

3. rapid weight gain from 1–6 years

4. characteristic facial features, such as narrow bifrontal diameter, almond-shaped palpebral fissures, narrow nasal bridge and down-turned mouth

5. hypogonadism

6. learning disability.

Minor criteria (one half point each):

1. decreased foetal movement/infantile lethargy

2. sleep disturbance and/or sleep apnoea

3. short stature for predicted height by mid-adolescence (if not on growth hormone treatment)

4. hypopigmentation

5. small hands and feet

6. narrow hands with straight ulnar border

7. esotropia/myopia

8. thick, viscous saliva

9. speech articulation defects

10. skin picking/rectal poking.

This is a disorder caused by defects in the functioning of genes on the short arm of chromosome 15, caused by loss of the paternal allele, either through deletion of this section of the paternal allele (70 per cent); through inheritance of both copies of the chromosome from the mother (uniparental idodisomy) (28 per cent); or, more rarely, through translocation, other structural alteration or deletion of the imprinting centre (two per cent).

It is equally common in both sexes, and no racial differences in prevalence are reported. There do; however, appear to be racial differences in the phenotype (Hudgins, Greer and Cassidy 1998).

It is often reported that the baby had diminished foetal movement. The typical clinical presentation is of clinical obesity, hypotonia, with a weak cry and poor sucking, learning disability, short stature, hypogonadotropic hypogonadism, strabismus, a 'shield-shaped' chest and small hands and feet. From early in the first year, hyperphagia is common, with progressive weight gain compared to the centile charts.

The development of pubic and body hair may be precocious, but other primary and secondary sexual characteristics tend to be delayed. Descent of the testes in boys and start of ovulation in girls can be extremely delayed.

Most PWS cases have growth hormone deficiency; however, this is variable. There does not appear to be a link between growth hormone levels and likelihood of obesity (Thacker et al. 1998).

Mild learning disability is seen in most cases. In addition, behavioural problems such as temper outbursts, obsession and compulsions often impair access to learning.

Hyperphagia is typical when access to food is not tightly controlled, and secondary problems such as impaired exercise tolerance, heart problems, type 2 diabetes and sleep apnoea are common.

Various factors may be directly related to the morbid obesity that typically accompanies PWS. Abnormalities of anterior pituitary hormone secretion such as insulin-like growth factor (IGF1) are reported in almost all cases, and structural abnormalities of the pituitary gland are seen in most cases (74 per cent vs eight per cent in controls). Similar profiles are seen in early-onset morbid obesity without PWS, and may be the basis to the obesity component of the condition (Miller et al. 2008). This could possibly provide an endocrine basis in the development of ASD similar to that in pituitary deficiency [58], despite the different genetic mechanisms involved.

Elevated levels of ghrelin, both when fasted and under normal conditions, are reported in PWS. Ghrelin acts both as a gastrointestinal hormone, modifying appetite, and as a neuropeptide, affecting brain levels of serotonin (Nonogaki, Ohashi-Nozue and Oka, 2006). Ghrelin abnormalities may be involved in the satiety problems that characterize those with PWS (see p.389).

Is there a link between PWS and ASD?

- Bolton *et al.* (2001) studied 21 people from six families with duplications of the 15q11–q13 region. Four of the people they studied had a pervasive developmental disorder, one being diagnosed as autistic. Most of the mutations giving rise to pervasive developmental disorders were maternal in origin, as would be seen in Angelman syndrome, not PWS. The authors concluded that developmental delay, but not specifically ASD, was associated with maternal inheritance of 15q11–q13 defects.

- Milner *et al.* (2005) studied a large sample of 96 PWS cases using various diagnostic tools. They compared cases where there was a maternally inherited uniparental disomy (where there had been no inheritance of a paternal chromosome 15 but both copies came from the mother) with cases where there was an inherited 15q11–q13 deletion on the paternally inherited chromosome. Their results indicated a strong association between paternally inherited 15q11–q13 deletions and ASD. Larger deletions were associated with lower intellectual level, but not with an increased likelihood of ASD diagnosis.

- Veltman, Craig and Bolton (2005), acknowledging the role of 15q11–q13 in ASD, reviewed the various studies of maternally and paternally inherited deletions and uniparental disomies. Based on the studies available to that time, all types of 15q11–q13 deletion, and uniparental disomy, conferred an increased risk of Angelman syndrome, but, in contrast, only maternally inherited uniparental disomy conveyed a significantly elevated risk of Prader-Willi syndrome.

- Descheemaeker *et al.* (2006) used a standardized scale to evaluate co-morbidity in 59 individuals with PWS and 59 matched controls with non-specific forms of learning disability, matched on gender, age and IQ. Most of those with PWS presented with a higher rate of autistic-like behaviour; however, using strict criteria (on DSM-III-R), 19 per cent of those with PWS were classified as having ASD, compared to 15 per cent of those with non-specific learning disabilities.

- Dimitropoulos and Schultz (2007) provide a further review of the evidence for genetic risk of ASD in those with PWS from loss or damage to 15q11–q13 and conclude, as did Veltman, Craig and Bolton (2005), that ASD appears to be most strongly linked to loss of the paternally inherited chromosome, particularly through inheritance of two copies of the maternal chromosome and none from the father (maternally inherited uniparental disomy).

Differential diagnosis: Genetic conditions affecting 15q11–q13 include Angelman syndrome [11] and oculocutaneous albinism [55], which should be considered. Neither condition is easily confused with PWS, as they result in markedly different phenotypes; however, genetic studies could suggest these conditions.

Biedl-Bardet syndrome [17], Cohen syndrome [23] and fragile-X syndrome [35] do; however, present with overlapping clinical phenotypes, and should also be included in the differential diagnosis.

Treatment and management: As PWS is a multi-system disorder with both structural and hormonal differences in the pituitary and other endocrine structures, good metabolic and imaging assessment are important as part of a comprehensive initial assessment. As a number of genetic factors can result in the clinical phenotype and may prove to be amenable to different approaches, ascertaining the genetic basis is also important. Treatment should be based on the outcome of such assessment.

A major practical problem for many with PWS is obesity due to overeating. This compounds the skeletal problems, in particular exacerbating difficulties due to scoliosis and increasing rates of sleep apnoea.

Early dietary intervention can be effective in controlling weight gain, but can result in short stature (Schmidt *et al.* 2008). It has been suggested that diet should therefore be coupled with growth hormone treatment. Unfortunately, the evidence to date is varied concerning clinical benefit (Mogul *et al.* 2008) and is coupled with a significant increase in obstructive sleep apnoea (Fillion, Deal and Van Vliet 2008). It may be that the differences in ghrelin production/metabolism are critical to the control of hunger.

As obesity is one of the major factors in morbidity and mortality for individuals with PWS, this is a critical aspect of ongoing care and management.

For an overview of management issues, see Butler, Lee and Whitman (2006).

As with Angelman syndrome [11] and oculocutaneous albinism [55], PWS shows evidence of dysfunction of the GABA system (Verhoeven and Tuinier 2006). The gamma-aminobutyric acid A receptor beta 3 (GABRB3), an inhibitory GABA receptor, is coded at 15q13–q15. Further elucidation of the nature of this abnormality and possible links to motor dysfunction and sleep problems may be important for future approaches to management.

Further information and support:

International:
International Prader-Willi Syndrome Organization
Website: www.ipwso.org

In Australia:
Prader-Willi Syndrome Association of Australia
E-mail: ellys@optusnet.com.au
Website: www.pws.asn.au/index.html

In Canada:
The Canadian Prader-Willi Syndrome Organization
2788 Bathurst St,
Suite 303
Toronto,
Ontario,
M6B 3A3
Tel.: 416-481-8657
E-mail: opwsa@rogers.com
Website: www.pwsacanada.com

In the UK:
Prader-Willi Syndrome Association (UK)
125a London Road
Derby
DE1 2QQ
Tel.: 01332 365676
Fax: 01332 360401
E-mail: admin@pwsa-uk.demon.co.uk (general enquiries)
Website: http://pwsa.co.uk/main.php

In the USA:
The Prader-Willi Syndrome Association (USA)
5700 Midnight Pass Rd
Sarasota,
Fla 34242
Toll-free: 800-926-4797
Tel.: 941-312-0400
Fax: 941-312-0142
E-mail: Reception@pwsausa.org
Web: www.pwsausa.org

62

Proteus syndrome

Gene locus: This has not yet been conclusively identified. There are suggestions of a link to PTEN defects (10q23) which have been reported in a number of cases (Smith J.M. *et al.* 2002; Zhou *et al.* 2000, 2001).

Key ASD reference: Butler *et al.* 2005

This syndrome is named after the Greek god Proteus, 'the old man of the sea', who was said to be able to change his shape to avoid being caught (Wiedemann *et al.* 1983). It is best known by the epithet of one of those who was most severely affected – the nineteenth-century 'Elephant Man' Joseph Merrick (Cohen 1988).

It occurs as a sporadic mutation, and the clinical picture is progressive throughout life.

How common is Proteus syndrome? Proteus syndrome is a rare condition with only around 200 cases reported so far worldwide (Orphanet 2008). There is no apparent difference in prevalence across racial groups. It is reported to be almost twice as common in males as in females (Turner, Cohen and Biesecker 2004).

Main clinical features: The main clinical features are macrocephaly, hamartomas and lipomas. Physical overgrowth is typically asymmetric. Overgrowth of the long bones in the arms and legs is typical (Nguyen *et al.* 2004) and scoliosis is common (del Rosario Barona-Mazuera *et al.* 1997). Tumours can occur in a range of body tissues (Jamis-Dow *et al.* 2004).

This is a hamartomatous overgrowth condition. Detailed discussion of such PTEN defects and their effects is provided in the sections outlines referred to in 'Differntial diagnosis' below and will not be repeated here.

Based on current consensus, these conditions are perhaps best grouped under a common heading of PHTSs (PTEN hamartoma–tumour syndrome) (Marsh *et al.* 1999; Waite and Eng 2002). There is marked variation in what is reported as Proteus syndrome in the published literature – Turner, Cohen and Biesecker (2004) reviewed 205 cases in the literature, of whom only 47.3 per cent would appear to meet current criteria.

Is there a link between Proteus syndrome and ASD?

- Butler *et al.* (2005) reviewed a series of 18 ASD cases with macrocephaly and identified three cases with previously unreported PTEN mutations.

Proteus syndrome is included here as one of the group of PTEN conditions with genotypic and phenotypic overlap reported in association with ASD.

Differential diagnosis: Differential diagnoses are as for the other PHTSs discussed – BRRS [15], BCNS [16] and Cowden syndrome [26].

Treatment and management: As for the other PHTSs, at the present time treatment is largely symptomatic.

Further information and support:

In the UK:
Proteus Family Network (UK)
31 Baswich Lane
Weeping Cross
Stafford
ST17 0BH
Tel.: 01785 254953
E-mail: info@proteus-uk.org
Web: www.proteus-uk.org

Proteus Syndrome Foundation
2 Watermill Close
Bexhill-on-Sea
East Sussex
TN39 5EJ
E-mail: tracy.whitewood_neal@virgin.net
Tel.: 01424 736640
Website: www.proteus-syndrome.org

In the USA:
Proteus Syndrome Foundation
4915 Dry Stone Dr
Colorado Springs,
CO 80918
Tel.: 719-264-8445 (day);
901-756-9375(day)
E-mail: kimkhoag@aol.com or jakebabs@aol.com
Website: www.proteus-syndrome.org

63a

Rett syndrome (RTT)

Gene loci: Xq28; 14q13

Key ASD references: Carney *et al.* 2003; Hagberg *et al.* 1983, 1985; Lam *et al.* 2000; Rett 1986

Rett syndrome is named after the Viennese paediatric neurologist Andreas Rett. He first described a group of girls who all presented with very similar difficulties, in a paper published in 1966. His initial findings were the result of chance observation of the similarities in two unrelated girls sitting in a clinic waiting area. One characteristic documented in these early cases but not replicated in later work was his report of raised blood ammonia levels (hyperammonaemia).

The biological basis to RTT has proved far more difficult to unravel than its clinical description.

A number of pairs of concordant identical twins have been reported (Partington 1988; Tariverdian, Kantner and Vogel 1987; Zoghbi *et al.* 1990), suggesting a probable genetic aetiology. However, although typically concordant for RTT diagnosis, clinical presentation and progression can vary across twins (Bruck *et al.* 1991), making it likely that environmental factors affect the expression of the genotype.

In a now classic genetics paper, Hudah Zoghbi's group from Baylor College in Houston showed that in some cases of RTT the defective gene was the X-linked methyl-CpG-binding protein 2 (MeCP2) (Amir *et al.* 1999).

A second gene has been identified at 14q13, the FOXG1 gene, which is affected in the 'congenital variant' of RTT (Ariani *et al.* 2008; Mencarelli *et al.* 2009). The phenotype in these first two types as reported to date appears to be almost identical. A third type of RTT presentation with early onset seizures is dealt with in a separate section [63b].

It has become clear that MeCP2 defects are also found in other clinical phenotypes, having been reported in neonatal onset encephalopathy, Angelman syndrome [11], other ASDs, and in non-specific X-linked mental retardation in males (Hammer *et al.* 2002). One study also suggests that boys with autism and a MeCP2 gene defect may be more likely to show evidence of developmental regression (Xi *et al.* 2007).

RTT is one of a group of human chromatin structure or modification disorders, many of which are linked to ASD. Others are ARX [13], Coffin-Lowry syndrome [21] and Rubinstein-Taybi syndrome [64] (reviewed in Hendrich and Bickmore 2001).

The clinical variation within the RTT group is also proving to be broader than had initially been thought, with some individuals showing development of skills such as writing and drawing and preservation of verbal ability into the teenage years, in contrast to the normal early regressive picture more typically described in the literature (Kerr *et al.* 2006).

Historically, more obviously similar, and more severely affected, clinical cases were most likely to be identified first (especially before a genetic test became clinically available). This perhaps led to greater apparent consistency in the clinical literature than may actually be the case.

Although much of the genetic literature has emerged since its publication, one of the most useful overviews of RTT remains Kerr and Witt Engerstrom's overview (2001).

How common is RTT? Several studies have provided prevalence estimates that are broadly similar:

- Suzuki, Hirayama and Arima (1989) report a rate of one in 20,000 girls affected in Tokyo.

- Hagberg (1995) estimated the overall prevalence in southern Sweden at around one in 15,000.

- Burd *et al.* (1990) estimated the 0–18 prevalence in girls in South Dakota as one in 19,786.

- In Texas, the prevalence has been estimated as one in 22,800 (Kozinetz *et al.* 1993).

The lack of good epidemiological studies is offset by the obvious clinical phenotype in many cases; however, the existence of mild RTT variants (Huppke *et al.* 2003, 2006) and of male cases (Maiwald *et al.* 2002; Philippart 1990; Schanen and Francke 1998) makes accurate estimation difficult.

Main clinical features: An early multi-centre European study (Hagberg *et al.* 1983) provided clinical details on 35 female patients from France, Portugal and Sweden. This paper essentially detailed the criteria used in describing the RTT phenotype. There is some variation across the cases described; however, all the girls showed a progressive encephalopathy. Development was reported as normal until age 7–18 months, at which point speech stopped (often after a small vocabulary had developed and functional hand use was lost. Where head circumference data was available, there was evidence of progressive microcephaly – the rate of head growth slowed, relative to normal growth charts. Rate of head growth is associated with developmental progression in RTT – larger head size and better early head growth is associated with greater likelihood of walking (Leonard and Bower 1998).

A large study looking for more pervasive genotype–phenotype associations was unable to identify any consistent pattern (Weaving et al. 2003).

Two studies have found consistent patterns. Schanen et al. (2004) studied a cohort of 85 RTT cases, 65 of whom had one of the eight main reported mutations. Missense mutations had the least effect – better language and lower overall symptom severity, with one particular mutation (R306C) being associated with the least impairment. A further large study of 524 females with RTT found marked differences in survival across the different reported mutations.

A study using the Australian RTT database (Robertson et al. 2006) found associations between particular behavioural characteristics and several of the specific RTT mutations. Jerky, ataxic movements were typical, with gradual loss of lower limb function such that most cases were confined to wheelchairs by their mid-teens, and onset of epilepsy during the second decade.

Hagberg (1995) reviewed 170 Swedish female cases, diagnosed on clinical phenotype, and aged between two and 52. Seventy-five per cent presented with the 'classic' Rett phenotype, while 25 per cent were 'atypical'. Today, a number of clinical variants are recognized, including the preserved speech variant (Renieri et al. 2009) – see below and the following section.

As the genotype is used as the gold standard for diagnosis, clinical variability in the phenotype is becoming greater. For example, a case with a novel frameshift deletion was described with macrocephaly (Oexle et al. 2005).

Reduced bone density seems common, being reported in 12/16 cases reported by Leonard et al. (1995).

Those affected with RTT typically have a frail build, rapid, energetic movements (including hand-wringing/washing and hand-biting), and bursts of rapid breathing. They have normal caloric intake and are hypometabolic compared to controls (Motil et al. 1994), suggesting that their growth failure is due to their level of involuntary activity.

There is no association between RTT and increased maternal age (Martinho et al. 1990).

A number of immune differences such as abnormal CD4+/CD8+ ratios and low levels of natural killer cells have been found, shown in a study of 20 RTT patients (Fiumara et al. 1999). Elevated levels of autoantibodies that selectively targeted nerve growth factor were found on repeated testing of five girls with RTT (Klushnik, Gratchev and Belichenko 2001).

The clearest evidence of consistent neuropathology in RTT is a reduction in dendritic branching, found on detailed ultrastructural examination of a series of 16 Rett brains (Armstrong *et al.* 1995): differences were largely confined neurons projecting from primary areas into association cortices and the limbic system. Developments in neuroimaging appear likely, in combination with neurogenetics, to be better able to predict RTT outcome (Mahmood *et al.* 2009).

Heart function is abnormal in many individuals with RTT. Ellaway *et al.* (1999), Guideri *et al.* (1999) and Sekul *et al.* (1994) have all reported prolonged QT intervals and reduced heart rate variability in patients with RTT, suggesting impairment of the autonomic nervous system (Glaze 2002).

Is there a link between RTT and ASD? RTT is a specific clinical subgroup within the autistic spectrum disorders. It does not really make sense to evaluate whether individuals with RTT have symptomology consistent with ASD, as it is a particular type of ASD with a known genetic basis. Prior to the introduction of agreed Rett criteria in 1994, individuals with Rett syndrome would typically have received a diagnosis of autism.

- Andreas Rett provided the first clinical descriptions of RTT in 1966. He reviewed the development of the concept in a paper published in 1986.

- Clinical criteria for RTT were published in 1985 (Hagberg *et al.* 1985). Delineation of the condition was based on a collaborative European series of cases (Hagberg *et al.* 1983).

- Lam *et al.* (2000) reported MeCP2 mutations in both RTT phenotypic female patients and in one four-year-old girl with a clinical diagnosis of infantile autism out of a screened group of 21 ASD cases.

- Carney *et al.* (2003) screened a population of 69 diagnosed ASD cases and found that two had *de novo* MeCP2 mutations.

The preserved speech variant of RTT: A number of reports describe the preserved speech variant (PSV) of RTT (De Bona *et al.* 2000; Zapella 1997; Zapella, Gillberg and Ehlers 1998). The PSV appears to have a broadly similar but slowed progression, with little evidence of seizure activity, muscle wastage or scoliosis, with preservation of communicative skills and often with recovery of functional hand use. One paper has outlined criteria and provided detailed clinical description of this preserved speech or 'Zapella' variant (Renieri *et al.* 2009).

All cases of PSV so far reported appear to be due to late truncating missense mutations (Zapella *et al.* 2001).

Male RTT: The initial view of RTT was that it was a condition found exclusively in females that may result in non-viable male conceptions. This view has had to be changed as a significant number of male cases have now been reported.

Mary Coleman (1990) reported one possible case of male RTT, and Philippart (1990) two such cases – these were reported as possible male Rett on the basis of the physical and behavioural phenotype, as the MeCP2 gene mutation was not identified until 1999. In 1998, Schanen *et al.* described two boys with neonatal encephalopathy born into families with RTT girls, suggesting a possible common genetic aetiology. A mildly affected male with MeCP2 somatic mosaicism and slow motor development has been reported (Clayton-Smith *et al.* 2000). Villard *et al.* (2000) presented two boys who died in infancy of severe neonatal encephalopathy and had a sister with classic RTT. The authors identified a missense mutation in the MeCP2 gene in the sister, tissue from one of the brothers, and on the inactive X chromosome in the mother. Topçu *et al.* (2002) reported a boy with a MeCP2 deletion and a 'classic' RTT phenotype. Zeev *et al.* (2005) described a brother and sister, both with MeCP2 mutations, where the sister had a classic Rett presentation and the brother a severe neonatal encephalopathy. Maiwald *et al.* (2002) described a phenotypic male with a 46,XX (female) karyotype and a MeCP2 deletion and phenotype. Leuzzi *et al.* (2004) reported on a 28-month-old boy with a MeCP2 mutation and neurophysiological findings consistent with reduced dendritic branching. Budden *et al.* (2005) and Dayer *et al.* (2007) present further single male Rett cases with mothers carrying mutated MeCP2 genes on their inactivated X chromosomes.

Differential diagnosis: As a regressive onset ASD with apparently normal early development and progressive microcephaly that typically affects females, most cases of RTT are easily identified, and MeCP2 screening is now widely available to confirm clinical suspicion. CDKL5 RTT [63b] and Angelman syndrome [11] are the two most likely alternative diagnoses. A number of conditions show similar patterns of early developmental regression. Those which could be confused on behavioural grounds are the various PTEN defects, such as BRRS [15] (but these are typically seen in association with macrocephaly), some of the inborn errors of metabolism [9] and [40], certain of the epilepsies [19], and Landau-Kleffner syndrome. Infantile neural ceroid lipofuscinosis (INCL) or Batten's disease (Wisniewski *et al.* 2000) can also show a similar early pattern; however, the progression is more rapid.

A male Rett case with a supernumerary paternally inherited X chromosome – Rett + Klinefeiter's syndrome – has been reported (Schwartzman *et al.* 1999).

Treatment and management: As RTT is a progressive disorder with apparently normal early development through the first year, the availability of MeCP2 screening both antenatally and in early infancy provides a window of opportunity for clinical intervention before the more obvious manifestations appear. Boys with a RTT-like phenotype are often not tested for MeCP2; however, the rising numbers of positive cases reported suggest that this should be a more regular part of diagnostic screening.

A number of treatment approaches have been found to have some efficacy in providing symptomatic improvements: magnesium supplementation has been found beneficial in the treatment of hyperventilation (Egger *et al.* 1992); melatonin may help with sleep difficulties (McArthur and Budden 1998); and l-carnitine has been reported to produce general improvements in well-being (Ellaway *et al.* 2001).

Prolonged QT intervals are noted in cardiac monitoring of individuals with RTT in general, and suggest that a range of medications that affect heart function should be avoided (see Weaving *et al.* 2005 for discussion).

Treatment of seizure activity is as for any other cases with similar seizures (Huppke *et al.* 2006). Seizure onset is often in adolescence, not like the Hanefeld variant where there is neonatal seizure onset in most cases. One study has suggested that levetiracetam may be beneficial in cases where seizure control is resistant to conventional antiepileptic medications (Specchio *et al.* 2009).

Scoliosis can often require corrective surgery and should be closely monitored in classic RTT cases, as secondary effects on breathing and organ restriction are common (Harrison and Webb 1990; Kerr *et al.* 2003).

A number of animal studies are showing the ability to reverse the effects of MeCP2 defects typically produced by the introduction of a 'Lox-STOP cassette' that can be displaced. A Lox-STOP cassette is a recombinant nucleic acid molecule that is incorporated into a gene of interest preventing it from functioning normally and that can be displaced restoring normal gene function. One animal study has shown that administration of insulin-like growth factor 1 (IGF1) can partially reverse much RTT symptomology. IGF1 levels have not been shown to be reduced in RTT (Riikonen 2003), and this approach has *not* been trialled in human RTT.

There is ongoing research on several possible treatments. Histone deacetylase inhibitors (HDACIs) are being trialled, but no published studies on this approach have yet appeared (see, for discussion, Abel and Zukin 2008; Kalin, Butler and Kozikowski 2009). Dextromethorphan, an NMDA glutamate receptor blocker, is also being investigated because of the reported increase in central nervous system glutamate receptors in RTT (Blue, Naidu and Johnston 1999) – but again, no studies have been reported (see Brkanac, Raskind and King 2008).

Further information and support:

International

International Rett Syndrome Association (IRSA)
9121 Piscataway Road, #2B
Clinton
Maryland
MD 20735
USA
Tel.: 800-818-RETT
Fax: 301-856-3336
E-mail: admin@rettsyndrome.org
Website: www.rettsyndrome.org

In the UK:

Rett Syndrome Association UK (RSAUK)
113 Friern Barnet Road
London
N11 3EU
Tel.: 0870 770 3266 (national);
020 8361 5161 (local)
Fax: 0870 770 3265 (national);
020 8368 6123 (local)
E-mail: info@rettsyndrome.org.uk
Website: www.rettsyndrome.org.uk

In the USA:

Rett Syndrome Research Foundation (RSRF) Office
4600 Devitt Drive
Cincinnati
Ohio
OH 45246
Tel.: 513-874-3020
Fax: 513-874-2520
Website: www.rsrf.org/index.html

63b

Rett syndrome (Hanefeld variant) (RSHV)

Gene locus: Xp22

Key ASD references: Goutieres and Aicardi 1986; Grosso *et al.* 2007a; Hagberg and Skjeldal 1994; Hanefeld 1985; Scala *et al.* 2005; Tao *et al.* 2004; Wearing *et al.* 2004

The Hanefeld variant was first described in a 1985 paper by Folker Hanefeld, and has been termed 'Rett syndrome (Hanefeld variant)'. The literature, somewhat confusingly, at times differentiates between 'serine/threonine kinase 9 defects', an 'early seizure variant of Rett syndrome' and 'Rett syndrome (Hanefeld variant)' (see, for example, the discussion in Bahi-Buisson *et al.* 2008a on the STK9 cases discussed in Kalscheuer *et al.* 2003). All three are reported with essentially the same early seizure onset and Rett symptomology in association with the same CDKL5 gene mutations at Xp22. It seems reasonable, given the synonymous gene defect and clinical presentation, to suggest that these three diagnoses are different terms for the same condition. This contrasts with the 'classic' Rett syndrome MeCP2 mutation at Xq28, and the 'congenital' variant FOXG1 mutation at 14q13, both of which typically have later onset of seizures.

RSHV is a variant of the phenotype found in typical Rett syndrome, and is due to a different gene defect at a different position on the X chromosome. It is similar in clinical presentation; however, typically, in addition to the Rett features (progressive microcephaly; loss of functional hand use; stereotyped hand movements), there is an early onset of seizure activity that is not seen in the MeCP2 form, with a fairly consistent pattern of seizure evolution (Bahi-Buisson *et al.* 2008a). One paper that reviewed the literature and presented three new cases found that 13 of 14 CDKL5 patients presented with seizures before three months of age (Evans *et al.* 2005).

CDKL5, like MeCP2, is a kinase (a type of enzyme that transfers phosphate groups from molecules such as adenosine triphosphate), and it is important in energy metabolism. It appears to affect the same physiological pathway as MeCP2 (Mari *et al.* 2005), which may explain the overlapping clinical phenotype.

A review of clinical cases of early infantile spasms, however, indicates that CDKL5 abnormalities are overrepresented in this broader clinical group, irrespective of Rett's phenotype (Archer *et al.* 2006). The genotype–phenotype association is not as strong as was initially suspected.

The gene defect involves cyclin-dependent kinase-like 5 (CDKL5), aka serine-threonine protein kinase 9 (STK9).

How common is Rett syndrome (Hanefeld variant)? The clinical phenotype is largely as for MeCP2 Rett syndrome, and this is classified on both ICD-10 and DSM-IV- Tr as an autistic spectrum disorder. No population screening has so far been conducted; however, from Bahi-Buisson *et al.* (2008b), it would appear to be commonly associated with the combination of otherwise unexplained seizures and learning disability in females.

Main clinical features: Early-onset seizures, usually within the first six weeks; severe early-onset hypotonia with delayed motor milestones; normal interictal EEG; other features as for Rett syndrome [63a].

Is there a link between Rett syndrome (Hanefeld variant) and ASD?

- In 1985, Folker Hanefeld described one child with infantile spasms who went on to develop the clinical phenotype of Rett syndrome. The girl's two sisters had already received a diagnosis of Rett syndrome. This suggested a different mechanism to MeCP2 in these cases.

- Goutieres and Aicardi (1986) described a series of seven girls who partially fulfilled criteria for Rett syndrome, but where the presentation was unusual. Five of the girls did not show normal early development, and two had early and intense seizure activity. At least two are likely to have been CDKL5 rather than MeCP2 cases.

- Hagberg and Skjeldal (1994) proposed a classification for atypical Rett syndrome variants and applied their criteria to 16 learning-disabled girls with 'partial' Rett syndrome. Two of the cases detailed as congenital variants had a history of early seizure as the principal feature of their initial presentation.

- Tao *et al.* (2004) were the first to identify CDKL5 defects in two unrelated female cases with a behavioural phenotype consistent with atypical Rett syndrome and with no defect in MeCP2. They also presented information on a pair of 41-year-old identical twin women with a Rett phenotype including episodic hyperventilation, marked hypotonia, scoliosis and a CDKL5 transversion. They point out in their review that ,while in 'classic' Rett cases the majority show evidence of MeCP2 mutation/deletion, this is true only of between 20 and 40 per cent of atypical cases.

- Weaving *et al.* (2004) reported on two families. In the first, there were three children with a single nucleotide CDKL5 deletion: a pair of 19-year-old identical twin girls, one with an atypical Rett phenotype, severe learning disability and a history of complex epilepsy, and one with autism and mild–moderate learning disability (IQ about 70) with good verbal ability and no history of seizures, and a brother with the same deletion who had had complex early-onset epilepsy and severe learning difficulties and had died at age 16 from aspiration pneumonia. The second family had two half-sisters, one with a CDKL5 deletion and a Rett-like phenotype, and the second had a 'classic' Rett phenotype and no seizures or evidence of either a CDKL5 or a MeCP2 deletion.

- Scala *et al.* (2005) report frameshift mutations in CDKL5 in two girls with a Rett phenotype but with early onset of epilepsy that in both cases was in the early weeks of life. MeCP2 and ARX mutations were screened for and excluded. The authors note that CDKL5 mutations have also been reported in West syndrome, another epileptic condition with early onset that has been linked to ASD, but usually with later onset of ASD symptomology (Erol, Alehan and Gümüs 2007; Kayaalp *et al.* 2007).

- Grosso *et al.* (2007a) review the 27 cases reported up to that point and present a case with sleep-related hyperkinetic seizures, suggesting that the range of seizure problems seen with CDKL5 mutation may be broader than had originally been thought.

- Bahi-Buisson *et al.* (2008a) screened a large population of 183 females with learning disability and early-onset seizures for CDKL5 mutations and identified 18 mutations in 20 unrelated cases. Eight had encephalopathy with Rett-like features, five had infantile spasms, and seven had encephalopathy with refractory epileptic seizures. The consistent pattern was of early-onset epilepsy and severe hypotonia, together with a normal EEG between seizures.

Differential diagnosis: MeCP2 Rett syndrome [63a] and Angelman syndrome [11] are the two most likely alternative diagnoses. The gene locus for Coffin-Lowry syndrome [21] is at Xp22.1–p22.2. A number of studies have described 'early infantile epileptic encephalopathy 2' with lesions at this site – this term seems to be synonymous with RTT (Hanefeld variant).

Netrin G1 translocation on chromosome 1 has been reported in a single case of early seizure variant Rett syndrome without a CDKL5 or MeCP2 mutation (Borg *et al.* 2005). Four non-pathogenic sequence variants but no further cases were found in a large case series screening of 115 Rett phenotype cases with neither CDKL5 or MeCP2 mutations, 52 of whom had early onset seizures (Archer *et al.* 2008). FOXG1 mutations were not screened in the Archer *et al.* study, and could account for some of their cases.

Treatment and management: As most studies to date on treatment have not looked specifically at the Hanefeld variant as a separate group, treatment should be as for classical Rett syndrome, in which a number of treatments have been found to have some efficacy: magnesium in the treatment of hyperventilation (Egger *et al.* 1992); melatonin for sleep difficulties (McArthur and Budden 1998); and l-carnitine which is reported to produce general improvements in well-being (Ellaway *et al.* 1999, 2001).

Specific approaches to the management of seizures should be as for other conditions resulting in infantile spasms. The treatment of choice, despite earlier concerns over visual field restriction, would still seem to be vigabatrin (see review and update in Willmore *et al.* 2009). Longer-term outcome studies of vigabatrin use in infancy show fewer effects on visual fields than had been predicted (Gaily, Jonsson and Lappi 2009).

Prolonged QT intervals are noted in cardiac monitoring of individuals with Rett syndrome in general and suggest that a range of medications that can affect heart function should be avoided (see Weaving *et al.* 2005 for discussion).

Further information and support: Although somewhat different in aetiology, the clinical presentation is the same as classic Rett syndrome, except for the nature and severity of the seizure problems. Support from the Rett syndrome associations is the same as for the MeCP2 and FOXG1 forms of the condition (see the listing in the previous section). In addition, the various national and international epilepsy associations may provide more specific help and advice concerning seizures.

International:
The International League Against Epilepsy
The International Bureau for Epilepsy
Both can be accessed through the Epilepsy.org
website at www.epilepsy.org.

Epilepsy Helpline
UK freephone: 0808 800 5050
International: +44 113 210 8850
E-mail: helpline@epilepsy.org.uk
Txt msg: 07797 805 390 info

In the UK:
Epilepsy Action
New Anstey House
Gate Way Drive
Yeadon
Leeds
LS19 7XY
Tel.: 0113 210 8800

In the USA:
Epilepsy Foundation of America
8301 Professional Place
Landover
MD 20785
Tel.: 800-332 1000
Fax: 301-918-2102
Website: www.epilepsyfoundation.org

64

Rubinstein-Taybi syndrome

aka • broad thumb hallux syndrome

Gene loci: 22q13; 16p13.3

Key ASD reference: Hellings *et al.* 2002

In Rubinstein-Taybi syndrome there are a number of distinctive features – a prominent nose, broad thumbs and broad big toes (this combination is the first to alert clinicians to the possible diagnosis). Infants affected by this syndrome are typically small for age, have feeding difficulties, fail to thrive, have frequent chest infections, exhibit congenital heart disease, and show evidence of developmental delay. Rubinstein-Taybi syndrome was first described in 1963 by Jack Herbert Rubinstein and Hooshang Taybi.

How common is Rubinstein-Taybi syndrome? The best current estimate is 1/100,000–1/125,000 (Hennekam *et al.* 1990). No differences in prevalence in different racial groups have been reported.

Main clinical features: Initial presentation is often of failure to thrive, as feeding difficulties are common and compounded by a slower rate of skeletal growth. A third of cases present with cardiac problems which often compound respiratory infections.

Motor and other developmental milestones are typically delayed, with an average IQ of 51 being reported. Speech development is often poor.

Broad thumbs and big toes are always seen. Other digits are also commonly enlarged, and in some there is syndactyly or polydactyly. Reduced development of the upper jaw (hypoplastic maxilla) with a narrow palate is typical. Most of those affected have a prominent 'beaked' nose, down-slanted eyelids and low-set ears. A third of cases have significantly smaller heads than normal for their overall body size.

Some 80 per cent of boys have undescended testes. Three-quarters of girls have excess body hair. Hypotonia is noted in around two-thirds of cases, as is some degree of strabismus.

Around one third of cases show EEG abnormalities, but no significant association with seizure activity has been reported.

There appear to be no differences in the rate at which males and females are affected.

Tumours of various types are seen in one in 20 cases.

Sleep problems such as sleep apnoea are reported to be common, but there is no systematic research on this issue (Zucconi *et al.* 1993).

Milder versions have been reported, typically described as 'incomplete Rubinstein-Taybi syndrome' (Zimmermann *et al.* 2007).

Is there a link between Rubinstein-Taybi syndrome and ASD?

- One paper suggests a possible link between Rubinstein-Taybi syndrome and ASD: Hellings *et al.* (2002) describe an adult female with a complex clinical presentation. She had a severe learning disability, overactivity, inattention and recurrent manic episodes with aggression, and had received a dual psychiatric diagnosis of bipolar mood disorder and autism. The authors suggest a possible link with GABA receptor or transmitter function, as abnormalities in GABAergic function have been linked to 16p13.3 deletion, a site implicated in Rubinstein-Taybi syndrome.

This suggestion would be consistent with other GABA mechanisms, such as the defect seen in OCA2 [55] at 15q11.2, that have been suggested in ASD (see DeLong 2007).

This mechanism may also account for the high level of side-effects with neuroleptic medication reported in this condition (Levitas and Reid 1998).

A second gene site at 22q13 (EP300) has been identified as sufficient to cause Rubinstein-Taybi phenotype (Roelfsema *et al.* 2005) and encodes a histone acetyltransferase important in cell proliferation and differentiation. A number of copy number variations linked to ASD have been reported at 22q13, and it is also the locus of the SHANK3 susceptibility gene at 22q13.3.

Differential diagnosis: Several other conditions that have been reported in association with ASD, or which overlap with ASD-associated conditions, can present with similar clinical features: Aarskog syndrome [8]; Simpson-Golabi-Behmel syndrome; and Weaver syndrome.

In addition, a number of other rare overgrowth conditions have a similar phenotype: Greig syndrome; Larsen syndrome; Pfeiffer syndrome (Cohen 1973, 1977) and Saethre-Chotzen syndrome (Cohen, Neri and Weksberg 2002).

Treatment and management: Wiley *et al.* (2003) have provided medical guidelines for clinical management and surveillance of patients with Rubinstein-Taybi syndrome.

The high level of side effects with conventional neuroleptic medication is noted above (Levitas and Reid 1998).

There can be problems with anaesthesia due to difficulties with intubation (Twigg and Cook 2002). There is a particular susceptibility to adverse reactions to certain anaesthetics, such as succinylcholine (Stirt 1981).

The specific nature of the physiological defects underlying Rubinstein-Taybi suggests that pharmacological approaches which modify the cyclic AMP response element binding protein (CREB) mapped to 16p13.3 may have direct effects on the cognitive and long-term memory problems seen in Rubinstein-Taybi (Hallam and Bourtchouladze 2006). This provides a specific focus for a novel therapeutic approach to this condition that addresses some of its core features.

There is ongoing research on the possible role of histone deacetylase inhibitors (HDACIs) in the treatment of Rubinstein-Taybi, but no published studies on this approach have yet appeared. (See, for discussion, Abel and Zukin 2008; Kalin, Butler and Kozikowski 2009.)

Further information and support:

International:
Umbrella International Rubenstein-Taybi website
www.rubinstein-taybi.org/index.html

In the UK:
Rubinstein Taybi Syndrome, UK Support Group
21 Cricketers Green
Yeadon
Leeds
LS19 7YS
Tel.: 0113 250 3778
E-mail: john.peat@tiscali.co.uk
Website: www.rtsuk.org

In the USA:
Rubinstein-Taybi Parent Group
PO Box 146
Smith Center
Kansas
KS 66967
Tel.: 888-447-2989

65

Schindler disease

aka • neuroaxonal dystrophy, Schindler type

• alpha-N-acetylgalactosaminidase deficiency, type I

• NAGA deficiency, type I

Gene loci: 22q11; 22q13.1(?)

Key ASD reference: Blanchon *et al.* 2002

Schindler disease is a lysosomal disease caused by lack of the enzyme alpha-N-acetylgalactosaminidase. It was first described by Schindler and colleagues from Rotterdam (Schindler *et al.* 1989; van Diggelen *et al.* 1988). Clinical variability may be partly due to a second gene anomaly in phospholipase A2 group VI (PLA2G6).

How common is Schindler disease? No epidemiological studies have been carried out, so prevalence is currently unknown; however, given its obvious and progressive course, it is an extremely rare presentation, with only a dozen reported cases in the world literature. On current understanding it seems unlikely that any benign or *forme fruste* variants of the condition will be identified (presentation of a condition that is distinguished by being mild or partial in comparison to what would be typical).

Main clinical features: There is considerable phenotypic variability and two types are recognized – type 1, which is infantile onset, and type 2, also known as Kanzaki disease, with onset in adulthood. The co-morbid case reported by Blanchon *et al.* is clearly type 1.

Schindler disease is a type of lysosomal storage disorder that is caused by a lesion to the alpha-N-acetylgalactosaminidase gene. In affected infants development appears normal in the early months of life, after which there is rapid deterioration with frequent myoclonic seizures, severe motor delay and cortical blindness. It is an infantile-onset neuroaxonal dystrophy with similar neuropathology to other neuraxonal dystrophies (Wolfe, Schindler and Desnick 1995).

It is thought that the variability in clinical features is due to the presence in some cases of a second genetic lesion in PLA2G6 (Westaway, Gregory and Hayflick 2007). This independently shows a range of neurodegenerative features (Kurian *et al.* 2008).

Is there a link between Schindler disease and ASD?

- To date, there is only a single case of Schindler disease that has been reported in association with ASD. This was a 12-year-old boy with an IQ of 48 with autistic disorder, reported in 2002 by a group from the Kanner Centre in Saint Etienne in France (Blanchon *et al.* 2002).

As the prevalence of Schindler disease is not known, it is unclear whether there is a true association, and a biological basis to any link can only be speculated about. As so many overlapping conditions associated with ASD are located at 22q11, the link could be due to contiguous-affected regions. Schindler disease is a rare cause of ASD.

Differential diagnosis: Predominantly other neuroaxonal dystrophies such as Seitelberger disease (see Wang *et al.* 1988).

Treatment and management: At present no specific treatments for Schindler disease have been found.

Further information and support:

In France:
Vaincre Les Maladies Lysosomales
2 ter avenue de France
Massy, 91300
Tel.: 01 69 75 40 30
Fax: 01 60 11 15 83
E-mail: accueil@vml-asso.org
Website: www.vml-asso.org

In the UK:
CLIMB (Children Living with Inherited Metabolic Diseases)
Climb Building
176 Nantwich Road
Crewe, Intl
CW2 6BG
Tel.: 0870 7700 325
Fax: 0870 7700 327
E-mail: info@climb.org.uk
Internet: www.CLIMB.org.uk

In the USA:
Hide and Seek Foundation
4123 Lankershim Boulevard
North Hollywood
California
CA 91602-2828
Tel.: 818-762-8621
E-mail: Info@hideandseek.org
Website: www.hideandseek.org/diseases.html
An umbrella group for children with lysosomal disease.

66

Smith-Lemli-Opitz syndrome (SLOS)

aka • RHS syndrome

Gene locus: 11q12–q13

A more severe form, 'Smith-Lemli-Opitz type II' (Curry *et al.* 1987), has not been associated with ASD and will not be discussed here.

Key ASD references: Aneja and Tierney 2008; Sikora *et al.* 2006; Tierney, Nwokoro and Kelley 2000; Tierney *et al.* 2001, 2006

Smith-Lemli-Opitz syndrome was first reported in a paper published in 1964 by David Weyhe Smith, John Marius Opitz and Luc Lemli (Smith, Lemli and Opitz 1964). It was the first metabolic syndrome reported to result in multiple congenital malformations and a distinct behavioural phenotype. It has an autosomal recessive pattern of inheritance.

SLOS results from a gene defect that affects the production of the enzyme 7-dehydrocholesterol reductase (Mobius *et al.* 1998; Tint *et al.* 1994). A number of useful overviews are available which deal with cholesterol biosynthesis and the problems seen in SLOS and other related conditions (Herman 2003; Salen *et al.* 1996). The gene has been mapped to 11q12-q13 (Wassif *et al.* 1998). General reviews on SLOS can be found in Irons (2007) and Porter (2008).

How common is SLOS? This is currently not firmly established. A review of all diagnosed cases in the UK from 1984 to 1998 suggested a rate of one in 60,000 (Ryan *et al.* 1998). The availability of reliable screening techniques (for example, Scalco *et al.* 2003) has considerably widened the reported clinical phenotype.

One US study (Battaile *et al.* 2001), screening 1,503 anonymous blood samples for one specific SLOS mutation (IVS8-1G-C), estimated the carrier frequency for all SLOS mutations to be as high as one in 30, with a predicted prevalence of SLOS of between one in 1,590 and one in 13,500. This is the most prevalent mutation in populations of Western European ancestry; however, in other populations, such as those of Czech and Slovak descent, it is uncommon (Kozak *et al.* 2000), and carrier frequency may be significantly lower in such groups. SLOS appears more common in Central European populations and in those descended from them (Witsch-Baumgartner *et al.* 2008).

Rates of SLOS in the Czech Republic have been estimated at one in 10,000 (Opitz 1999) and in Slovakia at between one in 15,000 and one in 20,000 (Bzduch, Beluchova and Skodova 2000).

Based on population prevalence of carriers for the gene in a Polish screening study of the most common mutations (Ciara *et al.* 2006), the prevalence of SLOS in this population is likely to be in the region of between one in 2,300 and one in 3,900.

One study comparing 59 British, Polish, German and Austrian cases found different patterns of mutation in the different populations (Witsch-Baumgartner *et al.* 2001).

Main clinical features: Smith-Lemli-Opitz syndrome is a condition that affects the DHCR7 (7-dehydrocholesterol reductase) gene that is critical to the body's production of cholesterol. There is now an extensive body of research on DHCR7 and on how it affects development (see Yu and Patel 2005 for a review). Defects in the gene can result in a range of physical abnormalities (Kelley 2000).

There is a wide range of severity reported in SLOS, and this is thought primarily to reflect dietary levels of cholesterol intake (Waye *et al.* 2002).

In the 25 cases reported by Ryan *et al.* (1998), 98 per cent had learning disability, 80 per cent had second and third toe syndactyly and 72 per cent had congenital cardiac problems. In this series, serum 7-dehydrocholesterol levels did not appear linked to clinical severity of the disorder.

Typical physical features include microcephaly with bi-temporal narrowing, ptosis, epicanthic folds and a short nose with anteverted nostrils, capillary haemangioma of the forehead, postaxial polydactyly and second and third toe syndactyly. Growth retardation is a common feature. A high-arched, narrow palate and cleft palate are commonly seen, and hypospadias is a frequent feature in males (Opitz *et al.* 2002). Ambiguous genital development has been reported in a number of genetically male cases (Bialer *et al.* 1987; Fukazawa *et al.* 1992; Lachman *et al.* 1991; Scarbrough, Huddleston and Finley 1986).

In infancy, poor sucking, irritability and failure to thrive are commonly noted (Pinsky and DiGeorge 1965).

The typical behavioural presentation includes learning disability. Some are in the low normal range of intelligence (Anderson *et al.* 1998; Langius *et al.* 2003; Mueller *et al.* 2003; Nowaczyk, Whelan and Hill 1998), and there may be behavioural abnormalities (Tierney *et al.* 2000, 2001).

Tactile, visual and auditory sensitivity are reported to be common problems (Anstey and Taylor 1999; Tierney, Nwokoro and Kelley 2000). Similar sensory hypersensitivities, particularly hyperacusis (sound sensitivity), are seen in other conditions such as Williams syndrome [77] (Attias *et al.* 2008). Sleep problems are reported to be a common feature, but lessen with age and are usually not significant after puberty. Self-injury and aggression are significant issues for many and may require specific approaches to management.

Structural brain anomalies are seen in around a third of those with SLOS. The main anomalies reported include central cerebellar vermal hypoplasia, partial or complete callosal dysgenesis, and hypoplasia of the frontal lobes (Gorlin, Cohen and Levin 1990). The brain is smaller than normal in some 84 per cent (see, for reviews, Hennekam 2005; Kelley and Hennekam 2000). Complete callosal agenesis, together with partial development of the frontal lobes, has also been reported (Kelley *et al.* 1996). Holoprosencephaly (a failure of development of the forebrain in the embryo, resulting in a small head and characteristic facial features) has been reported in a number of cases (Kelley 1998; McKeever and Young 1990; Nowaczyk *et al.* 2001).

The clinical features of SLOS are partly modified by the maternal genotype, and in particular by the effects of the ApoE genotype on transmission of cholesterol from the maternal blood supply to the developing embryo (Witsch-Baumgartner *et al.* 2004).

Antenatal screening demonstrates low maternal urinary oestriol (Jezela-Stanek *et al.* 2006) and elevated plasma oestriol levels (Shackleton *et al.* 1999) and can be useful in early detection of SLOS. Shackleton's group also demonstrated the presence of equine-type oestriols that are not normally found, but made up over half of the oestrogens detected in the mother carrying a foetus affected by SLOS. It has been speculated that the effects on oestriol levels may be due to abnormal development of the foetal adrenal glands (McKeever and Young 1990), and adrenal insufficiency has been found to be a complicating factor in some cases (Andersson *et al.* 1999).

Several other conditions show similar differences in urinary and blood marker oestriol levels, in particular Down syndrome [31] (Craig *et al.* 2006) and X-linked ichthyosis [80], but abnormalities can be found in a range of other presentations (Duric *et al.* 2003; Kim *et al.* 2000)

Is there a link between SLOS and ASD?

- The first published paper to suggest a link between SLOS and ASD appeared in 2000 (Tierney, Nwokoro and Kelley 2000). Tierney and colleagues reviewed their own and others' work and noted that six of 13 cases they had presented at an AACAP (American Academy of Child and Adolescent Psychiatry) meeting in 1999 had scored as autistic on both the ADI-R and on DSM-IV criteria.

- Tierney *et al.* (2001) used multiple age-dependent postal questionnaires and telephone interviews to evaluate the behavioural phenotype of 56 subjects with SLOS. Forty-seven were later followed up with direct observation and interview. The authors concluded that individuals with SLOS manifest a characteristic behavioural profile of cognitive delay, sensory hyperreactivity, irritability, language impairment, sleep-cycle disturbance, self-injurious behaviour, syndrome-specific motor movements, upper body opisthotonus (a muscular reaction where the infant arches backwards appearing to push away from someone who is holding them) and autism spectrum behaviours. Nine of the 17 subjects (53 per cent) who were assessed on the ADI-R met criteria for autistic disorder.

- In 2006, Sikora *et al.* published a study on 14 children with SLOS aged 3–16 using questionnaire, interview and direct observational measures. Depending on the measures used, between 71 and 86 per cent fulfilled criteria for an ASD, with some 50 per cent fulfilling criteria for autistic disorder.

- In a study of cholesterol in an unselected series of 100 ASD cases obtained from the AGRE specimen bank, Tierney *et al.* (2006) found low cholesterol levels (below the normal population fifth centile levels) in 19 cases. No cases had levels consistent with SLOS, but this report suggests that a significant proportion of ASD cases have abnormal sterol metabolism.

- The most recent paper on ASD and SLOS (Aneja and Tierney 2008) is a review of the role of cholesterol in autism, using SLOS as a paradigm case. It provides information on the various mechanisms by which sterol deficiencies can result in developmental abnormalities, namely:

- ○ the role of cholesterol in embryonic and foetal development (Tabin and McMahon 1997)
- ○ cholesterol as a precursor in the formation of neuroactive steroids (Marcos *et al.* 2004)
- ○ cholesterol's role in the formation of myelin (Saher *et al.* 2005)
- ○ cholesterol as a modulator of oxytocin receptors (Gimpl *et al.* 2002)
- ○ cholesterol as a modulator of serotonin 1A receptors (Chattopadhyay *et al.* 2005).

- One study has compared excretion levels of two compounds: 8-hydroxy-2-deoxyguanosine (8-OHdG) and 8-isoprostane-F2alpha (8-iso-PGF2alpha). The study compared 33 autistic children with 29 healthy group-matched controls. A slight overall group difference was found. The autistic group's distribution was bimodal and a small subgroup of the autistic children showed a far more marked elevation over controls, suggesting that a subgroup had a specific defect in sterol metabolism (Ming *et al.* 2005).

On the basis of some of the genetic screening studies (such as Ciara *et al.* 2006) the high prevalence of SLOS suggests that it could be a common cause of ASD in some populations. SLOS is thought to be more common in parts of Central Europe, so this finding may not generalize to other populations, as the different mutations have been reported to occur at very different rates.

Antenatal detection: Antenatal diagnosis of SLOS by biochemical profiling has been possible for some years (Johnson *et al.* 1994; McGaughran *et al.* 1994). Reliable diagnosis is possible (Irons and Tint 1998) from both testing of amniotic fluid (Dallaire *et al.* 1995; Kratz and Kelley 1999) and chorionic villus sampling (Kratz and Kelley 1999). Maternal urinary steroid levels can also prove a reliable diagnostic tool (Jezela-Stanek *et al.* 2006).

A number of abnormalities are detectable on ultrasound. Intrauterine growth retardation is most common, being seen in two-thirds of cases (Goldenberg *et al.* 2004).

Genetics: A large number of genetic factors have been identified as sufficient to result in SLOS, with more than 120 separate mutations so far having been described, the majority being missense mutations (well over 85 per cent are of this type), with smaller numbers of nonsense mutations, small deletions and insertions, and mutations that affect splicing or translation initiation (Yu and Patel 2005).

It seems likely that variations in the gene mutations involved relate to the biochemical differences in cholesterol synthesis and to the clinical phenotype (Neklason *et al.* 1999).

Differential Diagnosis: A marker found almost exclusively in SLOS is the particular pattern of (Y-shaped) syndactyly – with webbing between the upper portion of the second and third toes (Gofflot *et al.* 2003). It is reported in a high proportion of cases (79/80 in the series reported by Cunniff *et al.* 1997, and 40/55 of those reported by Johnson 1975).

Various SLOS features are seen in other conditions, and the phenotypic variability within SLOS is wide; however, the biochemical profile (Seller *et al.* 1997) and genetics are specific.

A number of other conditions present with similar abnormalities of sterol metabolism, including beta-sitosterolemia; CHILD syndrome; desmosterolosis; mevalonic aciduria, and X-linked dominant chondrodysplasia punctata.

A number of conditions present with varying combinations of features that overlap with those seen in SLOS, and some are reported as co-occurring in the same individuals: Dubowitz syndrome; Meckel-Gruber syndrome; Noonan syndrome [52]; Nguyen syndrome; Russell-Silver syndrome; Simpson-Golabi-Behmel syndrome; trisomy 13 syndrome (but note that both conditions can co-exist); trisomy 18 (Edwards) syndrome; pseudo-trisomy 13 syndrome; and Pallister-Hall syndrome.

Treatment and management: The following are important aspects.

Cholesterol supplementation: Antenatal cholesterol supplementation is feasible and produces *in utero* improvement in foetal plasma cholesterol and red cell volume (Irons *et al.* 1999). To date no reports have been published on the effects of this approach on subsequent development.

The age at which cholesterol supplementation and correction of 7-dehydrocholesterol build-up is addressed may be critical, as the effects on myelin development and blood–brain barrier function in the nervous system may be difficult to reverse (Morell and Jurevics 1996).

Irons *et al.* (1994) provided an early report on improvements in cholesterol levels in a severely affected girl with SLOS treated with bile salts and cholesterol. Post-treatment cholesterol levels, although improved, were still well below normal values.

In an early review, Kelley (1998) noted reports of marked improvements in physical growth and development, communication, self-injurious behaviour and agitation. Elias *et al.* (1997) reported similar results in six children they had treated, and, in addition, reduced skin sensitivity, bettered infection tolerance, reduced gastrointestinal symptomology and improved developmental progress, with no reported adverse reactions. Nwokoro and Mulvihill (1997) reported on bile acid and cholesterol replacement in six cases, with reported behavioural improvements and improvements in quality of life, but variable effects on plasma cholesterol levels. Irons *et al.* (1997) reported biochemical and clinical improvement (in growth and neurodevelopmental status) in 14 SLOS patients, in parallel with an increase in plasma cholesterol and percentage sterol as cholesterol, after treatment with cholesterol alone (3) or cholesterol in combination with bile acids (11).

Linck *et al.* (2000) were able to show reductions in 7-dehydrocholesterol and increases in cholesterol in serum through dietary cholesterol supplementation.

Sikora *et al.* (2004) reported no improvement in development in 14 SLOS cases who were followed up over a six-year period of cholesterol supplementation. This study did; however, find wide variation in the results obtained, with two cases reported as showing substantial improvement, but full data being obtained on only two cases. Initial cholesterol levels, not response to supplementation, seemed the best predictor of outcome.

Improvements in skin sensitivity to ultraviolet light have been documented in response to cholesterol supplementation (Azurdia, Anstey and Rhodes 2001; Starck, Lovegren-Sandblom and Bjorkhem 2002a).

Simvastatin: As part of the metabolic problem may result from the build-up of 7-dehydrocholesterol in body tissues, studies are being conducted on the use of simvastatin to reduce 7-dehydrocholesterol in parallel with cholesterol supplementation. Effects on development are mixed (Haas *et al.* 2007; Jira *et al.* 2000; Starck, Lovegren-Sandblom and Bjorkhem 2002b), but the combined treatment appears well tolerated and has the predicted metabolic effects (Chan *et al.* 2009).

Other aspects of care: A variety of management issues are discussed in Irons (2007) and in Kelley and Hennekan (2000).

There are minor issues in anaesthetic care where diagnostic imaging or surgical management is required (Choi and Nowaczyk 2000), and other issues in surgical management have been discussed (Craigie *et al.* 2005). Minor issues in dental treatment have also been reported (Muzzin and Harper 2003).

Haloperidol can exacerbate symptomology, as it can bind to the DHCR7 binding site leading to an excessive build-up of 7-dehydrocholesterol.

Further information and support:
In the USA:
Smith-Lemli-Opitz/RSH Foundation
PO Box 212
Georgetown,
MA 01833
Tel.: 978 352 5885
E-mail: cgold@smithlemliopitz.org;
sloinfo@smithlemliopitz.org (general information)
Website: www.smithlemliopitz.org

67

Smith-Magenis syndrome (SMS)

Gene locus: 17p11.2, typically with interstitial deletion, but also with specific mutation of RAI1

Key ASD references: Cohen *et al.* 2005; de Almeida, Reis and Martins 1989; Dykens, Finucane and Gayley 1997; Hicks *et al.* 2008; Lockwood *et al.* 1988; Mariner *et al.* 1986; Vostanis *et al.* 1994

The first paper to describe SMS was a clinical description of a series of nine cases with 17p11.2 deletions (Smith *et al.* 1986). A further paper describing a small series of six cases appeared later the same year (Stratton *et al.* 1986). All 15 cases were described as conforming to the same clinical phenotype – physically they were described as broad skulled, having flat faces and protruding jaws, and as being growth retarded. They had hoarse voices, speech delay, delayed milestones and behavioural difficulties.

For a review of Smith-Magenis syndrome, see Gropman *et al.* (2007).

Martin, Wolters and Smith (2006) highlight the high degree of maladaptive behaviour seen in individuals with SMS. Global cognitive functioning in SMS is delayed and is generally consistent with the person's communication and daily living skills, but socialization is often better than would be expected from overall intelligence.

The current view of SMS is that it is a microdeletion syndrome that results from a mutation/deletion including the retinoic-acid induced 1 (RAI1) gene which seems sufficient to produce the SMS phenotype (Slager *et al.* 2003), while larger deletions result in the variable heart and kidney problems seen in most cases. Over 90 per cent of cases carry the core genetic deletion – a 3.7-Mb interstitial deletion in chromosome 17p11.2 (Potocki *et al.* 2000b). The disorder can also be caused by specific mutations in the RAI1 (retinoic acid inducible) gene, which is also within the Smith-Magenis chromosome region (Girirajan *et al.* 2005).

How common is SMS? The best estimate is that the population prevalence of SMS is between one in 15,000 and one in 25,000 (Juyal *et al.* 1996; Smith *et al.* 2006). Prevalence of one in 600 has been found in a population with learning disability of unknown cause (Struthers *et al.* 2002).

Similar numbers of male and female cases are reported. There have been no reports of any association with racial group, and parental age does not appear to be an additional risk factor.

Main clinical features: The first clinical report of a child with Smith-Magenis syndrome (Patil and Bartley 1984) gave details of a four-year-old girl with a slight build (50th percentile for height and head circumference but fifth centile for weight). She had a significant learning disability, delayed speech and language, generalized hypotonia, small ears, and a conductive hearing loss. She was found to have an interstitial deletion of chromosome 17p11.2.

Commonly reported early features are infantile hypotonia and failure to thrive. Infant development does not seem to show autistic features, which become more apparent with age, typically between two and three years of age (Wolters *et al.* 2009).

A number of physical features are consistently seen: brachycephaly; a flattened midface; a broad bridge to the nose; a Mobius/Cupid's bow mouth shape and short stature (Lockwood *et al.* 1988).

Other commonly reported problems include: otolaryngolic abnormalities (94 per cent); ocular abnormalities (85 per cent); cleft lip/palate (75 per cent); peripheral nerve problems (75 per cent); scoliosis (65 per cent); heart defects (52 per cent); abnormal genitalia (35 per cent); and epilepsy (25 per cent) (Greenberg *et al.* 1991).

Learning disability is typically present, but of variable level, typically with an IQ of between 40 and 60, although the reported range is wider (Greenberg *et al.* 1996). Communication is typically impaired.

A number of behavioural features are thought to be characteristic, particularly self-mutilation and inserting objects into body orifices such as the ears (see, for example, Greenberg *et al.* 1991).

Sleep disturbance is seen in a high proportion of those with SMS, noted in 62 per cent of those reported by Greenberg *et al.* (1991), 75 per cent of those they reported on in 1996, 60 per cent of those studied by Dykens, Finucane and Gayley (1997), a series of 19 cases reported by Potocki et al. (2000b), 19 of whom had abnormal excretion of a melatonin metabolite, and a further series of 20 cases (De Leersnyder et al. 2001), 40 per cent of whom showed evidence of an abnormal pattern of melatonin release. Some have absent REM (rapid eye movement) sleep (2/32 cases studied by Greenberg et al. 1991).

Smith A.C.M et al. (2002) carried out lipid profiling on 49 SMS cases and noted that cholesterol levels were elevated above the 95th centile in 57 per cent.

It is possible that various aspects of the SMS phenotype, particularly hypotonia, seizure activity, learning disability and the behavioural phenotype, result from mitochondrial abnormalities due to mutation or deletion of the NT5M gene, which is in the SMS critical region of 17p11.2 (see Lucas et al. 2001; Rampazzo et al. 2000). NT5M is deoxyribonucleoside, which is imported into mitochondria where it is converted to a deoxyribonucleoside kinase and limits the accumulation of thymidine triphosphate.

Specific deletion of the RI1 gene can result in a phenotype without short stature or gastrointestinal involvement, but with the craniofacial differences – the broad head and flattened facial appearance and the behavioural components of SMS – self-injury, temper, and sleep disturbance (Girirajan et al. 2005). This is similar to the restricted SMS phenotype shown in animal models with selective retinoic acid induced gene 1 deletion (Walz et al. 2006).

Is there a link between SMS and ASD? A number of papers have so far been published reporting cases with Smith-Magenis syndrome and ASD:

- Mariner et al. (1986) published an early paper on autosomal gene defects associated with ASD and learning difficulties. One of the cases they describe is the first de novo 17p deletion reported in association with ASD.

- Lockwood et al. (1988) discussed three cases with 17p11.2 deletions, one of whom, a 17-year-old Caucasian girl with an IQ of 40, was described as having some autistic behaviour but good eye contact.

- De Almeida, Reis and Martins (1989) presented a further single SMS case: a three-year-old boy with delayed development, a broad face with hypoplastic midface, prognathism, and behavioural anomalies consistent with an ASD.

- Vostanis et al. (1994) described two autosomal genetic conditions in association with ASD. One of these cases, a 17-year-old boy, had an interstitial chromosome 17 deletion.

- Dykens, Finucane and Gayley (1997) published a study on the behavioural and cognitive profile of a small series of 12 individuals (ten male, two female) with SMS, who were aged between 14 and 51. From a variety of assessments, all that can be concluded here is that fewer than five of these people were scored as autistic.

- Hicks et al. (2008) reported on a pair of three-and-a-half-year-old identical male twins concordant for SMS, learning disability, communication delay, motor stereotypies and self-injurious behaviour and ASD. This is the first description of SMS in twins. The twins were divergent on a number of features – particularly the presence of cardiac and renal abnormalities and the extent of their language problems and behavioural issues.

Despite their zygosity, the twins had marked differences in presentation, including their divergent for cardiac anomalies (twin A had atrio- and ventriculo-septal defects and pulmonary stenosis, while twin B was normal) and renal anomalies (twin A had bilateral reflux, while twin B was normal), delayed expressive language development (more severe in twin A), and behavioural phenotype (destructive behavioural outbursts were markedly worse in twin B).

Differential Diagnosis: All of the differential diagnoses are other genetic conditions that have been linked to ASD.

The principal differential diagnosis to be considered is fragile-X [35]; other conditions that can sometimes present with a similar phenotype are 22q11.2 deletion syndrome [18, 20, 29a, 76]; Prader-Willi syndrome [61]; and Williams syndrome [77]. Down syndrome [31] can occasionally be confused in the neonatal period.

Treatment and management: In one study with nine children (De Leersnyder *et al.* 2001), acebutolol, a selective beta-1-adrenergic antagonist, was given early in the morning. A significant decrease in inappropriate behaviour and improved concentration were noted. In addition, delayed sleep onset, lengthened sleep and delayed waking were also seen.

There is clear evidence that hypercholesterolaemia is linked to SMS, as is an increased risk of cardiac malformation. Treatment strategies to lower LDL cholesterol in particular would seem advisable, and maintenance management with cholesterol-lowering agents may be useful to consider.

Sleep problems are common in SMS, and appear linked to a defect in the production of serotonin and abnormal circadian release of melatonin. This suggests that serotonin supplementation or supplementation with precursors may also be helpful.

There is a particular constellation of challenging behaviour difficulties that appear to result in an SMS-specific behavioural phenotype. The general literature on treatment of such behaviours in ASD suggests that consideration of medications such as risperidone may be warranted where behavioural strategies have proved ineffective; however, this needs to be carefully monitored, as side-effects can be significant (Yang and Tsai 2004).

Further information and support:

In the UK:
The Smith-Magenis Syndrome Foundation
24 Brook Road
Dersingham
King's Lynn
Norfolk
PE31 6LG
Tel.: 01328 730 782
E-mail: info@smith-magenis.co.uk
Website: www.smith-magenis.co.uk

In the USA:
PRISMS, Inc.
(Parents and Researchers Interested in Smith-Magenis Syndrome)
21800 Town Center Plaza
Suite #266A-633
Sterling,
VA 20164
Tel.: 972 231 0035
Fax: 413 826 6539
E-mail: info@prisms.org
Website: www.prisms.org/start.htm

68

Sotos syndrome

aka • cerebral gigantism

Gene locus: 5q35

Key ASD references: Cohen 2003; Finegan *et al.* 1994; Morrow, Whitman and Accardo 1990; Mouridsen and Hansen 2002; Rutter and Cole 1991; Zapella 1990

There are two Orphanet reviews of Sotos syndrome (Baujat and Cormier-Daire 2007; Tatton-Brown and Rahman 2007), and a further useful review can be found in Gosalakkal (2004).

The condition was first clearly described in 1964 by Juan Fernandez Sotos and colleagues. An earlier report (Schlesinger 1931) appears to document a remarkably similar phenotype, and may be the earliest account identified to date. The key features are accelerated bone ageing over the first four years, acromegaly and non-progressive neurological deficits.

The NSD1 gene (Nuclear Receptor-Binding Su-var, Enhancer of Zeste, and Trithorax Domain Protein 1) has been implicated in a high proportion of cases, with varying specific NSD1 defects in different populations (microdeletions appear particularly prevalent in the Japanese) (Rio *et al.* 2003). NSD1 defects do not appear to be common in other overgrowth conditions (Türkmen *et al.* 2003).

How common is Sotos syndrome? Sotos syndrome is assumed in the literature to be common, as a large number of clinical cases have been reported; however, no epidemiological studies have so far been carried out.

Main clinical features: In the initial paper (Sotos *et al.* 1964) five children were described who had a disorder characterized by excessively rapid growth, acromegalic features, and a nonprogressive cerebral disorder with learning disability. A high-arched palate and a prominent jaw were noted in several cases. The children were large at birth, their length being between the 90th and 97th centiles, with advanced bone age in most.

Sotos syndrome is an overgrowth condition – people who have it are significantly larger than would be expected for their families. They have a distinct facial appearance, a larger skull, and learning difficulties that can be varied in severity. In addition, advanced bone age is typical (a wrist X-ray to identify accelerated bone age was the diagnostic tool of choice before the 5q35 abnormality was identified). Seizures and curvature of the spine are also fairly common in Sotos syndrome.

The localization of Sotos syndrome to NSD1 at 5q35 is a fairly recent finding (Kurotaki *et al.* 2002). Clinical diagnosis based on phenotype (macrocephaly, facial features and size) is successful in identifying NSD1 Sotos syndrome in 99 per cent of cases, suggesting that the NSD1 phenotype can be reliably diagnosed in the majority of cases (Tatton-Brown et al. 2005).

The clinical characteristics of Sotos syndrome are detailed in Tatton-Brown and Rahman (2004). There are three key features: a typical facial gestalt which becomes more pronounced with age (with lengthening of the face and the jaw-line becoming more prominent – Allanson and Cole 1996), significant macrocephaly and learning difficulties, which are seen in over 90 per cent of cases (Tatton-Brown and Rahman 2004). Childhood physical overgrowth, advanced bone age, cardiac and kidney anomalies, neonatal jaundice, neonatal hypotonia, febrile convulsions, tumours and scoliosis are also all fairly common features.

Cardiac problems are reported in some 50 per cent of cases (Kaneko et al. 1987).

Cole and Hughes (1990) note that the somatic features tend to become less obvious with age.

Sotos can be found with normal intelligence (Cole and Hughes 1994; De Boer et al. 2004; van Haelst et al. 2005). The two series where IQ/DQ has been reported note a wide range of functioning, with mean scores in the high 70s (Cole and Hughes: mean 78, range 40–129 (78 cases); De Boer et al.: mean 76, range 47–105 (21 cases)).

Most cases arise as sporadic mutations with no family history. Both concordant (Hook and Reynolds 1967) and discordant (Brown et al. 1998) identical twin pairs have been reported. Where a family history is reported, the pattern of inheritance is typically consistent with autosomal dominant inheritance (van Haelst et al. 2005).

Sotos syndrome has also been reported in association with fragile-X syndrome [35] (see, for example, Verloes, Sacré and Geubelle 1987); however, no such cases have been reported to date with co-morbid ASD, and an NSD1 mutation was not tested for in these cases.

At the time of writing, studies are appearing in which Sotos-phenotype cases are being reported with other gene abnormalities, such as 11p15 (Baujat et al. 2004), and other clinical conditions (in addition to Weaver syndrome, which is phenotypically similar) are being reported with 5q35 defects (Baujat and Cormier-Daire 2007).

Is there a link between Sotos syndrome and ASD? Many of the early accounts of cerebral gigantism would be consistent with an ASD diagnosis. Kjellman in 1965, for example, described a girl with aggressive, wilful and avoidant behaviour who had apparently normal motor skills but was nonverbal.

As early as 1984, Varley and Crnic had documented social deficits in Sotos syndrome; however, none of the cases they described were thought to have an ASD.

- The first publication to suggest a link between Sotos syndrome and autism was a single case study published by Morrow, Whitman and Accardo in 1990. The paper described a four-year-and-eleven-month-old boy of normal intelligence (assessed on the Stanford-Binet), but with delayed early milestones, immediate and delayed echolalia, abnormal eye contact and self-injury (headbanging and hair-pulling). He fulfilled criteria for autistic disorder.

- In the same year (1990), Michele Zapella, a paediatric neurologist from Sienna in Northern Italy, published a similar case report.

- The following year, Rutter and Cole (1991) published a case series of 16 children with Sotos syndrome aged between 5 and 15. Two-thirds of these children had IQs in the normal range. A number of behaviours were seen as characteristic – tantrums, destructiveness, social withdrawal and eating and sleeping difficulties. Several of the children were said to display autistic tendencies, but no standardized assessments of ASD were carried out.

- Finegan et al. (1994) studied 27 cases of Sotos syndrome and compared their profiles to 20 other non-specific overgrowth cases. In the Sotos group, 21 had IQ scores in the average range – a greater proportion than in the comparison group. Expressive and receptive language levels were commensurate with IQ. The Sotos children were more likely to be irritable, had higher rates of stereotyped behaviour, had a high rate of ADHD (seen in 38 per cent) and were more socially withdrawn. Several were thought to be autistic.

- Mouridsen and Hansen (2002) described two Sotos cases, one of whom had low normal IQ, ADHD and autistic features, while the other had a moderate learning disability and met the tenth revision of the International Classification of Diseases (ICD-10) criteria for autistic disorder.

- Cohen (2003) reviewed the evidence on behavioural and cognitive phenotypes in the various overgrowth syndromes, including Sotos syndrome.

- A paper by Compton et al. (2004) presents a 20-year-old male case of Sotos syndrome who presented with apparent delusions and hallucinations and a long-standing history of learning disability, seizures, asthma, difficulties with peer relationships and temper outbursts.

Differential diagnosis: Differential diagnosis is between Sotos syndrome and a number of other overgrowth syndromes, some of which have been linked to ASD, such as Bannayan-Riley-Ruvalcaba syndrome [15]; basal cell naevus syndrome [16]; cortical dysplasia–focal epilepsy syndrome [19]; Cole-Hughes macrocephaly syndrome [24]; Cowden syndrome [26]; Orstavik 1997 syndrome [56]; and Proteus syndrome [62], and some which have not, such as Simpson-Golabi-Behmel syndrome type I and Weaver syndrome.

Weaver syndrome presents with the greatest degree of phenotypic similarity, but can usually be discriminated by the absence of an NSD1 defect – the genetic finding that is typically seen in Sotos syndrome. There are; however, cases reported as Weaver syndrome that also have NSD1 mutations (see, for example, Baujat et al. 2005).

Treatment and management: As a multisystem disorder, Sotos requires multidisciplinary review to identify difficulties in the individual case and put in place appropriate monitoring and treatment as required. As cardiac problems, kidney problems and scoliosis are potential areas that will require management, it is important that these are reviewed and treatment provided as required. See the discussion of general management issues in Baujat and Cormier-Daire (2007).

Further information and support:

In Canada:
Sotos Syndrome Support Association of Canada
1944 Dumfries
Montreal
Quebec
H3P 2R9
E-mail: info@sssac.com
Website: www.sssac.com

In the UK:
The Child Growth Foundation
2 Mayfield Avenue
Chiswick
London
W4 1PW

Tel.: 020 8995 0257
E-mail: Jenny.cgf@btopenworld.com
Websites: www.childgrowthfoundation.org;
www.heightmatters.org.uk

In the USA:
Sotos Syndrome Support Association
PO Box 4626
Wheaton
Illinois
IL 60189
Tel. (toll-free): 888-246-7772
E-mail: sssa@well.com
Website: www.well.com/~sssa

69

Succinic semialdehyde dehydrogenase (SSADH) deficiency

Gene locus: 6p22

Key ASD references: Knerr *et al.* 2008; Pearl *et al.* 2003

SSADH deficiency is an inborn error of metabolism that is a rare autosomal recessive disorder of gamma aminobutyric acid (GABA) metabolism. The missing mitochondrial enzyme, found in astrocytes, catalyses the transformation of succinic semialdehyde into succinic acid, which would normally then provide gamma-hydroxybutyrate as a key factor in the tricarboxylic/Krebs cycle.

The first case identified was reported in 1981 by Jakobs *et al.*, and was a Turkish child of consanguineous parents, with neurologic abnormalities and elevated urinary excretion of gamma-hydroxybutyrate (GHB). He had a mild learning difficulty but was markedly ataxic and hypotonic. The same child, when followed up at age five, had elevated levels of GABA in both urine and cerebrospinal fluid (Gibson *et al.* 1984). Various other affected children from consanguineous relationships have been reported, suggesting autosomal recessive inheritance (Gibson *et al.* 1997b).

How common is SSADH? SSADH has been described to date in over 400 cases in the literature, but at present there is no accurate estimate of the likely population prevalence (Pearl *et al.* 2003).

Main clinical features: The first large clinical series (N=23) to be described (Gibson *et al.* 1997a) noted delayed motor, cognitive and language development, hypotonia, ataxia, seizures, diminished reflexes, behavioural problems and EEG abnormalities as the most commonly reported features. These can be seen reflected in the series reported by Pearl *et al.* (2003) and Knerr *et al.* (2008), tabulated in Table B69 below.

Long-term follow-up, albeit limited, suggests that the behavioural phenotype is fairly static and does not worsen over time (Crutchfield *et al.* 2008).

Is there a link between SSADH and ASD?

- Pearl *et al.* (2003) reviewed 53 cases, all with early developmental delay, and over 80 per cent with learning disability at the time of review. Sleep disturbances were common, being seen in 68 per cent, and one case was described as having autistic behaviour – the age and sex are not specified in the paper.

- Knerr *et al.* (2008) reviewed 33 adolescent and adult cases, four of whom had a diagnosis of PDD or autism.

In total, these two papers describe a total of five cases of ASD in association with SSADH, giving a combined likelihood of about eight per cent. There may be a slight overlap in the cases in the two reports.

Table B69: Clinical features of SSADH deficiency

	Pearl *et al.* (2003)		Knerr *et al.* (2008)	
	N	%	N	%
Clinical findings	(N=53)		(N=33)	
• developmental delay	53	100	33	100
• mental retardation	43	81		
• hypotonia	35	66	15	45
• behavioural problems	37	70	27	82
• seizures	24	45	19	58
• ataxia	28	53	20	61
• language delay	18	34		
Neuropsychiatric problems	(N=37)	70	(N=27)	82
• aggression	6	16	6	18
• anxiety	11	30	12	36
• hallucinations	4	11	5	15
• hyperactivity	15	41	13	39
• inattention	19	51	18	55
• OCD	13	35	11	33

• sleep disturbance	25	68	15	45
• PDD/autism	1	3	4	12
Ataxia			(N=20)	60
• decreased balance			8	24
• uncoordinated movements			8	24
• wide-based gait			7	21
• uncoordinated walking			7	21
• hand tremors			6	18
• excessive movements			4	12
• tripping			2	6
Seizures	(N=25)	47	(N=19)	57
• generalized tonic-clonic	14	56	14	42
• absence	10	40	12	36
• myoclonic	5	20	3	9
• unspecified	3	12	9	27
• other (ALTE, atonic, partial, febrile)	7	28		
EEG studies	(N = 28)	53		
• background abnormal/slowing	7	25		
• spike discharges	8	29		
• ESES	1	4		
• photosensitivity	2	7		
• normal	10	36		
Neuroimaging	(N = 30)	57		
• increased T2 signal				
• globus pallidi	13	43		
• white matter	2	7		
• dentate nucleus	5	17		
• brainstem	2	7		
• cerebral atrophy	3	10		

These two series (Knerr *et al.* 2008; Pearl *et al.* 2003) review a total of 86 cases. The earlier study presented a collation of 14 newly reported cases, together with a review of previously published cases (age range 1–21 years), and the later one a series of adolescent and adult cases from the database maintained at the Children's National Medical Center in Washington.

The main autistic features that have been noted are withdrawn affect, poor eye contact, poor pretend play, stereotypies, inability to transition and a strong preference for routine (Pearl *et al.* 2009).

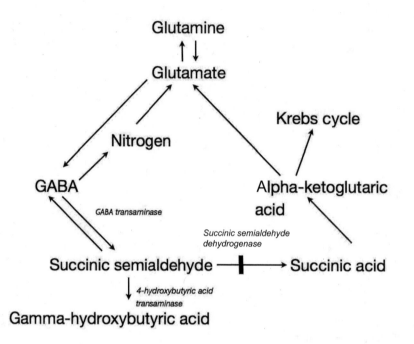

Figure B69: The neurochemistry of SSADH

Differential diagnosis: Differential diagnosis will be from other conditions that interfere with GABAergic systems, such as fragile-X syndrome [35, 36] and tuberous sclerosis [73], or present with delayed milestones together with ataxia, as in Joubert syndrome [44]. All of these are phenotypically distinct, and the genetics and biochemistry should easily identify SSADH.

Treatment and management: The principal metabolic abnormalities seen in SSADH are elevations in gamma aminobutyric acid (GABA) and gamma-hydroxybutyrate (GHB).

Treatments to date have largely involved the use of GABA inhibitors such as vigabatrin (Gropman 2003) and other medications that modulate the GABA system (Knerr *et al.* 2007) and amino acids such as taurine, which has the same receptor binding (Pearl and Gibson 2004; Pearl *et al.* 2009).

In an interesting report by Leuzzi *et al.* (2007) two brothers with SSADH deficiency developed dystonic movements that were brought on by exercise. In both cases the problem was improved with the use of vigabatrin, and in one there was a parallel improvement in walking and a reduction in seizure activity.

Further information and support:

In the USA:

The PND Association – Pediatric Neurotransmitter
Disease Association
6 Nathan Drive
Plainview
New York
NY 11803
Tel./Fax: 516-937-0049
E-mail: PND@PNDAssoc.org
Website: www.pndassoc.org

70

Timothy syndrome

Gene locus: 12p13.3

Key ASD references: Splawski *et al.* 2004, 2006

Timothy syndrome is a specific abnormality of calcium involved in nerve conduction known as (Cav 12). It is named after the American cardiologist Dr Katherine W. Timothy, who was instrumental in much of the early research on long QT syndromes. Timothy syndrome is one of ten such conditions. An overview of Timothy syndrome can be found in Splawski *et al.* (2008).

A helpful review of calcium signalling abnormalities seen in seizure disorders, migraine and ASD can be found in Gargus (2009).

How common is Timothy syndrome? Not currently established – only 20 cases have been reported to date worldwide, so the prevalence would appear to be low, given the clinical presentation.

Main clinical features: Timothy syndrome results from a defect on chromosome 12 that results in an abnormality of calcium metabolism. This is a single nucleotide substitution that results in an amino acid substitution of an arginine for a glycine. The gene defect affects calcium flow with a build-up of excess calcium in cells. Around half of the cases so far reported have dysmorphic facial features, typically with a flat nasal bridge, small upper jaw and low-set ears. Syndactyly (webbing) of the fingers and several toes seen in all cases, as are small teeth, and all are bald at birth. All individuals with this defect have cardiac involvement, with QT prolongation (the period of activation and recovery of the ventricular heart muscle calculated from an ECG reading) seen in all cases, and arrythmia in well over 90 per cent. One in three has an enlarged heart. More complex cardiac defects such as ventriculo-septal defects and Tetralogy of Fallot are seen in approximately one in four cases.

Only 25 per cent of those with Timothy syndrome have a learning disability and one in five will have a seizure disorder.

Recurrent infections are common, being seen in over 40 per cent of cases. Breathing difficulties are also common, with pneumonia or bronchitis being seen in just under half of the reported cases. One in three has a brisk gag reflex that complicates feeding. Low blood sugar levels are regularly recorded in one in three cases, as are low calcium levels.

Is there a link between Timothy syndrome and ASD?

- In 2004, Splawski and co-workers reviewed the literature and presented data on 17 clinical cases. This paper established that Timothy syndrome results in a multisystem disorder with a characteristic phenotype, including cardiac arrythmia in all cases, ASD in 80 per cent, and learning disability in 25 per cent. In every case, ASD was as a consequence of a *de novo* missense mutation at 12p13.3.

- Splawski *et al.* (2006) screened 461 individuals with ASD for evidence of the gene mutation CACNA1H at 12p13.3 that causes Timothy syndrome. Missense mutations were identified in six cases, and in none of 480 'ethnically matched' controls.

From the cases reported to date, some 80 per cent have an ASD and 60 per cent meet full criteria for autism.

Differential diagnosis: The principal differential diagnoses are the other long QT syndromes (Splawski *et al.* 2005), and other ASD syndromes which also present with syndactyly: BBS [17] and SLOS [66] are the two most likely. Having conjoined second and third toes is an unusual presentation seen in Timothy syndrome but is often assumed to be a phenotypic marker of SLOS.

Treatment and management: Studies to date on the use of calcium channel blocking agents that successfully treat angina in adults are showing some promising results (Jacobs *et al.* 2006; Napolitano, Bloise and Priori 2006).

An experimental model of the effects of Timothy syndrome on cardiac function at the cellular level is showing positive effects of a drug – ranolazine – but no clinical trials of its use have so far taken place (Sicouri *et al.* 2007).

Further information and support:
US-based, parent-maintained website:
Timothysyndrome.org
Website: www.timothysyndrome.org

71

Tourette syndrome (GTS)

aka • Gilles de la Tourette syndrome (GTS)

Gene loci: 7q31; 8q; 11q23; 13q31.1; 16p; 17q25

Key ASD references: Barabas and Matthews 1984; Baron-Cohen *et al.* 1999a, 1999b; Burd *et al.* 1987, 2009; Canitano and Vivanti 2007; Comings and Comings 1991; Healy 1965; Hebebrand *et al.* 1994; Kadesjo and Gillberg 2000; Kano, Ohta and Nagai 1987; Kano *et al.* 1988; Kerbeshian and Burd 1986, 1996; Nelson and Pribor 1993; Realmuto and Main 1982; Ringman and Jankovic 2000; Ritvo *et al.* 1990; Stern and Robertson 1997; Sverd 1991; Sverd, Montero and Gurevich 1993.

The condition is known as Gilles de la Tourette syndrome after the French clinician, a student of Charcot at the Salpetrière in Paris, who in 1885 wrote an early description of the condition (see discussion in Kushner 1995; Lees 1986). Tourette published his best known paper on the condition, '*Étude sur une affection nerveuse caractérisée par de l'incoordination motrice, acompagnée d'écholalie et de coprolalie*', in 1885. The first case to arouse interest was the Marquise de Dampierre, a Parisian aristocrat who was first described by Itard in 1825. The Marquise was the subject of Tourette's 1885 paper, but it is unlikely that Tourette ever met with or examined her (if still alive, she would have been 86 at the time of his first publication), and from the historical records Charcot also seems unlikely to have met or treated her (see Kurlan 2004; Teive *et al.* 2008).

Tourettte syndrome (GTS) is diagnosed on the basis of chronic vocal and motor tics. In its extreme form GTS can be socially disabling and include involuntary obscene vocalizations (coprolalia) and involuntary obscene gestures (copropraxia).

It can be caused by mutations in the SLITRK1 gene at 13q31; however, this is a rare cause, being seen in around one in 60 GTS cases (Abelson *et al.* 2005). Linkage of the Tourette phenotype to several other chromosomal sites has also been proposed.

A number of useful overviews of GTS have been produced: Comings (1990), Kurlan (2004), Leckman and Cohen (1999), Robertson (2000) and Singer (2005) remain amongst the most detailed and helpful. An excellent historical overview of the development of our understanding of GTS can be found in Kushner (1999).

How common is Tourette syndrome? A number of epidemiological studies have been published, giving a variety of prevalence rates. The rates reported range from 0.05 per cent of boys and 0.03 per cent of girls aged 16 to 17 years (Apter *et al.* 1992) through 1.05 per cent of boys and 0.1 per cent of girls aged 6 to 15 years (Comings, Himes and Comings 1990) to 3.3 per cent of children aged 13 to 14 years (Mason *et al.* 1998).

Kadesjo and Gillberg (2000) studied 409 11-year-old children in a total population cohort. Boys with TS were four times as prevalent as girls (N=5, 4:1), and two-thirds had significant co-morbidity. A second component to the paper was a study of 5–15-year-old children referred to a national GTS clinic over a three-year period. All attended mainstream school, and three were of borderline ability. ADHD was the most common co-morbid feature, affecting 64 per cent. Asperger disorder was diagnosed in three (five per cent) and PDD-NOS in 10 (17 per cent).

Khalifa and von Knorring (2003) carried out a questionnaire survey of 4,479 7–15-year-olds. In total, some 6.6 per cent had experienced some type of tic disorder in the preceding year, with 0.6 per cent fulfilling criteria for GTS.

Main clinical features: Tourette syndrome is a neurologic disorder in which the diagnostic features are major chronic motor and vocal tics with associated behavioural abnormalities. Approximately 80 per cent of cases are male and the majority of those diagnosed are children or adolescents. In around one in ten cases, there is a positive family history – an older first-degree relative has received the diagnosis.

Diagnosis of GTS is based on the clinical presentation of chronic major motor and vocal tics. Typically, the first symptoms are motor tics around the head or neck, and there is a gradual 'cephalocaudal' progression – the motor tics affect more and more of the body, moving from head to foot. (Tics are particularly prevalent in the child and adolescent population (with an estimated lifetime prevalence of around ten per cent). The majority of tics will spontaneously remit with age.) With progression of the disease other motor features may appear, such as echopraxia, and vocal tics such as echolalia, sniffing, coughing, grunting and coprolalia may develop. Coprolalia and copropraxia are not necessary features for diagnosis – copropraxia is seldom reported in the clinical literature, while coprolalia is seen in around eight per cent of current cases (Goldenberg, Brown and Weiner 1994). Prior to 1987, both coprolalia and copropraxia were necessary for diagnosis, and GTS was consequently far less commonly diagnosed. It is not uncommon for the affected person to be unaware of their own tics (Kurlan *et al.* 1987).

GTS is overrepresented in certain ethnic groups (such as the Ashkenazi Jewish population) and appears to be rare in others – for example, few Afro-Caribbean cases have been reported.

As with most neurodevelopmental disorders, there is a preponderance of males, with a 4:1 male to female ratio (Comings and Comings 1985). This could indicate that GTS is more prevalent in males, that the presentation is more severe, or that the presentation is different across the sexes.

From some of the studies carried out (Nee *et al.* 1980; Pauls and Leckman 1986; Pauls *et al.* 1988), there seems to be an association between GTS and a positive family history of tics, GTS and obsessive-compulsive disorder (OCD).

One study of a family with a paternal history of OCD and a boy and girl both with OCD and GTS, together with learning disability, identified an insertion/translocation involving chromosomes 2 and 7 which interrupted the CNTNAP2 gene (Verkerk *et al.* 2003). This is potentially important, as it is the first gene region to be identified as an ASD risk factor in several independent studies (Alarcón *et al.* 2008; Arking *et al.* 2008; Bakkaloglu *et al.* 2008; Rossi *et al.* 2008). It has also been shown to be a risk factor for CDFE syndrome [19] as a specific ASD condition associated with seizure problems and abnormal cortical development, and for communication problems (Alarcón *et al.* 2005a).

Comings (1990) has suggested that there may be a link between GTS and mutations in the tryptophan 2.3 dioxygenase gene. This enzyme is the first rate-limiting factor in the breakdown pathway from tryptophan to kynurenine and is involved in central nervous system development. It is interesting that an association has also been noted between mutations of this gene and ASD (Nabi *et al.* 2004). This mutation, where present, would be likely to result in elevated levels of serotonin.

Suggestions that a difference in dopamine systems is also important have come from studies which show benefits from the use of treatments that block the dopamine D2 receptor, such as haloperidol, and exacerbation of symptoms through medications that increase dopaminergic activity.

A family history where both parents have certain GTS features – tics, OCD or anxiety – is common. Walkup *et al.* (1996) found a positive family history for this broader phenotype in a high percentage of cases, with 19 per cent where both parents were or had been affected. Kurlan *et al.* (1994) found that, in families who had a significant history of GTS, the broader phenotype was seen in both parents in 41 per cent of cases.

Is there a link between Tourette syndrome and ASD? A large number of co-morbid cases are reported in the clinical literature.

- The first paper to suggest a link between GTS and ASD was an early Irish report of an adolescent boy (Healy 1965).

- Realmuto and Main (1982) also described a single co-morbid clinical case – a 15-year-old boy.

- Barabas and Matthews (1984) described another boy, diagnosed at age two with autism and additionally at 15 with GTS.

- Kerbeshian and Burd (1986) described six cases of atypical pervasive developmental disorder (also identified as fulfilling criteria for Asperger syndrome), three of whom also presented with co-morbid GTS.

- Burd *et al.* (1987) presented data on 59 patients with autism or PDD-NOS. Twelve of their series had co-morbid GTS which developed after their ASD symptomology. They noted that those who developed GTS had higher IQs and better expressive and receptive language than the rest of their group.

- Kano, Ohta and Nagai (1987) presented two cases of GTS with infantile autism, and took issue with the conclusion of Burd *et al.* that the development of GTS appears to parallel improvement in autistic symptomology.

- Kano *et al.* (1988) appears to be a re-presentation of data on the two boys described in Kano, Ohta and Nagai (1987).

- The study by Ritvo *et al.* (1990) of 233 people with autism in Utah, which looked specifically for medical co-morbidities, reported a number of cases with co-morbid GTS.

- Comings and Comings (1991) reviewed the literature on pervasive developmental disorder to that point, and identified 41 cases who would today be diagnosed as having ASD who were subsequently diagnosed with GTS. They report a further 16 cases with co-morbid presentations and three further families where both conditions were found. They also report a high incidence of other disorders in extended family of their cases and suggest a possible link to abnormalities of serotonin metabolism.

- Sverd (1991) presents a further ten cases of co-morbidity, suggesting that individuals with GTS alone may result from having a single copy of the critical gene involved, while homozygous inheritance (where the affected person carried two affected copies) could result in the reported co-morbid cases.

- Nelson and Pribor (1993) described the case of a calendrical calculator (someone who can, apparently without effort, link days of the week to dates) with ASD and GTS. The possibility that obsessive-compulsive features provide a critical link between the two conditions is raised by these authors.

- Sverd, Montero and Gurevich (1993) reported two children and two adults with autistic disorder, an additional schizophrenia-like psychosis, and tics or GTS. The authors suggest that co-morbid GTS may be a factor that increases the likelihood of ASD developing into a more schizophrenic type of psychotic presentation.

- In the first paper to provide evidence of a link between ASD, GTS and a specific genetic defect, Hebebrand *et al.* (1994) reported a partial trisomy 16p in a 14-year-old boy with an ASD and GTS. He had complex motor and vocal phenomena, including simple tics that had been present since childhood.

- Kerbeshian and Burd (1996) noted that both bipolar disorder and ASD had been reported in association with GTS. They identified four patients in North Dakota for whom these three diagnoses had been given, and the chronology: ASD diagnosis preceded GTS diagnosis, which preceded bipolar disorder diagnosis in all cases. The authors suggest that there may be common factors which underly the aetiology of this observed association.

- Stern and Robertson (1997) provided a review of the 90 or so cases of ASD co-morbid with GTS reported to that date, and the arguments for and against a biological association between the conditions.

- Kadesjo and Gillberg (2000) reported an epidemiological screening of 407 children (50 per cent of all 11-year-olds in a small town in central Sweden). This first study identified five children with GTS: four boys and one girl. The girl and one boy had no co-morbid diagnoses. The other boys had diagnoses of Asperger syndrome, DAMP (Disorders of Attention, Motor Control and Perception) and ADHD. A second study screened all children diagnosed with GTS from the same area aged 5–15 (N=58). A high rate of co-morbidity was found, particularly for ADHD (64 per cent), with ASD being seen in 22 per cent of cases (Asperger syndrome five per cent and PDD-NOS 17 per cent). As the majority of the cases identified in the 11-year-old screening had not been clinically identified, the second study is likely to suffer from ascertainment bias and may have elevated co-morbidity, as such cases are more likely to come to clinical attention.

- Ringman and Jankovic (2000) described a series of 12 ASD cases that had been referred to a movement disorders clinic in Texas. The authors discriminated Asperger syndrome cases on the basis of normal language development, and on this basis all of the GTS cases reported were classified as having Asperger syndrome. Three of their GTS cases had severe sensory deficits. The cases they classified as being autistic had complex motor stereotypies in addition to simple tics.

- Canitano and Vivanti (2007) described a survey of the prevalence of tic disorders in a sample of 105 people with ASD. Twenty-four showed evidence of significant tic disorders. Overall, tic disorders were seen in 22 per cent of the sample, with 11 per cent having chronic motor tics and 11 per cent having additional vocal tics sufficiently chronic to qualify for a diagnosis of GTS. In this sample, all of those examined had some degree of learning disability. There was an association between the severity of tics and the severity of learning disability.

- Burd *et al.* (2009) used an international database of 7,288 people with GTS to identify cases with co-morbid ASD (called in the paper 'pervasive developmental disorders'). A total of 334 co-morbid cases were identified, giving a rate of 4.6 per cent. As a group, these cases were more complex in their presentation. Some 98.8 per cent had additional co-morbidity, while this was only true of 13.2 per cent of those with GTS without ASD.

Two studies by the Cambridge ARC (Autism Research Centre) group have looked at the prevalence of GTS in ASD populations:

- Baron-Cohen *et al.* (1999a) reviewed 37 children attending an ASD school and found that three (8.1 per cent) met criteria for a co-morbid diagnosis of GTS.

- Baron-Cohen *et al.* (1999b) extended the initial study with a review of 497 pupils from nine further schools for ASD. Overall, 4.3 per cent had definite and 2.2 per cent probable GTS. Some 7.1 per cent of those with an autism diagnosis were co-morbid, 7.7 per cent of those with Asperger syndrome and five per cent of those with another ASD diagnosis.

In summary, there is a large body of both case report and clinical series evidence that suggests GTS and ASD co-occur at a significantly higher rate than would be expected unless there were some common underlying process in the two conditions.

Differential diagnosis: A number of conditions can present with similar features, but typically with later onset (as in Huntington's chorea) or with other obvious features (as in Wilson's disease and Hallevorden-Spatz syndrome). The only other condition that also significantly overlaps with ASD and may be confused with GTS is tuberous sclerosis [73].

Treatment and management: A wide range of pharmacological, behavioural, neurosurgical and 'alternative' treatment approaches have been tried. The literature on this topic is voluminous and cannot be covered in any detail here. The interested reader is referred to some helpful reviews (Lavenstein 2003; Silay and Jankovic 2005). Suffice it to say that there is a wide range of treatments that appear to have significantly benefited subgroups. As much of this literature predates the identification of the large number of apparently sufficient genes for the development of GTS, the possibility that particular genetic causes are selectively benefited by particular therapies has not yet been fully explored.

Risperidone, a medication which inhibits the re-uptake of serotonin, has proved beneficial in controlling tics in some cases (Dion *et al.* 2002; Scahill *et al.* 2003).

The most commonly used medications are haloperidol, clonidine and sulpiride.

Nicotine has been claimed to produce significant clinical benefits; however, the small amount of well-controlled research to date has shown limited effects (Howson *et al.* 2004).

Transcranial magnetic resonance stimulation has been advocated, but the results to date in well-controlled studies are also disappointing (Orth *et al.* 2005).

Deep brain stimulation with surgically implanted electrodes is an extreme treatment strategy that has proved beneficial in some cases, but could only be undertaken in neurosurgical centres with appropriate expertise (Skidmore *et al.* 2006).

At the present time there is nothing to suggest that any particular aetiology of GTS is more likely to be linked to ASD than any other. The effects, if any, of GTS co-morbidity on the approach that is likely to be most beneficial in management of ASD is currently unclear.

Further information and support:

Two useful books for families are:

Chowdhury, U. (2004) *Tics and Tourette Syndrome: A Handbook for Parents and Professionals.* London: Jessica Kingsley Publishers.

Robertson, M. and Cavanna, A. (2008) *Tourette Syndrome (The Facts)* (2nd edn). Oxford: Oxford University Press.

There is also a DVD which was produced on one of my patients and gives a useful vignette of someone affected with GTS (John does not have a co-morbid ASD):

John's Not Mad, BBC Q.E.D. Documentary, Fremantle Home Entertainment (2004).

In Australia:
Tourette Syndrome Association of Australia Inc.
PO Box 1173
Maroubra
NSW 2035
Tel.: (02) 9382 3726
Fax: (02) 9382 3764
E-mail: info@tourette.org.au
Website: www.tourette.org.au

In the UK:
Tourette Syndrome (UK) Association
Southbank House
Black Prince Road
London
SW1 7SJ
Helpline: 0845 458 1252
Office: 020 7793 2357
E-mail: help@tsa.org.uk
Website: www.tsa.org.uk

In the USA:
Tourette Syndrome Association Inc.
42–40 Bell Blvd.
Bayside
New York
NY 11361
Tel.: 718-224-2999
Fax: 718-279-9596
Website: www.tsa-usa.org

72

Trichothiodystrophy (TTD)

aka • brittle hair–intellectual impairment–decreased fertility–short stature (BIDS) syndrome

• onychotrichodysplasia

• chronic neutropaenia and mild mental retardation syndrome (ONMRS)

• Amish brittle hair syndrome

• hair–brain syndrome

• Polit syndrome

- Tay syndrome
- Sabinas syndrome

Gene locus: 19q13.2-q13.3, 6p25.3, 2q21

Key ASD reference: Schepis *et al.* 1997

Trichothiodystrophy is the term used for a rare group of genetic disorders – all of which affect organ systems (including the skin) that arise from the neuroectoderm (part of the developing embryo that goes on to form the peripheral nervous system) (Bergmann and Egly 2001). This is one of a range of defects involving DNA damage response that result in neurodevelopmental disorders (see Barzilai, Biton and Shiloh 2008).

How common is trichothiodystrophy? The prevalence of TTD is thought to be low, with some 20 cases reported in the clinical literature to date (Rossi and Cantisani 2004). As most cases have not been genotyped, the relative prevalence of the XPD and XPB forms is not known at this time. The TTD-A form has been characterized (Giglia-Mari *et al.* 2004) but is thought to be rare (Stefanini *et al.* 1993).

Main clinical features: The term 'trichothiodystrophy' (TTD) was introduced as a descriptive label for the combination of brittle hair, brittle nails and ichthyotic skin. Limited subcutaneous fat is also characteristic (Happle *et al.* 1984). One review suggested that low birthweight, small head circumference, small genitalia, cataracts and recurrent infection are also characteristic (Blomquist *et al.* 1991). Most cases, in addition, demonstrate delayed motor development and some degree of learning disability. Brittle hair and nails are due to sulphur deficiency (Price *et al.* 1980). Sensitivity to sunlight is also common, being noted in approximately half of the reported cases (Broughton *et al.* 2001).

Key features (adapted and extended from Bergmann and Egly 2001, p.280)

Skin abnormalities:

- brittle hair and nails
- ichthyosis (dried and crackled skin covered with thin adherent scales)
- collodion baby (transparent shiny skin at birth)
- erythroderma (exfoliative dermatitis), eczema
- photosensitivity (in some 50 per cent of cases, but without apparent increased cancer skin risk).

Physical features:

- growth retardation
- microcephaly
- skeletal deformations
- receding chin, protruding ears and thin, beaked nose
- impaired development of primary sexual characteristics
- decreased subcutaneous fat (with failure to form breast tissue in females)

- dental abnormalities and increased carie formation.

Neurological dysfunctions:

- learning disability
- spasticity/paralysis, ataxia, intention tremor
- impaired motor control
- prematurely aged facial features
- dysmyelination.

Ocular abnormalities:

- cataracts
- conjunctivitis.

Immune system:

- recurrent infections.

Although it is common to see a mild level of learning disability in individuals who show this constellation of features, presentation is variable, and normal intelligence has been reported (Verhage *et al.* 1987).

The first cases reported were a brother and a sister of Asian first-cousin parents (Tay 1971). Both showed ichthyosiform erythroderma, were growth-retarded and learning-disabled, and one died neonatally from an intestinal obstruction.

In one individual who has been followed for over a decade (Jorizzo *et al.* 1982; Stefanini *et al.* 1993), there was no indication of any progressive problems except for hand joint contractures, secondary to ichthyosiform involvement of the palms of the hands.

Is there a link between TTD and ASD?

- To date, only one case has been reported in the literature in association with ASD. This was an Italian boy, 14 years old at the time of the report, with autism associated with TTD, absence seizures with diffuse spike-and-wave discharges apparent on EEG, short stature, and learning disability (Schepis *et al.* 1997). The genotype in this case was not reported.

Given the low overall reported prevalence of TTD, it is impossible to comment on the extent to which the conditions are linked or whether this is a chance co-occurrence of unrelated factors.

The biological basis to TTD appears to be similar to that causing xeroderma pigmentosum [79], which, although not common, is significantly more prevalent. It is possible that defects in the transcription factor IIH (TFIIH) system, which is involved in repair of oxidative DNA damage, may prove to be a more general genetic factor in several forms of ASD.

TTD results from abnormalities of the TFIIH DNA transcription/repair system. As this system involves ten separate proteins, a number of separate genetic defects may prove to be involved, three of which have so far been reported, with two gene loci identified.

Differential diagnosis: The skin involvement is usually apparent within the first two months after birth and is not easily confused with other ASD conditions, the most common alternative causes being immunodeficiency, papulosquamous dermatitis and Netherton syndrome (see Pruzkowski *et al.* 2000). There are a number of other genetic ichthyoses (see, for example, Nakabayashi *et al.* 2005), all of which appear to operate through effects on DNA nucleotide excision repair (Kraemer *et al.* 2007).

There are a number of nucleotide excision repair syndromes. None is common, but all have been reported in association with ASDs, and there appears to be significant phenotypic overlap. Using complementation testing by cell fusion, two specific defects were identified in one study of TTD (Hoeijmakers 1994). A third complementation group has been identified in one child of a consanguineous marriage (Weeda *et al.* 1997).

A further form of TTD has been shown to result from reduced production of TFIIH (Vermeulen *et al.* 2000). This is also due to a small gene mutation that contributes to TFIIH stability and concentration (Cleaver 2005).

A particular form of TTD that seems to be exacerbated by temperature has been reported (Kleijer, Beemer and Boom 1994), and has been shown to be characterized by a specific TFIIH transcription factor mutation (Vermeulen *et al.* 2001).

Treatment and management: No specific treatment strategies have been reported to date. The characterization in the clinical description provided does not allow for any conclusions to be drawn concerning best management.

It is possible that advances in our understanding of nucleotide excision repair mechanisms will lead to targeted treatment approaches.

Further information and support: There is no specific support group, but TTD is covered by a foundation working with families of those with various skin disorders. Contact details are given below.

In the USA:
FIRST (The Foundation for Ichthyosis and Related Skin Types)
1364 Welsh Road G2
North Wales
Pennsylvania
PA 19454
Tel.: 215-619-0670
Fax: 215-619-0780
E-mail: info@scalyskin.org
Website: www.scalyskin.org/contactus.cfm

73

Tuberous sclerosis complex (TSC)

aka • Bourneville syndrome
• epiloia

Gene loci: 16p13.3 (TSC2), 12q14, 9q34 (TSC1)

Key ASD references: Asano *et al.* 2001; Baker, Piven and Sato 1998; Bolton *et al.* 2002; Critchley and Earl 1932; Curatolo *et al.* 2004; Datta, Mandal and Bhattacharya 2009; de Vries, Hunt and Bolton 2007; Gillberg, Gillberg and Ahlsen 1994; Humphrey *et al.* 2004; Hunt and Dennis 1987; Hunt and Shepherd 1993; Khare *et al.* 2001; Kothur, Ray and Malhi 2008; Lewis *et al.* 2004; Riikonen and Simell 1990; Seri *et al.* 1999; Smalley 1995; Smalley *et al.* 1992

The original term for this condition was 'Bourneville syndrome', after the French neurologist Désiré-Magloire Bourneville, who first described cases in 1880. The term 'tuberous sclerosis' was used to describe the appearance of the brain on autopsy – there was the clear appearance of swollen structures that resembled the tubers of a potato.

Individuals with TSC commonly present with four key features – epilepsy, learning difficulties, behaviour problems, and lesions to the skin ('depigmented macules'). Various kidney problems are also common (typically angiomyolipomas and renal cysts).

The term 'epiloia' was introduced as an acronym standing for 'epilepsy, low intelligence, and adenoma sebaceum'; however, this term has not superseded TSC in clinical use, partly because the term 'adenoma sebaceum' is not an accurate description of the cutaneous features.

The association of TSC with two principal genes – TSC1 and TSC2 – was clarified by two studies (Kandt *et al.* 1992; Povey *et al.* 1994). Taken together these studies indicate that just over half of cases are caused by each mutation. The mechanisms by which synapse development and the control of axonal guidance are affected in TSC are becoming much more clearly understood (Knox *et al.* 2007): this is through the effects of two principal abnormal gene products – hamartin (a TSC1 product) and tuberin (a TSC2 product).

For more detail on TSC than could easily be given here, the reader is referred to three sources – a clinical overview (Curatolo 2003), a detailed review of the biology (Crino, Nathanson and Henske 2006), and an overview of advances in our understanding of the neurobiology (Napolioni, Moavero and Curatolo 2009).

How common is tuberous sclerosis? The most recent prevalence estimate for TSC is one in 24,956 (Devlin *et al.* 2006). This is in broad agreement with earlier estimates. The rate in childhood is higher, at some one in 12,000 (Sampson *et al.* 1989). TSC is the second most common neurocutaneous disorder after neurofibromatosis type 1.

Main clinical features: TSC seems equally common in all races and both sexes. There is no association with increased age of either parent.

It first came to light because of the characteristic skin lesions that can occur without other major problems. As with many of the conditions noted here, the phenotype is broad, with varying levels of intelligence and varying severity of physical phenotype.

The skin lesions usually referred to as 'depigmented macules' were first clearly documented in the later 1960s (Fitzpatrick *et al.* 1968). They are typically present at birth in most cases, allowing early diagnosis, but may only be evident under a Wood's light examination (ultraviolet light examination in a dark room).

Infantile spasms, progressing to seizure activity, are seen in a significant proportion of TSC cases, with some 70 per cent of such cases being diagnosed with ASD.

Renal problems are common, with 60–80 per cent of cases having angiomyolipomas (benign growths in the fatty tissue of the kidney). Renal problems are frequently present, but often go unrecognized. In one review (Cook *et al.* 1996) of 139 cases, 61 per cent had evidence of renal damage on ultrasound. Some problems can be more severe, and kidney failure is amongst the leading causes of death in TSC.

There is a reported association between the extent of renal involvement and the level of learning disabilities (O'Callaghan, Noakes and Osborne 2000). This is likely to be an indication of the general severity of the condition (with more severe cases being more likely to have problems with kidney and with central nervous system function), rather than of any direct causal link between renal problems and intellectual function.

Pitting in the enamel of the teeth is a further common characteristic, seen in over 70 per cent of cases (Flanagan *et al.* 1997).

Is there a link between tuberous sclerosis and ASD?

- In 1932, well before autism was characterized by Kanner (1943), Critchley and Earl (1932) described 'a combination of intellectual defect and a primitive form of psychosis' in TSC.

- Riikonen and Amnell (1981) surveyed 192 Finnish children with infantile spasms. Twenty-four had ASD diagnoses, of which 14 were transient. They noted an association between infantile spasms and the co-occurrence of autism and tuberous sclerosis. Riikonen and Simell (1990) reviewed the association between TSC and infantile spasms in 24 cases, indicating that without appropriate therapy the prognosis was worse than for infantile spasms that are idiopathic; and that relapse rate was higher after stopping adrenocorticotropic hormone therapy.

- Hunt and Dennis (1987) described the psychiatric status of a sample of 90 children with TSC. Hyperkinetic behaviour was described in 59 per cent. Half of the sample had 'psychotic' behaviour and 13 per cent were severely aggressive. Of those with infantile spasms, 57 per cent were diagnosed as autistic.

- Smalley *et al.* (1992) reviewed the literature to that time, reporting that between 17 per cent and 58 per cent of TSC cases were noted to have ASD where the association had been looked for. In a series of seven co-morbid cases, the only clear discrimination from others with TSC appeared to be a higher proportion of males in the co-morbid group, with an even sex ratio in the rest of their TSC cases.

- Hunt and Shepherd (1993) interviewed the parents of 21 children with TSC and categorized five as having ASD and four (all girls) as having behaviour consistent with PDD-NOS.

- Gillberg, Gillberg and Ahlsen (1994) described a series of 28 TSC cases, 24 of whom had 'autistic features', and 17 of those fulfilled (DSM-III-R) criteria for autistic disorder.

- Bolton and Griffiths (1997) were the first to report on an association between the numbers of temporal lobe tubers and the likelihood of ASD diagnosis in TSC cases. They reported a strong association between increasing numbers of temporal tubers, decreased IQ and likelihood of ASD diagnosis, from a series of 18 referred TSC cases whose brain scans were reviewed.

- Baker, Piven and Sato (1998) screened a clinic sample of 20 TSC cases on the Autism Behavior Checklist (ABC) and then carried out the Autism Diagnostic Interview (ADI) and observational recording on the children who scored as likely cases. They 'conservatively' estimated ASD to be present in 20 per cent of their cases.

- Smalley (1998) suggested a possible association between maternal depression and genetic factors predisposing to ASD and TSC in offspring, with the finding that mothers who had co-morbid children were more likely to have experienced depression that antedated the conception of the affected child.

- In one of the only neurophysiological studies of TSC, Seri et al. (1999) compared brainstem auditory evoked responses between 14 children with TSC, seven with autistic disorder and seven without. The results indicated that those with autistic disorder had a central auditory processing disorder coupled with automatic memory problems, associated with unilateral or bilateral temporal lobe lesions.

- Asano et al. (2001) assessed nine autistic, nine learning-disabled non-autistic and eight non-learning-disabled children with TSC, using MRI and PET scanning. Bilateral temporal hypometabolism was associated with ASD and with communication difficulties, as was hypermetabolism in deep cerebellar nuclei.

- Khare et al. (2001) examined a family with a missense mutation affecting the TSC2 gene affecting 19/34 family members, 17 of whom had a TSC diagnosis. Two of those affected had a co-morbid ASD diagnosis – one of autism and one of PDD.

- The earlier findings of Bolton and Griffiths concerning temporal lobe tubers were confirmed in a more detailed but overlapping retrospective analysis (Bolton et al. 2002). This paper presented data from 53 TSC cases, 19 of whom had an ASD diagnosis.

- Askalan et al. (2003) published a small cross-over pilot study of the treatment of infantile spasms in nine infants aged 3–16 months. The study used two medications – corticotropin (ACTH) and vigabatrin. The study sample was too small to draw conclusions concerning treatment efficacy, but did find those with symptomatic spasms were more likely to develop epilepsy and to be autistic at follow-up (all were assessed on the ADOS-G (Autism Diagnostic Observation Scale – Generic) at two years of age). All of those with ASD had developed epilepsy, and all showed treatment response (two improved on vigabatrin, one on vigabatrin and adrenocorticotropic hormone in combination).

- In 2004, Humphrey et al. published on a male monozygotic twin pair with TSC. The twins were discordant for autism, and the affected twin had a lower IQ, earlier onset seizures and larger central nervous system tubers.

- In a study of 94 TSC patients, an association was found between TSC2 mutations, diagnosis of autism, presence of infantile spasms and lower IQ (Lewis et al. 2004). No such association was found for TSC1. This suggests that the TSC2 locus at 16p13.3 may be a specific susceptibility locus for ASD.

- De Vries, Hunt and Bolton (2007) carried out a postal survey of 265 families with TSC members. The overall rate of ASD was 48 per cent (119 of 246 returns): 66 per cent of those with co-morbid learning disability (96/146), but only 17 per cent (13/78) of those with reported normal intelligence. This indicated a strong association between likelihood of ASD diagnosis and learning disability in those with TSC.

- Kothur, Ray and Malhi (2008) described two Indian cases of ASD in TSC in association with temporal lobe tubers.

- Datta, Mandal and Bhattacharya (2009) described a six-year-old boy with a history of convulsions from the age of four months, who had both a learning disability and autism in combination with TSC. In this case it is not entirely clear how the diagnosis of autism was made, as the Conners' Rating Scale mentioned in the paper is an ADHD, not an ASD, rating measure.

There have been number of useful reviews of the association between ASD and TSC (see, for example, Curatolo *et al.* 2004; Wiznitzer 2004).

Just under half of all TSC cases would seem to fulfil criteria for an ASD, and the likelihood seems highest in those cases where there have been infantile spasms, where there is greater learning disability, and where there is more obvious neurological involvement. This is most likely to be in TSC2 cases and to relate to abnormal production of tuberin.

Differential diagnosis: The principal differential diagnoses would be neurofibromatosis (NF1) [51] and the various PTEN hamartoma tumour syndromes, such as BRRS [15], BCNS [16], Proteus syndrome [62] and Cowden syndrome [26].

Treatment and management: TSC in association with ASD appears to be more likely to be associated with the TSC2 susceptibility gene at 16p13.3, and to occur after infantile spasms and in association with learning disability, both of which are also more likely to be seen with the TSC2 mutation. From work on animals, it appears that seizure activity, learning and memory problems, and structural abnormalities of brain development can be minimized or prevented through early or prophylactic treatment.

The neurobiology of TSC predicts problems with GABAergic function. The beneficial effects reported from the limited trial data so far suggest that the treatment of infantile spasms with vigabatrin, or with vigabatrin and ACTH, can improve outcome (Askalan *et al.* 2003; Riikonen and Simell 1990). Vigabatrin prescription has reduced due to concerns over possible visual field defects, and such an approach would require careful regular monitoring for possible side effects.

The pathways involving hamartin and tuberin result in abnormal protein synthesis and involve a group of kinases known as TORs (targets of rapamycin). They had been identified as being affected by rapamycin, an antifungal agent that has largely fallen out of favour due to its immunosuppressive effects. Rapamycin has been shown to correct the abnormalities of behaviour and brain structure in animal TSC models. Two clinical studies to date provide evidence for some positive effects of rapamycin in patients. An initial study (Franz *et al.* 2006) found that in a small series treatment resulted in reduction in the size of astrocytomas (a type of central nervous system tumour that affects astrocytes – star-shaped glial cells found throughout the nervous system), but that when treatment was stopped, there was regrowth. One study demonstrated that renal and cardiac problems could also be improved, but that there was a high rate of side effects (Bissler *et al.* 2008).

Long-term treatment with rapamycin in humans can be difficult to maintain due to the high rate of side effects, including elevated blood lipid levels, mouth ulcers and increased susceptibility to infection. In adults, this has led to patients discontinuing long-term treatment in some 50 per cent of cases reported to date.

It would appear that prophylactic treatment might be possible; however, longer-term treatment has not yet been evaluated. The possible side effects from rapamycin are both predictable and treatable. While the results to date look promising, this is an urgent area for further systematic research, particularly to address the mechanism by which rapamycin alters nervous system, kidney and heart function, and whether approaches with fewer collateral problems could be developed.

Further information and support:

International:

Tuberous Sclerosis International
Secretariat TSI
Goudseweg 5
2411 HG Bodegraven
The Netherlands
Tel.: + 01726-51597
E-mail: info@stsn.nl
Website: www.stsn.nl/tsi/tsi.htm

In Canada:

Tuberous Sclerosis Canada
92 Caplan Ave
Suite 125
Barrie
Ontario
L9N 0Z7
Tel. English toll-free: 800-347-0252
Téléphone en Francais: 866-558-7278
Website: www.tscanada.ca/request.htm

In the UK:

Tuberous Sclerosis Association
PO Box 12979
Barnt Green
Birmingham
B45 5AN
Tel.: 0121 445 6970
Website: www.tuberous-sclerosis.org

In the USA:

Tuberous Sclerosis Alliance
801 Roeder Road
Suite 750
Silver Spring
Maryland
20910
Toll-free: 800-225-6872
Tel.: 301-562-9890
Fax: 301-562-9870
E-mail: info@tsalliance.org
Website: www.tsalliance.org

74

Turner syndrome

aka • Morgagni-Turner syndrome

• Morgagni-Turner-Albright syndrome

• Shereshevskii-Turner syndrome

- Turner-Albright syndrome
- Turner-Vary syndrome
- Morgagni-Shereshevskii-Turner-Albright syndrome
- Ullrich-Turner syndrome
- Bonnevie-Ullrich syndrome
- gonadal dysgenesis
- monosomy X

Gene locus: Xp22.33

Key ASD references: Creswell and Skuse 2000; Donnelly *et al.* 2000; Lewis *et al.* 1995; Skuse 2000; Skuse *et al.* 1997

Turner syndrome, which affects only females, is named after the American endocrinologist Henry Hubert Turner who described a series of seven cases in a paper published in 1938. Turner syndrome was identified at an early stage in clinical genetics, as it results from the absence of one copy of the X chromosome. It is a 'sex chromosome aneuploidy' – a condition resulting from an atypical number of sex chromosomes. It was easy to identify on karyotyping due to the gross nature of the difference.

Girls with the same condition had previously been described by several clinicians, including the Italian anatomist Giovanni Morgagni in 1768; in a Russian clinical paper by Nikolai Shereshevskii in 1925; and in the German clinical literature in 1930 in a paper by Otto Ullrich.

How common is Turner syndrome? Turner syndrome is a condition which affects only females and occurs in approximately one in 2,000 live births (Gravholt 2005a; Gravholt *et al.* 1996). It is a sex chromosome aneuploidy that results from the total or partial absence of the second sex chromosome, resulting in a 46,XO rather than 46,XX phenotype. There is a clear parent-of-origin effect – where the X chromosome is of paternal origin, girls with Turner syndrome have a higher likelihood of ocular abnormalities and a tendency to be of higher cognitive ability. Some 20 per cent of Turner syndrome cases inherit their X chromosome from their fathers (Sagi *et al.* 2007).

Main clinical features: The most common (i.e. frequency of 50 per cent or greater) physical abnormalities affecting girls with TS include short stature, infertility, oestrogen deficiency, hypertension, elevated hepatic enzymes, middle-ear infection, micrognathia, bone age retardation, decreased bone mineral content, *cubitus valgus* (a deformity of the arms in which the elbows are turned inwards and the forearm extends away from the body when extended), and poor physical development during the first postnatal year. Females with TS also have significantly higher risks for certain diseases compared to the general population, including hypothyroidism, diabetes, heart disease, osteoporosis, congenital malformations (heart, urinary system, face, neck, ears), neurovascular disease and cirrhosis of the liver, as well as colon and rectal cancers (Gravholt 2005b).

The typical physical features seen in Turner syndrome are: short stature (unless treated with growth hormone); a webbed neck; drooping eyelids; a broad, flat, shield-shaped chest; absent or incomplete development at puberty for both primary and secondary sexual characteristics (which can often be helped by growth hormone treatment); infertility; dry eyes; amenorrhoea; and vaginal dryness. Infants with Turner syndrome often have swollen hands and feet.

Is there a link between Turner syndrome and ASD? There have been four papers to date that suggest a link between Turner syndrome and ASD.

- Lewis et al. (1995) detailed a number of genetic disorders in a US psychiatric population. Included in their series were the first individuals to be reported with a co-morbid diagnosis of Turner syndrome and ASD.

- Skuse et al. (1997) reported on a series of 80 Turner syndrome cases, 55 with X chromosomes of maternal origin and 25 of paternal origin. Comparison of the two groups showed that those who had inherited a paternal X chromosome were better socially adjusted, had higher verbal IQ and better executive function skills than those who had inherited a maternal X chromosome. Three of those with maternally inherited X chromosomes fulfilled criteria for autism. This suggested that the X chromosome contains a gene or genes that is/are imprinted and not expressed by the maternal X chromosome. As males inherit their X chromosome almost exclusively from their mothers, this could help to explain the increased rates of developmental disorders of social cognition in boys.

- Creswell and Skuse (1999) presented five cases of autism in girls with Turner syndrome from a clinical population of 150 Turner cases. This would indicate a rate at least five times higher than in the general population, if the sample were representative of Turner syndrome. (The authors claim a 300 times increased likelihood of autism; however, they base this on a one in 10,000 rate for the general population.) All five cases had inherited a maternal X chromosome. It is unclear whether these cases are from an expanded cohort drawing on the earlier series reported by this group in 1997, or are from a newly ascertained series.

- Donnelly et al. (2000) presented a further case of autism in a girl with Turner syndrome with a maternally inherited X chromosome, strengthening the hypothesis of a parent-of-origin effect on social cognition.

- Skuse (2000) provides an overview of the evidence for imprinted X-linked genes in autism, based on his research group's work on Turner syndrome.

Parent-of-origin effects are not confined to the behavioural phenotype. A study on an Israeli series of 83 Turner syndrome cases (Sagi et al. 2007) found parent-of-origin effects, with kidney problems, higher body mass index (but lower LDL and total cholesterol) being found with a maternally inherited X chromosome, increased ocular problems and higher academic achievement being more common with inheritance of a paternal X chromosome.

A more general overview of X-chromosome factors in ASD, including updated information on Turner syndrome, can be found in Marco and Skuse (2006).

Differential diagnosis: The clinical presentation in Turner syndrome is usually quite distinctive and apparent.

There are a small number of rare alternative diagnoses: autoimmune thyroiditis; gonadal dysgenesis; lymphoedema; and XY gonadal agenesis syndrome. However, diagnosis should be simple on karyotyping except in mosaic cases.

Treatment and management: For most aspects of Turner syndrome with ASD, management is the same as for other ASD conditions. As it is a multisystem condition, those with Turner syndrome require help and treatment by a multidisciplinary team. A useful overview of the issues involved in ongoing treatment and management can be found in Hjerrild, Mortensen and Gravholt (2008).

Short stature is a matter of concern for many with Turner syndrome (Sutton *et al.* 2005); however, infertility and lack of development of sexual characteristics are viewed by many as the most difficult aspects of the condition.

Both physical growth and development of sexual characteristics can be promoted through the use of growth hormone treatment (Bakalov *et al.* 2007). Improved glucose tolerance and reduced risk of developing type II diabetes appear to be direct health consequences of growth hormone replacement (Wooten *et al.* 2008). Concerns over possible negative effects on heart development appear to be unsubstantiated (Matura *et al.* 2007).

Further information and support:

In Australia:
PO Box 112
Frenchs Forest
NSW 1640
Tel.: (02) 9452 4196
Fax: (02) 9975 4037
E-mail: turnersyn@netpro.net.au
Website: www.turnersyndrome.org.au

In Canada:
Turner's Syndrome Society of Canada
323 Chapel Street
Ottawa,
Ontario
K1N 7Z2
Toll-free 800-465-6744
Tel.: 613-321-2267
Fax: 613-321-2268
E-mail: tssincan@web.net
Website: www.turnersyndrome.ca

In France:
Association des Groupes Amitié Turner
AGAT C/O A.A.A.F.A
2 rue André Messager
B.P 5
75860 Paris Cedex 18
Tel.: 01 53 28 14 86
E-mail: association_agatts@yahoo.fr
Website: www.agat-turner.org

In Germany:
Ringstraße 18
D-53809 Ruppichteroth
Tel.: 02247 759750
Fax: 02247 759756
E-mail: geschaeftsstelle@turner-syndrom.de
Website: www.turner-syndrom.de

In the UK:
Turner Syndrome Support Society (TSSS)
13 Simpson Court,
11 South Ave
Clydebank Business Park
Clydebank G81 2NR
Tel.: 0141 952 8006
Helpline: 0845 230 7520
Fax: 0141 952 8025
E-mail: Turner.Syndrome@tss.org.uk
Website: www.tss.org.uk

In the USA:
Turner Syndrome Society of the United States
14450 TC Jester
Suite 260
Houston
Texas
TX 77014
Toll-free: 800-365-9944
Tel.: 832-249-9988
Fax: 832-249-9987
E-mail: tssus@turner-syndrome-us.org
Website: www.turner-syndrome-us.org

75

Unilateral cerebellar hypoplasia syndrome

Gene locus: No specific gene has been identified as linked to this presentation

Key ASD reference: Ramaekers *et al.* 1997

Unilateral cerebellar hypoplasia syndrome is a neurodevelopmental disorder. It is one of the more common presentations of cerebellar structural abnormalities, but does not have a clear genetic or metabolic pathogenesis (Ramaekers *et al.* 1997). It is typically associated with developmental delay (Patel and Barkovich 2002).

How common is unilateral cerebellar hypoplasia syndrome? There is no epidemiological information on the prevalence of this condition. It is assumed to be rare, with a prevalence of less than one in 100,000.

Main clinical features: At present, there is no clear aetiology to this presentation; however, it seems most likely to be genetic. As no clear basis has so far been identified, this pattern is not recognized in current classifications of cerebellar malformation (Patel and Barkovich 2002).

Is there a link between unilateral cerebellar hypoplasia syndrome and ASD?

- There is one report of two unrelated male cases of ASD in association with unilateral cerebellar hypoplasia. Both cases were microcephalic, and in both there was an associated ipsilateral choreido-retinal coloboma (Ramaekers *et al.* 1997).

Cases of cerebellar hypoplasia are well documented in the ASD literature (see, for example, Courchesne *et al.* 1994). Cases of unilateral cerebellar hypoplasia have been reported in association with a number of genetic conditions linked to ASD, including - Joubert [44] (Chance *et al.* 1999) and Mobius [48] (Harbord *et al.* 1989) syndromes.

Differential diagnosis: Unilateral cerebellar malformations are rare, with various causes of hypoplasia gradually becoming clarified (Poretti, Wolf and Boltshauser 2008). Some ASD cases are reported in association with Joubert [44] and Mobius [48] syndromes; however, the pathogenesis in the cases reported by Ramaekers *et al.* (1997) is unclear at this time and no genetic basis has been reported.

Treatment and management: No specific treatment or management approaches are known at this time. Cerebellar abnormalities are well-recognized concomitants of ASD and, given the reported pattern, are likely to result in both rapid classical conditioning of responses (giving rise to 'insistence on sameness') and to truncal ataxia. Where these result from a defect in embryological development, they are unlikely to be easily modifiable, but need to be recognized and accommodated to.

Further information and support:

In the UK:
Unique
Rare Chromosome Disorder Support Group
PO Box 2189
Surrey
CR3 5GN
Telephone helpline: 01883 330766
E-mail: info@rarechromo.org
Website: www.rarechromo.org/

In the USA:
National Organization for Rare Disorders (NORD)
55 Kenosia Avenue
PO Box 1968
Danbury
CT 06813-1968
Tel.: 203-744-0100
Toll-free: 800-999-6673 (voicemail only)
TDD Number: 203-797-9590
Fax: 203-798-2291
E-mail: orphan@rarediseases.org
Website: www.rarediseases.org/info/contact.html

76

Velocardiofacial syndrome (VCFS)

See also: CATCH 22 [18]; CHARGE syndrome [20]; DiGeorge syndrome I [29a]

Gene locus: 22q11.2

Key ASD references: Chudley *et al.* 1998; Kates *et al.* 2007a; 2007b; Kozma 1998; Niklasson *et al.* 2001;

VCFS has been included here for completeness, as the term is still in common use and there are support groups in the USA and Australia that use it. The core material has been covered in several other sections dealing with cases which have been identified as CATCH 22 [18], CHARGE syndrome [20] and DiGeorge syndrome I [29a], and will not be duplicated here. Turn to these other sections for further information that is relevant to people who have a diagnosis of VCFS.

A review of the history of work on VCFS can be found in Shprintzen (2008), which links to these other literatures.

How common is VCFS? It is estimated that 22q11.2 deletions are found in one in every 4,000 live births (Tézenas Du Montcel *et al.* 1996).

Main clinical features: See sections under CATCH 22 [18]; CHARGE syndrome [20]; and DiGeorge syndrome I [29].

Is there a link between VCFS and ASD?

• Chudley *et al.* (1998) documented a series of cases with 22q11 deletions and ASD. One of this original series has been reclassified as having a 22q13 defect and not a 22q11 deletion, as originally thought.

- Kozma (1998) presented a case of a girl with diagnoses of VCFS and ASD, a cardiac defect and profound learning disability.

- Niklasson et al. (2001) reviewed 32 children with '22q11 deletion syndrome'. Ninety-four per cent had associated learning disability, 28 per cent had ADHD alone, 15 per cent had ASD alone, and 16 per cent fulfilled criteria for ADHD and ASD.

- In a meticulous study using the ADI-R to compare five groups – ASD + VCFS children compared to VCFS alone; siblings of VCFS children; a group with idiopathic autism; and community controls – Kates et al. (2007a, 2007b) were able to show that there were a range of VCFS-specific behaviours which were seen irrespective of ASD co-morbidity, and a number of behaviours seen in idiopathic cases but not typically seen in those with 'VCFS autism'. In particular, difficulties sharing attention, limited gestural communication, difficulty in initiating conversation and the presence of circumscribed interests were seen in VCFS with or without ASD, suggesting that these behaviours are VCFS-specific. Limited fantasy play, increased ritualistic behaviour, presence of motor stereotypies and repetitive use of objects were *not* seen in the non-ASD VCFS cases, but were seen in idiopathic ASD and not seen in VCFS where there was no associated ASD.

This last study provides a helpful template to aid in evaluating the effects of treatment interventions, but also suggests caution in being overinclusive in diagnosis. In VCFS, particular features normally thought to be aspects of ASD (such as those detailed above), and which are assumed to be such when scoring on measures such as the ADOS and ADI-R, should be given less emphasis in arriving at a diagnosis.

Differential diagnosis: A variety of overlapping clinical disorders all associated with 22q11.2 defects are reported. The overlap in both phenotype and genotype suggest a variety of conditions should be considered: see Table A17.

Treatment and management: See below for VCFS supports and see also the earlier sections in this book on other 22q11.2 diagnoses (CATCH 22 [18], CHARGE syndrome [20] and DiGeorge syndrome I [29a] for further information on treatment and management.

Further information and support:

In Australia and Asia:
E-mail: secretary@vcfsfa.org.au
Website: www.vcfsfa.org.au

In France:
GENERATION 22
24 rue Constant Strohl
F-67000 Strasbourg
Tel./Fax: ++ 33 3 88 31 81 32
Website: www.generation22.fr/

In the UK:
Max Appeal!
Lansdowne House
13 Meriden Avenue
Wollaston
Stourbridge
West Midlands
DY8 4QN

Tel.: 01384 821227
E-mail: info@maxappeal.org.uk
Website: www.maxappeal.org.uk

In the USA
Velo-Cardio-Facial Syndrome Educational
Foundation, Inc.
PO Box 874
Milltown
NJ 08850
Tel.: 732-238-8803
Toll-free: 866-VCFSEF5
E-mail: info@vcfsef.org

77

Williams syndrome (WS)

aka • Williams-Beuren syndrome (WBS)

• infantile hypercalcaemia

Gene locus: 7q11.23

Key ASD references: Berg *et al.* 2007; Edelmann *et al.* 2007; Gillberg and Rasmussen 1994; Herguner and Mukaddes 2006; Klein-Tasman *et al.* 2007, 2009; Laws and Bishop 2004; Reiss *et al.* 1985

The syndrome was first identified in New Zealand by Dr J.C.P. Williams (Williams, Barratt-Boyes and Lowe 1961). Williams focused on the cardiac defect but felt that 'the association of supravalvular stenosis with the physical and mental characteristics here described may constitute a previously unrecognized syndrome' (p.1311). The four children in the study all had the rare heart defect supravalvular aortic stenosis (SVAS), learning difficulties and a particular constellation of facial features. They were all said to have acquired normal social habits.

WS arises from a deletion of 7q11.23. Typically the gene deletion found in WS is large (some 1.5–2.5 megabytes), and deletes 17 or more genes.

How common is WS? The population prevalence has been estimated as approximately one in 10,000 live births (Grimm and Wesselhoeft 1980). One Norwegian survey has arrived at a figure of one in 7,500 (Strømme *et al.* 2002a).

Main clinical features: Williams syndrome, as it typically presents, has a cardiac component (SVAS), peripheral cardiac artery narrowing, a elfin face, learning difficulties, short stature, differences in the formation of the teeth, and infantile hypercalcaemia (Grimm and Wesselhoeft 1980). There is often a 'stellate' or 'lacey' pattern to the iris (Holmstrom *et al.* 1990), and individuals are predominantly blue-eyed (77 per cent) (Winter *et al.* 1996).

Both boys and girls with WS tend to be smaller than average, mean height tracking the third centile. They have normal pubertal growth spurts, again achieving adult heights around the third centile. *In utero* growth is more typically within the normal range (Pankau *et al.* 1992).

Hyperacusis is a common feature, affecting 41/49 cases (84 per cent) in one series (Gothelf *et al.* 2006), and 54/54 (100 per cent) in another (Mari *et al.* 1995). It is thought that both the hyperacusis and high-frequency sensorineural hearing loss commonly seen in the same individuals could result from an abnormality of the auditory nerve. On functional brain imaging, people with WS show unusual patterns of activation to sounds, which may account for their hyperacusis (Levitin *et al.* 2003). Hyperacusis is commonly associated with fears and phobias in people with WS (seen in 58 per cent of a sample of

38 Swedish individuals with WS (Blomberg, Rosander and Andersson 2006), compared to 2.5 per cent of a control sample).

From the literature to date, the range of overall ability documented in WS is wide, ranging from severe learning disability to good average ability with a mean IQ in the mild learning disability range (Ewart *et al.* 1993; Plissart *et al.* 1994). A consistent finding is one of nonverbal learning disability, with a significant discrepancy in favour of verbal skills, and the differences in spatial ability reported (Mervis, Robinson and Pani 1999).

Concentration problems, motor restlessness and attention-seeking behaviour are commonly reported.

A hoarse/brassy voice has typically been described (Gosch, Stading and Pankau 1994). This may be a direct function of the abnormalities of elastin in the vocal chords (Vaux *et al.* 2003).

Muscle tone changes progressively from hypotonia to hypertonia with age (Chapman, du Plessis and Pober 1996). A neurological study of 47 WS cases (Gagliardi *et al.* 2007) documented problems with gross and fine motor control, mild cerebellar signs and a progressive pattern of soft extrapyramidal signs through late childhood into early adolescence.

Connective tissue abnormalities and both facial and general myopathy are common and well described in WS (Voit *et al.* 1991), typically with delayed motor milestones, muscle pains and hypotonia. In extreme cases, there may be joint contractures and scoliosis. Abnormalities of elastin are typically seen on skin biopsy and may prove to be a useful assessment of the extent of the elastin defect (Dridi *et al.* 1999).

These features are not always seen; however, and a number of pairs of MZ twins have been described where only one twin shows obvious features (Castorina *et al.* 1997; Pankau *et al.* 1993), and similar variability may be seen across genetically similar affected family members (Pankau *et al.* 2001).

Many of the clinical features of WS are associated with elastin defects. (Elastin is a protein which gives elasticity to skin and connective tissue in the body. It is a key factor in the efficient functioning of the vascular system.) From two studies looking in total at 104 WS cases, deletion of the elastin gene was found in over 90 per cent of the cases (Mari *et al.* 1995; Nickerson *et al.* 1995). Elastin defects result in supravalvular aortic stenosis (SVAS) (Li *et al.* 1998). Narrowing of both the cerebral arteries (Kaplan, Levinson and Kaplan 1995) and renal arteries (Biesecker, Laxova and Friedman 1987; Pober *et al.* 1993) are reported as elastin-related problems.

Cardiac problems are very common in WS. Not all people with WS have problems, but they are found in at least three-quarters of cases, and significant problems can go undetected (Jones and Smith 1975). Problems are more likely, and often more severe, in boys (Sadler *et al.* 2001). Surgical intervention can be required in around 20 per cent of cases (Wessel *et al.* 1994).

In one large series of 75 cases, SVAS was the most common cardiac diagnosis, being seen in 32/44 (73 per cent). Pulmonary arterial stenosis (PAS) was seen in 18/44 (41 per cent), an aortic or mitral valve defect in 5/44 (11 per cent) of cases, and tetralogy of Fallot was seen in one (2 per cent) case (Eronen *et al.* 2002).

Thyroid hypoplasia is common in WS, being seen in up to 75 per cent of cases, with 25 per cent having elevated levels of thyroid-stimulating hormone (Cherniske *et al.* 2004; Selicorni *et al.* 2006; Stagi *et al.* 2005).

Puberty is often advanced in WS, while emotional-social development is typically slowed. It has been argued that in some cases this may give grounds for the use of medication or hormonal interventions to delay sexual maturation. One case of extreme precocity has been documented (Scothorn and Butler 1997), in a girl with onset of puberty at 7.5 years and of menarche at 8.5 years; however, a large series of 86 girls with WS found a mean age at menarche of 11.5 years +/- 1.7 years compared to 12.9 +/- 1.1 years in a population sample of 759 girls (Partsch *et al.* 2002).

In an interesting study by Giannotti *et al.* (2001), six (9.5 per cent) out of a series of 63 WS patients, compared to only one (0.54 per cent) of 184 controls, tested positive for the presence of antiendomesial and antigliadin antibodies. The presence of these antibodies is indicative of *coeliac disease* suggesting a significantly increased risk of coeliac disease in WS.

With regard to the *central nervous system*: the WS brain is more symmetrical than normal (Schmitt *et al.* 2001). The posterior cortex and cerebellum are relatively well developed, while the frontal lobes are less well developed (Jernigan *et al.* 1993; Wang *et al.* 1992).

The *corpus callosum* (the large fibre tract which connects the two hemispheres of the brain) is often less well developed (Luders *et al.* 2007; Tomaiuolo *et al.* 2002), and the thalamus and parietal and occipital lobes are smaller (Boddaert *et al.* 2006; Reiss *et al.* 2004).

Epilepsy is not a recognized concomitant of WS. Three papers have documented infantile spasms in a total of four cases to date (Mizugishi *et al.* 1998; Morimoto *et al.* 2003; Tsao and Westman 1997).

Hypertension is a common problem in WS that is seen in approximately 50 per cent of cases (Broder *et al.* 1999; Del Campo *et al.* 2006). From examining a series of 96 WS cases, it was found that those people who lacked the NCF1 gene as part of their deletion were significantly less likely to be hypertensive. This was probably because they had reduced levels of oxidative stress. Based on these findings, Del Campo *et al.* suggest that antioxidant therapies focused on reducing NADPH oxidase activity may be beneficial, particularly for those WS cases who are hypertensive.

Is there a link between WS and ASD?

- In 1985 Alan Reiss and colleagues described two six-year-old cases of WS who fulfilled criteria for autism (Reiss *et al.* 1985).

- A Swedish paper by Gillberg and Rasmussen (1994) described four further cases of WS with autistic behaviour. All were preschool; there were two girls and two boys.

- In a study (Laws and Bishop 2004) of language use in 19 children and young adults with WS, compared to similar groups with Down syndrome [31] and specific language impairment, the broad conclusions were that 'individuals with Williams syndrome have pragmatic language impairments, poor social relationships and restricted interests. Far from representing the polar opposite of autism, as suggested by some researchers, Williams syndrome would seem to share many of the characteristics of autistic disorder.'

- Based on a case report of a 12-year-old boy with WS and ASD, and an accompanying literature review, Herguner and Mukaddes (2006) suggest that the defect in the elastin gene at 7q11.23 results in the core features seen in WS, and that co-morbid autistic symptomology may result from disruption to genes which flank the elastin locus. This notion is lent support by a molecular genetics study based on an atypical WS deletion in a six-and-a-half-year-old girl with ASD (Edelmann et al. 2007).

- A study of 29 children with WS aged between two and five years classified approximately half the group as being on the autistic spectrum, and three as having autism (Klein-Tasman et al. 2007). The same group has suggested that many young children with WS show social communicative difficulties, and suggest that there may be issues of diagnostic overshadowing (failing to pick up on the social difficulties due to identifying WS as the primary issue) (Klein-Tasman et al. 2009).

- One suggestion for the behavioural phenotype in WS duplication, based on discussion of a new 13-year-old female case, is a regionally selective defect in neural migration (Torniero et al. 2007).

From the above, it is clear that the co-occurrence of ASD and WS is now a well-established phenomenon, and that the communication pattern seen in WS is similar to that typically described in ASD. It seems likely that the genetic basis of the co-occurrence was due to genetic factors which overlap with 7q11.23 – a deletion in this region may be necessary but seems on its own not to be sufficient to result in an ASD.

Williams syndrome is associated with ASD in approximately 50 per cent of cases. Given the population prevalence of WS, this suggests that the combined condition occurs in approximately one in every 15,000 live births.

Unrecognized WS cases: It is possible for the presentation of WS to be benign and unnoticed until another family member is identified. One paper describes three families in which an affected parent was only identified as having WS once the child had been diagnosed (Morris, Thomas and Greenberg 1993).

WS locus duplication: If, instead of a microdeletion of the WS locus, there is a duplication, this produces a severe delay in expressive language, and a relative strength in visuospatial abilities – in contrast to the normal language fluency and hyperverbal pattern seen in WS (Berg et al. 2007; Depienne et al. 2007; Somerville et al. 2005). Eleven of the 27 WS duplication cases reported in the literature to date (41 per cent) have autistic spectrum disorders.

A first case of triplication of the WS locus has been reported (Beunders et al. 2009). Consistent with the effects reported in the duplication cases to date, triplication appears to result in learning difficulties, severe expressive language delay, behavioural problems, autistic features and dysmorphisms.

These studies strengthen the conclusion that there is a direct association between the WS region of chromosome 7 and the development of a specific range of language, nonverbal and social abilities.

Differential diagnosis: Two other genetic conditions present with similar abnormalities of connective tissue affecting the heart and other vascular structures – Ehlers-Danlos syndrome [34] and Marfan's syndrome (Grimm and Wesselhoeft 1980; Tantam, Evered and Hersov 1990). Neither has a similar physical phenotype in other respects. Although there are a number of other conditions reported with ASD that have a cardiac component (see Table A4), none of these is likely to be confused with WS.

A single case report of WS in association with Klinefelter syndrome describes a four-year-old Chinese boy co-morbid for the two conditions – an additional X chromosome together with a 7q11.23 deletion. He is growth-retarded despite adequate nutrition and presents with a ventriculo-septal heart defect (Lee le *et al.* 2006).

A number of other non-genetic factors can cause supravalvular aortic stenosis (SVAS) in association with ASD: rubella embryopathy (Chess 1971; Varghese, Izukawa and Rowe 1969) and thalidomide embryopathy (Jorgensen 1972; Miller *et al.* 2005) are the best documented.

Treatment and management: There are useful general overviews of treatment and management for WS aimed at both the primary care physician (Lashkari, Smith and Graham 1999) and those managing adult WS cases (Pober and Morris 2007).

There is now growing evidence for the efficacy of growth hormone therapy in addressing the short stature seen in those with WS (Kuijpers *et al.* 1999; Xekouki *et al.* 2005).

Infantile hypercalcaemia, a factor that is thought to be associated with the extent of cardiac problems, can be successfully treated through the use of biphosphonate (Cagle *et al.* 2004; Oliveri *et al.* 2004).

Treatments to address oxidative stress in those who present with hypertension may be of benefit (Del Campo *et al.* 2006); however, there is no intervention research to date that has addressed this issue.

Screening for coeliac disease should form part of the assessment of those with Williams syndrome, with appropriate dietary intervention where this is identified (Hill *et al.* 2005).

Thyroid function is abnormal in three-quarters of WS individuals and regular thyroid function testing is a recommended part of routine monitoring of WS cases (Cambiaso *et al.* 2007; Selicorni *et al.* 2006).

Although there is no systematic research on the issues, from the literature to date, it seems likely that both vitamin D and calcium supplementation would be contraindicated in those with WS.

The various problems associated with growth, hypercalcaemia, cardiac, thyroid and kidney function and coeliac disease are all important to keep under review and to manage and treat as appropriate.

Further information and support:

A best-practice genetic guideline has been published (Committee on Genetics, American Academy of Pediatrics 2001).

A useful overview can be found in the following short book:
Bellugi, U. and St George, M. (eds.) (2001) *Journey from Cognition to Brain to Gene: Perspectives from Williams Syndrome.* Massachusetts: MIT Press.

A fairly comprehensive list of National Williams syndrome support groups can be found at www.wsf.org/family/support/orgsint.htm; this is part of The Williams Syndrome Comprehensive Website: www.wsf.org.

In Australia:
Williams Syndrome Support Group of Victoria
43 Naroo Street,
Balwyn Vic 3103
Tel.: (03) 9859 4450
E-mail: jwan@enternet.com.au
Website: http://home.vicnet.net.au/~wsfsg

In Canada:
Canadian Association for Williams Syndrome (CAWS)
17-780 Thivierge
Pierresfonds
Quebec
H9J 3R6
Tel.: 514-620-7696
E-mail: cawschairs@shaw.ca
Website: www.caws-can.org

In the UK:
The Williams Syndrome Foundation (UK)
161 High Street
Tonbridge
Kent
TN9 1BX
Tel.: 01732 365152
Fax: 01732 360178
E-mail: John.nelson-wsfoundation@btinternet.com
Website: www.williams-syndrome.org.uk

In the USA:
Williams Syndrome Association
PO Box 297
Clawson,
MI 48017-0297
Tel.: 248-541-3630
Fax: 248-541-3631
E-mail: tmonkaba@aol.com
Website: www.williams-syndrome.org

Williams Syndrome Foundation
16211 N. Greenfield Drive
Klein
TX 77379
Tel.: 713-376-1626
Fax: 713-257-2718
E-mail: gbiescar@neosoft.com
Website: www.wsf.org

78

Hereditary xanthinuria type II

Gene locus: Not clearly established

Key ASD reference: Zannolli *et al.* 2003

This is a recently identified clinical condition with a specific biochemistry but no clear understanding of its genetic basis. It is thought to be an autosomal recessive condition.

How common is hereditary xanthinuria type II? It is a rare disorder with few reported cases (Simmonds 2003). It is thought to present with a similar frequency to classic or type I xanthinuria, of between one in 6,000 and one in 69,000.

Main clinical features: The clinical presentation is varied from around 20 per cent of cases who are asymptomatic to a small percentage at the opposite extreme who present with acute renal failure. Most cases have xanthine calculi (hard lumps of crystallized xanthine that forms in the kidneys) and crystalluria (crystals of xanthine excreted in urine). The presence of calcium salts in the kidneys is suggestive of hyperparathyroidism. Some ten per cent of cases present with duodenal ulcers, myopathy or arthropathy.

This is an autosomal recessive disorder which results in defects in two specific enzymes – xanthine dehydrogenase and aldehyde oxidase. The genes for these enzymes are both on chromosome 2 (at 2p22–p23 and 2q33 respectively), but their physical separation makes mutation of both unlikely. Individuals with this condition are unable to metabolize allopurinol because of the lack of aldehyde oxidase.

A defect in the gene for human molybdenum cofactor sulphatase (HMCS) has been identified in independent cases and results in defects in the production of xanthine dehydrogenase and aldehyde oxidase, with the additional inactivation of sulphite oxidase (Ichida *et al.* 2001).

Is there a link between hereditary xanthinuria type II and ASD?

- To date a single case has been reported in which the combination of xanthinuria type II and ASD features has been reported. The report was on an 11-year-old boy with learning disability, autistic features, vocal and motor tics, cortical and renal cysts, osteopaenia (low bone mineral density), hair and teeth defects, and a range of behavioural symptoms, including aggression with temper tantrums, and attention deficit hyperactivity disorder.

At the present time, there is no understanding of a biological basis that could underpin the co-occurrence of ASD and xanthinuria type II.

Differential diagnosis: Hereditary xanthinuria type I presents with similar physical problems, but a less complex metabolic profile, with a mutation in the gene for xanthine dehydrogenase *without* the mutation affecting aldehyde oxidase. There are no other conditions that present with the same clinical pattern.

Treatment and management: High fluid intake and purine restriction are the current recommended treatment (Simmonds 2003). Endocrine treatment for calcium build-up, where present, is also indicated.

Further information and support:

In the UK:
Unique
Rare Chromosome Disorder Support Group
P.O. Box 2189
Surrey
CR3 5GN
E-mail: info@rarechromo.org
Telephone helpline: 01883 330766
Website: www.rarechromo.org

In the USA:
National Organization for Rare Disorders (NORD)
55 Kenosia Avenue
PO Box 1968
Danbury,
CT 06813-1968
Tel.: 203-744-0100
Toll-free: 800-999-6673 (voicemail only)
TDD Number: 203-797-9590
Fax: 203-798-2291
E-mail: orphan@rarediseases.org
Website: www.rarediseases.org/info/contact.html

79

Xeroderma pigmentosum (Complementation group C)

Gene locus: 3p25

Key ASD reference: Khan *et al.* 1998

Xeroderma pigmentosum is a condition in which the skin cannot repair damage to DNA caused by ultraviolet light (Slor *et al.* 2000). It results in thinning of the skin, odd patterns of skin pigmentation, and telangectasia (spidery fine surface blood vessels). Basal cell carcinoma (cancer of the basal skin cells) is also common.

A summary of the genetic mechanisms involved in xeroderma pigmentosum can be found in Cleaver *et al.* (1999).

How common is xeroderma pigmentosum? The best current estimate of prevalence is one in 250,000 (Hedera and Fink 2007).

Main clinical features: Skin, eye and central nervous system effects should be monitored. The nature and extent of any such involvement is largely dependent on the extent of sun exposure. Lack of vitamin D can also result in brittle bones if not addressed.

Is there a link between xeroderma pigmentosum and ASD?

- To date, a single case – a four-year-old Korean boy with xeroderma pigmentosum complementation group C – has been reported in association with ASD (Khan *et al.* 1998). He was nonverbal, and showed evidence of ADHD and autistic features without any obvious neurologic involvement. He had delayed motor development, a cleft palate, and a duplex right kidney. His MRI was reported as normal. He was an adopted child and there was no available background history. He presented with numerous freckle-like pigmented lesions of sun-exposed areas of his face, lips and ears, which appeared after sun exposure at around nine months.

In general the complementation group C form of xeroderma pigmentosa appears to have the least neurological sequelae (Anttinen *et al.* 2008).

Differential diagnosis: A number of other genetic conditions can result in photosensitivity and increased risk of UV skin damage: xeroderma pigmentosum (XP) with neurologic abnormalities; Cockayne syndrome (CS) (including cerebrooculofacioskeletal syndrome (COFS)); the XP/CS complex; trichothiodystrophy (TTD) [72]; the XP/TTD complex; and the UV-sensitive syndrome.

Treatment and management: Protection from ultraviolet in sunlight is the primary treatment. UVC from some house lighting can also cause damage and levels should be checked. Where the condition is identified early in life there is a possibility of low vitamin

D levels, and supplementation should be considered. Given that only a single case has been described to date, no specific recommendations concerning the ASD aspects of xeroderma pigmentation can be given at this time.

Further information and support:

In the UK:

Xeroderma Pigmentosa Support Group
2 Strawberry Close
Prestwood
Great Missenden
Bucks
HP16 0SG
Tel.: 01494 890981
Fax: 01494 864439
E-mail: webmaster@xpsupportgroup.org.uk
Website: www.xpfamilysupport.com

In the USA:

XP Family Support Group
3006 Notre Dame Drive
Sacramento,

CA 95826
Orange County: 949-218-9401
Sacramento: 916-628-3814
E-mail: xpfamily@sbcglobal.net
Website: www.xpfamilysupport.com/contact.php

Share and Care Cockayne Syndrome Network Inc.
PO Box 570618
Dallas,
TX 75357
Tel.: 1 866-COCKAYNE (Toll-free)
Fax: 972-613-4590
E-mail: J93082@aol.com
Website: www.cockayne-syndrome.org

80

X-linked ichthyosis (XLI)

aka • steroid sulphatase deficiency

Gene locus: Xp22.32

Key ASD reference: Kent *et al.* 2008

XLI was first described by Wells and Kerr (1965) in a clinical study of 81 affected males. It is a condition that can be identified through antenatal screening. It is a dermatological condition that results from a defect of the steroid sulphatase (STS) gene at Xp22.32 (first reported by Jöbsis *et al.* 1980). It results from a deletion in 85 per cent of cases (Hernandez-Martin, Gonzales-Sarimiento and De Unamuno 1999) or a point mutation in the other 15 per cent. To date, six separate point mutations have been reported (Alperin and Shapiro 1997).

Most cases are thought to be transmitted from the mother. Consistent with maternal transmission of STS deletion, in the majority of reported cases mothers show reduced STS activity levels, consistent with carrier status, and there is no STS activity in the affected person (Cuevas-Covarrubias *et al.* 1995; Valdes-Flores *et al.* 2001).

In the cases where an ASD has been reported in XLI, there is a deletion of the contiguous NLGN4, gene which has been linked to ASD in non-XLI cases.

Monozygotic twins have been reported with a concordant phenotype (XLI, learning disability and grand mal epilepsy in both cases) (Gohlke *et al.* 2000).

How common is XLI? The best current estimate of prevalence is one in 5,043 males (Ingordo *et al.* 2003).

Main clinical features: XLI is typically noticed shortly after birth through peeling of large scales of skin. Scales are primarily on the neck, trunk, and backs of the hands and feet. The typical scaling on the neck gave rise to the term 'dirty neck disease'. The face, palms and soles are typically spared. XLI improves during the summer, while ichthyosis vulgaris does not. There is no apparent improvement with age. Some patients may present with additional features, such as undescended testes and testicular cancer. Corneal opacities are seen in between 50 and 100 per cent of cases, and in the majority of female carriers (Sever, Frost and Weinstein 1968). Both undescended tested (Lykkesfeldt *et al.* 1985) and hypogonadism (Pike *et al.* 1989) appear to be more common than would be expected in the general population.

Although epilepsy has been reported with ichthyosis (Quattrini *et al.* 1986), it is not clear whether any of the reported cases had XLI and prevalence is uncertain.

In a large early series of 50 affected families reported by Lykkesfeldt *et al.* (1985), 42 families had more than one affected member, strongly suggesting a genetic aetiology.

Is there a link between XLI and ASD?

- There has been only one study to date examining a possible link between XLI and ASD (Kent *et al.* 2008). This study screened 25 children with XLI who had been detected through antenatal screening of maternal urinary oestriol, a test that can identify steroid sulphatase deficiencies. The children were aged five years and above. Five children were found to have an ASD or language/ communication disorder. All of the children identified, in contrast to the other children screened, had large deletions that included deletion of the NLGN4 gene.

There are cases; however, with features of XLI and NLGN4 deletion, but without ASD symptomology (Macarov *et al.* 2007).

The gene responsible for XLI is contiguous to the NLGN4 gene. NLGN4 has been linked to ASD (see, for example, Lawson-Yuen *et al.* 2008), and often the NLGN4 gene is deleted in individuals with XLI.

A number of models for the possible role of NLGN4 in the genesis of ASD have been proposed (Bourgeron 2007; De Jaco *et al.* 2008; Talebizadeh *et al.* 2006).

Several studies have failed to replicate evidence of NLGN4 defects in ASD (Gauthier *et al.* 2005; Vincent *et al.* 2004; Ylisaukko-oja *et al.* 2005) suggesting that there may be variations in the prevalence of NLGN4 defects in different populations.

Differential diagnosis: XLI differs in various ways, both clinically and histologically, from autosomal dominant ichthyosis (Wells and Jennings 1967). The distribution of scaling can also be helpful in differentiating XLI from ichthyosis vulgaris (Okano *et al.* 1988).

The differential diagnosis of XLI is from the various other ichthyoses. These can be discriminated using skin biopsy staining (Lake *et al.* 1991).

None of the other ichthyotic conditions has been reported to date in association with ASD.

One case of ichthyosis in a girl with Turner syndrome [74] has been described (Solomon and Schoen 1971), in which there was a positive paternal family history. A specific Turner syndrome neurocognitive phenotype has been mapped to Xp22.3 by examining women with partial X-chromosome deletions (Zinn et al. 2007), and in one such case a son with the same partial deletion had XLI.

A clinical overlap between XLI and Kallmann syndrome, also an Xp22.3 condition, has been noted in a number of papers (see, for example, Krishnamurthy, Kapoor and Yadav 2007).

Wieacker et al. (1983) looked for linkage between the RC8 sequence at Xp21.2 implicated in Duchenne muscular dystrophy [33] and the STS locus in XLI. No cases of XLI together with Duchenne have so far been reported.

Treatment and management: Treatment and management of XLI is primarily directed at keeping the skin hydrated and supple to prevent scaling (Janniger and Schwartz 2008).

Good results have been reported in various studies using the topical application of cholesterol-based creams (Lykkesfeldt and Hoyer 1983; Zettersten et al. 1998), and retinoid creams (Shwayder 2004). It is thought that the formation of scales is a result of accumulation of undegraded cholesterol sulphate increasing corneodesmosome retention and reducing cholesterol synthesis (Elias et al. 1984, 2008).

Shapiro et al. (1978) showed that arylsulphatase deficiency is X-linked and that it is expressed in postnatal life as X-linked ichthyosis.

Freiberg et al. (1997) were able to demonstrate correction of steroid sulphatase (STS) expression and histology in skin cells from XLI patients grafted onto immunodeficient mice, where a retroviral expression vector was used to correct gene function. Spirito et al. (2001) have reviewed the evidence on such gene therapy approaches to the treatment of cutaneous diseases.

As antenatal detection is possible by screening and around one in five cases is co-morbid for ASD, screening would detect the one in 25,000 live births who are likely to have XLI and an ASD.

Treatment of the ASD should be as for other cases with NLGN4 deletion, coupled with management of the dermatological problems.

Further information and support:

In the UK:
Ichthyosis Support Group
PO Box 7913
Reading
RG6 4ZQ
Tel.: 0845 602 9202
E-mail: isg@ichthyosis.org.uk
Website: www.ichthyosis.org.uk/home.aspx

In the USA:
Foundation for Ichthyosis and Related Skin Types
1364 Welsh Road G2
North Wales
PA 19454
Tel.: 215 619 0670
Fax: 215 619 0780
(for general information about the Foundation or ichthyosis)
E-mail: info@scalyskin.org
Website: www.scalyskin.org/index.cfm

SECTION C

Some promising developments

1

Mitochondrial defects

Mitochondria are the energy-producing subcellular organelles found in cells throughout the body. The only exceptions are nerve cells, which lack mitochondria and are therefore both dependent on a continuous supply of external energy and exquisitely sensitive to the effects of energy deprivation. This occurs when key compounds are missing from the diet, fail to be made in the body's metabolic pathways, or when circulation is arrested.

To date, HEADD syndrome [39] is the only mitochondriopathy to have been reported specifically in association with ASD. Most studies have not tested individuals with ASD for possible mitochondrial dysfunction. Where such testing has been done, it is concluded that mitochondrial energy defects may be amongst the most commonly associated biological factors (Oliveira *et al.* 2005).

A large number of genes are involved in interaction with mitochondria, and a study on 22q11 candidate genes has identified six genes which encode mitochondrial proteins (Maynard *et al.* 2008). These genes may account in part for the phenotypic variability seen in 22q11 conditions and the difficulties that have been experienced in their classification (see, for example, Burn 1999).

It has been established that mitochondrial DNA mutations, previously thought to be rare, are common in the general population, with pathogenic mtDNA mutations being present in approximately one in 200 people (Elliott *et al.* 2008). It is unsurprising, therefore, that mitochondrial disorders appear to be at least as common in those with ASD (Weissman *et al.* 2008).

Mitochondria are fascinating and have potential relevance to ASD for many reasons.

1. They possess their own separate ring chromosome, one within each mitochondrion rather than in the cell nucleus like all other chromosomes and so have a different inheritance system.

2. They are almost always inherited exclusively from the mother, because the mitochondria in sperm are coiled around the tail, and the tail is shed as the sperm enters the egg for fertilization.

3. The numbers of mitochondria per cell vary, and, at cell division, which mitochondria go into each divided cell, and how they themselves subsequently multiply, is not yet fully understood.

4. As mitochondria are critical to energy production, mitochondrial defects are commonly seen in conditions where energy production within the organism is abnormal, such as epilepsy.

5. Mitochondrial defects are 'heteroplasmic': where a mitochondrial DNA defect arises, it is often found to differing extents in different cell lines within the body, depending on the proportion of abnormal mitochondria present.

6. Systematic mitochondrial DNA defects are found in some ASD conditions which were previously thought to be the result of nuclear DNA differences, as in Klinefelter's syndrome (Oikawa *et al.* 2002).

7. Mitochondrial dysfunctions are associated with oxidative stress (Sas *et al.* 2007), a factor which has been recognized as common in people with ASD (James *et al.* 2004, 2006).

A simple introduction to the role and importance of the mitochondria can be found in Nick Lane's excellent little tome (Lane 2005), and a general introduction to the issue of mitochondrial disorders and dysfunction can be found in Naviaux (2000).

The possibility that autism could be caused by a mitochondrial defect was first raised in 1998 (Lombard 1998), and a range of subsequent studies indicate problems with mitochondrial function in some people with ASD. In some cases this seems to be an indication of a mitochondrial gene defect (Chugani *et al.* 1999; Correia *et al.* 2006; Graf *et al.* 2000; Oliveira *et al.* 2005; Pons *et al.* 2004). In others, it may indicate a defect in nuclear DNA mechanisms which interact with mitochondrial function (as with the inverse duplication of chromosome 15q11–q13) (Filipek *et al.* 2003).

There have been a number of discussions of mitochondrial defects in ASD in the clinical literature (see, for example, Lerman-Sagie *et al.* 2004; Pons *et al.* 2004; Tsao and Mendell 2007), most of which present small case series, but with several different defects in mitochondrial DNA.

One case has received considerable attention, as it is a child with a regressive autistic presentation, growth failure, and clear evidence of a metabolic disturbance of mitochondrial function (Poling *et al.* 2006). This child has reduced levels of all of the biochemical markers of oxidative phosphorylation. The authors also presented data from a retrospective casenote review of clinic cases that suggested that approximately 40 per cent of ASD cases had test results (for aspartate aminotransferase and/or serum creatine kinase) that would be consistent with such defects.

A number of avenues for the treatment of mitochondrial gene defects currently show promise (see, for review, Swerdlow 2007; Wallace 2005).

2

Gene markers

Improvements in genetic technology and ease of access to clinical samples are resulting in regular reports of DNA differences that have not previously been noted. Often such differences are not associated with previously recognized clinical conditions. A number of the conditions we have discussed in the previous section of the book have been identified in this way. Where no such phenotype has been linked but the gene difference is associated with an increased liklihood of ASD, the difference is known as a gene marker. Gene markers are segments of DNA associated with specific genes or traits – in this case with ASD diagnosis. Typically, the role or function of the genes in the marker region itself is not known.

Table C2.1 lists the chromosomes and positions of known gene markers, the 'scan groups' (genetic research groups) who have described them, the strength of the association found (expressed as Lod scores), and the candidate gene locus where known/identified.

Table C2.1: Gene loci with linkage to ASD diagnoses

Chr	Position	Marker (at or near)	Scan group	MLS (multipoint Lod score)	Candidate gene locus
1	1p13.2	D1S1675	1	2.63+?	
	1q21–22	D1S1653	1	2.63	
	1q22	D1S2721	2	2.88	
	1q23.3	D1S484	2	3.58	
	1q42.2	D1S1656	3	3.06	
2	2q31.1	D2S2188	4 (but see 16)	4.80	DLX1/2
	2q31.1	D2S355	3 (but see 16)	3.32	DLX1/2
3	3p24.1	D3S2432	2	3.32	
	3p25.3	D3S3691	5	2.22	
	3q22.1	D3S3045–D3S1736	6	3.10	
	3q26.32	D3S3715–D3S3037	1	4.81	
4	4q23	D4S1647	3	2.87	
	4q27	D4S3250	3	2.73	
	4q32.3	D4S2368	2	2.82	
5	5p13.1	D5S2494	7	2.54	
	5p13.1	D5S2494	8	2.55	
6	6q14.3	D6S1270	3	2.61	
	6q16.3	D6S283	9	2.23	
7	7q21.2	D7S1813	10	2.20	PON1
	7q22.1	D7S477	4	3.55	RELN

			(but see 17)		
	7q32.1–34	D7S539–D7S684	11	3.55	WNT2
	7q34–36.2	D7S1824–D7S3058	6	2.98	EN2
	7q36.1	D7S483	12	2.37	
9	9p22.2	D9S157	4	3.11	
	9q34.3	D9S1826	4	3.59	
11	11p11.2–13	D11S1392/D11S1993	7	2.24	BDNF
13	13q12.3	D13S217/12229	10	2.30	
	13q22	D13S800	10	2.30	
	13q32.1–32.3	D13S793–D13S1271	2	2.86	
15	15q21.2	CYP19	4	2.21	
16	16p13	D16S3102	4	2.93	
	16p13.2	D16S407	4	2.22	
17	17p11.2	D17S1298–D17S1299	6	2.22	SLC6A4
	17q11.2	D17S1294–D17S798	13	4.30	SLC6A4
	17q11.2	D17S1294	5	2.85	SLC6A4
	17q11.2	D17S1800	7	2.83	SLC6A4
	17q11.2	HTTINT2	4	2.34	SLC6A4
	17q21.2	D17S1299	5	2.26	HOXB1
	17q21.32	D17S2180	14	4.41	HOXB1
	17q24.3	D17S1290–D17S1301	6	2.84	
19	19q	D19S433	8	[3.36]	
	19p13.11	D19S930	5	2.77	
	19p13.12	D19S714	8	2.77	
	19p13.12	D19S714	3	2.31	
21	21q21.1	D21S1437	12	3.40	
X	Xq21.33	DXS6789	1	2.54	
	Xq25	DXS1047	8	2.67	
	Xq	DXS1047	8	[2.27]	

Note: For ease of presentation and simplicity, I have adopted the standard convention of reporting only linkage Lod scores of 2.2 or greater (see Lander and Kruglyak 1995). It is more typical to take a Lod score of 3.0 or above (which would indicate a likelihood of 1,000 to 1 that the association was a chance one) as indicative of an association between the gene and the trait – in this case ASD.

Scan groups:

1. Auranen *et al.* 2002
2. Ylisaukko-oja *et al.* 2004
3. Buxbaum *et al.* 2004
4. International Molecular Genetic Study of Autism Consortium 2001
5. McCauley *et al.* 2005
6. Alarcón *et al.* 2005b
7. Yonan *et al.* 2003
8. Liu *et al.* 2001
9. Philippe *et al.* 1999
10. Barrett *et al.* 1999
11. International Molecular Genetic Study of Autism Consortium 1998
12. Mills *et al.* 2005
13. Stone *et al.* 2004
14. Cantor *et al.* 2005
15. Shao *et al.* 2002
16. Rabionet *et al.* 2004
17. Devlin *et al.* 2004
18. Dutta *et al.* 2008

Table C2.2 lists clinical syndromes (as they appear in Section B of this book), the genes known to be associated with these syndromes, and the specific genes at these loci where they are known.

Table C2.2: Syndromes, gene loci and genes

- A gene locus in plain type with no linked syndrome is one that has been reported in association with ASD, but with no known association to a specific clinical phenotype.
- *Italic type* indicates a close match of an associated *clinical* phenotype to a gene marker.
- ***Bold italic type*** indicates loci for associated *behavioural* phenotypes that are genetically contiguous with high lod score linkage sites.

Linked syndrome (if applicable)	Gene locus	Gene acronym
	1p13.2	
Dihydropyrimidine dehydrogenase (DPYS) deficiency [30]	1p22	
Down syndrome [31]	1p35.2–p33	
Ehlers-Danlos syndrome [34]	1p36.3–p36.2	
	1q21–22	
	1q22	
	1q23.3	
	1q42.2	
Down syndrome [31]	1q43	
Neurofibromatosis type 1 [51]	2p22–p21	
Hypothyrodism [43]	2q12–q14	
Joubert syndrome [44]	2q13	
Biedl-Bardet syndrome [17]	*2q31*	
Ehlers-Danlos syndrome [34]	*2q31*	
Ehlers-Danlos syndrome [34]	*2q31*	
	2q31.1	*DLX 1/2*
Ehlers-Danlos syndrome [34]	2q34	
Biedl-Bardet syndrome [17]	3p12–q13	
Pituitary deficiency [58]	3p21.2–p21.1	HESX1
	3p24.1	
Xeroderma pigmentosum [79]	*3p25*	
	3p25.3	
	3q22.3	
Fragile-X syndrome [35, 36]	3q28	
Phenylketonuria [57]	4p15.31	
Hyper IgE syndrome [41]	4q21	
	4q23	
	4q27	

	4q32.3	
Pituitary deficiency [58]	5p13–p12	
De Lange syndrome [27]	*5p13.1*	
	5p13.1	
Ehlers-Danlos syndrome [34]	5q23;	
Ehlers-Danlos syndrome [34]	5q35.2–q35.3	
Sotos syndrome [68]	5q35	
Lujan-Fryns syndrome [46]	5q terminal	
Congential adrenal hyperplasia [25]	6p21.3	
Ehlers-Danlos syndrome [34]	6p21.3	
Succinic semialdehyde dehydrogenase deficiency [69]	6p22	
Trichothiodystrophy [72]	6p25.3	
	6q14.3	
	6q16.3	
Joubert syndrome [44]	6q23.3	
Biedl-Bardet syndrome [17]	7p14	
	4q27	
Trichothiodystrophy [72]	7p14	
Cogenital adrenal hyperplasia [25]	7q11.2	
Williams syndrome [77]	7q11.23	
CHARGE [20]	7q21.1	
Ehlers-Danlos syndrome [34]	7q22.1	
	7q21.2	PON1
	7q22.1	RELN
	7q32.1–q34	WNT2
	7q34–q36.2	EN2
	7q36	
	7q36.1	EN2
Congenital adrenal hyperplasia [25]	8p11.2	
CHARGE [20]	8q12.1	
Congenital adrenal hyperplasia [25]	8q21	
Cohen syndrome [23]	8q22–q23	
	9p22.2	
Basal cell naevus syndrome [16]	9q22.3	
Biedl-Bardet syndrome [17]	9q31–q34.1	
Tuberous sclerosis [73]	9q34	
	9q34.3	

Pituitary deficiency [58]	*9q34.3*	
Joubert syndrome [44]	*9q34.3*	
Ehlers-Danlos syndrome [34]	*9q34.2–q34.3*	
Di George syndrome I [29a]	10p14–10p13	
Cowden syndrome [26]	10q22.3	
Cowden syndrome [26]	10q23.31	
Bannayan-Riley-Ruvalcaba syndrome [15]	10q23.31	
ALPS [14]	10q24.1	
Congenital adrenal hyperplasia [25]	10q24.3	
Apert syndrome [12]	10q26	
	11p13–11.2	BDNF
Joubert syndrome [44]	11p13.3–12	
Smith-Lemli-Opitz syndrome [66]	11q12–q13	
Biedl-Bardet syndrome [17]	11q13	
Tourette syndrome [71]	11q23	
Phenylketonuria [57]	11q22.3–q23.3	
Noonan syndrome [52]	12q12.1	
Timothy syndrome [70]	12p13.3	
Tuberous sclerosis [73]	12q14	
Duchenne's disease [33]	12q21	
Biedl-Bardet syndrome [17]	12q21.2	
Joubert syndrome [44]	12q21.3	
Phenylketonuria [57]	12q24.1	
Noonan syndrome [52]	12q24.1	
	13q12.3	
Mobius syndrome [48]	13q12.2–q13	
Fragile-X syndrome [35, 36]	13q14	
	13q22	
Tourette syndrome [71]	13q31	
	13q32.1–32.3	
L-2-hydroxyglutaric aciduria [40]	14q22.1	
Phenylketonuria [57]	14q22.1–q22.2	
Hypothyroidism [43]	14q31	
Goldenhar syndrome [38]	14q32	
Biedl-Bardet syndrome [17]	14q32.1	
Angelman syndrome [11]	15q11–q13	
Prader-Willi syndrome [61]	15q11–q13	

Prader-Willi syndrome [61]	15q12	
Oculocutaneous albinism [55]	15q11.2–q12	
	15q21.2	
Biedl-Bardet syndrome [17]	15q22.3–q23	
Congenital adrenal hyperplasia [25]	15q23–q24	
	16p13	
	16p13.2	
Tuberous sclerosis [73]	16p13.3	
Biedl-Bardet syndrome [17]	16q21	
Smith-Magenis syndrome [67]	*17p11.2*	
Potocki-Lupski syndrome [60]	*17p11.2*	
Fragile-X syndrome [35, 36]	17p13.1	
	17q11.2	*SLC6A4*
Neurofibromatosis type I [51]	*17q11.2*	
	17q21.2	HOXBI
	17q21.32	HOXBI
Ehlers-Danlos syndrome [34]	17q21.31–q22	
Pituitary deficiency [58]	*17q22–q24*	
	17q24.3	
	19p	
	19p13.11	
	19p13.12	
Myotonic dystrophy (MD1) [50]	19q13.2–q13.3	
GAMT deficiency [37]	19p13.3	
Trichothiodystrophy [72]	19q13.2–13.3	
Steinert myotonic dystrophy	19q13.2–q13.3	
Beidl-Bardet syndrome [17]	20p12	
	21q21.1	
Down syndrome [31]	21q22.1–q22.2	
Down syndrome [31]	21q22.3	
CATCH 22 [20]	*22q11.2*	
CHARGE [20]	*22q11.2*	
DiGeorge syndrome I [29a]	*22q11.2*	
Velocardiofacial syndrome [76]	*22q11.2*	
Adenylosuccinate lyase deficiency [9]	22q13.1	
Down syndrome [31]	22q22.2	
De Lange syndrome [27]	Xp11.21	
Down syndrome [31]	Xp11.23	

Hypomelanosis of Ito [42]	Xp11.30	
Ornithine carbamyltransferase deficiency [54]	Xp21.1	
Duchenne's disease [33]	Xp21.2	
Rett syndrome (Hanefield variant) [63b]	*Xp22*	*CDKL5*
Rett syndrome [63a]	*Xp22*	*MeCP2*
Coffin-Lowry syndrome [21]	Xp22.2–p22.1	
ARX gene mutations [13]	Xp22.13	
Oculocutaneous albinism [55]	Xp22.3	
X-linked ichthyosis [80]	Xp22.32	
	Xq	
Lujan-Fryns syndrome [46]	Xq13	
	Xq21.33	
	Xq25	
Fragile-X syndrome [35, 36]	*Xq27.3*	*FMR1*
Angelman syndrome [11]	Xq28	
Ehlers-Danlos syndrome [34]	Xq28	
Angelman syndrome [11]	*Xq28*	*UBE3A*
Rett syndrome [63a]	*Xq28*	*MeCP2*
Rett syndrome (Hanefeld variant) [63b]	*Xq28*	*CDKL5*
Fragile-X syndrome [35, 36]	*Xq28*	*FMR1*

Definitions of gene acronyms

- BDNF – brain-derived neurotrophic factor
- CDKL-5 – cyclin-dependent kinase-like 5
- DLX 1/2 – distal-less homeobox 1/2
- EN2 – engrailed 2
- FMR1 – fragile-X mental retardation protein 1
- HESX1 – homeobox gene expressed in ES cells
- HOXB1 – homeobox B1
- MeCP2 – methyl-CpG binding protein 2
- PON1 – paroxonase 1
- RELN – reelin
- SLC6A4 – solute carrier family 6 (neurotransmitter transporter, serotonin) member 4
- UBE3A – ubiquitin-protein ligase E3A
- WNT2 – wingless-type MMTV integration site family, member 2

Studies to date have not reported on Y chromosome abnormalities, except for the association with an extra Y chromosome in XYY syndrome [4]. Given the high male to female ratio for ASD, Y chromosome abnormalities could be an important factor in some forms of ASD. There is a high degree of homology between the functional areas of the Y chromosome and the X chromosome. There are Y-specific genes, such as the SRY gene

(Quintana-Murci and Fellous 2001), which could be important. Research on such factors is ongoing (Smith, Spence and Flodman 2009).

One gene marker (3q26.32) that we go on to discuss below is important in the metabolism of galactose. Galactose is a monosaccharide sugar which, along with glucose, is produced when lactose from cow's milk is digested by lactase. It is, to date, the candidate region with the strongest association to ASD diagnosis. This association may help to provide an alternative explanatory mechanism to the 'opioid hypothesis' for the beneficial effects reported in many cases from the removal of milk and milk products from the diet.

In addition to the genes identified in such screening studies, there are many other differences which have been reported in a proportion of those with ASDs, such as the MET receptor tyrosine kinase variant at 7q31 (Campbell et al. 2006). This pathway is under the control of a number of genetic factors (Campbell, Sutcliffe, et al. 2008).

A further study has highlighted the variability of clinical phenotypes, including one that is ASD-specific, associated with recurrent rearrangements of 1q21.1 (Mefford et al. 2008).

A number of reviews highlight many of the genotype–phenotype associations seen in ASD (see, for example, Aitken 2008; Benvenuto et al. 2009; Lintas and Persico 2008).

A further study has shown the importance of matching on behavioural phenotype rather than simply on ASD diagnosis, with high Lod scores being obtained using factors such as delayed onset of phrase speech and low IQ, which were not seen in overall ASD populations (Liu et al. 2008). The importance of differentiating within the ASD population rather than assuming that a common model will be appropriate for all cases continues to gain in empirical support.

3

Potential correction of 'nonsense' mutations

Nonsense mutations are mutations in a chromosome that prevent a ribosome from fully reading a given portion of DNA. The result is a block in the production of the appropriate RNA to manufacture a specific protein.

Nonsense mutations have been reported in a number of conditions and dysfunctions relevant to ASD.

Table C3: Nonsense mutations associated with ASD

Condition	Section/key references
ARX	[13]
Biedl-Bardet syndrome	[17]
Coffin-Lowry syndrome	[21]
Cohen syndrome	[23]
Cowden syndrome	[26]
Rett syndrome	[63a]
Neuroligin 3 and neuroligin 4 defects	Jamain *et al.* 2003
FDXP2	Gong *et al.* 2004
Creatine transporter defect	Poo-Arguelles *et al.* 2006

One study (Welch *et al.* 2007) has provided evidence for the possibility of correction of nonsense mutation defects. This finding opens up the possibility of identifying and correcting gene defects of this type which, when left untreated, result in metabolic abnormalities (for discussion, see Linde and Kerem 2008; Rowe and Clancy 2009).

4

Differences in the gastrin-releasing peptide receptor (GRPR) gene

Gene locus: Xp22.3–p21.2

Only one of each pair of chromosomes in a cell is active, and inactivation is normally random. This process is one of the key features in our biology which provides for the rich variation in human behaviour. Skewed or biased inactivation of one particular copy favouring expression of a defective copy is seen in many diseases and disorders.

A skewed pattern of X-chromosome inactivation is seen in many X-linked mental retardation conditions, such as Aarskog syndrome [8] and Williams syndrome [77] (see Plenge *et al.* 2002 for discussion). In female carriers of X-linked mental retardation conditions there is skewed inactivation of the affected chromosome. This results in the mutation being present on the preferentially inactive chromosome. Non-random X-chromosome inactivation is seen in females in many conditions related to ASD: in an unselected series of female cases diagnosed with autism (Talebizadeh *et al.* 2005); in four familial Rett syndrome cases without MeCP2 mutation (Villard *et al.* 2001) and in carriers of X-linked adrenoleukodystrophy (adrenomyeloneuropathy [10]) (Maier *et al.* 2002). It is thought that X-chromosome genes may be of particular importance in the development of autism, given the abnormal sex ratio, with approximately four times as many boys affected, and the presence of X-chromosome differences in many of the female cases reported.

GRPR (gastrin-releasing peptide receptor) is a gene that is widely expressed in various organ systems, including the central nervous system and the gastrointestinal tract. It is expressed early in embryonic development (Battey, Wada and Wray 1994). It is found on the short arm of the X chromosome, fairly close to the gene involved in ARX [13] and the gene for neuroligin 4 (Blasi *et al.* 2006; Chocholska *et al.* 2006; Laumonnier *et al.* 2004).

The first paper to suggest a link between autism and a break point in the X chromosome at the site of the GRPR gene was a single case study published in the 1990's (Rao *et al.* 1994).

A second case was reported shortly after (Bolton *et al.* 1995), where a GRPR abnormality was subsequently characterized (Ishikawa-Brush *et al.* 1997). These papers both describe the phenotype and genetic profile of a 27-year-old female patient who had multiple extoses (bony lumps on the long bones (of the legs, arms, fingers, toes), on the pelvis and on the shoulderblades) a learning disability (she had an IQ of 35), *grand mal* epilepsy, brachycephaly and short stature, in addition to her autism.

It is important to note that there may be large ethnic differences in the prevalence of GRPR differences. The polymorphic sites which appear to be significantly associated in North American studies appear far less prevalent in Japanese populations (Marui *et al.* 2004b).

Why might GRPR be relevant? A number of studies have shown abnormalities in such 'bombesin-like' peptides and their receptors in other conditions, such as schizophrenia and Alzheimer's disease (see Roesler *et al.* 2006a for a review). Gastrin-releasing peptide is called 'bombesin-like' because it is one of a structurally similar class of peptides, the first of which to be characterized was isolated from the skin of the frog '*Bombina bombina*'.

Studies in rodent models have shown that GRPRs in the hippocampus are important regulators of memory consolidation (Roesler *et al.* 2006b).

Presti-Torres *et al.* (2007) have shown that neonatal rats whose GRPR pathway was blockaded with bombesin were impaired in both social interaction and novel object memory. The study authors hypothesize that impairment in the action of gastrin-releasing peptide may be a useful model for neurodevelopmental disorders such as autism.

Defects in GRPR are involved in structural differences in the amygdala and in the development of heightened fear responses, both of which are common features in ASD. Shumyatsky *et al.* (2002) found that in mice gastrin-releasing peptide is strongly expressed both in the lateral nucleus of the amygdala – the region that conveys fearful auditory information to the GABAergic interneurons of the lateral nucleus – and the lateral nucleus itself. Gastrin-releasing peptide excited these interneurons and increased their inhibition of principal neurons. GRPR-deficient mice had more pronounced and persistent long-term fear memory.

As abnormality of interneuron function has been proposed as a basis of neurodevelopmental disorders (Levitt, Eagleson and Powell 2004), and structural defects in the amygdala have been proposed as core neuroanatomic abnormalities in ASD (Amaral, Bauman and Schumann 2003; Baron-Cohen *et al.* 2000a), the presence of GRPR defects in some ASD cases, and the direct effect of such defects on interneuron development within the amygdala, is potentially of great importance and warrants further systematic study.

Some animal work is beginning to emerge, demonstrating effects on memory consolidation of GRPR antagonists, which could have clinical implications for improving memory consolidation (Santos Dantas *et al.* 2006).

5

Differences in glutamate mechanisms and metabolism

Abnormalities of glutamate metabolism appear common in a number of the conditions linked to ASD that have been discussed. The biology is particularly well understood in fragile-X syndrome [35, 36] and in tuberous sclerosis [73], and in addition a number of gene differences affecting glutamatergic function have been identified as overrepresented in the ASD population.

The evidence concerning possible glutamate abnormalities in autism come from several sources.

- There are a number of genes implicated in glutamate metabolism which have been highlighted from various genome studies in autistic populations:
  - the glutamate G6 receptor gene GRIK2 at 6p21 (Jamain *et al.* 2002; Shuang *et al.* 2004)
  - the glutamate G5 receptor gene mGluR5 affected by the FMR1 site at Xq27.3 (Westmark and Malter 2007)
  - the glutamate G8 receptor gene GRM8 at 7q31 (Serajee *et al.* 2003).
- In animal models, at least, induction of central hypoglutamatergia through the use of antipsychotics can induce autistic-like behaviour (Nilsson *et al.* 2001).
- Elevated glutamate levels are seen as a consequence of anxiety, a common clinical feature in ASD (Gillott, Furniss and Walter 2001).

- With specific conditions such as fragile-X syndrome [35, 36] and tuberous sclerosis [73] it is clear that there is a problem due to the absence of specific components of the glutamate pathway (in fragile-X, through the absence of one specific glutamate receptor – mGluR5).

- Preliminary findings to date show some promise; however, early reports are of cases selected on ASD diagnosis, not concurrent anxiety (Niederhofer 2007).

6

Differences in oxytocin

Oxytocin is a sexually dimorphic neuropeptide expressed most in the female. There has been considerable discussion of its possible role in ASD (see Carter 2007; Hammock and Young 2006). Oxytocin is important as a modulator of the functioning of the hypothalamic-pituitary-adrenal axis in situations of social stress and social interaction (see Heinrichs and Gaab 2007 for an overview), and it has been found that intranasal administration of oxytocin significantly increases trust in social situations, and willingness to take social risks based on personal judgement (Kosfeld *et al.* 2005).

Oxytocin receptor gene (OXTR) abnormalities have been found to be overrepresented in both Caucasian (Jacob *et al.* 2007) and Chinese Beijing HapMap and Han ASD samples (Wu S. *et al.* 2005).

The OXTR is located at a linkage site for ASD (3p2–p25), identified by one study group (McCauley *et al.* 2005).

Several pieces of published evidence point to a role for oxytocin in the ASDs.

- The HOXA1 and EN2 genes which are implicated in autism are involved in the oxytocin system (for discussion, see Badcock and Crespi 2006).

- Plasma levels of oxytocin are lower in an unselected ASD population when compared to age-matched controls (Modahl *et al.* 1998).

- In one study, oxytocin infusion significantly reduced repetitive behaviours in a group of adults with diagnoses of autism and Asperger's syndrome, compared to the effects of sham infusion (Hollander *et al.* 2003).

- In a randomized, placebo-controlled study of 30 normal, non-ASD adults measuring performance on a task where subjects inferred the mental state of others from facial expression (the 'Reading the Mind in the Eyes' Test), a single 24 IU intranasal spray of oxytocin significantly improved performance on difficult-to-discriminate items (Domes *et al.* 2007).

- A large study used high-resolution techniques to identify copy number variants from 119 whole blood samples from individuals with ASD from multiplex autism families, extended family members and phenotypically normal unrelated controls. Postmortem brain tissue (temporal cortex) from nine cases and nine controls was also compared. Both comparisons demonstrated hypermethylation of a CpG island upstream of the OXTR gene coding for oxytocin in ASD, compared with controls, and the latter comparison showed a consequent decrease in OXTR expression (Gregory *et al.* 2009). These findings strongly suggest epigenetic regulation of reduced oxytocin levels in ASD.

7

Ghrelin differences

Gene locus: 3p26–p25

Ghrelin is a gastrointestinal hormone and neuropeptide which has been arousing much interest (see Anderson *et al.* 2005 for a general review). It is involved in central nervous system, immune and gastrointestinal function and seems, in animal studies at least, to be protective against stress-induced gastrointestinal dysfunction (Brzozowski *et al.* 2004).

In mice and rats, ghrelin affects both synapse formation and dopaminergic activity of the nucleus accumbens in the midbrain (Abizaid *et al.* 2006).

Abnormalities of ghrelin production have been implicated in a range of conditions which range from epilepsy (Berilgen *et al.* 2006) and irritable bowel disease (Peracchi *et al.* 2006) to immune dysfunction (Dixit and Taub 2005).

In animal models an association has been found between plasma ghrelin levels and brain levels of serotonin (Nonogaki, Ohashi-Nozue and Oka 2006). Given the extensive data on serotonergic defects in ASD, together with the immune and gastrointestinal components discussed earlier, ghrelin may prove to be of clinical importance in some of the cases who show this constellation of features.

8

Ciliopathies

Cilia can be viewed as sensory cellular antennae that coordinate signalling pathways, either to produce particular patterns of motility or to coordinate processes involved in cell division and differentiation. Cilia perform a wide variety of functions in mammals – clearing our lungs of debris; helping our intestines to process food; affording information to our senses; and providing the 'outboard motor' for sperm motility and for the movement of the egg out of the ovary. First described as early as 1835 (Purkinje and Valentin 1835), the various functions of cilia, their presence in a range of body systems, and their high degree of phylogenic preservation have only recently come to be appreciated.

We now know that defects in the genetics of cilia are involved in a number of human neurodevelopmental disorders, including Alstrom syndrome; Biedl-Bardet syndrome (BBS) [17] (Avidor-Reiss *et al.* 2004); Joubert syndrome [44] (Gorden *et al.* 2008); Meckel-Gruber syndrome; Løken-Senior syndrome; oral-facial-digital syndrome; and polycystic kidney disease. Abnormalities of the cilia are also now recognized to be involved in cancer, and particularly in the growth of tumours.

As both BBS [17] and Joubert syndrome [44] have been reported in association with ASD, while other ciliopathies such as oral-facial-digital syndrome have many features in common, it seems likely that for some ASD conditions this may provide a link for certain ASD presentations between the diagnosis and their associated gastrointestinal, sensory, respiratory and reproductive problems.

Our understanding of the abnormal proteins implicated in the development of BBS has come from discovering that these are variants of highly conserved ciliary proteins which are important factors in intracellular transport and are involved in formation of the basal bodies of ciliated cells. For a discussion of these developments, see Section B [17] in this book.

BBS cases have been reported with ciliary problems in lung function (Shah *et al.* 2008), and with both partial and complete anosmia (Iannaccone *et al.* 2005; Kulaga *et al.* 2004).

Specific mouse knockouts have been produced for several of the BBS genes: BBS1 (Kulaga *et al.* 2004), BBS2 (Nishimura *et al.* 2004), BBS4 (Kulaga *et al.* 2004, Mykytyn *et al.* 2004) and BBS6 (Fath *et al.* 2005; Ross A.J. *et al.* 2005). These have provided support for ciliary dysfunction in BBS. Several ciliary dysfunctions have been noted in these BBS mouse models: in sperm motility, retinal, lung and olfactory function.

9

Aquaporins

These are a family of genetic factors that regulate water-selective cell membrane channels, controlling fluid homeostasis and glycerol transport (Krane and Goldstein 2007). There is increasing interest in the role of aquaporins in bodily functions. They are critically involved in fluid balance in a range of body systems such as the eye, lungs, salivary and sweat glands, the gastrointestinal tract, and the kidneys.

Aquaporins are a class of compounds that form water channels in cell membranes. A range of factors are likely to alter aquaporin function. In animal models, aquaporin expression in the gastrointestinal system can be altered by the induction of a food allergy (Yamamoto, Kuramoto and Kadowaki 2007) that affects water absorption through the gut wall.

There is some system specificity to the various aquaporins so far discovered. Aquaporin-1, for example, appears to be erythrocyte (red blood cell) specific, while aquaporin-4 is central nervous system specific.

There is increasing interest in the role of certain of the aquaporin channels, and their controlling genes. Aquaporins 0, 1, 2, 4, 5, 6 and 8 are specific channels involved in water transport, while aquaporins 3, 7, 9 and 10 are involved in glycerol release and transport. Aquaporins 7 and 9 allow glycerol to move through cell membranes (Hara-Chikuma and Verkman 2006) and are implicated in various conditions, including type 2 diabetes, obesity and various other metabolic disorders (Hibuse *et al.* 2005; Wintour and Henry 2006).

Genetic defects in aquaporin-4 (Zhou *et al.* 2008) can affect blood–brain barrier development and function, and could increase the impact of peripheral glutamate levels on central nervous system glutamatergic function.

Viral exposure at certain critical points in early brain development can affect the functioning of aquaporin-4 (Fatemi *et al.* 2008a, 2008b). As aquaporin-4 is involved in the migration of glial cells, neural signal transduction and brain oedema (Verkman *et al.* 2006), it may have a major effect in neural development. To date this has not been linked to abnormalities of glutamatergic function.

Defects in aquaporin-4 are known to occur in some of the neuromuscular conditions that have been associated with ASD, such as Duchenne muscular dystrophy [33] and in epilepsy (Benga 2006; Obeid and Herrmann 2006).

Our recognition and partial understanding of aquaporins and their functions is very recent. Peter Agre of Johns Hopkins University in Baltimore shared the Nobel Prize for Chemistry in 2003 for the discovery and investigation of aquaporin channels (Agre 2006).

SECTION D

Appendices

The following lists of contacts and information resources are not comprehensive – new resources and new information become available all the time, but these are reasonably up-to-date at the time of publication. The charities working in this area have changed considerably during the time this book was being compiled. Treat this as a starting point, rather than a definitive listing.

Appendix I: National autism support groups

Many of the national society websites carry links (see, for example www.nas.org.uk), and many of the more general books on autism also list resources, link sites and national associations (see, for example, Exkorn 2005; Shore and Rastelli 2006; Sicile-Kira 2003).

For general information concerning ASDs, and for information on local supports the following may be helpful.

In Australia:

New South Wales
Autism Spectrum Australia (Aspect)
41 Cook St (PO Box 361)
Forestville
NSW 2087
Tel.: +61 (0) 2 8977 8300;
FREECALL 1800 06 99 78
Fax: +61 (0) 2 8977 8399
E-mail: contact@autismnsw.com.au
Website: www.autismnsw.com.au

Queensland
Autism Association Queensland
PO Box 363
437 Hellawell Road
Sunnybank Hills
Queensland 4109
Tel.: +61 (0) 73 273 0000
Fax: +61 (0) 73 273 8306
E-mail: mailbox@autismqld.asn.au

South Australia
Autism of South Australia
3 Fisher Street
Myrtle Bank
SA 5064
Postal address:
PO Box 339
Fullarton
SA 5063
Tel.: +61 (0) 8379 6976
Fax: +61 (0) 8338 1216
E-mail: admin@autismsa.org.au
Website: www.autismsa.org.au

Tasmania
Autism Tasmania
PO Box 1552
Launceston
TAS 7250
Tel.: +61 (0) 363 443 261
E-mail: autism@autismtas.org.au
Website: www.autismtas.org.au

Victoria
Autism Victoria
35 High Street
Glen Iris,
Victoria 3146
Postal address:
PO Box 235
Ashburton, 3147
Tel.: +61 (0) 3 98 85 0533
Fax: +61 (0) 3 98 85 0508
E-mail: autismav@vicnet.net.au
Website: www.autismvictoria.org.au/home/

Autistic Citizens Residential and Resources Society of Victoria Inc
PO Box 3015
Ripponlea
Victoria, 3185
Tel.: +61 (0) 417 384 454
E-mail: dcoates@asd.org.au
Website: www.asd.org.au

Western Australia
Autism Association of Western Australia (Inc)
37 Hay Street
Subiaco 6008
Postal Address:
Locked Bag 9
Post Office
West Perth
WA 6872
Tel.: +61 (08) 9489 8900
Fax: +61 (08) 9489 8999
E-mail: autismwa@autism.org.au
Website: www.autism.org.au

In Canada:
Autism Society Canada
Box 22017
1670 Heron Road
Ottawa
Ontario
K1V 0C2
Tel.: 613-789-9843 or 866-476-8440 (toll-free)
Fax: 613-789-6985
E-mail: info@autismsocietycanada.ca
Website: www.autismsocietycanada.ca

In England:
The National Autistic Society
393 City Road
London
EC1V 1NG
Tel.: 020 7833 2299
Fax: 020 7833 9666
E-mail: nas@nas.org.uk
Website: www.nas.org.uk

In Ireland:
Irish Autism Action
41 Newlands
Mullingar
Co. Westmeath
Tel./fax: +353 (0) 44 9331609
E-mail: kevin@autismireland.ie
Website: www.autismireland.ie

Irish Society for Autism
Unity Building
16/17 Lower O'Connell Street
Dublin 1
Tel.: +353 (01) 874 4684
Fax: +353 (01) 874 4224
E-mail: autism@isa.iol.ie
Website: www.autism.ie

Asperger Syndrome Association of Ireland
(ASPIRE)
Carmichael House
North Brunswick Street
Dublin 14
Tel.: +353 (01) 878 0027
Fax: +353 (01) 873 5737
E-mail: asperger@email.com
Website: www.aspire-irl.org

In Japan:
Autism Society Japan
6F, Da Vinci Tsukji 2
6–22 Akashicho
Chuo-ku
Tel.: +81 33 545 3380
Fax: +81 33 545 3381
E-mail: asj@autism.or.jp
Website: www.autism.or.jp

In Scotland:
Scottish Society for Autism
Hilton House
Alloa Business Park
The Whins
Alloa
FK10 3SA
Tel.: 01259 720044
Fax: 01259 720051
E-mail: info@autism-in-scotland.org.uk
Website: www.autism-in-scotland.org.uk

In Wales:
Autism Cymru
6 Great Darkgate Street
Aberystwyth
Ceredigion
SY23 1DE
Tel.: 01970 625256
Fax: 01970 639454
E-mail: sue@autismcymru.org
Website: www.autismcymru.org

In the USA:

Autism Society of America
7910 Woodmont Avenue
Suite 300
Bethesda
MD 20814
Tel.: 301-657-0881
Tel.: 800-3AUTISM
Fax: 301-657-0869
E-mail: info@autism-society.org or chapters@
autism-society.org
Website: www.autism-society.org

Other resources on particular aspects of ASD:

The Autism Research Institute
4182 Adams Avenue
San Diego
CA 92116
Fax: 619-563-6840
E-mail: media@autismresearchinstitute.com
Website: www.autism.com

Autism Research Unit
School of Health, Natural and Social Sciences
City Campus
University of Sunderland
Sunderland
SR1 3SD
UK
Tel.: 0191 510 8922
Fax: 0191 567 0420
E-mail: autism.unit@sunderland.ac.uk
Website: http://osiris.sunderland.ac.uk

UC Davis MIND Institute
(Medical Investigation of Neurodevelopmental
Disorders)
2825 50th Street
Sacramento
California
CA 95817
Tel.: 916-703-0280
Website: www.ucdmc.ucdavis.edu
An excellent resource is the series of recorded
talks in the MIND Institute lecture series on
neurodevelopmental disorders, which can be
viewed through University of California Television
at www.uctv.tv

Autism Research Centre
Section of Developmental Psychiatry
University of Cambridge
Douglas House
18b Trumpington Road
Cambridge
CB2 8AH
Tel.: 01223 746057
Fax: 01223 746033
E-mail: raj33@medschl.cam.ac.uk (ARC
administrator)
Website: www.autismresearchcentre.com

Appendix II: Autism research charities

In Canada:
Autism Speaks Canada
8 King Street East
Suite 1104
Toronto
Ontario
M5C 1B5
Tel.: 888-362-6227
E-mail: slanthier@autismspeaks.org
Website: www.autismspeaks.ca/

In the UK:
Autism Speaks
Autistica
Rotherfield House
7 Fairmile
Henley-on-Thames
Oxfordshire
RG9 2JR
Tel.: 01491 412311
Fax: 01491 571921
E-mail: info@autismspeaks.org.uk
Website: www.autismspeaks.org.uk/

In the USA:
Autism Speaks
2 Park Avenue
11th Floor
New York
NY 10016
Tel.: 212-252-8584
Fax: 212-252-8676
E-mail: contactus@autismspeaks.org
Website: www.autismspeaks.org

The Simons Foundation
101 Fifth Avenue
5th Floor
New York
NY 10003
E-mail: admin@simonsfoundation.org
Website: http://simonsfoundation.org

Appendix III: Some general autism information websites

- **Autismconnect**
  A free website which carries a wide range of information, links, details of forthcoming meetings and news on autism and autism-related conditions.
  Website: www.autismconnect.org

- **Autism One**
  A US not-for-profit organization set up by parents, which has a website and web-based radio station devoted to covering autism education and treatment issues.
  Website: www.autismone.org.uk/

- **Autism Cymru**
  A Welsh Assembly-sponsored site which carries a broad range of information on autism-related issues.
  Website: www.autismcymru.org

Appendix IV: Organizations and charities dealing with and funding research on related conditions

Bill and Melinda Gates Foundation
PO Box 23350
Seattle
WA 98102
USA
Tel.: 206-709-3100 (reception);
206-709-3140 (grant inquiries)
E-mail: info@gatesfoundation.org
Website: www.gatesfoundation.org

Medical Research Council
20 Park Crescent
London
W1B 1AL
UK
Tel.: 020 7636 5422
Fax: 020 7436 6179
E-mail: corporate@headoffice.mrc.ac.uk
Website: www.mrc.ac.uk

PACE (People Against Childhood Epilepsy)
7 East 85th Street
Suite A3
New York
NY 10028
USA
Tel.: 212-665 (PACE)-7223
Fax: 212-327-3075
E-mail: pacenyemail@aol.com
Website: www.paceusa.org

Tourettes Action
Southbank House
Black Prince Road
London
SE1 7SJ
UK
TS helpline: 0845 458 1252
E-mail: help@tourettes-action.org.uk
Administration: 020 7793 2356
E-mail: admin@tourettes-action.org.uk
Website: www.tourettes-action.org.uk

The Wellcome Trust
Gibbs Building
215 Euston Road
London
NW1 2BE
UK
Tel.: 020 7611 8888
Fax: 020 7611 8545
E-mail: contact@wellcome.ac.uk
Website: www.wellcome.ac.uk

Appendix V: Some relevant professional organizations

- **IMGSAC – The International Molecular Genetic Study of Autism Consortium**
  Contact links for most of those involved in this group are available on the website.
  Website: www.well.ox.ac.uk

- **INSAR – The International Society for Autism Research**
  INSAR is a professionals-only organization for those working in the area of autism research. The principal function of the Society at present is setting up and running the annual International Meeting for Autism Research.

  Specific requests for information on INSAR should be directed to Dr Nurit Yirmiya: NuritYirmiya@huji.ac.il

  The INSAR Conference homepage can be found on the website at www.cevs.ucdavis.edu

- **SSBP – The Society for the Study of Behavioural Phenotypes**
  This is an international organization that started in 1987 with a specific interest in investigating behavioural and emotional aspects of biologically determined clinical syndromes associated with intellectual disability.

  Administrative Secretary
  SSBP
  2nd Floor
  Douglas House
  18b Trumpington Road
  Cambridge
  CB2 8AH
  UK
  Tel.: 01223 746 100
  Fax: 01223 746 122
  E-mail: ssbpRobbie@aol.com
  Website: www.ssbp.co.uk

Appendix VI: General information on rare biomedical conditions

A range of self-help groups and organizations provide information and support for families with many of the conditions described in this volume, and many of these groups devote their efforts to a specific identified condition.

In addition to those condition-specific groups, several 'umbrella' groups exist, which help to support and work with a range of conditions. Others, such as NORD and Unique (see below), provide information on disorders that are not identified commonly enough for specific support groups to have been established.

In Australasia:
AGSA (The Association of Genetic Support of Australasia Inc.)
66 Albion Street
Surry Hills
NSW 2010
Australia
E-mail: info@agsa-geneticsupport.org.au
Website: www.agsa-geneticsupport.org.au

In Canada:
The London Health Sciences Centre
800 Commissioners Road East
PO Box 5010
London
Ontario
N6A 5W9
Tel.: 519-685-8500
Website: www.lhsc.on.ca
Maintains: the Canadian Directory of Genetic Support Groups.

In Europe:
The European Organisation for Rare Diseases (EURODIS)
Plateforme Maladies Rares
102 rue Didot
75014 Paris
France
Tel.: +33 (1) 56 53 52 10
Fax: +33 (1) 56 53 52 15
E-mail: eurordis@eurordis.org
Website: www.eurordis.org
EURODIS is a parent-driven alliance of patient organizations and individuals living with rare diseases.

In Sweden:
The Swedish Association of Rare Disorders
Sällsynta diagnoser
Box 1386
172 27 Sundbyberg
Tel.: 08764 49 99
Fax: 08546 40 494
Website: www.sallsyntadiagnoser.nu

In the UK:
Contact a Family
209–211 City Road
London
EC1V 1JN
Tel.: 020 7608 8700
Fax: 020 7608 8701
Helpline: 0808 808 3555
Textphone: 0808 808 3556
Freephone helpline for parents and families
(10am–4pm, Mon–Fri):
E-mail: info@cafamily.org.uk
Website: www.cafamily.org.uk/
Linking site for families with the same condition:
www.makingcontact.org/

Genetic Interest Group
Unit 4D
Leroy House
436 Essex Road
London
N1 3QP
Tel.: 020 7704 3141
Fax: 020 7359 1447
E-mail: mail@gig.org.uk
Website: www.gig.org.uk

Unique
Rare Chromosome Disorder Support Group
PO Box 2189
Surrey
CR3 5GN
Helpline: 01883-330766
E-mail: info@rarechromo.org
Website: www.rarechromo.org

In the USA:
The Children's Craniofacial Association (CCA.com)
13140 Coit Road
Suite 307
Dallas
Texas
TX 75240
Toll-free: 800-535-3643
Tel.: 214-570-9099
Fax: 214-570-8811
E-mail: contactCCA@ccakids.com
Website: www.ccakids.com

Genetic Alliance
4301 Connecticut Ave, NW
Suite 404
Washington, DC
20008-2304
Tel.: 202-966-5557
Fax: 202-966-8553
E-mail: info@geneticalliance.org
Website: www.geneticalliance.org

The MAGIC Foundation
Corporate Office
6645 W. North Avenue
Oak Park
IL 60302
Tel.: 708-383-0808
Toll-free parent help-line: 800-3MAGIC3 or
800-362-4423
Fax: 708-383-0899
Website: http://magicfoundation.org

National Organization for Rare Disorders (NORD)
55 Kenosia Avenue
PO Box 1968
Danbury
CT 06813-1968
Tel.: 203 744-0100
Toll-free: 800-999-6673 (voicemail only)
TDD Number: 203-797-9590
Fax: 203-798-2291
E-mail: orphan@rarediseases.org
Website: www.rarediseases.org

Appendix VII: Searching for further information

In addition to the materials noted at the end of each chapter in Section B, a variety of other resources can provide helpful information on specific conditions.

- **The Birth Disorder Information Directory**
  This directory provides a detailed list of clinical disorders with brief definitions.
  Website: www.bdid.com

- **Genetests**
  This website currently provides technical information on 373 genetic conditions, and international directories of genetic testing laboratories and diagnostic clinics.
  Website: www.genetests.org

- **The National Center for Biotechnology Information (NCBI)**
  Provided as a free resource by the National Institutes for Health in the USA, NCBI gives a rapid means of searching the medical literature by giving access to a number of databases. The most relevant is PubMed, which can search a huge proportion of the peer-reviewed medical literature (over 16 million papers at the time of writing). Searching on all databases through the NCBI search window accesses a large number of clinical and research papers as open-access PDF files.
  Website: www.ncbi.nlm.nih.gov

- **OMIM (Online Mendelian Inheritance in Man)**
  This is a catalogue of known human genetic disorders.
  Website: www.ncbi.nlm.nih.gov/omim

Appendix VIII: Relevant clinical journals

- *Autism*
  http://aut.sagepub.com/
- *Biological Psychiatry*
  www.journals.elsevierhealth.com
- *Brain and Development*
  www.elsevier.com
- *Development and Psychopathology*
  http://journals.cambridge.org
- *Developmental Medicine and Child Neurology (DMCN)*
  www.blackwellpublishing.com
- *Journal of the American Academy of Child and Adolescent Psychiatry (JAACAP)*
  www.jaacap.com
- *Journal of Autism and Developmental Disorders (JADD)*
  www.springer.com
- *Journal of Child Neurology*
  http://jcn.sagepub.com
- *Journal of Child Psychology and Psychiatry (JCPP)*
  www.blackwellpublishing.com
- *Journal of Inherited Metabolic Disease*
  www.springer.com
- *Mental Retardation and Developmental Disabilities Research Reviews (MRDDRR)*
  http://eu.wiley.com
- *Molecular Psychiatry*
  www.nature.com
- *Proceedings of the National Academy of Science (PNAS)*
  www.pnas.org

Appendix IX: List of clinical conditions

Many of the conditions we have discussed have several different names. This makes keeping up to date more complex, as the same condition might be talked of differently in different countries or at different times. This will be made even more complex with the proposed diagnostic revisions in the *Diagnostic and Statistical Manual* of the American Psychiatric Association, Fifth Revision (*DSM-V*). The *DSM-V* is the standard system for agreed diagnostic criteria in North American mental health practice.

The following listing of conditions covered in the book gives (where applicable) a reasonable cross-referencing of the possible terms used for the various disorders discussed. This should help when searching for new information.

Usual name of condition	Alternative name/s
• 15q11–q13 duplication	
• chromosome 2q deletion	
• XXY syndrome	Klinefelter's syndrome
• XYY syndrome	
• 10p terminal deletion	
• 45,X/46,XY mosaicism	
• 22q13 deletion syndrome	Phelan-McDermid syndrome
• Aarskog syndrome	Aarskog-Scott syndrome
• Aarskog-Scott syndrome	Aarskog syndrome
• adenylosuccinate lyase (ADSL) deficiency	
• adrenomyeloneuropathy	AMN
• alpha-thalassaemia/mental retardation syndrome, nondeletion type, X-linked; ATRX	mental retardation – hypotonic facies syndrome; Smith-Fineman-Myers syndrome; Carpenter-Waziri syndrome; Chudley-Lowry syndrome; Juberg-Marsidi syndrome; Holmes-Gang syndrome
• Amish brittle hair syndrome	brittle air–intellectual impairment–decreased fertility–short stature (BIDS) syndrome; hair–brain syndrome; trichothiodystrophy
• Angelman syndrome	happy puppet syndrome
• Apert syndrome	
• ARX gene mutations	

- Autism secondary to autoimmune lymphoproliferative syndrome (ALPS)

  Canale-Smith syndrome; Evans syndrome; autoimmune hemolytic anaemia; idiopathic thrombocytopenia; Coombs-positive hemolytic anaemia; immune thrombocytopenia

- autoimmune haemolytic anaemia

  autism secondary to autoimmune lymphoproliferative syndrome (ALPS); Canale-Smith syndrome; Evans syndrome; idiopathic thrombocytopenia; Coombs-positive haemolytic anaemia; immune thrombocytopenia

- Bannayan-Riley-Ruvalcaba syndrome

  BRRS; Bannayan-Zonana syndrome (BZS); macrocephaly, with multiple lipomas, and haemangiomata; macrocephaly with pseudopapilloedema, and multiple haemangiomata; Riley-Smith syndrome; Ruvalcaba-Myhre-Smith syndrome (RMSS)

- Bannayan-Zonana syndrome (BZS)

  Bannayan-Riley-Ruvalcaba syndrome (BRRS); macrocephaly, with multiple lipomas, and haemangiomata; macrocephaly with pseudopapilloedema, and multiple haemangiomata; Riley-Smith syndrome; Ruvalcaba-Myhre-Smith syndrome (RMSS)

- basal cell naevus syndrome

  epithéliomatose multiple généralisée; fifth phakomatosis; Gorlin syndrome; Gorlin-Goltz syndrome; hereditary cutaneomandibular polyoncosis; multiple basalioma syndrome; naevoid basal cell carcinoma syndrome

- Biedl-Bardet syndrome

- brittle hair–intellectual impairment–decreased fertility–short stature (BIDS) syndrome

  Amish brittle hair syndrome; hair–brain syndrome; trichothiodystrophy

- bulldog syndrome

  Simpson-Golabi-Behmel syndrome type 1 (SGBS1)

  Golabi-Rosen syndrome; Simpson dysmorphia syndrome (SDYS); dysplasia gigantism syndrome, X-linked (DGSX)

- Canale-Smith syndrome

  autism secondary to autoimmune lymphoproliferative syndrome (ALPS); Evans syndrome; autoimmune haemolytic anaemia; idiopathic thrombocytopenia; Coombs-positive haemolytic anaemia; immune thrombocytopenia

- carbohydrate-deficient glycoconjugate syndrome, type 1a

  olivopontocerebellar atrophy; Jaeken syndrome; phosphomannomutase 2 deficiency

- Carpenter-Waziri syndrome

  alpha-thalassaemia/mental retardation syndrome, nondeletion type, X-linked; ATRX; mental retardation – hypotonic facies syndrome; Smith-Fineman-Myers syndrome; Chudley-Lowry syndrome; Juberg-Marsidi syndrome; Holmes-Gang syndrome

- CATCH 22
- CHARGE syndrome   velocardiofacial syndrome
- Chudley-Lowry syndrome   Carpenter-Waziri syndrome; alpha-thalassaemia/ mental retardation syndrome, nondeletion type, X-linked; ATRX; mental retardation – hypotonic facies syndrome; Smith-Fineman-Myers syndrome; Juberg-Marsidi syndrome; Holmes-Gang syndrome
- Cockayne syndrome   xeroderma pigmentosum
- Coffin-Lowry syndrome
- Coffin-Siris syndrome
- Cohen syndrome
- Cole-Hughes macrocephaly syndrome   macrocephaly/autism syndrome
- congenital adrenal hyperplasia
- Coombs-positive haemolytic anaemia   autoimmune haemolytic anaemia; autism secondary to autoimmune lymphoproliferative syndrome (ALPS); Canale-Smith syndrome; Evans syndrome; idiopathic thrombocytopenia; immune thrombocytopenia
- cortical dysplasia–focal epilepsy (CDFE) syndrome
- Cowden syndrome
- Danon disease
- de Lange syndrome
- DiGeorge syndrome (phenotypic overlap)
- dihydropyrimidine dehydrogenase (DPYS) deficiency   *uraciluria thyminuria*
- Down syndrome
- Dravet's syndrome
- Duchenne's disease
- dysplasia gigantism syndrome, X-linked (DGSX)   bulldog syndrome; Simpson-Golabi-Behmel syndrome type 1 (SGBS1); Golabi-Rosen syndrome; Simpson dysmorphia syndrome (SDYS)
- Ehlers-Danlos syndrome
- epiloia   tuberous sclerosis
- *epithéliomatose multiple généralisée*   basal cell naevus syndrome; fifth phakomatosis; Gorlin syndrome; Gorlin-Goltz syndrome; hereditary cutaneomandibular polyoncosis; multiple basalioma syndrome; naevoid basal cell carcinoma syndrome

- Evans syndrome

  autism secondary to autoimmune lymphoproliferative syndrome (ALPS); Canale-Smith syndrome; autoimmune haemolytic anaemia; idiopathic thrombocytopenia; Coombs-positive haemolytic anaemia; immune thrombocytopenia

- fifth phakomatosis

  basal cell naevus syndrome; *epithéliomatose multiple généralisée*; Gorlin syndrome; Gorlin-Goltz syndrome; hereditary cutaneomandibular polyoncosis; multiple basalioma syndrome; naevoid basal cell carcinoma syndrome

- fragile-X syndrome
- fragile-X permutation (partial methylation defects)
- GAMT deficiency (guanidinoacetate methyltransferase deficiency)
- Golabi-Rosen syndrome

  dysplasia gigantism syndrome, X-linked (DGSX); bulldog syndrome; Simpson-Golabi-Behmel syndrome type 1 (SGBS1); Simpson dysmorphia syndrome (SDYS)

- Goldenhar syndrome
- Gorlin syndrome

  basal cell naevus syndrome; *epithéliomatose multiple généralisée*; fifth phakomatosis; Gorlin-Goltz syndrome; hereditary cutaneomandibular polyoncosis; multiple basalioma syndrome; naevoid basal cell carcinoma syndrome

- Gorlin-Goltz syndrome

  basal cell naevus syndrome; *epithéliomatose multiple généralisée*; fifth phakomatosis; Gorlin syndrome; hereditary cutaneomandibular polyoncosis; multiple basalioma syndrome; naevoid basal cell carcinoma syndrome

- Gurrieri syndrome
- hair–brain syndrome

  Amish brittle hair syndrome; brittle hair–intellectual impairment–decreased fertility–short stature (BIDS) syndrome; trichothiodystrophy

- happy puppet syndrome   Angelman syndrome
- HEADD syndrome
- hemihyperplasia
- Hereditary cutaneomandibular polyoncosis

  basal cell naevus syndrome; *epithéliomatose multiple généralisée*; fifth phakomatosis; Gorlin syndrome; Gorlin-Goltz syndrome; multiple basalioma syndrome; naevoid basal cell carcinoma syndrome

- Holmes-Gang syndrome

    Chudley-Lowry syndrome; Carpenter-Waziri syndrome; alpha-thalassaemia/mental retardation syndrome, nondeletion type, X-linked; ATRX; mental retardation – hypotonic facies syndrome; Smith-Fineman-Myers syndrome; Juberg-Marsidi syndrome

- hyper IgE syndrome with autism
- L-2-hydroxyglutaric aciduria
- Hypomelanosis of Ito
- hypothyroidism
- idiopathic thrombocytopenia

    autoimmune haemolytic anaemia; autism secondary to autoimmune lymphoproliferative syndrome (ALPS); Canale-Smith syndrome; Coombs-positive haemolytic anaemia; Evans syndrome; immune thrombocytopenia

- Jaeken syndrome

    carbohydrate-deficient glycoconjugate syndrome, type 1a; olivopontocerebellar atrophy; phosphomannomutase 2 deficiency

- Job syndrome

    hyper IgE syndrome with autism

- Joubert syndrome
- Juberg-Marsidi syndrome

    Holmes-Gang syndrome; Chudley-Lowry syndrome; Carpenter-Waziri syndrome; alpha-thalassaemia/mental retardation syndrome, nondeletion type, X-linked; ATRX; mental retardation – hypotonic facies syndrome; Smith-Fineman-Myers syndrome

- Kabuki syndrome
- Kleine-Levin syndrome
- Klinefelter's syndrome

    XXY syndrome

- Lujan-Fryns syndrome
- macrocephaly/autism syndrome

    Cole-Hughes macrocephaly syndrome

- macrocephaly, with multiple lipomas, and haemangiomata

    Bannayan-Riley-Ruvalcaba syndrome (BRRS); Bannayan-Zonana syndrome (BZS); macrocephaly with pseudopapilledoema, and multiple haemangiomata; Riley-Smith syndrome; Ruvalcaba-Myhre-Smith syndrome (RMSS)

- macrocephaly with pseudopapilledaema, and multiple haemangiomata

    Bannayan-Riley-Ruvalcaba syndrome (BRRS); Bannayan-Zonana syndrome (BZS); macrocephaly, with multiple lipomas, and haemangiomata; Riley-Smith syndrome; Ruvalcaba-Myhre-Smith syndrome (RMSS)

- mental retardation – hypotonic facies syndrome

  Juberg-Marsidi syndrome; Holmes-Gang syndrome; Chudley-Lowry syndrome; Carpenter-Waziri syndrome; alpha-thalassaemia/mental retardation syndrome, nondeletion type, X-linked; ATRX; Smith-Fineman-Myers syndrome

- 2-methylbutyryl-CoA dehydrogenase deficiency
- methylenetetrahydrofolate reductase deficiency (+/- homocystinuria)
- Mobius syndrome
- MOMO syndrome
- multiple basalioma syndrome

  basal cell naevus syndrome; *epithéliomatose multiple généralisée*; fifth phakomatosis; Gorlin syndrome; Gorlin-Goltz syndrome; hereditary cutaneomandibular polyoncosis; naevoid basal cell carcinoma syndrome

- Myhre syndrome
- naevoid basal cell carcinoma syndrome

  basal cell naevus syndrome; *epithéliomatose multiple généralisée*; fifth phakomatosis; Gorlin syndrome; Gorlin-Goltz syndrome; hereditary cutaneomandibular polyoncosis; multiple basalioma syndrome

- neurofibromatosis type 1

  von Recklinghausen disease

- Noonan syndrome
- oculocutaneous albinism
- olivopontocerebellar atrophy

  carbohydrate-deficient glycoconjugate syndrome, type 1a; Jaeken syndrome; phosphomannomutase 2 deficiency

- onychotrichodysplasia, chronic neutropaenia and mild mental retardation syndrome (ONMRS)

  trichothiodystrophy; brittle hair–intellectual impairment–decreased fertility–short stature (BIDS) syndrome; Amish brittle hair syndrome; hair–brain syndrome; Polit syndrome; Tay syndrome; Sabinas syndrome

- ornithine carbamyltransferase deficiency
- Orstavik 1997 syndrome
- PEHO syndrome (progressive hypsarrythmia and optic atrophy)
- Phelan-McDermid syndrome

  22q13 deletion syndrome

- phenylketonuria
- phosphomannomutase 2 deficiency

  olivopontocerebellar atrophy carbohydrate-deficient glycoconjugate syndrome, type 1a; Jaeken syndrome

- pituitary deficiency
- Polit syndrome — brittle hair–intellectual impairment–decreased fertility–short stature (BIDS) syndrome; Amish brittle hair syndrome; hair–brain syndrome; onychotrichodysplasia, chronic neutropaenia and mild mental retardation syndrome (ONMRS); Tay syndrome; trichothiodystrophy; Sabinas syndrome

- Prader-Willi syndrome
- Proteus syndrome
- Rett syndrome
- Rett syndrome (Hanefeld variant)
- Riley-Smith syndrome — Bannayan-Riley-Ruvalcaba syndrome (BRRS); Bannayan-Zonana syndrome (BZS); macrocephaly, with multiple lipomas, and haemangiomata; macrocephaly with pseudopapilloedaema, and multiple haemangiomata; Ruvalcaba-Myhre-Smith syndrome (RMSS)

- Rubinstein-Taybi syndrome
- Ruvalcaba-Myhre-Smith syndrome (RMSS) — Bannayan-Riley-Ruvalcaba syndrome (BRRS); Bannayan-Zonana syndrome (BZS); macrocephaly, with multiple lipomas, and haemangiomata; macrocephaly with pseudopapilloedaema, and multiple haemangiomata; Riley-Smith syndrome

- Sabinas syndrome — brittle hair–intellectual impairment–decreased fertility–short stature (BIDS) syndrome; Amish brittle hair syndrome; hair–brain syndrome; onychotrichodysplasia, chronic neutropaenia and mild mental retardation syndrome (ONMRS); Polit syndrome; trichothiodystrophy; Tay syndrome

- Schindler disease
- Simpson dysmorphia syndrome (SDYS) — Golabi-Rosen syndrome; dysplasia gigantism syndrome, X-linked (DGSX); bulldog syndrome; Simpson-Golabi-Behmel syndrome type 1 (SGBS1)

- Simpson-Golabi-Behmel syndrome type 1 (SGBS1) — bulldog syndrome; dysplasia gigantism syndrome, X-linked (DGSX); Golabi-Rosen syndrome; Simpson dysmorphia syndrome (SDYS)

- Smith-Fineman-Myers syndrome — mental retardation – hypotonic facies syndrome; Juberg-Marsidi syndrome; Holmes-Gang syndrome; Chudley-Lowry syndrome; Carpenter-Waziri syndrome; alpha-thalassaemia/mental retardation syndrome, nondeletion type, X-linked; ATRX

- Smith-Lemli-Opitz syndrome
- Smith-Magenis syndrome

- Sotos syndrome (also see Weaver syndrome)
- Sturge-Weber syndrome
- succinic semialdehyde dehydrogenase (SSADH) deficiency
- Tay syndrome

  brittle hair–intellectual impairment–decreased fertility–short stature (BIDS) syndrome; Amish brittle hair syndrome; hair–brain syndrome; onychotrichodysplasia, chronic neutropaenia and mild mental retardation syndrome (ONMRS); Polit syndrome; Sabinas syndrome; trichothiodystrophy

- Timothy syndrome
- Tourette syndrome
- trichothiodystrophy

  Amish brittle hair syndrome; brittle hair–intellectual impairment–decreased fertility–short stature (BIDS) syndrome; hair–brain syndrome

- tuberous sclerosis   epiloia
- Turner syndrome
- unilateral cerebellar hypoplasia syndrome
- velocardiofacial syndrome   CHARGE syndrome
- von Recklinghausen disease   neurofibromatosis type 1
- Weaver syndrome   Weaver-Smith syndrome (see also Sotos syndrome)
- Weaver-Smith syndrome   Weaver syndrome (see also Sotos syndrome)
- Williams syndrome
- xeroderma pigmentosum   Cockayne syndrome
- X-linked ichthyosis

Appendix X: Further genetic information and support

- **The Autism Genetic Database** can be accessed at http://wren.bcf.ku.edu/
  It is a site established in 2009 by the Bioinformatics Department of the University of Kansas. It provides a reasonably comprehensive searchable database of autism susceptibility genes. Information on the site and how to use it can be found at: Matuszek, G. and Talabizadeh, Z. (2009) 'Autism Genetic Database: A comprehensive database for autism susceptibility gene-CNVs integrated with known noncoding RNAs and fragile sites.' *BMC Medical Genetics*, 10:102. The digital object identifier is doi:10.1186/1471-2350-10-102. This paper can be downloaded from www.biomedcentral.com.

- **Chromosome Help-Station** is a general link site for support for people and families with rare chromosome disorders. It can be accessed at: www.chromosomehelpstation.com/

- Another useful site for families with members who have been found to have rarer genetic differences such as deletions, duplications, trisomies, inversions, translocations or ring chromosomes is:

  Chromosome Deletion Outreach, Inc.
  PO Box 724
  Boca Raton
  Florida
  FL 33429-0724
  USA
  Family helpline: 561-395-4252
  E-mail: info@chromodisorder.org
  Website: www.chromodisorder.org

- **CLIMB (Children Living with Inherited Metabolic Diseases)**
  Climb Building
  176 Nantwich Road
  Crewe
  CW2 6BG
  UK
  Tel.: 0800 652 3181 or 0845 241 2172 Mon–Fri 10.00am–4.00pm GMT
  E-mail: info.svcs@climb.org.uk
  Website: www.climb.org.uk/

CLIMB provides an excellent information resource covering a wide range of inherited metabolic disorders. It also provides disease-specific information and family support.

- **The Genetic and Rare Diseases Information Center**
  PO Box 8126
  Gaithersburg
  Maryland
  MD 20898-8126
  USA
  Tel.: 888-205-2311 (phone)
  888-205-3223 (TTY)
  301-519-3194 (International Telephone Access Number)
  Fax: 240-632-9164
  E-mail: GARDinfo@nih.gov
  Website: http://rarediseases.info.nih.gov

This service, established by the National Human Genome Research Institute (NHGRI) and the Office of Rare Diseases (ORD), provides information to the public and to clinical and research professionals on genetic and rare diseases.

- Another excellent website for clinical and genetic information can be found at: **GeneTests: Medical Genetics Information Resource** (online database) Copyright, University of Washington, Seattle. 1993–2007. Available at www.genetests.org.

- **The Council for Responsible Genetics**
  5 Upland Road
  Suite 3
  Cambridge
  MA 02140
  USA
  Tel.: 617-868-0870
  Fax: 617-491-5344
  E-mail: crg@genewatch.org
  Website: www.genewatch.org

This site is dedicated to monitoring the development of genetic and biotechnology advances and their ethical implications. An interesting section on autism can currently be found at www.genewatch.org.

- **geneimprint**
  This site was established in 1997 and is run by the Jirtle Laboratory at Duke University. It provides access to a wide range of material on genomic imprinting.
  Website: either www.geneimprint.com or www.geneimprint.org

- **GOLD (Genetics of Learning Disability)**
  The GOLD study is a project based at the Cambridge Institute for Medical Research in England. It is investigating genetic causes of learning disabilities in families with more than one affected family member, using a range of techniques.
  Website: http://goldstudy.cimr.cam.ac.uk

- **Human-Mouse Gene Searcher**
  This is a more technical site that allows people to search for genetic information on human and mouse behavioural and physical phenotypes, and look at similarities. A quick search for mouse genes equivalent to those that have been linked to human autistic neuroanatomy yielded 1,556 references.
  Website: www.ich.ucl.ac.uk

- **The Jackson Laboratory**
  This is the world's largest mammalian genetics research institute. The website gives access to information on a wide range of research, and to a bibliography on ongoing work in areas such as neurodevelopment.
  Website: www.jax.org

Glossary of terms

Many terms and labels are used in descriptions of people with neurodevelopmental disorders and reports written about them. The glossary covers many of the terms that are used in this volume and aims to de-mystify some of the more technical jargon.

acrocentric – with the centromere closer to one end of the chromosome (giving rise to one long and one short arm)

adrenocorticotrophic hormone – a peptide hormone produced by the anterior pituitary gland. It stimulates production of glucocorticoids by the adrenal cortex

aerophagy – air swallowing

agenesis – failure to develop

alexithymia – difficulty a person has in recognizing and describing their own emotions

amaurosis – blindness due to a brain (rather than an ocular) problem

amenorrhoea – absence of menstruation

amygdala – an 'almond-shaped' component of the limbic system, located deep in the temporal lobes. It is involved in a range of basic emotions (sometimes known as 'fight-or-flight' responses) like stress, panic and aggression

aneuploidy – having an uneven number of chromosomes (typically used in describing a missing or additional X or Y)

anosmia – inability to sense smells

aquaporin – water channels in cell membranes

arachnoid – the 'spider's-web-like' membrane covering the brain and spinal cord

aristaless – a homeobox gene deletion that results in a loss of bristles on the antennae of fruitflies, and learning disability and epilepsy in humans

astrocytomas – a type of central nervous system tumour that affects astrocytes (star-shaped glial cells found throughout the nervous system)

ataxia – poor coordination and unsteadiness

athetosis – slow, writhing, involuntary movements

atonic – with loss of normal muscle tone and strength

atresia – lacking a normal opening

autosome – involving any chromosome except for the sex chromosomes

brachy- – short

brachycephalic – a head shape with a short front-to-back length relative to the width of the skull

brachymetaphalangism – shortened bones in the fingers and/or toes

café-au-lait spots – flat skin spots more than 1.5cm in diameter, the colour of milky coffee; more than six such spots may indicate neurofibromatosis

callosal agenesis – failure of development of the corpus callosum (the major fibre tract connecting the two hemispheres of the brain)

calvaria cells – cells that become osteoblasts, the precursors from which bone is formed

calyceal – affecting a ball-shaped structure. Here it is used to describe calyceal clubbing – a shortening of the glomeruli in the kidney

cardiomyopathy – a disease affecting the heart muscle

caruncle – the small red area at the corner of the eye, containing sweat and sebaceous glands

centaurin-gamma-2 (CENTG2) – a gene found at 2q37.3 that is involved in membrane trafficking

centimorgan – a measure of the extent to which two genes are likely to appear together. One centimorgan is equivalent to 1 million base-pairs

centromere – a condensed section of a chromosome, to which spindle fibres attach during mitosis

channelopathy – disorders caused by disruption to ion channels

choanae – the apertures between the back of the nasal cavity and the throat

chorea – rapid, jerky, irregular, involuntary movements

choreoathetoid – abnormal movements that combine chorea and athetosis

chorionic villous sample – a tissue sample taken from the vascular supply to the placenta, which enables the genotyping of the foetus

choroid – the vascular membrane between the retina and the sclera that provides the retinal blood supply

chromatids – one of the two copies of each chromosome, which are joined at the centromere

Chromatin – the mass of genetic material and associated proteins distributed through the nucleus of a cell that condense to form chromosomes before cell division takes place

Chromatin remodelling – the epigenetic process that changes how chromatin is unwound through the cell, regulating how RNA transcription takes place

clonic – sudden involuntary muscle contractions

cohesin – the protein complex that binds chromatids during mitosis

coloboma – a hole in any of the primary structures of the eye

CNVs – copy number variations are variations in the number of copies of small segments of repeating DNA at a given sequence on a chromosome

concordance – the presence of the same trait in both members of a twin pair

conotruncal – affecting the conotruncal septum in the heart (found most commonly in tetralogy of Fallot)

craniosynostosis – premature closure of the sutures of the skull

cubitus valgus – a deformity of the arms in which the elbows are turned inwards and the forearm extends away from the body when extended

cutis marmorata – a pink-coloured, marbled skin mottling

cytogenetic arrays – tests that can allow the simultaneous assessment of large numbers of SNPs (single nucleotide polymorphisms) and CNVs (copy number variations)

dendritic – affecting dendrites (the small extensions from nerve cells which carry impulses from other nerve cells towards the cell body)

dentatorubral-pallidoluysian – combined degeneration of the *dentatorubral* system (a nerve fibre system beginning in the dentate nucleus in the cerebellum and projecting to the red nucleus in the midbrain) and the *pallidoluysian* system (which projects from the globus pallidus (part of the lentiform nucleus in the midbrain) to subthalamic nuclei

dermoid – a benign, skin-like growth

diabetes – a chronic condition interfering with energy metabolism due to lack of insulin secretion

DNA – deoxyribonucleic acid (the long chains of nucleic acid pairs found in the nucleus of cells that specify the biological instructions for their development and metabolic function)

DNA methylation – the addition of a methyl group to DNA, thereby altering gene expression

DNA methylation profiling – using a sequence of molecular probes to identify the methylation status of particular cells

dysarthria – difficulty controlling the pitch, volume, rhythm and affective qualities of the voice, caused by paralysis, weakness or poor coordination of the muscles of the mouth

dysmorphic – any physical characteristic that has not formed normally

dystonia – abnormal heightened muscle tension that can result in jerking and twisting movement

EEG – ElectroEncephaloGraphy (a method of recording the electrical activity of the brain through electrodes placed on the scalp)

encephalocoele – where a portion of brain tissue has herniated (pushed through) a lesion in the skull

endophenotype – genetically based behavioural phenotype

epigenetic – a biological characteristic which does not involve a change in DNA sequence but influences the expression of DNA

epigenetic imprinting – various epigenetic mechanisms, such as genomic imprinting, histone deacetylation and telomere modification, that exercise epigenetic control over gene expression

epiphyseal – concerning the growth plates at the end of the long bones of the arms and legs

equinovarus – '*talipes equinovarus*' is the term for club foot

evidence-based medicine – systematic evaluation of the research literature to inform clinical practice

exon – a DNA sequence that encodes for protein synthesis

falx – the strong membrane that extends down between and divides the two hemispheres of the brain

folate (folic acid/vitamin B9) – a water-soluble essential vitamin that is critical for the synthesis of DNA

folinic acid – a more stable, less easily oxidized form of folic acid that is commonly used in pharmaceutical preparations

frameshift mutation – a mutation where the number of nucleotides inserted or deleted is not a multiple of 3, so that all of the material after the shift is incorrectly read

gastro-esophageal – to do with the stomach and oesophagus (the throat)

gastrointestinal – to do with the stomach and intestines

gastrostomy – surgical insertion of a tube into the stomach to allow feeding or drainage

genetic duplications – when additional copies of genes arise through misalignment during cell division

genomic imprinting – where particular genes are expressed when inherited from one parent (a 'parent-of-origin effect')

genotype – the genetic constitution of an individual

glia – the cells within the nervous system that provide supportive functions to the neurons: Schwann cells, astrocytes, oligodendrocytes and ependymal cells

globus pallidus – a structure in the basal ganglia that filters relevant from irrelevant information from the senses

glucocorticoid – any of several steroid hormones produced by the adrenal cortex that regulate food digestion and inflammation

glutathione – a polypeptide which is widely involved in Redox reactions (a chemical reaction in which the oxidation state of the molecules involved is altered)

glycerol kinase – an enzyme involved in fat metabolism that transfers phosphorus from adenosine triphosphate to glycerol, producing glycerol phosphate

haemangioma – a skin lesion with dense masses of blood vessels

haemolytic – destroying red blood cells

hamartoma – an abnormally large mass of tissue

haplotype – a set of closely linked genes on a chromosome, that tend to be inherited together

haploinsufficiency – where mutation has inactivated one copy of a gene resulting in insufficient production of the gene product (which is normally a protein)

hepatitis – inflammation of the liver, usually due to infection or toxic exposure

hepatoblastoma – malignant growth in the liver

hepatosplenomegaly – enlargement of the liver and spleen

hemizygous – where there is a single gene copy, either because the gene is on a sex chromosome or because of deletion or mutation of the second copy on an autosome

hippocampus – a structure in the centre of the brain that is crucial for the formation of new memories and is sometimes damaged by lack of oxygen or by seizure activity

hirsutism – excessive growth of face and/or body hair

histone – a small, disc-like protein structure that DNA coils around to form chromatin

histone deacetylation – a process that increases the binding between histones and DNA, thereby reducing transcription and modifying gene expression

homeobox – involved in the formation of a specific body segment during development. Homeobox genes are highly conserved across species

homeodomain – a highly conserved DNA sequence which includes a homeobox gene

Huntington – a protein that is important in nerve development and programmed cell death, which is absent/abnormal in Huntington's chorea

hydranencephaly – a condition in which there is lack of development of the frontal and parietal lobes of the brain and the skull

hydrometrocolpos – distension of the uterus and vagina due to fluid retention

hyperbaric oxygen treatment – inhalation of oxygen while under increased atmospheric pressure

hyperlaxity – excessive joint mobility

hypernasal – a specific vocal quality resulting from excessive air passing through the nose

hyperpigmentation – excessive skin pigmentation resulting in darker skin than would be normal

hypertelorism – wide spacing of paired organs such as the eyes

hypoglossia – having a shorter, more poorly developed tongue than normal

hypoparathyroidism – reduced production of parathyroid hormone, a factor important in control of calcium levels in the blood. Reduced levels result in hypocalcaemia

hypopigmentation – reduced skin pigmentation resulting in lighter skin than would be normal

hypospadias – an anomaly where the urethra opens either on the underside of the penis in boys, or into the vagina in girls

hypotonia – reduced muscle tone

hypsrrythmia – infantile spasms (a type of early onset seizure)

ileo-colonic nodular hyperplasia – enlarged nodules forming on the lining of the ileum and colon

incidence – the number of new cases which occur within a given population over a given time (usually per year)

intracytoplasmic – within the cell contents, between the outer cell membrane and the nucleus

isodicentric – where a person has additional genetic material from a particular chromosome. This can occur in mosaicism

isodisomy – where both copies of a chromosome are inherited from a single parent

jugular foraminal stenosis – narrowing of the gap in the base of the skull carrying the jugular vein. Narrowing of this space, seen in craniosynostosis, can significantly increase blood pressure

keratocysts – cysts formed in the sebaceous glands at the hair follicles

ketogenic – involving the formation of ketones (organic compounds like acetone), as seen in diabetes and through dietary carbohydrate restriction

kilobase – a unit of measurement equivalent to 1,000 DNA base pairs

lamina propria – a thin layer containing blood vessels which is below the outer layer of any organ

lentiform nucleus – a lentil-shaped or bi-convex structure in the midbrain that includes the globus pallidus and putamen, and is involved in a variety of aspects of emotional processing

leptin – a hormone produced by adipose tissue that signals the level of fat in the body

ligament – tough, fibrous tissue with lateral flexibility that connects bones and ligaments at joints

linoleic acid – an essential omega-6 polyunsaturated fatty acid

linolenic acid – an omega oil (in its cis form it is an omega-6 and in its alpha form an omega-3)

lissencephaly – where the surface of the brain has a smooth appearance due to reduced numbers of nerve cells

Lod score – a measure of the likelihood of genes being linked which is reported as the logarithm of the odds of an observed association compared to what would be expected were the genes unrelated

lupus erythematosus – an autoimmune condition where the body's own tissues are attacked by its immune system

lymphoedema – swelling of body tissues due to inadequate drainage of lymphatic fluids

lymphoproliferative – a term used for the accumulation of lymph cells in the bloodstream (as in acute lymphoblastic leukaemia), or with enlargement of parts of the lymphatic system

macrocephaly – enlargement of the brain

macro-orchidism – enlargement of the testes

macule – an area of differently coloured skin that is not elevated, depressed or different in texture to the skin surrounding it

megabase – a unit of measurement equivalent to 1 million DNA base pairs

megacaryoblastic – concerning cells found in the bone marrow

membrane trafficking – the movement of material across cell membranes including neurotransmitters (such as serotonin, dopamine, norepinephrine and gamma aminobutyric acid); adenosine triphosphate; nitric oxide; and water

meningocoele – a form of spina bifida in which the meninges (the protective sheath which surrounds the spinal column) protrudes through the vertebrae but remains beneath the skin

microcephaly – small-brained

microdeletion – deletion of a small piece of chromosomal material not detectable by conventional techniques

missense mutation – a gene mutation that is within a coding sequence of DNA and results in insertion of a different amino acid in the protein

mitochondria – sub-cellular organelles with their own separate DNA. Mitochondria use oxygen and produce energy by oxidative phosphorylation

molecular epidemiology – the use of molecular techniques in medical epidemiology

mosaicism – where cells of genetically different types are found in the same organism

mulitiple families – families with more than one affected member

murine – concerning mice

myelopathy – pathology of the spinal column

myoclonic – sudden involuntary muscle twitching

myopathy – diseases of the skeletal or voluntary muscles not due to a neurological condition, that result in muscle wasting or weakness

naevi – purplish-red areas of skin due to abnormal vasculature, sometimes called port-wine stains

nephronophthisis – a wasting disease of the kidneys that results in fibrosis and cysts. It is the most common genetic cause of childhood kidney failure

neural ceroid lipofuscinosis – also known as Batten disease, and previously as 'familial cerebromacular degeneration' and 'juvenile amaurotic idiocy': a common group of storage disorders (nine separate genetic variants have so far been identified), typically affecting lysosomes. NCL is typically degenerative, affecting the central nervous system and visual function, with early and rapid developmental regression, visual loss and severe epilepsy

neurexin – a class of type 1 membrane proteins that help nerve cells to connect at synapses

neuroectoderm – the part of the developing embryo that goes on to form the peripheral nervous system

neuroligin – a class of type 1 membrane proteins that help nerve cells to connect at synapses

neuropeptides – small, opioid-like neurotransmitters

neurotransmitter – a neurochemical, dopmine, serotonin, gamma-aminobutyric acid (GABA), nitrous oxide and adenosine triphosphte (ATP) being the best known, that modifies signalling from and between nerve cells

neutropaenia – low levels of neutrophils, a particular class of white blood cells

nodes of Ranvier – the gap between two Schwann cells (fatty cells that wrap around the axons of nerve cells allowing electrical signals to be transmitted faster) on the axon of a myelinated nerve that allows faster 'saltatory' electrical nerve conduction

no disjunction – failure of paired chromosomes to separate at cell division

nonsense mutation – a gene mutation or deletion which results in the lack of a particular amino acid which would normally be part of a protein produced by that gene

non-syndromal – not associated with a recognized genetic syndrome

nuchal translucency – a measure taken from foetal ultrasound that is normally carried out at 11–14 weeks post-conception. It estimates the amount of fluid at the back of the baby's neck and is a test that can help to identify Down syndrome

nucleus accumbens – a central region of the midbrain, situated deep in the frontal lobes between the caudate and the putamen

oligodendrocyte – a variety of glial cells found exclusively in the central nervous system

opisthotonus – a muscular reaction where the infant arches backwards, appearing to push away from anyone who is holding them

orchidopexy – a surgical procedure to correct undescended testes

ornithine transcarbamylase – an enzyme involved in the urea cycle in mitochondria

osteoblast – a bone-forming cell

osteodystrophy – a condition that affects bone growth

osteoporosis – reduction in bone mass due to loss of calcium and protein

oxytocin – a chemical produced in the hypothalamus that acts as both a hormone and a neurotransmitter. It is involved in a range of positive social behaviours

papiloma – a benign tumour derived from the skin

peroxisome – enzyme-containing organelles produced by the endoplasmic reticulum found in all human cells

phacomatoses – conditions characterized by the presence of harmatomas in multiple body tissues

phenotype – the characteristics of an individual. Typcially used to refer to characteristics related to a particular genotype

phenotypic variability – the variation in phenotype seen across people with the same genotype

photic – using light

pleiotropy – multiple effects resulting from the same gene

polyalanine expansion – an expansion in alanine tracts (particular trinucleotide sequences found most commonly in homeobox genes)

polyclonia – multiple clonic spasms

polydactyly – the presence of additional fingers and/or toes

polydipsia – excessive drinking of fluids

polygenic – a characteristic controlled by the interaction of genes

polymicrogyria – the presence of larger than normal numbers of cerebral convolutions/gyri

polyuria – excessive production of urine

posterior fossa – the part at the base of the skull that links to the spinal column

prevalence – the number of cases which are present within a given population

primitive neuroectodermal (PNET) tumour – a type of central nervous system tumour that develops from early nerve foetal cells. These tumours can be found in a variety of tissues, but predominantly form in the brain, and as medulloblastomas in the hindbrain

proband – the particular individual being studied

prognathism – abnormal protrusion of the lower jaw

proprioceptive – orientation in space through attention to internal stretch and balance receptors

proteinuria – the presence of protein in the urine

purpura – small haemorrhages on the skin and mucus membranes, typically as an allergic reaction

putamen – a structure in the basal ganglia involved in various types of learning and emotional response

pyloric stenosis – narrowing of the opening from the stomach into the ileum/small intestine

retinochoroid – concerning the vascular choroid membrane of the eye between the retina and the sclera

RNA – there are several forms of RNA (ribonucleic acid). These provide the nucleotide mechanism by which the DNA code is translated into an amino acid sequence producing functional proteins

RNA associated gene silencing (aka RNAi/RNA interference) – RNA associated gene silencing in the incorporation of an otherwise active DNA sequence into heterochromatin (non-active sequences of chromatin important for cell differentiation). This is achieved by a process known as RITS (RNA-induced transcriptional silencing)

Robertsonian translocation – where two long arms of acrocentric chromosomes fuse. It is the most common type of chromosome translocation seen in humans. Seen with translocations of chromosomes 13, 14, 15, 21 and 22, but primarily between 13 and 14, 13 and 21 and 21 and 22. A balanced translocation has no phenotypic effect, whereas unbalanced translocation can cause multiple malformations and learning disability. Unbalanced translocations between 14 and 21 and between 21 and 22 can result in Down syndrome [31]

savant – someone who is exceptionally gifted, often in a specialized field of knowledge such as mathematics. The term is typically applied to someone who also has an autistic spectrum disorder

scoliosis – excessive curvature of the spine

sensorineural – involving the sensory nerves

septum pellucidum – the thin membrane which forms the central division in the brain between the cerebral hemispheres

status epilepticus – prolonged, generalized epileptic seizures

stereotactic – refers to surgery where the structures operated on are located precisely in three dimensions (normally applied to precise forms of neurosurgery)

supernumary – additional

sylvian fissure – the largest cortical fissure, between the frontal and temporal lobes

syndactyly – where two or more fingers and/or toes are joined together

syndromal – a characteristic group of signs and symptoms that consistently occur together

synophrys – a single, unbroken eyebrow

synostosis – fusion of bones that are normally separate

synteny – genetic conservation across species

telomere – small recurrent sequence of DNA at the end of chromosome, that acts as a protective cap

tetralogy of Fallot – a complex congenital heart defect that compounds five of the major defects arising simultaneously

thanatophoric – short-limbed

thrombocytopenia – an abnormally low platelet count that would lead to limited coagulation and blood clotting

transcription – production of a complementary RNA sequence to a gene on a sequence of chromosomal DNA

translocation – movement of a segment of DNA to a position where it was not normally located

trichilemmomas – a benign tumour formed from a hair follicle

ulna – the longer of the two bones in the forearm

uniparental isodisomy – where both copies of one chromosome are inherited from a single parent

urethra – the tube that carries urine from the bladder

urticaria – raised itchy areas of skin, also known as hives, usually caused by an allergic reaction

References

A number of references appear with the term doi and an alphanumeric string after it at the end of the reference citation rather than the more usual volume–issue number–pages format. These references are to electronic journals that are available over the internet rather than to paper journals. For example, typing doi:10.1371/journal.pgen.1000253 takes you to the relevant article by Aguilar-Fuentes *et al.* in the on-line journal *PLoS Genetics.*

A

Aarskog, D. (1970) 'A familial syndrome of short stature associated with facial dysplasia and genital anomalies.' *Journal of Pediatrics*, 77:856–861.

Abel, T. and Zukin, R.S. (2008) 'Epigenetic targets of HDAC inhibition in neurodegenerative and psychiatric disorders.' *Current Opinion in Pharmacology*, 8: 57–64.

Abelson, J.F., Kwan, K.Y., O'Roak, B.J., Baek, D.Y. *et al.* (2005) 'Sequence variants in SLITRK1 are associated with Tourette's syndrome.' *Science*, 310: 317–320.

Abitbol, M., Menini, C., Delezoide, A.-L., Rhyner, T. *et al.* (1993) 'Nucleus basalis magnocellularis and hippocampus are the major sites of FMR-1 expression in the human fetal brain.' *Nature Genetics*, 4: 147–153.

Abizaid, A., Liu, Z.-W., Andrews, Z.B., Shanabrough, M. *et al.* (2006) 'Ghrelin modulates the activity and synaptic input organization of midbrain dopamine neurons while promoting appetite.' *Journal of Clinical Investigation* 116, 12: 3229–3239.

Aboulghar, H., Aboulghar, M., Mansour, R., Serour, G. *et al.* (2001) 'A prospective controlled study of karyotyping for 430 consecutive babies conceived through intracytoplasmic sperm injection.' *Fertility and Sterility*, 76: 249–253.

Abraham, I., Juhasz, G., Kekesi, K.A. and Kovacs, K.J. (1998) 'Corticosterone peak is responsible for stress-induced elevation of glutamate in the hippocampus.' *Stress*, 2: 171–181.

Abramsky, L. and Chapple, J. (1997) '47,XXY (Klinefelter syndrome) and 47,XYY: estimated rates of and indication for postnatal diagnosis with implications for prenatal counselling.' *Prenatal Diagnosis*, 17: 363–368.

Adams, J.B. and Holloway, C. (2004) 'Pilot study of a moderate dose multivitamin/mineral supplement for children with autistic spectrum disorder.' *Journal of Alternative and Complementary Medicine*, 10: 1033–1039.

Adams, M., Lucock, M., Stuart, J., Fardell, S. *et al.* (2007) 'Preliminary evidence for involvement of the folate gene polymorphism 19 bp deletion-DHFR in occurrence of autism.' *Neuroscience Letters*, 422: 24–29.

Afzal, N., Murch, S., Thirrupathy, K., Berger, L. *et al.* (2003) 'Constipation with acquired megarectum in children with autism.' *Pediatrics*, 112: 939–942.

Aguirre, D., Nieto, K., Lazos, M., Pena, Y.R. *et al.* (2006) 'Extragonadal germ cell tumors are often associated with Klinefelter syndrome.' *Human Pathology*, 37: 477–480.

Agostoni, C., Massetto, N., Biasucci, G., Rottoli, A. *et al.* (2000) 'Effects of long-chain polyunsaturated fatty acid supplementation on fatty acid status and visual function in treated children with hyperphenylalaninemia.' *Journal of Pediatrics*, 137: 504–509.

Agostoni, C., Verduci, E., Massetto, N., Fiori, L. *et al.* (2003) 'Long-term effects of long-chain polyunsaturated fats in hyperphenylalaninemic children.' *Archives of Disease in Childhood*, 88: 582–583.

Agre, P. (2006) 'Aquaporin water channels: from atomic structure to clinical medicine.' *Nanomedicine: Nanotechnology, Biology, and Medicine*, 2: 266–267.

Airaksinen, E.M. (1974) 'Tryptophan treatment of infants with Down's syndrome.' *Annals of Clinical Research* 6, 1: 33–39.

Aitken, K.J. (1991) 'Examining the evidence for a common structural basis to autism.' *Developmental Medicine and Child Neurology*, 33: 930–934.

Aitken, K.J. (1998) 'Behavioural phenotypes.' *Association for Child Psychology and Psychiatry Occasional Papers Series*, 15: 5–20.

Aitken, K.J. (2008) 'Intersubjectivity, affective neuroscience, and the neurobiology of autistic spectrum disorders: a systematic review.' *The Keio Medical Journal* 57, 1: 15–36.

Aitken, K.J. (2009) *Dietary Interventions in the ASDs – Why They Work When They Do, Why They Don't When They Don't.* London: Jessica Kingsley Publishers.

Akaboshi, S., Ruiters, J., Wanders, R.J.A., Andresen, B.S. *et al.* (2001) 'Divergent phenotypes in siblings with confirmed 2-methylbutyry-CoA dehydrogenase (2-MBAD) deficiency.' *Journal of Inherited Metabolic Disease*, 24 (Suppl.1): 58.

Akbarnia, B.A., Gabriel, K.R., Beckman, E. and Chalk, D. (1992) 'Prevalence of scoliosis in neurofibromatosis.' *Spine*, 17 (Suppl.): S244–S248.

Akefeldt, A. and Gillberg, C. (1991) 'Hypomelanosis of Ito in three cases with autism and autistic-like conditions.' *Developmental Medicine and Child Neurology*, 33: 737–743.

Akefeldt, A., Gillberg, C. and Larsson, C. (1991) 'Prader-Willi syndrome in a Swedish rural county: epidemiological aspects.' *Developmental Medicine and Child Neurology*, 33: 715–721.

Akenside, M. (1768) 'Observations on cancers.' *Medical Transactions of the Royal College of Physicians of London*, 1: 64–92.

Akhondzadeh, S., Tajdar, H., Mohammadi, M.R., Mohammadi, M. *et al.* (2008) 'A double-blind placebo-controlled trial of piracetam added to risperidone in patients with autistic disorder.' *Child Psychiatry and Human Development* 39, 3: 237–245.

Al-Ahmari, A., Shah, N., Sung, L., Zipursky, A. and Hitzler, J. (2006) 'Long-term results of an ultra low-dose cytarabine-based regimen for the treatment of acute megakaryoblastic leukaemia in children with Down syndrome.' *British Journal of Haematology* 133, 6: 646–648.

Alarcón, M., Abrahams, B.S., Stone, J.L., Duvall, J.A. *et al.* (2008) 'Linkage, association, and gene-expression analyses identify CNTNAP2 as an autism-susceptibility gene.' *American Journal of Human Genetics* 82, 1: 150–159.

Alarcón, M., Cantor, R.M., Liu, J., Gilliam, T.C., Geschwind, D.H., and the AGRE Consortium (2005a). 'Evidence for a language quantitative trait locus on chromosome 7q in multiplex autism families.' *American Journal of Human Genetics*, 70: 60–71.

Alarcón, M., Yonan, A.L., Gilliam, T.C., Cantor, R.M. and Geschwind, D.H. (2005b) 'Quantitative genome scan and ordered-subsets analysis of autism endophenotypes support language QTLs.' *Molecular Psychiatry*, 10: 747–757.

Alberti, A., Pirrone, P., Elia, M., Waring, R.H. and Romano, C. (1999) 'Sulphation deficit in "low–functioning" autistic children: a pilot study.' *Biological Psychiatry 46*, 3: 420–424.

Alcántara, M.A., Villarreal, M.T., Del Castillo, V., Gutiérrez, G. *et al.* (1999) 'High frequency of de novo deletions in Mexican Duchenne and Becker muscular dystrophy patients: Implications for genetic counselling.' *Clinical Genetics 55*, 5: 376–380.

Aldred, S., Moore, K.M., Fitzgerald, M. and Waring, R.H. (2003) 'Plasma amino acid levels in children with autism and their families.' *Journal of Autism and Developmental Disorders 33*, 1: 93–97.

Allanson, J.E. (1987) 'Noonan syndrome.' *Journal of Medical Genetics*, 24: 9–13.

Allanson, J.E. and Cole, T.R.P. (1996) 'Sotos syndrome: evolution of facial phenotype subjective and objective assessment.' *American Journal of Medical Genetics*, 65: 13–20.

Allanson, J.E., Hennekam, R.C. and Ireland, M. (1997) 'De Lange syndrome: subjective and objective comparison of the classical and mild phenotypes.' *Journal of Medical Genetics*, 34: 645–650.

Allanson, J.E., Upadhyaya, M., Watson, G.H., Partington, M. *et al.* (1991) 'Watson syndrome: is it a subtype of type 1 neurofibromatosis?' *Journal of Medical Genetics*, 28: 752–756.

Allen, E.G., Sherman, S., Abramowitz, A., Leslie, M. *et al.* (2005) 'Examination of the effect of the polymorphic CGG repeat in the FMR1 gene on cognitive performance.' *Behavioral Genetics*, 35: 435–445.

Allingham-Hawkins, D.J., Babul-Hirji, R., Chitayat, D., Holden, J.J.A. *et al.* (1999) 'Fragile-X premutation is a significant risk factor for premature ovarian failure: the international collaborative POF in fragile-X study – preliminary data.' *American Journal of Medical Genetics*, 83: 322–325.

Allport, S. (2006) 'The Queen of Fats: why Omega-3s were removed from the Western diet and what we can do to replace them.' Berkeley: University of California Press.

Almeida, L.S., Vilarinho, L., Darmin, P.S., Rosenberg, E.H. *et al.* (2007) 'A prevalent pathogenic GAMT mutation (c.59G>C) in Portugal.' *Molecular Genetics and Metabolism*, 91: 1–6.

Alperin, E.S. and Shapiro, L.J. (1997) 'Characterization of point mutations with X-linked ichthyosis: effects on the structure and function of the steroid sulfatase protein.' *Journal of Biological Chemistry*, 272: 20756–20763.

Alsdorf, R. and Wyszynski, D.F. (2005) 'Teratogenicity of sodium valproate.' *Expert Opinion on Drug Safety 4*, 2: 345–353.

Alvarez Retuerto, A.I., Cantor, R.M., Gleeson, J.G., Ustaszewska, A. et al. (2008) 'Association of common variants in the Joubert syndrome gene (AHI1) with autism.' *Human Molecular Genetics*, 17: 3887–3896.

Alwan, S., Tredwell, S.J. and Friedman, J.M. (2005) 'Is osseous dysplasia a primary feature of neurofibromatosis 1 (NF1)?' *Clinical Genetics 67*, 5: 378–390.

Amaral, D.G., Bauman, M.D. and Schumann, C.M. (2003) 'The amygdala and autism: implications from non-human primate studies.' *Genes, Brain and Behavior*, 2: 295–302.

Amir, N. and Gross-Tzur, V. (1994) 'Paradoxical normalization in childhood epilepsy.' *Epilepsia 35*, 5: 1060–1064.

Amir, R.E., Van den Veyver, I.B., Wan, M., Tran, C.Q. *et al.* (1999) 'Rett syndrome is caused by mutations in X-linked MECP2, encoding methyl-CpG-binding protein 2.' *Nature Genetics 2*, 3: 185–188.

Amiri, K., Hagerman, R.J. and Hagerman, P.J. (2008) 'Fragile X-associated tremor/ataxia syndrome: an aging face of the fragile-X gene.' *Archives of Neurology 65*, 1: 19–23.

Amlashi, S.F., Riffaud, L., Brassier, G. and Morandi, X. (2003) 'Nevoid basal cell carcinoma syndrome: relation with desmoplastic medulloblastoma in infancy. A population-based study and review of the literature.' *Cancer*, 98: 618–624.

Amminger, G.P., Berger, G.E., Schafer, M.R., Klier, C. *et al.* (2006) 'Omega-3 fatty acids supplementation in children with autism: a double-blind randomized, placebo-controlled pilot study.' *Biological Psychiatry 61*, 4: 551–553.

Amon, M., Menapace, R. and Kirnbauer, R. (1990) 'Ocular symptomatology in familial Hypomelanosis of Ito. Incontinentia pigmenti achromians.' *Ophthalmologica 200*, 1: 1–6.

Anderlid, B.M., Schoumans, J., Anneren, G., Tapia-Paez, I. *et al.* (2002) 'FISH-mapping of a 100-kb terminal 22q13 deletion.' *Human Genetics*, 110: 439–443.

Anderson, A.J., Stephan, M.J., Walker, W.O. and Kelley, R.I. (1998) 'Variant RSH/Smith-Lemli-Opitz syndrome with atypical sterol metabolism.' *American Journal of Medical Genetics*, 78: 413–418.

Anderson, G.M., Jacobs-Stannard, A., Chawarska, K., Volkmar, F.R. and Kliman, H.J. (2007) 'Placental trophoblast inclusions in Autism Spectrum Disorder.' *Biological Psychiatry*, 61, 487–49.

Anderson, L.L., Jeftinija, S., Scanes, C.G., Stromer, M.H. *et al.* (2005) 'Physiology of ghrelin and related peptides.' *Domestic Animal Endocrinology*, 29: 111–144.

Anderson, P.J. and David, D.J. (2005) 'Spinal anomalies in Goldenhar syndrome.' *The Cleft Palate–Craniofacial Journal 42*, 5: 477–480.

Anderson, R.J., Bendell, D.J., Garnett, I., Groundwater, P.W. *et al.* (2002) 'Identification of indolyl-3-acryloylglycine in the urine of people with autism.' *Journal of Pharmacy and Pharmacology*, 54: 295–298.

Andersson, H.C., Frentz, J., Martinez, J.E., Tuck-Muller, C.M. and Bellizaire, J. (1999) 'Adrenal insufficiency in Smith-Lemli-Opitz syndrome.', *American Journal of Medical Genetics*, 82: 382–384.

Andres, E., Loukili, N.H., Noel, E., Kaltenbach, G. *et al.* (2004) 'Vitamin B12 (cobalamin) deficiency in elderly patients.' *Canadian Medical Association Journal*, 171: 251–259.

Andresen, B.S., Christensen, E., Corydon, T.J., Bross, P. *et al.* (2000) 'Isolated 2-methylbutyrylglycinuria caused by short/branched-chain acyl-CoA dehydrogenase deficiency: identification of a new enzyme defect, resolution of its molecular basis, and evidence for distinct acyl-CoA dehydrogenases in isoleucine and valine metabolism.' *American Journal of Human Genetics*, 67: 1095–1103.

Aneja, A. and Tierney, E. (2008) 'Autism: the role of cholesterol in treatment.' *International Review of Psychiatry 20*, 2: 165–170.

Angell, M. (2004) *The Truth About the Drug Companies: How They Deceive Us and What to Do About It.* New York: Random House.

Angelman, H. (1965) "Puppet children": a report of three cases.' *Developmental Medicine and Child Neurology*, 7: 681–688.

Angkustsiri, K., Wirojanan, J., Deprey, L.J., Gane, L.W. and Hagerman, R.J. (2008) 'Fragile-X syndrome with anxiety disorder and exceptional verbal intelligence.' *American Journal of Medical Genetics*, 146A: 376–379.

Ani, C., Grantham-McGregor, S. and Muller, D. (2000) 'Nutritional supplementation in Down syndrome: theoretical considerations and current status.' *Developmental Medicine and Child Neurology*, 42: 207–213.

Anstey, A.V. and Taylor, C.R. (1999) 'Photosensitivity in the Smith-Lemli-Opitz syndrome: the US experience of a new congenital photosensitivity syndrome.' *Journal of the American Academy of Dermatology*, 41: 121–123.

Antar, L.N., Afroz, R., Dictenberg, J.B., Carroll, R.C. and Bassell, G.J. (2004) 'Metabotropic glutamate receptor activation regulates fragile-X mental retardation protein and *Fmr1* mRNA localization differentially in dendrites and synapses.' *The Journal of Neuroscience*, 24: 2648–2655.

Antila, E. and Westermarck, T. (1989) 'On the etiopathogenesis and therapy of Down syndrome.' *International Journal of Developmental Biology*, 33: 183–188.

Antila, E., Nordberg, U.R., Syväoja, E.L. and Westermarck, T. (1990) 'Selenium therapy in Down syndrome (DS): a theory and a clinical trial.' *Advances in Experimental Medicine and Biology*, 264: 183–186.

Antshel, K.M., Aneja, A., Strunge, L., Peebles, J. *et al.* (2007) 'Autistic Spectrum Disorders in velocardiofacial syndrome (22q11.2 deletion).' *Journal of Autism and Developmental Disorders*, 37: 1776–1786.

Antshel, K.M., Kates, W.R., Roizen, N., Fremont, W. and Shprintzen, R.J. (2005) '22q11.2 deletion syndrome: genetics, neuroanatomy and cognitive/behavioral features keywords.' *Child Neuropsychology*, 11: 5–19.

Anttinen, A., Koulu, L., Nikoskelainen, E., Portin, R. *et al.* (2008) 'Neurological symptoms and natural course of xeroderma pigmentosum.' *Brain 131*, 8: 1979–1989.

Aoki, M., Abe, K., Kameya, T., Watanabe, M. and Itoyama, Y. (1994) 'Maternal anticipation of DRPLA.' *Human Molecular Genetics*, 3: 1197–1198.

Apert, M.E. (1906) 'De l'acrocéphalosyndactylie.' *Bulletins et mémoires de la Société médicale des hôpitaux de Paris*, 23: 1310–1330.

Apter, A., Pauls, D.L., Bleich, A., Zohar, A.H. *et al.* (1992) 'A population-based epidemiological study of Tourette syndrome among adolescents in Israel.' *Advances in Neurology*, 58: 61–65.

Arakawa, M., Shiozuka, M., Nakayama, Y., Hara, T. *et al.* (2003) 'Negamycin restores dystrophin expression in skeletal and cardiac muscles of mdx mice.' *Journal of Biochemistry (Tokyo) 134*, 5: 751–758.

Araneta, M.R.G., Moore, C., Olney, R.S., Edmonds, L.D. *et al.* (2002) 'Goldenhar syndrome among infants born in military hospitals to Gulf War veterans.' *Teratology 56*, 4: 244–251.

Archer, H.L., Evans, J.C., Edwards, S., Colley, J. *et al.* (2006) 'CDKL5 mutations cause infantile spasms, early onset seizures and severe mental retardation in female patients.' *Journal of Medical Genetics*, 12: 729–734.

Archer, H.L., Evans, J.C., Millar, D.S., Thompson, P.W. *et al.* (2008) '*NTNG1* mutations are a rare cause of Rett syndrome.' *American Journal of Medical Genetics A, 140*, 7: 691–694.

Ariani, F., Hayek, G., Rondinella, D., Artuso, R. *et al.* (2008) 'FOXG1 is responsible for the congenital variant of Rett syndrome.' *American Journal of Human Genetics*, 83: 89–93.

Arias-Dimas, A., Vilaseca, M.A., Artuch, R., Ribes, A. and Campistol, J. (2006) 'Diagnosis and treatment of brain creatine deficiency syndromes' [article in Spanish]. *Revista de Neurologia 43*, 5: 302–308.

Arking, D.E., Cutler, D.J., Brune, C.W., Teslovich, T.M. *et al.* (2008) 'A common genetic variant in the neurexin superfamily member CNTNAP2 increases familial risk of autism.' *American Journal of Human Genetics 82*, 1: 160–164.

Arlt, C.F. von (1881) *Klinische Darstellung der Krankheiten des Auges zunächst der Binde-, Horn- und Lederhaut, dann der Iris und des Ciliarkörpers*. Wien: Braumüller.

Armstrong, D., Dunn, J.K., Antalffy, B. and Trivedi, R. (1995) 'Selective dendritic alterations in the cortex of Rett syndrome.' *Journal of Neuropathology and Experimental Neurology*, 54: 195–201.

Arnold, G.L., Hyman, S.L., Mooney, R.A. and Kirby, R.S. (2003) 'Plasma amino acids profiles in children with autism: potential risk of nutritional deficiencies.' *Journal of Autism and Developmental Disorders 33*, 4: 449–454.

Arnulf, I., Zeitzer, J.M., File, J., Farber, N. and Mignot, E. (2005) 'Kleine-Levin syndrome: a systematic review of 186 cases in the literature.' *Brain, 128*: 2763–2776.

Arriola-Pereda, G., Verdú-Pérez, A. and de Castro-De Castro, P. (2009) 'Cerebral polymicrogyria and 22q11 deletion syndrome' [Article in Spanish]. *Revista de Neurologia 48*, 4: 188–190.

Ars, E., Kruyer, H., Morell, M., Pros, E. *et al.* (2003) 'Recurrent mutations in the NF1 gene are common among neurofibromatosis type 1 patients.' *Journal of Medical Genetics*, 40: e82.

Arts, H.H., Doherty, D., van Beersum, S.E.C., Parisi, M.A. et al. (2007) 'Mutations in the gene encoding the basal body protein RPGRIP1L, a nephrocystin-4 interactor, cause Joubert syndrome.' *Nature Genetics*, 39: 882–888.

Asano, E., Chugani, D.C., Muzik, O., Behen, M. et al. (2001) 'Autism in tuberous sclerosis complex is related to both cortical and subcortical dysfunction.' *Neurology*, 57: 1269–1277.

Ashrafi, M.R., Shabanian, R., Abbaskhanian, A., Nasirian, A. *et al.* (2007a) 'Selenium and intractable epilepsy: is there any correlation?' *Pediatric Neurology*, 36: 25–29.

Ashrafi, M.R., Shabanian, R., Mohammadi, M. and Kavusi, S. (2006) 'Extensive Mongolian spots: a clinical sign merits special attention.' *Pediatric Neurology 34*, 2: 143–145.

Ashrafi, M.R., Shams, S., Nouri, M., Mohseni, M. *et al.* (2007b) 'A probable causative factor for an old problem: selenium and glutathione peroxidase appear to play important roles in epilepsy pathogenesis.' *Epilepsia 48*, 9: 1750–1755.

Ashwood, P., Wills, S. and Van de Water, J. (2006) 'The immune response in autism: a new frontier for autism research.' *Journal of Leukocyte Biology 80*, 1: 1–15.

Askalan, R., Mackay, M., Brian, J., Otsubo, H. *et al.* (2003) 'Prospective preliminary analysis of the development of autism and epilepsy in children with infantile spasms.' *Journal of Child Neurology*, 18: 165–170.

Assumpcao, F., Santos, R.C., Rosario, M. and Mercadante, M. (1999) 'Brief report: autism and Aarskog syndrome.' *Journal of Autism and Developmental Disorders*, 29: 179–181.

Attias, J., Raveh, E., Ben-Naftali, N.F., Zarchi, O. and Gothelf, D. (2008) 'Hyperactive auditory efferent system and lack of acoustic reflexes in Williams syndrome.' *Journal of Basic Clinical Physiology and Pharmacology 19*, 3–4: 193–207.

Attwell, D. (2000) 'Brain uptake of glutamate: food for thought.' *Journal of Nutrition*, 130: 1023S–1025S.

August, G.J. and Lockhart, L.H. (1984) 'Familial autism and the fragile-X chromosome.' *Journal of Autism and Developmental Disorders*, 14: 197–204.

Auranen, M., Vanhala, R., Varilo, T., Ayers, K. *et al.* (2002) 'A genome-wide screen for autism-spectrum disorders: evidence for a major susceptibility locus on chromosome 3q25–27.' *American Journal of Human Genetics*, 71: 777–790.

Ausio, J., Levin, D.B., De Amorim, G.V., Bakker, S. and Macleod, P.M. (2003) 'Syndromes of disordered chromatin remodeling.' *Clinical Genetics*, 64: 83–95.

Austin, D.W. and Shandley, K. (2008) 'An investigation of porphyrinuria in Australian children with autism.' *Journal of Toxicology and Environmental Health, Part A*, 71: 1349–1351.

Autism Genome Project Consortium (2007) 'Mapping autism risk loci using genetic linkage and chromosomal rearrangements.' *Nature Genetics*. Online 18 Feb. 2007, doi:10.1038/ng1985.

Avidor-Reiss, T., Maer, A.M., Koundakjian, E., Polyanovsky, A. *et al.* (2004) 'Decoding cilia function: defining specialized genes required for compartmentalized cilia biogenesis.' *Cell*, 117: 527–539.

Awaya, Y., Satoh, F., Oguni, H., Miyamoto, M. *et al.* (1990) 'Study of the mechanism of seizures induced by hot bathing – ictal EEG of hot bathing induced seizures in severe myoclonic epilepsy in infancy (SMEI).' [Article in Japanese.] In M. Seino and S. Ohtahara (eds.) *Annual Report of the Japanese Epilepsy Research Foundation* (Osaka), 2: 103–110.

Aymé, S. (2000) 'Bridging the gap between molecular genetics and metabolic medicine: access to genetic information.' *European Journal of Pediatrics 159*: Supp. 3: S183–S185.

Azurdia, R.M., Anstey, A.V. and Rhodes, L.E. (2001) 'Cholesterol supplementation objectively reduces photosensitivity in the Smith-Lemli-Opitz syndrome.' *British Journal of Dermatology*, 144: 143–145.

B

Baala, L., Romano, S., Khaddour, R., Saunier, S. *et al.* (2007) 'The Meckel-Gruber syndrome gene, MKS3, is mutated in Joubert syndrome.' *American Journal of Human Genetics*, 80: 186–194.

Babovic-Vuksanovic, D., Ballman, K., Michels, V., McGrann, P. *et al.* (2006) 'Phase II trial of pirfenidone in adults with neurofibromatosis type 1.' *Neurology*, 67: 1860–1862.

Bachner-Melman, R., Dina, C., Zohar, A.H., Constantini, N. *et al.* (2005) 'AVPR1a and SLC6A4 gene polymorphisms are associated with creative dance performance.' *PLoS Genetics*, 1: e42.

Backes, M., Genc, B., Schreck, J., Doerfler, W. *et al.* (2000) 'Cognitive and behavioral profile of fragile-X boys: correlations to molecular data.' *American Journal of Medical Genetics*, 95: 150–156.

Bäckman, B., Grevér-Sjölander, A.C., Bengtsson, K., Persson, J. and Johansson, I. (2007) 'Children with Down syndrome: oral development and morphology after use of palatal plates between 6 and 48 months of age.' *International Journal of Paediatric Dentistry 17*, 1: 19–28.

Backman, E. and Henriksson, K.G. (1995) 'Low-dose prednisolone treatment in Duchenne and Becker muscular dystrophy.' *Neuromuscular Disorders*, 5: 233–241.

Badcock, C. and Crespi, B. (2006) 'Imbalanced genomic imprinting in brain development: an evolutionary basis for the aetiology of autism.' *Journal of Evolutionary Biology 19*, 4: 1007–1032.

Badhwar, A., Andermann, F., Valerio, R.M. and Andermann, E. (2000) 'Founder effect in Joubert syndrome.' *Annals of Neurology*, 48: 435–436.

Baghdadi, A., Picot, M.C., Pascal, C., Pry, R. and Aussilloux, C. (2003) 'Relationship between age of recognition of first disturbances and severity in young children with autism.' *European Journal of Child and Adolescent Psychiatry*, 12: 122–127.

Bagni, C. and Greenough, W.T. (2005) 'From mRNP trafficking to spine dysmorphogenesis: the roots of fragile-X syndrome.' *Nature Reviews Neuroscience 6*, 5: 376–387.

BaHammam, A.S., Gad El Rab, M., Owais, S.M., Alswat, K. and Hamam, K.D. (2007) 'Clinical characteristics and HLA typing of a family with Kleine-Levin syndrome.' *Sleep Medicine 9*, 5: 575–578.

Bahi-Buisson, N., Kaminska, A., Boddaert, N., Rio, M. *et al.* (2008a) 'The three stages of epilepsy in patients with *CDKL5* mutations.' *Epilepsia 49*, 6: 1027–1037.

Bahi-Buisson, N., Nectoux, J., Rosas-Vargas, H.E., Milh, M. *et al.* (2008b) 'Key clinical features to identify girls with CDKL5 mutations.' *Brain*, 131: 2647–2661.

Baieli, S., Pavone, L., Meli, C., Fiumara, A. and Coleman, M. (2003) 'Autism and phenylketonuria.' *Journal of Autism and Developmental Disorders*, 33: 201–204.

Bakalov, V.K., Shawker, T., Ceniceros, I. and Bondy, C.A. (2007) 'Uterine development in Turner syndrome.' *Journal of Pediatrics 151*, 5: 528–531.

Bakare, M.O. and Ikegwuonu, N.N. (2008) 'Childhood autism in a 13-year-old boy with oculocutaneous albinism: a case report.' *Journal of Medical Case Reports 2*, 56 doi:10.1186/1752-1947-2-56.

Baker, P., Piven, J. and Sato, Y. (1998) 'Autism and tuberous sclerosis complex: prevalence and clinical features.' *Journal of Autism and Developmental Disorders 28*, 4: 279–285.

Baker, P., Piven, J., Schwartz, S. and Patil, S. (1994) 'Duplication of chromosome 15q11–13 in two individuals with autistic disorder.' *Journal of Autism and Developmental Disorders*, 24: 529–535.

Bakkaloglu, B., O'Roak, B.J., Louvi, A., Gupta, A.R. *et al.* (2008) 'Molecular cytogenetic analysis and resequencing of contactin associated protein–like 2 in Autism Spectrum Disorders.' *American Journal of Human Genetics*, 82: 165–173.

Balci, S., Engiz, O., Yilmaz, Z. and Baltaci, V. (2006) 'Partial trisomy (11;22) syndrome with manifestations of Goldenhar sequence due to maternal balanced t(11;22).' *Genetic Counselling 17*, 3: 281–289.

Bamshad, M. and Guthery, S.L. (2007) 'Race, genetics and medicine: does the color of a leopard's spots matter?' *Current Opinion in Pediatrics*, 19: 613–618.

Bandim, J.M., Ventura, L.O., Miller, M.T., Almeida, H.C. and Costa, A.E.S. (2003) 'Autism and Mobius sequence: an exploratory study of children in northeastern Brazil.' *Arquivos de Neuro-psiquiatrica 61*, 2-A: 181–185.

Barabas, G. and Matthews, W.S. (1983) 'Coincident infantile autism and Tourette syndrome: a case study.' *Journal of Developmental and Behavioural Pediatrics*, 4: 280–282.

Baraitser, M. (1977) 'Genetics of Möbius syndrome.' *Journal of Medical Genetics 14*, 6: 415–417 .

Baraitser, M. (1982) 'Heterogeneity and pleiotropism in the Moebius syndrome.' Letter, *Clinical Genetics*, 21: 290.

Baraitser, M., Patton, M., Lam, S.T.S., Brett, E.M. and Wilson, J. (1987) 'The Angelman (happy puppet) syndrome: is it autosomal recessive?' *Clinical Genetics*, 31: 323–330.

Baranek, G.T., Danko, C.D., Skinner, M.L., Bailey, D.B. Jr. *et al.* (2005) 'Video analysis of sensory-motor features in infants with fragile-X syndrome at 9–12 months of age.' *Journal of Autism and Developmental Disorders 35*, 5: 645–656.

Barbosa-Gonçalves, A., Vendrame-Goloni, C.B., Martins, A.L. and Fett-Conte, A.C. (2008) 'Subtelomeric region of chromosome 2 in patients with autism spectrum disorders.' *Genetics and Molecular Research 7*, 2: 527–533.

Bardet, G. (1920) 'Sur un syndrome d'obedite congenitale avec polydactylie at retinite pigmentaire (contribution a l'etude des lormes cliniques de l'obesite typophysaire)' (thesis). Paris.

Barisic, I., Tokic, V., Loane, M., Bianchi, F. *et al.* (2008) 'Descriptive epidemiology of Cornelia de Lange syndrome in Europe.' *American Journal of Medical Genetics A, 146A*, 1: 51–59.

Barkovich, A.J., Hevner, R. and Guerrini, R. (1999) 'Syndromes of bilateral symmetrical polymicrogyria.' *American Journal of Neuroradiology*, 20: 1814–1821.

Barkovich, A.J., Kuzniecky, R.I., Jackson, G.D., Guerrini, R. and Dobyns, W.B. (2001) 'Classification system for malformations of cortical development: update.' *Neurology*, 57: 2168–2178.

Barnett, S., Reilly, S., Carr, L., Ojo, I. *et al.* (2002) 'Behavioural phenotype of Bardet-Biedl syndrome.' *Journal of Medical Genetics* 39: e76: www.jmedgenet

Barnevik-Olsson, M., Gillberg, C. and Fernell, E. (2008) 'Prevalence of autism in children born to Somali parents living in Sweden: a brief report.' *Developmental Medicine and Child Neurology 50*, 8: 598–601.

Baron-Cohen, S. (2002) 'The extreme male brain theory of autism.' *Trends in Cognitive Science*, 6: 248–254.

Baron-Cohen, S., Mortimore, C., Moriarty, J., Izaguirre, J. and Robertson, M. (1999a) 'The prevalence of Gilles de la Tourette's syndrome in children and adolescents with autism.' *Journal of Child Psychology and Psychiatry*, 40: 213–218.

Baron-Cohen, S., Ring, H.A., Bullmore, E.T., Wheelwright, S. *et al.* (2000) 'The amygdala theory of autism.' *Neuroscience and Biobehavioural Reviews*, 24: 355–364.

Baron-Cohen, S., Scahill, V.L., Izaguirre, J., Hornsey, H. and Robertson, M.M. (1999b) 'The prevalence of Gilles de la Tourette syndrome in children and adolescents with autism: a large-scale study.' *Psychological Medicine 29*, 5: 1151–1159.

Baron-Cohen, S., Wheelwright, S., Cox, A., Baird, G. *et al.* (2000) 'Early identification of autism by the Checklist for Autism in Toddlers (CHAT).' *Journal of the Royal Society of Medicine 93*, 10: 521–525.

Barrett, S., Beck, J.C., Bernier, R., Bisson, E. *et al.* (1999) 'An autosomal genomic screen for autism: collaborative linkage study of autism.' *American Journal of Medical Genetics*, 88: 609–615.

Barth, P.G. (1993) 'Pontocerebellar hypoplasias: an overview of a group of inherited neurodegenerative disorders with fetal onset.' *Brain and Development*, 15: 411–422.

Barth, P.G., Hoffmann, G.F., Jaeken, J., Lehnert, W. et al. (1992) 'L-2-hydroxyglutaric acidemia: a novel inherited neurometabolic disease.' *Annals of Neurology*, 32: 66–71.

Barton, B. and North, K. (2004) 'Social skills of children with neurofibromatosis type 1.' *Developmental Medicine and Child Neurology*, 46: 553–563.

Bartsch, O., Nemecková, M., Kocárek, E., Wagner, A. *et al.* (2003) 'DiGeorge/velocardiofacial syndrome: FISH studies of chromosomes 22q11 and 10p14, and clinical reports on the proximal 22q11 deletion.' *American Journal of Medical Genetics A, 117A,* 1: 1–5.

Barzilai, A., Biton, S. and Shiloh, Y. (2008) 'The role of the DNA damage response in neuronal development, organization and maintenance.' *DNA Repair*, 7: 1010–1027.

Basile, E., Villa, L., Selicorni, A. and Molteni, M. (2007) 'The behavioural phenotype of Cornelia de Lange syndrome: a study of 56 individuals.' *Journal of Intellectual Disability Research 51*, 9: 671–681.

Baskin, E., Kayiran, S.M., Oto, S., Alehan, F. *et al.* (2002) 'Cerebellar vermis hypoplasia in a patient with Bardet-Biedl syndrome.' *Journal of Child Neurology*, 17: 385–387.

Bassett, A.S., Chow, E.W., Husted, J., Weksberg, R. et al. (2005) 'Clinical features of 78 adults with 22q11 deletion syndrome.' *American Journal of Medical Genetics A*, 138: 307–313.

Batra, P., Kharbanda, O.P., Duggal, R., Reddy, P. and Parkash, H. (2003) 'Orthodontic treatment of a case of Aarskog syndrome.' *Journal of Clinical Pediatric Dentistry*, 27: 229–233.

Battaglia, A. and Carey, J.C. (2006) 'Etiologic yield of autistic spectrum disorders: a prospective study.' *American Journal of Medical Genetics Part C – Seminars in Medical Genetics, 142C,* 1: 3–7.

Battaile, K.P., Battaile, B.C., Merkens, L.S., Maslen, C.L. and Steiner, R.D. (2001) 'Carrier frequency of the common mutation IVS8-1G>C in DHCR7 and estimate of the expected incidence of Smith-Lemli-Opitz syndrome.' *Molecular Genetics and Metabolism*, 72: 67–71.

Battey, J., Wada, E. and Wray, S. (1994) 'Bombesin receptor gene expression during mammalian development.' *Annals of the New York Academy of Science*, 739: 244–252.

Battini, R., Alessandrì, M.G., Leuzzi, V., Moro, F. *et al.* (2006) 'Arginine:glycine amidinotransferase (AGAT) deficiency in a newborn: early treatment can prevent phenotypic expression of the disease.' *Journal of Pediatrics 148*, 6: 828–830.

Baujat, B., Krastinova–Lolov, D., Blumen, M., Baglin, A.C. *et al.* (2006) 'Radiofrequency in the treatment of craniofacial plexiform neurofibromatosis: a pilot study.' *Plastic and Reconstructive Surgery*, 117: 1261–1268.

Baujat, G. and Cormier–Daire, V. (2004) 'Sotos syndrome.' *Orphanet Encyclopaedia.* www.orpha.net

Baujat, G. and Cormier-Daire, V. (2007) 'Sotos syndrome.' *Orphanet Journal of Rare Diseases 2,* 36 doi:10.1186/1750-1172-2-36.

Baujat, G., Rio, M., Rossignol, S., Sanlaville, D. *et al.* (2004) 'Paradoxical NSD1 mutations in Beckwith-Wiedemann syndrome and 11p15 anomalies in Sotos syndrome.' *American Journal of Human Genetics*, 74: 715–720.

Baujat, G., Rio, M., Rossignol, S., Sanlaville, D. *et al.* (2005) 'Clinical and molecular overlap in overgrowth syndromes.' *American Journal of Medical Genetics C, 137C,* 1: 4–11.

Bauman, M. (ed.) (2005) *The Neurology of Autism.* Oxford: Oxford University Press.

Bay, C., Mauk, J., Radcliffe, J. and Kaplan, P. (1993) 'Mild Brachmann-de Lange syndrome: delineation of the clinical phenotype, and characteristic behaviors in a six-year-old boy.' *American Journal of Medical Genetics*, 47: 965–968.

Beales, P.L. (2005) 'Lifting the lid on Pandora's box: the Bardet-Biedl syndrome.' *Current Opinion in Genetics and Development*, 15: 315–323.

Bear, M.F. (2005) 'Therapeutic implications of the mGluR theory of fragile-X mental retardation.' *Genes, Brain and Behavior 4*, 6: 393–398.

Bear, M.F., Huber, K.M. and Warren, S.T. (2004) 'The mGluR theory of fragile-X mental retardation.' *Trends in the Neurosciences*, 27: 370–377.

Bearden, C.E. and Freimer, N.B. (2006) 'Endophenotypes for psychiatric disorders: ready for primetime?' *Trends in Genetics 22*, 6: 306–313.

Bearden, C.E., Reus, V.I. and Freimer, N.B. (2004) 'Why genetic investigation of psychiatric disorders is so difficult.' *Current Opinion in Genetics and Development 14*, 3: 280–286.

Becerra-Solano, L.E., D?az-Rodriguez, M., Nastasi-Catanese, J.A., Toscano-Flores, J.J. et al. (2008) 'The fifth female patient with Myhre syndrome: further delineation.' *Clinical Dysmorphology*, 17: 113–117.

Beenakker, E.A., Fock, J.M., Van Tol, M.J., Maurits, N.M. *et al.* (2005) 'Intermittent prednisone therapy in Duchenne muscular dystrophy: a randomized controlled trial.' *Archives of Neurology*, 62: 128–132.

Beggs, A.H. (1997) 'Dystrophinopathy, the expanding phenotype: dystrophin abnormalities in X-linked dilated cardiomyopathy.' *Circulation*, 95: 2344–2347.

Beighton, P. (1969) 'Cardiac abnormalities in the Ehlers-Danlos syndrome.' *British Heart Journal 31*, 2: 227–232.

Beighton, P., De Paepe, A., Steinmann, B., Tsipouras, P. and Wenstrup, R.J. (1998) 'Ehlers-Danlos syndromes: revised nosology, Villefranche, 1997. Ehlers-Danlos National Foundation (USA) and Ehlers-Danlos Support Group (UK).' *American Journal of Medical Genetics*, 77: 31–37.

Bell, J.G., Sargent, J.R., Tocher, D.R. and Dick, J.R. (2000) 'Red blood cell fatty acid compositions in a patient with autistic spectrum disorder: a characteristic abnormality in neurodevelopmental disorders?' *Prostaglandins Leukotrienes and Essential Fatty Acids*, 63: 21–25.

Bell, J.G., MacKinlay, E.E., Dick, J.R., MacDonald, D.J. *et al.* (2004) 'Essential fatty acids and phospholipase A2 in autistic spectrum disorders.' *Prostaglandins Leukotrienes and Essential Fatty Acids*, 71: 201–204.

Belmonte, M.K. and Bourgeron, T. (2006) 'Fragile-X syndrome and autism at the intersection of genetic and neural networks.' *Nature Neuroscience 9*, 10: 1221–1225.

Benaron, L.D. (2003) 'Commentary: inclusion to the point of dilution.' *Journal of Autism and Developmental Disorders*, 33: 355–359.

Benasayag, S., Rittler, M., Nieto, F., Torres de Aguirre, N. *et al.* (2001) '47,XYY karyotype and normal SRY in a patient with a female phenotype.' *Journal of Pediatric Endocrinology and Metabolism*, 14: 797–801.

Bender, B., Fry, E., Pennington, B., Puck, M. *et al.* (1983) 'Speech and language development in 41 children with sex chromosome anomalies.' *Pediatrics 71*, 2: 262–267.

Benga, I. (2006) 'Priorities in the discovery of the implications of water channels in epilepsy and Duchenne muscular dystrophy.' *Cellular and Molecular Biology (Noisy-le-grand) 52*, 7: 46–50.

Bennett, R.R., den Dunnen, J., O'Brien, K.F., Darras, B.T. and Kunkel, L.M. (2001) 'Detection of mutations in the dystrophin gene via automated DHPLC screening and direct sequencing.' *BMC Genetics*, 2: 17.

Ben-Shachar, S., Ou, Z., Shaw, C.A., Belmont, J.W. *et al.* (2008) '22q11.2 distal deletion: a recurrent genomic disorder distinct from DiGeorge syndrome and velocardiofacial syndrome.' *American Journal of Human Genetics*, 82: 214–221.

Benvenuto, A., Moavero, R., Alessandrelli, R., Manzi, B. and Curatolo, P. (2009) 'Syndromic autism: causes and pathogenetic pathways.' *World Journal of Pediatrics 5*, 3: 169–176.

Berg, J.S., Brunetti-Pierri, N., Peters, S.U., Kang, S.H. *et al.* (2007) 'Speech delay and autism spectrum behaviors are frequently associated with duplication of the 7q11.23 Williams-Beuren syndrome region.' *Genetics in Medicine 9*, 7: 427–441.

Berger, R., Stoker-de Vries, S.A., Wadman, S.K., Duran, M. *et al.* (1984) 'Dihydropyrimidine dehydrogenase deficiency leading to thymine-uraciluria. an inborn error of pyrimidine metabolism.' *Clinica Chimica Acta 141*, 2–3: 227–234.

Bergink, V., van Megen, H.J.G.M. and Westenberg, H.G.M. (2004) 'Glutamate and anxiety.' *European Neuropsychopharmacology*, 14: 175–183.

Bergmann, C., Zerres, K., Senderek, J., Rudnik-Schoneborn, S. *et al.* (2003) 'Oligophrenin 1 (OPHN1) gene mutation causes syndromic X-linked mental retardation with epilepsy, rostral ventricular enlargement and cerebellar hypoplasia.' *Brain*, 126: 1537–1544.

Bergmann, E. and Egly, J.-M. (2001) 'Trichothiodystrophy, a transcription syndrome.' *Trends in Genetics 17*, 5: 279–286.

Berilgen, M.S., Mungen, B., Ustundag, B. and Demira, C. (2006) 'Serum ghrelin levels are enhanced in patients with epilepsy.' *Seizure*, 15: 106–111.

Berry-Kravis, E. (2008) 'Fragile-X research: a status report.' *The National Fragile-X Foundation Quarterly*, 31: 12–16.

Berry-Kravis, E. and Potanos, K. (2004) 'Psychopharmacology in fragile-X syndrome – present and future.' *Mental Retardation and Developmental Disabilities Research Reviews*, 10: 42–48.

Berry-Kravis, E., Potanos, K., Weinberg, D., Zhou, L. and Goetz, C.G. (2005) 'Fragile X-associated tremor/ataxia syndrome in sisters related to X-inactivation.' *Annals of Neurology*, 57: 144–147.

Berry-Kravis, E., Sumis, A., Hervey, C., Nelson, M. *et al.* (2008) 'Open-label treatment trial of lithium to target the underlying defect in fragile-X syndrome.' *Journal of Developmental and Behavioral Pediatrics*, 29: 293–302.

Berthier, M.L., Santamaria, J., Encabo, H. and Tolosa, E.S. (1992) 'Recurrent hypersomnia in two adolescent males with Asperger's syndrome.' *Journal of the American Academy of Child and Adolescent Psychiatry*, 31: 735–738.

Bertola, D.R., Pereira, A.C., Passetti, F., de Oliveira, P.S. *et al.* (2005) 'Neurofibromatosis–Noonan syndrome: molecular evidence of the concurrence of both disorders in a patient.' *American Journal of Medical Genetics A*, 136: 242–245.

Betancur, C., Leboyer, M. and Gillberg, C. (2002) 'Increased rate of twins among affected sibling pairs with autism.' *American Journal of Human Genetics*, 70: 1381–1383.

Bettelheim, B. (1955) *Truants From Life: The Rehabilitation of Emotionally Disturbed Children.* Glencoe, IL: Free Press.

Bettelheim, B. (1967) *The Empty Fortress: Infantile Autism and the Birth of the Self.* New York: Free Press.

Betz, R., Rensing, C., Otto, E., Mincheva, A. *et al.* (2000) 'Children with ocular motor apraxia type Cogan carry deletions in the gene (NPHP1) for juvenile nephronophthisis.' *Journal of Pediatrics*, 136: 828–831.

Beunders, G., van de Kamp, J.M., Veenhoven, R.H., van Hagen, J.M. *et al.* (2009) 'A triplication of the Williams-Beuren syndrome region in a patient with mental retardation, a severe expressive language delay, behavioural problems and dysmorphisms.' *Journal of Medical Genetics, JMG Online*, doi:10.1136/jmg.2009.070490.

Beuten, J., Hennekam, R.C.M., Van Roy, B., Mangelschots, K. *et al.* (1996) 'Angelman syndrome in an inbred family.' *Human Genetics*, 97: 294–298.

Bhuiyan, Z., Klein, M. Hammond, P., Mannens, M.M. *et al.* (2006) 'Genotype–phenotype correlations of 39 patients with Cornelia de Lange syndrome: the Dutch experience.' *Journal of Medical Genetics*, 43: 237–250.

Bialer, M.G., Penchaszadeh, V.B., Kahn, E., Libes, R. *et al.* (1987) 'Female external genitalia and Mullerian duct derivatives in a 46,XY infant with the Smith-Lemli-Opitz syndrome.' *American Journal of Medical Genetics*, 28: 723–731.

Bickel, H. (1996) 'The first treatment of phenylketonuria.' *European Journal of Pediatrics 155*, Suppl. 1: 2–3.

Biedl, A. (1922) 'Ein Geschwisterpaar mit adipose-genitaler Dystrophie.' *Deutsche Medizinische Wochenschrift*, 48: 1630.

Biesecker, L.G., Laxova, R. and Friedman, A. (1987) 'Renal insufficiency in Williams syndrome.' *American Journal of Medical Genetics*, 28: 131–135.

Biggar, W.D., Politano, L., Harris, V.A., Passamano, L. *et al.* (2004) 'Deflazacort in Duchenne muscular dystrophy: a comparison of two different protocols.' *Neuromuscular Disorders*, 14: 476–482.

Bilora, F., Petrobelli, F., Boccioletti, V. and Pomerri, F. (2000) 'Moderate-dose intravenous immunoglobulin treatment of Job's disease: case report.' *Minerva Medica*, 91: 113–116.

Bissler, J.J., McCormack, F.X., Young, L.R., Elwing, J.M. et al. (2008) 'Sirolimus for angiomyolipoma in tuberous sclerosis complex or lymphangioleiomyomatosis.' *New England Journal of Medicine*, 358: 140–151.

Bittigau, P. and Ikonomidou, C. (1997) 'Glutamate in neurologic diseases.' *Journal of Child Neurology*, 12: 471–485.

Blanchon, Y.C., Gay, C., Gibert, G. and Lauras, B. (2002) 'A case of N-acetyl galactosaminidase deficiency (Schindler disease) associated with autism.' *Journal of Autism and Developmental Disorders*, 32: 145–146.

Blank, C.E. (1960) 'Apert's syndrome (a type of acrocephalosyndactyly): observations on a British series of thirty-nine cases.' *Annals of Human Genetics*, 24: 151–164.

Blasco, M.A. (2007) 'The epigenetic regulation of mammalian telomeres.' *Nature Reviews: Genetics*, 8, 299–309.

Blasi, F., Bacchelli, E., Pesaresi, G., Carone, S. *et al.* (2006) 'Absence of coding mutations in the X-linked genes neuroligin 3 and neuroligin 4 in individuals with autism from the IMGSAC collection.' *American Journal of Medical Genetics B Neuropsychiatric Genetics 141*, 3: 220–221.

Bird A. (2007) 'Perceptions of epigenetics.' *Nature Insight 447*, 7143: 396–398.

Bird, T.D. (2007) (update) 'Myotonic dystrophy type 1 (Steinert's disease).' *GeneReviews* www.ncbi.nlm.nih.gov

Björkstén, B., Bäck, O., Gustavson, K.H., Hallmans, G. *et al.* (1980) 'Zinc and immune function in Down's syndrome.' *Acta Paediatrica Scandinavica 69*, 2: 183–187.

Blake, K.D. and Prasad, C. (2006) 'CHARGE syndrome.' *Orphanet Journal of Rare Diseases*, 1:34 doi: 10.1186/1750-1172-1-34, www.ojrd.com.

Blau, H.M. (2008) 'Cell therapies for muscular dystrophy.' *New England Journal of Medicine 359*, 13: 1403–1405.

Blaxill, M.X. (2004) 'What's going on? The question of time trends in autism.' *Public Health Reports 119*, 6: 536–551.

Bleesing, J.J. (2003) 'Autoimmune lymphoproliferative syndrome (ALPS).' *Current Pharmaceutical Design*, 9: 265–278.

Bleesing, J.J.H., Johnson, J. and Zhang, K. (2007) 'Autoimmune lymphoproliferative syndrome.' *GeneReviews* www.ncbi.nlm.nih.gov

Blomberg, S., Rosander, M. and Andersson, G. (2006) 'Fears, hyperacusis and musicality in Williams syndrome.' *Research in Developmental Disabilities*, 27: 668–680.

Blomquist, H.K., Back, O., Fagerlund, M., Holmgren, G. and Stecksen-Blicks, C. (1991) 'Tay or IBIDS syndrome: a case with growth and mental retardation, congenital ichthyosis and brittle hair.' *Acta Paediatrica Scandinavica*, 80: 1241–1245.

Blomquist, H.K., Bohman, M., Edvinsson, S.O., Gillberg, C. *et al.* (1985) 'Frequency of the fragile-X syndrome in infantile autism: a Swedish multicenter study.' *Clinical Genetics*, 27: 113–117.

Blondis, T.A., Cook, E. Jr., Koza-Taylor, P. and Finn, T. (1996) 'Asperger syndrome associated with Steinert's myotonic dystrophy.' *Developmental Medicine and Child Neurology*, 38: 840–847.

Blount, B.C. and Ames, B.N. (1995) 'DNA damage in folate deficiency.' *Bailliere's Clinical Haematology 8*, 3: 461–478.

Blue, M.E., Naidu, S. and Johnston, M.V. (1999) 'Altered development of glutamate and GABA receptors in the basal ganglia of girls with Rett syndrome.' *Experimental Neurology 156*, 2: 345–352.

Boccone, L., Dessi, V., Zappu, A., Piga, S. *et al.* (2006) 'Bannayan-Riley-Ruvalcaba syndrome with reactive nodular lymphoid hyperplasia and autism and a PTEN mutation' (letter). *American Journal of Medical Genetics*, 140A: 1965–1969.

Boddaert, N., Belin, P., Chabane, N., Poline, J-B. *et al.* (2003) 'Perception of complex sounds: abnormal pattern of cortical activation in autism.' *American Journal of Psychiatry*, 160: 2057–2060.

Boddaert, N., Chabane, N., Belin, P., Bourgeois, M. *et al.* (2004) 'Perception of complex sounds in autism: abnormal auditory cortical processing in children.' *American Journal of Psychiatry*, 161: 2117–2120.

Boddaert, N., Mochel, F., Meresse, I., Seidenwurm, D. *et al.* (2006) 'Parieto-occipital grey matter abnormalities in children with Williams syndrome.' *NeuroImage*, 30, 721–725.

Bodfish, J.W. (2004) 'Treating the core features of autism: are we there yet?' *Mental Retardation and Developmental Disabilities Research Reviews 10*, 4: 318–326.

Bodrug, S.E., Ray, P.N., Gonzalez, I.L., Schmickel, R.D. et al. (1987) 'Molecular analysis of a constitutional X-autosome translocation in a female with muscular dystrophy.' *Science*, 237: 1620–1624.

Boeckers, T.M., Bockmann, J., Kreutz, M.R. and Gundelfinger, E.D. (2002) 'ProSAP/Shank prot.' *Journal of Neurochemistry*, 81: 903–910.

Boles, D.J., Bodurtha, J. and Nance, W.E. (1987) 'Goldenhar complex in discordant monozygotic twins: a case report and review of the literature.' *American Journal of Medical Genetics*, 28: 103–109.

Bolton, P.F. and Griffiths, P.D. (1997) 'Association of tuberous sclerosis of temporal lobes with autism and atypical autism.' *Lancet 349*, 9049: 392–395.

Bolton, P.F., Dennis, N.R., Browne, C.E., Thomas, N.S. *et al.* (2001) 'The phenotypic manifestations of interstitial duplications of proximal 15q with special reference to the autistic spectrum disorders.' *American Journal of Medical Genetics 105*, 8: 675–685.

Bolton, P.F., Park, R.J., Higgins, J.N., Griffiths, P.D. and Pickles, A. (2002) 'Neuro-epileptic determinants of autism spectrum disorders in tuberous sclerosis complex.' *Brain 125*, 6: 1247–1255.

Bolton, P.F., Powell, J., Rutter, M., Buckle, V. *et al.* (1995) 'Autism, mental retardation, multiple exostoses and short stature in a female with 46,X,t(X;8) (p22.13;q22.1).' *Psychiatric Genetics 5*, 2: 51–55.

Bolton, P.F., Veltman, M.W., Weisblatt, E., Holmes, J.R. *et al.* (2004) 'Chromosome 15q11–13 abnormalities and other medical conditions in individuals with autism spectrum disorders.' *Psychiatric Genetics*, 14: 131–137.

Bonamico, M., Mariani, P., Danesi, H.M., Crisogianni, M. *et al.* (2001) 'Prevalence and clinical picture of celiac disease in Italian Down syndrome patients: a multicenter study.' *Journal of Pediatric Gastroenterology and Nutrition 33*, 2: 139–143.

Bonati, M.T., Russo, S., Finelli, P., Valsecchi, M.R. *et al.* (2007) 'Evaluation of autism traits in Angelman syndrome: a resource to unfold autism genes.' *Neurogenetics 8*, 3: 169–178.

Bonthron, D.T., Fitzpatrick, D.R., Porteous, M.E.M. and Trainer, A.H. (1998) *Clinical Genetics: A Case-Based Approach*. London: W.B. Saunders

Boog, G., Sagot, F., Winer, N., David, A. and Nomballais, M.F. (1999) 'Brachmann-de Lange syndrome: a cause of early symmetric fetal growth delay.' *European Journal of Obstetrics, Gynecology and Reproductive Biology*, 85: 173–177.

Borck, G., Redon, R., Sanlaville, D., Rio, M. *et al.* (2004) 'NIPBL mutations and genetic heterogeneity in Cornelia de Lange syndrome.' *Journal of Medical Genetics*, 41: e128.

Borg, I., Freude, K., Kubart, S., Hoffmann, K. *et al.* (2005) 'Disruption of Netrin G1 by a balanced chromosome translocation in a girl with Rett syndrome.' *European Journal of Human Genetics*, 13: 921–927.

Borges, W.G., Augustine, N.H. and Hill, H.R. (2000) 'Defective IL–12/interferon-gamma pathway in patients with hyperimmunoglobulinemia E syndrome.' *Journal of Pediatrics 136*, 2: 176–180.

Borges, W.G., Hensley, T., Carey, J.C., Petrak, B.A. and Hill, H.R. (1998) 'The face of Job.' *Journal of Pediatrics 133*, 2: 303–305.

Boris, M., Goldblatt, A., Galanko, J. and James, S.J. (2004) 'Association of MTHFR Gene Variants with Autism.' *Journal of American Physicians and Surgeons, 9*, 4: 106–108.

Boris, M., Kaiser, C.C., Goldblatt, A., Elice, M.W. et al (2007) 'Effect of pioglitazone treatment on behavioral symptoms in autistic children.', *Journal of Neuroinflammation*. 4:3. doi: 10.1186/1742-2094-4-3.

Botez, M.I., Botez, T., Ross-Chouinard, A. and Lalonde, R. (1993) 'Thiamine and folate treatment of chronic epileptic patients: a controlled study with the Wechsler IQ scale.' *Epilepsy 16*, 2: 157–163.

Botto, L.D. and Yang, Q. (2000) '5,10-Methylenetetrahydrofolate Reductase Gene Variants and Congenital Anomalies: A HuGE Review.', *American Journal of Epidemiology, 151*: 862–877.

Bourgeron, T. (2007) 'The possible interplay of synaptic and clock genes in autism spectrum disorders.' *Cold Spring Harbour Symposia in Quantative Biology*, 72: 645–654.

Bouzas, E.A., Caruso, R.C., Drews-Bankiewicz, M.A. and Kaiser-Kupfer, M.I. (1994) 'Evoked potential analysis of visual pathways in human albinism.' *Ophthalmology*, 101: 309–314.

Bowden, J.A. and McArthur, C.L. III (1972) 'Possible biochemical model for phenylketonuria.' *Nature*, 235: 230.

Bower, B.D. and Jeavons, P.M. (1967) 'The "happy puppet" syndrome.' *Archives of Diseases in Childhood*, 42: 298–301.

Boycott, K.M., Flavelle, S., Bureau, A., Glass, H.C. *et al.* (2005) 'Homozygous deletion of the very low density lipoprotein receptor gene causes autosomal recessive cerebellar hypoplasia with cerebral gyral simplification.' *American Journal of Human Genetics*, 77: 477–483.

Braam, W., Didden, R., Smits, M.G. and Curfs, L.M. (2008) 'Melatonin for chronic insomnia in Angelman syndrome: a randomized placebo-controlled trial.' *Journal of Child Neurology 23*, 6: 649–654.

Braddock, B.A., Farmer, J.E., Deldrick, K.M., Iverson, J.M. *et al.* (2006) 'Oromotor and Communication in Joubert Syndrome: Further Evidence of Mulisystem Apraxia.' *Journal of Child Neurology, 21*: 130–163.

Bradford, Y., Haines, J., Hutcheson, H., Gardiner, M. *et al.* (2001) 'Incorporating language phenotypes strengthens evidence of linkage to autism.' *American Journal of Medical Genetics*, 105: 539–547.

Bradstreet, J., Geier, D.A., Kartzinel, J.J., Adams, J.B. and Geier, M.R. (2003) 'A case-control study of mercury burden in children with autistic spectrum disorders.' *Journal of American Physicians and Surgeons 8*, 3: 76–79.

Bradstreet, J.J., Smith, S., Granpeesheh, D., El-Dahr, J.M. and Rossignol, D. (2007) 'Spironolactone might be a desirable immunologic and hormonal intervention in autism spectrum disorders.' *Medical Hypotheses*, 68: 979–987.

Brancati, F., Travaglini, L., Zablocka, D., Boltshauser, E. et al. (2008) 'RPGRIP1L mutations are mainly associated with the cerebello-renal phenotype of Joubert syndrome-related disorders.' *Clinical Genetics*, 74: 164–170.

Braun, K., Van, N., Yeargin-Allsopp, M., Schendel, D. and Fernhoff, P. (2003) 'Long-term developmental outcomes of children identified through a newborn screening program with a metabolic or endocrine disorder: a population-based approach.' *Journal of Pediatrics*, 143: 236–242.

Bregman, J.D. and Volkmar, F.R. (1988) 'Autistic social dysfunction and Down syndrome.' *Journal of the American Academy of Child and Adolescent Psychiatry*, 27: 440–441.

Brenner, M. and Hearing, V.J. (2008) 'Modifying skin pigmentation – approaches through intrinsic biochemistry and exogenous agents.' *Drug Discovery Today: Disease Mechanisms 5*, 2: e189–e199.

Brenton, D.P. and Lilburn, M. (1996) 'Maternal phenylketonuria: a study from the United Kingdom.' *European Journal of Pediatrics*, 155 (Suppl. 1): 177–180.

Bresolin, N., Castelli, E., Comi, G.P., Felisari, G. *et al.* (1994) 'Cognitive impairment in Duchenne muscular dystrophy.' *Neuromuscular Disorders*, 4: 359–369.

Bretherick, K.L., Fluker, M.R. and Robinson, W.P. (2005) 'FMR1 repeat sizes in the gray zone and high end of the normal range are associated with premature ovarian failure.' *Human Genetics*, 117: 376–382.

Briegel, W. (2006) 'Neuropsychiatric findings of Moebius sequence – a review.' *Clinical Genetics*, 70: 91–97.

Briegel, W., Hofmann, C. and Schwab, K.O. (2007) 'Moebius sequence: behavior problems of preschool children and parental stress.' *Genetic Counselling*, 18: 267–275.

Brieger, P., Bartel-Friedrich, S., Haring, A. and Marneros, A. (1998) 'Oculo-auriculo-vertebral spectrum disorder (Goldenhar 'Syndrome') coexisting with schizophreniform disorder' (letter). *Journal of Neurology, Neurosurgery and Psychiatry 65*, 1: 135–136.

Brierre de Boismont, A. (1862) *Des hallucinations* (third edn). Germer Baillere (ed.), Paris.

Brkanac, Z., Raskind, W.H. and King, B.H. (2008) 'Pharmacology and genetics of autism: implications for diagnosis and treatment.' *Personalized Medicine 5*, 6: 599–607.

Broder, K., Reinhardt, E., Ahern, J., Lifton, R. *et al.* (1999) 'Elevated ambulatory blood pressure in 20 subjects with Williams syndrome.' *American Journal of Medical Genetics*, 83: 356–360.

Broughton, B.C., Berneburg, M., Fawcett, H., Taylor, E.M. *et al.* (2001) 'Two individuals with features of both xeroderma pigmentosum and trichothiodystrophy highlight the complexity of the clinical outcomes of mutations in the XPD gene.' *Human Molecular Genetics*, 10: 2539–2547.

Brown, A., Phelan, M.C., Patil, S., Crawford, E. *et al.* (1996) 'Two patients with duplication of 17p11.2: the reciprocal of the Smith-Magenis syndrome deletion?' *American Journal of Medical Genetics*, 63: 373–377.

Brown, W.T., Friedman, E., Jenkins, E.C., Brooks, J. *et al.* (1982a) 'Association of fragile-X syndrome with autism.' *Lancet 319*, 8263: 100.

Brown, W.T., Jenkins, E.C., Friedman, E., Brooks, J. *et al.* (1982b) 'Autism is associated with the fragile-X syndrome.' *Journal of Autism and Developmental Disorders*, 12: 303–308.

Brown, W.T., Wisniewski, K.E., Sudhalter, V., Keogh, M. *et al.* (1998) 'Identical twins discordant for Sotos syndrome.' *American Journal of Medical Genetics*, 79: 329–333.

Browne, C.E., Dennis, N.R., Maher, E., Long, F.L. *et al.* (1997) 'Inherited interstitial duplications of proximal 15q: genotype–phenotype correlations.' *American Journal of Human Genetics*, 61: 1342–1352.

Bruck, I., Philippart, M., Giraldi, D. and Antoniuk, S. (1991) 'Difference in early development of presumed monozygotic twins with Rett syndrome.' *American Journal of Medical Genetics*, 39: 415–417.

Brussino, A., Gellera, C., Saluto, A., Mariotti, C. *et al.* (2005) 'FMR1 gene premutation is a frequent genetic cause of late-onset sporadic cerebellar ataxia.' *Neurology*, 64: 145–147.

Bryson, Y., Sakati, N., Nyhan, W.L. and Fish, C.H. (1971) 'Self mutilative behavior in the Cornelia de Lange syndrome.' *American Journal of Mental Deficiency*, 76: 319–324.

Brzozowski, T., Konturek, P.C., Konturek, S.J., Kwiecien, S. *et al.* (2004) 'Exogenous and endogenous ghrelin in gastroprotection against stress-induced gastric damage.' *Regulatory Peptides*, 120: 39–51.

Bucci, I., Napolitano, G., Giuliani, C., Lio, S. *et al.* (1999) 'Zinc sulphate supplementation improves thyroid hypofunction in hypozincemic Down children.' *Biological Trace Element Research*, 67: 257–268.

Bucci, I., Napolitano, G., Giuliani, C., Lio, S. *et al.* (2001) 'Concerns about using Zn supplementation in Down's syndrome (DS) children.' *Biological Trace Element Research 82*, 1–3: 273–275.

Buckley, R.H., Dinno, N. and Weber, P. (1998) 'Angelman syndrome: are the estimates too low?' *American Journal of Medical Genetics*, 80: 385–390.

Buckley, R.H., Wray, B.B. and Belmaker, E.Z. (1972) 'Extreme hyperimmunoglobulinemia E and undue susceptibility to infection.' *Pediatrics 49*, 1: 59–70.

Buckley, S.J. (2005) 'Autism and Down syndrome.' *Down Syndrome News and Update 4*, 4: 114–120.

Budden, S.S., Dorsey, H.C., Robert, D. and Steiner, R.D. (2005) 'Clinical profile of a male with Rett syndrome.' *Brain and Development*, 27: S69–S71.

Buie, T., Campbell, B., Fuchs, G.J. III, Furuta, G.T. et al. (2010a) 'Evaluation, diagnosis, and treatment of gastrointestinal disorders in individuals with ASDs: a consensus report.' *Pediatrics*, 125: S1–S19.

Buie, T., Fuhs, G.J. III, Furuta, G.T., Kooros, K. et al. (2010b) 'Recommendations for evaluation and treatment of common gastrointestinal problems in children with ASDs.' *Pediatrics*, 125: S19–S29.

Buiting, K., Dittrich, B., Gross, S., Lich, C. *et al.* (1998) 'Sporadic imprinting defects in Prader-Willi syndrome and Angelman syndrome: implications for imprint-switch models, genetic counseling, and prenatal diagnosis.' *American Journal of Human Genetics*, 63: 170–180.

Buiting, K., Saitoh, S., Gross, S., Dittrich, B. *et al.* (1995) 'Inherited microdeletions in the Angelman and Prader-Willi syndromes define an imprinting centre on human chromosome 15.' *Nature Genetics*, 9: 395–400.

Bull, M.J., Fitzgerald, J.F., Heifetz, S.A. and Brei, T.J. (1993) 'Gastrointestinal abnormalities: a significant cause of feeding difficulties and failure to thrive in Brachmann-de Lange syndrome.' *American Journal of Medical Genetics*, 47: 1029–1034.

Bundey, S., Hardy, C., Vickers, S., Kilpatrick, M.W. and Corbett, J.A. (1994) 'Duplication of the 15q11–13 region in a patient with autism, epilepsy and ataxia.' *Developmental Medicine and Child Neurology*, 36: 736–742.

Buntinx, I.M., Hennekam, R.C.M., Brouwer, O.F., Stroink, H. *et al.* (1995) 'Clinical profile of Angelman syndrome at different ages.' *American Journal of Medical Genetics*, 56: 176–183.

Buoni, S., Zannolli, R., de Santi, M., Macucci, F. *et al.* (2006) 'Neurocutaneous syndrome with mental delay, autism, blockage in intracellular vesicular trafficking and melanosome defects.' *European Journal of Neurology 13*, 8: 42–851.

Burck, U. (1983) 'Genetic aspects of hemifacial microsomia.' *Human Genetics*, 64: 291–296.

Burd, L., Fisher, W.W., Kerbeshian, J. and Arnold, M.E. (1987) 'Is development of Tourette disorder a marker for improvement in patients with autism and other pervasive developmental disorders?' *Journal of the American Academy of Child and Adolescent Psychiatry 26*, 2: 162–165.

Burd, L., Li, Q., Kerbeshian, J., Klug, M.G. and Freeman, R.D. (2009) 'Tourette syndrome and comorbid pervasive developmental disorders.' *Journal of Child Neurology 24*, 2: 170–175.

Burd, L., Vesely, B., Martsolf, J. and Kerbeshian, J. (1990) 'Prevalence study of Prader-Willi syndrome in North Dakota.' *American Journal of Medical Genetics*, 37: 97–99.

Burger, R.A. and Warren, R.P. (1998) 'Possible immunogenetic basis for autism.' *Mental Retardation and Developmental Disabilities Research Reviews*, 4: 137–141.

Burglen, L., Heron, D., Moerman, A., Dieux-Coeslier, A. *et al.* (2003) 'Myhre syndrome: new reports, review, and differential diagnosis.' *Journal of Medical Genetics*, 40: 546–551.

Burke, B.A., Johnson, D., Gilbert, E.F., Drut, R.M. et al. (1987) 'Thyrocalcitonin-containing cells in the Di George anomaly.' *Human Pathology*, 18: 355–360.

Burke, J.R., Enghild, J.J., Martin, M.E., Jou, Y.-S. *et al.* (1996) 'Huntingtin and DRPLA proteins selectively interact with the enzyme GAPDH.' *Nature Medicine*, 2: 347–350.

Burusnukul, P., de los Reyes, E.C., Yinger, J. and Boue, D.R. (2008) 'Danon disease: an unusual presentation of autism.' *Pediatric Neurology 39*, 1: 52–54.

Burn, J. (1999) 'Closing time for CATCH22.' *Journal of Medical Genetics*, 36: 737–738.

Burn, J., Wilson, D.I., Cross, I., Atif, U. et al. (1995) 'The Clinical Significance of 22q11 Deletion.' In E.B. Clark, R.R. Markwald and A. Takao (eds.) *Developmental Mechanisms of Heart Disease.* New York: Futura Publishers.

Bushby, K.M. (1999) 'The limb-girdle muscular dystrophies – multiple genes, multiple mechanisms.' *Human Molecular Genetics,* 8: 1875–1882.

Bushby, K.M. and Gardner-Medwin, D. (1993) 'The clinical, genetic and dystrophin characteristics of Becker muscular dystrophy. I: Natural history.' *Journal of Neurology,* 240: 98–104.

Bushby, K.M., Thambyayah, M. and Gardner-Medwin, D. (1991) 'Prevalence and incidence of Becker muscular dystrophy.' *Lancet 337,* 8748: 1022–1024.

Buske, A., Gewies, A., Lehmann, R., Ruther, K. *et al.* (1999) 'Recurrent NF1 gene mutation in a patient with oligosymptomatic neurofibromatosis type 1 (NF1).' *American Journal of Medical Genetics,* 86: 328–330.

Butler, M.G., Dasouki, M.J., Zhou, X.P., Talebizadeh, Z. *et al.* (2005) 'Subset of individuals with autism spectrum disorders and extreme macrocephaly associated with germline PTEN tumour suppressor gene mutations.' *Journal of Medical Genetics,* 42: 318–321.

Butler, M.G., Lee, P.D.K. and Whitman, B.Y. (eds.) (2006) *Management of Prader-Willi Syndrome* (third edn). New York: Springer.

Buxbaum, J.D., Silverman, J., Keddache, M., Smith, C.J. *et al.* (2004) 'Linkage analysis for autism in subset families with obsessive-compulsive behaviors: evidence for an autism susceptibility gene on chromosome 1 and further support for susceptibility genes on chromosomes 6 and 19.' *Molecular Psychiatry,* 9: 144–150.

Buyse, M.E. (ed.) (1990) 'Chromosome X, Chromosome XYY.' In *Birth Defects Encyclopedia,* 400–401. Cambridge, MA: Blackwell Scientific Publications.

Buyske, S., Williams, T.A., Mars, A.E., Stenroos, E.S. *et al.* (2006) 'Analysis of case–parent trios at a locus with a deletion allele: association of GSTM1 with autism.' *BMC Genetics 7,* 8, doi:10.1186/1471-2156-7-8.

Bzduch, V., Beluchova, D. and Skodova, J. (2000) 'Incidence of Smith-Lemli-Opitz syndrome in Slovakia.' *American Journal of Medical Genetics,* 90: 260.

C

Cabanlit, M., Wills, S., Goines, P., Ashwood, P. and Van de Water, J. (2007) 'Brain-specific autoantibodies in the plasma of subjects with autistic spectrum disorder.' *Annals of the New York Academy of Science,* 1107: 92–103.

Cagianut, B., Schnebli, H.P., Rhyner, K. and Furrer, J. (1984) 'Decreased thiosulfate sulfur transferase (rhodanese) in Leber's hereditary optic atrophy.' *Journal of Molecular Medicine 62,* 18: 850–854.

Cagle, A.P., Waguespack, S.G., Buckingham, B.A., Shankar, R.R. and Dimeglio, L.A. (2004) 'Severe infantile hypercalcemia associated with Williams syndrome successfully treated with intravenously administered pamidronate.' *Pediatrics 114,* 4: 1091–1095.

Caldeira Araujo, H., Smit, W., Verhoeven, N.M., Salomons, G.S. *et al.* (2005) 'Guanidinoacetate methyltransferase deficiency identified in adults and a child with mental retardation.' *American Journal of Medical Genetics,* 133A: 122–127.

Caldwell, H.K. and Young, W.S.3rd (2006) 'Oxytocin and Vasopressin: Genetics and Behavioral Implications.' In R.Lim (ed.) *Handbook of Neurochemistry and Molecular Neurobiology: Neuroactive Proteins and Peptides* (third edn). New York: Springer Verlag.

Cambiaso, P., Orazi, C., Digilio, M.C., Loche, S. et al. (2007) 'Thyroid morphology and subclinical hypothyroidism in children and adolescents with Williams syndrome.' *Journal of Pediatrics,* 150: 62–65.

Campbell, C. and Jacob, P. (2003) 'Deflazacort for the treatment of Duchenne dDystrophy: a systematic review.' *BMC Neurology,* 3: 7.

Campbell, D.B., Buie, T.M., Winter, H., Bauman, M. *et al.* (2009) 'Distinct genetic risk based on association of MET in families with co-occurring autism and gastrointestinal conditions.' *Pediatrics 123,* 3: 1018–1024.

Campbell, D.B., Li, C., Sutcliffe, J.S., Persico, A.M. and Levitt, P. (2008) 'Genetic evidence implicating multiple genes in the MET receptor tyrosine kinase pathway in autism spectrum disorder.' *Autism Research 1,* 3: 159–168.

Campbell, D.B., Sutcliffe, J.S., Ebert, P.J., Militerni, R. *et al.* (2006) 'A genetic variant that disrupts MET transcription is associated with autism.' *Proceedings of the National Academy of Science USA 103,* 45: 16834–16839.

Canale, V.C. and Smith, C.H. (1967) 'Chronic lymphadenopathy simulating malignant lymphoma.' *Journal of Pediatrics,* 70: 891–899.

Canitano, R. and Vivanti, G. (2007) 'Tics and Tourette syndrome in autism spectrum disorders.' *Autism 11,* 1: 19–28.

Cantagrel, V., Silhavy, J.L., Bielas, S.L., Swistun, D. et al. (2008) 'Mutations in the cilia gene ARL13B lead to the classical form of Joubert syndrome.' *American Journal of Human Genetics,* 83: 170–179.

Cantor, R.M., Kono, N., Duvall, J.A., Alvarez-Retuerto, A. *et al.* (2005) 'Replication of autism linkage: fine-mapping peak at 17q21.' *American Journal of Human Genetics,* 76: 1050–1056.

Cantor, R.M., Yoon, J.L., Furr, J. and Lajonchere, C.M. (2007) 'Paternal age and autism are associated in a family-based sample' (letter). *Molecular Psychiatry,* 12: 419–423.

Caraballo, R.H. and Fejerman, N. (2006) 'Dravet syndrome: study of 53 patients.' *Epilepsy Research,* 70, Supp. 1: S231–S238.

Caraballo, R.H., Cersosimo, R.O., Sakr, D., Cresta, A. *et al.* (2005) 'Ketogenic diet in patients with Dravet syndrome.' *Epilepsia 46,* 9: 1539–1544.

Caraballo, R.H., Tripoli, J., Escobal, L., Cersosimo, R. *et al.* (1998) 'Ketogenic diet: efficacy and tolerability in childhood intractable epilepsy.' *Revista de Neurologia,* 26: 61–64.

Carethers, J.M., Furnari, F.B., Zigman, A.F., Lavine, J.E. *et al.* (1998) 'Absence of PTEN/MMAC1 germ-line mutations in sporadic Bannayan-Riley-Ruvalcaba syndrome.' *Cancer Research,* 58: 2724–2726.

Carey, J.C. (1998) 'Neurofibromatosis-Noonan syndrome.' *American Journal of Medical Genetics,* 75: 263–264.

Carlson, N.R. (2001) *Physiology of Behavior* (7th ed). Boston: Allyn and Bacon.

Carney, R.M., Wolpert, C.M., Ravan, S.A., Shahbazian, M. *et al.* (2003) 'Identification of MeCP2 mutations in a series of females with autistic disorder.' *Pediatric Neurology,* 28: 205–211.

Carothers, A.D., Hecht, C.A. and Hook, E.B. (1999) 'International variation in reported livebirth prevalence rates of Down syndrome, adjusted for maternal age.' *Journal of Medical Genetics,* 36: 386–393.

Carper, R.A. and Courchesne, E. (2005) 'Localized enlargement of the frontal cortex in early autism.' *Biological Psychiatry,* 57: 126–133.

Carr, R., Wasdell, M.B., Hamilton, D., Weiss, M.D. *et al.* (2007) 'Long-term effectiveness outcome of melatonin therapy in children with treatment-resistant circadian rhythm sleep disorders.' *Journal of Pineal Research,* 43: 351–359.

Carotti, A., Digilio, M.C., Piacentini, G., Saffirio, C. et al. (2008) 'Cardiac defects and results of cardiac surgery in 22q11.2 deletion syndrome.' *Developmental Disabilities Research Reviews,* 14: 35–42.

Carter, C.S. (2007) 'Sex differences in oxytocin and vasopressin: implications for autism spectrum disorders?' *Behavioural Brain Research,* 176: 170–186.

Carter, J.A., Lees, J.A., Goma, J.K., Murira, G. *et al.* (2006) 'Severe falciparum malaria and acquired childhood language disorder.' *Developmental Medicine and Child Neurology,* 48: 51–57.

Carter, J.C., Capone, G.T., Gray, R.M., Cox, C.S. and Kaufmann, W.E. (2007) 'Autistic-spectrum disorders in Down syndrome: further delineation and distinction from other behavioral abnormalities.' *American Journal of Medical Genetics, B Neuropsychiatric Genetics 144,* 1: 87–94.

Cartier, N. and Aubourg, P. (2008) 'Hematopoietic stem cell gene therapy in Hurler syndrome, globoid cell leukodystrophy, metachromatic leukodystrophy and X-adrenoleukodystrophy.' *Current Opinion in Molecular Therapeutics 10,* 5: 471–478.

Cartier, N., Hacein-Bey-Abina, S., Bartholomae, C.C., Veres, G. *et al.* (2009) 'Hematopoietic stem cell gene therapy with a lentiviral vector in X-linked adrenoleukodystrophy.' *Science 326* 5954: 818–823.

Cartlidge, P.H. and Curnock, D.A. (1986) 'Specific malabsorption of vitamin B12 in Down's syndrome.' *Archives of Disease in Childhood 61,* 5: 514–515.

Casella, E.B., Valente, M., de Navarro, J.M. and Kok, F. (2005) 'Vitamin B12 deficiency in infancy as a cause of developmental regression.' *Brain and Development 27,* 8: 1–3.

Cass, H., Sekaran, D. and Baird, G. (2006) 'Medical investigation of children with autistic spectrum disorders.' *Child: Care, Health and Development 32,* 5: 521–533.

Castaño, G., Etchart, C. and Sookoian, S. (2006) 'Vitamin A toxicity in a physical culturist patient: a case report and review of the literature.' *Annals of Hepatology 5,* 4: 293–295.

Castori, M., Brancati, F., Rinaldi, R., Adami, L. *et al.* (2006) 'Antenatal presentation of the oculo-auriculo-vertebral spectrum (OAVS).' *American Journal of Medical Genetics,* 140A: 1573–1579.

Castori, M., Valente, E.M., Donati, M.A., Salvi, S. et al. (2005) 'NPHP1 gene deletion is a rare cause of Joubert syndrome related disorders.' *Journal of Medical Genetics,* 42: e9.

Castorina, P., Selicorni, A., Bedeschi, F., Dalpra, L. and Larizza, L. (1997) 'Genotype–phenotype correlation in two sets of monozygotic twins with Williams syndrome.' *American Journal of Medical Genetics,* 69: 107–111.

Castre, M., Lampinen, K.E., Miettinen, R., Koponen, E. *et al.* (2002) 'BDNF regulates the expression of fragile-X mental retardation protein mRNA in the hippocampus.' *Neurobiology of Disease,* 11: 221–229.

Caughey, A.B., Washington, A.E., Gildengorin, V. and Kuppermann, M. (2004) 'Assessment of demand for prenatal diagnostic testing using willingness to pay.' *Obstetrics and Gynecology 103,* 3: 539–545.

Cavaille, J., Buiting, K., Kiefmann, M., Lalande, M. *et al.* (2000) 'Identification of brain-specific and imprinted small nucleolar RNA genes exhibiting an unusual genomic organization.' *Proceedings of the National Academy of Science USA,* 97: 14311–14316.

Cavaille, J., Seitz, H., Paulsen, M., Ferguson-Smith, A.C. and Bachellerie, J.P. (2002) 'Identification of tandemly-repeated C/D snoRNA genes at the imprinted human 14q32 domain reminiscent of those at the Prader-Willi/Angelman syndrome region.' *Human Molecular Genetics,* 11: 1527–1538.

Cazzullo, A.G., Musetti, M.C., Musetti, L., Bajo, S. *et al.* (1999) 'B-endorphin levels in peripheral blood mononuclear cells and long-term naltrexone treatment in autistic children.' *European Neuropsychopharmacology 94,* 4: 361–366.

Centerwall, S.A. and Centerwall, W.R. (2000) 'The discovery of phenylketonuria: the story of a young couple, two retarded children, and a scientist.' *Pediatrics 105,* 1: 89–103.

Ceponiene, R., Lepisto, T., Shestakova, A., Vanhala, R. *et al.* (2003) 'Speech–sound–selective auditory impairment in children with autism: they can perceive but do not attend.' *Proceedings of the National Academy of Science USA 100,* 9: 5567–5572.

Ceulemans, B.P.G.M., Claes, L.R.F. and Lagae, L.G. (2004) 'Clinical correlations of mutations in the *SCN1A* gene: from febrile seizures to severe myoclonic epilepsy in infancy.' *Pediatric Neurology 30,* 4: 236–243.

Chae, Y.-J., Chung, C.-E., Kim, B.-J., Lee, M.-H. and Lee, H. (1998) 'The gene encoding guanidinoacetate methyltransferase (GAMT) maps to human chromosome 19 at band p13.3 and to mouse chromosome 10.' *Genomics,* 49: 162–164.

Challman, T.D., Barbaresi, W.J., Katusic, S.K. and Weaver, A. (2003) 'The yield of the medical evaluation of children with pervasive developmental disorders.' *Journal of Autism and Developmental Disorders 33,* 2: 187–192.

Chan, Y.M., Merkens, L.S., Connor, W.E., Roullet, J.B. (2009) 'Effects of dietary cholesterol and simvastatin on cholesterol synthesis in Smith-Lemli-Opitz syndrome.' *Pediatric Research 65,* 6: 681–685.

Chance, P.F., Cavalier, L., Satran, D., Pellegrino, J.E. *et al.* (1999) 'Clinical nosologic and genetic aspects of Joubert and related syndromes.' *Journal of Child Neurology,* 14: 660–666.

Chandana, S.R., Behen, M.E., Juhasz, C., Muzik, O. *et al.* (2005) 'Significance of abnormalities in developmental trajectory and asymmetry of cortical serotonin synthesis in autism.' *International Journal of Developmental Neuroscience,* 23: 171–182.

Chandler, K.E., Kidd, A., Al-Gazali, L., Kolehmainen, J. *et al.* (2003) 'Diagnostic criteria, clinical characteristics, and natural history of Cohen syndrome.' *Journal of Medical Genetics,* 40: 233–241.

Chang, B.S., Ly, J., Appignani, B., Bodell, A. *et al.* (2005) 'Reading impairment in the neuronal migration disorder of periventricular nodular heterotopia.' *Neurology,* 64: 799–803.

Chao, P.H., Chao, M.C., Hwang, K.P. and Chung, M.Y. (2009) 'Hypocalcemia impacts heart failure control in DiGeorge 2 syndrome.' *Acta Paediatrica 98,* 1: 195–198.

Chapman, C.A., du Plessis, A. and Pober, B.R. (1996) 'Neurologic findings in children and adults with Williams syndrome.' *Journal of Child Neurology 11,* 1: 63–65.

Charlton, N. and Wallace, K.L. (2009) 'Post-chelator challenge urinary metal testing.' American College of Medical Toxicology Position Statement on Post-chelator Challenge Urinary Metal Testing. www.acmt.net

Chartrand, J.-P., Filon-Bilodeau, S. and Belin, P. (2007) 'Brain response to birdsongs in bird experts.' *NeuroReport 18,* 4: 335–340.

Chaste, P., Nygren, G., Anckarsäter, H., Råstam, M. *et al.* (2007) 'Mutation screening of the ARX gene in patients with autism.' *American Journal of Medical Genetics B Neuropsychiatric Genetics 144B,* 2: 228–230.

Chattopadhyay, A., Jafurulla, M., Kalipatnapu, S., Pucadyil, T.J. and Harikumar, K.G. (2005) 'Role of cholesterol in ligand binding and G-protein coupling of serotonin1A receptors solubilized from bovine hippocampus.' *Biochemical and Biophysical Research Communications,* 327: 1036–1041.

Chauhan, A., Chauhan, V., Brown, W.T. and Cohen, I. (2004a) 'Oxidative stress in autism: increased lipid peroxidation and reduced serum levels of ceruloplasmin and transferrin – the antioxidant proteins.' *Life Sciences,* 75: 2539–2549.

Chauhan, V., Chauhan, A., Cohen, I.L., Brown, W.T. and Sheikh, A. (2004b) 'Alteration in amino-glycerophospholipids levels in the plasma of children with autism: a potential biochemical diagnostic marker.' *Life Sciences,* 74: 1635–1643.

Chawarska, K., Paul, R., Klin, I., Hannigen, S. *et al.* (2007) 'Parental recognition of developmental problems in toddlers with autism spectrum disorders.' *Journal of Autism and Developmental Disorders,* 37: 62–72.

Chehimi, J., Elder, M., Greene, J., Noroski, L. et al. (2001) 'Cytokine and chemokine dysregulation in hyper-IgE syndrome.' *Clinical Immunology,* 100: 49–56.

Chen, C.H. and Hsiao, K.J. (1989) 'A Chinese classic phenylketonuria manifested as autism.' *British Journal of Psychiatry,* 155: 251–253.

Chen, I. and Toth, M. (2001) 'Fragile-X mice develop sensory hyperreactivity to auditory stimuli.' *Neuroscience 103,* 4: 1043–1050.

Chen, L., Tracy, T. and Nam, C.I. (2007) 'Dynamics of postsynaptic glutamate receptor targeting.' *Current Opinion in Neurobiology,* 17: 53–58.

Chen, Z., Karaplis, A.C., Ackerman, S.L., Pogribny, I.P. *et al.* (2001) 'Mice deficient in methylenetetrahydrofolate reductase exhibit hyperhomocysteinemia and decreased methylation capacity, with neuropathology and aortic lipid deposition.' *Human Molecular Genetics,* 10: 433–443.

Cherniske, E.M., Carpenter, T.O., Klaiman, C., Young, E. *et al.* (2004) 'Multisystem study of 20 older adults with Williams syndrome.' *American Journal of Medical Genetics,* 131A: 255–264.

Chess, S. (1971) 'Autism in children with congenital rubella.' *Journal of Autism and Childhood Schizophrenia 1,* 1: 33–47.

Chez, M.B., Memon, S. and Hung, P.C. (2004) 'Neurologic treatment strategies in autism: an overview of medical intervention strategies.' *Seminars in Pediatric Neurology*, 11: 229–235.

Chez, M.G., Chang, M., Krasne, V., Coughlan, C. *et al.* (2006) 'Frequency of epileptiform EEG abnormalities in a sequential screening of autistic patients with no known clinical epilepsy from 1996 to 2005.' *Epilepsy and Behavior*, 8: 267–271.

Chiang, A.P., Nishimura, D., Searby, C., Elbedour, K. et al. (2004) 'Comparative genomic analysis identifies an ADP-ribosylation factor-like gene as the cause of Bardet-Biedl syndrome (BBS3).' *American Journal of Human Genetics*, 75: 475–484.

Chieffo, C., Garvey, N., Gong, W., Roe, B. *et al.* (1997) 'Isolation and characterization of a gene from the DiGeorge chromosomal region homologous to the mouse Tbx1 gene.' *Genomics*, 43: 267–277.

Chilosi, A., Leuzzi, V., Battini, R., Tosetti, M. *et al.* (2008) 'Treatment with l-arginine improves neuropsychological disorders in a child with creatine transporter defect.' *Neurocase 14*, 2: 151–161.

Chinnery, P., Majamaa, K., Turnbull, D. and Thorburn, D. (2006) 'Treatment for mitochondrial disorders.' *Cochrane Database of Systematic Reviews*, Issue 1. Art. No.: CD004426, doi: 10.1002/14651858.CD004426.pub2.

Chiron, C., Marchand, M.C., Tran, A., Rey, E. *et al.* (2000) 'Stiripentol in severe myoclonic epilepsy in infancy: a randomized placebo-controlled syndrome-dedicated trial. STICLO study group.' *Lancet 356*, 9242: 1638–1642.

Chisolm, J.J. Jr. (2001) 'The road to primary prevention of lead toxicity in children.' *Pediatrics, 107*, 3: 581–583.

Chiu, S., Wegelin, J.A., Blank, J., Jenkins, M. *et al.* (2007) 'Early acceleration of head circumference in children with fragile-X syndrome and autism.' *Journal of Developmental and Behavioral Pediatrics 28*, 1: 31–35.

Chiurazzi, P., Tabolacci, E. and Neri, G. (2004) 'X-linked mental retardation (XLMR): from clinical condition to cloned gene.' *Critical Reviews in Clinical and Laboratory Science*, 41: 117–158.

Cho, H. and Tapscott, S.J. (2007) 'Myotonic dystrophy: emerging mechanisms for DM1 and DM2.' *Biochimica et Biophysica Acta*, 1772: 195–204.

Chocholska, S., Rossier, E., Barbi, G. and Kehrer-Sawatzki, H. (2006) 'Molecular cytogenetic analysis of a familial interstitial deletion Xp22.2–22.3 with a highly variable phenotype in female carriers.' *American Journal of Medical Genetics A, 140*, 6: 604–610.

Choi, P.T. and Nowaczyk, M.J. (2000) 'Anesthetic considerations in Smith-Lemli-Opitz syndrome.' *Canadian Journal of Anaesthesiology*, 47: 556–561.

Choong, Y.F., Watts, P., Little, E. and Beck, L. (2003) 'Goldenhar and cri-du-chat syndromes: a contiguous gene deletion syndrome?' *Journal of the American Academy for Pediatric Ophthalmology and Strabismus*, 7: 226–227.

Chowdhury, U. (2004) *Tics and Tourette Syndrome: A Handbook for Parents and Professionals*. London: Jessica Kingsley Publishers.

Christian, S.L., Brune, C.W., Sudi, J., Kumar, R.A. *et al.* (2008) 'Novel submicroscopic chromosomal abnormalities detected in autism spectrum disorder.' *Biological Psychiatry*, 15: 1111–1117.

Chudley, A.E., Gutierrez, E., Jocelyn, L.J. and Chodirker, B.N. (1998) 'Outcomes of genetic evaluation in children with developmental disorder.' *Journal of Developmental and Behavioral Pediatrics*, 19: 321–325.

Chugani, D.C., Sundram, B.S., Behen, M., Lee, M. and Moore, G.J. (1999) 'Evidence of altered energy metabolism in autistic children.' *Progress in Neuro-Psychopharmacology and Biological Psychiatry*, 23: 635–641.

Chugani, H.T., Juhász, C., Behen, M.E., Ondersma, R. and Muzik, O. (2007) 'Autism with facial port-wine stain: a new syndrome?' *Pediatric Neurology*, 37: 192–199.

Chun, H.J., Zheng, L., Ahmad, M., Wang, J. et al. (2002) 'Pleiotropic defects in lymphocyte activation caused by caspase-8 mutations lead to human immunodeficiency.' *Nature*, 419: 395–399.

Chung, J.H. and Eng, C. (2005) 'Nuclear-cytoplasmic partitioning of phosphatase and tensin homologue deleted on chromosome 10 (PTEN) differentially regulates the cell cycle and apoptosis.' *Cancer Research*, 65: 8096–8100.

Ciaccio, M., Piccione, M., Giuffrè, M., Macaione, V. *et al.* (2003) 'Aminoacid profile and oxidative status in children affected by Down syndrome before and after supplementary nutritional treatment.' *Italian Journal of Biochemistry 52*, 2: 72–79.

Ciani, F., Poggi, G.M., Pasquini, E., Donati, M.A. and Zammarchi, E. (2000) 'Prolonged exclusive breast-feeding from vegan mother causing an acute onset of isolated methylmalonicaciduria due to a mild mutase deficiency.' *Clinical Nutrition 19*, 2: 137–139.

Ciara, E., Popowska, E., Piekutowska-Abramczuk, D., Jurkiewicz, D. *et al.* (2006) 'SLOS carrier frequency in Poland as determined by screening for Trp151X and Val326Leu DHCR7 mutations.' *European Journal of Medical Genetics 49*, 6: 499–504.

Cideciyan, A.V., Aleman, T.S., Boye, S.L., Schwartz, S.B. et al. (2008) 'Human gene therapy for RPE65 isomerase deficiency activates the retinoid cycle of vision but with slow rod kinetics.' *Proceedings of the National Academy of Science USA*, 105: 15112–15117.

Claes, L., Del-Favero, J., Ceulemans, B., Lagae, L. *et al.* (2001) 'De novo mutations in the sodium-channel gene SCN1A cause severe myoclonic epilepsy of infancy.' *American Journal of Human Genetics 68*, 6: 1327–1332.

Clarke, D.F., Roberts, W., Daraksan, M., Dupuis, A. *et al.* (2005) 'The prevalence of autistic spectrum disorder in children surveyed in a tertiary care epilepsy clinic.' *Epilepsia*, 46: 1970–1977.

Clark-Taylor, T. and Clark-Taylor, B.E. (2004) 'Is autism a disorder of fatty acid metabolism? Possible dysfunction of mitochondrial beta-oxidation by long chain acyl-CoA dehydrogenase.' *Medical Hypotheses*, 62: 970–975.

Clayton, P.T. (2006) 'B6-responsive disorders: a model of vitamin dependency.' *Journal of Inherited Metabolic Disease 29*, 2–3: 317–326.

Clayton-Smith, J., Watson, P., Ramsden, S. and Black, G.C.M. (2000) 'Somatic mutation in MECP2 as a non-fatal neurodevelopmental disorder in males.' *Lancet 356*, 9232: 830–832.

Cleaver, J.E. (2005) 'Splitting hairs – discovery of a new DNA repair and transcription factor for the human disease trichothiodystrophy.' *DNA Repair*, 4: 285–287.

Cleaver, J.E., Thompson, L.H., Richardson, A.S. and States, J.C. (1999) 'A summary of mutations in the UV-sensitive disorders: xeroderma pigmentosum, Cockayne syndrome, and trichothiodystrophy.' *Human Mutation*, 14: 9–22.

Cleves, M.A., Hobbs, C.A., Cleves, P.A., Tilford, J.M. *et al.* (2007) 'Congenital defects among liveborn infants with Down syndrome.' *Birth Defects Research A Clinical and Molecular Teratology 79*, 9: 657–663.

Coffee, B., Ikeda, M., Budimirovic, D.B., Hjelm, L.N. *et al.* (2008) 'Mosaic FMR1 deletion causes fragile-X syndrome and can lead to molecular misdiagnosis: a case report and review of the literature.' *American Journal of Medical Genetics A, 146A*, 10: 1358–1367.

Coffin, G.S. and Siris, E. (1970) 'Mental retardation with absent fifth fingernail and terminal phalanx.' *American Journal of Diseases of Children*, 119: 433–439.

Coffin, G.S., Siris, E. and Wegienka, L.C. (1966) 'Mental retardation with osteocartilaginous anomalies.' *American Journal of Diseases of Childhood*, 112: 205–213.

Cogulu, O., Aykuta, A., Kutukculera, N., Ozkinayb, C. and Ozkinaya, F. (2007) 'Two cases of macrocephaly and immune deficiency.' *Clinical Dysmorphology*, 16: 81–84.

Cohen, D., Pichard, N., Tordjman, S., Baumann, C. *et al.* (2005) 'Specific genetic disorders and autism: clinical contribution towards their identification.' *Journal of Autism and Developmental Disorders*, 35: 103–116.

Cohen, I.L., Sudhalter, V., Pfadt, A., Jenkins, E.C. *et al.* (1991) 'Why are autism and the fragile-X syndrome associated? Conceptual and methodological issues.' *American Journal of Human Genetics*, 48: 195–202.

Cohen, L.H., Vamos, E., Heinrichs, C., Toppet, M. et al. (1997) 'Growth failure, encephalopathy, and endocrine dysfunctions in two siblings, one with 5-oxoprolinase deficiency.' *European Journal of Pediatrics*, 156: 935–938.

Cohen, M.M. Jr. (1973) 'An etiologic and nosologic overview of craniosynostosis syndromes.' *Birth Defects Original Articles Series XI*, 2: 137–189.

Cohen, M.M. Jr. (1977) 'Genetic perspectives on craniosynostosis and syndromes with craniosynostosis.' *Journal of Neurosurgery*, 47: 886–898.

Cohen, M.M. Jr. (1988) 'Further diagnostic thoughts about the Elephant Man.' *American Journal of Medical Genetics*, 29: 777–782.

Cohen, M.M. Jr. (1990) 'Bannayan-Riley-Ruvalcaba syndrome: renaming three formerly recognized syndromes as one etiologic entity' (letter). *American Journal of Medical Genetics*, 35: 291.

Cohen, M.M. Jr. (2003) 'Mental deficiency, alterations in performance, and CNS abnormalities in overgrowth syndromes.' *American Journal of Medical Genetics C Seminars in Medical Genetics*, 117: 49–56.

Cohen, M.M. Jr. and Kreiborg, S. (1993) 'Visceral anomalies in the Apert syndrome.' *American Journal of Medical Genetics*, 45: 758–760.

Cohen, M.M. Jr. and Kreiborg, S. (1995) 'Hands and feet in the Apert syndrome.' *American Journal of Medical Genetics*, 57: 82–96.

Cohen, M.M. Jr., Hall, B.D., Smith, D.W., Graham, C.B. and Lampert, K.J. (1973) 'A new syndrome with hypotonia, obesity, mental deficiency, and facial, oral, ocular and limb anomalies.' *Journal of Pediatrics*, 83: 280–284.

Cohen, M.M. Jr., Neri, G. and Weksberg, R. (2002) *Overgrowth Syndromes*. Oxford Monographs in Medical Genetics, 43. Oxford: Oxford University Press.

Cole, T.R.P. and Hughes, H.E.(1990) 'Sotos syndrome.' *Journal of Medical Genetics*, 27: 571–576.

Cole, T.R.P. and Hughes, H.E. (1991) 'Autosomal dominant macrocephaly: benign familial macrocephaly or a new syndrome?' *American Journal of Medical Genetics*, 41: 115–124.

Cole, T.R.P. and Hughes, H.E. (1994) 'Sotos syndrome: a study of the diagnostic criteria and natural history.' *Journal of Medical Genetics*, 31: 20–32.

Coleman, M. (1990) 'Is classical Rett syndrome ever present in males?' *Brain and Development*, 12: 31–32.

Coleman, M. (ed.) (2005) *The Neurology of Autism*. Oxford: Oxford University Press.

Coleman, M. and Gillberg, C. (1985) *The Biology of the Autistic Syndromes*. New York: Praeger Publishing.

Coleman, M., Sobel, S., Bhagavan, H.N., Coursin, D. *et al.* (1985) 'A double blind study of vitamin B6 in Down's syndrome infants. Part 1 – Clinical and biochemical results.' *Journal of Mental Deficiency Research*, 29: 233–240.

Collier, D.A. (2008) 'Schizophrenia: the polygene princess and the pea.' *Psychological Medicine*, 38: 1687–1691.

Collis, M.S. (1951) *The Discovery of LS Lowry*. London: Alex Reid and Lefevre.

Comery, T.A., Harris, J.B., Willems, P.J., Oostra, B.A. *et al.* (1997) 'Abnormal dendritic spines in fragile-X knockout mice: maturation and pruning deficits.' *Proceedings of the National Academy of Science USA*, 94: 5401–5404.

Comi, A.M. (2006) 'Advances in Sturge-Weber syndrome.' *Current Opinion in Neurology*, 19: 124–128.

Comi, A.M. (2007) 'Update on Sturge-Weber syndrome: diagnosis, treatment, quantitative measures, and controversies.' *Lymphatic Research and Biology* 5, 4: 257–264.

Comi, A.M., Zimmerman, A.W., Frye, V.H., Law, P.A. and Peeden, J.N. (1999) 'Familial clustering of autoimmune disorders and evaluation of medical risk factors in autism.' *Journal of Child Neurology* 14, 6: 388–394.

Comings, D.E. (1990) *Tourette Syndrome and Human Behavior*. Duarte: Hope Press.

Comings, D.E. and Comings, B.G. (1985) 'Tourette syndrome: clinical and psychological aspects of 250 cases.' *American Journal of Human Genetics*, 37: 435–450.

Comings, D.E. and Comings, B.G. (1991) 'Clinical and genetic relationships between autism–pervasive developmental disorder and Tourette syndrome: a study of 19 cases.' *American Journal of Medical Genetics*, 39: 180–191.

Comings, D.E., Himes, J.A. and Comings, B.G. (1990) 'An epidemiologic study of Tourette's syndrome in a single school district.' *Journal of Clinical Psychiatry* 51, 11: 463–469.

Commission on Classification and Terminology of the International League Against Epilepsy (1989) 'Proposal for revised classification of epilepsies and epileptic syndromes.' *Epilepsia*, 30: 289–299.

Compton, M.T., Celentana, M., Brian Price, B. and Furman, A.C. (2004) 'A case of Sotos syndrome (cerebral gigantism) and psychosis.' *Psychopathology*, 37: 190–194.

Conciatori, M., Stodgell, C.J., Hyman, S.L., O'Bara, M. *et al.* (2004) 'Association between the HOXA1 A218G polymorphism and increased head circumference in patients with autism.' *Biological Psychiatry*, 55: 413–441.

Condon, W.S. and Sander, L.W. (1974) 'Synchrony demonstrated between movements of the neonate and adult speech.' *Child Development*, 45: 456–462.

Conley, C.L., Krevans, J.R., Chow, B.F., Barrows, C. and Lang, C.A. (1951) 'Observations on the absorption, utilization and excretion of vitamin B12.' *Journal of Laboratory and Clinical Medicine*, 38: 84–94.

Connarty, M., Dennis, N.R., Patch, C., Macpherson, J.N. and Harvey, J.F. (1996) 'Molecular re-investigation of patients with Huntington's disease in Wessex reveals a family with dentatorubral and pallidoluysian atrophy.' *Human Genetics*, 97: 76–78.

Connolly, A.M., Chez, M.G., Pestronk, A., Arnold, S.T. *et al.* (1999) 'Serum autoantibodies to brain in Landau-Kleffner variant, autism, and other neurologic disorders.' *The Journal of Pediatrics 134*, 5: 607–613.

Connolly, A.M., Chez, M., Streif, E.M., Keeling, R.M. *et al.* (2006) 'Brain-derived neurotrophic factor and autoantibodies to neural antigens in sera of children with autistic spectrum disorders, Landau-Kleffner syndrome, and epilepsy.' *Biological Psychiatry 59*, 4: 354–363.

Connor, J.M. and Fernandez, C. (1984) 'Genetic aspects of hemifacial microsomia' (letter). *Human Genetics*, 68: 349.

Conte, G. and Gioia, L. (1836) 'Scrofola del sistema muscolare.' *Annali Clinici dell'Ospedale degli Incurabili, Napoli*, 66.

Conway, B.R. (2007) 'Colour vision: mice see hue too.' *Science 17*, 12: R457–R560.

Cook, E.H. Jr., Lindgren, V., Leventhal, B.L., Courchesne, R. *et al.* (1997) 'Autism or atypical autism in maternally but not paternally derived proximal 15q duplication.' *American Journal of Human Genetics 60*, 4: 928–934.

Cook, J.A., Oliver, K., Mueller, R.F. and Sampson, J. (1996) 'A cross-sectional study of renal involvement in tuberous sclerosis.' *Journal of Medical Genetics*, 33: 480–484.

Coppola, G., Capovilla, G., Montagnini, A., Romeo, A. *et al.* (2002) 'Topiramate as add-on drug in severe myoclonic epilepsy in infancy: an Italian multicenter open trial.' *Epilepsy Research 49*, 1: 45–48.

Corbett, B.A., Kantor, A.B., Schulman, H., Walker, W.L. *et al.* (2007) 'A proteomic study of serum from children with autism showing differential expression of apolipoproteins and complement proteins.' *Molecular Psychiatry*, 12: 292–306.

Cornish, K.M., Turk, J., Wilding, J., Sudhalter, V. *et al.* (2004) 'Annotation: Deconstructing the attention deficit in fragile-X syndrome: a developmental neuropsychological approach.' *Journal of Child Psychology and Psychiatry 45*, 6: 1042–1053.

Correia, C., Coutinho, A.M., Diogo, L., Grazina, M. *et al.* (2006) 'Brief report. High frequency of biochemical markers for mitochondrial dysfunction in autism: no association with the mitochondrial aspartate/glutamate carrier SLC25A12 gene.' *Journal of Autism and Developmental Disorders*, 36: 1137–1140.

Cossu, G. and Sampaolesi, M. (2007) 'New therapies for Duchenne muscular dystrophy: challenges, prospects and clinical trials.' *TRENDS in Molecular Medicine 13*, 12: 520–526.

Courchesne, E. (1997) 'Brainstem, cerebellar and limbic neuroanatomical abnormalities in autism.' *Current Opinion in Neurobiology 7*, 2: 269–278.

Cousley, R.R. and Calvert, M.L. (1997) 'Current concepts in the understanding and management of hemifacial microsomia.' *British Journal of Plastic Surgery,* 50: 536–551.

Cowan, R., Hoban, P., Kelsey, A., Birch, J.M. *et al.* (1997) 'The gene for the naevoid basal cell carcinoma syndrome acts as a tumour-suppressor gene in medulloblastoma.' *British Journal of Cancer,* 76: 141–145.

Coward, R.J., Risdon, R.A., Bingham, C., Hattersley, A.T. *et al.* (2001) 'Kidney disease in Hypomelanosis of Ito.', *Nephrology, Dialysis, Transplantation, 16* 6: 1267–1269.

Cox, E.V. and White, A.M. (1962) 'Methylmalonic acid excretion: index of vitamin Bq12 deficiency.' *Lancet 280,* 7261: 853–856.

Cox, G.F. and Kunkel, L.M. (1997) 'Dystrophies and heart disease.' *Current Opinion in Cardiology,* 12: 329–343.

Craig, W.Y., Haddow, J.E., Palomaki, G.E., Kelley, R.I. *et al.* (2006) 'Identifying Smith-Lemli-Opitz syndrome in conjunction with prenatal screening for Down syndrome.' *Prenatal Diagnosis 26,* 9: 842–849.

Craigie, R.J., Ba'ath, M., Fryer, A. and Baillie, C. (2005) 'Surgical implications of the Smith-Lemli-Opitz syndrome.' *Pediatric Surgery International 21,* 6: 482–484.

Creak, E.M. (1963) 'Childhood psychosis: a review of 100 cases.' *British Journal of Psychiatry,* 109: 84–89.

Creange, A., Zeller, J., Rostaing-Rigattieri, S., Brugieres, P. *et al.* (1999) 'Neurological complications of neurofibromatosis type 1 in adulthood.' *Brain 122,* 3: 473–481.

Creel, D., O'Donnell, F.E. Jr. and Witkop, C.J. Jr. (1978) 'Visual system anomalies in human ocular albinos.' *Science,* 201: 931–933.

Cremin, J.D. Jr., Luck, M.L., Laughlin, N.K. and Smith, D.R. (1999) 'Efficacy of succimer chelation for reducing brain lead in a primate model of human lead exposure.' *Toxicology and Applied Pharmacology 161,* 3: 283–293.

Creswell, C.S. and Skuse, D.H. (1999) 'Autism in association with Turner syndrome: Genetic implications for male vulnerability to pervasive developmental disorders.', *Neurocase, 5,* 6: 511–518.

Creswell, C. and Skuse, D. (2000) 'Autism in association with Turner syndrome: implications for male vulnerability.' *Neurocase,* 5: 511–518.

Crino, P.B., Nathanson, K.L. and Henske, E.P. (2006) 'The tuberous sclerosis complex.' *New England Journal of Medicine,* 355: 1345–1356.

Critchley, M. and Earl, C.J.C. (1932) 'Tuberose sclerosis and allied conditions.' *Brain,* 55: 311–346.

Critchley, M. and Hoffman, H.L. (1942) 'The syndrome of periodic somnolence and morbid hunger (Kleine-Levin syndrome).' *British Medical Journal. 137:* 137–139.

Croen, L.A., Goines, P., Braunschweig, D., Yolken, R. *et al.* (2008) 'Brain-derived neurotrophic factor and autism: maternal and infant peripheral blood levels in the Early Markers for Autism (EMA) Study.' *Autism Research 1,* 2: 130–137.

Croen, L.A., Najjar, D.V., Fireman, B. and Grether, J.K. (2007) 'Maternal and paternal age and risk of autism spectrum disorders.' *Archives of Pediatric and Adolescent Medicine,* 161: 334–340.

Croft, J.B. and Swift, M. (1990) 'Obesity, hypertension, and renal disease in relatives of Bardet-Biedl syndrome sibs.' *American Journal of Medical Genetics,* 36: 37–42.

Crow, T.J. (2008) 'The emperors of the schizophrenia polygene have no clothes.' *Psychological Medicine,* 38: 1681–1685.

Crutchfield, S.R., Haas, R.H., Nyhan, W.L. and Gibson, K.M. (2008) 'Succinic semialdehyde dehydrogenase deficiency: phenotype evolution in an adolescent patient at 20-year follow-up.' *Developmental Medicine and Child Neurology 50,* 11: 880–881.

Cuevas-Covarrubias, S.A., Kofman-Alfaro, S., Orozco Orozco, E. and Diaz-Zagoya, J.C. (1995) 'The biochemical identification of carrier state in mothers of sporadic cases of X-linked recessive ichthyosis.' *Genetic Counselling,* 6: 103–107.

Cundiff, D.K. and Harris, W. (2006) 'Case report of 5 siblings: malnutrition? rickets? DiGeorge syndrome? developmental delay?' *Nutrition Journal,* 5: 1, doi: 10.1186/1475-2891-5-1.

Cunniff, C., Kratz, L.E., Moser, A., Natowicz, M.R. and Kelley, R.I. (1997) 'Clinical and biochemical spectrum of patients with RSH/Smith-Lemli-Opitz syndrome and abnormal cholesterol metabolism.' *American Journal of Medical Genetics,* 68: 263–269.

Curatolo, P. (ed.) (2003) *Tuberous Sclerosis Complex: From Basic Science to Clinical Phenotypes.* Cambridge: MacKeith Press.

Curatolo, P., Porfirio, M.C., Manzi, B. and Seri, S. (2004) 'Autism in tuberous sclerosis.' *European Journal of Paediatric Neurology,* 8: 327–332.

Curry, C.J., Stevenson, R.E., Aughton, D., Byrne, J. et al. (1997) 'Evaluation of mental retardation. Recommendations of a consensus conference: American College of Medical Genetics.' *American Journal of Medical Genetics,* 72: 468–477.

Curry, C.J.R., Carey, J.C., Holland, J.S., Chopra, D. *et al.* (1987) 'Smith-Lemli-Opitz syndrome-type II: multiple congenital anomalies with male pseudohermaphroditism and frequent early lethality.' *American Journal of Medical Genetics,* 26: 45–57.

Cusmano-Ozog, K., Manning, M.A. and Hoyme, H.E. (2007) '22q13.3 deletion syndrome: a recognizable malformation syndrome associated with marked speech and language delay.' *American Journal of Medical Genetics C: Seminars in Medical Genetics 145C,* 4: 393–398.

Cyran, S.E., Martinez, R., Daniels, S., Dignan, P.S.J. and Kaplan, S. (1987) 'Spectrum of congenital heart disease in CHARGE association.' *Journal of Pediatrics,* 110: 576–580.

Cyrulnik, S.E., Fee, R.J., De Vivo, D.C., Goldstein, E. and Hinton, V.J. (2007) 'Delayed developmental language milestones in children with Duchenne's muscular dystrophy.' *Journal of Pediatrics 150,* 5: 474–478.

Czyzyk, E., Jozwiak, S., Roszkowski, M. and Schwartz, R.A. (2003) 'Optic pathway gliomas in children with and without neurofibromatosis 1.' *Journal of Child Neurology,* 18: 471–478.

D

Dallaire, L., Mitchell, G., Giguere, R., Lefebvre, F. *et al.* (1995) 'Prenatal diagnosis of Smith-Lemli-Opitz syndrome is possible by measurement of 7-dehydrocholesterol in amniotic fluid.' *Prenatal Diagnosis,* 15: 855–858.

D'Aloia, A., Vizzardi, E., Zanini, G., Antonioli, E. *et al.* (2008) 'Young woman affected by a rare form of familial connective tissue disorder associated with multiple arterial pulmonary stenosis and severe pulmonary hypertension.' *Circulation Journal,* 72: 164–167.

Dalton, P., Deacon, R., Blamire, A., Pike, M. *et al.* (2003) 'Maternal neuronal antibodies associated with autism and a language disorder.' *Annals of Neurology 53,* 4: 533–537.

D'Amelio, M., Ricci, I., Sacco, R., Liu, X. *et al.* (2005) 'Paraoxonase gene variants are associated with autism in North America, but not in Italy: possible regional specificity in gene–environment interactions.' *Molecular Psychiatry,* 10: 1006–1016.

Dan, B. (2008) *Angelman Syndrome: Clinics in Developmental Medicine.* London: MacKeith Press, Wiley-Blackwell.

Danfors, T., von Knorring, A.L., Hartvig, P., Langstrom, B. *et al.* (2005) 'Tetrahydrobiopterin in the treatment of children with autistic disorder: a double-blind placebo-controlled crossover study.' *Journal of Clinical Psychopharmacology 25,* 5: 485–489.

Danks, D.M. (1978) 'Pteridines and phenylketonuria: report of a workshop. Introductory comments.' *Journal of Inherited Metabolic Disease 1,* 2: 47–48.

Danlos, H-A. (1908) 'Un cas de cutis laxa avec tumeurs par contusion chronique des coudes et des genoux (xanthome juvénile pseudo-diabetique de MM Hallopeau et Macé de Lépinay).' *Bulletin de la Societé francaise de dermatologie et de syphiligraphie,* Paris, 19: 70–72.

Darendeliler, F., Larsson, P., Neyzi, O., Price, A.D. *et al.* (2003) 'Growth hormone treatment in Aarskog syndrome: analysis of the KIGS (Pharmacia International Growth Database) data.' *Journal of Pediatric Endocrinology and Metabolism 16,* 8: 1137–1142.

Darras, B.T. and Francke, U. (1988) 'Myopathy in complex glycerol kinase deficiency patients is due to 3' deletions of the dystrophin gene.' *American Journal of Human Genetics,* 43: 126–130.

Datta, A.K., Mandal, S. and Bhattacharya, S. (2009) 'Autism and mental retardation with convulsion in tuberous sclerosis: a case report.' *Cases Journal*, 2: 7061, doi: 10.4076/1757-1626-2-7061.

Daumas-Duport, C., Scheithauer, B.W., Chodkiewicz, J.P., Laws, E.R. Jr. and Vedrenne, C. (1988) 'Dysembryoplastic neuroepithelial tumor: a surgically curable tumor of young patients with intractable partial seizures. Report of thirty-nine cases.' *Neurosurgery*, 23: 545–556.

Dauvilliers, Y., Mayer, G., Lecendreux, M., Neidhart, E. *et al.* (2002) 'Kleine-Levin syndrome: an autoimmune hypothesis based on clinical and genetic analyses.' *Neurology*, 59: 1739–1745.

Davalos, D.B., Merikangas, J. and Bender, S. (2001) 'Psychosis in Hypomelanosis of Ito.' *Journal of the Royal Society of Medicine 94*, 3: 140–141.

Davenport, S.L.H., Hefner, M.A. and Mitchell, J.A. (1986) 'The spectrum of clinical features in CHARGE syndrome.' *Clinical Genetics*, 29: 298–310.

David, O., Fiorucci, G.C., Tosi, M.T., Altare, F. *et al.* (1996) 'Hematological studies in children with Down syndrome.' *Pediatric Hematology and Oncology 13*, 3: 271–275.

Davidson, Z.E. and Truby, H. (2009) 'A review of nutrition in Duchenne muscular dystrophy.' *Journal of Human Nutrition and Dietetics 22*, 5: 383–393.

Davis, S.D., Schaller, J. and Wedgwood, R.J. (1966) 'Job's syndrome: recurrent, "cold", staphylococcal abscesses.' *Lancet 287*, 7445: 1013–1015.

Dawson, G., Munson, J., Webb, S.J., Nalty, T. *et al.* (2007) 'Rate of head growth decelerates and symptoms worsen in the second year of life in autism.' *Biological Psychiatry*, 61: 458–464.

Day, R.E. and Schutt, W.H. (1979) 'Normal children with large heads-benign familial megalencephaly.' *Archives of Disease in Childhood 54*, 7: 512–517.

Dayer, A.G., Bottani, A., Bouchardy, I., Fluss, J. *et al.* (2007) 'MECP2 mutant allele in a boy with Rett syndrome and his unaffected heterozygous mother.' *Brain and Development*, 29: 47–50.

de Almeida, J.C., Reis, D.F. and Martins, R.R. (1989) 'Interstitial deletion of (17) (p11.2:) a microdeletion syndrome. Another example.' *Annals of Genetics*, 32: 184–186.

Deardorff, M.A., Kaur, M., Yaeger, D., Rampuria, A. et al. (2007) 'Mutations in cohesin complex members SMC3 and SMC1A cause a mild variant of Cornelia de Lange syndrome with predominant mental retardation.' *American Journal of Human Genetics*, 80: 485–494.

Deb, S., Braganza, J., Norton, N., Williams, H. *et al.* (2000) 'APOE epsilon 4 influences the manifestation of Alzheimer's disease in adults with Down's syndrome.' *British Journal of Psychiatry*, 176: 468–472.

de Baulny, H.O. and Saudubray, J.M. (2002) 'Branched-chain organic aciduria.' *Seminars in Neonatology*, 7: 65–74.

de Baulny, H.O., Benoist, J.F., Rigal, O., Touati, G. *et al.* (2005) 'Methylmalonic and propionic acidaemias: management and outcome.' *Journal of Inherited Metabolic Disorders*, 28: 415–423.

DeBella, K., Poskitt, K., Szudek, J. and Friedman, J.M. (2000) 'Use of "unidentified bright objects" on MRI for diagnosis of neurofibromatosis 1 in children.' *Neurology*, 54: 1646–1651.

DeBella, K., Szudek, J. and Friedman, J.M. (2000) 'Use of the National Institutes of Health criteria for diagnosis of neurofibromatosis 1 in children.' *Pediatrics*, 105: 608–614.

De Boer, L., Kant, S.G., Karperien, M., Van Beers, L. *et al.* (2004) 'Psychosocial, cognitive, and motor dysfunctioning in patients with suspected Sotos syndrome: a comparison genotype–phenotype correlation in patients suspected of having Sotos syndrome.' *Hormone Research*, 62: 197–207.

De Bona, C., Zapella, M., Hayek, G., Meloni, I. et al. (2000) 'Preserved speech variant is allelic of classic Rett syndrome.' *European Journal of Human Genetics*, 8: 325–330.

De Decker, H.P. and Lawrenson, J.B. (2001) 'The 22q11.2 deletion: from diversity to a single gene theory.' *Genetics in Medicine 3*, 1: 2–5.

De Giacomo, A. and Fombonne, E. (1998) 'Parental recognition of developmental abnormalities in autism.' *European Child and Adolescent Psychiatry 7*, 3: 131–136.

De Hert, M., Steemans, D., Theys, P., Fryns, J.-P. and Peuskens, J. (1996) 'Lujan-Fryns syndrome in the differential diagnosis of schizophrenia.' *American Journal of Medical Genetics*, 67: 212–214.

De Jaco, A., Comoletti, D., King, C.C. and Taylor, P. (2008) 'Trafficking of cholinesterases and neurolignins mutant proteins: an association with autism.' *Chemico-Biological Interactions*, 175: 349–351.

DeJong, G. and Nelson, M.M. (1992) 'Choanal atresia in two unrelated patients with the Coffin-Siris syndrome.' *Clinical Genetics*, 42: 320–322.

Dekaban, A.S. (1969) 'Hereditary syndrome of congenital retinal blindness (Leber), polycystic kidneys and maldevelopment of the brain.' *American Journal of Ophthalmology*, 68: 1029–1037.

de Knecht-van Eekelen, A. and Hennekam, R.C. (1994) 'Historical study: Cornelia C. de Lange (1871–1950) – a pioneer in clinical genetics.' *American Journal of Medical Genetics*, 52: 257–266.

de la Chapelle, A., Herva, R., Koivisto, M. and Aula, P. (1981) 'A deletion in chromosome 22 can cause DiGeorge syndrome.' *Human Genetics*, 57: 253–256.

De-la-Torre, R., Casado, A., Lopez-Fernandez, E., Carrascosa, D. *et al.* (1996) 'Overexpression of copper–zinc superoxide dismutase in trisomy 21.' *Experientia*, 52: 871–873.

de la Tourette, G.A.E.B. (1885) 'Étude sur une affection nerveuse, characterisée par l'incoordination motrice accompagnée de l'écholalie et de coprolalie.' *Archives of Neurology*, 9: 158–200.

Delaunoy, J.P., Dubos, A., Marques Pereira, P. and Hanauer, A. (2006) 'Identification of novel mutations in the RSK2 gene (RPS6KA3) in patients with Coffin-Lowry syndrome.' *Clinical Genetics*, 70: 161–166.

Delabar, J.M., Theophile, D., Rahmani, Z., Chettouh, Z. *et al.* (1993) 'Molecular mapping of twenty-four features of Down syndrome on chromosome 21.', *European Journal of Human Genetics, 1*: 114–124.

Del Campo, M., Antonell, A., Magano, L.F., Munoz, F.J. *et al.* (2006) 'Hemizygosity at the NCF1 gene in patients with Williams-Beuren syndrome decreases their risk of hypertension.' *American Journal of Human Genetics*, 78: 533–542.

Del Campo, M., Jones, M.C., Veraksa, A.N., Curry, C.J. *et al.* (1999) 'Monodactylous limbs and abnormal genitalia are associated with hemizygosity for the human 2q31 region that includes the HOXD cluster.' *American Journal of Human Genetics*, 65: 104–110.

De Leersnyder, H., de Blois, M.-C., Vekemans, M., Sidi, D. *et al.* (2001) 'Beta-1-adrenergic antagonists improve sleep and behavioural disturbances in a circadian disorder, Smith-Magenis syndrome.' *Journal of Medical Genetics*, 38: 586–590.

Delgado-Escueta, A.V. and Bourgeois, B.F. (2008) 'Debate: does genetic information in humans help us treat patients? PRO – genetic information in humans helps us treat patients. CON – genetic information does not help at all.' *Epilepsia 49*, Suppl. 9: 13–24.

DeLong, R. (2007) 'GABA (A) receptor alpha 5 subunit as a candidate gene for autism and bipolar disorder: a proposed endophenotype with parent-of-origin and gain-of-function features, with or without oculocutaneous albinism.' *Autism 11*, 2: 135–147.

Delous, M., Baala, L., Salomon, R., Laclef, C. *et al.* (2007) 'The ciliary gene RPGRIP1L is mutated in cerebello-oculo-renal syndrome (Joubert syndrome type B) and Meckel syndrome.' *Nature Genetics*, 39: 875–881.

del Rosario Barona-Mazuera, M., Hidalgo-Galvan, L.R., de la Luz Orozco-Covarrubias, M., Duran-McKinster, C. *et al.* (1997) 'Proteus syndrome: new findings in seven patients.' *Pediatric Dermatology 14*, 1: 1–5.

De Luca, A., Bottillo, I., Sarkozy, A., Carta, C. *et al.* (2005) 'NF1 gene mutations represent the major molecular event underlying neurofibromatosis-Noonan syndrome.' *American Journal of Human Genetics*, 77: 1092–1101.

Demczuk, S., Levy, A., Aubry, M., Croquette, M.-F. *et al.* (1995) 'Excess of deletions of maternal origin in the DiGeorge/velo-cardio-facial syndromes: a study of 22 new patients and review of the literature.' *Human Genetics*, 96: 9–13.

Dementieva, Y.A., Vance, D.D., Donnelly, S.L., Elston, L.A. *et al.* (2005) 'Accelerated head growth in early development of individuals with autism.' *Pediatric Neurology*, 32: 102–108.

Den Dunnen, J.T., Grootscholten, P.M., Bakker, E., Blonden, L.A. *et al.* (1989) 'Topography of the Duchenne muscular dystrophy (DMD) gene: FIGE and cDNA analysis of 194 cases reveals 115 deletions and 13 duplications.' *American Journal of Human Genetics*, 45: 835–847.

den Hollander, A.I., Roepman, R., Koenekoop, R.K. and Cremers, F.P.M. (2008) 'Leber congenital amaurosis: genes, proteins and disease mechanisms.' *Progress in Retinal and Eye Research*, 27: 391–419.

Dennis, M., Lockyer, L., Lazenby, A.L., Donnelly, R.E. *et al.* (1999) 'Intelligence patterns among children with high-functioning autism, phenylketonuria, and childhood head injury.' *Journal of Autism and Developmental Disorders 29*, 1: 5–17.

Deon, M., Sitta, A., Barschak, A.G., Coelho, D.M. *et al.* (2007) 'Induction of lipid peroxidation and decrease of antioxidant defenses in symptomatic and asymptomatic patients with X-linked adrenoleukodystrophy.' *International Journal of Developmental Neuroscience*, 25: 441–444.

Deonna, T. and Roulet, E. (2006) 'Autistic spectrum disorder: evaluating a possible contributing or causal role of epilepsy.' *Epilepsia 47*, Suppl. 2, 79–82.

Deonna, T. and Ziegler, A.L. (1993) 'Cognitive development and behavior in Joubert syndrome.' *Biological Psychiatry*, 33: 854–855.

De Paepe, A., Devereux, R.B., Dietz, H.C., Hennekam, R.C.M. and Pyeritz, R.E. (1996) 'Revised diagnostic criteria for the Marfan syndrome.' *American Journal of Medical Genetics*, 62: 417–426.

Depienne, C., Héron, D., Betancur, C., Benyahia, B. *et al.* (2007) 'Autism, language delay and mental retardation in a patient with 7q11 duplication.' *Journal of Medical Genetics 44*, 7: 452–458.

Derbent, M., Yilmaz, Z., Baltaci, V., Saygili, A. *et al.* (2003) 'Chromosome 22q11.2 deletion and phenotypic features in 30 patients with conotruncal heart defects.' *American Journal of Medical Genetics,* 116A: 129–135.

Descheemaeker, M.J., Govers, V., Vermeulen, P. and Fryns, J.-P. (2006) 'Pervasive developmental disorders in Prader-Willi syndrome: the Leuven experience in 59 subjects and controls.' *American Journal of Medical Genetics 140*, 11: 1136–1142.

DeScipio, C., Kaur, M., Yaeger, D., Innis, J.W. *et al.* (2005) 'Chromosome rearrangements in Cornelia de Lange syndrome (CdLS): Report of a der(3) t(3;12)(p25.3;p13.3) in two half sibs with features of CdLS and review of reported CdLS cases with chromosome rearrangements.' *American Journal of Medical Genetics A*, 137: A276–282.

DeSilva, S., Drachman, D.B., Mellits, D. and Kuncl, R.W. (1987) 'Prednisone treatment in Duchenne muscular dystrophy: long-term benefit.' *Archives of Neurology*, 44: 818–822.

Devlin, B., Bennett, P., Dawson, G., Figlewicz, D.A. *et al.* (2004) 'Alleles of a Reelin CGG repeat do not convey liability to autism in a sample from the CPEA Network.' *American Journal of Medical Genetics B Neuropsychiatric Genetics*, 126B: 46–50.

Devlin, L.A., Shepherd, C.H., Crawford, H. and Morrison, P.J. (2006) 'Tuberous sclerosis complex: clinical features, diagnosis, and prevalence within Northern Ireland.' *Developmental Medicine and Child Neurology*, 48: 495–499.

de Vries, B.B.A., Robinson, H., Stolte-Dijkstra, I., Tjon Pian Gi, C.V. *et al.* (1995) 'General overgrowth in the fragile-X syndrome: variability in the phenotypic expression of the FMR1 gene mutation.' *Journal of Medical Genetics*, 32: 764–769.

de Vries, P.J., Hunt, A. and Bolton, P.F. (2007) 'The psychopathologies of children and adolescents with tuberous sclerosis complex (TSC): a postal survey of UK families.' *European Child and Adolescent Psychiatry 16*, 1: 16–24.

Devys, D., Lutz, Y., Rouyer, N., Bellocq, J.-P. and Mandel, J.-L. (1993) 'The FMR-1 protein is cytoplasmic, most abundant in neurons and appears normal in carriers of a fragile-X premutation.' *Nature Genetics*, 4: 335–340.

DeWitt, C.A., Bishop, A.B., Buescher, L.S. and Stone, S.P. (2006) 'Hyperimmunoglobulin E syndrome: two cases and a review of the literature.' *Journal of the American Academy of Dermatology*, 54: 855–865.

Dhar, S.U., Scaglia, F., Li, F.-Y., Smith, L. *et al.* (2009) 'Expanded clinical and molecular spectrum of guanidinoacetate methyltransferase (GAMT) deficiency.' *Molecular Genetics and Metabolism*, 96: 38–43.

Dhond, J.-L., Ardouin, P., Hayte, J.-M. and Farriaux J.-P. (1981) 'Developmental aspects of pteridine metabolism and relationships with phenylalanine metabolism.' *Clinica Chimica Acta*, 116: 143–152.

Diano, S. and Horvath, T.L. (2008) 'Anticonvulsant effects of leptin in epilepsy.' *Journal of Clinical Investigation 118*, 1: 26–28.

Dietz, C., Swinkels, S., Van Daalen, E., Van Engeland, H. and Buitelaar, J. (2006) 'Screening for autistic spectrum disorder in children aged 14–15 months, II: population screening with the Early Screening of Autistic Traits Questionnaire (ESAT), design and general findings.' *Journal of Autism and Developental Disorders*, 36: 713–722.

Dietz, H.C. (2007) 'Marfan syndrome: from molecules to medicines.' *American Journal of Human Genetics*, 81: 662–667.

DiGeorge, A.M. (1965) 'Discussions on a new concept of the cellular basis of immunology.' *Journal of Pediatrics*, 67: 907.

Digilio, M.C., Calzolari, F., Capolino, R., Toscano, A. *et al.* (2008) 'Congenital heart defects in patients with oculo-auriculo-vertebral spectrum (Goldenhar syndrome).' *American Journal of Medical Genetics A, 146A*, 14: 1815–1819.

DiMagno, E.P., Lowe, J.E., Snodgrass, P.J. and Jones, J.D. (1986) 'Ornithine transcarbamylase deficiency – a cause of bizarre behavior in a man.' *New England Journal of Medicine*, 315: 744–747.

Dimitropoulos, A. and Schultz, R.T. (2007) 'Autistic-like symptomatology in Prader-Willi syndrome: a review of recent findings. *Current Psychiatry Reports 9*, 2: 159–164.

Ding, Z., Harding, C.O. and Thöny, B. (2004) 'State-of-the-art 2003 on PKU gene therapy.' *Molecular Genetics and Metabolism*, 81: 3–8.

Dion, Y., Annable, L., Sandor, P. and Chouinard, G. (2002) 'Risperidone in the treatment of Tourette syndrome: a double-blind, placebo-controlled trial.' *Journal of Clinical Psychopharmacology*, 22: 31–39.

Dionisi-Vici, C., Deodato, F., Roschinger, W., Rhead, W. and Wilcken, B. (2006) '"Classical" organic acidurias, propionic aciduria, methylmalonic aciduria and isovaleric aciduria: long-term outcome and effects of expanded newborn screening using tandem mass spectrometry.' *Journal of Inherited Metabolic Disease*, 29: 383–389.

Dixit, V.D. and Taub, D.D. (2005) 'Mini review. Ghrelin and immunity: a young player in an old field.' *Experimental Gerontology*, 40: 900–910.

Dixon-Salazar, T., Silhavy, J.L., Marsh, S.E., Louie, C.M. et al. (2004) 'Mutations in the AHI1 gene, encoding jouberin, cause Joubert syndrome with cortical polymicrogyria.' *American Journal of Human Genetics*, 75: 979–987.

Dobson, C.M., Wai, T., Leclerc, D., Kadir, H. *et al.* (2002) 'Identification of the gene responsible for the cblB complementation group of vitamin B12-dependent methylmalonic aciduria.' *Human Molecular Genetics*, 11: 3361–3369.

Doherty, D., Glass, I.A., Siebert, J.R., Strouse, P.J. *et al.* (2005) 'Prenatal diagnosis in pregnancies at risk for Joubert syndrome by ultrasound and MRI.' *Prenatal Diagnosis*, 25: 442–447.

Dolen, G. and Bear, M.F. (2005) 'Courting a cure for fragile-X.' *Neuron*, 45: 642–644.

Dolinoy, D.C., Weidman, J.R. and Jirtle, R.L. (2007) 'Epigenetic gene regulation: linking early developmental environment to adult disease.' *Reproductive Toxicology*, 23: 297–307.

Dolinsky, L.C., de Moura-Neto, R.S. and Falcao-Conceicao, D.N. (2002) 'DGGE analysis as a tool to identify point mutations, *de novo* mutations and carriers of the dystrophin gene.' *Neuromuscular Disorders*, 12: 845–848.

Domes, G., Heinrichs, M., Michel, A., Berger, C. and Herpertz, S.C. (2007) 'Oxytocin improves "mind-reading" in humans.' *Biological Psychiatry 61*, 6: 731–733.

Donnai, D., Read, A.P., McKeown, C. and Andrews, T. (1988) 'Hypomelanosis of Ito: a manifestation of mosaicism or chimerism.' *Journal of Medical Genetics 25*, 12: 809–818.

Donnelly, S.L., Wolpert, C.M., Menold, M.M., Bass, M.P. *et al.* (2000) 'Female with autistic disorder and monosomy X (Turner syndrome): parent-of-origin effect of the X chromosome.' *American Journal of Medical Genetics 96*, 3: 312–316.

Doose, H., Lunau, H., Castiglione, E. and Waltz, S. (1998) 'Severe idiopathic generalized epilepsy of infancy with generalized tonic-clonic seizures.' *Neuropediatrics*, 2: 229–238.

Dosman, C.F., Brian, J.A., Drmic, I.E., Senthilselvan, A. *et al.* (2007) 'Children with autism: effect of iron supplementation on sleep and ferritin.' *Pediatric Neurology*, 36: 152–158.

dos Santos, L.L., Magalhães, M. de C., Januário, J.N., Burle de Aguiar, M.J. and Carvalho, M.R.S. (2006) 'The time has come: a new scene for PKU treatment.' *Genetics and Molecular Research 5*, 1: 33–44.

Down, J.L.H. (1867) 'Observations on an ethnic classification of idiots.' [*London Hospital Clinical Lecture Reports* (1866) 3: 259. [First printed in *The Journal of Mental Science*] 1867. Reproduced in: *Mental Retardation 33* (1995): 54–56.

Down, J.L.H. (1887) *On Some of the Mental Affections of Childhood and Youth.* London: Churchill.

Drappa, J., Vaishnaw, A.K., Sullivan, K.E., Chu, J.-L. and Elkon, K.B. (1996) 'Fas gene mutations in the Canale-Smith syndrome, an inherited lymphoproliferative disorder associated with autoimmunity.' *New England Journal of Medicine*, 335: 1643–1649.

Dravet, C. (1978) 'Les epilepsies graves de l'enfant.' *Vie Medicale au Canada Francais*, 8: 543–548.

Dravet, C., Bureau, M., Guerrini, R., Giraud, N. and Roger, J. (1992) 'Severe Myoclonic Epilepsy in Infants.' In J. Roger, C. Dravet, M. Bureau, F.E. Dreifuss, A. Perret and P. Wolf (eds.) *Epileptic Syndromes in Infancy, Childhood and Adolescence* (2nd edn). London: John Libbey.

Dravet, C., Bureau, M., Oguni, H., Fukuyama, Y. and Cokar, O. (2005) 'Severe Myoclonic Epilepsy in Infancy (Dravet Syndrome).' In:J. Roger, M. Bureau, C. Dravet, P. Genton, C.A. Tassinari and P. Wolf (eds). *Epileptic Syndromes in Infancy, Childhood and Adolescence* (4th edn). London: John Libbey.

Dridi, S.M., Ghomrasseni, S., Bonnet, D., Aggoun, Y. *et al.* (1999) 'Skin elastic fibers in Williams syndrome.' *American Journal of Medical Genetics*, 87: 134–138.

Drogari, E. and Leonard, J.V. (1988) 'Late onset ornithine carbamoyl transferase deficiency in males.' *Archives of Disease in Childhood*, 63: 1363–1367.

Drogari, E., Smith, I., Beasley, M. and Lloyd, J.K. (1987) 'Timing of strict diet in relation to fetal damage in maternal phenylketonuria: an international collaborative study by the MRC/DHSS phenylketonuria register.' *Lancet 330*, 8565: 927–930.

Duboc, D., Meune, C., Pierre, B., Wahbi, K. *et al.* (2007) 'Perindopril preventive treatment on mortality in Duchenne muscular dystrophy: 10 years' follow-up.' *American Heart Journal 154*, 3: 596–602.

Dugoff, L. and Sujansky, E. (1996) 'Neurofibromatosis type 1 and pregnancy.' *American Journal of Medical Genetics*, 66: 7–10.

Dumars, S., Andrews, C., Chan, W.M., Engle, E.C. and Demer, J.L. (2008) 'Magnetic resonance imaging of the endophenotype of a novel familial Möbius-like syndrome.' *Journal of the American Academy of Pediatric Ophthalmology and Strabismus*, 12: 381–389.

Duncan, P.A. and Shapiro, L.R. (1993) 'Interrelationships of the hemifacial microsomia–VATER, VATER, and sirenomelia phenotypes.' *American Journal of Medical Genetics*, 47: 75–84.

Dunlap, G., Robbins, F.R. and Darrow, M.A. (1994) 'Parents' reports of their children's challenging behaviors: results of a statewide survey.' *Mental Retardation 32*, 3: 206–212.

Duran, M., Dorland, L., Meuleman, E.E., Allers, P. and Berger, R. (1997) 'Inherited defects of purine and pyrimidine metabolism: laboratory methods for diagnosis.' *Journal of Inherited Metabolic Disease*, 20: 227–236.

Durelli, L., Mutani, R. and Fassio, F. (1983) 'The treatment of myotonia: evaluation of chronic oral taurine therapy.' *Neurology 33*, 5: 599–603.

Duric, K., Skrablin, S., Lesin, J., Kalafatic, D. *et al.* (2003) 'Second trimester total human chorionic gonadotropin, alpha-fetoprotein and unconjugated estriol in predicting pregnancy complications other than fetal aneuploidy.' *European Journal of Obstetrics, Gynecology and Reproductive Biology 110*, 1: 12–15.

Durkin, M.S., Maenner, M.J., Newschaffer, C.J., Lee, L.-C. et al. (2008) 'Advanced parental age and the risk of autism spectrum disorder.' *American Journal of Epidemiology*, 168: 1268–1276.

Durmowicz, A.G. (2001) 'Pulmonary edema in 6 children with Down syndrome during travel to moderate altitudes.' *Pediatrics*, 108: 443–447.

Dutta, S., Sinha, S., Ghosh, S., Chatterjee, A., Ahmed, S. and Usha, R. (2008) 'Genetic analysis of reelin gene (RELN) SNPs: no association with autism spectrum disorder in the Indian population.' *Neuroscience Letters*, 441: 56–60.

Dykens, E.M. and Volkmar, F.R. (1997) 'Medical Conditions Associated with Autism.' In D.J. Cohen and F.R. Volkmar (eds.) *Handbook of Autism and Pervasive Developmental Disorders*. New York: John Wiley and Sons.

Dykens, E.M., Finucane, B.M. and Gayley, C. (1997) 'Brief report: cognitive and behavioral profiles in persons with Smith-Magenis syndrome.' *Journal of Autism and Developmental Disorders*, 27: 203–210.

Dziobek, I., Gold, S.M., Wolf, O.T. and Convit, A. (2007) 'Hypercholesterolemia in Asperger syndrome: independence from lifestyle, obsessive-compulsive behavior, and social anxiety.' *Psychiatry Research*, 149: 321–324.

E

Ebbesen, F. and Petersen, W. (1982) 'Goldenhar's syndrome: discordance in monozygotic twins and unusual anomalies.' *Acta Paediatrica Scandinavica*, 71: 685–687.

Edelmann, L., Prosnitz, A., Pardo, S., Bhatt, J. *et al.* (2007) 'An atypical deletion of the Williams-Beuren syndrome interval implicates genes associated with defective visuospatial processing and autism.' *Journal of Medical Genetics*, 44: 136–143.

Edery, P., Chabrier, S., Ceballos-Picot, I., Marie, S. *et al.* (2003) 'Intrafamilial variability in the phenotypic expression of adenylosuccinate lyase deficiency: a report on three patients.' *American Journal of Medical Genetics*, 120A: 185–190.

Eerola, I., Boon, L.M., Mulliken, J.B., Burrows, P.E. *et al.* (2003) 'Capillary malformation-arteriovenous malformation, a new clinical and genetic disorder caused by RASA1 mutations.' *American Journal of Human Genetics 73*, 6: 1240–1249.

Egelton, R.D. and Davis, T.P. (2005) 'Development of neuropeptide drugs that cross the blood–brain barrier.' *NeuroRx 2*, 1: 44–53.

Egger, J., Hofacker, N., Schiel, W. and Holthausen, H. (1992) 'Magnesium for hyperventilation in Rett's syndrome.' *Lancet 340*, 8819: 621–622.

Ehlers, E.L. (1901) 'Cutis laxa. Neigung zu Haemorrhagien in der Haut, Lockerung mehrerer Artikulationen.' *Dermatologische Zeitschrift* (Berlin), 8: 173–174.

Ehninger, D., Li, W., Fox, K., Stryker, M.P. and Silva, A.J. (2008) 'Reversing neurodevelopmental disorders in adults.' *Neuron*, 60: 950–960.

Eichler, E.E., Richards, S., Gibbs, R.A. and Nelson, D.L. (1993) 'Fine structure of the human FMR1 gene.' *Human Molecular Genetics 2*, 1: 1147–1153. [Published erratum: *Human Molecular Genetics 3*, 4 (1994): 684–685.]

Eidinow, J. and Edmonds, D. (2002) *Wittgenstein's Poker*. London: Faber & Faber.

Ekström, A.-B., Hakenäs-Plate, L., Samuelsson, L., Tulinius, M. and Wentz, E. (2008) 'Autism spectrum conditions in myotonic dystrophy type 1: a study on 57 individuals with congenital and childhood forms.' *American Journal of Medical Genetics Part B, 147B*, 6: 918–926.

Ekström, A.-B., Hakenäs-Plate, L., Tulinius, M. and Wentz, E. (2009) 'Cognition and adaptive skills in myotonic dystrophy type 1: a study of 55 individuals with congenital and childhood forms.' *Developmental Medicine and Child Neurology*, 51: 982–990

El Hajj, T., Nasreddine, W., Korri, H., Atweh, S. and Beydoun, A. (2009) 'A case of Kleine-Levin syndrome with a complete and sustained response to carbamazepine.' *Epilepsy and Behavior 15*, 3: 391–392.

Elias, E.R., Irons, M.B., Hurley, A.D., Tint, G.S. and Salen, G. (1997) 'Clinical effects of cholesterol supplementation in six patients with the Smith-Lemli-Opitz syndrome (SLOS).' *American Journal of Medical Genetics*, 68: 305–310.

Elias, P.M., Williams, M.L., Holleran, W.M., Jiang, Y.J. and Schmuth, M. (2008) 'Pathogenesis of permeability barrier abnormalities in the ichthyoses: inherited disorders of lipid metabolism.' *Journal of Lipid Research*, 49: 697–714.

Elias, P.M., Williams, M.L., Maloney, M.E., Bonifas, J.A. *et al.* (1984) 'Stratum corneum lipids in disorders of cornification: steroid sulfatase and cholesterol sulfate in normal desquamation and the pathogenesis of recessive X-linked ichthyosis.' *Journal of Clinical Investigation*, 74: 1414–1421.

Ellaway, C., Williams, K., Leonard, H., Higgins, G. *et al.* (1999) 'Rett syndrome: randomized controlled trial of L-carnitine.' *Journal of Child Neurology*, 14: 162–167.

Ellaway, C.J., Peat, J., Williams, K., Leonard, H. and Christodoulou, J. (2001) 'Medium-term open label trial of L-carnitine in Rett syndrome.' *Brain and Development*, 23 (Suppl.1): S85–89.

Elliott, H.R., Samuels, D.C., Eden, J.A., Relton, C.L. and Chinnery, P.F. (2008) 'Pathogenic mitochondrial DNA mutations are common in the general population.' *The American Journal of Human Genetics*, doi:10.1016/j.ajhg.2008.07.004.

Ellis, J.M., Tan, H.K., Gilbert, R.E., Muller, D.P.R. *et al.* (2008) 'Supplementation with antioxidants and folinic acid for children with Down's syndrome: randomised controlled trial.' *British Medical Journal*, 336: 594–597.

Emanuele, E., Lossano, C., Politi, P. and Barale, F. (2007) 'Pioglitazone as a therapeutic agent in autistic spectrum disorder.' *Medical Hypotheses 69*, 3: 699.

Eng, C. (2003) 'PTEN: one gene, many syndromes.' *Human Mutation*, 22: 183–198.

Engel, E. (1993) 'Uniparental disomy revisited: the first twelve years.' *American Journal of Medical Genetics*, 46: 670–674.

Engelhardt, M., Neumann, G., Berbalk, A. and Reuter, I. (1998) 'Creatine supplementation in endurance sports.' *Medicine and Science in Sport and Exercise 30*, 7: 1123–1129.

Enns, G.M., O'Brien, W.E., Kobayashi, K., Shinzawa, H. and Pellegrino, J.E. (2005) 'Postpartum psychosis in mild argininosuccinate synthetase deficiency.' *Obstetrics and Gynecology*, 105: 1244–1246.

Epstein, R.A. (2006) *Overdose: How Excessive Government Regulation Stifles Pharmaceutical Innovation*. New Haven and London: Yale University Press.

Erickson, C.A., Mullett, J.E. and McDougle, C.J. (2009) 'Open-label memantine in fragile-X syndrome.' *Journal of Autism and Developmental Disorders*, 39: 1629–1635.

Erickson, C.A., Stigler, K.A., Corkins, M.R., Posey, D.J. *et al.* (2005) 'Gastrointestinal factors in autistic disorder: a critical review.' *Journal of Autism and Developmental Disorders*, 35: 713–727.

Erlandsen, H. and Stevens, R.C. (2001) 'A structural hypothesis for BH(4) responsiveness in patients with mild forms of hyperphenylalaninaemia and phenylketonuria.' *Journal of Inherited Metabolic Disease*, 24: 213–230.

Erol, I., Alehan, F. and Gümüs, A. (2007) 'West syndrome in an infant with vitamin B12 deficiency in the absence of macrocytic anaemia.' *Developmental Medicine and Child Neurology*, 49: 774–776.

Eronen, M., Peippo, M., Hiippala, A., Raatikka, M. *et al.* (2002) 'Cardiovascular manifestations in 75 patients with Williams syndrome.' *Journal of Medical Genetics*, 39: 554–558.

Escayg, A., Heils, A., MacDonald, B.T., Haug, K. *et al.* (2001) 'A novel SCN1A mutation associated with generalized epilepsy with febrile seizures plus – and prevalence of variants in patients with epilepsy.' *American Journal of Human Genetics*, 68: 866–873.

Esch, B.E. and Carr, J.E. (2004) 'Secretin as a treatment for autism: a review of the evidence.' *Journal of Autism and Developmental Disorders 34*, 5: 543–556.

Evangeliou, A., Vasilaki, K., Karagianni, P. and Nikolai, N. (2009) 'Clinical applications of creatine supplementation on paediatrics.' *Current Pharmaceutical Biotechnology*, 10: 683–690.

Evangeliou, A., Vlachonikolis, I., Mihailidou, H., Spilioti, M. et al. (2003) 'Application of a ketogenic diet in children with autistic behavior: pilot study.' *Journal of Child Neurology*, 18: 113–118.

Evans, D. (2003) *Placebo: The Belief Effect*. London: HarperCollins.

Evans, D.G., Baser, M.E., McGaughran, J., Sharif, S. *et al.* (2002) 'Malignant peripheral nerve sheath tumours in neurofibromatosis 1.' *Journal of Medical Genetics*, 39: 311–314.

Evans, D.G., Birch, J.M. and Orton, C.I. (1991) 'Brain tumours and the occurrence of severe invasive basal cell carcinoma in first-degree relatives with Gorlin syndrome.' *British Journal of Neurosurgery*, 5: 643–646.

Evans, D.G., Ladusans, E.J., Rimmer, S., Burnell, L.D. *et al.* (1993) 'Complications of the naevoid basal cell carcinoma syndrome: results of a population based study.' *Journal of Medical Genetics 30*, 6: 460–464.

Evans, J.C., Archer, H.L., Colley, J.P., Ravn, K. *et al.* (2005) 'Early onset seizures and Rett-like features associated with mutations in CDKL5.' *European Journal of Human Genetics*, 13: 1113–1120.

Evers, L.J.M., Vermaak, M.P., Engelen, J.J.M. and Curfs, L.M.G. (2006) 'The velocardiofacial syndrome in older age: dementia and autistic features.' *Genetic Counselling*, 17: 333–340.

Ewart, A.K., Morris, C.A., Atkinson, D., Jin, W. et al. (1993) 'Hemizygosity at the elastin locus in a developmental disorder, Williams syndrome.' *Nature Genetics*, 5: 11–16.

Exkorn, K.S. (2005) *The Autism Sourcebook: Everything You Need to Know about Diagnosis, Treatment, Coping and Healing*. New York: HarperCollins.

Ezzeldin, H. and Diasio, R. (2004) 'Dihydropyrimidine dehydrogenase deficiency, a pharmacogenetic syndrome associated with potentially life-threatening toxicity following 5-fluorouracil administration.' *Clinical Colorectal Cancer 4*, 3: 181–189.

F

Facher, J.J., Regier, E.J., Jacobs, G.H., Siwik, E. *et al.* (2004) 'Cardiomyopathy in Coffin-Lowry syndrome.' *American Journal of Medical Genetics*, 128A: 176–178.

Fackenthal, J.D., Marsh, D.J., Richardson, A.L., Cummings, S.A. *et al.* (2001) 'Male breast cancer in Cowden syndrome patients with germline PTEN mutations.' *Journal of Medical Genetics*, 38: 159–164.

Falk, M.J., Feiler, H.S., Neilson, D.E., Maxwell, K. *et al.* (2004) 'Cohen syndrome in the Ohio Amish.' *American Journal of Medical Genetics*, 128A: 23–28.

Falk, M.J., Wang, H. and Traboulski, E.I. (2006) 'Cohen Syndrome.' In: *GeneReviews at GeneTests: Medical Genetics Information Resource* [database online]. Copyright, University of Washington, Seattle, 1997–2006. Available at www.genetests.org

Falk, R.E. and Casas, K.A. (2007) 'Chromosome 2q37 deletion: clinical and molecular aspects.' *American Journal of Medical Genetics 145C*, 4: 357–371.

Falls, J.G., Pulford, F.J., Wylie, A.A. and Jirtle, R.L. (1999) 'Review. Genomic imprinting: implications for human disease.' *American Journal of Pathology*, 154: 635–647.

Falter, C.M., Plaisted, K.C. and Davis, G. (2008) 'Male brains, androgen, and the cognitive profile in autism: convergent evidence from 2D: D and congenital adrenal hyperplasia.' *Journal of Autism and Developmental Disorders 38*, 5: 997–998.

Farmer, J.E., Deidrick, K.M., Gitten, J.C., Fennell, E.B. and Maria, B.L. (2006) 'Parenting stress and its relationship to the behavior of children with Joubert syndrome.' *Journal of Child Neurology*, 21: 163–167.

Farzin, F., Perry, H., Hessl, D., Loesch, D. *et al.* (2006) 'Autism spectrum disorders and attention-deficit/hyperactivity disorder in boys with the fragile-X premutation.' *Developmental and Behavioral Pediatrics 27*, 2: S137–S144.

Fatemi, S.H., Folsom, T.D., Reutiman, T.J. and Lee, S. (2008a) 'Expression of astrocytic markers aquaporin 4 and connexin 43 is altered in brains of subjects with autism.' *Synapse 62*, 7: 501–507.

Fatemi, S.H., Folsom, T.D., Reutiman, T.J. and Sidwell, R.W. (2008b) 'Viral regulation of aquaporin 4, connexin 43, microcephalin and nucleolin.' *Schizophrenia Research 98*, 1–3: 163–177.

Fatemi, S.H., Halt, A.R., Stary, J.M., Kanodia, R. *et al.* (2002) 'Glutamic acid decarboxylase 65 and 67 kDa proteins are reduced in autistic parietal and cerebellar cortices.' *Biological Psychiatry*, 52: 805–810.

Fath, M.A., Mullins, R.F., Searby, C., Nishimura, D.Y. *et al.* (2005) 'Mkks-null mice have a phenotype resembling Bardet-Biedl syndrome.' *Human Molecular Genetics 14*, 9: 1109–1118.

Fehlow, P., Bernstein, K., Tennstedt, A. and Walther, F. (1993) ['Early infantile autism and excessive aerophagy with symptomatic megacolon and ileus in a case of Ehlers-Danlos syndrome.'] (Article in German.) *Pädiatrie und Grenzgebiete 31*, 4: 259–267.

Feinstein, C. and Reiss, A.L. (1998) 'Autism: the point of view from fragile-X syndrome.' *Journal of Autism and Developmental Disorders*, 28: 393–405.

Feldman, R. (2007) 'Parent–infant synchrony and the construction of shared timing: physiological precursors, developmental outcomes, and risk conditions.' *Journal of Child Psychology and Psychiatry 48*, 3/4: 329–354.

Felisari, G., Martinelli Boneschi, F., Bardoni, A., Sironi, M. *et al.* (2000) 'Loss of Dp140 dystrophin isoform and intellectual impairment in Duchenne dystrophy.' *Neurology*, 55: 559–564.

Fenichel, G., Pestronk, A., Florence, J., Robison, V. and Hemelt, V. (1997) 'A beneficial effect of oxandrolone in the treatment of Duchenne muscular dystrophy: a pilot study.' *Neurology*, 48: 1225–1226.

Fenichel, G.M., Florence, J.M., Pestronk, A., Mendell, J.R. *et al.* (1991) 'Long-term benefit from prednisone therapy in Duchenne muscular dystrophy.' *Neurology*, 41: 1874–1877.

Fenichel, G.M., Griggs, R.C., Kissel, J., Kramer, T.I. *et al.* (2001) 'A randomized efficacy and safety trial of oxandrolone in the treatment of Duchenne dystrophy.' *Neurology*, 56: 1075–1079.

Ferguson-Smith, M.A. and Yates, J.R. (1984) 'Maternal age specific rates for chromosome aberrations and factors influencing them: report of a collaborative European study on 52, 965 amniocenteses.' *Prenatal Diagnosis*, 4: 5–44.

Ferland, R.J., Eyaid, W., Collura, R.V., Tully, L.D. et al. (2004) 'Abnormal cerebellar development and axonal decussation due to mutations in AHI1 in Joubert syndrome.' *Nature Genetics*, 36: 1008–1013.

Ferlini, A., Sewry, C., Melis, M.A., Mateddu, A. and Muntoni, F. (1999) 'X-linked dilated cardiomyopathy and the dystrophin gene.' *Neuromuscular Disorders*, 9: 339–346.

Fernández, L., Lapunzina, P., Pajares, I.L., Criado, G.R. et al. (2005) 'Higher frequency of uncommon 1.5–2 Mb deletions found in familial cases of 22q11.2 deletion syndrome.' *American Journal of Medical Genetics A*, 136: 71–75.

Fernell, E., Fagerberg, U.L. and Hellstrom, P.M. (2007) 'No evidence for a clear link between active intestinal inflammation and autism based on analyses of faecal calprotectin and rectal nitric oxide.' *Acta Paediatrica 96*, 7: 1076–1079.

Fernell, E., Olsson, V.A., Karlgren-Leitner, C., Norlin, B. *et al.* (1999) 'Autistic disorders in children with CHARGE association.' *Developmental Medicine and Child Neurology*, 41: 270–272.

Fernell, E., Watanabe, Y., Adolfsson, I., Tani, Y. *et al.* (1997) 'Possible effects of tetrahydrobioterin treatment in six children with autism – clinical and positron emission tomography data: a pilot study.' *Developmental Medicine and Child Neurology 39*, 5: 313–318.

Ferner, R.E. (2007) 'Neurofibromatosis 1.' *European Journal of Human Genetics*, 15: 131–138.

Feuk, L., Carson, A.R. and Scherer, S.W. (2006) 'Structural variation in the human genome.' *Nature Reviews: Genetics*, 7: 85–97.

Filipek, P.A., Juranek, J., Nguyen, M.T., Cummings, C. and Gargus, J.J. (2004) 'Relative carnitine deficiency in autism.' *Journal of Autism and Developmental Disorders 34*, 6: 615–623.

Filipek, P.A., Juranek, J., Smith, M., Mays, L.Z. *et al.* (2003) 'Mitochondrial dysfunction in autistic patients with 15q inverted duplication.' *Annals of Neurology*, 53: 801–804.

Fillano, J.J., Goldenthal, M.J., Rhodes, C.H. and Marin-Garcia, J. (2002) 'Mitochondrial dysfunction in patients with hypotonia, epilepsy, autism, and developmental delay: HEADD syndrome.' *Journal of Child Neurology*, 17: 435–439.

Fillion, M., Deal, C. and Van Vliet, G. (2008) 'Retrospective study of the potential benefits and adverse events during growth hormone treatment in children with Prader-Willi syndrome.' *Journal of Pediatrics*, 154: 230–233.

Fine, S.E., Weissman, A., Gerdes, M., Pinto-Martin, J. *et al.* (2005) 'Autism spectrum disorders and symptoms in children with molecularly confirmed 22q11.2 deletion syndrome.' *Journal of Autism and Developmental Disorders 35*, 4: 461–470.

Finegan, J.K., Cole, T.R.P., Kingwell, E., Smith, M.L. *et al.* (1994) 'Language and behavior in children with Sotos syndrome.' *Journal of the American Academy of Child and Adolescent Psychiatry*, 33: 1307–1315.

Finegold, S.M., Molitoris, D., Song, Y. Liu, C. *et al.* (2002) 'Gastrointestinal microflora studies in late-onset autism.' *Clinical Infectious Diseases*, 35 (Suppl. 1): S6–16.

Finsterer, J. (2004) 'Mitochondriopathies.' *European Journal of Neurology 11*, 3: 163–186.

Finsterer, J. and Stollberger, C. (2003) 'The heart in human dystrophinopathies.' *Cardiology*, 99: 1–19.

Fisch, G.S., Cohen, I.L., Wolf, E.G., Brown, W.T. *et al.* (1986) 'Autism and the fragile-X syndrome.' *American Journal of Psychiatry 143*, 1: 71–73.

Fischer, S., Ludecke, H.-J., Wieczorek, D., Bohringer, S. et al. (2006) 'Histone acetylation dependent allelic expression imbalance of BAPX1 in patients with the oculo-auriculo-vertebral spectrum.' *Human Molecular Genetics 15*, 4: 581–587.

Fisher, J.L. (2008) 'The anti-convulsant stiripentol acts directly on the GABAA receptor as a positive allosteric modulator.' *Neuropharmacology 56*, 1: 190–197.

Fisher, S.E. and Scharff, C. (2009) 'FOXP2 as a molecular window into speech and language.' *Trends in Genetics 25*, 4: 166–177.

Fitzgerald, M. (2004) *Artistic Creativity: Is There a Link between Autism in Men and Exceptional Ability?* Hove: Brunner-Routledge.

Fitzgerald, M. (2005) *The Genesis of Artistic Creativity.* London: Jessica Kingsley Publishers.

Fitzpatrick, M. (2008) *Defeating Autism: A Damaging Delusion.* Abingdon: Routledge.

Fitzpatrick, T.B., Szabo, G., Hori, Y., Simone, A.A. *et al.* (1968) 'White leaf-shaped macules.' *Archives of Dermatology*, 98: 1–6.

Flejter, W.L., Bennett-Baker, P.E., Ghaziuddin, M., McDonald, M. *et al.* (1996) 'Cytogenetic and molecular analysis of inv dup(15) chromosomes observed in two patients with autistic disorder and mental retardation.' *American Journal of Medical Genetics*, 61: 182–187.

Flanagan, N., O'Connor, W.J., McCartan, B., Miller, S. *et al.* (1997) 'Developmental enamel defects in tuberous sclerosis: a clinical genetic marker?' *Journal of Medical Genetics*, 34: 637–639.

Flanigan, K.M., von Niederhausern, A., Dunn, D.M., Alder, J. *et al.* (2003) 'Rapid direct sequence analysis of the dystrophin gene.' *American Journal of Human Genetics*, 72: 931–939.

Fleck, B.J., Pandya, A., Vanner, L., Kerkering, K. and Bodurtha, J. (2001) 'Coffin-Siris syndrome: review and presentation of new cases from a questionnaire study.' *American Journal of Medical Genetics*, 99: 1–7.

Fiumara, A., Sciotto, A., Barone, R., D'Asero, G. *et al.* (1999) 'Peripheral lymphocyte subsets and other immune aspects in Rett syndrome.' *Pediatric Neurology*, 21: 619–621.

Fokstuen, S., Vrticka, K., Riegel, M., Da Silva, V. *et al.* (2001) 'Velofacial hypoplasia (Sedlackova syndrome): a variant of velocardiofacial (Shprintzen) syndrome and part of the phenotypical spectrum of del 22q11.2.' *European Journal of Pediatrics*, 160: 54–57.

Folling, A. (1934) 'Ueber Ausscheidung von Phenylbrenztraubensaeure in den Harn als Stoffwechselanomalie in Verbindung mit Imbezillitaet.' *Zeitschrift fur Physiologische Chemie*, 227: 169–176.

Folstein, S. and Rutter, M. (1988) 'Autism: familial aggregation and genetic implications.' *Journal of Autism and Developmental Disorders 18*, 1: 3–30.

Folstein, S.E. and Rosen-Sheidley, B. (2001) 'Genetics of autism: complex aetiology for a heterogeneous disorder.' *Nature Reviews/Genetics*, 2: 943–955.

Fombonne, E. (2005) 'Epidemiology of autistic disorder and other pervasive developmental disorders.' *Journal of Clinical Psychiatry*, 66, Suppl. 10: 3–8.

Fombonne, E., Du Mazaubrun, C., Cans, C. and Grandjean, H. (1997) 'Autism and associated medical disorders in a French epidemiological survey.' *Journal of the American Academy of Child and Adolescent Psychiatry*, 36: 1561–1569.

Fombonne, E., Zakarian, R., Bennett, A., Meng, L. and McLean-Heywood, D. (2006) 'Pervasive developmental disorders in Montreal, Quebec, Canada: prevalence and links with immunizations.' *Pediatrics 118*, 1: e139–150. [Includes disclosure of conflict of interest declaration not in original paper.]

Fon, E.A., Sarrazin, J., Meunier, C., Alarcia, J. *et al.* (2005) 'Adenylosuccinate lyase (ADSL) and infantile autism: absence of previously reported point mutation.' *American Journal of Medical Genetics*, 60: 554–557.

Forest, M.G. (2004) 'Recent advances in the diagnosis and management of congenital adrenal hyperplasia due to 21-hydroxylase deficiency.' *Human Reproduction Update*, 10: 469–485.

Formigari, R., Michielon, G., Digilio, M.C., Piacentini, G. *et al.* (2009) 'Genetic syndromes and congenital heart defects: how is surgical management affected?' *European Journal of Cardio-Thoracic Surgery, 35*: 606–614.

Fossali, E., Signorini, E., Intermite, R.C., Casalini, E. *et al.* (2000) 'Renovascular disease and hypertension in children with neurofibromatosis.' *Pediatric Nephrology*, 14: 806–810.

Fox, J.W., Lamperti, E.D., Eksioglu, Y.Z., Hong, S.E. *et al.* (1998) 'Mutations in filamin 1 prevent migration of cerebral cortical neurons in human periventricular heterotopia.' *Neuron*, 21: 1315–1325.

Franceschini, P., Silengo, M.C., Bianco, R., Biagioli, M. *et al.* (1986) 'The Coffin-Siris syndrome in two siblings.' *Pediatric Radiology*, 16: 330–333.

Francke, U., Harper, J.F., Darras, B.T., Cowan, J.M. et al. (1987) 'Congenital adrenal hypoplasia, myopathy, and glycerol kinase deficiency: molecular genetic evidence for deletions.' *American Journal of Human Genetics*, 40: 212–227.

Francke, U., Ochs, H.D., de Martinville, B., Giacalone, J. *et al.* (1985) 'Minor Xp21 chromosome deletion in a male associated with expression of Duchenne muscular dystrophy, chronic granulomatous disease, retinitis pigmentosa, and McLeod syndrome.' *American Journal of Human Genetics*, 37: 250–267.

Franz, D.N., Leonard, J., Tudor, C., Chuck, G. *et al.* (2006) 'Rapamycin causes regression of astrocytomas in tuberous sclerosis complex.' *Annals of Neurology*, 59: 490–498.

Frauli, M., Neuville, P., Vol, C., Pin, J.-P. and Prezeau, L. (2006) 'Among the twenty classical l-amino acids, only glutamate directly activates metabotropic glutamate receptors.' *Neuropharmacology*, 50: 245–253.

Freeman, A.F., Collura-Burke, C.J., Patronas, N.J., Ilcus, L.S. *et al.* (2007) 'Brain abnormalities in patients with hyperimmunoglobulin E syndrome.' *Pediatrics*, online, April 16, doi:10.1542/peds.2006-2649.

Freiberg, R.A., Choate, K.A., Deng, H., Alperin, E.S. *et al.* (1997) 'A model of corrective gene transfer in X-linked ichthyosis.' *Human Molecular Genetics*, 6: 927–933.

Freitag, C.M. (2007) 'The genetics of autistic disorders and its clinical relevance: a review of the literature.' *Molecular Psychiatry*, 12: 2–22.

Fridman, C., Varela, M.C., Kok, F., Diament, A. and Koiffmann, C.P. (2000) 'Paternal UPD15: further genetic and clinical studies in four Angelman syndrome patients.' *American Journal of Medical Genetics*, 92: 322–327.

Friedman, J.M. (1999) 'Vascular and Endocrine Abnormalities.' In J.M. Friedman, D.H. Gutmann, M. MacCollin and V.M. Riccardi (eds.) *Neurofibromatosis: Phenotype, Natural History, and Pathogenesis*. Baltimore: Johns Hopkins University Press.

Friedman, J.M. (2007) 'Neurofibromatosis 1.' Online review in GeneReviews, accessible at www.ncbi.nlm.nih.gov.

Friedman, J.M. and Birch, P.H. (1997) 'Type 1 neurofibromatosis: a descriptive analysis of the disorder in 1,728 patients.' *American Journal of Medical Genetics*, 70: 138–143.

Friedman, J.M., Arbiser, J., Epstein, J.A., Gutmann, D.H. *et al.* (2002) 'Cardiovascular disease in neurofibromatosis 1: report of the NF1 Cardiovascular Task Force.' *Genetics in Medicine 4*, 3: 105–111.

Frints, S.G., Froyen, G., Marynen, P., Willekens, D. et al. (2002) 'Re-evaluation of MRX36 family after discovery of an ARX gene mutation reveals mild neurological features of Partington syndrome.' *American Journal of Medical Genetics*, 112: 427–428.

Fritschy, J.M. (2008) 'Epilepsy, E/I balance and GABA(A) receptor plasticity.' *Frontiers in Molecular Neuroscience*, 1: 5.

Fritz, B., Kuster, W., Orstavik, K.H., Naumova, A., Spranger, J. and Rehder, H. (1998) 'Pigmentary mosaicism in Hypomelanosis of Ito: further evidence for functional disomy of Xp.' *Human Genetics 103*, 4: 441–449.

Froster, U.G. and Gortner, L. (1993) 'Thrombocytopenia in the Brachmann-de Lange syndrome.' *American Journal of Medical Genetics*, 46: 730–731.

Fryburg, J.S., Breg, W.R. and Lindgren, V. (1991) 'Diagnosis of Angelman syndrome in infants.' *American Journal of Medical Genetics*, 38: 58–64.

Fryburg, J.S., Lin, K.Y. and Golden, W.L. (1996) 'Chromosome 22q11.2 deletion in a boy with Opitz (G/BBB) syndrome.', *American Journal of Medical Genetics, 62*: 274–275.

Fryns, J.-P. (1986) 'On the nosology of the Cornelia de Lange and Coffin-Siris syndromes' (letter). *Clinical Genetics*, 29: 263–264.

Fryns, J.-P. (1992) 'Aarskog syndrome: the changing phenotype with age.' *American Journal of Genetics*, 43: 420–427.

Fryns, J.-P., Borghgraef, M., Brown, T.W., Chelly, J. *et al.* (2000) '9th International Workshop on fragile-X syndrome and X-linked mental retardation.' *American Journal of Medical Genetics*, 94: 345–360.

Fryns, J.-P., Kleczkowska, A., Kubien, E. and Van den Berghe, H. (1995) 'XYY syndrome and other Y chromosome polysomies: mental status and psychosocial functioning.' *Genetic Counselling*, 6: 197–206.

Fryns, J.-P., Lemaire, J., Timmermans, J., Soekarman, D. and van den Berghe, H. (1993) 'The association of hemifacial microsomia, homolateral micro/anophthalmos, hemihypotrophy, dental anomalies, submucous cleft palate, CNS malformations and hypopigmented skin lesions following Blaschko's lines in two unrelated female patients: further evidence for a lethal mutation surviving in mosaic form in "Hypomelanosis of Ito".' *Genetic Counselling*, 4: 63–67.

Fryns, J.-P., Moerman, F., Goddeeris, P., Bossuyt, C. and Van den Berghe, H. (1979) 'A new lethal syndrome with cloudy cornea, diaphragmatic defects and distal limb deformities.' *Human Genetics*, 50: 65–70.

Fryns, J.-P. and Vinken, L. (1994) 'Thrombocytopenia in the Brachmann-de Lange syndrome.' *American Journal of Medical Genetics*, 49: 360.

Fuhrmann-Rieger, A., Kohler, A. and Fuhrmann, W. (1984) 'Duplication or insertion in 15q11–13 associated with mental retardation–short stature and obesity – Prader-Willi or Cohen syndrome?' *Clinical Genetics*, 25: 347–352.

Fujiwara, T. (2006) 'Clinical spectrum of mutations in SCN1A gene: severe myoclonic epilepsy in infancy and related epilepsies.' *Epilepsy Research*, 70S: S223–S230.

Fujiwara, T., Nakamura, H., Watanabe, M., Yagi, K. *et al.* (1990) 'Clinicoelectrographic concordance between monozygotic twins with severe myoclonic epilepsy in infancy.' *Epilepsia*, 31: 281–286.

Fukazawa, R., Nakahori, Y., Kogo, T., Kawakami, T. *et al.* (1992) 'Normal Y sequences in Smith-Lemli-Opitz syndrome with total failure of masculinization.' *Acta Paediatrica*, 81: 570–572.

Fukuma, G., Oguni, H., Shirasaka, Y., Watanabe, K. *et al.* (2004) 'Mutations of neuronal voltage-gated Na+ channel 1 subunit gene SCN1A in core severe myoclonic epilepsy in infancy (SMEI) and in borderline SMEI(SMEB).' *Epilepsia*, 45: 140–148.

Fukushima, Y., Ohashi, H., Wakui, K., Nishida, T. *et al.* (1992) 'DiGeorge syndrome with del(4)(q21.3q25): possibility of the fourth chromosome region responsible for DiGeorge syndrome' (abstract). *American Journal of Human Genetics*, 51 (Suppl.) A80.

G

Gabis, L., Pomeroy, J. and Andriola, M.R. (2005) 'Autism and epilepsy: cause, consequence, comorbidity, or coincidence?' *Epilepsy and Behavior*, 7: 652–656.

Gagliardi, C., Martelli, S., Burt, M.D. and Borgatti, R. (2007) 'Evolution of neurologic features in Williams syndrome.' *Pediatric Neurology*, 36: 301–306.

Gaily, E., Jonsson, H. and Lappi, M. (2009) 'Visual fields at school-age in children treated with vigabatrin in infancy.' *Epilepsia 50*, 2: 206–216.

Galli-Carminati, G., Chauvet, I. and Deriaz, N. (2006) 'Prevalence of gastrointestinal disorders in adult clients with pervasive developmental disorders.' *Journal of Intellectual Disability Research 50*, 10: 711–718.

Galvagni, F., Saad, F.A., Danieli, G.A., Miorin, M. *et al.* (1994) 'A study on duplications of the dystrophin gene: evidence of a geographical difference in the distribution of breakpoints by intron.' *Human Genetics*, 94: 83–87.

Galván-Manso, M., Campistol, J., Conill, J. and Sanmartí, F.X. (2005) 'Analysis of the characteristics of epilepsy in 37 patients with the molecular diagnosis of Angelman syndrome.' *Epileptic Disorders*, 7: 19–25.

Ganesan, V., Johnson, A., Connelly, A., Eckhardt, S. and Surtees, R.A. (1997) 'Guanidinoacetate methyltransferase deficiency: new clinical features.' *Pediatric Neurology*, 17: 155–157.

Gantois, I. and Kooy, R.F. (2002) 'Targeting fragile-X.' *Genome Biology 3*, 5: 1–5.

Garber, K., Smith, K.T., Reines, D. and Warren, S.T. (2006) 'Transcription, translation and fragile-X syndrome.' *Current Opinion in Genetics and Development*, 16: 270–275.

Garces, M.E., Perez, W. and Salvador, M. (2005) 'Oxidative stress and hematologic and biochemical parameters in individuals with Down syndrome.' *Mayo Clinic Proceedings 80*, 12: 1607–1611.

Garcia-Cruz, D., Figuera, L.E., Feria-Velazco, A., Sanchez-Corona, J. *et al.* (1993) 'The Myhre syndrome: report of two cases.' *Clinical Genetics*, 44: 203–207.

Gargus, J.J. (2009) 'Genetic calcium signaling abnormalities in the central nervous system: seizures, migraine and autism.' *Annals of the New York Academy of Science*, 1151: 133–156.

Garrod, A. (1909) *Inborn Errors of Metabolism.* The Croonian lectures delivered before the Royal College of Physicians of London in June 1908. London: Oxford University Press.

Garrod, A.E. (1902) 'The incidence of alkaptonuria, a study in chemical individuality.' *Lancet 160*, 4137: 1616–1620.

Garrod, A.E. (1931) *Inborn Factors in Disease.* Oxford: Oxford University Press.

Garstang, J. and Wallis, M. (2006) 'Randomized controlled trial of melatonin for children with autistic spectrum disorders and sleep problems.' *Child: Care, Health and Development 32*, 5: 585–589.

Garty, B.Z., Laor, A. and Danon, Y.L. (1994) 'Neurofibromatosis type 1 in Israel: survey of young adults.' *Journal of Medical Genetics*, 31: 853–857.

Gasparini, F., Lingenhöhl, K., Stoehr, N., Flor, P.J. et al. (1999) '2-methyl-6-(phenylethynyl)-pyridine (MPEP), a potent, selective and systemically active mGlu5 receptor antagonist.' *Neuropharmacology*, 38: 1493–1503.

Gauthier, J., Bonnel, A., St-Onge, J., Karemera, L. *et al.* (2005) 'NLGN3/NLGN4 gene mutations are not responsible for autism in the Quebec population.' *American Journal of Medical Genetics B: Neuropsychiatric Genetics 132B*, 1: 74–75.

Gecz, J., Cloosterman, D. and Partington, M. (2006) 'ARX: a gene for all seasons.' *Current Opinion in Genetics and Development*, 16: 308–316.

Geerts, M., Steyaert, J. and Fryns, J.-P. (2003) 'The XYY syndrome: a follow-up study on 38 boys.' *Genetic Counselling*, 14: 267–279.

Gennery, A.R., Flood, T.J., Abinun, M. and Cant, A.J. (2000) 'Bone marrow transplantation does not correct the hyper IgE syndrome.' *Bone Marrow Transplant 25*, 12: 1303–1305.

Gentile, M., Di Carlo, A., Susca, F., Gambotto, A. *et al.* (1996) 'COACH syndrome: report of two brothers with congenital hepatic fibrosis, cerebellar vermis hypoplasia, oligophrenia, ataxia, and mental retardation.' *American Journal of Medical Genetics*, 64: 514–520.

Genton, P., Semah, F. and Trinka, E. (2006) 'Valproic acid in epilepsy: pregnancy-related issues.' *Drug Safety 29*, 1: 1–21.

Gerevini, V.D., Di Caruso, A., Cappuccio, I., Vitiani, L.R. *et al.* (2004) 'The mGlu5 metabotropic glutamate receptor is expressed in zones of active neurogenesis of the embryonic and postnatal brain.' *Developmental Brain Research*, 150: 17–22.

Gerlai, J. and Gerlai, R. (2003) 'Autism: a large unmet medical need and a complex research problem.' *Physiology and Behavior*, 79: 461–470.

Geschwind, D.H. and Levitt, P. (2007) 'Autism spectrum disorders: developmental disconnection syndromes.' *Current Opinion in Neurobiology*, 17: 103–111.

Geschwind, N. and Galaburda, A.M. (1985a) 'Cerebral lateralisation: biological mechanisms, associations and pathology. I: A hypothesis and program for research.' *Archives of Neurology 42*, 5: 428–459.

Geschwind, N. and Galaburda, A.M. (1985b) 'Cerebral lateralisation: biological mechanisms, associations and pathology. II: A hypothesis and program for research.' *Archives of Neurology 42*, 6: 521–552.

Geschwind, N. and Galaburda, A.M. (1985c) 'Cerebral lateralisation: biological mechanisms, associations and pathology. III: A hypothesis and a program for research.' *Archives of Neurology*, 42: 634–654.

Geubel, A.P., De Galocsy, C., Alves, N., Rahier, J. and Dive, C. (1991) 'Liver damage caused by therapeutic vitamin A administration: estimate of dose-related toxicity in 41 cases.' *Gastroenterology 100*, 6: 1701–1709.

Ghaziuddin, M. (1997) 'Autism in Down's syndrome: family history correlates.' *Journal of Intellectual Disability Research 41*, 1: 87–91.

Ghaziuddin, M. (2000) 'Autism in Down's syndrome: a family history study.' *Journal of Intellectual Disability Research 44*, 5: 562–566.

Ghaziuddin, M., Bolyard, B. and Alessi, N. (1994) 'Autistic disorder in Noonan syndrome.' *Journal of Intellectual Disability Research*, 38: 67–72.

Ghaziuddin, M., Tsai, L.Y. and Ghaziuddin, N. (1992) 'Autism in Down's syndrome: presentation and diagnosis.' *Journal of Intellectual Disability Research*, 36: 449–456.

Giannotti, A., Digilio, M.C., Marino, B., Mingarelli, R. and Dallapiccola, B. (1994) 'Cayler cardiofacial syndrome and del 22q11: part of the CATCH22 phenotype.' *American Journal of Medical Genetics*, 53: 303–304.

Giannotti, A., Tiberio, G., Castro, M., Virgilii, F., Colistro, F. *et al.* (2001) 'Coeliac disease in Williams syndrome.' *Journal of Medical Genetics*, 38: 767–768.

Gibbs, M.V. and Thorpe, J.G. (1983) 'Personality stereotype of noninstitutinalized Down syndrome children.' *American Journal of Mental Deficiency* 87, 6: 601–605.

Gibson, G. and Muse, S.V. (2004) *A Primer of Genome Science* (2nd edn.) Massachusetts: Sinauer Associates Ltd.

Gibson, K.M., Burlingame, T.G., Hogema, B., Jakobs, C. *et al.* (2000) '2-methylbutyryl-coenzyme A dehydrogenase deficiency: a new inborn error of L-isoleucine metabolism.' *Pediatric Research 47*, 6: 830–833.

Gibson, K.M., Christensen, E., Jakobs, C., Fowler, B. *et al.* (1997a) 'The clinical phenotype of succinic semialdehyde dehydrogenase deficiency (4-hydroxybutyric aciduria): case reports of 23 new patients.' *Pediatrics*, 99: 567–574.

Gibson, K.M., Doskey, A.E., Rabier, D., Jakobs, C. and Morlat, C. (1997b) 'Differing clinical presentation of succinic semialdehyde dehydrogenase deficiency in adolescent siblings from Lifu Island, New Caledonia.' *Journal of Inherited Metabolic Disease*, 20: 370–374.

Gibson, K.M., Jansen, I., Sweetman, L., Nyhan, W.L. *et al.* (1984) '4-hydroxybutyric aciduria: a new inborn error of metabolism. III: Enzymology and inheritance.' *Journal of Inherited Metabolic Disorders*, 7 (Suppl. 1): 95–96.

Gibson, K.M., Sacks, M., Kiss, D, Pohowalla, P. *et al.* (1999) '2-methylbutyrylglycinuria in a neonate with CNS dysfunction: evidence for isolated 2-methylbutyryl-CoA dehydrogenase deficiency, and inborn error of L-isoleucine metabolism.' *Journal of Inherited Metabolic Disease*, 22 (Suppl. 1): 16.

Giglia-Mari, G., Coin, F., Ranish, J.A., Hoogstraten, D. *et al.* (2004) 'A new, tenth subunit of TFIIH is responsible for the DNA repair syndrome trichothiodystrophy group A.' *Nature Genetics*, 36: 714–719.

Gilbert, D.L. (2007) 'Regarding "Omega-3 fatty acids supplementation in children with autism: a double-blind randomized, placebo-controlled pilot study".' *Biological Psychiatry*, e-print, doi:10.1016/j.biopsych.2007.03.028.

Gillberg, C. (1983) 'Identical triplets with infantile autism and the fragile-X syndrome.' *British Journal of Psychiatry*, 143: 256–260.

Gillberg, C. (1992) 'Subgroups in autism: are there behavioural phenotypes typical of underlying medical conditions?' *Journal of Intellectual Disability Research 36*, 3: 201–214.

Gillberg, C. and Billstedt, E. (2000) 'Autism and Asperger syndrome: coexistence with other clinical disorders.' *Acta Psychiatrica Scandinavica*, 102: 321–330.

Gillberg, C. and Coleman, M. (1996) 'Autism and medical disorders: a review of the literature.' *Developmental Medicine and Child Neurology*, 38: 191–202.

Gillberg, C. and Rasmussen, P. (1994) 'Brief report: four case histories and a literature review of Williams syndrome and autistic behaviour.' *Journal of Autism and Developmental Disorders 24*, 3: 381–393.

Gillberg, C. and Steffenburg, S. (1989) 'Autistic behaviour in Moebius syndrome.' *Acta Paediatrica Scandinavica*, 78: 314–316.

Gillberg, C. and Wahlstrom, J. (1985) 'Chromosome abnormalities in infantile autism and other childhood psychoses: a population study of 66 cases.' *Developmental Medicine and Child Neurology*, 27: 293–304.

Gillberg, C. and Winnergard, I. (1984) 'Childhood psychosis in a case of Moebius syndrome.' *Neuropediatrics 15*, 3: 147–149.

Gillberg, C., Winnergard, I. and Wahlstrom, J. (1984) 'The sex chromosomes – one key to autism? An XYY case of infantile autism.' *Applied Research in Mental Retardation*, 5: 353–360.

Gillberg, I.C., Gillberg, C. and Ahlsen, G. (1994) 'Autistic behaviour and attention deficits in tuberous sclerosis: a population-based study.' *Developmental Medicine and Child Neurology 36*, 1: 50–56.

Gillberg, I.C., Gillberg, C. and Kopp, S. (1992) 'Hypothyroidism and autism spectrum disorders.' *Journal of Child Psychology and Psychiatry*, 33: 531–542.

Gillessen-Kaesbach, G., Demuth, S., Thiele, H., Theile, U. *et al.* (1999) 'A previously unrecognised phenotype characterised by obesity, muscular hypotonia, and ability to speak in patients with Angelman syndrome caused by an imprinting defect.' *European Journal of Human Genetics*, 7: 638–644.

Gillis, L.A., McCallum, J., Kaur, M., DeScipio, C. et al. (2004) 'NIPBL mutational analysis in 120 individuals with Cornelia de Lange syndrome and evaluation of genotype–phenotype correlations.' *American Journal of Human Genetics*, 75: 610–623.

Gillott, A., Furniss, F. and Walter, A. (2001) 'Anxiety in high-functioning children with autism.' *Autism 5*, 3: 277–286.

Gimpl, G., Wiegand, V., Burger, K. and Fahrenholz, F. (2002) 'Cholesterol and steroid hormones: modulators of oxytocin receptor function.' *Progress in Brain Research*, 139: 43–55.

Gingell, K., Parmar, R. and Sungum-Paliwal, S. (1996) 'Autism and multiple pituitary deficiency. '*Developmental Medicine and Child Neurology*, 38: 545–549.

Girirajan, S., Elsas, L.J. II, Devriendt, K. and Elsea, S.H. (2005) 'RAI1 variations in Smith-Magenis syndrome patients without 17p11.2 deletions.' *Journal of Medical Genetics*, 42: 820–828.

Giunco, C.T., Moretti-Ferreira, D., Silva, A.E., Rocha, S.S. and Fett-Conte, A.C. (2008) 'MOMO syndrome associated with autism: a case report.' *Genetic and Molecular Research 7*, 4: 1223–1225.

Glaser, R.L., Broman, K.W., Schulman, R.L., Eskenazi, B. *et al.* (2003) 'The paternal-age effect in Apert syndrome is due, in part, to the increased frequency of mutations in sperm.' *American Journal of Human Genetics*, 73: 939–947.

Glaser, R.L., Jiang, W., Boyadjiev, S.A., Tran, A.K. *et al.* (2000) 'Paternal origin of FGFR2 mutations in sporadic cases of Crouzon syndrome and Pfeiffer syndrome.' *American Journal of Human Genetics*, 66: 768–777.

Glasson, E.J., Bower, C., Petterson, B., de Klerk, N. *et al.* (2004) 'Perinatal factors and the development of autism: a population study.' *Archives of General Psychiatry*, 61: 618–627.

Glaze, D.G. (2002) 'Neurophysiology of Rett syndrome.' *Mental Retardation and Developmental Disability Research Reviews 8*, 2: 66–71.

Gleeson, J.G., Keeler, L.C., Parisi, M.A., Marsh, S.E. *et al.* (2004) 'Molar tooth sign of the midbrain–hindbrain junction: occurrence in multiple distinct syndromes.' *American Journal of Medical Genetics A*, 125: 125–134.

Glover, M.T., Brett, E.M. and Atherton, D.J. (1989) 'Hypomelanosis of Ito: spectrum of the disease.' *Journal of Pediatrics 115*, 1: 75–80.

Godel, V., Regenbogen, L., Goya, V. and Goodman, R.M. (1982) 'Autosomal dominant Goldenhar syndrome.' *Birth Defects Original Articles Series 18*, 6: 621–628.

Goffin, A., Hoefsloot, L.H., Bosgoed, E., Swillen, A. and Fryns, J.-P. (2001) 'PTEN mutation in a family with Cowden syndrome and autism.' *American Journal of Medical Genetics*, 105: 521–524.

Gofflot, F., Hars, C., Illien, F., Chevy, F. *et al.* (2003) 'Molecular mechanisms underlying limb anomalies associated with cholesterol deficiency during gestation: implications of hedgehog signaling.' *Human Molecular Genetics 12*, 10: 1187–1198.

Goh, Y.I., Bollano, E., Einarson, T.R. and Koren, G. (2006) 'Prenatal multivitamin supplementation and rates of congenital anomalies: a meta-analysis.' *Journal of Obstetrics and Gynaecology Canada 28*, 8: 680–689.

Gohlke, B.C., Haug, K., Fukami, M., Friedl, W. *et al.* (2000) 'Interstitial deletion in Xp22.3 is associated with X linked ichthyosis, mental retardation, and epilepsy.' *Journal of Medical Genetics*, 37: 600–602.

Goin-Kochel, R.P., Myers, B.J. and Mackintosh, V.H. (2007) 'Parental reports on the use of treatments and therapies for children with autism spectrum disorders.' *Research in Autism Spectrum Disorders 11*, 1: 195–209.

Goizet, C., Excoffier, E., Taine, L., Taupiac, E. *et al.* (2000) 'Case with autistic syndrome and chromosome 22q13.3 deletion detected by FISH.' *American Journal of Medical Genetics*, 96: 839–844.

Gokcay, G., Baykal, T., Gokdemir, Y. and Demirkol, M. (2006) 'Breast-feeding in organic acidaemias.' *Journal of Inherited Metabolic Disease*, 29: 304–310.

Goldacre, B. (2009) *Bad Science.* London: Fourth Estate.

Goldberg-Stern, H., Strawsburg, R.H., Patterson, B., Hickey, F. *et al.* (2001) 'Seizure frequency and characteristics in children with Down syndrome.' *Brain and Development*, 23: 375–378.

Golden, G.S. (1984) 'Controversies in therapies for children with Down syndrome.' *Pediatrics in Review*, 6: 116–120.

Goldenberg, A., Wolf, C., Chevy, F., Benachi, A. *et al.* (2004) 'Antenatal manifestations of Smith-Lemli-Opitz (RSH) syndrome: a retrospective survey of 30 cases.' *American Journal of Medical Genetics*, 124A: 423–426.

Goldenberg, J.N., Brown, S.B. and Weiner, W.J. (1994) 'Coprolalia in younger patients with Gilles de la Tourette syndrome.' *Movement Disorders 9*, 6: 622–625.

Goldenhar, M. (1952) 'Associations malformatives de l'oeil et de l'oreille: en particulier, le syndrome: dermoide epibulbaire-appendices auriculaires-fistula auris congenita et ses relations avec la dysostose mandibulo-faciale.' *Journal de Genetique Humaine*, 1: 243–282.

Goldstone, A.P. and Beales, P.L. (2008) 'Genetic obesity syndromes.' *Frontiers in Hormone Research*, 36: 37–60.

Gomez, L., Le Deist, F., Blanche, S., Cavazzana-Calvo, M. *et al.* (1995) 'Treatment of Omenn syndrome by bone marrow transplantation.' *Journal of Pediatrics*, 127: 76–81.

Gomez-Lado, C., Eiris-Punal, J., Blanco-Barca, O., del Rio-Latorre, E. *et al.* (2004) 'Hipomelanosis de Ito. Un sindrome neurocutaneo heterogeneo y posiblemente infradiagnosticado.' [Article in Spanish: 'Hypomelanosis of Ito. A possibly under-diagnosed heterogeneous neurocutaneous syndrome.'] *Revista de Neurologia 38*, 3: 223–228.

Gong, X., Jia, M., Ruan, Y., Shuang, M. et al. (2004) 'Association between the FOXP2 gene and autistic disorder in Chinese population.' *American Journal of Medical Genetics B: Neuropsychiatric Genetics*, 127: 113–116.

Goncalves, M.A.F.V., Holkers, M., van Nierop, G.P., Wieringa, R. *et al.* (2008) 'Human genome by a fiber-modified high-capacity adenovirus-based vector system.' *PLoS ONE 3*, 8: e3084, doi:10.1371/journal.pone.0003084.

Gonzalez, F.J. and Fernandez-Salguero, P. (1995) 'Diagnostic analysis, clinical importance and molecular basis of dihydropyrimidine dehydrogenase deficiency.' *Trends in Pharmacological Science*, 16: 325–327.

Goodey, C.F. (2006) 'Behavioural phenotypes in disability research: historical perspectives.' *Journal of Intellectual Disability Research 50*, 6: 397–403.

Goodlin-Jones, B.L., Tassone, F., Gane, L.W. and Hagerman, R.J. (2004) 'Autistic spectrum disorder and the fragile-X premutation.' *Journal of Developmental and Behavioral Pediatrics*, 25: 392–398.

Goodship, J., Cross, I., LiLing, J. and Wren, C. (1998) 'A population study of chromosome 22q11 deletions in infancy.' *Archives of Disease in Childhood*, 79: 348–351.

Gorden, N.T., Arts, H.H., Parisi, M.A., Coene, K.L.M. *et al.* (2008) 'CC2D2A is mutated in Joubert syndrome and interacts with the ciliopathy-associated basal body protein CEP290.' *American Journal of Human Genetics 83*, 5: 559–571.

Gorker, I. and Tuzun, U. (2005) 'Autistic-like findings associated with a urea cycle disorder in a 4-year-old girl.' *Journal of Psychiatry and Neuroscience*, 30: 133–135.

Gorlin, R.J. (1990) 'Branchial Arch and Oro-acral Disorders.' In J.J. Gorlin, M.M.Jr. Cohen, and L.S. Levin (eds.) *Syndromes of the Head and Neck* (3rd ed.). Oxford: Oxford University Press.

Gorlin, R.J., Cohen, M.M. and Levin, L.S. (1990) *Syndromes of the Head and Neck* (3rd Edn). Oxford: Oxford University Press.

Gosalakkal, J.A. (2004) 'Sotos syndrome (cerebral gigantism): a review of neurobehavioral, developmental and neurological manifestations.' *International Pediatrics 19*, 3: 147–151.

Gosch, A., Stading, G. and Pankau, R. (1994) 'Linguistic abilities in children with Williams-Beuren syndrome.' *American Journal of Medical Genetics*, 52: 291–296.

Gosden, R.G. and Feinberg, A.P. (2007) 'Genetics and epigenetics – Nature's pen-and-pencil set.' *New England Journal of Medicine 356*, 7: 731–733.

Gosselin, J., Lebon-Labich, B., Lucron, H., Marçon, F. and Leheup, B. (2004) 'Syndrome de délétion 22 q 11 et maladie de basedow. À propos de trois observations pédiatriques.' [Article in French: 'Grave's disease in children with 22q11 deletion. Report of three cases.'] *Archives de Pediatrie*, 11: 1468–1471.

Gotham, K., Pickles, A. and Lord, C. (2008) 'Standardizing ADOS scores for a measure of severity in autism spectrum disorders.' *Journal of Autism and Developmental Disorders*, 39: 693–705.

Gothelf, D., Farber, N., Raveh, E., Apter, A. and Attias, J. (2006) 'Hyperacusis in Williams syndrome: characteristics and associated neuroaudiologic abnormalities.' *Neurology*, 66: 390–395.

Gottfried, O.N., Viskochil, D.H., Fults, D.W. and Couldwell, W.T. (2006) 'Molecular, genetic, and cellular pathogenesis of neurofibromas and surgical implications.' *Neurosurgery*, 58: 1–16.

Gottlieb, S., Driscoll, D.A., Punnett, H.H., Sellinger, B. *et al.* (1998) 'Characterization of 10p deletions suggests two nonoverlapping regions contribute to the DiGeorge syndrome phenotype.' *American Journal of Human Genetics 62*, 2: 495–498.

Gould, E.L., Loesch, D.Z., Martin, M.J., Hagerman, R.J. *et al.* (2000) 'Melatonin profiles and sleep characteristics in boys with fragile-X syndrome: a preliminary study.' *American Journal of Medical Genetics*, 95: 307–315.

Goutieres, F. and Aicardi, J. (1986) 'Atypical forms of Rett syndrome.' *American Journal of Medical Genetics* (Suppl. 1): 183–194.

Graf, A., Landolt, M.A., Mori, A.C. and Boltshauser, E. (2006) 'Quality of life and psychological adjustment in children and adolescents with neurofibromatosis type 1.' *Journal of Pediatrics*, 149: 348–353.

Graf, W.D., Marin-Garcia, J., Gao, H.G., Pizzo, S. *et al.* (2000) 'Autism associated with mitochondrial DNA G8363A transfer RNA (Lys) mutation.' *Journal of Child Neurology*, 15: 357–361.

Graham, J.M. Jr., Rosner, B., Dykens, E. and Visootsak, J. (2005) 'Behavioral features of CHARGE syndrome (Hall-Hittner syndrome): comparison with Down syndrome, Prader-Willi syndrome, and Williams syndrome.' *American Journal of Medical Genetics A*, 133: 240–247.

Granpeesheh, D., Tarbox, J. and Dixon, D.R. (2009) 'Applied behavior analytic interventions for children with autism: a description and review of treatment research.' *Annals of Clinical Psychiatry 21*, 3: 162–173.

Gräsbeck, R. (2006) 'Imerslund-Gräsbeck syndrome (selective vitamin B12 malabsorption with proteinuria).' '*ORPHANET Journal of Rare Diseases*,' 1: 17, doi:10.1186/1750-1172-1-17.

Gravholt, C.H. (2005a) 'Epidemiological, endocrine and metabolic features in Turner syndrome.' *Arquivos Brasilleries Endocrinologin e metabologia*, 49: 145–156.

Gravholt, C.H. (2005b) 'Clinical practice in Turner syndrome.' *Nature Clinical Practice in Endocrinology and Metabolism 1*, 1: 41–52.

Gravholt, C.H., Juul, S., Naeraa, R.W. and Hansen, J. (1996) 'Prenatal and postnatal prevalence of Turner's syndrome: a registry study.' *British Medical Journal*, 312: 16–21.

Gray, K.M. and Tonge, B.J. (2001) 'Are there early features of autism in infants and preschool children?' *Journal of Paediatrics and Child Health*, 37: 221–226.

Greco, D., Romano, C., Reitano, S., Barone, C. *et al.* (2008) 'Three new patients with dup(17)(p11.2p11.2) without autism' (letter). *Clinical Genetics,* 73: 294–296.

Greenberg, F., Elder, F.F.B., Haffner, P., Northrup, H. and Ledbetter, D.H. (1988) 'Cytogenetic findings in a prospective series of patients with DiGeorge anomaly.' *American Journal of Human Genetics,* 43: 605–611.

Greenberg, F., Guzzetta, V., Montes de Oca-Luna, R., Magenis, R.E. *et al.* (1991) 'Molecular analysis of the Smith-Magenis syndrome: a possible contiguous-gene syndrome associated with del(17)(p11.2).' *American Journal of Human Genetics,* 49: 1207–1218.

Greenberg, F., Lewis, R.A., Potocki, L., Glaze, D. *et al.* (1996) 'Multi-disciplinary clinical study of Smith-Magenis syndrome (deletion 17p11.2).' *American Journal of Medical Genetics,* 62: 247–254.

Greenstein, M.A. (1990) 'Prader-Willi and Angelman syndromes in one kindred with expression consistent with genetic imprinting' (abstract). *American Journal of Human Genetics,* 47 (Suppl.): A59.

Greenwood, R.S., Tupler, L.A., Whitt, J.K., Buu, A. *et al.* (2005) 'Brain morphometry, T2-weighted hyperintensities, and IQ in children with neurofibromatosis type 1.' *Archives of Neurology,* 62: 1904–1908.

Greeves, L.G., Patterson, C.C., Carson, D.J., Thom, R. *et al.* (2000) 'Effect of genotype on changes in intelligence quotient after dietary relaxation in phenylketonuria and hyperphenylalaninaemia.' *Archives of Disease in Childhood,* 82: 216–221.

Gregorevic, P. and Chamberlain, J.S. (2003) 'Gene therapy for muscular dystrophy.' *Expert Opinion on Biological Therapy,* 3: 803–814.

Gregory, S.G., Connelly, J.J., Towers, A.J., Johnson, J. *et al.* (2009) 'Genomic and epigenetic evidence for oxytocin receptor deficiency in autism.' *BMC Medicine,* 7: 62, doi:10.1186/1741-7015-7-62.

Griebel, V., Krageloh-Mann, I. and Michaelis, R. (1989) 'Hypomelanosis of Ito – report of four cases and survey of the literature.' *Neuropediatrics,* 20: 234–237.

Grier, R.E., Farrington, F.H., Kendig, R. and Mamunes, P. (1983) 'Autosomal dominant inheritance of the Aarskog syndrome.' *American Journal of Medical Genetics,* 15: 39–46.

Griffiths, P.V., Demellweek, C., Fay, N., Robinson, P.H. and Davidson, D.C. (2000) 'Wechsler subscale IQ and subtest profile in early treated phenylketonuria.' *Archives of Disease in Childhood,* 82: 209–215.

Griggs, R.C., Kingston, W., Herr, B.E., Forbes, G. and Moxley, R.T. 3rd (1985) 'Lack of relationship of hypogonadism to muscle wasting in myotonic dystrophy.' *Archives of Neurology 42,* 9: 881–885.

Griggs, R.C., Moxley, R.T. 3rd, Mendell, J.R., Fenichel, G.M. *et al.* (1993) 'Duchenne dystrophy: randomized, controlled trial of prednisone (18 months) and azathioprine (12 months).' *Neurology,* 43: 520–527.

Grimbacher, B., Dutra, A.S., Holland, S.M., Fischer, R.E. *et al.* (1999a) 'Analphoid marker chromosome in a patient with hyper-IgE syndrome, autism, and mild mental retardation.' *Genetics in Medicine,* 1: 213–218.

Grimbacher, B., Holland, S.M., Gallin, J.I., Malech, H.L. *et al.* (1999b) 'Hyper-IgE syndrome with recurrent infections – an autosomal dominant multisystem disorder.' *New England Journal of Medicine 340,* 9: 692–702.

Grimbacher, B., Holland, S.M. and Puck, J.M. (2005) 'Hyper-IgE syndromes.' *Immunological Reviews,* 203: 244–250.

Grimbacher, B., Schaffer, A.A., Holland, S.M., Davis, J. *et al.* (1999c) 'Genetic linkage of hyper-IgE syndrome to chromosome 4.' *American Journal of Human Genetics 65,* 3: 735–744.

Grimm, T. and Wesselhoeft, H. (1980) 'Zur Genetik des Williams-Beuren-Syndroms und der isolierten Form der supravalvulaeren Aortenstenose (Untersuchungen von 128 Familien).' *Zeitschrift für Kardiologie,* 69: 168–172.

Grinker, R.R. (2007) *Unstrange Minds: A Father, a Daughter and a Search for New Answers – Remapping the World of Autism.* New York: Basic Books.

Groen, W.B., Swinkels, S.H., van der Gaag, R.J. and Buitelaar, J.K. (2007) 'Finding effective screening instruments for autism using Bayes theorem.' *Archives of Pediatric and Adolescent Medicine,* 161: 415–416.

Grompe, M., Jones, S.N. and Caskey, C.T. (1990) 'Molecular detection and correction of ornithine transcarbamylase deficiency.' *Trends in Genetics 6,* 10: 335–339.

Grønskov, K., Ek, J. and Brondum-Nielsen, K. (2007) 'Oculocutaneous albinism.' *Orphanet Journal of Rare Diseases,* 2: 43, doi:10.1186/1750-1172-2-43.

Grønskov, K., Hjalgrim, H., Nielsen, I.-M. and Brondum-Nielsen, K. (2004) 'Screening of the ARX gene in 682 retarded males.' *European Journal of Human Genetics,* 12: 701–705.

Gropman, A. (2003) 'Vigabatrin and newer interventions in succinic semialdehyde dehydrogenase deficiency.' *Annals of Neurology,* 54 (Suppl. 6) : S66–S72.

Gropman, A.L., Elsea, S., Duncan, W.C. Jr and Smith, A.C.M. (2007) 'New developments in Smith-Magenis syndrome (del 17p11.2).' *Current Opinion in Neurology,* 20: 125–134.

Grosso, S., Brogna, A., Bazzotti, S., Renieri, A. *et al.* (2007) 'Seizures and electroencephalographic findings in CDKL5 mutations: case report and review.' *Brain and Development,* 29: 239–242.

Grosso, S., Lasorella, G., Russo, A., Galluzzi, P. *et al.* (2007) 'Aicardi syndrome with favourable outcome: case report and review.' *Brain and Development 29,* 7: 443–446.

Gryder, D.S. and Rogawski, M.A. (2003) 'Selective antagonism of GluR5 kainate receptor-mediated synaptic currents by topiramate in rat basolateral amygdala neurons.' *Journal of Neuroscience,* 23: 7069–7074.

Gueant, J.-L., Anello, G., Bosco, P., Gueant-Rodriguez, R.-M. *et al.* (2005) 'Homocysteine and related genetic polymorphisms in Down's syndrome IQ.' *Journal of Neurology, Neurosurgery and Psychiatry,* 76: 706–709.

Guerrini, R., Dravet, C., Genton, P., Belmonte, A. *et al.* (1998) 'Lamotrigine and seizure aggravation in severe myoclonic epilepsy.' *Epilepsia,* 39: 508–512.

Guideri, F., Acampa, M., Hayek, G., Zapella, M. and Di Perri, T. (1999) 'Reduced heart rate variability in patients affected with Rett syndrome: a possible explanation for sudden death.' *Neuropediatrics,* 30: 146–148.

Guldager, B., Jørgensen, P.J. and Grandjean, P. (1996) 'Metal excretion and magnesium retention in patients with intermittent claudication treated with intravenous disodium EDTA.', *Clinical Chemistry, 42,* 12: 1938–1942.

Gurrieri, F. and Neri, G. (1991) 'A girl with the Lujan-Fryns syndrome' (letter). *American Journal of Medical Genetics,* 38: 290–291.

Guldberg, P., Rey, F., Zschocke, J., Romano, V. *et al.* (1998) 'A European multicenter study of phenylalanine hydroxylase deficiency: classification of 105 mutations and a general system for genotype-based prediction of metabolic phenotype.' *American Journal of Human Genetics,* 63: 71–79.

Gussoni, E., Bennett, R.R., Muskiewicz, K.R., Meyerrose, T. *et al.* (2002) 'Long-term persistence of donor nuclei in a Duchenne muscular dystrophy patient receiving bone marrow transplantation.' *Journal of Clinical Investigation,* 110: 807–814.

Gussoni, E., Blau, H.M. and Kunkel, L.M. (1997) 'The fate of individual myoblasts after transplantation into muscles of DMD patients.' *Nature Medicine,* 3: 970–977.

Gussoni, E., Soneoka, Y., Strickland, C.D., Buzney, E.A. *et al.* (1999) 'Dystrophin expression in the mdx mouse restored by stem cell transplantation.' *Nature,* 401: 390–394.

Gustafson, S., Zbuk, K.M., Scacheri, C. and Eng, C. (2007) 'Cowden syndrome.' *Seminars in Oncology 34,* 5: 428–434.

Guthrie, R. (1996) 'The introduction of newborn screening for phenylketonuria: a personal history.' *European Journal of Pediatrics,* 155 (Suppl. 1): 4–5.

Guthrie, R. and Susi, A. (1963) 'A simple phenylalanine method for detecting phenylketonuria in large populations of newborn infants.' *Pediatrics*, 32: 338–343.

Guttler, F., Azen, C., Guldberg, P., Romstad, A. *et al.* (1999) 'Relationship among genotype, biochemical phenotype, and cognitive performance in females with phenylalanine hydroxylase deficiency: report from the maternal phenylketonuria collaborative study.' *Pediatrics*, 104: 258–262.

Guttman, B., Griffiths, A., Suzuki, D. and Cullis, T. (2002) *Genetics: A Beginner's Guide*. London: OneWorld Books.

H

Haargaard, B. and Fledelius, H.C. (2006) 'Down's syndrome and early cataract.' *British Journal of Ophthalmology*, 90: 1024–1027.

Haas, D., Garbade, S.F., Vohwinkel, C., Muschol, N. et al. (2007) 'Effects of cholesterol and simvastatin treatment in patients with Smith-Lemli-Opitz syndrome (SLOS).' *Journal of Inherited Metabolic Disease 30*, 3: 375–387.

Hagberg, B. (1995) 'Rett syndrome: clinical peculiarities and biological mysteries.' *Acta Paediatrica 84*, 9: 971–976.

Hagberg, B., Aicardi, J., Dias, K. and Ramos, O. (1983) 'A progressive syndrome of autism, dementia, ataxia, and loss of purposeful hand use in girls: Rett's syndrome. Report of 35 cases.' *Annals of Neurology*, 14: 471–479.

Hagberg, B., Goutieres, F., Hanefeld, F., Rett, A. and Wilson, J. (1985) 'Rett syndrome: criteria for inclusion and exclusion. *Brain and Development*, 7: 372–373.

Hagberg, B.A. and Skjeldal, O.H. (1994) 'Rett variants: a suggested model for inclusion criteria.' *Pediatric Neurology 11*, 1: 5–11.

Hagerman, R. (1999) *Neurodevelopmental Disorders: Diagnosis and Treatment.* Oxford: Oxford University Press.

Hagerman, R.J. (1997) 'Fragile X syndrome: molecular and clinical insights and treatment issues.' *Western Medical Journal*, 166: 129–137.

Hagerman, R.J. (2006) 'Lessons from fragile-X regarding neurobiology, autism, and neurodegeneration.' *Journal of Developmental and Behavioral Pediatrics 27*, 1: 63–74.

Hagerman, R.J. and Cronister, A. (1996) *Fragile-X Syndrome: Diagnosis, Treatment and Research* (2nd edn). Baltimore: Johns Hopkins Press.

Hagerman, R.J. and Hagerman, P.J. (2002a) *Fragile-X Syndrome: Diagnosis, Treatment, and Research* (3rd edn). Baltimore: Johns Hopkins University Press.

Hagerman, R.J. and Hagerman, P.J. (2002b) 'The fragile-X premutation: into the phenotypic fold.' *Current Opinion in Genetics and Development*, 12: 278–283.

Hagerman, R.J. and Hagerman, P.J. (2008) 'Testing for fragile-X gene mutations throughout the life span.' *Journal of the American Medical Association 300*, 20: 2419–2421.

Hagerman, R.J. and Synhorst, D.P. (1984) 'Mitral valve prolapse and aortic dilatation in the fragile-X syndrome.' *American Journal of Medical Genetics*, 17: 123–131.

Hagerman, R.J., Berry-Kravis, E., Hessl, D., Coffey, S. et al. (2008) 'Trial of fenobam, an mGluR5 antagonist, in adults with fragile-X syndrome.' *Journal of Intellectual Disability Research 52*, 10: 814.

Hagerman, R.J., Berry-Kravis, E., Kaufmann, W.E., Ono, M.Y. et al. (2009) 'Advances in the treatment of fragile-X syndrome.' *Pediatrics 123*, 1: 378–390.

Hagerman, R.J., Hull, C.E., Safanda, J.F., Carpenter, I. et al. (1994a) 'High-functioning fragile-X males: demonstration of an unmethylated fully expanded FMR-1 mutation associated with protein expression.' *American Journal of Medical Genetics,* 51: 298–308.

Hagerman, R.J., Jackson, A.W., Levitas, A., Braden, M. et al. (1986) 'Oral folic acid versus placebo in the treatment of males with the fragile-X syndrome.' *American Journal of Medical Genetics 23*, 1–2: 241–262.

Hagerman, R.J., Leavitt, B.R., Farzin, F., Jacquemont, S. et al. (2004) 'Fragile-X-associated tremor/ataxia syndrome (FXTAS) in females with the FMR1 premutation.' *American Journal of Human Genetics*, 74: 1051–1056.

Hagerman, R.J., Ono, M.Y. and Hagerman, P.J. (2005) 'Recent advances in fragile-X: a model of autism and neurodegeneration.' *Current Opinion in Psychiatry*, 18: 490–496.

Hagerman, R.J., van Housen, K., Smith, A.C.M. and McGavran, L. (1984) 'Consideration of connective tissue dysfunction in the fragile-X syndrome.' *American Journal of Medical Genetics*, 17: 111–121.

Hagerman, R.J., Wilson, P., Staley, L.W., Lang, K.A. et al. (1994b) 'Evaluation of school children at high risk for fragile-X syndrome utilizing buccal cell FMR-1 testing.' *American Journal of Medical Genetics*, 51: 474–481.

Hahn, A. and Neubauer, B.A. (2005) 'Autismus und Stoffwechselerkrankungen – was ist gesichert?' [Article in German: 'Autism and metabolic disorders – a rational approach'] *Zeitschrift fur Kinder und Jugendpsychiatrie und Psychotherapie*, 33: 259–271.

Haibach, H., Burns, T.W., Carlson, H.E., Burman, K.D. and Deftos, L.J. (1992) 'Multiple hamartoma syndrome (Cowden's disease) associated with renal cell carcinoma and primary neuroendocrine carcinoma of the skin (Merkel cell carcinoma).' *American Journal of Clinical Pathology*, 97: 705–712.

Halder, A., Jain, M., Kabra, M. and Gupta, N. (2008) 'Mosaic 22q11.2 microdeletion syndrome: diagnosis and clinical manifestations of two cases.' *Molecular Cytogenetics*, 1: 18, doi:10.1186/1755-8166-1-18.

Hall, B.D. (1979) 'Choanal atresia and associated multiple anomalies.' *Journal of Pediatrics*, 95: 395–398.

Hall, J.G. (1993) 'CATCH 22.' *Journal of Medical Genetics*, 30: 801–802.

Hallam, T.M. and Bourtchouladze, R. (2006) 'Rubinstein-Taybi syndrome: molecular findings and therapeutic approaches to improve cognitive dysfunction.' *Cellular and Molecular Life Sciences 63*, 15: 1725–1735.

Hals, J., Bjerve, K.S., Nilsen, H., Svalastog, A.G. and Ek, J. (2000) 'Essential fatty acids in the nutrition of severely neurologically disabled children.' *British Journal of Nutrition*, 83: 219–225.

Hamed, S.A. (2006) 'Drug evaluation: PTC-124 – a potential treatment of cystic fibrosis and Duchenne muscular dystrophy.' *IDrugs 9*, 11: 783–789.

Hamel, B.C., Smits, A.P., de Graaff, E., Smeets, D.F. et al. (1994) 'Segregation of FRAXE in a large family: clinical, psychometric, cytogenetic, and molecular data.' *American Journal of Human Genetics*, 55: 923–931.

Hammen, A., Wagner, B., Berkhoff, M. and Donati, F. (1998) 'A paradoxical rise of neonatal seizures after treatment with vitamin B6.' *European Journal of Paediatric Neurology*, 2: 319–322.

Hammer, S., Dorrani, N., Dragich, J., Kudo, S. and Schanen, C. (2002) 'The phenotypic consequences of MECP2 mutations extend beyond Rett syndrome.' *Mental Retardation and Developmental Disabilities Research Reviews 8*, 2: 94–98.

Hammock, E.A. and Young, L.J. (2006) 'Oxytocin, vasopressin and pair bonding: implications for autism.' *Philosophical Transactions of the Royal Society of London B Biological Sciences 361*, 1476: 2186–2198.

Hammond, L.S., Macias, M.M., Tarleton, J.C. and Shashidhar Pai, G. (1997) 'Fragile-X syndrome and deletions in FMR1: new case and review of the literature.' *American Journal of Medical Genetics*, 72: 430–434.

Han, M. and Criado, E. (2005) 'Renal artery stenosis and aneurysms associated with neurofibromatosis.' *Journal of Vascular Surgery*, 41: 539–543.

Hanauer, A. (2001) 'Coffin-Lowry syndrome (CLS).' *Orphanet Encyclopaedia*, www.orpha.net.

Hanefeld, F. (1985) 'The clinical pattern of the Rett syndrome.' *Brain and Development*, 7: 320–325.

Hanley, W.B., Koch, R., Levy, H.L., Matalon, R. et al. (1996) 'The North American Maternal Phenylketonuria Collaborative Study, developmental assessment of the offspring: preliminary report.' *European Journal of Pediatrics*, 155 (Suppl. 1): 169–172.

Hanley, W.B., Lee, A.W., Hanley, A.J.G., Lehotay, D.C. *et al.* (2000) 'Hypotyrosinemia in phenylketonuria.' *Molecular Genetics and Metabolism*, 69: 286–294.

Hansteen, I.L., Varslot, K., Steen-Johnsen, J. and Langard, S. (1982) 'Cytogenetic screening of a newborn population.' *Clinical Genetics*, 21: 309–314.

Happé, F., Ronald, A. and Plomin, R. (2006) 'Time to give up on a single explanation for autism.' *Nature Neuroscience*, 9: 1218–1220.

Happle, R., Traupe, H., Grobe, H. and Bonsmann, G. (1984) 'The Tay syndrome (congenital ichthyosis with trichothiodystrophy).' *European Journal of Pediatrics*, 141: 147–152.

Happle, R. and Vakilzadeh, F. (1982) 'Hamartomatous dental cusps in Hypomelanosis of Ito.' *Clinical Genetics*, 21: 65–68.

Harach, H.R., Soubeyran, I., Brown, A., Bonneau, D. and Longy, M. (1999) 'Thyroid pathologic findings in patients with Cowden disease.' *Annals of Diagnostic Pathology*, 3: 331–340.

Hara-Chikuma, M. and Verkman, A.S. (2006) 'Physiological roles of glycerol-transporting aquaporins: the aquaglyceroporins.' *Cellular and Molecular Life Sciences*, 63: 1386–1392.

Harbord, M.G., Finn, J.P., Hall-Craggs, M.A., Brett, E.M. and Baraitser, M. (1989) 'Mobius' syndrome with unilateral cerebellar hypoplasia.' *Journal of Medical Genetics*, 26: 579–582.

Harrell, R.F., Capp, R.H., Davis, D.R., Peerless, J. and Ravitz, L.R. (1981) 'Can nutritional supplements help mentally retarded children? An exploratory study.' *Proceedings of the National Academy of Science USA* 78, 1: 574–578.

Harris, J.C. (2006) *Intellectual Disability: Understanding its Development, Causes, Classification, Evaluation and Treatment.* Oxford: Oxford University Press.

Harrison, D.J. and Webb, P.J. (1990) 'Scoliosis in the Rett syndrome: natural history and treatment.' *Brain and Development 12*, 1: 154–156.

Harrison, K.L. and Pheasant, A.E. (1995) 'Analysis of urinary pterins in autism.' *Biochemical Society Transactions 23*, 4: 603S.

Hartsfield, J.K. Jr., Hall, B.D., Grix, A.W., Kousseff, B.G. *et al.* (1993) 'Pleiotropy in Coffin-Lowry syndrome: sensorineural hearing deficit and premature tooth loss as early manifestations.' *American Journal of Medical Genetics*, 45: 552–557.

Hartshorne, T.S., Grialou, T.L. and Parker, K.R. (2005) 'Autistic-like behavior in CHARGE syndrome.' *American Journal of Medical Genetics A*, 133: 257–261.

Hartshorne, T.S., Hefner, M.A. and Davenport, S.L. (2005) 'Behavior in CHARGE syndrome: introduction to the special topic.' *American Journal of Medical Genetics*, 133A: 228–231.

Hartshorne, T.S., Nicholas, J., Grialou, T.L. and Russ, J.M. (2007) 'Executive function in CHARGE syndrome.' *Child Neuropsychology 13*, 4: 333–344.

Harum, K.H., Alemi, L. and Johnston, M.V. (2001) 'Cognitive impairment in Coffin-Lowry syndrome correlates with reduced RSK2 activation.' *Neurology*, 56: 207–214.

Hashimoto, T. (1999) 'Peroxisomal β-oxidation enzymes.' *Neurochemical Research*, 24: 551–563.

Haspeslagh, M., Fryns, J.P. and van den Berghe, H. (1984) 'The Coffin-Siris syndrome: report of a family and further delineation.' *Clinical Genetics*, 26: 374–378.

Hatton, D.D., Sideris, J., Skinner, M., Mankowski, J. *et al.* (2006) 'Autistic behavior in children with fragile-X syndrome: prevalence, stability, and the impact of FMRP.' *American Journal of Medical Genetics A*, 140: 1804–1813.

Havlovicova, M., Novotna, D., Kocarek, E., Novotna, K. *et al.* (2007) 'Clinical report: a girl with neurofibromatosis type 1, atypical autism and mosaic ring chromosome 17.' *American Journal of Medical Genetics Part A*, 143A: 76–81.

Hayashi, M.L., Shankaranarayana Rao, B.S., Seo, J.-S., Choi, H.-S. et al. (2007) 'Inhibition of p21-activated kinase rescues symptoms of fragile X syndrome in mice.' *Proceedings of the National Academy of Science*, 104: 11489–11494.

Hayden, D. (2003) *Pox: Genius, Madness and the Mysteries of Syphilis.* New York: Basic Books.

Healy, N.M. (1965) 'Gilles de la Tourette syndrome in an autistic child.' *Journal of the Irish Medical Association*, 57: 93–94.

Hebebrand, J., Martin, M., Korner, J., Roitzheim, B. *et al.* (1994) 'Partial trisomy 16p in an adolescent with autistic disorder and Tourette's syndrome.' *American Journal of Medical Genetics 54*, 3: 268–270.

Hecht, F. and Glover, T.W. (1983) 'Antibiotics containing trimethoprim and the fragile-X chromosome' (letter). *New England Journal of Medicine*, 308: 285–286.

Hedera, P. and Fink, J.K. (2007) 'Xeroderma pigmentosum.' *eMedicine*, www.emedicine.com.

Heilstedt, H.A., Ballif, B.C., Howard, L.A., Kashork, C.D. and Shaffer, L.G. (2003) 'Population data suggest that deletions of 1p36 are a relatively common chromosome abnormality.' *Clinical Genetics*, 64: 310–316.

Heinrichs, M. and Gaab, J. (2007) 'Neuroendocrine mechanisms of stress and social interaction: implications for mental disorders.' *Current Opinion in Psychiatry*, 20: 158–162.

Hellings, J.A., Hossain, S., Martin, J.K. and Baratang, R.R. (2002) 'Psychopathology, GABA, and the Rubinstein-Taybi syndrome: a review and case study.' *American Journal of Medical Genetics*, 114: 190–195.

Henderson, S. (1987) *The Test of Motor Impairment* (revised). London: Department of Educational Psychology, Institute of Education.

Hendrich, B. and Bickmore, W. (2001) 'Human diseases with underlying defects in chromatin structure and modification.' *Human Molecular Genetics*, 10: 2233–2242.

Hendriks, Y.M., Verhallen, J.T., van der Smagt, J.J., Kant, S.G. *et al.* (2003) 'Bannayan-Riley-Ruvalcaba syndrome: further delineation of the phenotype and management of PTEN mutation – positive cases.' *Familial Cancer 2*, 2: 79–85.

Hendriksen, J.G. and Vles, J.S. (2008) 'Neuropsychiatric disorders in males with Duchenne muscular dystrophy: Frequency rate of attention-deficit hyperactivity disorder (ADHD), autism spectrum disorder, and obsessive-compulsive disorder. *Journal of Child Neurology, 23*: 477–481.

Hennekam, R.C., Van Den Boogaard, M.J., Sibbles, B.J. and Van Spijker, H.G. (1990) 'Rubinstein-Taybi syndrome in The Netherlands.' *American Journal of Medical Genetics*, 6 (Supplement): 17–29.

Hennekam, R.C.M. (2005) 'Congenital brain anomalies in distal cholesterol biosynthesis defects.' *Journal of Inherited Metabolic Disorders*, 28: 385–392.

Hennies, H.C., Rauch, A., Seifert, W., Schumi, C. *et al.* (2004) 'Allelic heterogeneity in the COH1 gene explains clinical variability in Cohen syndrome.' *American Journal of Human Genetics*, 75: 138–145.

Herbert, J.D., Sharp, I.R. and Gaudiano, B.A. (2002) 'Separating fact from fiction in the etiology and treatment of autism: a scientific review of the evidence.' *The Scientific Review of Mental Health Practice 1*, 1: 23–43.

Herguner, S. and Mukaddes, N.M. (2006) 'Autism and Williams syndrome: a case report.' *World Journal of Biological Psychiatry 7*, 3: 186–188.

Herman, G.E. (2003) 'Disorders of cholesterol biosynthesis: prototypic metabolic malformation syndromes.' *Human Molecular Genetics 12* (Spec. No. 1): R75–88.

Herman, G.E., Greenberg, F. and Ledbetter, D.H. (1988) 'Multiple congenital anomaly/mental retardation (MCA/MR) syndrome with Goldenhar complex due to a terminal del(22q).' *American Journal of Medical Genetics 29*, 4: 909–915.

Herman, G.E., Henninger, N., Ratliff-Schaub, K., Pastore, M. *et al.* (2007) 'Genetic testing in autism: how much is enough?' *Genetics in Medicine 9*, 5: 268–274.

Hermida-Prieto, A., Eirís-Puñal, J., Álvarez-Moreno, A., Alonso-Martín, A., Barreiro Conde, J. and Castro-Gago, M. (1997) 'Hipomelanosis de Ito: autismo, dilatación segmentaria del colon y hallazgo inusual en neuroimagen.' [Article in Spanish.] *Revista de Neurología*, 25: 71–74.

Hernandez, R.N., Feinberg, R.L., Vaurio, R., Passanante, N.M. *et al.* (2009) 'Autism spectrum disorder in fragile-X syndrome: a longitudinal evaluation.' *American Journal of Medical Genetics A, 149A,* 6: 1125–1137.

Hernandez-Martin, A., Gonzalez-Sarmiento, R. and De Unamuno, P. (1999) 'X-linked ichthyosis: an update.' *British Journal of Dermatology,* 141: 617–627.

Herrmann, D.N. (2008) 'Experimental therapeutics in hereditary neuropathies: the past, the present, and the future.' *Neurotherapeutics,* 5: 507–515.

Hersh, J.H., Bloom, A.S. and Weisskopf, B. (1982) 'Childhood autism in a female with Coffin-Siris syndrome.' *Journal of Developmental and Behavioral Pediatrics,* 3: 249–251.

Hertz-Picciotto, I. and Delwiche, L. (2009) 'The rise in autism and the role of age at diagnosis.' *Epidemiology 20,* 1: 84–90.

Hessl, D., Rivera, S.M. and Reiss, A.L. (2004) 'The neuroanatomy and neuroendocrinology of fragile-X syndrome.' *Mental Retardation and Developmental Disabilities Research Reviews 10,* 1: 17–24.

Hibuse, T., Maeda, N., Funahashi, T., Yamamoto, K. *et al.* (2005) 'Aquaporin 7 deficiency is associated with development of obesity through activation of adipose glycerol kinase.' *Proceedings of the National Academy of Science USA,* 102: 10993–10998.

Hicks, M., Ferguson, S., Bernier, F. and Lemay, J.-F. (2008) 'A case report of monozygotic twins with Smith-Magenis syndrome.' *Journal of Developmental and Behavioural Pediatrics,* 29: 42–46.

Hide, W.A., Babenko, V.N., van Heusden, P.A., Seoighe, C. and Kelso, J.F. (2001) 'The contribution of exon-skipping events on chromosome 22 to protein coding diversity.' *Genome Research,* 11: 1848–1853.

Hill, I.D., Dirks, M.H., Liptak, G.S., Colletti, R.B. *et al.* (2005) 'Guideline for the diagnosis and treatment of celiac disease in children: recommendations of the North American Society for Pediatric Gastroenterology, Hepatology and Nutrition.' *Journal of Pediatric Gastroenterology and Nutrition 40,* 1: 1–19.

Hinton, V.J., De Vivo, D.C., Nereo, N.E., Goldstein, E. and Stern, Y. (2000) 'Poor verbal working memory across intellectual level in boys with Duchenne dystrophy.' *Neurology,* 54: 2127–2132.

Hinton, V.J., De Vivo, D.C., Nereo, N.E., Goldstein, E. and Stern, Y. (2001) 'Selective deficits in verbal working memory associated with a known genetic etiology: the neuropsychological profile of Duchenne muscular dystrophy.' *Journal of the International Neuropsychological Society,* 7: 45–54.

Hinton, V.J., Fee, R.J., De Vivo, D.C. and Goldstein, E. (2006) 'Poor facial affect recognition among boys with duchenne muscular dystrophy.' *Journal of Autism and Developmental Disorders 37,* 10: 1925–1933.

Hirawat, S., Welch, E.M., Elfring, G.L., Northcutt, V.J. *et al.* (2007) 'Safety, tolerability, and pharmacokinetics of PTC124, a nonaminoglycoside nonsense mutation suppressor, following single- and multiple-dose administration to healthy male and female adult volunteers.' *Journal of Clinical Pharmacology,* 47: 430–444.

Hirayama, K., Iizuka, R., Maehara, K. and Watanabe, T. (1981) 'Clinicopathological study of dentatorubro-pallidoluysian atrophy. Part 1: Its clinical form and analysis of symptomatology.' *Shinkei Kenkyu no Shinpo,* 25: 725–736.

Hiriashi, Y., Kato, S., Ishihara, T. and Takano, T. (1992) 'Quantitative Southern blot analysis in the dystrophin gene of Japanese patients with Duchenne or Becker muscular dystrophy: a high frequency of duplications.' *Journal of Medical Genetics,* 29: 897–901.

Hirose, S. (2006) 'A new paradigm of channelopathy in epilepsy syndromes: intracellular trafficking abnormality of channel molecules.' *Epilepsy Research,* 70 (Suppl.): S206–S217.

Hitchins, M.P., Rickard, S., Dhalla, F., de Vries, B.B.A. *et al.* (2004) 'Investigation of UBE3A and MECP2 in Angelman syndrome (AS) and patients with features of AS.' *American Journal of Medical Genetics,* 125A: 167–172.

Hittner, H.M., Hirsch, N.J., Kreh, G.M. and Rudolph, A.J. (1979) 'Colobomatous microphthalmia, heart disease, hearing loss, and mental retardation – a syndrome.' *Journal of Pediatric Ophthalmology and Strabismus,* 16: 122–128.

Hitzler, J.K., Cheung, J., Li, Y., Scherer, S.W. and Zipursky, A. (2003) 'GATA1 mutations in transient leukemia and acute megakaryoblastic leukemia of Down syndrome.' *Blood,* 101: 4301–4304.

Hjerrild, B.E., Mortensen, K.H. and Gravholt, C.H. (2008) 'Turner syndrome and clinical treatment.' *British Medical Bulletin,* 86: 77–93.

Ho, A., Todd, R.D. and Constantino, J.N. (2005) 'Brief report: autistic traits in twins vs. non-twins – a preliminary study.' *Journal of Autism and Developmental Disorders,* 35: 129–133.

Hobbs, K., Kennedy, A., DuBray, M., Bigler, E.D. *et al.* (2007) 'A retrospective fetal ultrasound study of brain size in autism.' *Biological Psychiatry,* 62: 1048–1055, doi:10.1016/j.biopsych.2007.03.020

Hodgkin, D.C., Kamper, J., MacKay, M., Pickworth, J. *et al.* (1956) 'Structure of vitamin B12.' *Nature 178,* 4524: 64–66.

Hodgkins, P.R., Harris, C.M., Shawkat, F.S., Thompson, D.A. *et al.* (2004) 'Joubert syndrome: long-term follow-up.' *Developmental Medicine and Child Neurology,* 46: 694–699.

Hoeijmakers, J.H.J. (1994) 'Human nucleotide excision repair syndromes: molecular clues to unexpected intricacies.' *European Journal of Cancer,* 30A: 1912–1921.

Hofstra, R.M., Mulder, I.M., Vossen, R., de Koning-Gans, P.A. *et al.* (2004) 'DGGE-based whole-gene mutation scanning of the dystrophin gene in Duchenne and Becker muscular dystrophy patients.' *Human Mutation,* 23: 57–66.

Hogart, A., Leung, K.N., Wang, N.J., Wu, D.J. *et al.* (2008a) 'Chromosome 15q11–13 duplication syndrome brain reveals epigenetic alterations in gene expression not predicted from copy number.' *Journal of Medical Genetics,* doi:10.1136/jmg.2008.061580.

Hogart, A., Wu, D, LaSalle, J.M. and Schanen, N.C. (2008b) 'The comorbidity of autism with the genomic disorders of chromosome 15q11.2–q13.' *Neurobiology of Disease,* doi:10.1016/j.nbd.2008.08.011.

Hohoff, A., Joos, U., Meyer, U., Ehmer, U. and Stamm, T. (2007) 'The spectrum of Apert syndrome: phenotype, particularities in orthodontic treatment, and characteristics of orthognathic surgery.' *Head and Face Medicine 3,* 10: 1–24.

Hoksbergen, R., ter Laak, J., Rijk, K., van Dijkum, C. and Stoutjesdijk, F. (2005) 'Post-institutional autistic syndrome in Romanian adoptees.' *Journal of Autism and Developmental Disorders 35,* 5: 615–623.

Holder-Espinasse, M., Marie, S., Bourrouillou, G., Ceballos-Picot, I. *et al.* (2002) 'Towards a suggestive facial dysmorphism in adenylosuccinate lyase deficiency?' (letter). *Journal of Medical Genetics,* 39: 440–442.

Holland, S.M., DeLeo, F.R., Elloumi, H.Z., Hsu, A.P. *et al.* (2007) 'STAT3 mutations in the hyper-IgE syndrome.' *New England Journal of Medicine 357,* 16: 1608–1619.

Hollander, E., Novotny, S., Hanratty, M., Yaffe, R. *et al.* (2003) 'Oxytocin infusion reduces repetitive behaviors in adults with autistic and Asperger's disorders.' *Neuropsychopharmacology,* 28: 193–198.

Holliday, R. (2006) 'Epigenetics: a historical overview.' *Epigenetics 1,* 2: 76–80.

Hollowell, J.G., Staehling, N.W., Flanders, W.D., Hannon, W.H. et al. (2002) 'Serum TSH, T(4), and thyroid antibodies in the United States population (1988 to 1994): National Health and Nutrition Examination Survey (NHANES III).' *Journal of Clinical Endocrinology and Metabolism,* 87: 489–499.

Holm, V.A., Cassidy, S.B., Butler, M.G., Hanchett, J.M. *et al.* (1993) 'Prader-Willi syndrome: consensus diagnostic criteria.' *Pediatrics 91,* 2: 398–402.

Holmes, A.S., Blaxill, M.F. and Hayley, B.E. (2003) 'Reduced levels of mercury in first baby haircuts of autistic children.' *International Journal of Toxicology,* 22: 277–285.

Holmstrom, G., Almond, G., Temple, K., Taylor, D. and Baraitser, M. (1990) 'The iris in Williams syndrome.' *Archives of Diseases in Childhood,* 65: 987–989.

Holroyd, S., Reiss, A.L. and Bryan, R.N. (1991) 'Autistic features in Joubert syndrome: a genetic disorder with agenesis of the cerebellar vermis.' *Biological Psychiatry*, 29: 287–294.

Honda, H., Shimizu, Y. and Rutter, M. (2005) 'No effect of MMR withdrawal on the incidence of autism: a total population study.' *Journal of Child Psychology and Psychiatry 46*, 6: 572–579.

Hong, S.E., Shugart, Y.Y., Huang, D.T., Shahwan, S.A. *et al.* (2000) 'Autosomal recessive lissencephaly with cerebellar hypoplasia is associated with human RELN mutations.' *Nature Genetics*, 26: 93–96.

Hoo, J. and Shrimpton, A.E. (2005) 'Familial hyper- and hypopigmentation with age - related pattern change' (letter). *American Journal of Medical Genetics*, 132A: 215–218.

Hoogerwaard, E.M., Bakker, E., Ippel, P.F., Oosterwijk, J.C. *et al.* (1999) 'Signs and symptoms of Duchenne muscular dystrophy and Becker muscular dystrophy among carriers in the Netherlands: a cohort study.' *Lancet 353*, 9170: 2116–2119.

Hook, E.B. and Reynolds, J.W. (1967) 'Cerebral gigantism: endocrinological and clinical observations of six patients including a congenital giant, concordant monozygotic twins, and a child who achieved adult gigantic size.' *Journal of Pediatrics*, 70: 900–914.

Hook, E.B., Cross, P.K. and Schreinemachers, D.M. (1983) 'Chromosomal abnormality rates at amniocentesis and in live-born infants.' *Journal of the American Medical Association*, 249: 2034–2038.

Horgan, J.E., Padwa, B.L., LaBrie, R.A. and Mulliken, J.B. (1995) 'OMENS-plus: analysis of craniofacial and extracraniofacial anomalies in hemifacial microsomia.' *The Cleft Palate–Craniofacial Journal 32*, 5: 405–412.

Hornig, M., Briese, T., Buie, T., Bauman, M.L. et al. (2008) 'Lack of association between measles virus vaccine and autism with enteropathy: a case-control study.' *PLoS One*, 3: e3140.

Hornig, M. and Lipkin, W.I. (2001) 'Infectious and immune factors in the pathogenesis of neurodevelopmental disorders: epidemiology, hypotheses, and animal models.' *Mental Retardation and Developmental Disabilities Research Reviews*, 7: 200–210.

Hornig, M., Chian, D. and Lipkin, W.I. (2004) 'Neurotoxic effects of postnatal thimerosal are mouse strain dependent.' *Molecular Psychiatry*, 9: 833–845.

Horrobin, D. (2001) *The Madness of Adam and Eve: How Schizophrenia Shaped Humanity*. London: Bantam Press.

Horrobin, D.F. (2003) 'Are large clinical trials in rapidly lethal diseases usually unethical?' (personal paper). *Lancet 361*, 9358: 695–697

Horvath, K. and Perman, J. A. (2002a) 'Autism and gastrointestinal symptoms.' *Current Gastroenterology Reports*, 4: 251–258.

Horvath, K. and Perman, J.A. (2002b) 'Autistic disorder and gastrointestinal disease.' *Current Opinion in Pediatrics*, 14: 583–587.

Horvath, K., Medeiros, L. and Rabszytn, A. (2000) 'High prevalence of gastrointestinal symptoms in autistic children with autistic spectrum disorder.' *Journal of Pediatric Gastroenterology and Nutrition*, 31: S174.

Horvath, K., Papadimitriou, J.C., Rabsztyn, A., Drachenberg, C. and Tildon, J.T. (1999) 'Gastrointestinal abnormalities in children with autistic disorder.' *Journal of Pediatrics*, 135: 559–563.

Horvath, K., Stefanatos, G., Sokolski, K.N., Wachtel, R., Nabors, L. and Tildon, J.T. (1998) 'Improved social and language skills after secretin administration in patients with autistic spectrum disorders.' *Journal of the Association of the Academy of Minority Physicians 9*, 1: 9–15.

Hoshino, Y., Watanabe, M., Tachibana, R., Kaneko, M. and Kumashiro, H. (1984) 'The hypothalamo-pituitary function in autistic children.' *Neurosciences*, 10: 285–291.

Hoskins, J.A., Jack, G., Wade, H.E., Peiris, R.J.D. *et al.* (1980) 'Enzymatic control of phenylalanine intake in phenylketonuria.' *Lancet 316*, 8165: 392–394.

Howlin, P. (1997) 'Prognosis in autism: do specialist treatments affect long-term outcome?', *European Child and Adolescent Psychiatry, 6*, 2: 55–72.

Howlin, P. (1998) 'Practitioner review: psychological and educational treatments for autism.' *Journal of Child Psychology and Psychiatry 39*, 3: 307–322.

Howlin, P. (2001) 'Autistic features in Cohen syndrome: a preliminary report.' *Developmental Medicine and Child Neurology*, 43: 692–696.

Howlin, P. (2003) 'Can early interventions alter the course of autism?' *Novartis Foundation Symposium*, 251: 250–259.

Howlin, P., Karpf, J. and Turk, J. (2005) 'Behavioural characteristics and autistic features in individuals with Cohen syndrome.' *European Journal of Child and Adolescent Psychiatry*, 14: 57–64.

Howlin, P., Wing, L. and Gould, J. (1995) 'The recognition of autism in children with Down syndrome – implications for intervention and some speculations about pathology.' *Developmental Medicine and Child Neurology*, 37: 406–414.

Howson, A.L., Batth, S., Ilivitsky, V., Boisjoli, A. *et al.* (2004) 'Clinical and attentional effects of acute nicotine treatment in Tourette's syndrome.' *European Psychiatry 19*, 2: 102–112.

Hsu, C.-L., Lin, D.C.Y., Chen, C.-L., Wang, C.-M. and Wong, A.M.K. (2009) 'The effects of a gluten- and casein-free diet in children with autism: a case report.' *Chang Gung Medical Journal*, 32: 459–465.

Hu, J.F., Oruganti, H., Vu, T.H. and Hoffman, A.R. (1998) 'The role of histone acetylation in the allelic expression of the imprinted human insulin-like growth factor 11 gene.' *Biochemical and Biophysical Research Communications*, 251: 403–408.

Hu, J.F., Vu, T.H. and Hoffman, A.R. (1996) 'Promoter-specific modulation of insulin-like growth factor II genomic imprinting by inhibitors of DNA methylation.' *Journal of Biological Chemistry*, 271: 18253–18262.

Huang, W.H. and Porto, M. (2002) 'Abnormal first-trimester fetal nuchal translucency and Cornelia de Lange syndrome.' *Obstetrics and Gynecology*, 99: 956–958.

Huber, K.M., Gallagher, S.M., Warren, S.T. and Bear, M.F. (2002) 'Altered synaptic plasticity in a mouse model of fragile-X mental retardation.' *Proceedings of the National Academy of Science USA*, 99: 7746–7750.

Hudgins, L., Geer, J.S. and Cassidy, S.B. (1998) 'Phenotypic differerences in African Americans with Prader-Willi syndrome.' *Genetics in Medicine 1*, 1: 49–51.

Hudson, L.L., Markert, M.L., Devlin, B.H., Haynes, B.F. and Sempowski, G.D. (2007) 'Human T cell reconstitution in DiGeorge syndrome and HIV-1 infection.' *Seminars in Immunology 19*, 5: 297–309.

Huerta, P.T., Kowal, C., DeGiorgio, L.A., Volpe, B.T. and Diamond, B. (2006) 'Immunity and behavior: antibodies alter emotion.' *Proceedings of the National Academy of Science USA 103*, 3: 678–683.

Huffmeier, U., Zenker, M., Hoyer, J., Fahsold, R. and Rauch, A. (2006) 'A variable combination of features of Noonan syndrome and neurofibromatosis type I are caused by mutations in the NF1 gene.' *American Journal of Medical Genetics A*, 140: 2749–2756.

Huijbregts, S.C.J., De Sonneville, L.M.J., Licht, R., van Spronsen, F.J. and Sergeant, J.A. (2002) 'Short-term dietary interventions in children and adolescents with treated phenylketonuria: effects on neuropsychological outcome of a well-controlled population.' *Journal of Inherited Metabolic Disease*, 25: 419–430.

Hulinsky, R., Byrne, J.L., Lowichik, A. and Viskochil, D.H. (2005) 'Fetus with interstitial del(5)(p13.1p14.2) diagnosed postnatally with Cornelia de Lange syndrome.' *American Journal of Medical Genetics A*, 137: 336–338.

Hulten, M., Armstrong, S., Challinor, P., Gould, C. *et al.* (1991) 'Genomic imprinting in an Angelman and Prader-Willi translocation family' (letter). *Lancet 338*, 8767: 638–639.

Hultman, C.M., Sparen, P. and Cnattingius, S. (2002) 'Prenatal risk factors for infantile autism.' *Epidemiology*, 13: 417–423.

Humphrey, A., Higgins, J.N.P., Yates, J.R.W. and Bolton, P.F. (2004) 'Monozygotic twins with tuberous sclerosis discordant for the severity of developmental deficits.' *Neurology*, 62: 795–798.

Hundscheid, R.D., Smits, A.P., Thomas, C.M., Kiemeney, L.A. and Braat, D.D. (2003) 'Female carriers of fragile-X premutations have no increased risk for additional diseases other than premature ovarian failure.' *American Journal of Medical Genetics*, 117: 6–9.

Hunsucker, S.A., Mitchell, B.S. and Spychala, J. (2005) 'The 5'-nucleotidases as regulators of nucleotide and drug metabolism.' *Pharmacology and Therapeutics*, 107: 1–30.

Hunt, A. and Dennis, J. (1987) 'Psychiatric disorder among children with tuberous sclerosis.' *Developmental Medicine and Child Neurology 29*, 2: 190–198.

Hunt, A. and Shepherd, C. (1993) 'A prevalence study of autism in tuberous sclerosis.' *Journal of Autism and Developmental Disorders 23*, 2: 323–339.

Hunter, A.G.W. (2002) 'Coffin-Lowry syndrome: a 20-year follow-up and review of long-term outcomes.' *American Journal of Medical Genetics*, 111: 345–355.

Hunter, A.G.W., Schwartz, C.E. and Abidi, F.E. (2007) 'Coffin-Lowry syndrome.' *GeneReviews*, http://clsf.info.

Hunter, L.C., O'Hare, A., Herron, W.J., Fisher, L.A. and Jones, G.E. (2003) 'Opioid peptides and dipeptidyl peptidase in autism.' *Developmental Medicine and Child Neurology*, 45: 121–128.

Huntley, C.C. and Stevenson, R.E. (1969) 'Maternal phenylketonuria: course of two pregnancies.' *Obstetrics and Gynecology*, 34: 694–700.

Huppke, P., Held, M., Laccone, F. and Hanefeld, F. (2003) 'The spectrum of phenotypes in females with Rett syndrome.' *Brain and Development 25*, 5: 346–351.

Huppke, P., Maier, E.M., Warnke, A., Brendel, C., Laccone, F. and Gartner, J. (2006) 'Very mild cases of Rett syndrome with skewed X inactivation.' *Journal of Medical Genetics*, 43: 814–816.

Hurmerinta, K., Pirinen, S., Kovero, O. and Kivitie-Kallio, S. (2002) 'Craniofacial features in Cohen syndrome: an anthropometric and cephalometric analysis of 14 patients.' *Clinical Genetics*, 62: 157–164.

Hurst, D.L. (1990) 'Epidemiology of severe myoclonic epilepsy of infancy.' *Epilepsia 31*, 4: 397–400.

Hus, V., Pickles, A., Cook, E.H. Jr., Risi, S. and Lord, C. (2007) 'Using the Autism Diagnostic Interview – Revised to increase phenotypic homogeneity in genetic studies of autism.' *Biological Psychiatry*, 61: 438–448.

Huson, S.M., Compston, D.A.S., Clark, P. and Harper, P.S. (1989) 'A genetic study of von Recklinghausen neurofibromatosis in south east Wales. 1: Prevalence, fitness, mutation rate, and effect of parental transmission on severity.' *Journal of Medical Genetics*, 26: 704–711.

Hussman, J.P. (2001) 'Suppressed GABAergic inhibition as a common factor in suspected etiologies of autism.' *Journal of Autism and Developmental Disorders*, 31: 247–248.

Hvas, A.-M., Ellegaard, J. and Nexø, E. (2001) 'Vitamin B12 treatment normalizes metabolic markers but has limited clinical effect: a randomized placebo-controlled study. *Clinical Chemistry*, 47: 1396–1404.

Hwa, H.L., Chang, Y.Y., Chen, C.H., Kao, Y.S. *et al.* (2007) 'Multiplex ligation-dependent probe amplification identification of deletions and duplications of the Duchenne muscular dystrophy gene in Taiwanese subjects.' *Journal of the Formosan Medical Association 106*, 5: 339–346.

I

Iannaccone, A., Mykytyn, K., Persico, A.M., Searby, C.C. *et al.* (2005) 'Clinical evidence of decreased olfaction in Bardet-Biedl syndrome caused by a deletion in the BBS4 gene.', *American Journal of Medical Genetics A, 132*: 343-346.

Ibarra, B., Rivas, F., Medina, C., Franco, M.E. *et al.* (1990) 'Hematological and biochemical studies in children with Down syndrome.' *Annals of Genetics 33*, 2: 84–87.

Ichida, K., Matsumura, T., Sakuma, R., Hosoya, T. and Nishino, T. (2001) 'Mutation of human molybdenum cofactor sulfurase gene is responsible for classical xanthinuria type II.' *Biochemical and Biophysical Research Communications*, 282: 1194–1200.

Iizuka, R., Hirayama, K. and Maehara, K. (1984) 'Dentatorubro-pallidoluysian atrophy: a clinico-pathological study.' *Journal of Neurology, Neurosurgery and Psychiatry*, 47: 1288–1298.

Ikeda, K., Schiltz, E., Fujii, T., Takahashi, M. *et al.* (2005) 'Phenylalanine ammonia-lyase modified with polyethylene glycol: potential therapeutic agent for phenylketonuria.' *Amino Acids 29*, 3: 283–287.

Ikeuchi, T., Onodera, O., Oyake, M., Koide, R. *et al.* (1995) 'Dentatorubral-pallidoluysian atrophy (DRPLA): close correlation of CAG repeat expansions with the wide spectrum of clinical presentations and prominent anticipation.' *Seminars in Cell Biology 6*, 1: 37–44.

Imai, T., Hattori, H., Miyazaki, M., Higuchi, Y. *et al.* (2001) 'Dandy-Walker variant in Coffin-Siris syndrome.' *American Journal of Medical Genetics*, 100: 152–155.

Imamura, Y., Fujikawa, Y., Komaki, H., Nakagawa, E. *et al.* (2007) 'A case of Möbius syndrome presenting with symptoms of severe infantile form of congenital muscular disorder.' *No To Hattatsu 39*, 1: 59–62.

Ingordo, V., D'Andria, G., Gentile, C., Decuzzi, M. *et al.* (2003) 'Frequency of X-linked ichthyosis in coastal southern Italy: a study on a representative sample of a young male population.' *Dermatology 207*, 2: 148–150.

Ingudomnukul, E., Baron-Cohen, S., Wheelwright, S. and Knickmeyer, R. (2007) 'Elevated rates of testosterone-related disorders in women with autism spectrum conditions.' *Hormones and Behavior 51*, 5: 597–604.

Insel, T.R. and Fenton, W.S. (2005) 'Psychiatric epidemiology: it's not just about counting anymore.' *Archives of General Psychiatry 62*, 6: 590–592.

International Molecular Genetic Study of Autism Consortium (1998) 'A full genome screen for autism with evidence for linkage to a region on chromosome 7q.' *Human Molecular Genetics*, 7: 571–578.

International Molecular Genetic Study of Autism Consortium (2001) 'A genomewide screen for autism: strong evidence for linkage to chromosomes 2q, 7q, and 16p.' *American Journal of Human Genetics*, 69: 570–581.

Ireland, M., English, C., Cross, I., Lindsay, S. and Strachan, T. (1995) 'Partial trisomy 3q and the mild Cornelia de Lange syndrome phenotype.' *Journal of Medical Genetics*, 32: 837–838.

Irons, M. (2007) 'Smith-Lemli-Opitz syndrome.' *GeneReviews*, downloadable from www.ncbi.nlm.nih.gov.

Irons, M., Elias, E.R., Abuelo, D., Bull, M.J. *et al.* (1997) 'Treatment of Smith-Lemli-Opitz syndrome: results of a multicenter trial.' *American Journal of Medical Genetics*, 68: 311–314.

Irons, M., Elias, E.R., Tint, G.S., Salen, G. *et al.* (1994) 'Abnormal cholesterol metabolism in the Smith-Lemli-Opitz syndrome: report of clinical and biochemical findings in four patients and treatment in one patient.' *American Journal of Medical Genetics*, 50: 347–352.

Irons, M.B. and Tint, G.S. (1998) 'Prenatal diagnosis of Smith-Lemli-Opitz syndrome.' *Prenatal Diagnosis*, 18: 369–372.

Irons, M.B., Nores, J., Stewart, T.L., Craigo, S.D. *et al.* (1999) 'Antenatal therapy of Smith-Lemli-Opitz syndrome.' *Fetal Diagnosis and Therapy 14*, 3: 133–137.

Irwin, S.A., Galvez, R. and Greenough, W.T. (2000) 'Dendritic spine structural anomalies in fragile-X mental retardation syndrome.' *Cerebral Cortex, 10*: 1038–1044.

Ishikawa-Brush, Y., Powell, J.F., Bolton, P., Miller, A.P. *et al.* (1997) 'Autism and multiple exostoses associated with an X;8 translocation occurring within the GRPR gene and 3' to the SDC2 gene.' *Human Molecular Genetics 6*, 8: 1241–1250.

Ishmael, H.A., Cataldi, D., Begleiter, M.L., Pasztor, L.M. *et al.* (2003) 'Five new subjects with ring chromosome 22.' *Clinical Genetics*, 63: 410–414.

Israel, J., Lessick, M., Szego, K. and Wong, P. (1991) 'Translocation 19;Y in a child with Bannayan-Zonana phenotype.' *Journal of Medical Genetics*, 28: 427–428.

Issekutz, K.A., Graham, J.M. Jr., Prasad, C., Smith, I.M. and Blake, K.D. (2005) 'An epidemiological analysis of CHARGE syndrome: preliminary results from a Canadian study.' *American Journal of Medical Genetics, 133A,* 3: 309–317.

Item, C.B., Stockler-Ipsiroglu, S., Stromberger, C., Muhl, A. *et al.* (2001) 'Arginine: glycine amidinotransferase deficiency: the third inborn error of creatine metabolism in humans.' *American Journal of Human Genetics* 69: 1127–1133.

Ito, M. (1952) 'Studies on melanin.' *Tohoku Journal of Experimental Medicine,* 55: 1–104.

Ito, M. (2004) '"Nurturing the brain" as an emerging research field involving child neurology.' *Brain and Development,* 26: 429–433.

J

Jablonka, E. and Lamb, M.J. (2005) *Evolution in Four Dimensions: Genetic, Epigenetic, Behavioral and Symbolic Variation in the History of Life.* Cambridge MA: MIT Press.

Jacob, A.G., Driscoll, D.J., Shaughnessy, W.J., Stanson, A.W. et al. (1998) 'Klippel-Trénaunay syndrome: spectrum and management.' *Mayo Clinic Proceedings,* 73: 28–36.

Jacob, S., Brune, C.W., Carter, C.S., Leventhal, B.L. *et al.* (2007) 'Association of the oxytocin receptor gene (OXTR) in Caucasian children and adolescents with autism.' *Neuroscience Letters,* doi:10.1016/j.neulet.2007.02.001.

Jacobs, A., Knight, B.P., McDonald, K.T. and Burke, M.C. (2006) 'Verapamil decreases ventricular tachyarrhythmias in a patient with Timothy syndrome (LQT8).' *Heart Rhythm 3,* 8: 967–970.

Jacobs, P.A. and Hassold, T.J. (1995) 'The origin of numerical chromosome abnormalities.' *Advances in Genetics,* 33: 10133.

Jacobs, P.A., Brunton, M., Melville, M.M., Brittain, R.P. and McClemont, W.F. (1965) 'Aggressive behavior, mental sub-normality and the XYY male.' *Nature,* 208: 1351–1352.

Jacobs, P.A., Melville, M., Ratcliffe, S., Keay, A.J. and Syme, J. (1974) 'A cytogenetic survey of 11,680 newborn infants.' *Annals of Human Genetics,* 37: 359–376.

Jackman, C., Horn, N.D., Molleston, J.P. and Sokol, D.K. (2009) 'Gene associated with seizures, autism, and hepatomegaly in an Amish girl.' *Pediatric Neurology,* 40: 310–313.

Jackson, C.E., Weiss, L., Reynolds, W.A., Forman, T.F. and Peterson, J.A. (1976) 'Craniosynostosis midface hypoplasia, and foot abnormalities: an autosomal dominant phenotype in a large Amish kindred.' *Journal of Pediatrics,* 88: 963–968.

Jackson, L., Kline, A.D., Barr, M.A. and Koch, S. (1993) 'De Lange syndrome: a clinical review of 310 individuals.' *American Journal of Medical Genetics,* 47: 940–946.

Jacquot, S., Zeniou, M., Touraine, R. and Hanauer, A. (2002) 'X-linked Coffin-Lowry syndrome (CLS, MIM 303600, RPS6KA3 gene, protein product known under various names: pp90rsk2, RSK2, ISPK, MAPKAP1).' *European Journal of Human Genetics,* 10: 2–5.

Jaeken, J. and Hagberg, B. (1991) 'Clinical presentation and natural course of the carbohydrate-deficient glycoprotein syndrome.' *Acta Paediatrica Scandinavica,* Suppl. 375: 6–13.

Jaeken, J. and van den Berghe, G. (1984) 'An infantile autistic syndrome characterized by the presence of succinylpurines in body fluids.' *Lancet 324,* 8411: 1058–1061.

Jaeken, J., van den Bergh, F., Vincent, M.F., Casaer, P. and van den Berghe, G. (1992) 'Adenylosuccinase deficiency: a newly recognized variant. *Journal of Inherited Metabolic Disease,* 15: 416–418.

Jaeken, J., Wadman, S.K., Duran, M., van Sprang, F.J. et al. (1988) 'Adenylosuccinase deficiency: an inborn error of purine nucleotide synthesis.' *European Journal of Pediatrics,* 148: 126–131.

Jaenisch, R. and Bird, A. (2003) 'Epigenetic regulation of gene expression: how the genome integrates intrinsic and environmental signals.' *Nature Genetics Supplement,* 33: 243–254.

Jakobs, C., Bojasch, M., Monch, E., Rating, D. *et al.* (1981) 'Urinary excretion of gamma-hydroxybutyric acid in a patient with neurological abnormalities: the probability of a new inborn error of metabolism.' *Clinica et Chimica Acta,* 111: 169–178.

Jamain, S., Betancur, C., Quach, H., Philippe, A. *et al.* (2002) 'Paris Autism Research International Sibpair (PARIS) Study, 2002: linkage and association of the glutamate receptor 6 gene with autism.' *Molecular Psychiatry,* 7: 302–310.

Jamain, S., Quach, H., Betancur, C., Rastam, M. *et al.* (2003) 'Mutations of the X-linked genes encoding neuroligins NLGN3 and NLGN4 are associated with autism.' *Nature Genetics 34,* 1: 27–29.

James, A., Culver, C. and Golabi, M. (2006) 'Simpson-Golabi-Behmel syndrome.' *GeneReviews,* www.genetests.org.

James, J.B., George, F. and Audhya, T. (2006) 'Abnormally high plasma levels of vitamin B6 in children with autism not taking supplements compared to controls not taking supplements.' *Journal of Alternative and Comparative Medicine 12,* 1: 59–63.

James, S.J., Cutler, P., Melnyk, S., Jernigan, S. *et al.* (2004) 'Metabolic biomarkers of increased oxidative stress and impaired methylation capacity in children with autism.' *American Journal of Clinical Nutrition,* 80: 1611–1617.

James, S.J., Melnyk, S., Jernigan, S., Cleves, M.A. *et al.* (2006) 'Metabolic endophenotype and related genotypes are associated with oxidative stress in children with autism.' *American Journal of Medical Genetics B, Neuropsychiatric Genetics,* doi:10.1002/amjg.b.30366.

Jamis-Dow, C.A., Turner, J., Biesecker, L.G. and Choyke, P.L. (2004) 'Radiologic manifestations of Proteus syndrome.' *Radiographics 24,* 4: 1051–1068.

Jamison, K.R. (1993) *Touched with Fire: Manic-Depressive Illness and the Artistic Temperament.* New York: Simon and Schuster.

Janniger, C.K. and Schwartz, R.A. (2008) 'Ichthyosis, X-linked.' *EMedicine,* downloadable from http://emedicine.medscape.com.

Janssen, P.J. and van der Heijden, C.A. (1988) 'Aspartame: review of recent experimental and observational data.' *Toxicology,* 50: 1–26.

Jarbrink, K. and Knapp, M. (2001) 'The economic impact of autism.' *Autism 5,* 1: 7–22.

Jarbrink, K., McCrone, P., Fombonne, E., Zanden, H. and Knapp, M. (2007) 'Cost-impact of young adults with high-functioning autistic spectrum disorder.' *Research in Developmental Disabilities,* 28: 94–104.

Javitt, D.C. (2004) 'Glutamate as a therapeutic target in psychiatric disorders.' *Molecular Psychiatry,* 9: 984–997.

Jawad, A.F., McDonald-McGinn, D.M., Zackai, E. and Sullivan, K.E. (2001) 'Immunologic features of chromosome 22q11.2 deletion syndrome (DiGeorge syndrome/velocardiofacial syndrome).' *Journal of Pediatrics,* 139: 715–723.

Jedele, K.B. (2007) 'The overlapping spectrum of Rett and Angelman syndromes: a clinical review.' *Seminars in Pediatric Neurology,* 14: 108–117.

Jeffries, A.R., Curran, S., Elmslie, F., Sharma, A. *et al.* (2005) 'Molecular and phenotypic characterization of ring chromosome 22.' *American Journal of Medical Genetics A,* 137: 139–147.

Jepson, B. and Johnson, J. (2007) *Changing the Course of Autism: A Scientific Approach for Parents and Physicians.* Boulder, CO: Sentient Publications.

Jernigan, T.L., Bellugi, U., Sowell, E., Doherty, S. and Hesselink, J.R. (1993) 'Cerebral morphologic distinctions between Williams and Down syndromes.' *Archives of Neurology 50,* 2: 186–191.

Jervis, G.A. (1947) 'Studies on phenylpyruvic oligophrenia: the position of the metabolic error.' *Journal of Biological Chemistry,* 169: 651–656.

Jezela-Stanek, A., Malunowicz, E.M., Ciara, E., Popowska, E. *et al.* (2006) 'Maternal urinary steroid profiles in prenatal diagnosis of Smith-Lemli-Opitz syndrome: first patient series comparing biochemical and molecular studies.' *Clinical Genetics,* 69: 77–85.

Jha, P., Sheth, D. and Ghaziuddin, M. (2007) 'Autism spectrum disorder and Klinefelter syndrome.' *European Journal of Child and Adolescent Psychiatry,* March 30 [e-print], doi:10.1007/s00787-007-0601-8

Jiang, Y., Tsai, T.-F., Bressler, J. and Beaudet, A.L. (1998) 'Imprinting in Angelman and Prader-Willi syndromes.' *Current Opinion in Genetics and Development,* 8: 334–342.

Jiang, Y.-H., Bresler, J. and Beaudet, A.L. (2004) 'Epigenetics and human disease.' *Annual Review of Genomics and Human Genetics,* 5: 479–510.

Jin, P., Zarnescu, D.C., Ceman, S., Nakamoto, M. et al. (2004) 'Biochemical and genetic interaction between the fragile X mental retardation protein and the microRNA pathway.' *Nature Neuroscience,* 7: 113–117.

Jira, P.E., Wevers, R.A., de Jong, J., Rubio-Gozalbo, E. *et al.* (2000) 'Simvastatin: a new therapeutic approach for Smith-Lemli-Opitz syndrome.' *Journal of Lipid Research 41,* 8: 1339–1346.

Jirtle, R.L. and Skinner, M.K. (2007) 'Environmental epigenomics and disease susceptibility.' *Nature Review: Genetics,* 8: 253–262.

Jirtle, R.L., Sander, M. and Barrett, J.C. (2000) 'Genomic imprinting and environmental disease susceptibility.' *Environmental Health Perspectives 108,* 3: 271–278.

Jöbsis, A.C., De Groot, W.P., Tigges, A.J., De Bruijn, H.W. et al. (1980) 'X-linked ichthyosis and X-linked placental sulfatase deficiency: a disease entity. Histochemical observations.' *American Journal of Pathology 99,* 2: 279–289.

Johansson, M., Billstedt, E., Danielsson, S., Strömland, K. *et al.* (2007) 'Autism spectrum disorder and underlying brain mechanism in the oculoauriculovertebral spectrum.' *Developmental Medicine and Child Neurology 49,* 4: 280–288.

Johansson, M., Gillberg, C. and Råstam, M. (2009) 'Autism spectrum conditions in individuals with Möbius sequence, CHARGE syndrome and oculo-auriculo-vertebral spectrum: diagnostic aspects.' *Research in Developmental Disabilities,* 31: 9–24.

Johansson, M., Råstam, M., Billstedt, E., Danielsson, S. *et al.* (2006) 'Autism spectrum disorders and underlying brain pathology in CHARGE association.' *Developmental Medicine and Child Neurology,* 48: 40–50.

Johansson, M., Wentz, E., Fernell, E., Stromland, K. *et al.* (2001) 'Autistic spectrum disorders in Möbius sequence: a comprehensive study of 25 individuals.' *Developmental Medicine and Child Neurology 43,* 5: 338–345.

Johnson, H., Wiggs, L., Stores, G. and Huson, S.M. (2005) 'Psychological disturbance and sleep disorders in children with neurofibromatosis type 1.' *Developmental Medicine and Child Neurology,* 47: 237–242.

Johnson, H.G., Ekman, P., Friesen, W., Nyhan, W.L. and Fish, C.H. (1976) 'Behavioral phenotype in the Cornelia de Lange syndrome.' *Pediatric Research,* 10: 843–850.

Johnson, J.A., Aughton, D.J., Comstock, C.H., von Oeyen, P.T. *et al.* (1994) 'Prenatal diagnosis of Smith-Lemli-Opitz syndrome, type II.' *American Journal of Medical Genetics,* 49: 240–243.

Johnson, V.P. (1975) 'Smith-Lemli-Opitz syndrome: review and report of two affected siblings.' *Zeitschrift für Kinderheilkunde,* 119: 221–234.

Joncourt, F., Neuhaus, B., Jostarndt-Foegen, K., Kleinle, S. *et al.* (2004) 'Rapid identification of female carriers of DMD/BMD by quantitative real-time PCR.' *Human Mutation,* 23: 385–391.

Jones, K.L. and Smith, D.W. (1975) 'The Williams elfin facies syndrome: a new perspective.' *Journal of Pediatrics,* 186: 718–723.

Jongbloet, P.H. (1987) 'Goldenhar syndrome and overlapping dysplasias, in vitro fertilisation and ovopathy.' *Journal of Medical Genetics,* 24: 616–620.

Jongmans, M.C.J., Admiraal, R.J., van der Donk, K.P., Vissers, L.E.L.M. *et al.* (2006) 'CHARGE syndrome: the phenotypic spectrum of mutations in the CHD7 gene.' *Journal of Medical Genetics,* 43: 306–314.

Jongmans, M.C.J., van Ravenswaaij-Arts, C.M.A., Pitteloud, N., Ogata, T. *et al.* (2009) 'CHD7 mutations in patients initially diagnosed with Kallmann syndrome – the clinical overlap with CHARGE syndrome.' *Clinical Genetics,* 75: 65–71.

Jorgensen, G. (1972) 'Befunde bei speziellen angeborenen Angiokardiopathien (II).' In P.E. Becker (ed.) *Humangenetik: Ein kurzes Handbuch in fünf Bänden.* Stuttgart: Thieme.

Jorgensen, O.S., Mellerup, E.T. and Rafelsen, O.J. (1970) 'Amino acid excretion in urine of children with various psychiatric diseases – a thin layer chromatrographic study.' *Danish Medical Bulletin,* 17: 166–170.

Jorizzo, J.L., Atherton, D.J., Crounse, R.G. and Wells, R.S. (1982) 'Ichthyosis, brittle hair, impaired intelligence, decreased fertility and short stature (IBIDS syndrome).' *British Journal of Dermatology,* 106: 705–710.

Joubert, M., Eisenring, J.J., Robb, J.P. and Andermann, F. (1969) 'Familial agenesis of the cerebellar vermis: a syndrome of episodic hyperpnea, abnormal eye movements, ataxia, and retardation.' *Neurology,* 19: 813–825.

Journel, H., Roussey, M. and Le Marec, B. (1989) 'MCA/MR syndrome with oligodactyly and Moebius anomaly in first cousins: new syndrome or familial facial-limb disruption sequence?' *American Journal of Medical Genetics,* 34: 506–510.

Jovanovic, S.V., Clements, D. and MacLeod, K. (1998) 'Biomarkers of oxidative stress are significantly elevated in Down syndrome.' *Free Radical Biology and Medicine,* 25: 1044–1048.

Junien, C. (2006) 'Impact of diets and nutrients/drugs on early epigenetic programming.' *Journal of Inherited Metabolic Disease,* 29: 359–365.

Juranek, J., Filipek, P.A., Berenji, G.R., Modahl, C. *et al.* (2006) 'Association between amygdala volume and anxiety level: magnetic resonance imaging (MRI) study in autistic children.' *Journal of Child Neurology,* 21: 1051–1058.

Jure, R., Rapin, I. and Tuchman, R.F. (1991) 'Hearing-impaired autistic children.' *Developmental Medicine and Child Neurology,* 33: 1062–1072.

Jurecka, A. (2009) 'Inborn errors of purine and pyrimidine metabolism.' *Journal of Inherited Metabolic Disease,* 32: 247–263.

Jurecka, A., Tylki-Szymanska, A., Zikanova, M., Krijt, J. and Kmoch, S. (2008) 'D-ribose therapy in four Polish patients with adenylosuccinate lyase deficiency: absence of positive effect.' *Journal of Inherited Metabolic Disease,* July 12, doi:10.1007/s10545-008-0904-z.

Jurkiewicz, E., Mierzewska, H. and Kusmierska, K. (2007) 'Adenylosuccinate lyase deficiency: the first identified Polish patient.' *Brain and Development,* 29: 600–602.

Juyal, R.C., Figuera, L.E., Hauge, X., Elsea, S.H. et al. (1996) 'Molecular analyses of 17p11.2 deletions in 62 Smith-Magenis syndrome patients.' *American Journal of Human Genetics,* 58: 998–1007.

K

Kadesjo, B. and Gillberg, C. (2000) 'Tourette's disorder: epidemiology and comorbidity in primary school children.' *Journal of the American Academy of Child and Adolescent Psychiatry 39,* 5: 548–555.

Kadrabová, J., Madáric, A., Sustrová, M. and Ginter, E. (1996) 'Changed serum trace element profile in Down's syndrome.' *Biological Trace Element Research 54,* 3: 201–206.

Kaffman, A. and Meaney, M.J. (2007) 'Neurodevelopmental sequelae of postnatal maternal care in rodents: clinical and research implications of molecular insights.' *Journal of Child Psychology and Psychiatry 48,* 3/4: 224–244.

Kagan-Kushnir, T., Roberts, S.W. and Snead, O.C. 3rd (2005) 'Screening electroencephalograms in autism spectrum disorders: evidence-based guideline.' *Journal of Child Neurology,* 20: 197–206.

Kahwash, S.B., Fung, B., Savelli, S., Bleesing, J.J. and Qualman, S.J. (2007) 'Autoimmune lymphoproliferative syndrome (ALPS): a case with congenital onset.' *Pediatric and Developmental Pathology 10,* 4: 315–319.

Kalin, J.H., Butler, K.V. and Kozikowski, A.P. (2009) 'Creating zinc monkey wrenches in the treatment of epigenetic disorders.' *Current Opinion in Chemical Biology 13,* 3: 263–271.

Kallen, K., Robert, E., Castilla, E.E., Mastroiacovo, P. and Kallen, B. (2004) 'Relation between oculo-auriculo-vertebral (OAV) dysplasia and three other non-random associations of malformations (VATER, CHARGE, and OEIS).' *American Journal of Medical Genetics,* 127A: 26–34.

Kallen, K., Robert, E., Mastroiacovo, P., Castilla, E.E. and Kallen, B. (1999) 'CHARGE association in newborns: a registry-based study.' *Teratology*, 60: 334–343.

Kalscheuer, V.M., Tao, J., Donnelly, A., Hollway, G. *et al.* (2003) 'Disruption of the serine/threonine kinase 9 gene causes severe X-linked infantile spasms and mental retardation.' *American Journal of Human Genetics*, 72: 1401–1411.

Kaminski, R.M., Banerjee, M. and Rogawski, M.A. (2004) 'Topiramate selectively protects against seizures induced by ATPA, a GluR5 kainate receptor agonist.' *Neuropharmacology*, 46: 1097–1104.

Kanaumi, T., Takashima, S., Hirose, S., Kodama, T. and Iwasaki, H. (2006) 'Neuropathology of methylmalonic acidemia in a child.' *Pediatric Neurology*, 34: 156–159.

Kanavin, O.J., Woldseth, B., Jellum, E., Tvedt, B. *et al.* (2007) '2-methylbutyryl-CoA dehydrogenase deficiency associated with autism and mental retardation: a case report.' *Journal of Medical Case Reports*, 1: 98, doi:10.1186/1752-1947-1-98.

Kanazawa, I. (1998) 'Dentatorubral-pallidoluysian atrophy or Naito-Oyanagi disease.' *Neurogenetics*, 2: 1–17.

Kanazawa, O. and Shirane, S. (1999) 'Can early zonisamide medication improve the prognosis in the core and peripheral types of severe myoclonic epilepsy in infants?' *Brain and Development*, 21: 503.

Kandel, E. (1979) 'Psychotherapy and the single synapse: the impact of psychiatric thought on neurobiological research.' *New England Journal of Medicine*, 301: 1028–1037.

Kandel, E.R. (2006) *In Search of Memory: The Emergence of a New Science of Mind.* New York: Norton.

Kandel, E.R., Schwartz, J.H. and Jessell, T.M. (eds.) (1991) *Principles of Neuroscience.* New York: Elsevier.

Kandel, E.R., Schwartz, J.H. and Jessell, T.M. (1995) *Essentials of Neural Science and Behavior.* Norwalk, CT: Appleton and Lange.

Kaneko, H., Tsukahara, M., Tachibana, H., Kurashige, H. *et al.* (1987) 'Congenital heart defects in Sotos sequence.' *American Journal of Medical Genetics*, 26: 569–576.

Kang, H.C., Kwon, J.W., Lee, Y.M., Kim, H.D. *et al.* (2007) 'Nonspecific mitochondrial disease with epilepsy in children: diagnostic approaches and epileptic phenotypes.' *Child's Nervous System 23*, 11: 1301–1307.

Kandt, R.S., Haines, J.L., Smith, M., Northrup, H. *et al.* (1992) 'Linkage of a major gene locus for tuberous sclerosis to a chromosome 16 marker for polycystic kidney disease' (abstract). *American Journal of Human Genetics*, 51, Suppl.: A4.

Kanner, A.M. (2004) 'Recognition of the various expressions of anxiety, psychosis, and aggression in epilepsy.' *Epilepsia*, 45, Suppl. 2: 22–27.

Kanner, L. (1943) 'Autistic disturbances of affective contact.' *Nervous Child*, 2: 217–250.

Kano, Y., Ohta, M. and Nagai, Y. (1987) 'Two case reports of autistic boys developing Tourette's disorder: indications of improvement?' *Journal of the American Academy of Child and Adolescent Psychiatry 26*, 6: 937–938.

Kano, Y., Ohta, M., Nagai, Y., Yokota, K. and Shimizu, Y. (1988) 'Tourette's disorder coupled with infantile autism: a prospective study of two boys.' *Japanese Journal of Psychiatry and Neurology 42*, 1: 49–57.

Kaplan, P., Levinson, M. and Kaplan, B.S. (1995) 'Cerebral artery stenoses in Williams syndrome cause strokes in childhood.' *Journal of Pediatrics*, 126: 943–945.

Kaplan, S., Itzkovitz, S. and Shapiro, E. (2007) 'A universal mechanism ties genotype to phenotype in trinucleotide diseases.' *PLoS Computational Biology 3*, 11: e235, doi:10.1371/ journal.pcbi.0030235.

Kapoor, S., Mukherjee, S.B., Paul, R. and Dhingra, B. (2005) 'OMTNS-Plus Syndrome.', *Indian Journal of Pediatrics, 72*, 8: 707–708.

Kar, P.S., Ogoe, B., Poole, R. and Meeking, D. (2005) 'Di-George syndrome presenting with hypocalcaemia in adulthood: two case reports and a review.' *Journal of Clinical Pathology 58*, 6: 655–657.

Karpf, J., Turk, J. and Howlin, P. (2004) 'Cognitive, language, and adaptive behavior profiles in individuals with a diagnosis of Cohen syndrome.' *Clinical Genetics*, 65: 327–332.

Kassaï, B., Chiron, C., Augier, S., Cucherat, M. *et al.* (2008) 'Severe myoclonic epilepsy in infancy: a systematic review and a meta-analysis of individual patient data.' *Epilepsia 49*, 2: 343–348.

Kates, W.R., Antshel, K.M., Fremont, W.P., Shprintzen, R.J. *et al.* (2007a) 'Comparing phenotypes in patients with idiopathic autism to patients with velocardiofacial syndrome (22q11 DS) with and without autism.' *American Journal of Medical Genetics A, 143*, 22: 2642–2650.

Kates, W.R., Antshel, K., Willhite, R., Bessette, B.A. *et al.* (2005) 'Gender-moderated dorsolateral prefrontal reductions in 22q11.2 deletion syndrome: implications for risk for schizophrenia.' *Child Neuropsychology 11*, 1, 73–85.

Kates, W.R., Krauss, B.R., AbdulSabur, N., Colgan, D. *et al.* (2007b) 'The neural correlates of non-spatial working memory in velocardiofacial syndrome (22q11.2 deletion syndrome).' *Neuropsychologia*, 45: 2863–2873.

Kates, W.R., Miller, A.M., Abdulsabur, N., Antshel, K.M. *et al.* (2006) 'Temporal lobe anatomy and psychiatric symptoms in velocardiofacial syndrome (22q11.2 deletion syndrome).' *Journal of the American Academy of Child and Adolescent Psychiatry 45*, 5: 587–595.

Kato, M., Das, S., Petras, K., Kitamura, K. et al. (2004) 'Mutations of ARX are associated with striking pleiotropy and consistent genotype–phenotype correlation.' *Human Mutation*, 23: 147–159.

Kato, M., Das, S., Petras, K., Sawaishi, Y. et al. (2003) 'Polyalanine expansion of ARX associated with cryptogenic West syndrome.' *Neurology*, 61: 267–276.

Kato, M., Saitoh, S., Kamei, A., Shiraishi, H. et al. (2007) 'A longer polyalanine expansion mutation in the ARX gene causes early infantile epileptic encephalopathy with suppression-burst pattern (Ohtahara syndrome).' *American Journal of Human Genetics, 81*: 361–366.

Kato, T., Hattori, H., Yorifuji, T., Tashiro, Y. and Nakahata, T. (2001) 'Intracranial aneurysms in Ehlers-Danlos syndrome type IV in early childhood.' *Pediatric Neurology*, 25: 336–339.

Katsanis, N. (2004) 'The oligogenic properties of Bardet-Biedt syndrome.' *Human Molecular Genetics*, 13 (Special No. 1): R65–R71.

Katsanis, N., Ansley, S.J., Badano, J.L., Eichers, E.R. *et al.* (2001) 'Triallelic inheritance in Bardet-Biedl syndrome, a Mendelian recessive disorder.' *Science*, 293: 2256–2259.

Katz, J.D. and Ropper, A.H. (2002) 'Familial Kleine-Levin syndrome: two siblings with unusually long hypersomnic spells.' *Archives of Neurology*, 59: 1959–1961.

Kau, A.S.M., Tierney, E., Bukelis, I., Stump, M.H. *et al.* (2004) 'Social behavior profile in young males with fragile-X syndrome: characteristics and specificity.' *American Journal of Medical Genetics*, 126A: 9–17.

Kaufman, S., Max, E.E. and Kang, E.S. (1975) 'Phenylalanine hydroxylase activity in liver biopsies from hyperphenylalaninemia heterozygotes: deviation from proportionality with gene dosage.' *Pediatric Research*, 9: 632–634.

Kaufmann, D., Muller, R., Bartelt, B., Wolf, M. *et al.* (2001) 'Spinal neurofibromatosis without café-au-lait macules in two families with null mutations of the NF1 gene.' *American Journal of Human Genetics*, 69: 1395–1400.

Kaufmann, W.E. and Moser, H.W. (2000) 'Dendritic anomalies in disorders associated with mental retardation.' *Cerebral Cortex*, 10: 981–991.

Kaufmann, W.E., Cortell, R., Kau, A.S.I., Tierney, E. *et al.* (2004) 'Autism spectrum disorder in fragile-X syndrome: communication, social interaction, and specific behaviors.' *American Journal of Medical Genetics A*, 129: 225–234.

Kaur, M., Descipio, C., McCallum, J., Yaeger, D. *et al.* (2005) 'Precocious sister chromatid separation (PSCS) in Cornelia de Lange syndrome.' *American Journal of Medical Genetics A*, 138: A27–31.

Kawame, H., Adachi, M., Tachibana, K., Kurosawa, K. *et al.* (2001) 'Graves' disease in patients with 22q11.2 deletion.' *Journal of Pediatrics*, 139: 892–895.

Kawamura, T., Chen, J., Takahashi, T., Ichitani, Y. and Nakahara, D. (2006) 'Prenatal stress suppresses cell proliferation in the early developing brain.' *NeuroReport 17*, 14: 1515–1518.

Kayaalp, L., Dervent, A., Saltik, S., Uluduz, D. *et al.* (2007) 'EEG abnormalities in West syndrome: correlation with the emergence of autistic features.' *Brain and Development*, 29: 336–345.

Kaye, C.I., Martin, A.O., Rollnick, B.R., Nagatoshi, K. *et al.* (1992) 'Oculoauriculovertebral anomaly: segregation analysis.' *American Journal of Medical Genetics*, 43: 913–917.

Kaye, C.I., Rollnick, B.R., Hauck, W.W., Martin, A.O. *et al.* (1989) 'Microtia and associated anomalies: statistical analysis.' *American Journal of Medical Genetics 34*, 4: 574–578.

Keegan, C.E., Mulliken, J.B., Wu, B.-L. and Korf, B.R. (2001) 'Townes-Brocks syndrome versus expanded spectrum hemifacial microsomia: review of eight patients and further evidence of a "hot spot" for mutation in the SALL1 gene.' *Genetics and Medicine*, 3: 310–313.

Keeler, L.C., Marsh, S.E., Leeflang, E.P., Woods, C.G. et al. (2003) 'Linkage analysis in families with Joubert syndrome plus oculo-renal involvement identifies the CORS2 locus on chromosome 11p12–q13.3.' *American Journal of Human Genetics*, 73: 656–662.

Keenan, G.F., Sullivan, K.E., McDonald-McGinn, D.M. and Zackai, E.H. (1997) 'Arthritis associated with deletion of 22q11.2: more common than previously suspected' [letter; comment]. *American Journal of Medical Genetics*, 71: 488.

Kelberman, D., Tyson, J., Chandler, D.C., McInerney, A.M. *et al.* (2001) 'Hemifacial microsomia: progress in understanding the genetic basis of a complex malformation syndrome.' *Human Genetics*, 109: 638–645.

Keller, C., Reynolds, A., Lee, B. and Garcia-Prats, J. (1998) 'Congenital myotonic dystrophy requiring prolonged endotracheal and noninvasive assisted ventilation: not a uniformly fatal condition.' *Pediatrics*, 101: 704–706.

Kelley, R.I. (1998) 'RSH/Smith-Lemli-Opitz syndrome: mutations and metabolic morphogenesis' (editorial). *American Journal of Human Genetics*, 63: 322–326.

Kelley, R.I. (2000) 'Inborn errors of cholesterol biosynthesis.' *Advances in Pediatrics*, 47: 1–53.

Kelley, R.I. and Hennekam, R.C.M. (2000) 'The Smith-Lemli-Opitz syndrome.' *Journal of Medical Genetics*, 37: 321–335.

Kelley, R.I., Zackai, E.H., Emanuel, B.S., Kistenmacher, M. *et al.* (1982) 'The association of the DiGeorge anomaly with partial monosomy of chromosome 22.' *Journal of Pediatrics*, 101: 197–200.

Kelley, R.L., Roessler, E., Hennekam, R.C., Feldman, G.L. et al. (1996) 'Holoprosencephaly in RSH/Smith-Lemli-Opitz syndrome: does abnormal cholesterol metabolism affect the function of Sonic Hedgehog?' *American Journal of Medical Genetics*, 66: 478–484.

Kent, L., Emerton, J., Bhadravathi, V., Weisblatt, E. et al. (2008) 'X-linked ichthyosis (steroid sulfatase deficiency) is associated with increased risk of attention deficit hyperactivity disorder, autism and social communication deficits.' *Journal of Medical Genetics*, 45: 519–524.

Kent, L., Perry, D. and Evans, J. (1998) 'Autism in Down's syndrome: three case reports.' *Autism*, 2: 259–361.

Kerbeshian, J. and Burd, L. (1986) 'Asperger's syndrome and Tourette syndrome: the case of the pinball wizard.' *British Journal of Psychiatry*, 148: 731–736.

Kerbeshian, J. and Burd, L. (1996) 'Case study: comorbidity among Tourette's syndrome, autistic disorder, and bipolar disorder.' *Journal of the American Academy of Child and Adolescent Psychiatry 35*, 5: 681–685.

Kerr, A.M. and Witt Engerstrom, I. (eds.) (2001) *Rett Disorder and the Developing Brain*. Oxford: Oxford University Press.

Kerr, A.M., Archer, H.L., Evans, J.C., Prescott, R.J. and Gibbon, F. (2006) 'People with MECP2 mutation-positive Rett disorder who converse.' *Journal of Intellectual Disability Research 50*, 5: 386–394.

Kerr, A.M., Webb, P., Prescott, R.J. and Milne, Y. (2003) 'Results of surgery for scoliosis in Rett syndrome.' *Journal of Child Neurology 18*, 10: 703–708.

Kerrigan, J.F., Shields, W.D., Nelson, T.Y., Bluestone, D.L. *et al.* (2000) 'Ganaxolone for treating intractable infantile spasms: a multicenter, open-label, add-on trial.' *Epilepsy Research 42*, 2/3: 133–139.

Kesler, S.R., Simensen, R.J., Voeller, K., Abidi, F. *et al.* (2007) 'Altered neurodevelopment associated with mutations of RSK2: a morphometric MRI study of Coffin-Lowry syndrome.' *Neurogenetics 8*, 2: 143–148.

Khalifa, N. and von Knorring, A.L. (2003) 'Prevalence of tic disorders and Tourette syndrome in a Swedish school population.' *Developmental Medicine and Child Neurology 45*, 5: 315–319.

Khan, S.G., Levy, H.L., Legerski, R., Quackenbush, E. *et al.* (1998) 'Xeroderma pigmentosum group C splice mutation associated with autism and hypoglycinemia.' *Journal of Investigative Dermatology*, 111: 791–796.

Khare, L., Strizheva, G.D., Bailey, J.N., Au, K.-S. *et al.* (2001) 'A novel missense mutation in the GTPase activating protein homology region of TSC2 in two large families with tuberous sclerosis complex.' *Journal of Medical Genetics*, 38: 347–349.

Khoshnood, B., Pryde, P., Wall, S., Singh, J. *et al.* (2000) 'Ethnic differences in the impact of advanced maternal age on birth prevalence of Down syndrome.' *American Journal of Public Health*, 90: 1778–1781.

Khoshnood, B., De Vigan, C., Vodovar, V., Goujard, J. and Goffinet, F. (2004) 'A population-based evaluation of the impact of antenatal screening for Down's syndrome in France, 1981-2000.', *British Journal of Obstetrics and Gynacology, 111*, 5: 485–490.

Kim, S.Y., Kim, S.K., Lee, J.S., Kim, I.K. and Lee, K. (2000) 'The prediction of adverse pregnancy outcome using low unconjugated estriol in the second trimester of pregnancy without risk of Down's syndrome.' *Yonsei Medical Journal 41*, 2: 226–229.

Kim, W., Erlandsen, H., Surendran, S., Stevens, R.C. *et al.* (2004) 'Trends in enzyme therapy for phenylketonuria.' *Molecular Therapy*, 10: 220–224.

Kimata, H. (1995) 'High-dose intravenous gamma-globulin treatment for hyperimmunoglobulinemia E syndrome.' *Journal of Allergy and Clinical Immunology 95*, 3: 771–774.

King, B.H. and Bostic, J.Q. (2006) 'An update on pharmacologic treatments for autism spectrum disorders.' *Child and Adolescent Psychiatric Clinics of North America*, 15: 161–175.

King, M.D., Fountain, C., Dakhlallah, D. and Bearman, P.S. (2009) 'Estimated autism risk and older reproductive age.' *American Journal of Public Health*, 99: 1673–1679.

King, R.A. and Oetting, W.S. (2007) 'Oculocutaneous albinism type 2.' Downloadable from *GeneReviews* at www.ncbi.nlm.nih.gov.

King, R.A., Wiesner, G.L., Townsend, D. and White, J.G. (1993) 'Hypopigmentation in Angelman syndrome.' *American Journal of Medical Genetics*, 46: 40–44.

Kishino, T., Lalande, M. and Wagstaff, J. (1997) 'UBE3A/E6-AP mutations cause Angelman syndrome.' *Nature Genetics*, 15: 70–73.

Kitamura, K., Yanazawa, M., Sugiyama, N., Miura, H. et al. (2002) 'Mutation of ARX causes abnormal development of forebrain and testes in mice and X-linked lissencephaly with abnormal genitalia in humans.' *Nature Genetics*, 32: 359–369.

Kitanovski, L., Ovcak, Z. and Jazbec, J. (2009) 'Multifocal hepatoblastoma in a 6-month-old girl with trisomy 18: a case report.' *Journal of Medical Case Reports*, 3: 8319, doi:10.4076/1752-1947-3-8319.

Kivitie-Kallio, S., Autti, T., Salonen, O. and Norio, R. (1998) 'MRI of the brain in the Cohen syndrome: a relatively large corpus callosum in patients with mental retardation and microcephaly.' *Neuropediatrics*, 29: 298–301.

Kivitie-Kallio, S., Larsen, A., Kajasto, K. and Norio, R. (1999) 'Neurological and psychological findings in patients with Cohen syndrome: a study of 18 patients aged 11 months to 57 years.' *Neuropediatrics*, 30: 181–189.

Kjellman, B. (1965) 'Cerebral gigantism.' *Acta Paediatrica Scandinavica*, 54: 603–609.

Klauck, S.M., Munstermann, E., Bieber-Martig, B., Ruhl, D. *et al.* (1997) 'Molecular genetic analysis of the FMR-1 gene in a large collection of autistic patients.' *Human Genetics*, 100: 224–229.

Klavdieva, M.M. (1996) 'The history of neuropeptides IV.' *Frontiers in Neuroendocrinology*, 17: 247–280.

Kleijer, W.J., Beemer, F.A. and Boom, B.W. (1994) 'Intermittent hair loss in a child with PIBI(D)S syndrome and trichothiodystrophy with defective DNA repair-xeroderma pigmentosum group D.' *American Journal of Medical Genetics*, 52: 227–230.

Klein, D. and Ammann, F. (1969) 'The syndrome of Laurence-Moon-Bardet-Biedl and allied diseases in Switzerland: clinical, genetic and epidemiological studies.' *Journal of Neurological Sciences*, 9: 479–513.

Kleine, W. (1925) 'Periodische Schlafsucht.' *Monatsschrift für Psychiatrie und Neurologie*, 57: 285.

Klein-Tasman, B.P., Mervis, C.B., Lord, C. and Phillips, K.D. (2007) 'Socio-communicative deficits in young children with Williams syndrome: performance on the autism diagnostic observation schedule.' *Child Neuropsychology 13*, 5: 444–467.

Klein-Tasman, B.P., Phillips, K.D., Lord, C., Mervis, C.B. and Gallo, F.J. (2009) 'Overlap with the autism spectrum in young children with Williams syndrome.' *Journal of Developmental and Behavioural Pediatrics*, 30: 289–299.

Kline, A.D., Barr, M. and Jackson, L.G. (1993) 'Growth manifestations in the Brachmann-de Lange syndrome.' *American Journal of Medical Genetics*, 47: 1042–1049.

Kline, A.D., Stanley, C., Belevich, J., Brodsky, K. *et al.* (1993) 'Developmental data on individuals with the Brachmann-de Lange syndrome.' *American Journal of Medical Genetics*, 47: 1053–1058.

Klushnik, T.P., Gratchev, V.V. and Belichenko, P.V. (2001) 'Brain-directed autoantibodies levels in the serum of Rett syndrome patients.' *Brain and Development*, 23 (Suppl. 1): 113–117.

Kluwe, L., Siebert, R., Gesk, S., Friedrich, R.E. *et al.* (2004) 'Screening 500 unselected neurofibromatosis 1 patients for deletions of the NF1 gene.' *Human Mutation*, 23: 111–116.

Kluwe, L., Tatagiba, M., Funsterer, C. and Mautner, V.F. (2003) 'NF1 mutations and clinical spectrum in patients with spinal neurofibromas.' *Journal of Medical Genetics*, 40: 368–371.

Kmoch, S., Hartmannova, H., Stiburkova, B., Krijt, J. *et al.* (2000) 'Human adenylosuccinate lyase (ADSL), cloning and characterization of full-length cDNA and its isoform, gene structure and molecular basis for ADSL deficiency in six patients.' *Human Molecular Genetics*, 9: 1501–1513.

Knapp, M., Romeo, R. and Beecham, J. (2009) 'Economic cost of autism in the UK.' *Autism 13*, 3: 317–336.

Knerr, I., Gibson, K.M., Jakobs, C. and Pearl, P.L. (2008) 'Neuropsychiatric morbidity in adolescent and adult succinic semialdehyde dehydrogenase deficiency patients.' *CNS Spectrums 13*, 7: 598–605.

Knerr, I., Pearl, P.L., Bottiglieri, T., Carter Snead, O. *et al.* (2007) 'Therapeutic concepts in succinate semialdehyde dehydrogenase (SSADH; ALDH5a1) deficiency (g-hydroxybutyric aciduria): hypotheses evolved from 25 years of patient evaluation, studies in ALDH5a1j/j mice and characterization of g-hydroxybutyric acid pharmacology.' *Journal of Inherited Metabolic Disease*, 30: 279–294.

Knickmeyer, R.C. and Baron-Cohen, S. (2006) 'Fetal testosterone and sex differences in typical social development and in autism.' *Journal of Child Neurology 21*, 10: 825–845.

Knickmeyer, R.C., Baron-Cohen, S., Fane, B.A., Wheelwright, S. *et al.* (2006) 'Androgens and autistic traits: a study of individuals with congenital adrenal hyperplasia.' *Hormones and Behavior*, 50: 148–153.

Knivsberg, A.M., Reichelt, K.L., Hoien, T. and Nodland, M. (2002) 'A randomised controlled study of dietary intervention in autistic syndromes.' *Nutritional Neuroscience 5*, 4: 251–261.

Knoll, J.H.M., Nicholls, R.D., Magenis, R.E., Graham, J.M. Jr. *et al.* (1989) 'Angelman and Prader-Willi syndromes share a common chromosome 15 deletion but differ in parental origin of the deletion.' *American Journal of Medical Genetics*, 32: 285–290.

Knox, S., Ge, H., Dimitroff, B.D., Ren, Y. *et al.* (2007) 'Mechanisms of TSC-mediated control of synapse assembly and axonal guidance.' *PLoS ONE 2*, 4: e375, 1–13, doi:10.1371/journal.pone.0000375.

Kobrynski, L., Chitayat, D., Zahed, L., McGregor, D. *et al.* (1993) 'Trisomy 22 and facioauriculovertebral (Goldenhar) sequence.' *American Journal of Medical Genetics*, 46: 68–71.

Kobylinski, O. (1883) 'Über eine Flughautähnliche Ausbreitung am Haise.' *Archives of Anthropology*, 14: 342–811.

Koch, M.C., Grimm, T., Harley, H.G. and Harper, P.S. (1991) 'Genetic risks for children of women with myotonic dystrophy.' *American Journal of Human Genetics*, 48: 1084–1091.

Koch, R., Burton, B., Hoganson, G., Peterson, R. *et al.* (2002) 'Phenylketonuria in adulthood: a collaborative study.' *Journal of Inherited Metabolic Disorders*, 25: 333–346.

Koch, R., Moats, R., Guttler, F., Guldberg, P. and Nelson, M. Jr. (2000) 'Blood–brain phenylalanine relationships in persons with phenylketonuria.' *Pediatrics*, 106: 1093–1096.

Koch, R., Moseley, K.D., Moats, R., Yano, S. *et al.* (2003a) 'Danger of high-protein dietary supplements to persons with hyperphenylalaninaemia.' *Journal of Inherited Metabolic Disease 26*, 4: 339–342.

Koch, R., Moseley, K.D., Yano, S., Nelson, M. Jr. and Moats, R.A. (2003b) 'Large neutral amino acid therapy and phenylketonuria: a promising approach to treatment.' *Molecular Genetics and Metabolism*, 79: 110–113.

Koide, R., Ikeuchi, T., Onodera, O., Tanaka, H. *et al.* (1994) 'Unstable expansion of CAG repeat in hereditary dentatorubral-pallidoluysian atrophy (DRPLA).' *Nature Genetics*, 6: 9–13.

Kolehmainen, J., Black, G.C.M., Saarinen, A., Chandler, K. *et al.* (2003) 'Cohen syndrome is caused by mutations in a novel gene, COH1, encoding a transmembrane protein with a presumed role in vesicle-mediated sorting and intracellular protein transport.' *American Journal of Human Genetics*, 72: 1359–1369.

Kolehmainen, J., Wilkinson, R., Lehesjoki, A.-E., Chandler, K. *et al.* (2004) 'Delineation of Cohen syndrome following a large-scale genotype–phenotype screen.' *American Journal of Human Genetics*, 75: 122–127.

Kolevzon, A., Gross, R. and Reichenberg, A. (2007) 'Prenatal and perinatal risk factors for autism: a review and integration of findings.' *Archives of Pediatric and Adolescent Medicine*, 161: 326–333.

Kolevzon, A., Smith, C.J., Schmeidler, J., Buxbaum, J.D. and Silverman, J.M. (2004) 'Familial symptom domains in monozygotic siblings with autism.' *American Journal of Medical Genetics (Neuropsychiatric Genetics)*, 129B: 76–81.

Komoto, J., Usui, S., Otsuki, S. and Terao, A. (1984) 'Infantile autism and Duchenne muscular dystrophy.' *Journal of Autism and Developmental Disorders 14*, 2: 91–95.

Komrower, G.M., Sardharwalla, I.B., Coutts, J.M.J. and Ingham, D. (1979) 'Management of maternal phenylketonuria: an emerging clinical problem.' *British Medical Journal*, I: 1383–1387.

Komure, O., Sano, A., Nishino, N., Yamauchi, N. *et al.* (1995) 'DNA analysis in hereditary dentatorubral-pallidoluysian atrophy: correlation between CAG repeat length and phenotypic variation and the molecular basis of anticipation.' *Neurology*, 45: 143–149.

Kondo, I., Nagataki, S. and Miyagi, N. (1990) 'The Cohen syndrome: does mottled retina separate a Finnish and a Jewish type?' *American Journal of Medical Genetics*, 37: 109–113.

Kooy, R.F., Willemsen, R. and Oostra, B.A. (2000) 'Fragile-X syndrome at the turn of the century.' *Molecular Medicine Today*, 6: 193–198.

Korman, S.H. (2006) 'Inborn errors of isoleucine degradation: a review.' *Molecular Genetics and Metabolism*, 89: 289–299.

Kornhuber, J., Mack-Burhardt, F., Konradi, C. *et al.* (1989) 'Effect of antemortem and postmortem factors on [3H]MK-801 binding in the human brain: transient elevation during early childhood.' *Life Science*, 45: 745–749.

Kosfeld, M., Heinrichs, M., Zak, P.J., Fishbacher, U. and Fehr, E. (2005) 'Oxytocin increases trust in humans' (letter). *Nature*, 435: 673–676.

Kothur, K., Ray, M. and Malhi, P. (2008) 'Correlation of autism with temporal tubers in tuberous sclerosis complex.' *Neurology India* 56, 1: 74–76.

Kousseff, B.G., Thomson-Meares, J., Newkirk, P. and Root, A.W. (1993) 'Physical growth in Brachmann-de Lange syndrome.' *American Journal of Medical Genetics*, 47: 1050–1052.

Kozak, L., Francova, H., Hrabnicova, E., Prochazkova, D. *et al.* (2000) 'Smith-Lemli-Opitz syndrome: molecular-genetic analysis of ten families.' *Journal of Inherited Metabolic Disease*, 23: 409–412.

Kozinetz, C.A., Skender, M.L., MacNaughton, N., Almes, M.J. *et al.* (1993) 'Epidemiology of Rett syndrome: a population-based registry.' *Pediatrics* 91, 2: 445–450.

Kozma, C. (1998) 'On cognitive variability in velocardiofacial syndrome: profound mental retardation and autism.' *American Journal of Medical Genetics*, 81: 269–270.

Krab, L.C., de Goede-Bolder, A., Aarsen, F.K., Pluijm, S.M. *et al.* (2008) 'Effect of simvastatin on cognitive functioning in children with neurofibromatosis type 1: a randomized controlled trial.' *Journal of the American Medical Association 300*, 3: 287–294.

Kraemer, K.H., Patronas, N.J., Schiffman, R., Brooks, B.P. *et al.* (2007) 'Xeroderma pigmentosum, trichothiodystrophy and Cockayne syndrome: a complex genotype–phenotype relationship.' *Neuroscience*, 145: 1388–1396.

Krane, C.M. and Goldstein, D.L. (2007) 'Comparative functional analysis of aquaporins/glyceroporins in mammals and anurans.' *Mammalian Genome*, 18: 452–462.

Krantz, I.D., McCallum, J., DeScipio, C., Kaur, M. *et al.* (2004) 'Cornelia de Lange syndrome is caused by mutations in NIPBL, the human homolog of drosophila melanogaster nipped-B.' *Nature Genetics*, 36: 631–635.

Kratz, L.E. and Kelley, R.I. (1999) 'Prenatal diagnosis of the RSH/Smith-Lemli-Opitz syndrome.', *American Journal of Medical Genetics, 82*, 5: 376–381.

Krishnamurthy, S., Kapoor, S. and Yadav, S. (2007) 'Nephrotic syndrome with X-linked ichthyosis, Kallmann syndrome and unilateral renal agenesis.' *Indian Pediatrics 44*, 4: 301–303.

Krivit, K., Lockman, L.A., Watkins, P.A., Hirsch, J. and Shapiro, E.G. (1995) 'The future for treatment by bone marrow transplantation for adrenoleukodystrophy, metachromatic leukodystrophy, globoid cell leukodystrophy and Hurler syndrome.' *Journal of Inherited Metabolic Disease*, 18: 398–412.

Kroll, J.S. (1985) 'Pyridoxine for neonatal seizures: an unexpected danger.' *Developmental Medicine and Child Neurology 985*, 27: 377–379.

Kröll-Seger, J., Portilla, P., Dulac, O. and Chiron, C. (2006) 'Topiramate in the treatment of highly refractory patients with Dravet syndrome.' *Neuropediatrics 37*, 6: 325–329.

Kuhl, P.K. (2000) 'A new view of language acquisition.' *Proceedings of the National Academy of Science 97*, 22: 11850–11857.

Kuhl, P.K., Coffey-Corina, S., Padden, D. and Dawson, G. (2005) 'Links between social and linguistic processing of speech in preschool children with autism: behavioral and electrophysiological measures.' *Developmental Science 8*, 1: F1–F12.

Kuijpers, G.M., De Vroede, M., Knol, H.E. and Jansen, M. (1999) 'Growth hormone treatment in a child with Williams-Beuren syndrome: a case report.' *European Journal of Pediatrics 158*, 6: 451–454.

Kujat, A., Schulz, M.D., Strenge, S. and Froster, U.G. (2006) 'Renal malformations in deletion 22q11.2 patients' (letter). *American Journal of Medical Genetics*, 140A: 1601–1602.

Kulaga, H.M., Leitch, C.C., Eichers, E.R., Badano, J.L. et al. (2004) 'Loss of BBS proteins causes anosmia in humans and defects in olfactory cilia structure and function in the mouse.' *Nature Genetics*, 36: 994–998.

Kumagai, T., Miura, K., Ohki, T., Matsumoto, A. *et al.* (2001) ['Central nervous system involvements in Duchenne/Becker muscular dystrophy']. *No To Hattatsu 33*, 6: 480–486.

Kurian, M.A., Morgan, N.V., MacPherson, L., Foster, K. *et al.* (2008) 'Phenotypic spectrum of neurodegeneration associated with mutations in the PLA2G6 gene (PLAN).' *Neurology*, 70: 1623–1629.

Kurlan, R. (2004) *Handbook of Tourette's Syndrome and Related Tic and Behavioral Disorder.* New York: Marcel Dekker.

Kurlan, R., Behr, J., Medved, L., Shoulson, I., Pauls, D. and Kidd, K.K. (1987) 'Severity of Tourette's syndrome in one large kindred: implication for determination of disease prevalence rate.' *Archives of Neurology*, 44: 268–269.

Kurlan, R., Eapen, V., Stern, J., McDermott, M.P. and Robertson, M.M. (1994) 'Bilineal transmission in Tourette's syndrome families.' *Neurology*, 44: 2336–2342.

Kurotaki, N., Imaizumi, K., Harada, N., Masuno, M. *et al.* (2002) 'Haploinsufficiency of NSD1 causes Sotos syndrome.' *Nature Genetics*, 30: 365–366.

Kushner, H.I. (1995) 'Medical Fictions: the case of the cursing Marquise and the (re)construction of Gilles de la Tourette's syndrome.' *Bulletin of the History of Medicine*, 69: 225–254.

Kushner, H.I. (1999) *A Cursing Brain? The Histories of Tourette Syndrome.* Cambridge, MA: Harvard University Press.

Kuzminski, A.M., Del Giacco, E.J., Allen, R.H., Stabler, S.P. and Lindenbaum, J. (1998) 'Effective treatment of cobalamin deficiency with oral cobalamin.' *Blood 92*, 4: 1191–1198.

Kyllerman, M. (1995) 'On the prevalence of Angelman syndrome.' *American Journal of Medical Genetics 59*, 3: 405.

Kyttala, M., Tallila, J., Salonen, R., Kopra, O. *et al.* (2006) 'MKS1, encoding a component of the flagellar apparatus basal body proteome, is mutated in Meckel syndrome.' *Nature Genetics*, 38: 155–157.

L

Lacassie, Y. and Arriaza, M.I. (1996) 'Opitz GBBB syndrome and the 22q11.2 deletion.' *American Journal of Medical Genetics*, 62: 318.

Lachlan, K.L., Lucassen, A.M., Bunyan, D. and Temple, I.K. (2007) 'Cowden syndrome and Bannayan-Riley-Ruvalcaba syndrome represent one condition with variable expression and age-related penetrance: results of a clinical study of PTEN mutation carriers.' *Journal of Medical Genetics*, 44: 579–585.

Lachman, M.F., Wright, Y., Whiteman, D.A.H., Herson, V. and Greenstein, R.M. (1991) 'Brief clinical report: a 46,XY phenotypic female with Smith-Lemli-Opitz syndrome.' *Clinical Genetics*, 39: 136–141.

Lacombe, D., Bonneau, D., Verloes, A., Couet, D. *et al.* (1993) 'Lujan-Fryns syndrome (X-linked mental retardation with marfanoid habitus, report of three cases and review.' *Genetic Counseling*, 4: 193–198.

Lajeunie, E., Cameron, R., El Ghouzzi, V., de Parseval, N. *et al.* (1999) 'Clinical variability in patients with Apert's syndrome.' *Journal of Neurosurgery*, 90: 443–447.

Lajiness-O'Neill, R.R., Beaulieu, I., Titus, J.B., Asamoah, A. *et al.* (2005) 'Memory and learning in children with 22q11.2 deletion syndrome: evidence for ventral and dorsal stream disruption?' *Neuropsychological Development and Cognition C Child Neuropsychology*, 11: 55–71.

Lake, B.D., Smith, V.V., Judge, M.R., Harper, J.I. and Besley, G.T.N. (1991) 'Hexanol dehydrogenase activity shown by enzyme histochemistry on skin biopsies allows differentiation of Sjogren-Larsson syndrome from other ichthyoses.' *Journal of Inherited Metabolic Disease*, 14: 338–340.

Lalande, M. and Calciano, M.A. (2007) 'Molecular epigenetics of Angelman syndrome.' *Cellular and Molecular Life Sciences 64*, 7/8: 947–960.

Lalani, S.R., Safiullah, A.M., Fernbach, S.D., Harutyunyan, K.G. *et al.* (2006) 'Spectrum of CHD7 mutations in 110 individuals with CHARGE syndrome and genotype–phenotype correlation.' *American Journal of Human Genetics*, 78: 303–314.

Lalani, S.R., Safiullah, A.M., Molinari, L.M., Fernbach, S.D. *et al.* (2004) 'SEMA3E mutation in a patient with CHARGE syndrome.' *Journal of Medical Genetics*, 41: e94.

Lalatta, F., Livini, E., Selicorni, A., Briscioli, V. *et al.* (1991) 'X-linked mental retardation with marfanoid habitus: first report of four Italian patients.' *American Journal of Medical Genetics*, 38: 228–232.

Lam, C.W., Yeung, W.L., Ko, C.H., Poon, P.M. *et al.* (2000) 'Spectrum of mutations in the MECP2 gene in patients with infantile autism and Rett syndrome.' *Journal of Medical Genetics*, 3: E41.

Lam, K.S.L., Aman, M.G. and Arnold, E. (2005) 'Neurochemical correlates of autistic disorder: a review of the literature.' *Research in Developmental Disabilities*, 27: 254–289.

Lama, G., Graziano, L., Calabrese, E., Grassia, C. *et al.* (2004) 'Blood pressure and cardiovascular involvement in children with neurofibromatosis type1.' *Pediatric Nephrology*, 19: 413–418.

Lammert, M., Friedman, J.M., Kluwe, L. and Mautner, V.F. (2005) 'Prevalence of neurofibromatosis 1 in German children at elementary school enrollment.' *Archives of Dermatology*, 141: 71–74.

Lamson, S.H. and Hook, E.B. (1980) 'A simple function for maternal-age-specific rates of Down syndrome in the 20-to-49-year age range and its biological implications.' *American Journal of Human Genetics*, 32: 743–753.

Landa, R.J., Holman, K.C. and Garrett-Mayer, E. (2007) 'Social and communication development in toddlers with early and later diagnosis of autism spectrum disorders.' *Archives of General Psychiatry 64*, 7: 853–864.

Lander, E. and Kruglyak, L. (1995) 'Genetic dissection of complex traits: guidelines for interpreting and reporting linkage results.' *Nature Genetics*, 11: 241–247.

Landgren, M., Gillberg, C. and Stromland, K. (1992) 'Goldenhar syndrome and autistic behaviour.' *Developmental Medicine and Child Neurology*, 34: 999–1005.

Landmark, C.J. and Johannessen, S.I. (2008) 'Pharmacological management of epilepsy: recent advances and future prospects.' *Drugs 68*, 14: 1925–1937.

Lane, N. (2005) *Power, Sex, Suicide: Mitochondria and the Meaning of Life.* Oxford: Oxford University Press.

Langius, F.A., Waterham, H.R., Romeijn, G.J., Oostheim, W. et al. (2003) 'Identification of three patients with a very mild form of Smith-Lemli-Opitz syndrome.' *American Journal of Medical Genetics*, 122A: 24–29.

Lashkari, A., Smith, A.K. and Graham, J.M. Jr. (1999) 'Williams-Beuren syndrome: an update and review for the primary physician.' *Clinical Pediatrics (Philadelphia) 38*, 4: 189–208.

Laumonnier, F., Bonnet-Brilhault, F., Gomot, M., Blanc, R. *et al.* (2004) 'X-linked mental retardation and autism are associated with a mutation in the NLGN4 gene, a member of the neuroligin family.' *American Journal of Human Genetics 74*, 3: 552–557.

Laurence, J.Z. and Moon, R.C. (1866) 'Four cases of retinitis pigmentosum occurring in the same family and accompanied by general imperfection of development.' *Ophthalmological Review*, 2: 32–41.

Lauritsen, M.B. and Ewald, H. (2001) 'The genetics of autism.' *Acta Psychiatrica Scandinavica*, 103: 411–427.

Lauritsen, M.B., Mors, O., Mortensen, P.B. and Ewald, H. (2002) 'Medical disorders among inpatients with autism in Denmark according to *icd-8*: a nationwide register-based study.' *Journal of Autism and Developmental Disorders 32*, 2: 115–119.

Lavenstein, B.L. (2003) 'Treatment approaches for children with Tourette's syndrome.' *Current Neurology and Neuroscience Reports 3*, 2: 143–148.

Laws, G. and Bishop, D. (2004) 'Pragmatic language impairment and social deficits in Williams syndrome: a comparison with Down's syndrome and specific language impairment.' *International Journal of Language and Communication Disorders*, 39: 45–64.

Lawson-Yuen, A., Saldivar, J.S., Sommer, S. and Picker, J. (2008) 'Familial deletion within NLGN4 associated with autism and Tourette syndrome.' *European Journal of Human Genetics*, 16: 614–618.

Lazo, O., Contreras, M., Hashmi, M., Stanley, W. *et al.* (1988) 'Peroxisomal lignoceroyl-CoA ligase deficiency in childhood adrenoleukodystrophy and adrenomyeloneuropathy.' *Proceedings of the National Academy of Science USA*, 85: 7647–7651.

Le Ber, I., Brice, A. and Durr, A. (2005) 'New autosomal recessive cerebellar ataxias with oculomotor apraxia.' *Current Neurology and Neuroscience Reports*, 5: 411–417.

Leckman, J.F. and Cohen, D.J. (eds.) (1999) *Tourette's Syndrome: Tics, Obsessions and Compulsions.* New York: John Wiley.

Ledbetter, D.H. (2008) 'Cytogenetic technology – genotype and phenotype.' *New England Journal of Medicine 359*, 16: 1728–1730.

Ledbetter, D.H., Riccardi, V.M., Airhart, S.D., Strobel, R.J. *et al.* (1981) 'Deletions of chromosome 15 as a cause of the Prader-Willi syndrome.' *New England Journal of Medicine 304*, 6: 325–329.

Le Deist, F. (2004) 'Autoimmune lymphoproliferative syndrome.' *Orphanet Encyclopaedia*, www.orpha.net.

Lee, D.A., Portnoy, S., Hill, P., Gillberg, C. and Patton, M.A. (2005) 'Psychological profile of children with Noonan syndrome.' *Developmental Medicine and Child Neurology*, 47: 35–38.

Lee, M.J. and Stephenson, D.A. (2007) 'Recent developments in neurofibromatosis type 1.' *Current Opinion in Neurology 20*, 2: 135–141.

Lee, S.-J. (2007) 'Sprinting without myostatin: a genetic determinant of athletic prowess.' *Trends in Genetics 23*, 10: 475–477.

Lee, W.T., Weng, W.C., Peng, S.F. and Tzen, K.Y. (2009) 'Neuroimaging findings in children with paediatric neurotransmitter diseases.' *Journal of Inherited Metabolic Disease 32*, 3: 361–370.

Lee Ie, Y., Quek, S.C., Chong, S.S., Tan, A.S. *et al.* (2006) 'Clinical report: a case of Williams syndrome and Klinefelter syndrome.' *Annals of the Academy of Medicine of Singapore 35*, 12: 901–904.

Lees, A.J. (1986) 'Georges Gilles de la Tourette: the man and his times.' *Revue Neurologique* (Paris), 142: 808–816.

Ledley, F.D., Koch, R., Jew, K., Beaudet, A. et al. (1988) 'Phenylalanine hydroxylase expression in liver of a fetus with phenylketonuria.' *Journal of Pediatrics*, 113: 463–468.

Legius, E., Schrander-Stumpel, C., Schollen, E., Pulles-Heintzberger, C. *et al.* (2002) 'PTPN11 mutations in LEOPARD syndrome.' *Journal of Medical Genetics*, 39: 571–574.

Legius, E., Wu, R., Eyssen, M., Marynen, P. *et al.* (1995) 'Encephalocraniocutaneous lipomatosis with a mutation in the NF1 gene.' *Journal of Medical Genetics*, 32: 316–319.

Legum, C., Godel, V. and Nemet, P. (1981) 'Heterogeneity and pleiotropism in the Moebius syndrome.' *Clinical Genetics*, 20: 254–259.

Leibowitz, D. and Dubowitz, V. (1981) 'Intellect and behaviour in Duchenne muscular dystrophy.' *Developmental Medicine and Child Neurology*, 23: 577–590.

Leisti, E.L., Pyhtinen, J. and Poyhonen, M. (1996) 'Spontaneous decrease of a pilocytic astrocytoma in neurofibromatosis type 1.' *AJNR American Journal of Neuroradiology*, 17: 1691–1694.

Lejeune, J., Gautier, M. and Turpin, R. (1959) 'Étude des chromosomes somatiques de neuf enfants mongoliens.' *Comptes Rendus de l'Academie des Sciences*, 248: 1721–1722.

Lejeune, J., Legrand, N., Lafourcade, J., Rethore, M.-O. *et al.* (1982) 'Fragilité du chromosome X et effets de la trimethoprime.' *Annales de Genetique*, 25: 149–151.

Leonard, H. and Bower, C. (1998) 'Is the girl with Rett syndrome normal at birth?' *Developmental Medicine and Child Neurology*, 40: 115–121.

Leonard, H., de Klerk, N., Bourke, J. and Bower, C. (2006) 'Maternal health in pregnancy and intellectual disability in the offspring: a population-based study.' *Annals of Epidemiology 16*, 6: 448–454.

Leonard, H., Thomson, M., Bower, C., Fyfe, S. and Constantinou, J. (1995) 'Skeletal abnormalities in Rett syndrome: increasing evidence for dysmorphogenetic defects.' *American Journal of Medical Genetics*, 58: 282–285.

Leonardi, M.L., Pai, G.S., Wilkes, B. and Lebel, R.R. (2001) 'Ritscher-Schinzel cranio-cerebello-cardiac (3C) syndrome: report of four new cases and review.' *American Journal of Medical Genetics*, 102: 237–242.

Le Parc, J.-M. (2005) 'Marfan syndrome.' *Orphanet Encyclopaedia*. Downloadable from: www.orpha.net.

Lerma-Carrillo, I., Molina, J.D., Cuevas-Duran, T., Julve-Correcher, C. *et al.* (2006) 'Psychopathology in the Lujan-Fryns syndrome: report of two patients and review.' *American Journal of Medical Genetics*, 140A: 2807–2811.

Lerman-Sagie, T., Leshinsky-Silver, E., Watemberg, N. and Lev, D. (2004) 'Should autistic children be evaluated for mitochondrial disorders?' *Journal of Child Neurology 19*, 5: 379–381.

Leuzzi, V. (2002) 'Inborn errors of creatine metabolism and epilepsy: clinical features, diagnosis, and treatment.' *Journal of Child Neurology*, 17: Suppl. 3, S89–S97.

Leuzzi, V., Bianchi, M.C., Tosetti, M., Carducci, C. *et al.* (2000) 'Clinical significance of brain phenylalanine concentration assessed by *in vivo* proton magnetic resonance spectroscopy in phenylketonuria.' *Journal of Inherited Metabolic Disease*, 23: 563–570.

Leuzzi, V., Di Sabato, M.L., Deodato, F., Rizzo, C. *et al.* (2007) 'Vigabatrin improves paroxysmal dystonia in succinic semialdehyde dehydrogenase deficiency.' *Neurology*, 68: 1320–1321.

Leuzzi, V., Di Sabato, M.L., Zollino, M., Montanaro, M.L. and Seri, S. (2004) 'Early-onset encephalopathy and cortical myoclonus in a boy with MECP2 gene mutation.' *Neurology*, 63: 1968–1970.

Levin, A.V., Seidman, D.J., Nelson, L.B. and Jackson, L.G. (1990) 'Ophthalmologic findings in the Cornelia de Lange syndrome.' *Journal of Pediatric Ophthalmology and Strabismus*, 27: 94–102.

Levin, M. (1929) 'Narcolepsy (Gelineau's syndrome) and other varieties of morbid somnolence.' *Archives of Neurology and Psychiatry*, 22: 1172–1200.

Levin, M. (1936) 'Periodic somnolence and morbid hunger: a new syndrome.' *Brain*, 59: 494–504.

Levine, T.M., Materek, A., Abel, J., O'Donnell, M. and Cutting, L.E. (2006) 'Cognitive profile of neurofibromatosis type 1.' *Seminars in Pediatric Neurology*, 13: 8–20.

Levitas, A.S. and Reid, C.S. (1998) 'Rubinstein-Taybi syndrome and psychiatric disorders.' *Journal of Intellectual Disability Research 42*, 4: 284–292.

Levitin, D.J., Menon, V., Schmitt, J.E., Eliez, S. *et al.* (2003) 'Neural correlates of auditory perception in Williams syndrome: an fMRI study.' *Neuroimage 18*, 1: 74–82.

Levitt, P., Eagleson, K.L. and Powell, E.M. (2004) 'Regulation of neocortical interneuron development and the implications for neurodevelopmental disorders.' *Trends in the Neurosciences 27*, 7: 400–406.

Levy, A., Michel, G., Lemerrer, M. and Philip, N. (1997) 'Idiopathic thrombocytopenic purpura in two mothers of children with DiGeorge sequence: a new component manifestation of deletion 22q11?' *American Journal of Medical Genetics*, 169: 356–359.

Levy, H.L., Guldberg, P., Guttler, F., Hanley, W.B. *et al.* (2001) 'Congenital heart disease in maternal phenylketonuria: report from the Maternal PKU Collaborative Study.' *Pediatric Research*, 49: 636–642.

Levy, H.L., Karolkewicz, V., Houghton, S.A. and MacCready, R.A. (1970) 'Screening the "normal" population in Massachusetts for phenylketonuria.' *New England Journal of Medicine*, 282:1455–1458.

Levy, H.L., Lobbregt, D., Barnes, P.D. and Poussaint, T.Y. (1996) 'Maternal phenylketonuria: magnetic resonance imaging of the brain in offspring.' *Journal of Pediatrics*, 128: 770–775.

Levy, H.L., Waisbren, S.E., Lobbregt, D., Allred, E. *et al.* (1995) 'Maternal mild hyperphenylalaninaemia: an international survey of offspring outcome.' *Obstetrical and Gynecological Survey 50*, 6: 430–431.

Levy, S.E. and Hyman, S.L. (2005) 'Novel treatments for autistic spectrum disorders.' *Mental Retardation and Developmental Disabilities Research Reviews*, 11: 131–142.

Levy, S.E., Mandell, D.S., Merhar, S., Ittenbach, R.F. and Pinto-Martin, J.A. (2003) 'Use of complementary and alternative medicine among children recently diagnosed with autistic spectrum disorder.' *Journal of Developmental and Behavioral Pediatrics 24*, 6: 418–423.

Levy, S.E., Mandell, D.S. and Schultz, R.T. (2009) 'Autism.' *The Lancet 374*, 9071: 1627–1638.

Levy, S.E., Souders, M.C., Ittenbach, R.F., Giarelli, E. *et al.* (2007) 'Relationship of dietary intake to gastrointestinal symptoms in children with autistic spectrum disorders.' *Biological Psychiatry*, 61: 492–497.

Lewis, J.C., Thomas, H.V., Murphy, K.C. and Sampson, J.R. (2004) 'Genotype and psychological phenotype in tuberous sclerosis' (letter). *Journal of Medical Genetics*, 41: 203–207.

Lewis, K.E., Lubetsky, M.J., Wenger, S.L. and Steele, M.W. (1995) 'Chromosomal abnormalities in a psychiatric population.' *American Journal of Medical Genetics*, 60: 53–54.

Li, D.Y., Brooke, B., Davis, E.C., Mecham, R.P. *et al.* (1998) 'Elastin is an essential determinant of arterial morphogenesis.' *Nature 393*, 6682: 276–280.

Lian, G. and Sheen, V. (2006) 'Cerebral developmental disorders.' *Current Opinion in Pediatrics*, 18: 614–620.

Licht, D.J. and Lynch, D.R. (2002) 'Juvenile dentatorubral-pallidoluysian atrophy: new clinical features.' *Pediatric Neurology 26*, 1: 51–54.

Liebermann, F. and Korf, B.R. (1999) 'Emerging approaches toward the treatment of neurofibromatoses.' *Genetics and Medicine*, 1: 158–164.

Lightdale, J.R., Siegel, B. and Heyman, M.B. (2001) 'Gastrointestinal symptoms in autistic children.' *Clinical Perspectives on Gastroenterology*, 1: 56–58.

Lilienfeld, S.O. (2005) 'Scientifically unsupported and supported interventions for childhood psychopathology: a summary.' *Pediatrics*, 115: 761–764.

Lima, M.D.M., Marques, Y.M.F.S., Alves-Júnior, S.M., Ortega, K.L. *et al.* (2007) 'Distraction osteogenesis in Goldenhar syndrome: case report and 8-year follow-up.' *Medicina Oral, Patologia Oral Y Cirugia Bucal 12*, 7: E528–531.

Limperopoulos, C., Bassan, H., Sullivan, N.R., Soul, J.S. et al. (2008) 'Positive screening for autism in ex-preterm infants: prevalence and risk factors.' Pediatrics, 121: 758–765.

Lin, A.E., Birch, P.H., Korf, B.R., Tenconi, R. et al. (2000) 'Cardiovascular malformations and other cardiovascular abnormalities in neurofibromatosis 1.' *American Journal of Medical Genetics*, 95: 108–117.

Lin, A.E., Siebert, J.R. and Graham, J.M. Jr. (1990) 'Central nervous system malformations in the CHARGE association.' *American Journal of Medical Genetics*, 37: 304–310.

Linck, L.M., Lin, D.S., Flavell, D., Connor, W.E. and Steiner, R.D. (2000) 'Cholesterol supplementation with egg yolk increases plasma cholesterol and decreases plasma 7-dehydrocholesterol in Smith-Lemli-Opitz syndrome.' *American Journal of Medical Genetics*, 93: 360–365.

Linde, L. and Kerem, B. (2008) 'Introducing sense into nonsense in treatments of human genetic diseases.' *Trends in Genetics 24*, 11: 552–563.

Linden, M.G. and Bender, B.G. (2002) 'Fifty-one prenatally diagnosed children and adolescents with sex chromosome abnormalities.' *American Journal of Medical Genetics*, 110: 118.

Linden, M.G., Bender, B.G. and Robinson, A. (1996) 'Intrauterine diagnosis of sex chromosome aneuploidy.' *Obstetric and Gynecology*, 87: 468–475.

Linden, M.G., Tassone, F., Gane, L.W., Hills, J.L. *et al.* (1999) 'Compound heterozygous female with fragile-X syndrome.' *American Journal of Medical Genetics*, 83: 318–321.

Lindor, N.M., Kasperbauer, J.L., Hoffman, A.D., Parisi, J.E. et al. (2002) 'Confirmation of existence of a new syndrome: LAPS syndrome.' American Journal of Medical Genetics 109, 2: 93–99.

Linnell, J.C. and Matthews, D.M. (1984) 'Cobalamin metabolism and its clinical aspects.' Clinical Science 66, 2: 113–121.

Lintas, C. and Persico, A.M. (2008) 'Autistic phenotypes and genetic testing: state-of-the-art for the clinical geneticist.' Journal of Medical Genetics, doi:10.1136/jmg.2008.060871.

Lion-François, L., Cheillan, D., Pitelet, G., Acquaviva-Bourdain, C. et al. (2006) 'High frequency of creatine deficiency syndromes in patients with unexplained mental retardation.' Neurology 67, 9: 1713–1714.

Lisk, D.R. (2009) 'Kleine-Levin syndrome.' Practical Neurology 9, 1: 42–45.

Liu, J., Nyholt, D.R., Magnussen, P., Parano, E. et al. (2001) 'A genome-wide screen for autism susceptibility loci.' American Journal of Human Genetics, 69: 327–340.

Liu, X., Dietrich, K.N., Radcliffe, J., Ragan, N.B. et al. (2002) 'Do children with falling blood lead levels have improved cognition?' Pediatrics 110, 4: 787–791.

Liu, X., Hubbard, J.A., Fabes, R.A. and Adam, J.B. (2006) 'Sleep disturbances and correlates of children with autism spectrum disorders.' Child Psychiatry and Human Development 37, 2: 179–191.

Liu, X.-Q., Paterson, A.D., Szatmari, P. and the Autism Genome Project Consortium (2008) 'Genome-wide linkage analyses of quantitative and categorical autism subphenotypes.' Biological Psychiatry, 64: 561–570.

Lockwood, D., Hecht, F., Dowman, C., Hecht, B.K. et al. (1988) 'Chromosome subband 17p11.2 deletion: a minute deletion syndrome.' Journal of Medical Genetics, 25: 732–737.

Loesch, D.Z., Bui, Q.M., Dissanayake, C., Clifford, S. et al. (2007) 'Molecular and cognitive predictors of the continuum of autistic behaviours in fragile-X.' Neuroscience and Biobehavioral Reviews, 31: 315–326.

Løken, A.A., Hanssen, O., Halvorsen, S. and Jolster, N.J. (1961) 'Hereditary renal dysplasia and blindness.' Acta Paediatrica, 50: 177–184.

Lombard, J. (1998) 'Autism: a mitochondrial disorder?' Medical Hypotheses, 50: 497–500.

Look, A.T. (2002) 'A leukemogenic twist for GATA1.' Nature Genetics, 32: 83–84.

Lopez-Bendito, G., Shigemoto, R., Fairen, A. and Lujan, R. (2002) 'Differential distribution of group 1 metabotropic glutamate receptors during rat cortical development.' Cerebral Cortex, 12: 625–638.

Lossie, A.C., Whitney, M.M., Amidon, D., Dong, H.J. et al. (2001) 'Distinct phenotypes distinguish the molecular classes of Angelman syndrome.' Journal of Medical Genetics, 38: 834–845.

Louis, M., Lebacq, J., Poortmans, J.R., Belpaire-Dethiou, M.C. et al. (2003) 'Beneficial effects of creatine supplementation in dystrophic patients.' Muscle and Nerve, 27: 604–610.

Lowe, T.L., Tanaka, K., Seashore, M.R., Young, J.G. and Cohen, D.J. (1980) 'Detection of phenylketonuria in autistic and psychotic children.' Journal of the American Medical Association, 243: 126–128.

Lowe, X., Eskenazi, B., Nelson, D.O., Kidd, S. et al. (2001) 'Frequency of XY sperm increases with age in fathers of boys with Klinefelter syndrome.' American Journal of Human Genetics, 69: 1046–1054.

Lu, Z., Zhang, R. and Diasio, R.B. (1993) 'Dihydropyrimidine dehydrogenase activity in human peripheral blood mononuclear cells and liver: population characteristics, newly identified deficient patients, and clinical implication in 5-fluorouracil chemotherapy.' Cancer Research, 53: 5433–5438.

Lu, Z., Zhang, R., Carpenter, J.T. and Diasio, R.B. (1998) 'Decreased dihydropyrimidine dehydrogenase activity in a population of patients with breast cancer: implication for 5-fluorouracil-based chemotherapy.', Clinical Cancer Research, 4, 2: 325–329.

Lubs, H.A. Jr. (1969) 'A marker X chromosome.' American Journal of Human Genetics, 21: 231–244.

Lucas, R.E., Vlangos, C.N., Das, P., Patel, P.I. and Elsea, S.H. (2001) 'Genomic organisation of the ~1.5 Mb Smith-Magenis syndrome critical interval: transcription map, genomic contig, and candidate gene analysis.' European Journal of Human Genetics, 9: 892–902.

Luciani, J.J., de Mas, P., Depetris, D., Mignon-Ravix, C. et al. (2003) 'Telomeric 22q13 deletions resulting from rings, simple deletions, and translocations: cytogenetic, molecular, and clinical analyses of 32 new observations.' Journal of Medical Genetics, 40: 690–696.

Luders, E., Di Paola, M., Tomaiuolo, F., Thompson, P.M. et al. (2007) 'Callosal morphology in Williams syndrome: a new evaluation of shape and thickness.' Neuroreport 18, 3: 203–207.

Ludwig, M., Katalinic, A., Gross, S., Sutcliffe, A. et al. (2005) 'Increased prevalence of imprinting defects in patients with Angelman syndrome born to subfertile couples.' Journal of Medical Genetics, 42: 289–291.

Lujan, J.E., Carlin, M.E. and Lubs, H.A. (1984) 'A form of X-linked mental retardation with marfanoid habitus.' American Journal of Medical Genetics, 17: 311–322.

Lukusa, T., Vermeesch, J.R., Holvoet, M., Fryns, J.P. and Devriendt, K. (2004) 'Deletion 2q37.3 and autism: molecular cytogenetic mapping of the candidate region for autistic disorder.' Genetic Counselling 15, 3: 293–301.

Lumley, M.A., Jordan, M., Rubenstein, R., Tsipouras, P. and Evans, M.I. (1994) 'Psychosocial functioning in the Ehlers-Danlos syndrome.' American Journal of Medical Genetics 53, 2: 149–152.

Lumley, M.A., Ovies, T., Stettner, L., Wehmer, F. and Lakey, B. (1996) 'Alexithymia, social support and health problems.' Journal of Psychosomatic Research 41, 6: 519–530.

Lund, P.M., Puri, N., Durham-Pierre, D., King, R.A. and Brilliant, M.H. (1997) 'Oculocutaneous albinism in an isolated Tonga community in Zimbabwe.' Journal of Medical Genetics, 34: 733–735.

Lykkesfeldt, G. and Hoyer, H. (1983) 'Topical cholesterol treatment of recessive X-linked ichthyosis.' Lancet 322, 8363: 1337–1338.

Lykkesfeldt, G., Bennett, P., Lykkesfeldt, A.E., Micic, S. et al. (1985) 'Abnormal androgen and oestrogen metabolism in men with steroid sulphatase deficiency and recessive X-linked ichthyosis.' Clinical Endocrinology, 23: 385–393.

Lynch, D.R., McDonald-McGinn, D.M., Zackai, E.H., Emanuel, B.S. et al. (1995) 'Cerebellar atrophy in a patient with velocardiofacial syndrome.' Journal of Medical Genetics, 32: 561–563.

Lynch, N.E., Lynch, S.A., McMenamin, J. and Webb, D. (2009) 'Bannayan-Riley-Ruvalcaba syndrome: a cause of extreme macrocephaly and neurodevelopmental delay.' Archives of Disease in Childhood 94, 7: 553–554.

M

Ma, D.Q., Whitehead, P.L., Menold, M.M., Martin, E.R. et al. (2005) 'Identification of significant association and gene–gene interaction of GABA receptor subunit genes in autism.' American Journal of Human Genetics, 77: 377–388.

Maaswinkel-Mooij, P.D., Laan, L.A.E.M., Onkenhout, W., Brouwer, O.F. et al. (1997) 'Adenylosuccinase deficiency presenting with epilepsy in early infancy.' Journal of Inherited Metabolic Disease, 20: 606–607.

Macarov, M., Zeigler, M., Newman, J.P., Strich, D. et al. (2007) 'Deletions of VCX-A and NLGN4: a variable phenotype including normal intellect.' Journal of Intellectual Disability Research 51, 5: 329–333.

Mahfoud, A., Domínguez, C.L., Pérez, A., Rodríguez, T. et al. (2004) ['L-2-hydroxyglutaric aciduria: clinical, biochemical and neuroradiological findings in two Venezuelan patients.'] [Article in Spanish.] Revista de Neurologia, 39: 343–346.

McArthur, A.J. and Budden, S.S. (1998) 'Sleep dysfunction in Rett syndrome: a trial of exogenous melatonin treatment.' *Developmental Medicine and Child Neurology*, 40: 186–192.

McBride, S.M.J., Choi, C.H., Wang, Y., Leibelt, D. et al. (2005) 'Pharmacological rescue of synaptic plasticity, courtship behaviour, and mushroom body defects in a drosophila model of fragile X syndrome.' *Neuron*, 45: 753–764.

McCandless, J. (2007) *Children with Starving Brains: A Medical Treatment Guide for Autism Spectrum Disorder* (3rd ed). North Bergen, NJ: Bramble Books.

McCauley, J.L., Li, C., Jiang, L., Olson, L.M. et al. (2005) 'Genome-wide and ordered-subset linkage analyses provide support for autism loci on 17q and 19p with evidence of phenotypic and interlocus genetic correlates.' *BMC Medical Genetics*, 6: 1–11, doi:10.1186/1471-2350-6-1.

McClung, C.A. and Nestler, E.J. (2007) 'Neuroplasticity mediated by altered gene expression.' *Neuropsychopharmacology Reviews*, 1–15, doi:10.1038/sj.npp.1301544.

MacCollin, M., Willett, C., Heinrich, B., Jacoby, L.B. et al. (2003) 'Familial Schwannomatosis: exclusion of the NF2 locus as the germline event.' *Neurology*, 60: 1968–1974.

MacDermott, S., Williams, K., Ridley, G., Glasson, E. and Wray, J. (2007) 'The prevalence of autism in Australia: can it be established from existing data?' Overview and report. Australian Advisory Board on Autism Spectrum Disorders, www.autismaus.com.au.

Macdonald, A., Daly, A., Davies, P., Asplin, D. et al. (2004) 'Protein substitutes for PKU: what's new?' *Journal of Inherited Metabolic Disease*, 27: 363–371.

MacDonald, M.R., Schaefer, G.B., Olney, A.H., Tamayo, M. and Frias, J.L. (1993) 'Brain magnetic resonance imaging findings in the Opitz G/BBB syndrome: extension of the spectrum of midline brain anomalies.' *American Journal of Medical Genetics*, 46: 706–711.

MacDonald, T.T. and Domizio, P. (2007) 'Autistic enterocolitis: is it a histopathological entity?' *Histopathology*, 50: 371–379, doi:10.1111/j.1365-2559.2007.02606.x.

McDonald-McGinn, D.M., Driscoll, D.A., Bason, L., Christensen, K. et al. (1995) 'Autosomal dominant "Opitz" GBBB syndrome due to a 22q11.2 deletion.' *American Journal of Medical Genetics*, 59: 103–113.

McDonald-McGinn, D.M., Kirschner, R., Goldmuntz, E., Sullivan, K. et al. (1999) 'The Philadelphia story: the 22q11.2 deletion: report on 250 patients.' *Genetic Counselling*, 10: 11–24 .

McDonald-McGinn, D.M., Tonnesen, M.K., Laufer-Cahana, A., Finucane, B. et al. (2001) 'Phenotype of the 22q11.2 deletion in individuals identified through an affected relative: cast a wide FISHing net!' *Genetics in Medicine*, 3: 23–29.

McDougle, C.J., Naylor, S.T., Cohen, D.J., Aghajanian, G.K. et al. (1996) 'Effects of tryptophan depletion in drug-free adults with autistic disorder.' *Archives of General Psychiatry 53*, 11: 993–1000.

MacFabe, D.F., Cain, D.P., Rodriguez-Capote, K., Franklin, A.E. et al. (2007) 'Neurobiological effects of intraventricular propionic acid in rats: possible role of short chain fatty acids on the pathogenesis and characteristics of autism spectrum disorders.' *Behavioral Brain Research*, 176: 149–169.

McFadden, S.A. (1996) 'Phenotypic variation in xenobiotic metabolism and adverse environmental response: focus on sulfur-dependent detoxification pathways.' *Toxicology 111*, 1/3: 43–65.

McGaughran, J., Donnai, D., Clayton, P. and Mills, K. (1994) 'Diagnosis of Smith-Lemli-Opitz syndrome' (letter). *New England Journal of Medicine*, 330: 1685–1686.

McGhee, E.M., Klump, C.J., Bitts, S.M., Cotter, P.D. and Lammer, E.J. (2000) 'Candidate region for Coffin-Siris syndrome at 7q32–34.' *American Journal of Medical Genetics*, 93: 241–243.

McGue, M. and Bouchard, T.J. Jr. (1998) 'Genetic and environmental influences on human behavioral differences.' *Annual Review of Neuroscience*, 21: 1–24.

McKeever, K., Shepherd, C.W., Crawford, H. and Morrison, P.J. (2008) 'An epidemiological, clinical and genetic survey of neurofibromatosis type 1 in children under sixteen years of age.' *Ulster Medical Journal*, 77: 160–163.

McKeever, P.A. and Young, I.D. (1990) 'Smith-Lemli-Opitz syndrome II: a disorder of the fetal adrenals?' *Journal of Medical Genetics*, 27: 465–466.

MacKenzie, J.J., Sumargo, I. and Taylor, S.A.M. (2006) 'A cryptic full mutation in a male with a classical fragile-X phenotype.' *Clinical Genetics*, 70: 39–42.

McKenzie, O., Ponte, M., Mangelsdorf, M., Finnis, G. et al. (2007) 'Aristaless-related homeobox gene, the gene responsible for West syndrome and related disorders, is a Groucho/transducin-like enhancer of split dependent transcriptional repressor.' *Neuroscience*, doi:10.1016/j.neuroscience.2007.01.038.

MacLean, J.E., Teshima, I.E., Szatmari, P. and Nowaczyk, M.J. (2000) 'Ring chromosome 22 and autism: report and review.' *American Journal of Medical Genetics 90*, 5: 382–385.

Maclean, K., Field, M.J., Colley, A.S., Mowat, D.R. et al. (2004) 'Kousseff syndrome: a causally heterogeneous disorder.' *American Journal of Medical Genetics*, 124A: 307–312.

McLean-Tooke, A., Barge, D., Spickett, G.P. and Gennery, A.R. (2008) 'Immunologic defects in 22q11.2 deletion syndrome.' Journal of Allergy and Clinical Immunology, 122: 362–367.

McNairn, A.J. and Gerton, J.L. (2008a) 'The chromosome glue gets a little stickier.' *Trends in Genetics 24*, 8: 382–389.

McNairn, A.J. and Gerton, J.L. (2008b) 'Cohesinopathies: one ring, many obligations.' *Mutation Research 647*, 1/2: 103–111.

McPherson, E.W., Laneri, G., Clemens, M.M., Kochmar, S.J. and Surti, U. (1997) 'Apparently balanced t(1;7)(q21.3;q34) in an infant with Coffin-Siris syndrome.' *American Journal of Medical Genetics*, 71: 430–433.

Maddalena, A., Sosnoski, D.M., Berry, G.T. and Nussbaum, R.L. (1988) 'Mosaicism for an intragenic deletion in a boy with mild ornithine transcarbamylase deficiency.' *New England Journal of Medicine*, 319: 999–1003.

Maddocks, J. and Reed, T. (1989) 'Urine test for adenylosuccinase deficiency in autistic children' (letter). *Lancet 333*, 8630: 158–159.

Madsen, P.P., Kibaek, M., Roca, X., Sachidanandam, R. et al. (2006) 'Short/branched-chain acyl-CoA dehydrogenase deficiency due to an IVS3+3A–G mutation that causes exon skipping.' *Human Genetics*, 118: 680–690.

Magenis, R.E., Toth-Fejel, S., Allen, L.J., Black, M. et al. (1990) 'Comparison of the 15q deletions in Prader-Willi and Angelman syndromes: specific regions, extent of deletions, parental origin, and clinical consequences.' *American Journal of Medical Genetics*, 35: 333–349.

Magenis, R.E., Toth-Fejel, S., Allen, L.J., Cohen, R. et al. (1988) 'Angelman, happy puppet and Prader-Willi syndromes: do they share an identical deletion?' (abstract). *American Journal of Human Genetics*, 43: A113.

Mahmood, A., Bibat, G., Zhan, A.-L., Izbudak, I. et al. (2009) 'White matter impairment in Rett syndrome: diffusion tensor imaging study with clinical correlations.' *American Journal of Neuroradiology*, 31: 295–299.

Maier, E.M., Kammerer, S., Muntau, A.C., Wichers, M. et al. (2002) 'Symptoms in carriers of adrenoleukodystrophy relate to skewed X inactivation.' *Annals of Neurology*, 52: 683–688.

Maillot, F., Lilburn, M., Baudin, J., Morley, D.W. and Lee, P.J. (2008) 'Factors influencing outcomes in the offspring of mothers with phenylketonuria during pregnancy: the importance of variation in maternal blood phenylalanine.' *American Journal of Clinical Nutrition 88*, 3: 700–705.

Maimburg, R.D. and Vaeth, M. (2006) 'Perinatal risk factors and infantile autism.' *Acta Psychiatrica Scandinavica 114*, 4: 257–264.

Mainardi, P.C. (2006) 'Cri du Chat syndrome.' *Orphanet Journal of Rare Diseases*, 1:33, doi:10.1186/1750-1172-1-33.

Maiwald, R., Bonte, A., Jung, H., Bitter, P. et al. (2002) 'De novo MECP2 mutation in a 46,XX male patient with Rett syndrome' (letter). *Neurogenetics*, 4: 107–108.

Mak, C.M., Siu, T.S., Lam, C.W., Chan, G.C. *et al.* (2007) 'Complete recovery from acute encephalopathy of late-onset ornithine transcarbamylase deficiency in a 3-year-old boy.' *Journal of Inherited Metabolic Disease 30*, 6: 981.

Makedonski, K., Abuhatzira, L., Kaufman, Y., Razin, A. and Shemer, R. (2005) 'MeCP2 deficiency in Rett syndrome causes epigenetic aberrations at the PWS/AS imprinting center that affects UBE3A expression.' *Human Molecular Genetics 14*, 8: 1049–1058.

Malcolm, S., Clayton-Smith, J., Nichols, M., Robb, S. *et al.* (1991) 'Uniparental paternal disomy in Angelman's syndrome.' *Lancet 337*, 8743: 694–697.

Malini, S.S. and Ramachandra N.B. (2006) 'Influence of advanced age of maternal grandmothers on Down syndrome.' *BMC Medical Genetics*, 7:4, doi:10.1186/1471-2350-7-4. Available from www.biomedcentral.com.

Mallin, S.R. and Walker, F.A. (1972) 'Effects of the XYY karyotype in one of two brothers with congenital adrenal hyperplasia.' *Clinical Genetics 3*, 6: 490–494.

Malvy, J., Barthélémy, C., Damie, D., Lenoir, P. *et al.* (2004) 'Behaviour profiles in a population of infants later diagnosed as having autistic disorder.' *European Journal of Child and Adolescent Psychiatry*, 13: 115–122.

Mankoski, R.E., Collins, M., Ndosi, N.K., Mgalla, E.H. *et al.* (2006) 'Etiologies of autism in a case-series from Tanzania.' *Journal of Autism and Developmental Disorders*, 36: 1039–1051.

Manning, M.A., Cassidy, S.B., Clericuzio, C., Cherry, A.M. *et al.* (2004) 'Terminal 22q deletion syndrome: a newly recognized cause of speech and language disability in the autism spectrum.' *Pediatrics*, 114: 451–457.

Manouvrier-Hanu, S., Amiel, J., Jacquot, S., Merienne, K. *et al.* (1999) 'Unreported RSK2 missense mutation in two male sibs with an unusually mild form of Coffin-Lowry syndrome.' *Journal of Medical Genetics*, 36: 775–778.

Mantilla-Capacho, J.M., Arnaud, L., Diaz-Rodriguez, M. and Barros-Nunez, P. (2005) 'Apert syndrome with preaxial polydactyly showing the typical mutation Ser252Trp in the FGFR2 gene.' *Genetic Counselling*, 16: 403–406.

Manto, M.U. (2005) 'The wide spectrum of spinocerebellar ataxias (SCAs).' *Cerebellum*, 4: 2–6.

Manzur, A.Y., Kuntzer, T., Pike, M. and Swan, A. (2008) 'Glucocorticoid corticosteroids for Duchenne muscular dystrophy' (update). *Cochrane Database Systematic Reviews*, 1: CD003725.

Mao, J.-R. and Bristow, J. (2001) 'The Ehlers-Danlos syndrome: on beyond collagens.' *The Journal of Clinical Investigation 107*, 9: 1063–1069.

Marco, E.J. and Skuse, D.H. (2006) 'Autism – lessons from the X chromosome.' *SCAN (Social Cognitive and Affective Neuroscience)*, 1: 183–193.

Marcos, J., Guo, L.W., Wilson, W.K., Porter, F.D. and Shackleton, C. (2004) 'The implications of 7-dehydrosterol-7-reductase deficiency (Smith-Lemli-Opitz syndrome) to neurosteroid production.' *Steroids*, 69: 51–60.

Margallo-Lana, M.L., Moore, P.B., Kay, D.W., Perry, R.H. *et al.* (2007) 'Fifteen-year follow-up of 92 hospitalized adults with Down's syndrome: incidence of cognitive decline, its relationship to age and neuropathology.' *Journal of Intellectual Disability Research 51*, 6: 463–477.

Mari, A., Amati, F., Mingarelli, R., Giannotti, A. *et al.* (1995) 'Analysis of the elastin gene in 60 patients with clinical diagnosis of Williams syndrome.' *Human Genetics*, 96: 444–448.

Mari, F., Azimonti, S., Bertani, I., Bolognese, F. *et al.* (2005) 'CDKL5 belongs to the same molecular pathway of MeCP2 and it is responsible for the early-onset seizure variant of Rett syndrome.' *Human Molecular Genetics*, 14: 1935–1946.

Marie, S., Cuppens, H., Heutersepreute, M., Jaspers, M. *et al.* (1999) 'Mutation analysis in adenylosuccinate lyase deficiency: eight novel mutations in the re-evaluated full ADSL coding sequence.' *Human Mutation*, 13: 197–202.

Marinaki, A.M., Champion, M., Kurian, M.A., Simmonds, H.A. *et al.* (2004) 'Adenylosuccinate lyase deficiency – first British case.' *Nucleosides, Nucleotides and Nucleic Acids*, 23: 1231–1233.

Mariner, R., Jackson, A., Levitas, A., Hagerman, R. *et al.* (1986) 'Autism, mental retardation and chromosomal abnormalities.' *Journal of Autism and Developmental Disorders*, 16: 425–440.

Marino, B., Digilio, M.C., Toscano, A., Anaclerio, S. *et al.* (2001) 'Anatomic patterns of conotruncal defects associated with deletion 22q11.' *Genetics in Medicine 3*, 1: 45–48.

Markert, M.L., Boeck, A., Hale, L.P., Kloster, A.L *et al.* (1999) 'Transplantation of thymus tissue in complete DiGeorge syndrome.' *New England Journal of Medicine*, 341: 1180–1189.

Markert, M.L., Devlin, B.H., Alexieff, M.J., Li, J. *et al.* (2007) 'Review of 54 patients with complete DiGeorge anomaly enrolled in protocols for thymus transplantation: outcome of 44 consecutive transplants.' *Blood 109*, 10: 4539–4547.

Marsh, D.J., Coulon, V., Lunetta, K.L., Rocca-Serra, P. *et al.* (1998) 'Mutation spectrum and genotype–phenotype analyses in Cowden disease and Bannayan-Zonana syndrome, two hamartoma syndromes with germline PTEN mutation.' *Human Molecular Genetics*, 7: 507–515.

Marsh, D.J., Kum, J.B., Lunetta, K.L., Bennett, M.J. et al. (1999) 'PTEN mutation spectrum and genotype–phenotype correlations in Bannayan-Riley-Ruvalcaba syndrome suggest a single entity with Cowden syndrome.' *Human Molecular Genetics*, 8: 1461–1472.

Marsh, R.W. and Cabaret, J.J. (1972) 'Down's syndrome treated with a low phenylalanine diet: case report.' *New Zealand Medical Journal 75*, 481: 364–365.

Marshall, C.R., Noor, A., Vincent, J.B., Lionel, A.C. *et al.* (2008) 'Structural variation of chromosomes in autism spectrum disorder.' *American Journal of Human Genetics 82*, 2: 477–488.

Marshall, P.D. and Galasko, C.S. (1995) 'No improvement in delay in diagnosis of Duchenne muscular dystrophy' [letter]. *Lancet*, 345: 590–591.

Martin, C.L. and Ledbeter, D.H. (2007) 'Autism and cytogenetic abnormalities: solving autism one chromosome at a time.' *Current Psychiatry Reports*, 9: 141–147.

Martin, D.M., Sheldon, S. and Gorski, J.L. (2001) 'CHARGE association with choanal atresia and inner ear hypoplasia in a child with a *de novo* chromosome translocation t(2;7)(p14;q21.11).' *American Journal of Medical Genetics*, 99: 115–119.

Martin, J.P. and Bell, J. (1943) 'A pedigree of mental defect showing sex-linkage.' *Journal of Neurology and Psychiatry*, 6: 154–157.

Martin, S.C., Wolters, P.L. and Smith, A.C. (2006) 'Adaptive and maladaptive behavior in children with Smith-Magenis syndrome.' *Journal of Autism and Developmental Disorders*, 36: 541–552.

Martins, S., Matama, T., Guimaraes, L., Vale, J. et al. (2003) 'Portuguese families with dentatorubropallidoluysian atrophy (DRPLA) share a common haplotype of Asian origin.' *European Journal of Human Genetics*, 11: 808–811.

Martinho, P.S., Otto, P.G., Kok, F., Diament, A. *et al.* (1990) 'In search of a genetic basis for the Rett syndrome.' *Human Genetics*, 86: 131–134.

Marui, T., Hashimoto, O., Nanba, E., Kato, C. *et al.* (2004a) 'Association between the neurofibromatosis-1 (NF1) locus and autism in the Japanese population.' *American Journal of Medical Genetics B Neuropsychiatric Genetics*, 131: 43–47.

Marui, T., Hashimoto, O., Nanba, E., Kato, C. *et al.* (2004b) 'Gastrin-releasing peptide receptor (GRPR) locus in Japanese subjects with autism.' *Brain and Development 26*, 1: 5–7.

Masi, G., Favilla, L. and Millepiedi, S. (2000) 'The Kleine-Levin syndrome as a neuropsychiatric disorder: a case report.' *Psychiatry 63*, 1: 93–100.

Maslen, C., Babcock, D., Robinson, S.W., Bean, L.J.H. *et al.* (2006) 'CRELD1 mutations contribute to the occurrence of cardiac atrioventricular septal defects in Down syndrome.' *American Journal of Medical Genetics*, 140A: 2501–2505.

Mason, A., Banerjee, S., Eapen, V., Zeitlin, H. and Robertson, M.M. (1998) 'The prevalence of Tourette syndrome in a mainstream school population.' *Developmental Medicine and Child Neurology 40*, 5: 292–296.

Matalon, R., Koch, R., Michals-Matalon, K., Moseley, K. *et al.* (2004) 'Biopterin responsive phenylalanine hydroxylase deficiency.' *Genetics in Medicine*, 6: 27–32.

Matalon, R., Surendran, S., Matalon, K.M., Tyring, S. *et al.* (2003) 'Future role of large neutral amino acids in transport of phenylalanine into the brain.' *Pediatrics*, 112: 1570–1574.

Matsuda, I., Matsuura, T., Nishiyori, A., Komaki, S. *et al.* (1996) 'Phenotypic variability in male patients carrying the mutant ornithine transcarbamylase (OTC) allele, arg40his, ranging from a child with an unfavourable prognosis to an asymptomatic older adult.' *Journal of Medical Genetics*, 33: 645–648.

Matsuura, K., Morimoto, Y., Sugimura, M., Taki, K. *et al.* (2009) ['Case report of dentatorubral pallidoluysian atrophy in a patient on a ketogenic diet.'] [Article in Japanese.] *Masui*, 58, 6: 762–764.

Matsuura, T., Sutcliffe, J.S., Fang, P., Galjaard, R.-J. *et al.* (1997) '*De novo* truncating mutations in E6-AP ubiquitin-protein ligase gene (UBE3A) in Angelman syndrome.' *Nature Genetics*, 15: 74–77.

Mattick, J.S. (2004) 'RNA regulation: a new genetics?' *Nature Reviews: Genetics*, 5: 316–323.

Mattison, L.K., Fourie, J., Desmond, R.A., Modak, A. *et al.* (2006) 'increased prevalence of dihydropyrimidine dehydrogenase deficiency in African-Americans compared with Caucasians.' *Clinical Cancer Research*, 12 5491–5495.

Mattson, R., Gallagher, B.B., Reynolds, E.H. and Glass D. (1973) 'Folate therapy in epilepsy, a controlled study.' *Archives of Neurology*, 29:78.

Matura, L.A., Sachdev, V., Bakalov, V.K., Rosing, D.R. and Bondy, C.A. (2007) 'Growth hormone treatment and left ventricular dimensions in Turner syndrome.' *Journal of Pediatrics 150*, 6: 587–591.

Maynard, T.M., Haskell, G.T., Peters, A.Z., Sikich, L. *et al.* (2003) 'A comprehensive analysis of 22q11 gene expression in the developing and adult brain.' *Proceedings of the National Academy of Science 100*, 24: 14433–14438.

Maynard, T.M., Meechan, D.W., Dudevoir, M.L., Gopalakrishna, D. *et al.* (2008) 'Mitochondrial localization and function of a subset of 22q11 deletion syndrome candidate genes.' *Molecular and Cellular Neuroscience 39*, 3: 439–451.

Mazzoni, D.S., Ackley, R.S. and Nash, D.J. (1994) 'Abnormal pinna type and hearing loss correlations in Down's syndrome.' *Journal of Intellectual Disability Research*, 38: 549–560.

Mbarek, O., Marouillat, S., Martineau, J., Barthélémy, C. *et al.* (2000) 'Association study of the NF1 gene and autistic disorder.' *American Journal of Medical Genetics Part C: Seminars in Medical Genetics 88*, 6: 729–732.

McFee, R.B. and Caraccio, T.R. (2001) 'Intravenous mercury injection and ingestion: clinical manifestations and management.' *Journal of Toxicology and Clinical Toxicology, 39*, 7: 733–738.

Mefford, H., Sharp, A., Baker, C., Itsara, A. *et al.* (2008) 'Recurrent rearrangements of chromosome 1q21.1 and variable pediatric phenotypes.' *New England Journal of Medicine 359*, 16: 1685–1699.

Megson, M.N. (2000) 'Is autism a G-alpha protein defect reversible with natural vitamin A?' *Medical Hypotheses 54*, 6: 979–983.

Meguid, N.A., Atta, H.M., Gouda, A.S. and Khalil, R.O. (2008) 'Role of polyunsaturated fatty acids in the management of Egyptian children with autism.' *Clinical Biochemistry 41*, 13: 1044–1048.

Mehta, P.D., Capone, G., Jewell, A. and Freedland, R.L. (2007) 'Increased amyloid beta protein levels in children and adolescents with Down syndrome.' *Journal of Neurological Science 254*, 1/2: 22–27.

Meldrum B.S. and Rogawski, M.A. (2007) 'Molecular targets for antiepileptic drug development.' *Neurotherapeutics 4*, 1: 18–61.

Melke, J., Goubran Botros, H., Chaste, P., Betancur, C. *et al.* (2007) 'Abnormal melatonin synthesis in autism spectrum disorders.' *Molecular Psychiatry*, 15 May 2007, doi:10.1038/sj.mp.4002016.

Melmed, R.D., Schneider, C.K., Fabes, R.A., Phillips, J. and Reichelt, K. (2000) 'Metabolic markers and gastrointestinal symptoms in children with autism and related disorders.' *Journal of Pediatric Gastroenterology and Nutrition*, 3: S31–S32.

Mencarelli, M.A., Kleefstra, T., Katzaki, E., Papa, F.T. *et al.* (2009) '14q12 microdeletion syndrome and congenital variant of Rett syndrome.' *European Journal of Medical Genetics*, 52: 148–152.

Mendell, J.R., Moxley, R.T., Griggs, R.C., Brooke, M.H. *et al.* (1989) 'Randomized, double-blind six-month trial of prednisone in Duchenne's muscular dystrophy.' *New England Journal of Medicine*, 320: 1592–1597.

Mensink, K.A., Ketterling, R.P., Flynn, H.C., Knudson, R.A. *et al.* (2006) 'Connective tissue dysplasia in five new patients with NF1 microdeletions: further expansion of phenotype and review of the literature.' *Journal of Medical Genetics 43*: e8.

Mercimek-Mahmutoglu, S., Stoeckler-Ipsiroglu, S., Adami, A., Appleton, R. *et al.* (2006) 'GAMT deficiency: features, treatment, and outcome in an inborn error of creatine synthesis.' *Neurology*, 67: 480–484.

Merhar, S.L. and Manning-Courtney, P. (2007) 'Two boys with 47, XXY and autism.' *Journal of Autism and Developmental Disorders 37*, 5: 840–846.

Merlini, L., Cicognani, A., Malaspina, E., Gennari, M. *et al.* (2003) 'Early prednisone treatment in Duchenne muscular dystrophy.' *Muscle and Nerve*, 27: 222–227.

Mervis, C.B., Robinson, B.F. and Pani, J.R. (1999) 'Visuospatial construction.' *American Journal of Human Genetics*, 65: 1222–1229.

Meryash, D.L., Szymanski, L.S. and Gerald, P.S. (1982) 'Infantile autism associated with the fragile-X syndrome.' *Journal of Autism and Developmental Disorders 12*, 3: 295–301.

Mesa, L.E., Dubrovsky, A.L., Corderi, J., Marco, P. and Flores, D. (1991) 'Steroids in Duchenne muscular dystrophy – deflazacort trial.' *Neuromuscular Disorders*, 1: 261–266.

Messahel, S., Pheasant, A.E., Pall, H., Ahmed-Choudhury, J. *et al.* (1998) 'Urinary levels of neopterin and biopterin in autism.' *Neuroscience Letters 241*, 1: 17–20.

Mestroni, L., Rocco, C., Gregori, D., Sinagra, G. et al. (1999) 'Familial dilated cardiomyopathy: evidence for genetic and phenotypic heterogeneity. Heart Muscle Disease Study Group.' *Journal of the American College of Cardiology*, 34: 181–190.

Meyer, G., Varoqueaux, F., Neeb, A., Oschlies, M. and Brose, N. (2004) 'The complexity of PDZ domain-mediated interactions at glutamatergic synapses: a case study on neuroligin.' *Neuropharmacology*, 47: 724–733.

Meyers, R.L. and Grua, J.R. (2000) 'Bilateral laparoscopic adrenalectomy: a new treatment for difficult cases of congenital adrenal hyperplasia.' *Journal of Pediatric Surgery*, 35: 1586–1590.

Mila, M., Castellvi-Bel, S., Gine, R., Vazquez, C. *et al.* (1996) 'A female compound heterozygote (pre- and full mutation) for the CGG FMR1 expansion.' *Human Genetics*, 98: 419–421.

Miladi, N., Larnaout, A., Kaabachi, N., Helayem, M. and Ben Hamida, M. (1992) 'Phenylketonuria: an underlying etiology of autistic syndrome. A case report.' *Journal of Child Neurology 7*, 1: 22–23.

Miles, J.H., Takahashi, T.N., Haber, A. and Hadden, L. (2003) 'Autism families with a high incidence of alcoholism.' *Journal of Autism and Developmental Disorders*, 33: 403–415.

Miller, G. (2006) 'Fragile X's unwelcome relative.' *Science*, 312: 518–521.

Miller, J.L., Goldstone, A.P., Couch, J.A., Shuster, J. *et al.* (2008) 'Pituitary abnormalities in Prader-Willi syndrome and early onset morbid obesity.' *American Journal of Medical Genetics A, 146A*, 5: 570–575.

Miller, M.T., Stromland, K., Ventura, L., Johansson, M. *et al.* (2004) 'Autism with ophthalmologic malformations: the plot thickens.' *Transactions of the American Ophthalmologic Society*, 102: 107–121.

Miller, M.T., Stromland, K., Ventura, L., Johansson, M. *et al.* (2005) 'Autism associated with conditions characterized by developmental errors in early embryogenesis: a mini review.' *International Journal of Developmental Neuroscience*, 23: 201–219.

Mills, P.B., Surtees, R.A.H., Champion, M.P., Beesley, C.E. *et al.* (2005) 'Neonatal epileptic encephalopathy caused by mutations in the PNPO gene encoding pyridox(am)ine 50-phosphate oxidase.' *Human Molecular Genetics 14,* 8: 1077–1086.

Milner, K.M., Craig, E.E., Thompson, R.J., Veltman, M.W. *et al.* (2005) 'Prader-Willi syndrome: intellectual abilities and behavioural features by genetic subtype.' *Journal of Child Psychology and Psychiatry,* 46: 1089–1096.

Minassian, B.A., DeLorey, T.M., Olsen, R.W., Philippart, M. *et al.* (1998) 'Angelman syndrome: correlations between epilepsy phenotypes and genotypes.' *Annals of Neurology,* 43: 485–493.

Ming, X., Stein, T.P., Brimacombe, M., Johnson, W.G. *et al.* (2005) 'Increased excretion of a lipid peroxidation biomarker in autism.' *Prostaglandins, Leukotrienes and Essential Fatty Acids,* 73: 379–384.

Mitchell, T.N., Free, S.L., Williamson, K.A., Stevens, J.M. *et al.* (2003) 'Polymicrogyria and absence of pineal gland due to PAX6 mutation.' *Annals of Neurology,* 53: 658–663.

Mizugishi, K., Yamanaka, K., Kuwajima, K. and Kondo, I. (1998) 'Interstitial deletion of chromosome 7q in a patient with Williams syndrome and infantile spasms.' *Journal of Human Genetics,* 43: 178–181.

MMWR (2001) 'Racial disparities in median age at death of persons with Down syndrome – United States, 1968–1997.' *Morbidity and Mortality Weekly Reports 50,* 22: 463–465.

MMWR (2006) 'Deaths associated with hypocalcaemia from chelation therapy – Texas, Pennsylvania, and Oregon, 2003–2005.' *Morbidity and Mortality Weekly Report,* 55: 204–207.

MMWR (2007a) 'Prevalence of autism spectrum disorders – Autism and Developmental Disabilities Monitoring Network, six sites, United States.' *Morbidity and Mortality Weekly Report,* 56: SS-1, 1–11.

MMWR (2007b) 'Prevalence of autism spectrum disorders – Autism and Developmental Disabilities Monitoring Network, 14 sites, United States, 2002.' *Morbidity and Mortality Weekly Report,* 56: SS-1, 12–28.

MMWR (2007c) 'Evaluation of a methodology for a collaborative multiple source surveillance network for autism spectrum disorders – Autism and Developmental Disabilities Monitoring Network, 14 sites, United States, 2002.' *Morbidity and Mortality Weekly Report,* 56: SS–1: 29–40.

Mobius, F.F., Fitzky, B.U., Lee, J.N., Paik, Y.-K. and Glossmann, H. (1998) 'Molecular cloning and expression of the human delta-7-sterol reductase.' *Proceedings of the National Academy of Science USA,* 95: 1899–1902.

Mochizuki, H., Miyatake, S., Suzuki, M., Shigeyama, T. *et al.* (2008) 'Mental retardation and lifetime events of Duchenne muscular dystrophy in Japan.' *Internal Medicine 47,* 13: 1207–1210.

Modahl, C., Green, L., Fein, D., Morris, M. *et al.* (1998) 'Plasma oxytocin levels in autistic children.' *Biological Psychiatry,* 43: 270 –277.

Moessner, R., Marshall, C.R., Sutcliffe, J.S., Skaug, J. *et al.* (2007) 'Contribution of SHANK3 mutations to autism spectrum disorder.' *American Journal of Human Genetics,* 81: 1289–1297.

Mogul, H.R., Lee, P.D., Whitman, B.Y., Zipf, W.B. *et al.* (2008) 'Growth hormone treatment of adults with Prader-Willi syndrome and growth hormone deficiency improves lean body mass, fractional body fat, and serum triiodothyronine without glucose impairment: results from the United States multicenter trial.' *Journal of Clinical Endocrinology and Metabolism 93,* 4: 1238–1245.

Mohammad, N.S., Jain, J.M.N., Chintakindi, K.P., Singh, R.P., Naik, U. and Akella, R.R.D. (2009) 'Aberrations in folate metabolic pathway and altered susceptibility to autism.' *Psychiatric Genetics,* 19: 171–176.

Moizard, M.P., Billard, C., Toutain, A., Berret, F. *et al.* (1998) 'Are Dp71 and Dp140 brain dystrophin isoforms related to cognitive impairment in Duchenne muscular dystrophy?' *American Journal of Medical Genetics,* 80: 32–41.

Molfetta, G.A., Munoz, M.V.R., Santos, A.C., Silva, W.A. Jr. *et al.* (2004) 'Discordant phenotypes in first cousins with UBE3A frameshift mutation.' *American Journal of Medical Genetics,* 127A: 258–262.

Molloy, C.A., Keddache, M. and Martin, L.J. (2005) 'Evidence for linkage on 21q and 7q in a subset of autism characterized by developmental regression.' *Molecular Psychiatry,* 10: 741–746.

Molloy, C.A. Morrow, A.L., Meinzen-Derr, J., Dawson, G. *et al.* (2006) 'Familial autoimmune thyroid disease as a risk factor for regression in children with autism spectrum disorder: A CPEA Study.' *Journal of Autism and Developmental Disorders 36,* 3: 317–324.

Moloney, D.M., Slaney, S.F., Oldridge, M., Wall, S.A. *et al.* (1996) 'Exclusive paternal origin of new mutations in Apert syndrome.' *Nature Genetics,* 13: 48–53.

Monaco, A.P., Bertelson, C.J., Liechti-Gallati, S., Moser, H. and Kunkel, L.M. (1988) 'An explanation for the phenotypic differences between patients bearing partial deletions of the DMD locus.' *Genomics,* 2: 90–95.

Moncla, A., Malzac, P., Voelckel, M.-A., Auquier, P. *et al.* (1999) 'Phenotype–genotype correlation in 20 deletion and 20 non-deletion Angelman syndrome patients.' *European Journal of Human Genetics,* 7: 131–139.

Montagu, A. (1986) *Touching: The Human Significance of the Skin.* New York: Harper and Row.

Moog, U., Engelen, J.J., Weber, B.W., van Gelderen, M. *et al.* (2004) 'Hereditary motor and sensory neuropathy (HMSN) IA, developmental delay and autism related disorder in a boy with duplication (17)(p11.2p12).' *Genetic Counselling,* 15: 73–80.

Moore, C.J., Daly, E.M., Schmitz, N., Tassone, F. *et al.* (2004) 'A neuropsychological investigation of male premutation carriers of fragile-X syndrome.' *Neuropsychologia,* 42: 1934–1947.

Moore, J.L. (2005) 'The significance of folic acid for epilepsy patients.' *Epilepsy and Behavior,* 7: 172–181.

Moore, S.J., Green, J.S., Fan, Y., Bhogal, A.K. *et al.* (2005) 'Clinical and genetic epidemiology of Bardet-Biedl syndrome in Newfoundland: a 22-year prospective, population-based, cohort study.' *American Journal of Medical Genetics A,* 132: 352–360.

Moran, C.N., Scott, R.A., Adams, S.M., Warrington, S.J. *et al.* (2004) 'Y chromosome haplotypes of elite Ethiopian endurance runners.' *Human Genetics,* 115: 492–497.

Morava, E., Cser, B., Karteszi, J., Huijben, K. *et al.* (2004) 'Screening for CDG type Ia in Joubert syndrome.' *Medical Science Monitor,* 10: 469–472.

Morey-Canellas, J., Sivagamasundari, U. and Barton, H. (2003) 'A case of autism in a child with Apert's syndrome.' *European Journal of Child and Adolescent Psychiatry,* 12: 100–102.

Morgagni, G.B. (1768) *Epistola anatomica medica XLVII,* article 20.

Morimoto, M., An, B., Ogami, A., Sin, N. *et al.* (2003) 'Infantile spasms in a patient with Williams syndrome and craniosynostosis.' *Epilepsia 44,* 11: 1459–1462.

Moro, F., Pisano, T., Bernardina, B.D., Polli, R. *et al.* (2006) 'Periventricular heterotopia in fragile-X syndrome.' *Neurology 67,* 4: 713–715.

Morell, P. and Jurevics, H. (1996) 'Origin of cholesterol in myelin.', *Neurochemical Research, 21,* 4: 463–470.

Morris, J.K. and Alberman, E. (2009) 'Trends in Down's syndrome live births and antenatal diagnoses in England and Wales from 1989 to 2008: analysis of data from the National Down Syndrome Cytogenetic Register.', *BMJ,* 339: b3794 doi:10.1136/bmj.b3794.

Morris, C.A., Thomas, I.T. and Greenberg, F. (1993) 'Williams syndrome: autosomal dominant inheritance.' *American Journal of Medical Genetics,* 47: 478–481.

Morrison, G.B., Bastian, A., Dela Rosa, T., Diasio, R.B. and Takimoto, C.H. (1997) 'Dihydropyrimidine dehydrogenase deficiency: a pharmacogenetic defect causing severe adverse reactions to 5-fluorouracil-based chemotherapy.' *Oncology Nursing Forum,* 24: 83–88.

Morrison, P.J., Mulholland, H.C., Craig, B.G. and Nevin, N.C. (1992) 'Cardiovascular abnormalities in the oculo-auriculo-vertebral spectrum (Goldenhar syndrome).' *American Journal of Medical Genetics,* 44: 425–428.

Morrow, E.M., Yoo, S.-Y., Flavell, S.W., Kim, T.-K. *et al.* (2008) 'Identifying autism loci and genes by tracing recent shared ancestry.' *Science 321*, 5886: 218–223.

Morrow, J.D., Whitman, B.Y. and Accardo, P.J. (1990) 'Autistic disorder in Sotos syndrome. a case report.' *European Journal of Pediatrics 149*, 8: 567–569.

Moser, H.W., Loes, D.J., Melhem, E.R., Raymond, G.V. *et al.* (2000) 'X-linked adrenoleukodystrophy: overview and prognosis as a function of age and brain magnetic resonance imaging abnormality. A study involving 372 patients.' *Neuropediatrics*, 31: 227–239.

Moser, H.W., Moser, A.B., Hollandsworth, K., Brereton, N.H. and Raymond, G.V. (2007) '"Lorenzo's Oil" therapy for X-linked adrenoleukodystrophy: rationale and current assessment of efficacy.' *Journal of Molecular Neuroscience 33*, 1: 105–113.

Moser, H.W., Moser, A.B., Smith, K.D., Bergin, A. *et al.* (1992) 'Adrenoleukodystrophy: phenotypic variability. Implications for therapy.' *Journal of inherited Metabolic Disease*, 15: 645–664.

Moser, H.W., Raymond, G.V., Lu, S.-E., Muenz, L.R. *et al.* (2005) 'Follow-up of 89 asymptomatic patients with adrenoleukodystrophy treated with Lorenzo's Oil.' *Archives of Neurology*, 62: 1073–1080.

Mosher, D.S., Quignon, P., Bustamante, C.D., Sutter, N.B. *et al.* (2007) 'A mutation in the myostatin gene increases muscle mass and enhances racing performance in heterozygote dogs.' *PLoS Genetics*, 3: e79, doi:10.1371/journal.pgen.0030079.

Moss, E., Wang, P.P., McDonald-McGinn, D.M., Gerdes, M. *et al.* (1995) 'Characteristic cognitive profile in patients with a 22q11.2 deletion: verbal IQ exceeds nonverbal IQ.' *American Journal of Human Genetics*, 57, Supplement: A20.

Moss, J. and Howlin, P. (2009) 'Autism spectrum disorders in genetic syndromes: implications for diagnosis, intervention and understanding the wider autism spectrum disorder population.' *Journal of Intellectual Disability Research*, 53: 852–873.

Moss, J.F., Oliver, C., Berg, K., Kaur, G. *et al.* (2008) 'Prevalence of autism spectrum phenomenology in Cornelia de Lange and cri du chat syndromes.' *American Journal of Mental Retardation 113*, 4: 278–291.

Motil, K.J., Schultz, R., Brown, B., Glaze, D.G. and Percy, A.K. (1994) 'Altered energy balance may account for growth failure in Rett syndrome.' *Journal of Child Neurology*, 9: 315–319.

Moulin-Romsee, C., Verdonck, A., Schoenaers, J. and Carels, C. (2004) 'Treatment of hemifacial microsomia in a growing child: the importance of co-operation between the orthodontist and the maxillofacial surgeon.' *Journal of Orthodontics 31*, 3: 190–200.

Mouridsen, S.E. and Hansen, M.-B. (2002) 'Neuropsychiatric aspects of Sotos syndrome: a review and two case illustrations.' *European Journal of Child and Adolescent Psychiatry*, 11: 43–48.

Mouridsen, S.E., Andersen, L.B., Sorensen, S.A., Rich, B. and Isager, T. (1992) 'Neurofibromatosis in infantile autism and other types of childhood psychoses.' *Acta Paedopsychiatrica*, 55: 15–18.

Mouridsen, S.E., Rich, B. and Isager, T. (1993) 'Brief report: parental age in infantile autism, autistic-like conditions, and borderline childhood psychosis.' *Journal of Autism and Developmental Disorders 23*, 2: 387–396.

Mouridsen, S.E., Rich, B., Isager, T. and Nedergaard, N.J. (2007) 'Autoimmune diseases in parents of children with infantile autism: a case-control study.' *Developmental Medicine and Child Neurology*, 49: 429–432.

Mousain-Bosc, M., Roche, M., Polge, A., Pradal-Prat, D. *et al.* (2006a) 'Improvement of neurobehavioral disorders in children supplemented with magnesium-vitamin B6. I: Attention deficit hyperactivity disorders.' *Magnesium Research 19*, 1: 46–52.

Mousain-Bosc, M., Roche, M., Polge, A., Pradal-Prat, D. *et al.* (2006b) 'Improvement of neurobehavioral disorders in children supplemented with magnesium-vitamin B6. II: Pervasive developmental disorder–autism.' *Magnesium Research 19*, 1: 53–62.

MRC (2001) *MRC Review of Autism Research: Epidemiology and Causes.* London: Medical Research Council, www.mrc.ac.uk

Mueller, C., Patel, S., Irons, M., Antshel, K. *et al.* (2003) 'Normal cognition and behavior in a Smith-Lemli-Opitz syndrome patient who presented with hirschsprung disease.' *American Journal of Medical Genetics A*, 123: 100–106.

Muhle, R., Trentacoste, S.V. and Rapin, I. (2004) 'The genetics of autism.' *Pediatrics*, 113: 472–486.

Mukaddes, N.M. and Herguner, S. (2007) 'Autistic disorder and 22q11.2 duplication.' *World Journal of Biological Psychiatry*, 8: 127–130.

Mukaddes, N.M., Alyanak, B., Kora, M.E. and Polvan, O. (1999) 'The psychiatric ssymptomatology in Kleine-Levin syndrome.' *Child Psychiatry and Human Development 29*, 3: 253–258.

Mukaddes, N.M., Fateh, R. and Kilincasian, A. (2008) 'Kleine-Levin syndrome in two subjects with diagnosis of autistic disorder.' *World Journal of Biological Psychiatry*, Feb.6: 1–6.

Mulley, J.C., Yu, S., Loesch, D.Z., Hay, D.A. *et al.* (1995) 'FRAXE and mental retardation.' *Journal of Medical Genetics*, 32: 162–169.

Munke, M., McDonald, D.M., Cronister, A., Stewart, J.M. et al. (1990) 'Oral-facial-digital syndrome type VI (Varadi syndrome): further clinical delineation.' *American Journal of Medical Genetics*, 35: 360–369.

Muntau, A.C., Roschinger, W., Habich, M., Demmelmair, H. *et al.* (2002) 'Tetrahydrobiopterin as an alternative treatment for mild phenylketonuria.' *New England Journal of Medicine*, 347: 2122–2132.

Muntoni, F. and Wells, D. (2007) 'Genetic treatments in muscular dystrophies.' *Current Opinion in Neurology*, 20: 590–594.

Muratori, F., Bertini, N. and Masi, G. (2002) 'Efficacy of lithium treatment in Kleine-Levin syndrome.' *European Psychiatry*, 17: 232–233.

Muntoni, F., Torelli, S. and Ferlini, A. (2003) 'Dystrophin and mutations: one gene, several proteins, multiple phenotypes.' *Lancet Neurology*, 2: 731–740.

Murch, S. (2003) 'Separating speculation from inflammation in autism.' *The Lancet 362*, 9394: 1498–1499.

Murgatroyd, C., Patchev, A.V., Wu, Y., Micale, V. *et al.* (2009) 'Dynamic DNA methylation programs persistent adverse effects of early-life stress.' *Nature Neuroscience*, 12: 1559–1566.

Murphy, S.K. and Jirtle, R.L. (2000) 'Imprinted genes as potential genetic and epigenetic toxicologic targets.' *Environmental Health Perspectives*, 108, Supplement 1: 5–11.

Musio, A., Selicorni, A., Focarelli, M.L., Gervasini, C. *et al.* (2006) 'X-linked Cornelia de Lange syndrome owing to SMC1L1 mutations.' *Nature Genetics*, 38: 528–530.

Muzzin, K.B. and Harper, L.F. (2003) 'Smith-Lemli-Opitz syndrome: a review, case report and dental implications.' *Special Care in Dentistry*, 23: 22–27.

Myhre, S.A., Ruvalcaba, R.H.A. and Graham, C.B. (1981) 'A new growth deficiency syndrome.' *Clinical Genetics*, 20: 1–5.

Mykytyn, K., Mullins, R.F., Andrews, M., Chiang, A.P. et al. (2004) 'Bardet-Biedl syndrome type 4 (BBS4)-null mice implicate Bbs4 in flagella formation but not global cilia assembly.' *Proceedings of the National Academy of Science USA*, 101: 8664–8669.

N

Nabi, R., Serajee, F.J., Chugani, D.C., Zhong, H. and Huq, A.H. (2004) 'Association of tryptophan 2,3 dioxygenase gene polymorphism with autism.' *American Journal of Medical Genetics B*, *125B*, 1: 63–68.

Nadeau, J.H. (2001) 'Modifier genes in mice and humans.' *Nature Review: Genetics*, 2: 165–174.

Nadesan, M.H. (2005) *Constructing Autism: Unravelling the 'Truth' and Understanding the Social.* Abingdon: Routledge.

Naito, H. and Oyanagi, S. (1982) 'Familial myoclonus epilepsy and choreoathetosis: hereditary dentatorubral-pallidoluysian atrophy.' *Neurology*, 32: 798–807.

Nakabayashi, K., Amann, D., Ren, Y., Saarialho-Kere, U. *et al.* (2005) 'Identification of *C7orf11* (*TTDN1*) gene mutations and genetic heterogeneity in nonphotosensitive trichothiodystrophy.' *American Journal of Human Genetics*, 76: 510–516.

Nakamine, A., Ouchanov, L., Jimenez, P., Manghi, E.R. *et al.* (2008) 'Duplication of 17(p11.2p11.2) in a male child with autism and severe language delay. *American Journal of Medical Genetics A*, 146A, 5: 636–643.

Nakamoto, M., Nalavadi, V., Epstein, M.P., Narayanan, U. *et al.* (2007) 'Fragile-X mental retardation protein deficiency leads to excessive mGluR5-dependent internalization of AMPA receptors.' *Proceedings of the National Academy of Science USA*, 104: 15537–15542.

Nanba, Y., Oka, A. and Ohno, K. (2007) ['Severe diarrhea associated with X-linked lissencephaly with absent corpus callosum and abnormal genitalia: a case report of successful treatment with the somatostatin analogue octreotide.'] *No To Hattatsu*, 39: 379–382.

Napolioni, V., Moavero, R. and Curatolo, P. (2009) 'Recent advances in neurobiology of tuberous sclerosis complex.' *Brain and Development 31*, 2: 104–113.

Napolitano, C., Bloise, R. and Priori, S.G. (2006) 'Gene-specific therapy for inherited arrhythmogenic diseases.' *Pharmacology and Therapeutics*, 110: 1–13.

Naqvi, S., Cole, T. and Graham, J.M. Jr. (2000) 'Cole-Hughes macrocephaly syndrome and associated autistic manifestations.' *American Journal of Medical Genetics*, 94: 149–152.

Nash, K., Sheard, E., Rovet, J. and Koren, G. (2008) 'Understanding fetal alcohol spectrum disorders (FASD): toward identification of a behavioral phenotype.' *Scientific World Journal*, 8: 873–882.

Nassogne, M.-C., Henrot, B., Aubert, G., Bonnier, C. *et al.* (2000) 'Adenylsuccinase deficiency: an unusual cause of early-onset epilepsy associated with acquired microcephaly.' *Brain and Development*, 22: 383–386.

Nataf, R., Skorupka, C., Amet, L., Lam, A. *et al.* (2006) 'Porphyrinuria in childhood autistic disorder: implications for environmental toxicity.' *Toxicology and Applied Pharmacology*, 214: 99–108.

National Initiative for Autism: Screening and Assessment (NIASA) (2003) *National Autism Plan for Children*. Report produced in collaboration with the Royal College of Paediatrics and Child Health, the Royal College of Psychiatrists, and the All-Party Parliamentary Group on Autism (APPGA). London: NAS.

Naviaux, R.K. (2000) 'Mitochondrial DNA disorders.' *European Journal of Pediatrics*, 159 (Supplement 3): S219–S226.

Neal, E.G., Chaffe, H., Schwartz, R.H., Lawson, M.S. *et al.* (2008) 'The ketogenic diet for the treatment of childhood epilepsy: a randomised controlled trial.' *Lancet Neurology 7*, 6: 500–506.

Nebesio, T.D., Ming, W., Chen, S., Clegg, T. *et al.* (2007) 'Neurofibromin-deficient Schwann cells have increased lysophosphatidic acid dependent survival and migration – implications for increased neurofibroma formation during pregnancy.' *Glia 55*, 5: 527–536.

Nee, L.E., Caine, E.D., Polinsky, R.J., Eldridge, R. and Ebert, M.H. (1980) 'Gilles de la Tourette syndrome: clinical and family study of 50 cases.' *Annals of Neurology*, 7: 41–49.

Need, A.C., Ge, D., Weale, M.E., Maia, J. *et al.* (2009) 'A genome-wide investigation of SNPs and CNVs in schizophrenia.' *PLoS Genetics 5*, 2: e1000373.

Nehal, K.S., PeBenito, R. and Orlow, S.J. (1996) 'Analysis of 54 cases of hypopigmentation and hyperpigmentation along the lines of Blaschko.' *Archives of Dermatology 132*, 10: 1167–1170.

Neisworth, J.T. and Wolfe, P.S. (2005) *The Autism Encyclopedia*. Baltimore: Paul H. Brookes/London: Jessica Kingsley Publishers.

Neklason, D.W., Andrews, K.M., Kelley, R.I. and Metherall, J.E. (1999) 'Biochemical variants of Smith-Lemli-Opitz syndrome.' *American Journal of Medical Genetics*, 85: 517–523.

Nelen, M.R., Kremer, H., Konings, I.B., Schoute, F. et al. (1999) 'Novel PTEN mutations in patients with Cowden disease: absence of clear genotype–phenotype correlations.' *European Journal of Human Genetics*, 7: 267–273.

Nelson, E.C. and Pribor, E.F. (1993) 'A calendar savant with autism and Tourette syndrome: response to treatment and thoughts on the interrelationships of these conditions.' *Annals of Clinical Psychiatry 5*, 2: 135–140.

Nelson, K.B., Grether, J.K., Croen, L.A., Dambrosia, J.M. *et al.* (2001) 'Neuropeptides and neurotrophins in neonatal blood of children with autism or mental retardation.' *Annals of Neurology 49*, 5: 597–606.

Nelson, P.G., Kuddo, T., Song, E.Y., Dambrosia, J.M. *et al.* (2006) 'Selected neurotrophins, neuropeptides, and cytokines: developmental trajectory and concentrations in neonatal blood of children with autism or Down syndrome.' *International Journal of Developmental Neuroscience 24*, 1: 73–80.

Nelson, S.F., Crosbie, R.H., Miceli, M.C. and Spencer M.J. (2009) 'Emerging genetic therapies to treat Duchenne muscular dystrophy.' *Current Opinion in Neurology 22*, 5: 532–538.

Nereo, N.E., Fee, R.J. and Hinton, V.J. (2003) 'Parental stress in mothers of boys with Duchenne muscular dystrophy.' *Journal of Pediatric Psychology 28*, 7: 473–484.

Neri, M., Torelli, S., Brown, S., Ugo, I. *et al.* (2007) 'Dystrophin levels as low as 30% are sufficient to avoid muscular dystrophy in the human.' *Neuromuscular Disorders*, 17: 913–918.

Neves-Pereira, M., Müller, B., Massie, D., Williams, J.H. et al. (2009) 'Deregulation of EIF4E: a novel mechanism for autism.' *Journal of Medical Genetics*, 46: 759–765.

New, M.I. (2004) 'An update of congenital adrenal hyperplasia.' *Annals of the New York Academy of Science*, 1038: 14–43.

Nguyen, D., Turner, J.T., Olsen, C., Biesecker, L.G. and Darling, T.N. (2004) 'Cutaneous manifestations of Proteus syndrome: correlations with general clinical severity.' *Archives of Dermatology 140*, 8: 947–953.

Nicholls, A.C., Oliver, J.E., McCarron, S., Harrison, J.B. *et al.* (1996) 'An exon-skipping mutation of a type V collagen gene (COL5A1) in Ehlers-Danlos syndrome.' *Journal of Medical Genetics*, 33: 940–946.

Nickerson, E., Greenberg, F., Keating, M.T., McCaskill, C. and Shaffer, L.G. (1995) 'Deletions of the elastin gene at 7q11.23 occur in approximately 90% of patients with Williams syndrome.' *American Journal of Human Genetics*, 56: 1156–1161.

Nicoletti, F., Bruno, V., Copani, A., Casabona, G. and Knöpfel, T. (1996) 'Metabotropic glutamate receptors: a new target for the therapy of neurodegenerative disorders?' *Trends in the Neurosciences*, 19: 267–271.

Nicolson, R., Bhalerao, S. and Sloman, L. (1998) '47,XYY karyotypes and pervasive developmental disorders.' *Canadian Journal of Psychiatry*, 43: 619–622.

Niederhofer, H. (2007) 'Glutamate antagonists seem to be slightly effective in psychopharmacologic treatment of autism' (letter). *Journal of Clinical Psychopharmacology 27*, 3: 317.

Nielsen, J. and Videbech, P. (1984) 'Diagnosing of chromosome abnormalities in Denmark.' *Clinical Genetics*, 26: 422–428.

Nielsen, J. and Wohlert, M. (1991) 'Chromosome abnormalities found among 34,910 newborn children: results from a 13-year incidence study in Arhus, Denmark.' *Human Genetics*, 87: 81–83.

Nielsen, J., Pelsen, B. and Sorensen, K. (1988) 'Follow-up of 30 Klinefelter males treated with testosterone.' *Clinical Genetics*, 33: 262–269.

Nienhuis, A.W., Dunbar, C.E. and Sorrentino, B.P. (2006) 'Genotoxicity of retroviral integration in hematopoietic cells.' *Molecular Therapy 13*, 6: 1031–1049.

Nigro, G., Comi, L.I., Politano, L. and Bain, R.J. (1990) 'The incidence and evolution of cardiomyopathy in Duchenne muscular dystrophy.' *International Journal of Cardiology*, 26: 271–277.

Nijhawan, N., Morad, Y., Seigel-Bartelt, J. and Levin, A.V. (2002) 'Caruncle abnormalities in the oculo-auriculo-vertebral spectrum.' *American Journal of Medical Genetics*, 113: 320–325.

Niklasson, L., Rasmussen, P., Oskarsdottir, S. and Gillberg, C. (2001) 'Neuropsychiatric disorders in the 22q11 deletion syndrome.' *Genetics in Medicine*, 3: 79–84.

Niklasson, L., Rasmussen, P., Oskarsdottir, S. and Gillberg, C. (2002) 'Chromosome 22q11 deletion syndrome (CATCH 22): neuropsychiatric and neuropsychological aspects.' *Developmental Medicine and Child Neurology*, 44: 44–50.

Nilsson, M., Waters, S., Waters, N., Carlsson, A. and Carlsson, M.L. (2001) 'A behavioural pattern analysis of hypoglutamatergic mice – effects of four different antipsychotic agents.' *Journal of Neural Transmission*, 108: 1181–1196.

Nishimura, D.Y., Fath, M., Mullins, R.F., Searby, C. et al. (2004) 'Bbs2-null mice have neurosensory deficits, a defect in social dominance, and retinopathy associated with mislocalization of rhodopsin.' *Proceedings of the National Academy of Science USA*, 101: 16588–16593.

Nishimura, D.Y., Swiderski, R.E., Searby, C.C., Berg, E.M. et al. (2005) 'Comparative genomics and gene expression analysis identifies BBS9, a new Bardet-Biedl syndrome gene.' *American Journal of Human Genetics*, 77: 1021–1033.

Nolan, M.A., Jones, O.D., Pedersen, R.L. and Johnston, H.M. (2003) 'Cardiac assessment in childhood carriers of Duchenne and Becker muscular dystrophies.', *Neuromuscular Disorders*, 13: 129–132.

Nolin, S.L., Brown, W.T., Glicksman, A., Houck, G.E. et al. (2003) 'Expansion of the fragile-X CGG repeat in females with pre-mutation or intermediate alleles.' *American Journal of Human Genetics*, 72: 454–464.

Nolin, S.L., Glicksman, A., Houck, G.E. Jr., Brown, W.T. and Dobkin, C.S. (1994) 'Mosaicism in fragile-X-affected males.' *American Journal of Medical Genetics*, 51: 509–512.

Nonogaki, K., Ohashi-Nozue, K. and Oka, Y. (2006) 'A negative feedback system between brain serotonin systems and plasma active ghrelin levels in mice.' *Biochemical and Biophysical Research Communications*, 341: 703–707.

Noonan, J.A. (2002) 'Noonan syndrome: a historical perspective.' *Heart Views 3*, 2: 102–106.

Noordam, C., Peer, P.G., Francois, I., De Schepper, J. et al. (2008) 'Long-term GH treatment improves adult height in children with Noonan syndrome with and without mutations in protein tyrosine phosphatase, non-receptor-type 11.' *European Journal of Endocrinology 159*, 3: 203–208.

Norio, R. (2003) 'The Finnish disease heritage. I: Characteristics, causes, background.' *Human Genetics*, 112: 441–456.

Norremolle, A., Nielsen, J.E., Sorensen, S.A. and Hasholt, L. (1995) 'Elongated CAG repeats of the B37 gene in a Danish family with dentato-rubro-pallido-luysian atrophy.' *Human Genetics*, 95: 313–321.

North, K. (1999) 'Cognitive Function and Academic Performance.' In J.M. Friedman, D.H. Gutmann, M. MacCollin, and V.M. Riccardi (eds.) *Neurofibromatosis: Phenotype, Natural History, and Pathogenesis.* Baltimore: Johns Hopkins University Press.

North, K.N., Riccardi, V., Samango-Sprouse, C., Ferner, R. et al. (1997) 'Cognitive function and academic performance in neurofibromatosis. 1: Consensus statement from the NF1 Cognitive Disorders Task Force.' *Neurology 48*, 4: 1121–1127.

Nowaczyk, M.J.M., Heshka, T., Eng, B., Feigenbaum, A.J. and Waye, J.S. (2001) 'DHCR7 genotypes of cousins with Smith-Lemli-Opitz syndrome.' *American Journal of Medical Genetics*, 100: 162–163.

Nowaczyk, M.J.M., Whelan, D.T. and Hill, R.E. (1998) 'Smith-Lemli-Opitz syndrome: phenotypic extreme with minimal clinical findings.' *American Journal of Medical Genetics*, 78: 419–423.

Nowak, C.B. (2007) 'The phacomatoses: dermatologic clues to neurologic anomalies.' *Seminars in Pediatric Neurology*, 14: 140–149.

Nowak, K.J. and Davies, K.E. (2004) 'Duchenne muscular dystrophy and dystrophin: pathogenesis and opportunities for treatment.' *EMBO Reports*, 5: 872–876.

Nwokoro, N.A. and Mulvihill, J.J. (1997) 'Cholesterol and bile acid replacement therapy in children and adults with Smith-Lemli-Opitz (SLO/RSH) syndrome.' *American Journal of Medical Genetics*, 68: 315–321.

O

Obeid, R. and Herrmann, W. (2006) 'Priorities in the discovery of the implications of water channels in epilepsy and Duchenne muscular dystrophy.' *Cellular and Molecular Biology (Noisy-le-grand) 52*, 5: 16–20.

Oberholzer, V.G., Levin, B., Burgess, E.A. and Young, W.F. (1967) 'Methylmalonic aciduria: an inborn error of metabolism leading to chronic metabolic acidosis.' *Archives of Diseases in Childhood*, 42: 492–504.

O'Brien, G. and Yule, W. (eds.) (1996) *Behavioural Phenotypes: Clinics in Developmental Medicine 138.* Cambridge: Cambridge University Press.

O'Callaghan, F.J.K., Noakes, M. and Osborne, J.P. (2000) 'Renal angiomyolipomata and learning difficulties in tuberous sclerosis complex.' *Journal of Medical Genetics*, 37: 156–157.

O'Donovan, M.C., Craddock, N. and Owen, M.J. (2008) 'Schizophrenia: complex genetics, not fairy tales.' *Psychological Medicine*, 38: 1697–1699.

Oexle, K., Thamm-Mucke, B., Mayer, T. and Tinschert, S. (2005) 'Macrocephalic mental retardation associated with a novel C-terminal MECP2 frameshift deletion.' *European Journal of Pediatrics*, 164: 154–157.

Ogawa, M., Moriya, N., Ikeda, H., Tanae, A. et al. (2004) 'Clinical evaluation of recombinant human growth hormone in Noonan syndrome.' *Endocrinology Journal*, 51: 61–68.

Ogilvie, C.M., Crouch, N.S., Rumsby, G., Creighton, S.M. et al. (2006) 'Congenital adrenal hyperplasia in adults: a review of medical, surgical and psychological issues.' *Clinical Endocrinology (Oxford)*, 64: 2–11.

Ogino, T., Ohtsuka, Y., Yamatogi, Y., Oka, E. and Ohtahara, S. (1989) 'The epileptic syndrome sharing common characteristics during early childhood with severe myoclonic epilepsy in infancy.', *Japanese Journal of Psychiatry and Neurology, 43*: 479–481.

Ogura, K. (2006) ['Dihydropyrimidine dehydrogenase activity and its genetic aberrations.'] [Article in Japanese.] *Gan To Kagaku Ryoho 33*, 8: 1041–1048.

Ohki, T., Watanabe, K., Negoro, T., Aso, K. et al. (1997) 'Severe myoclonic epilepsy in infancy: evolution of seizures.' *Seizure*, 6: 219–224.

Ohtsuka, Y., Maniwa, S., Ogino, T., Yamatogi, Y. and Ohtahara, S. (1991) 'Severe myoclonic epilepsy in infancy: a long-term follow-up study.' *Japanese Journal of Psychiatry and Neurology 45*, 2: 416–418.

Oikawa, H., Tun, Z., Young, D.R., Ozawa, H. et al. (2002) 'The specific mitochondrial DNA polymorphism found in Klinefelter's syndrome.' *Biochemical and Biophysical Research Communications*, 297: 341–345.

Okano, M., Kitano, Y., Yoshikawa, K., Nakamura, T. et al. (1988) 'X-linked ichthyosis and ichthyosis vulgaris: comparison of their clinical features based on biochemical analysis.' *British Journal of Dermatology 119*, 6: 777–783.

Okten, A., Kalyoncu, M. and Yaris, N. (2002) 'The ratio of second- and fourth-digit lengths and congenital adrenal hyperplasia due to 21-hydroxylase deficiency.' *Early Human Development 70*, 1/2: 47–54.

Oldendorf, W.H. and Szabo, J. (1976) 'Amino acid assignment to one of three blood–brain barrier amino acid carriers.' *American Journal of Physiology*, 230: 94–98.

O'Leary, D.M., Movsesyan, V., Vicini, S. and Faden, A.I. (2000) 'Selective mGluR5 antagonists MPEP and SIB-1893 decrease NMDA or glutamate-mediated neuronal toxicity through actions that reflect NMDA receptor antagonism.' *British Journal of Pharmacology*, 131: 1429–1437.

Oliveira, G., Diogo, L., Grazina, M., Garcia, P. et al. (2005) 'Mitochondrial dysfunction in autism spectrum disorders: a population-based study.' *Developmental Medicine and Child Neurology*, 47: 185–189.

Oliver, C., Moss, J., Petty, J., Arron, K. *et al.* (2003) *Self-injurious Behaviour in Cornelia de Lange Syndrome: A Guide for Parents and Carers.* Coventry: Trident Communications Ltd.

Oliveri, B., Mastaglia, S.R., Mautalen, C., Gravano, J.C. and Pardo Argerich, L. (2004) 'Long-term control of hypercalcaemia in an infant with Williams-Beuren syndrome after a single infusion of biphosphonate (pamidronate).' *Acta Paediatrica 93,* 7: 1002–1003.

Oliveira, M.M., Conti, C., Saconato, H. and Fernandes do Prado, G. (2009) 'Pharmacological treatment for Kleine-Levin syndrome.' *Cochrane Database Systematic Reviews,* 2: CD006685.

Olsson, G.M., Montgomery, S.M. and Alm, J. (2007) 'Family conditions and dietary control in phenylketonuria.' *Journal of Inherited Metabolic Disease,* 30, doi: 10.1007/s10545-007-0493-2.

O'Malley, M.R., Kaylie, D.M., Van Himbergen, D.J., Bennett, M.L. and Jackson, C.G. (2007) 'Chronic ear surgery in patients with syndromes and multiple congenital malformations.' *The Laryngoscope 117,* 111: 1993–1998.

Omgreen, M., Olsen, D. and Vissing, J. (2005) 'Aerobic training in patients with myotonic dystrophy type 1.' *Annals of Neurology,* 57: 754–757.

Onishi, A., Hasegawa, J., Imai, H., Chisaka, O. *et al.* (2005) 'Generation of knock-in mice carrying third cones with spectral sensitivity different from S and L cones.' *Zoological Science,* 22: 1145–1156.

Opitz, J.M. (1985) 'The Brachmann-de Lange syndrome.' *American Journal of Medical Genetics,* 22: 89–102.

Opitz, J.M. (1999) 'RSH (so-called Smith-Lemli-Opitz) syndrome.' *Current Opinion in Pediatrics,* 11: 353–362.

Opitz, J.M., Gilbert-Barness, E., Ackerman, J. and Lowichik, A. (2002) 'Cholesterol and development: the RSH ('Smith-Lemli-Opitz') syndrome and related conditions.' *Pediatric Pathology and Molecular Medicine,* 21: 153–181.

Opitz, J.M., Summitt, R.L., Smith, D.W. and Sarto, G.E. (1965) 'Noonan's syndrome in girls: a genocopy of the Ullrich-Turner syndrome' (abstract). *Journal of Pediatrics 5,* 2: 968.

Opitz, J.M., Westphal, J.M. and Daniel, A. (1984) 'Discovery of a connective tissue dysplasia in the Martin-Bell syndrome.' *American Journal of Medical Genetics,* 17: 101–109.

O'Riordan, S., Patton, M. and Schon, F. (2006) 'Treatment of drop episodes in Coffin-Lowry syndrome.' *Journal of Neurology,* 253: 109–110.

Ornitz, E.M. (1973) 'Childhood autism: a review of the clinical and experimental literature.' *California Medicine: The Western Journal of Medicine,* 118: 21–47.

Ornitz, E.M., Guthrie, D. and Farley, A.H. (1977) 'The early development of autistic children.' *Journal of Autism and Childhood Schizophrenia,* 7: 207–229.

Orphanet (2008) Prevalence of Rare Diseases: Bibliographic Data. May www.orpha.net.

Orphanet Reports Series No 1 (2009) 'Prevalence of rare diseases.' Available at http://www.orpha.net/orphacom/cahiers/docs/GB/Prevalence_of_rare_diseases_by_alphabetical_list.pdf accessed 6 May 2010.

Orrico, A., Galli, L., Cavaliere, M.L., Garavelli, L. *et al.* (2004) 'Phenotypic and molecular characterisation of the Aarskog-Scott syndrome: a survey of the clinical variability in light of FGD1 mutation analysis in 46 patients.' *European Journal of Human Genetics,* 12: 16–23.

Orrico, A., Hayek, G. and Burroni, L. (1999) 'Autosomal recessive syndrome of growth and mental retardation, seizures, retinal abnormalities, and osteodysplasia with similarity to the Gurrieri syndrome.' *American Journal of Medical Genetics,* 82: 84–87.

Orstavik, K.H., Stromme, P., Ek, J., Torvik, A. and Skjeldal, O.H. (1997) 'Macrocephaly, epilepsy, autism, dysmorphic features, and mental retardation in two sisters: a new autosomal recessive syndrome?' *Journal of Medical Genetics,* 34: 849–851.

Orth, M., Kirby, R., Richardson, M.P., Snijders, A.H. *et al.* (2005) 'Subthreshold rTMS over pre-motor cortex has no effect on tics in patients with Gilles de la Tourette syndrome.' *Clinical Neurophysiology 116,* 4: 764–768.

Ospina, M.B., Krebs, S.J., Clark, B., Karkhaneh, M., Hartling, L. *et al.* (2008) 'Behavioural and developmental interventions for autism spectrum disorder: a clinical systematic review.' *PLoS ONE 3,* 11: e3755, doi:10.1371/journal.pone.0003755.

Ostergaard, J.R., Sunde, L. and Okkels, H. (2005) 'Neurofibromatosis von Recklinghausen type I phenotype and early onset of cancers in siblings compound heterozygous for mutations in MSH6.' *American Journal of Medical Genetics A, 139A,* 2: 96–105.

Otto, E.A., Loeys, B., Khanna, H., Hellemans, J. et al. (2005) 'Nephrocystin-5, a ciliary IQ domain protein, is mutated in Senior-Loken syndrome and interacts with RPGR and calmodulin.' *Nature Genetics,* 37: 282–288.

Otto, E.A., Schermer, B., Obara, T., O'Toole, J.F. et al. (2003) 'Mutations in INVS encoding inversin cause nephronophthisis type 2, linking renal cystic disease to the function of primary cilia and left–right axis determination.' *Nature Genetics,* 34: 413–420.

Ouldim, K., Natiq, A., Jonveaux, P. and Sefiani, A. (2007) 'Case report: tetrasomy 15q11–q13 diagnosed by FISH in a patient with autistic disorder.' *Journal of Biomedicine and Biotechnology,* Article ID 61538, doi:10.1155/2007/61538.

Ousley, O., Rockers, K., Dell, M.L., Coleman, K. and Cubells, J.F. (2007) 'A review of neurocognitive and behavioral profiles associated with 22q11 deletion syndrome: implications for clinical evaluation and treatment.' *Current Psychiatry Reports,* 9: 148–158.

Ozonoff, S., Williams, B.J., Gale, S. and Miller, J.N. (1999) 'Autism and autistic behavior in Joubert syndrome.' *Journal of Child Neurology,* 14: 636–641.

P

Packer, R.J. and Rosser, T. (2002) 'Therapy for plexiform neurofibromas in children with neurofibromatosis 1: an overview.' *Journal of Child Neurology,* 17: 638–641.

Packer, R.J., Gutmann, D.H., Rubenstein, A., Viskochil, D. *et al.* (2002) 'Plexiform neurofibromas in NF1: toward biologic-based therapy.' *Neurology,* 58: 1461–1470.

Packham, E.A. and Brook, J.D. (2003) 'T-box genes in human disorders.' *Human Molecular Genetics,* 12 (Review Issue 1): R37–R44.

Page, P.Z., Page, G.P., Ecosse, E., Korf, B.R. *et al.* (2006) 'Impact of neurofibromatosis 1 on quality of life: a cross-sectional study of 176 American cases.' *American Journal of Medical Genetics A,* 140: 1893–1898.

Page, T. (2000) 'Metabolic approaches to the treatment of autism spectrum disorders.' *Journal of Autism and Developmental Disorders,* 30: 463–469.

Page, T. and Coleman, M. (2000) 'Purine metabolism abnormalities in a hyperuricosuric subclass of autism.' *Biochimica et Biophysica Acta,* 1500: 291–296.

Page, T. and Moseley, C. (2002) 'Metabolic treatment of hyperuricosuric autism.' *Progress in Neuropsychopharmacology and Biological Psychiatry,* 26: 397–400.

Page, T., Yu, A., Fontanesi, J. and Nyhan, W.L. (1997) 'Developmental disorder associated with increased nucleotidase activity.' *Proceedings of the National Academy of Sciences USA,* 94: 11601–11606.

Paine, R.S. (1957) 'The variability in manifestations of untreated patients with phenylketonuria (phenylpyruvic aciduria).' *Pediatrics 20,* 2: 290–302.

Palacios, J., Gamallo, C., Garcia, M. and Rodriguez, J.I. (1993) 'Decrease in thyrocalcitonin-containing cells and analysis of other congenital anomalies in 11 patients with DiGeorge anomaly.' *American Journal of Medical Genetics,* 46: 641–646.

Pallanti, S., Lassi, S., La Malfa, G., Campigli, M. *et al.* (2005) 'Short report. Autistic gastrointestinal and eating symptoms treated with secretin: a subtype of autism.' *Clinical Practice and Epidemiology in Mental Health,* 1: 24, doi:10.1186/1745-0179-1-24.

Palmer, S. (1978) 'Influence of vitamin A nutriture on the immune response: findings in children with Down's syndrome.' *International Journal of Vitamin and Nutrition Research 48,* 2: 188–216.

Palmini, A. and Luders, H.O. (2002) 'Classification issues in malformations caused by abnormalities of cortical development.' *Neurosurgical Clinics of North America*, 13: 1–16.

Palmucci, L., Mongini, T., Chiado-Piat, L., Doriguzzi, C. and Fubini, A. (2000) 'Dystrophinopathy expressing as either cardiomyopathy or Becker dystrophy in the same family.' *Neurology*, 54: 529–530.

Palomo, R., Belinchon, M. and Ozonoff, M. (2006) 'Autism and family home movies: a comprehensive review.' *Developmental and Behavioral Pediatrics*, 27: S59–S68.

Pandi-Perumal, S., Srinivasan, V., Poeggeler, B., Hardeland, R. and Cardinali, D.P. (2007) 'Drug insight: the use of melatonergic agonists for the treatment of insomnia – focus on ramelteon.' *Nature Clinical Practice: Neurology 3*, 4: 221–228.

Pankau, R., Gosch, A., Simeon, E. and Wessel, A. (1993) 'Williams-Beuren syndrome in monozygotic twins with variable expression.' *American Journal of Medical Genetics*, 47: 475–477.

Pankau, R., Partsch, C.-J., Gosch, A., Oppermann, H.C. and Wessel, A. (1992) 'Statural growth in Williams-Beuren syndrome.' *European Journal of Pediatrics*, 151: 751–755.

Pankau, R., Siebert, R., Kautza, M., Schneppenheim, R. *et al.* (2001) 'Familial Williams-Beuren syndrome showing varying clinical expression.' *American Journal of Medical Genetics*, 98: 324–329.

Papadimos, T.J. and Marco, A.P. (2003) 'Cornelia de Lange syndrome, hyperthermia and a difficult airway.' *Anaesthesia*, 58: 924–925.

Parisi, M.A., Bennett, C.L., Eckert, M.L., Dobyns, W.B. et al. (2004) 'The NPHP1 gene deletion associated with juvenile nephronophthisis is present in a subset of individuals with Joubert syndrome.' *American Journal of Human Genetics*, 75: 82–91.

Parisi, M.A., Doherty, D., Eckert, M.L., Shaw, D.W.W. et al. (2006) 'AHI1 mutations cause both retinal dystrophy and renal cystic disease in Joubert syndrome.' *Journal of Medical Genetics*, 43: 334–339.

Parisi, M.A. and Glass, I.A. (2007) 'Joubert syndrome.' *GeneReviews*, accessible at www.ncbi.nlm.nih.gov

Parisi, M.A., Doherty, D., Chance, P.F. and Glass, I.A. (2007) 'Joubert syndrome (and related disorders).' *European Journal of Human Genetics*, 1–11, doi: 10.1038/sj.ejhg.5201648.

Park, B.K. and Kitteringham, N.R. (1988) 'Relevance and Means of Assessing Induction and Inhibition of Drug Metabolism in Man.' In G.G. Gibson (ed.) *Progress in Drug Metabolism, 11.* New York: Taylor and Francis.

Park, Y.D. (2003) 'The effects of vagus nerve stimulation therapy on patients with intractable seizures and either Landau-Kleffner syndrome or autism.' *Epilepsy and Behavior*, 4: 286–290.

Parkes, J.D. (1999) 'Genetic factors in human sleep disorders with special reference to Norrie disease, Prader-Willi syndrome and Moebius syndrome.' *Journal of Sleep Research*, 8 (Supp. 1): 14–22.

Parry, G.J. and Bredesen, D.E. (1985) 'Sensory neuropathy with low-dose pyridoxine.' *Neurology 35*, 10: 1466–1468.

Parsa, C.F., Hoyt, C.S., Lesser, R.L., Weinstein, J.M. *et al.* (2001) 'Spontaneous regression of optic gliomas: thirteen cases documented by serial neuroimaging.' *Archives of Ophthalmology*, 119: 516–529.

Partington, M.W. (1988) 'Rett syndrome in monozygotic twins.' *American Journal of Medical Genetics*, 29: 633–637.

Partington, M.W. and MacDonald, M.R. (1971) '5-hydroxytryptophan (5-HTP) in Down's syndrome.' *Developmental Medicine and Child Neurology 13*, 3: 362–372.

Partington, M.W., Mulley, J.C., Sutherland, G.R., Hockey, A. *et al.* (1988) 'X-linked mental retardation with dystonic movements of the hands.' *American Journal of Medical Genetics*, 30: 251–262.

Partington, M.W., Turner, G., Boyle, J. and Gecz, J. (2004) 'Three new families with X-linked mental retardation caused by the 428–451dup(24bp) mutation in ARX.' *Clinical Genetics*, 66: 39–45.

Partsch, C.-J., Japing, I., Siebert, R., Gosch, A. *et al.* (2002) 'Central precocious puberty in girls with Williams syndrome.' *Journal of Pediatrics*, 141: 441–444.

Pascual-Castroviejo, I., Lopez-Rodriguez, L., de la Cruz Medina, M., Salamanca-Maesso, C. and Roche Herrero, C. (1988) 'Hypomelanosis of Ito: neurological complications in 34 cases.' *Canadian Journal of Neurological Science 15*, 2: 124–129.

Pascual-Castroviejo, I., Roche, C., Martinez-Bermejo, A., Arcas, J. *et al.* (1998) 'Hypomelanosis of Ito: a study of 76 infantile cases.' *Brain and Development 20*, 1: 36–43.

Pasterski, V., Hindmarsh, P., Geffner, M., Brook, C. *et al.* (2007) 'Increased aggression and activity level in 3- to 11-year-old girls with congenital adrenal hyperplasia.' *Hormones and Behavior 52*, 3: 368–374.

Patel, S. and Barkovich, A.J. (2002) 'Analysis and classification of cerebellar malformations.' *American Journal of Neuroradiology*, 23: 1074–1087.

Patil, S.R. and Bartley, J.A. (1984) 'Interstitial deletion of the short arm of chromosome 17.' *Human Genetics*, 67: 237–238.

Patton, M.A. and Afzal, A.R. (2002) 'Robinow syndrome.' *Journal of Medical Genetics 39*, 5: 305–310.

Patton, M.A., Goodship, J., Hayward, R. and Lansdown, R. (1988) 'Intellectual development in Apert's syndrome: a long-term follow-up of 29 patients.' *Journal of Medical Genetics*, 25: 164–167.

Patwardhan, A.J., Brown, W.E., Bender, B.G., Linden, M.G. *et al.* (2002) 'Reduced size of the amygdala in individuals with 47,XXY and 47,XXX karyotypes.' *American Journal of Medical Genetics 114*, 1: 93–98.

Paul, M. and Allington-Smith, P. (1997) 'Asperger syndrome associated with Steinert's myotonic dystrophy.' *Developmental Medicine and Child Neurology*, 39: 280–281.

Paul, R., Cohen, D.J. and Volkmar, F.R. (1983) 'Autistic behaviors in a boy with Noonan syndrome.' *Journal of Autism and Developmental Disorders 13*, 4: 433–434.

Pauls, D.L. and Leckman, J.F. (1986) 'The inheritance of Gilles de la Tourette's syndrome and associated behaviors: evidence for autosomal dominant transmission.' *New England Journal of Medicine*, 315: 993–997.

Pauls, D.L., Leckman, J.F., Raymond, C.L., Hurst, C.R. and Stevenson, J.M. (1988) 'A family study of Tourette's syndrome: evidence against the hypothesis of association with a wide range of psychiatric phenotypes' (abstract). *American Journal of Human Genetics*, 43: A64.

Pavol, M., Hiscock, M., Massman, P., Moore III, B. *et al.* (2006) 'Neuropsychological function in adults with von Recklinghausen's neurofibromatosis.' *Developmental Neuropsychology*, 29: 509–526.

Pavone, P., Incorpora, G., Fiumara, A., Parano, E. *et al.* (2004) 'Epilepsy is not a prominent feature of primary autism.' *Neuropediatrics 35*, 4: 207–210.

Pavone, P., Parano, E., Rizzo, R. and Trifiletti, R.R. (2006) 'Autoimmune neuropsychiatric disorders associated with streptococcal infection: Sydenham chorea, PANDAS, and PANDAS variants.' *Journal of Child Neurology*, 21: 727–736.

Paylor, R., Glaser, B., Mupo, A., Ataliotis, P. *et al.* (2006) 'Tbx1 haploinsufficiency is linked to behavioral disorders in mice and humans: implications for 22q11 deletion syndrome.' *Proceedings of the National Academy of Science USA*, 103: 7729–7734.

Peake, D., Notghi, L.M. and Philip, S. (2006) 'Management of epilepsy in children with autism.' *Current Paediatrics*, 16: 489–494.

Pearl, P.L. and Gibson, K.M. (2004) 'Clinical aspects of the disorders of GABA metabolism in children.' *Current Opinion in Neurology 17*, 2: 107–113.

Pearl, P.L., Capp, P.K., Novotny, E.J. and Gibson, K.M. (2005) 'Inherited disorders of neurotransmitters in children and adults.' *Clinical Biochemistry*, 38: 1051–1058.

Pearl, P.L., Gibson, K.M., Acosta, M.T., Vezina, L.G. *et al.* (2003) 'Clinical spectrum of succinic semialdehyde dehydrogenase deficiency.' *Neurology* 60, 9: 1413–1417.

Pearl, P.L., Gibson, K.M., Cortez, M.A., Wu, Y. *et al.* (2009) 'Succinic semialdehyde dehydrogenase deficiency: lessons from mice and men.' *Journal of Inherited Metabolic Disease,* doi: 10.1007/s10545-009-1034-y.

Pearson, C.E., Edamura, K.N. and Cleary, J.D. (2005) 'Repeat instability: mechanisms of dynamic mutations.' *Nature Review: Genetics,* 6: 729–742.

Pedersen, C.B., Kølvraa, S., Kølvraa, A., Stenbroen, V. *et al.* (2008) 'The ACADS gene variation spectrum in 114 patients with short-chain acyl-CoA dehydrogenase (SCAD) deficiency is dominated by missense variations leading to protein misfolding at the cellular level.' *Human Genetics 124,* 1: 43–56.

Peek, F. (1997) *The Real Rainman: Kim Peek.* Ogden: Harkness Publishing Consultants.

Peek, F. and Hanson, L.L. (2007) *The Life and Message of the Real Rain Man: The Journey of a Mega-Savant.* Port Chester, New York: Dude Publishing.

Pelc, K., Cheron, G. and Dan, B. (2008) 'Behavior and neuropsychiatric manifestations in Angelman syndrome.' *Neuropsychiatric Disease and Treatment* 4, 3: 577–584.

Pellegrino, J.E., Lensch, M.W., Muenke, M. and Chance, P.F. (1996) 'Clinical and molecular analysis in Joubert syndrome.' *American Journal of Medical Genetics A 72,* 1: 59–62.

Pellegrino, J.E., Schnur, R.E., Kline, R., Zackai, E.H. and Spinner, N.B. (1995) 'Mosaic loss of 15q11q13 in a patient with Hypomelanosis of Ito: is there a role for the P gene?' *Human Genetics 96,* 4: 485–489.

Pennebaker, J.W. (1982) *The Psychology of Physical Symptoms.* New York: Springer.

Penrose, L.S. (1933) 'The relative effects of paternal and maternal age in mongolism.' *Journal of Genetics,* 27: 219–224.

Penrose, L. and Questel, J.H. (1937) 'Metabolic studies in phenylketonuria.' *Biochemical Journal,* 31: 266–274.

Peracchi, M., Bardella, M.T., Caprioli, F., Massironi, S. *et al.* (2006) 'Circulating ghrelin levels in patients with inflammatory bowel disease.' *Gut,* 55: 432–433.

Pericak-Vance, M.A., Wolpert, C.M., Menold, M.M., Bass, M.P. *et al.* (1997) 'Linkage evidence supports the involvement of chromosome 15 in autistic disorder (AUT)' (abstract). *American Journal of Human Genetics,* 61 (Supplement): A40.

Perilongo, G., Moras, P., Carollo, C., Battistella, A. *et al.* (1999) 'Spontaneous partial regression of low-grade glioma in children with neurofibromatosis-1: a real possibility.' *Journal of Child Neurology,* 14: 352–356.

Perlman, S.L. (2002) 'Spinocerebellar degenerations: an update.' *Current Neurology and Neuroscience Reports,* 2: 331–341.

Persaud, R. (2007) 'Failure to replicate gene–environment interactions in psychopathology' (letter to the editor). *Biological Psychiatry,* doi:10.1016/j.biopsych.2006.10.032.

Petek, E., Kroisel, P.M., Schuster, M., Zierler, H. and Wagner, K. (1999) 'Mosaicism in a fragile-X male including a *de novo* deletion in the FMR1 gene.' *American Journal of Medical Genetics,* 84: 229–232.

Peters, S.U., Beaudet, A.L., Madduri, N. and Bacino, C.A. (2004) 'Autism in Angelman syndrome: implications for autism research.' *Clinical Genetics* 66, 6: 530–536.

Petersen, M.B., Adelsberger, P.A., Schinzel, A.A., Binkert, F. *et al.* (1991) 'Down syndrome due to *de novo* Robertsonian translocation t14;21: DNA polymorphism analysis suggests that the origin of the extra 21q is maternal.' *American Journal of Human Genetics,* 49: 529–536.

Petre-Quadens, O. and de Lee, C. (1975) '5-hydroxytryptophan and sleep in Down's syndrome.' *Journal of the Neurological Sciences,* 26: 443–453.

Petryk, A., Richton, S., Sy, J.P. and Blethen, S.L. (1999) 'The effect of growth hormone treatment on stature in Aarskog syndrome.' *Journal of Pediatric Endocrinology and Metabolism 12,* 2: 161–165.

Pey, A.L., Perez, B., Desviat, L.R., Martinez, M.A. *et al.* (2004) 'Mechanisms underlying responsiveness to tetrahydrobiopterin in mild phenylketonuria mutations.' *Human Mutation,* 24: 388–399.

Pfaendner, N.H., Reuner, G., Pietz, J., Jost, G. *et al.* (2005) 'MR imaging-based volumetry in patients with early-treated phenylketonuria.' *The American Journal of Neuroradiology,* 26: 1681–1685.

Phelan, M.C. (2008) 'Deletion 22q13.3 syndrome.' *Orphanet Journal of Rare Diseases,* 3: 14, doi:10.1186/1750-1172-3-14.

Philippart M. (1990) 'The Rett syndrome in males.' *Brain and Development,* 12: 33–36.

Philippe, A., Martinez, M., Guilloud-Bataille, M., Gillberg, C. *et al.* (1999) 'Genome-wide scan for autism susceptibility genes: Paris Autism Research International Sibpair Study.' *Human Molecular Genetics,* 8: 805–812.

Phillips, L. and Appleton, R.E. (2004) 'Systematic review of melatonin treatment in children with neurodevelopmental disabilities and sleep impairment.' *Developmental Medicine and Child Neurology,* 46: 771–775.

Philofsky, A., Hepburn, S.L., Hayes, A., Hagerman, R. and Rogers, S.J. (2004) 'Linguistic and cognitive functioning and autism symptoms in young children with fragile-X syndrome.' *American Journal of Mental Retardation 109,* 3: 208–218.

Pietrobono, R., Tabolacci, E., Zalfa, F., Zito, I. *et al.* (2005) 'Molecular dissection of the events leading to inactivation of the FMR1 gene.' *Human Molecular Genetics,* 14: 267–277.

Pietz, J., Rupp, A., Ebinger, F., Rating, D. *et al.* (2003) 'Cerebral energy metabolism in phenylketonuria: findings by quantitative in vivo (31)P MR spectroscopy.' *Pediatric Research,* 53: 654–662.

Pike, M.G., Hammerton, M., Edge, J., Atherton, D.J. and Grant, D.B. (1989) 'A family with X-linked ichthyosis and hypogonadism.' *European Journal of Pediatrics,* 148: 442–444.

Pinsky, L. and DiGeorge, A.M. (1965) 'A familial syndrome of facial and skeletal anomalies associated with genital abnormality in the male and normal genitals in the female: another cause of male pseudohermaphroditism.' *Journal of Pediatrics,* 66: 1049–1054.

Piqueras, B., Lavenu-Bombled, C., Galicier, L., Bergeron-van der Cruyssen, F. et al. (2003) 'Common variable immunodeficiency patient classification based on impaired B cell memory differentiation correlates with clinical aspects.' *Journal of Clinical Immunology,* 23: 385–400.

Plank, S.M., Copeland-Yates, S.A., Sossey-Alaoui, K., Bell, J.M. *et al.* (2001) 'Lack of association of the (AAAT)6 allele of the GXAlu tetranucleotide repeat in intron 27b of the NF1 gene with autism.' *American Journal of Medical Genetics 105,* 5: 404–405.

Platt, S.R. (2007) 'The role of glutamate in central nervous system health and disease – a review.' *The Veterinary Journal 173,* 2: 278–286.

Plenge, R.M., Stevenson, R.A., Lubs, H.A., Schwartz, C.E. and Willard, H.F. (2002) 'Skewed X-chromosome inactivation is a common feature of X-linked mental retardation disorders.' *American Journal of Human Genetics,* 71: 168–173.

Pletnikov, M.V., Moran, T.H. and Carbone, K. (2002) 'Borna disease virus infection of the neonatal rat: developmental brain injury model of autism spectrum disorders.' *Frontiers in Bioscience,* 7: d513–607.

Plissart, L., Borghgraef, M., Volcke, P., Van den Berghe, H. and Fryns, J.-P. (1994) 'Adults with Williams-Beuren syndrome: evaluation of the medical, psychological and behavioral aspects.' *Clinical Genetics,* 46: 161–167.

Pober, B.R. and Morris, C.A. (2007) 'Diagnosis and management of medical problems in adults with Williams-Beuren syndrome.' *American Journal of Medical Genetics C: Seminars in Medical Genetics 145,* 3: 280–290.

Pober, B.R., Lacro, R.V., Rice, C., Mandell, V. and Teele, R.L. (1993) 'Renal findings in 40 individuals with Williams syndrome.' *American Journal of Medical Genetics,* 46: 271–274.

Poirier, K., Eisermann, M., Caubel, I., Kaminska, A. *et al.* (2008) 'Combination of infantile spasms, non-epileptic seizures and complex movement disorder: a new case of ARX-related epilepsy.' *Epilepsy Research,* 80: 224–228.

Poirier, K., Lacombe, D., Gilbert-Dussardier, B., Raynaud, M. *et al.* (2006) 'Screening of ARX in mental retardation families: consequences for the strategy of molecular diagnosis.' *Neurogenetics*, 7: 39–46.

Poliak, S. and Peles, E. (2003) 'The local differentiation of myelinated axons at nodes of Ranvier.' *Nature Reviews Neuroscience*, 4: 968–980.

Poling, J.S., Frye, R.E., Shoffner, J. and Zimmerman, A.W. (2006) 'Developmental regression and mitochondrial dysfunction in a child with autism.' *Journal of Child Neurology 21*, 2: 170–172.

Polizzi, A., Pavone, P., Iannetti, P., Manfre, L. and Ruggieri, M. (2006) 'Septo-optic dysplasia complex: a heterogeneous malformation syndrome.' *Pediatric Neurology 34*, 1: 66–71.

Plomin, R. and Davis, O.S.P. (2009) 'The future of genetics in psychology and psychiatry: microarrays, genome-wide association, and non-coding RNA.' *Journal of Child Psychology and Psychiatry 50*, 1–2: 63–71.

Pons, R., Andreu, A.L., Checcarelli, N., Vila, M.R. *et al.* (2004) 'Mitochondrial DNA abnormalities and autistic spectrum disorders.' *Journal of Pediatrics*, 144: 81–85.

Poo-Arguelles, P., Arias, A., Vilaseca, M.A., Ribes, A. *et al.* (2006) 'X-linked creatine transporter deficiency in two patients with severe mental retardation and autism.' *Journal of Inherited Metabolic Disease 29*, 1: 220–223.

Poon, C.C., Meara, J.G. and Heggie, A.A. (2003) 'Hemifacial microsomia: use of the OMENS-plus classification at the Royal Children's Hospital of Melbourne.' *Plastic and Reconstructive Surgery 111*, 3: 1011–1018.

Poot, M., Beyer, V., Schwaab, I., Damatova, N. et al. (2009) 'Disruption of CNTNAP2 and additional structural genome changes in a boy with speech delay and autism spectrum disorder.' *Neurogenetics*, July 7 [epub ahead of print].

Popper, J.S., Hsia, Y.E., Rogers, T. and Yuen, J. (1980) 'Familial hibernation (Kleine-Levin) syndrome' (abstract). *American Journal of Human Genetics*, 32: 123A.

Poretti, A., Wolf, N. and Boltshauser, E. (2008) 'Differential diagnosis of cerebellar atrophy in childhood.' *European Journal of Paediatric Neurology*, 12: 155–167.

Porter, F.D. (2002) 'Malformation syndromes due to inborn errors of cholesterol synthesis.' *The Journal of Clinical Investigation 110*, 6: 715–724.

Porter, F.D. (2008) 'Smith-Lemli-Opitz syndrome: pathogenesis, diagnosis and management.' *European Journal of Human Genetics 16*, 5: 535–541.

Potocki, L., Bi, W., Treadwell-Deering, D., Carvalho, C.M. *et al.* (2007) 'Characterization of Potocki-Lupski syndrome (dup(17)(p11.2p11.2)) and delineation of a dosage-sensitive critical interval that can convey an autism phenotype.' *American Journal of Human Genetics 80*, 4: 633–649.

Potocki, L., Chen, K.S., Park, S.S., Osterholm, D.E. *et al.* (2000a) 'Molecular mechanism for duplication 17p11.2–the homologous recombination reciprocal of the Smith-Magenis microdeletion.' *Nature Genetics*, 24: 84–87.

Potocki, L., Glaze, D., Tan, D.-X., Park, S.-S. *et al.* (2000b) 'Circadian rhythm abnormalities of melatonin in Smith-Magenis syndrome.' *Journal of Medical Genetics*, 37: 428–433.

Pott, J.W. and Wong, K.H. (2006) 'Leber's hereditary optic neuropathy and vitamin B12 deficiency.' *Graefe's Archive for Clinical and Experimental Ophthalmology 244*, 10: 1357–1359.

Potter, N.T. (1996) 'The relationship between (CAG)n repeat number and age of onset in a family with dentatorubral-pallidoluysian atrophy (DRPLA): diagnostic implications of confirmatory and predictive testing.' *Journal of Medical Genetics*, 33: 168–170.

Povey, S., Burley, M.W., Attwood, J., Benham, F. *et al.* (1994) 'Two loci for tuberous sclerosis: one on 9q34 and one on 16p13.' *Annals of Human Genetics*, 58: 107–127.

Powell, B.R., Budden, S.S. and Buist, N.R.M. (1993) 'Dominantly inherited megalencephaly, muscle weakness, and myoliposis: a carnitine-deficient myopathy within the spectrum of the Ruvalcaba-Myhre-Smith syndrome.' *Journal of Pediatrics*, 123: 70–75.

Powers, J.M., DeCiero, D.P., Ito, M., Moser, A.B. and Moser, H.W. (2000) 'Adrenomyeloneuropathy: a neuropathologic review featuring its noninflammatory myelopathy.' *Neuropathology and Experimental Neurology 59*, 2: 89–102.

Poysky, J. (2007) 'Behavior patterns in Duchenne muscular dystrophy: report on the Parent Project Muscular Dystrophy Behavior Workshop 8–9 December 2006, Philadelphia, USA.' *Neuromuscular Disorders*, 17: 986–994.

Prader, A., Labhart, A. and Willi, H. (1956) 'Ein syndrome von Adipositas, Kleinwuchs, Kryptochismus und Oligophrenie nach myatonieartigem Zustand in Neugeborenenalter.' *Schweizerische Medizinische Wochenschrift*, 86: 1260–1261.

Prasad, C. and Galbraith, P.A. (2005) 'Sir Archibald Garrod and alkaptonuria – "story of metabolic genetics".' *Clinical Genetics*, 68: 199–203.

Prasad, C., Prasad, A.N., Chodirker, B.N., Lee, C. *et al.* (2000) 'Genetic evaluation of pervasive developmental disorders: the terminal 22q13 deletion syndrome may represent a recognizable phenotype.' *Clinical Genetics*, 57: 103–109.

Prasher, V.P. (1994) 'Screening for medical problems in adults with Down syndrome.' *Down Syndrome Research and Practice 2*, 2: 59–66.

Prasher, V.P. (1999) 'Down syndrome and thyroid disorders: a review.' *Down Syndrome Research and Practice*, 6: 25–42.

Prasher, V.P. (2004) 'Review of donepezil, rivastigmine, galantamine and memantine for the treatment of dementia in Alzheimer's disease in adults with Down syndrome: implications for the intellectual disability population.' *International Journal of Geriatric Psychiatry*, 19: 509–515.

Prasher, V.P. and Clarke, D.J. (1996) 'Case report: challenging behaviour in a young adult with Down's syndrome and autism.' *British Journal of Learning Disabilities*, 24: 167–169.

Preece, P.M. and Mott, J. (2006) 'Multidisciplinary assessment at a child development centre: do we conform to recommended standards?' *Child: Care, Health and Development*, 32: 559–563.

Preis, S., Majewski, F., Hantschmann, R., Schumacher, H. and Lenard, H.G. (1996) 'Goldenhar, Möbius and hypoglossia-hypodactyly anomalies in a patient: syndrome or association?' *European Journal of Pediatrics 155*, 5: 385–389.

Presti-Torres, J., de Lima, M.N., Scalco, F.S., Caldana, F. *et al.* (2007) 'Impairments of social behavior and memory after neonatal gastrin-releasing peptide receptor blockade in rats: implications for an animal model of neurodevelopmental disorders.' *Neuropharmacology*, 52: 724–732.

Price, V.H., Odom, R.B., Ward, W.H. and Jones, F.T. (1980) 'Trichothiodystrophy: sulfur-deficient brittle hair as a marker for a neuroectodermal symptom complex.' *Archives of Dermatology*, 116: 1375–1384.

Pridjian, G., Gill, W.L. and Shapira, E. (1995) 'Goldenhar sequence and mosaic trisomy 22.' *American Journal of Medical Genetics 59*, 4: 411–413.

Pruszkowski, A., Bodemer, C., Fraitag, S., Teillac-Hamel, D. et al. (2000) 'Neonatal and infantile erythrodermas: a retrospective study of 51 patients.', *Archives of Dermatology, 136*, 7: 875–880.

Procter, M., Phillips, J.A. III and Cooper, S. (1998) 'The molecular genetics of growth hormone deficiency.' *Human Genetics*, 103: 255–272.

Proud, V.K., Levine, C. and Carpenter, N.J. (1992) 'New X-linked syndrome with seizures, acquired micrencephaly, and agenesis of the corpus callosum.' *American Journal of Medical Genetics*, 43: 458–466.

Pueschel, S.M. (2006) 'The effect of acetyl-L-carnitine administration on persons with Down syndrome.' *Research in Developmental Disabilities*, 27: 599–604.

Pueschel, S.M., Reed, R.B., Cronk, C.E. and Goldstein, B.I. (1980) '5-hydroxytryptophan and pyridoxine: the effects in young children with Down's syndrome.' *American Journal of Diseases of Children*, 134: 838–844.

Purandare, K.N. and Markar, T.N. (2005) 'Psychiatric symptomatology of Lujan-Fryns syndrome: an X-linked syndrome displaying marfanoid symptoms with autistic features, hyperactivity, shyness and schizophreniform symptoms.' *Psychiatric Genetics*, 15: 229–231.

Purcell, A.E., Jeon, O.H., Zimmerman, A.W., Blue, M.E. and Pevsner, J. (2001) 'Postmortem brain abnormalities of the glutamate neurotransmitter system in autism.' *Neurology*, 57: 1618–1628.

Purkinje, J.E. and Valentin, G. (1835) 'De phaenomeno generali et fundamentali motus vibratorii continui in membranis cum externis tum internis animalium plurimorum et superiorum et inferiorum ordinum obvii: commentatio physiologica.' In: A. Schulz (ed.) *Commentatio Physiologica.* Wratislaviae: Sumptibus.

Purushottam, M., Ram Murthy, A., Shubha, G.N., Gayathri, N. and Nalini, A. (2008) 'Paternal inheritance or a *de novo* mutation in a Duchenne muscular dystrophy pedigree from South India.' *Journal of the Neurological Sciences* 268, 1/2: 179–182.

Puumala, S.E., Ross, J.A., Olshan, A.F., Robison, L.L. *et al.* (2007) 'Reproductive history, infertility treatment, and the risk of acute leukemia in children with Down syndrome: a report from the children's oncology group.' *Cancer 110,* 9: 2067–2074.

Puvabanditsin, S., Garrow, E. and Augustin, G. (2005) 'Poland–Möbius syndrome and cocaine abuse: a relook at vascular etiology.' *Pediatric Neurology 32,* 4: 285–287.

Pyeritz, R.E., Stamberg, J., Thomas, G.H., Bell, B.B. *et al.* (1982) 'The marker Xq28 syndrome (fragile-X syndrome) in a retarded man with mitral valve prolapse.' *Johns Hopkins Medical Journal,* 151: 231–237.

Q

Quattrini, A., Ortenzi, A., Silvestri, R., Paggi, A. *et al.* (1986) 'Ichthyosis accompanied by neurological symptoms with special reference to epilepsy.' *Italian Journal of Neurological Science 7,* 2: 233–242.

Quinlivan, R., Ball, J., Dunckley, M., Thomas, D.J. et al. (1995) 'Becker muscular dystrophy presenting with complete heart block in the sixth decade.' *Journal of Neurology,* 242: 398–400.

Quintana-Murci, L. and Fellous, M. (2001) 'The human Y chromosome: the biological role of a "functional wasteland".' *Journal of Biomedicine and Biotechnology 1,* 1: 18–24.

Quintero-Rivera, F., Robson, C.D., Reiss, R.E., Levine, D. *et al.* (2006) 'Intracranial anomalies detected by imaging studies in 30 patients with Apert syndrome' (letter). *American Journal of Medical Genetics,* 140A: 1337–1338.

Quisling, R.G., Barkovich, A.J. and Maria, B.L. (1999) 'Magnetic resonance imaging features and classification of central nervous system malformations in Joubert syndrome.' *Journal of Child Neurology,* 14: 628–635.

R

Rabionet, R., Jaworski, J.M., Ashley-Koch, A.E., Martin, E.R. *et al.* (2004) 'Analysis of the autism chromosome 2 linkage region: GAD1 and other candidate genes.' *Neuroscience Letters,* 372: 209–214.

Race, V., Marie, S., Vincent, M.-F. and van den Berghe, G. (2000) 'Clinical, biochemical and molecular genetic correlations in adenylosuccinate lyase deficiency.' *Human Molecular Genetics,* 9: 2159–2165.

Rae, C., Digney, A.L., McEwan, S.R. and Bates, T.C. (2003) 'Oral creatine monohydrate supplementation improves brain performance: a double-blind, placebo-controlled, cross-over trial.' *Proceedings of the Royal Society B: Biological Sciences,* 270: 2147–2150.

Rahman, T., Ramanathan, R., Stroud, S., Sample, W. *et al.* (2001) 'Towards the control of a powered orthosis for people with muscular dystrophy.' *IMechE Journal of Engineering in Medicine 215,* H: 267–274.

Rai, A.K., Singh, S., Mehta, S., Kumar, A. *et al.* (2006) 'MTHFR C677T and A1298C polymorphisms are risk factors for Down's syndrome in Indian mothers.' *Journal of Human Genetics,* 51: 278–283, doi: 10.1007/s10038-005-0356-3.

Raja, M. and Azzoni, A. (2008) 'Comorbidity of Asperger's syndrome and bipolar disorder.' *Clinical Practice and Epidemiology in Mental Health,* 4: 26, doi:10.1186/1745-0179-4-26.

Rajesh, R. and Girija, A.S. (2003) 'Pyridoxine-dependent seizures: a review.' *Indian Pediatrics 40,* 7: 633–638.

Ramackers, G.J. (2002) 'Rho proteins, mental retardation and the cellular basis of cognition.' *Trends in the Neurosciences,* 25: 191–199.

Ramaekers, V.T., Heimann, G., Reul, J., Thron, A. and Jaeken, J. (1997) 'Genetic abnormalities and cerebellar structural abnormalities in childhood.' *Brain,* 120: 1739–1751.

Rampazzo, C., Gallinaro, L., Milanesi, E., Frigimelica, E. *et al.* (2000) 'A deoxyribonucleotidase in mitochondria: involvement in regulation of dNTP pools and possible link to genetic disease.' *Proceedings of the National Academy of Science USA 97,* 15: 8239–8244.

Rao, P.N., Klinepeter, K., Stewart, W., Hayworth, R. *et al.* (1994) 'Molecular cytogenetic analysis of a duplication Xp in a male: further delineation of a possible sex-influencing region on the X chromosome.' *Human Genetics,* 94: 149–153.

Rapin, I. and Ruben, R.J. (1976) 'Patterns of anomalies in children with malformed ears.' *Laryngoscope,* 86: 1469–1502.

Rasmussen, P., Borjesson, O., Wentz, E. and Gillberg, C. (2001) 'Autistic disorders in Down syndrome: background factors and clinical correlates.' *Developmental Medicine and Child Neurology 43,* 11: 750–754.

Rasmussen, S.A. and Friedman, J.M. (2000) 'NF1 gene and neurofibromatosis 1.' *American Journal of Epidemiology 151,* 1: 33–40.

Rasmussen, S.A., Yang, Q. and Friedman, J.M. (2001) 'Mortality in neurofibromatosis 1: an analysis using US death certificates.' *American Journal of Human Genetics,* 68: 1110–1118.

Ratcliffe, S.G., Butler, G.E. and Jones, M. (1990) 'Edinburgh study of growth and development of children with sex chromosome abnormalities, IV.' *Birth Defects Original Articles Series,* 26: 1–44.

Raux, G., Bumsel, E., Hecketsweiler, B., van Amelsvoort, T. *et al.* (2007) 'Involvement of hyperprolinemia in cognitive and psychiatric features of the 22q11 deletion syndrome.' *Human Molecular Genetics 16,* 1: 83–91.

Raymond, G.V., Bauman, M.L. and Kemper, T.L. (1996) 'Hippocampus in autism: a Golgi analysis.' *Acta Neuropathologica (Berlin),* 91: 117–119.

Raynes, H.R., Shanske, A., Goldberg, S., Burde, R. and Rapin, I. (1999) 'Joubert syndrome: monozygotic twins with discordant phenotypes.' *Journal of Child Neurology,* 14: 649–654.

Reading, R. (2006) 'Prevalence of disorders of the autism spectrum in a population cohort of children in South Thames: the Special Needs and Autism Project (SNAP).' *Child Care Health and Development 32,* 6: 752–753.

Realmuto, G.M. and Main, B. (1982) 'Coincidence of Tourette's disorder and infantile autism.' *Journal of Autism and Developmental Disorders 12,* 4: 367–372.

Reardon, W., Harbord, M.G., Hall-Craggs, M.A., Kendall, B. *et al.* (1989) 'Central nervous system malformations in Mohr's syndrome.' *Journal of Medical Genetics,* 26: 659–663.

Recklinghausen, F.C. von (1882) *Ueber die multiplen Fibromen der Haut und ihre Beziehung zu den multiplen Neuromen.* Berlin: Hirschwald.

Redcay, E. and Courchesne, E. (2005) 'When is the brain enlarged in autism? A meta-analysis of all brain size reports.' *Biological Psychiatry,* 58: 1–9.

Reddy, K.S. (2005) 'Cytogenetic abnormalities and fragile-X syndrome in autism spectrum disorder.' *BMC Medical Genetics,* 6: 3, doi:10.1186/1471-2350-6-3.

Redon, R., Ishikawa, S., Fitch, K.R., Feuk, L. *et al.* (2006) 'Global variation in copy number in the human genome.' *Nature,* 444: 444–452, doi:10.1038/nature05329.

Regenbogen, L., Godel, V., Goya, V. and Goodman, R.M. (1982) 'Further evidence for an autosomal dominant form of oculoauriculovertebral dysplasia.' *Clinical Genetics,* 21: 161–167.

Reichelt, K.L. and Knivsberg, A.M. (2003) 'Can the pathophysiology of autism be explained by the nature of the discovered urine peptides?' *Nutritional Neuroscience,* 6: 19–28.

Reichenberg, A., Gross, R., Weiser, M., Bresnahan, M. *et al.* (2006) 'Advancing paternal age and autism.' *Archives of General Psychiatry 63*, 9: 1026–1032.

Reilley, P.R. (2006) *The Strongest Boy in the World: How Genetic Information is Reshaping Our Lives.* New York: Cold Spring Harbour Laboratory Press.

Reilly, C. (2009) 'Autism spectrum disorders in Down syndrome: a review.' *Research in Autism Spectrum Disorders,* 3: 829–839.

Reiner, D., Arnaud, E., Cinalli, G., Sebag, G. *et al.* (1996) 'Prognosis for mental function in Apert's syndrome.' *Journal of Neurosurgery:* 85, 66–72.

Reiner, O. and Coquelle, F.M. (2005) 'Missense mutations resulting in type 1 lissencephaly.' *Cellular and Molecular Life Sciences 62*, 4: 425–434.

Reiner, O., Coquelle, F.M., Peter, B., Levy, T. *et al.* (2006) 'The evolving doublecortin (DCX) superfamily.' *BMC Genomics,* 7: 188, doi:10.1186/1471-2164-7-188.

Reis, A., Dittrich, B., Greger, V., Buiting, K. *et al.* (1994) 'Imprinting mutations suggested by abnormal DNA methylation patterns in familial Angelman and Prader-Willi syndromes.' *American Journal of Human Genetics,* 54: 741–747.

Reiss, A.L. (2009) 'Childhood developmental disorders: an academic and clinical convergence point for psychiatry, neurology, psychology and pediatrics.' *Journal of Child Psychology and Psychiatry 50*, 1–2: 87–98.

Reiss, A.L. and Hall, S.S. (2007) 'Fragile-X syndrome: assessment and treatment implications.' *Child and Adolescent Psychiatric Clinics of North America,* 16: 663–675.

Reiss, A.L., Aylward, E., Freund, L.S., Joshi, P.K. and Bryan, R.N. (1991) 'Neuroanatomy of fragile-X syndrome: the posterior fossa.' *Annals of Neurology,* 29: 26–32.

Reiss, A.L., Eckert, M.A., Rose, F.E., Karchemskiy, A. *et al.* (2004) 'An experiment of nature: brain anatomy parallels cognition and behavior in Williams syndrome.' *The Journal of Neuroscience 24*, 21: 5009–5015.

Reiss, A.L., Feinstein, C., Rosenbaum, K.N., Borengasser-Caruso, M.A. and Goldsmith, B.M. (1985) 'Autism associated with Williams syndrome.' *Journal of Pediatrics 106*, 2: 247–249.

Reiss, A.L., Lee, J. and Freund, L. (1994) 'Neuroanatomy of fragile-X syndrome: the temporal lobe.' *Neurology,* 44: 1317–1324.

Reiter, R.J., Barlow-Walden, L., Poeggeler, B., Heiden, S.M. and Clayton, R.J. (1996) 'Twenty-four hour urinary excretion of 6-hydroxymelatonin sulfate in Down syndrome subjects.' *Journal of Pineal Research 20*, 1: 45–50.

Relling, M.V., Lin, J.S., Ayers, G.D. and Evans, W.E. (1992) 'Racial and gender differences in N-acetyltransferase, xanthine oxidase, and CYP1A2 activities.' *Clinical and Pharmacological Therapy,* 52: 643–658.

Renier, W.O. and Renkawek, K. (1990) 'Clinical and neuropathologic findings in a case of severe myoclonic epilepsy of infancy.' *Epilepsia,* 31: 287–291.

Renieri, A., Mari, F., Mencarelli, M.A., Scala, E. *et al.* (2009) 'Diagnostic criteria for the Zapella variant of Rett syndrome (the preserved speech variant).' *Brain and Development,* 31: 208–216.

Renner, E.D., Puck, J.M., Holland, S.M., Schmitt, M. *et al.* (2004) 'Autosomal recessive hyperimmunoglobulin E syndrome: a distinct disease entity.' *Journal of Pediatrics 144*, 1: 93–99.

Rett, A. (1966) 'Ueber ein eigenartiges hirnatrophisches Syndrom bei Hyperammoniamie in Kindesalter.' *Wiener Medizinische Wochenschrift,* 116: 723–738.

Rett, A. (1986) 'Rett syndrome: history and general overview.' *American Journal of Medical Genetics,* Supplement 1: 21–25.

Rhodes, L.E., de Rie, M.A., Leifsdottir, R., Yu, R.C. *et al.* (2007) 'Five-year follow-up of a randomized, prospective trial of topical methyl aminolevulinate photodynamic therapy vs surgery for nodular basal cell carcinoma.' *Archives of Dermatology 143*, 9: 1131–1136.

Riccardi, V.M. (1999) 'Historical Background and Introduction.' In J.M. Friedman, D.H. Gutmann, M. MacCollin, and V.M. Riccardi (eds.) *Neurofibromatosis: Phenotype, Natural History, and Pathogenesis.* Baltimore: Johns Hopkins University Press.

Rich, P.M., Cox, T.S. and Hayward, R.D. (2003) 'The jugular foramen in complex and syndromic craniosynostosis and its relationship to raised intracranial pressure.' *American Journal of Neuroradiology,* 24: 45–51.

Richards, C.S., Watkins, S.C., Hoffman, E.P., Schneider, N.R. *et al.* (1990) 'Skewed X inactivation in a female MZ twin results in Duchenne muscular dystrophy.' *American Journal of Human Genetics,* 46: 672–681.

Richdale, A.L. and Schreck, K.A. (2009) 'Sleep problems in autism spectrum disorders: prevalence, nature, and possible biopsychosocial aetiologies.' *Sleep Medicine Reviews,* 13: 403–411.

Richieri-Costa, A., Monteleone-Neto, R. and Gonzales, M.L. (1986) 'Coffin-Siris syndrome in a Brazilian child with consanguineous parents.' *Revista brasileira de genética,* IX: 169–177.

Richter-Unruh, A., Knauer-Fischer, S., Kaspers, S., Albrecht, B. *et al.* (2004) 'Short stature in children with an apparently normal male phenotype can be caused by 45,X/46,XY mosaicism and is susceptible to growth hormone treatment.' *European Journal of Pediatrics,* 163: 4–5, 251–256.

Ridge, S.A., Sludden, J., Brown, O., Robertson, L. *et al.* (1998) 'Dihydropyrimidine dehydrogenase pharmacogenetics in Caucasian subjects.' *British Journal of Clinical Pharmacology 46*, 2: 151–156.

Riikonen, R. (2003) 'Neurotrophic factors in the pathogenesis of Rett syndrome.' *Journal of Child Neurology 18*, 10: 693–697.

Riikonen, R. and Amnell, G. (1981) 'Psychiatric disorders in children with earlier infantile spasms.' *Developmental Medicine and Child Neurology,* 23: 747–760.

Riikonen, R. and Simell, O. (1990) 'Tuberous sclerosis and infantile spasms.' *Developmental Medicine and Child Neurology 32*, 3: 203–209.

Rimland, B. (1964) *Infantile Autism: The Syndrome and its Implications for a Neural Theory of Behavior.* New York: Appleton-Century-Crofts.

Ringman, J.M. and Jankovic, J. (2000) 'Occurrence of tics in Asperger's syndrome and autistic disorder.' *Journal of Child Neurology 15*, 6: 394–400.

Rio, M., Clech, L., Amiel, J., Faivre, L., Lyonnet, S. *et al.* (2003) 'Spectrum of NSD1 mutations in Sotos and Weaver syndromes.' *Journal of Medical Genetics 40*, 6: 436–440.

Ritvo, E.R., Mason-Brothers, A., Freeman, B.J., Pingree, C. *et al.* (1990) 'The UCLA–University of Utah epidemiologic survey of autism: the etiologic role of rare diseases.' *American Journal of Psychiatry,* 147: 1614–1621.

Rivera, S.M., Menon, V., White, C.D., Glaser, B. and Reiss, A.L. (2002) 'Functional brain activation during arithmetic processing in females with fragile-X syndrome is related to FMR1 protein expression.' *Human Brain Mapping,* 16: 206–218.

Robb, S.A., Pohl, K.R.E., Baraitser, M., Wilson, J. and Brett, E.M. (1989) 'The "happy puppet" syndrome of Angelman: review of the clinical features.' *Archives of Diseases in Childhood,* 64: 83–86.

Roberts, K.B. and Hall, J.G. (1971) 'Apert's acrocephalosyndactyly in mother and daughter: cleft palate in the mother.' *Birth Defects Original Articles Series VII,* 7: 262–264.

Robertson, L., Hall, S.E., Jacoby, P., Ellaway, C. *et al.* (2006) 'The association between behavior and genotype in Rett syndrome, using the Australian Rett syndrome Database.' *American Journal of Medical Genetics,* 141B: 177–183.

Robertson, M. and Cavanna, A. (2008) *Tourette Syndrome (The Facts)* (2nd edn). Oxford: Oxford University Press.

Robertson, M.M. (2000) 'Tourette syndrome, associated conditions and the complexities of treatment.' *Brain,* 123: 425–462.

Robin, N.H. (2006) 'It does matter: the importance of making the diagnosis of a genetic syndrome.' *Current Opinion in Pediatrics 18*, 6: 595–597.

Robin, N.H., Taylor, C.J., McDonald-McGinn, D.M., Zackai, E.H. *et al.* (2006) 'Polymicrogyria and deletion 22q11.2 syndrome: window to the etiology of a common cortical malformation.' *American Journal of Medical Genetics,* 140A: 2416–2425.

Robins, D.L., Fein, D., Barton, M.L. and Green, J.A. (2001) 'The Modified Checklist for Autism in Toddlers: an initial study investigating the early detection of autism and pervasive developmental disorders.' *Journal of Autism and Developmental Disorders 31*, 2: 131–144.

Robinson, A., Bender, B.G., Linden, M.G. and Salbenblatt, J.A. (1990) 'Sex chromosome aneuploidy: the Denver Prospective Study.' *Birth Defects Original Articles Series*, 26: 59–115.

Robinson, L.L. (1992) 'Down syndrome and leukemia.' *Leukemia*, 6: 5–7.

Rodenhiser, D. and Mann, M. (2006) 'Epigenetics and human disease: translating basic biology into clinical applications.' *Canadian Medical Association Journal*, 174: 341–348.

Rodier, P.M., Ingram, J.L., Tisdale, B., Nelson, S. and Romano, J. (1996) 'Embryological origin for autism: developmental anomalies of the cranial nerve motor nuclei.' *Journal of Comparative Neurology 370*, 2: 247–261.

Rodriguez, C., Mayo, J.C., Sainz, R.M., Antolin, I. *et al.* (2004) 'Regulation of antioxidant enzymes: a significant role for melatonin.' *Journal of Pineal Research*, 36: 1–9.

Rodríguez-Bujaldón, A.L., Vázquez-Bayo, C., Jiménez-Puya, R.J., Moreno-Giménez, J.C. (2008) 'Sturge-Weber syndrome and type 1 neurofibromatosis: a chance association?' [Article available in English and Spanish.] *Actas Dermosifiliográficas*, 99: 313–314.

Rodriguez-Viciana, P., Tetsu, O., Tidyman, W.E., Estep, A.L. *et al.* (2006) 'Germline mutations in genes within the MAPK pathway cause cardio-facio-cutaneous syndrome.' *Science*, 311: 1287–1290.

Roecker, G.O. and Huethner, C.A. (1983) 'An analysis for paternal-age effect in Ohio's Down syndrome births, 1970–1980.' *American Journal of Human Genetics*, 35: 1297–1306.

Roelfsema, J.H., White, S.J., Ariyurek, Y., Bartholdi, D. *et al.* (2005) 'Genetic heterogeneity in Rubinstein-Taybi syndrome: mutations in both the CBP and EP300 genes cause disease.' *American Journal of Human Genetics*, 76: 572–580.

Roesch, C., Steinbicker, V., Korb, C., von Rohden, L. and Schmitt, J. (2001) 'Goldenhar anomaly in one triplet derived from intracytoplasmic sperm injection (ICSI).' *American Journal of Medical Genetics 101*, 1: 82–83.

Roesler, R., Henriques, J.A.P. and Schwartzmann, G. (2006a) 'Gastrin-releasing peptide receptor as a molecular target for psychiatric and neurological disorders.' *CNS and Neurological Disorders – Drug Targets*, 5: 197–204.

Roesler, R., Luft, T., Oliveira, S.H.S., Farias, C.B. *et al.* (2006b) 'Molecular mechanisms mediating gastrin-releasing peptide receptor modulation of memory consolidation in the hippocampus.' *Neuropharmacology*, 51: 350–357.

Rogawski, M.A., Funderburk, S.J. and Cederbaum, S.D. (1978) 'Oculocutaneous albinism and mental disorder: a report of two autistic boys.' *Human Heredity*, 28: 81–85.

Rogawski, M.A., Gryder, D., Castaneda, D., Yonekawa, W. *et al.* (2003) 'GluR5 kainate receptors, seizures and the amygdala.' *Annals of the New York Academy of Science*, 985: 150–162.

Roger, J., Bureau, M., Dravet, C., Genton, P. *et al.* (eds.) (2005) *Epileptic Syndromes in Infancy, Childhood and Adolescence.* (4th edn). London: John Libbey.

Rogers, S.J. and Newhart-Larson, S. (1989) 'Characteristics of infantile autism in five children with Leber's congenital amaurosis.' *Developmental Medicine and Child Neurology 31*, 5: 598–608.

Rogers, S.J., Wehner, D.E. and Hagerman, R. (2001) 'The behavioral phenotype in fragile-X: symptoms of autism in very young children with fragile-X syndrome, idiopathic autism, and other developmental disorders.' *Journal of Developmental and Behavioral Pediatrics 22*, 6: 409–417.

Roizen, N.J. (2005) 'Complementary and alternative therapies for Down syndrome.' *Mental Retardation and Developmental Disabilities Research Reviews*, 11: 149–155.

Rollnick, B.R. (1988) 'Male transmission of Apert syndrome.' *Clinical Genetics*, 33: 87–90.

Rollnick, B.R. and Kaye, C.I. (1983) 'Hemifacial microsomia and variants: pedigree data.' *American Journal of Medical Genetics*, 15: 233–253.

Rollnick, B.R., Kaye, C.I., Nagatoshi, K., Hauck, W. and Martin, A.O. (1987) 'Oculoauriculovertebral dysplasia and variants: phenotypic characteristics of 294 patients.' *American Journal of Medical Genetics*, 26: 361–375.

Román, G.C. (2007) 'Autism: transient in utero hypothyroxinemia related to maternal flavonoid ingestion during pregnancy and to other environmental antithyroid agents.' *Journal of Neurological Sciences 262*, 1/2: 15–26.

Romano, C., Smout, S., Miller, J.K. and O'Malley, K.L. (2002) 'Developmental regulation of metabotropic glutamate receptor 5b protein in rodent brain.' *Neuroscience*, 111: 693–698.

Romo, T. 3rd, Fozo, M.S. and Sclafani, A.P. (2000) 'Microtia reconstruction using a porous polyethylene framework.' *Facial Plastic Surgery*, 16: 15–22.

Romo, T. 3rd, Presti, P.M. and Yalamanchili, H.R. (2006) 'Medpor alternative for microtia repair.' *Facial Plastic Surgery Clinics of North America*, 14: 129–136.

Roohi, J., Montagna, C., Tegay, D.H., Palmer, L.E. *et al.* (2008) 'Disruption of contactin 4 in three subjects with autism spectrum disorder.' *Journal of Medical Genetics.* Published online 18 Mar. 2008, doi:10.1136/jmg.2008.057505.

Ropers, H.-H. (2006) 'X-linked mental retardation: many genes for a complex disorder.' *Current Opinion in Genetics and Development*, 16: 260–269.

Ropers, H.-H. (2007) 'New perspectives for the elucidation of genetic disorders.' *American Journal of Human Genetics*, 81: 199–207.

Roposch, A., Bhaskar, A.R., Lee, F., Adedapo, S. *et al.* (2004) 'Orthopaedic manifestations of Brachmann-de Lange syndrome: a report of 34 patients.' *Journal of Pediatric Orthopedics B*, 13, 2: 118–122.

Rosenblatt, D.S., Duschens, E.A., Hellstrom, F.V., Goldick, M.S. *et al.* (1985) 'Folic acid blinded trial in identical twins with fragile-X syndrome.' *American Journal of Human Genetics*, 37: 543–552.

Ross, A.J. and Beales, P.L. (2007) 'Bardet-Biedl syndrome.' *GeneReviews*, www.ncbi.nlm.nih.gov.

Ross, A.J., May-Simera, H., Eichers, E.R., Kai, M. *et al.* (2005) 'Disruption of Bardet-Biedl syndrome ciliary proteins perturbs planar cell polarity in vertebrates.' *Nature Genetics*, 37: 1135–1140.

Ross, J.A., Blair, C.K., Olshan, A.F., Robison, L.L. *et al.* (2005) 'Periconceptional vitamin use and leukemia risk in children with Down syndrome – a children's oncology group study.' *Cancer 104*, 2: 405–410.

Rosser, T. and Packer, R.J. (2002) 'Intracranial neoplasms in children with neurofibromatosis 1.' *Journal of Child Neurology*, 17: 630–637.

Rossi, A. and Cantisani, C. (2004) 'Trichothiodystrophy.' *Orphanet Encyclopaedia* www.orpha.net.

Rossi, E., Verri, A.P., Patricelli, M.G., Destefani, V. *et al.* (2008) 'A 12Mb deletion at 7q33–q35 associated with autism spectrum disorders and primary amenorrhea.' *European Journal of Medical Genetics 51*, 6: 631–638.

Roubertie, A., Semprino, M., Chaze, A.M., Rivier, F. *et al.* (2001) 'Neurological presentation of three patients with 22q11 deletion (CATCH 22 syndrome).' *Brain and Development*, 23: 810–814.

Rouse, B., Azen, C., Koch, R., Matalon, R. *et al.* (1997) 'Maternal phenylketonuria collaborative study (MPKUCS) offspring: facial anomalies, malformations, and early neurological sequelae.' *American Journal of Medical Genetics*, 69: 89–95.

Rouse, B., Matalon, R., Koch, R., Azen, C. *et al.* (2000) 'Maternal phenylketonuria syndrome: congenital heart defects, microcephaly, and developmental outcomes.' *Journal of Pediatrics*, 136: 57–61.

Rousseau, F., Robb, L.J., Rouillard, P. and Der Kaloustian, V.M. (1994) 'No mental retardation in a man with 40% abnormal methylation at the FMR-1 locus and transmission of sperm cell mutations as premutations.' *Human Molecular Genetics*, 3: 927–930.

Rousseau, F., Rouillard, P., Morel, M.-L., Khandjian, E.W. and Morgan, K. (1995) 'Prevalence of carriers of permutation-size alleles of the FMR1 gene – and implications for the population genetics of the fragile-X syndrome.' *American Journal of Human Genetics*, 57: 1006–1018.

Rowe, S.M. and Clancy, J.P. (2009) 'Pharmaceuticals targeting nonsense mutations in genetic diseases: progress in development.' *BioDrugs 23*, 3: 165–174.

Roze, E., Gervais, D., Demeret, S., de Baulny, H.O. *et al.* (2003) 'Neuropsychiatric disturbances in presumed late-onset cobalamin C disease.' *Archives of Neurology*, 60: 1457–1462.

Rubenstein, J.L.R. and Merzenich, M.M. (2003) 'Model of autism: increased ratio of excitation/inhibition in key neural systems.' *Genes, Brain and Behavior*, 2: 255–267.

Rubinstein, J.H. and Taybi, H. (1963) 'Broad thumbs and toes and facial abnormalities.' *American Journal of Diseases in Childhood*, 105: 588–608.

Rubinsztein, D.C., Hon, J., Stevens, F., Pyrah, I. *et al.* (1999) 'Apo E genotypes and risk of dementia in Down syndrome.' *American Journal of Medical Genetics 88*, 4: 344–347.

Rubinsztein, D.C., Leggo, J., Chiano, M., Dodge, A. *et al.* (1997) 'Genotypes at the GluR6 kainate receptor locus are associated with variation in the age of onset of Huntington disease.' *Proceedings of the National Academy of Science USA*, 94: 3872–3876.

Rueda, J.-R., Ballesteros, J. and Tejada, M.-I. (2009) 'Systematic review of pharmacological treatments in fragile-X syndrome.' *BMC Neurology*, 9: 53, doi:10.1186/1471-2377-9-53.

Rugarli, E.I. (1999) 'Kallmann syndrome and the link between olfactory and reproductive development.' *American Journal of Human Genetics 65*, 4: 943–948.

Ruggieri, M. and McShane, M.A. (1998) 'Parental view of epilepsy in Angelman syndrome: a questionnaire study.' *Archives of Disease in Childhood*, 79: 423–426.

Ruggieri, M. and Pavone, L. (2000) 'Hypomelanosis of Ito: clinical syndrome or just phenotype?' *Journal of Child Neurology*,15: 635–644.

Rulli, I., Ferrero, G.B., Belligni, E., Delmonaco, A.G. *et al.* (2005) 'Myhre's syndrome in a girl with normal intelligence' (letter). *American Journal of Medical Genetics*, 134A: 100–102.

Rush, T., Hjelmhaug, J. and Lobner, D. (2008) 'Effects of chelators on mercury, iron, lead neurotoxicity in cortical culture.' *Neurotoxicology*, doi:10.1016/j.neuro.2008.10.009.

Russo, S., Briscioli, V., Cogliati, F., Macchi, M. *et al.* (1998) 'An unusual fragile-X sibship: female compound heterozygote and male with a partially methylated full mutation.' *Clinical Genetics*, 54: 309–314.

Rutter, M. (1968) 'Concepts of autism: review of research.' *Journal of Child Psychology and Psychiatry*, 9: 1–25.

Rutter, M. (1983) 'Low Level Lead Exposure: Sources, Effects and Implications.' In M. Rutter and R. Russell Jones (eds.) *Lead versus Health: Sources and Effects of Low Level Lead Exposure*. Chichester: John Wiley.

Rutter, M. (1991) 'Nature, nurture and psychopathology: a new look at an old topic.' *Development and Psychopathology*, 3: 125–136.

Rutter, M. (2006) 'Autism: its recognition, early diagnosis, and service implications.' *Journal of Developmental and Behavioral Pediatrics*, 27, Supplement 2: S54–S58.

Rutter, M. and Schopler, E. (1988) 'Autism and Pervasive Developmental Disorders.' In M. Rutter, A. Hussain, I. Tuma and S. Lann (eds.) *Assessment and Diagnosis in Child Psychopathology*. London.David Fulton Publishers,

Rutter, M., Andersen-Wood, L., Beckett, C., Bredenkamp, D. *et al.* (1999) 'Quasi-autistic patterns following severe early global privation. English and Romanian Adoptees (ERA) Study Team.' *Journal of Child Psychology and Psychiatry 40*, 4: 537–549.

Rutter, S.C. and Cole, T.R. (1991) 'Psychological characteristics of Sotos syndrome.' *Developmental Medicine and Child Neurology 33*, 10: 898–902.

Ruvalcaba, R.H.A., Myhre, S. and Smith, D.W. (1980) 'Sotos syndrome with intestinal polyposis and pigmentary changes of the genitalia.' *Clinical Genetics*, 18: 413–416.

Ruyter, B., Rosjo, C., Einen, O. and Thomassen, M.S. (2000) 'Essential fatty acids in Atlantic salmon: time course of changes in fatty acid composition of liver, blood and carcass induced by a diet deficient in n-3 and n-6 fatty acids.' *Aquaculture Nutrition 6*, 2: 109–117.

Ryall, R.G., Callen, D., Cocciolone, R., Duvnjak, A. *et al.* (2001) 'Karyotypes found in the population declared at increased risk of Down syndrome following maternal serum screening.' *Prenatal Diagnosis*, 21: 553–557.

Ryan, A.K., Bartlett, K., Clayton, P., Eaton, S. *et al.* (1998) 'Smith-Lemli-Opitz syndrome: a variable clinical and biochemical phenotype.' *Journal of Medical Genetics*, 35: 558–565.

Rzem, R., Veiga-da-Cunha, M., Noël, G., Goffette, S. et al. (2004) 'A gene encoding a putative FAD-dependent L-2-hydroxyglutarate dehydrogenase is mutated in L-2-hydroxyglutaric aciduria.' *Proceedings of the National Academy of Science USA*, 101: 16849–16854.

Rzeski, M., Kuran, W., Mierzewska, H., Vreken, P. *et al.* (1999) 'Adrenomieloneuropatia – jedna z postaci adrenoleukodystrofii sprzezonej z chromosomem X – badania rodziny.' [Adrenomyeloneuropathy: a form of X-linked adrenoleukodystrophy. Report of a family.] [Article in Polish.] *Neurologia i Neurochirugia Polska 33*, 5: 1173–1185.

S

Saal, H.M., Samango-Sprouse, C.A., Rodnan, L.A., Rosenbaum, K.N. and Custer, D.A. (1993) 'Brachmann-de Lange syndrome with normal IQ.' *American Journal of Medical Genetics*, 47: 995–998.

Saar, K., Al-Gazali, L., Sztriha, L., Rueschendorf, F. et al. (1999) 'Homozygosity mapping in families with Joubert syndrome identifies a locus on chromosome 9q34.3 and evidence for genetic heterogeneity.' *American Journal of Human Genetics*, 65: 1666–1671.

Sacco, R., Militerni, R., Frolli, A., Bravaccio, C. *et al.* (2007) 'Clinical, morphological, and biochemical correlates of head circumference in autism.' *Biological Psychiatry*, 62: 1038–1047.

Sacks, B. and Buckley, F. (1998) 'Multi-nutrient formulas and other substances as therapies for Down syndrome: an overview.' *Down Syndrome News and Update 1*, 2: 70–83.

Sadler, L.S., Pober, B.R., Grandinetti, A., Scheiber, D. *et al.* (2001) 'Differences by sex in cardiovascular disease in Williams syndrome.' *Journal of Pediatrics*, 139: 849–853.

Saemundsen, E., Ludvigsson, P., Hilmarsdottir, I. and Rafnsson, V. (2007) 'Autism spectrum disorders in children with seizures in the first year of life – a population-based study.' *Epilepsia 48*, 9: 1724–1730.

Sagi, L., Zuckerman-Levin, N., Gawlik, A., Ghizzoni, L. *et al.* (2007) 'Clinical significance of the parental origin of the X chromosome in Turner syndrome.' *Journal of Clinical Endocrinology and Metabolism 92*, 3: 846–852.

Saher, G., Brugger, B., Lapper-Siefke, C., Mobius, W. *et al.* (2005) 'High cholesterol level is essential for myelin membrane growth.' *Nature Neuroscience*, 8: 468–475.

Saif, M.W., Mattison, L., Carollo, T., Ezzeldin, H. and Diasio, R.B. (2006) 'Dihydropyrimidine dehydrogenase deficiency in an Indian population.' *Cancer Chemotherapy and Pharmacology 58*, 3: 396–401.

Saitoh, S., Buiting, K., Cassidy, S.B. and Conroy, J.M. (1997) 'Clinical spectrum and molecular diagnosis of Angelman and Prader-Willi syndrome patients with an imprinting mutation.' *American Journal of Medical Genetics 68*, 2: 195–206.

Saitoh, S., Harada, N., Jinno, Y., Hashimoto, K. *et al.* (1994) 'Molecular and clinical study of 61 Angelman syndrome patients.' *American Journal of Medical Genetics*, 52: 158–163.

Saitoh, S., Kubota, T., Ohta, T., Jinno, Y. *et al.* (1992) 'Familial Angelman syndrome caused by imprinted submicroscopic deletion encompassing GABAA receptor beta 3-subunit gene.' *Lancet 339*, 8789: 366–367.

Saitoh, S., Momoi, M.Y., Yamagata, T., Miyao, M. and Suwa, K. (1998) 'Clinical and electroencephalographic findings in juvenile type DRPLA.' *Pediatric Neurology*, 18: 265–268.

Sajedi, E., Gaston-Massuet, C., Signore, M., Andoniadou, C.L. et al. (2008) 'Analysis of mouse models carrying the I26T and R160C substitutions in the transcriptional repressor HESX1 as models for septo-optic dysplasia and hypopituitarism.' *Disease Models and Mechanics*, 1: 241–254.

Salen, G., Shefer, S., Batta, A.K., Tint, G.S. *et al.* (1996) 'Abnormal cholesterol biosynthesis in the Smith-Lemli-Opitz syndrome.' *Journal of Lipid Research*, 37: 1169–1180.

Salerno, C., D'Euphemia, P., Finocchiaro, R., Celli, M. *et al.* (1999) 'Effect of D-ribose on purine synthesis and neurological symptoms in a patient with adenylsuccinase deficiency.' *Biochimica Biophysica Acta*, 1453: 135–140.

Salman, M.S. (2002) 'Systematic review of the effect of therapeutic dietary supplements and drugs on cognitive function in subjects with Down syndrome.' *European Journal of Paediatric Neurology*, 6: 213–219.

Salomons, G.J., van Dooren, S.J.M., Verhoeven, N.M., Cecil, K.M. *et al.* (2001) 'X-linked creatine transporter (SLC6A8 gene) defect: a new creatine deficiency syndrome.' *American Journal of Human Genetics*, 68: 1497–1500.

Sampson, J.R., Scahill, S.J., Stephenson, J.B.P., Mann, L. and Connor, J.M. (1989) 'Genetic aspects of tuberous sclerosis in the west of Scotland.' *Journal of Medical Genetics*, 26: 28–31.

Samuraki, M., Komai, K., Hasegawa, Y., Kimura, M. *et al.* (2008) 'A successfully treated adult patient with L-2-hydroxyglutaric aciduria.' *Neurology* 70, 13: 1051–1052.

Sanchez-Albisua, I., Borell-Kost, S., Mau-Holzmann, U.A., Licht, P. and Krägeloh-Mann, I. (2007) 'Increased frequency of severe major anomalies in children conceived by intracytoplasmic sperm injection.' *Developmental Medicine and Child Neurology* 49, 2: 129–134.

Sandanam, T., Beange, H., Robson, L., Woolnough, H. *et al.* (1997) 'Manifestations in institutionalised adults with Angelman syndrome due to deletion.' *American Journal of Medical Genetics*, 70: 415–420.

Sanlaville, D. and Verloes, A. (2007) 'CHARGE syndrome: an update.' *European Journal of Human Genetics*, 15: 389–399.

Santos Dantas, A., Luft, T., Henriques, J.A.P., Schwartsmann, G. and Roesler, R. (2006) 'Opposite effects of low and high doses of the gastrin-releasing peptide receptor antagonist RC-3095 on memory consolidation in the hippocampus: possible involvement of the GABAergic system.' *Peptides*, 27: 2307–2312.

Saraiva, J.M. and Baraitser, M. (1992) 'Joubert syndrome: a review.' *American Journal of Medical Genetics*, 43: 726–731.

Sari, B.A., Karaer, K., Bodur, S. and Soysal, A.S. (2008) 'Case report: autistic disorder in Kabuki syndrome.' *Journal of Autism and Developmental Disorders*, 38: 198–201.

Sarimski, K. (1997) 'Communication, social-emotional development and parenting stress in Cornelia-de-Lange syndrome.' *Journal of Intellectual Disability Research*, 41: 70–75.

Sarkissian, C.N. and Gámez, A. (2005) 'Phenylalanine ammonia lyase, enzyme substitution therapy for phenylketonuria, where are we now?' *Molecular Genetics and Metabolism*, 86: S22–S26.

Sarkissian, C.N., Shao, Z., Blain, F., Peevers, R. *et al.* (1999) 'A different approach to treatment of phenylketonuria: phenylalanine degradation with recombinant phenylalanine ammonia lyase.' *Proceedings of the National Academy of Science*, 96: 2339–2344.

Sas, K., Robotka, H., Toldi, J. and Vécseia, L. (2007) 'Mitochondria, metabolic disturbances, oxidative stress and the kynurenine system, with focus on neurodegenerative disorders.', *Journal of the Neurological Sciences*, doi:10.1016/j.jns.2007.01.033

Sataloff, R.T., Spiegel, J.R., Hawkshaw, M., Epstein, J.M. and Jackson, L. (1990) 'Cornelia de Lange syndrome: otolaryngologic manifestations.' *Archives of Otolaryngology, Head and Neck Surgery*, 116: 1044–1046.

Satran, D., Pierpont, M.E. and Dobyns, W.B. (1999) 'Cerebello-oculo-renal syndromes including Arima, Senior-Loken and COACH syndromes: more than just variants of Joubert syndrome.' *American Journal of Medical Genetics*, 86: 459–469.

Saucy, P., Eidus, L. and Keeley, F. (1980) 'Perforation of the colon in a 15-year-old girl with Ehlers-Danlos syndrome type IV.' *Journal of Pediatric Surgery 25*, 11: 1180–1182.

Sayer, J.A., Otto, E.A., O'Toole, J.F., Nurnberg, G. et al. (2006) 'The centrosomal protein nephrocystin-6 is mutated in Joubert syndrome and activates transcription factor ATF4.' *Nature Genetics*, 38: 674–681.

Scahill, L., Leckman, J.F., Schultz, R.T., Katsovich, L. and Peterson, B.S. (2003) 'A placebo-controlled trial of risperidone in Tourette syndrome.' *Neurology*, 60: 1130–1135.

Scala, E., Ariani, F., Mari, F., Caselli, R. *et al.* (2005) 'CDKL5/STK9 is mutated in Rett syndrome variant with infantile spasms.' *Journal of Medical Genetics*, 42: 103–107.

Scalco, F.B., Cruzes, V.M., Vendramini, R.C., Brunetti, I.L. and Moretti-Ferreira, D. (2003) 'Diagnosis of Smith-Lemli-Opitz syndrome by ultraviolet spectrophotometry.' *Brazilian Journal of Medical and Biological Research 36*, 10: 1327–1332.

Scambler, P.J. (2000) 'The 22q11 deletion syndromes.' *Human Molecular Genetics 9*, 16: 2421–2426.

Scambler, D.J., Hepburn, S.L. and Rogers, S.J. (2006) 'A two-year follow-up on risk status identified by the Checklist for Autism in Toddlers.' *Journal of Developmental and Behavioral Pediatrics*, 27: 104–110.

Scarbrough, P.R., Huddleston, K. and Finley, S.C. (1986) 'An additional case of Smith-Lemli-Opitz syndrome in a 46,XY infant with female external genitalia.' *Journal of Medical Genetics*, 23: 174–175.

Scattone, A., Caruso, G., Marzullo, A., Piscitelli, D. *et al.* (2003) 'Neoplastic disease and deletion 22q11.2: a multicentric study and report of two cases.' *Pediatric Pathology and Molecular Medicine*, 22: 323–341.

Schaefer, G.B. and Lutz, R.E. (2006) 'Diagnostic yield in the clinical genetic evaluation of autism spectrum disorders.' *Genetics in Medicine 8*, 9: 549–556.

Schaefer, G.B. and Mendelsohn, N.J. (2008) 'Genetics evaluation for the etiologic diagnosis of autism spectrum disorders.' *Genetics in Medicine 10*, 1: 4–12.

Schaffer, J.V. and Bolognia, J.L. (2003) 'The treatment of hypopigmentation in children.' *Clinics in Dermatology*, 21: 296–310.

Schalkwijk, J., Zweers, M.C., Steijlen, P.M., Dean, W.B. *et al.* (2001) 'A recessive form of the Ehlers-Danlos syndrome caused by tenascin-X deficiency.' *New England Journal of Medicine*, 345: 1167–1175.

Schanen, C. and Francke, U. (1998) 'A severely affected male born into a Rett syndrome kindred supports X-linked inheritance and allows extension of the exclusion map' (letter). *American Journal of Human Genetics*, 63: 267–269.

Schanen, C., Houwink, E.J., Dorrani, N., Lane, J., *et al.* (2004) 'Phenotypic manifestations of MECP2 mutations in classical and atypical Rett syndrome.', *American Journal of Medical Genetics A., 126A*, 2: 129–40.

Schanen, N.C., Kurczynski, T.W., Brunnelle, D., Woodcock, M.M., Dure, L.S. IV and Percy, A.K. (1998) 'Neonatal encephalopathy in two boys in families with recurrent Rett syndrome.' *Journal of Child Neurology*, 13: 229–231.

Schara, U., Benedikt, G.H. and Schoser, B.G.H. (2006) 'Myotonic dystrophies type 1 and 2: a summary on current aspects.' *Seminars in Pediatric Neurology*, 13: 71–79.

Schauerte, E.W. and St-Aubin, P.M. (1966) 'Progressive synostosis in Apert's syndrome (acrocephalosyndactyly): with a description of roentgenographic changes in the feet.' *American Journal of Roentgenology*, 97: 67–73.

Schaumburg, H., Kaplan, J., Windebank, A., Vick, N. *et al.* (1983) 'Sensory neuropathy from pyridoxine abuse. A new megavitamin syndrome.' *New England Journal of Medicine 309*, 8: 445–448.

Scheffer, I.E., Wallace, R.H., Phillips, F.L., Hewson, P. *et al.* (2002) 'X-linked myoclonic epilepsy with spasticity and intellectual disability: mutation in the homeobox gene ARX.' *Neurology*, 59: 348–356.

Schenck, C.H., Arnulf, I. and Mahowald, M.W. (2007) 'Sleep and sex: what can go wrong? A review of the literatures on sleep related disorders and abnormal sexual behaviors and experiences.' *Sleep 30*, 6: 683–702.

Schendel, D. and Bhasin, T.K. (2008) 'Birth weight and gestational age characteristics of children with autism, including a comparison with other developmental disabilities.' *Pediatrics 121*, 6: 1155–1164.

Schepis, C., Elia, M., Siragusa, M. and Barbareschi, M. (1997) 'A new case of trichothiodystrophy associated with autism, seizures, and mental retardation.' *Pediatric Dermatology*, 14: 125–128.

Schindler, D., Bishop, D.F., Wolfe, D.E., Wang, A.M. *et al.* (1989) 'Neuroaxonal dystrophy due to lysosomal alpha-N-acetylgalactosaminidase deficiency.' *New England Journal of Medicine*, 320: 1735–1740.

Schlesinger, B. (1931) 'Gigantism (acromegalic in type).' *Proceedings of the Royal Society of Medicine*, 24: 1352–1353.

Schmandt, S.M., Packer, R.J., Vezina, L.G. and Jane, J. (2000) 'Spontaneous regression of low-grade astrocytomas in childhood.' *Pediatric Neurosurgery*, 32: 132–136.

Schmidt, C., Hofmann, U., Kohlmuller, D., Murdter, T. *et al.* (2005) 'Comprehensive analysis of pyrimidine metabolism in 450 children with unspecific neurological symptoms using high-pressure liquid chromatography-electrospray ionization tandem mass spectrometry.' *Journal of Inherited Metabolic Disease*, 28: 1109–1122.

Schmidt, H., Pozza, S.B., Bonfig, W., Schwarz, H.P. and Dokoupil, K. (2008) 'Successful early dietary intervention avoids obesity in patients with Prader-Willi syndrome: a ten-year follow-up.' *Journal of Pediatric Endocrinology and Metabolism 21*, 7: 651–655.

Schmitt, J.E., Eliez, S., Bellugi, U. and Reiss, A.L. (2001) 'Analysis of cerebral shape in Williams syndrome.' *Archives of Neurology*, 58: 283–287.

Schoepp, D.D., Jane, D.E. and Monn, J.A. (1999) 'Pharmacological agents acting at subtypes of metabotropic glutamate receptors.' *Neuropharmacology*, 38: 1431–1476.

Schopler, E., Reichler, R.J., DeVellis, R. and Daly, K. (1980) 'Towards objective classification of childhood autism: Childhood Autism Rating Scale (CARS).' *Journal of Autism and Developmental Disorders*, 10: 91–103.

Schrager, C.A., Schneider, D., Gruener, A.C., Tsou, H.C. and Peacocke, M. (1998) 'Clinical and pathological features of breast disease in Cowden's syndrome: an underrecognized syndrome with an increased risk of breast cancer.' *Human Pathology*, 29: 47–53.

Schrander-Stumpel, C.T.R.M., de Die-Smulders, C.E.M., Hennekam, R.C.M., Fryns, J.-P. *et al.* (1992) 'Oculoauriculovertebral spectrum and cerebral anomalies.' *Journal of Medical Genetics*, 29: 326–331.

Schroer, R.J., Phelan, M.C., Michaelis, R.C., Crawford, E.C. *et al.* (1998) 'Autism and maternally derived aberrations of chromosome 15q.' *American Journal of Medical Genetics*, 76: 327–336.

Schubbert, S., Zenker, M., Rowe, S.L., Boll, S. *et al.* (2006) 'Germline KRAS mutations cause Noonan syndrome.' *Nature Genetics*, 38: 331–336.

Schuelke, M., Wagner, K.R., Stolz, L.E., Hübner, C. *et al.* (2004) 'Myostatin mutation associated with gross muscle hypertrophy in a child.' *New England Journal of Medicine*, 350: 2682–2688.

Schuffenhauer, S., Lichtner, P., Peykar-Derakhshandeh, P., Murken, J. *et al.* (1998) 'Deletion mapping on chromosome 10p and definition of a critical region for the second DiGeorge syndrome locus (DGS2).' *European Journal of Human Genetics*, 6: 213–225.

Schulkin, J. (2007) 'Autism and the amygdala: an endocrine hypothesis.' *Brain and Cognition*, 65: 87–99.

Schultz, S.T., Klonoff-Cohen, H.S., Wingard, D.L., Akshoomoff, N.A. *et al.* (2006) 'Breastfeeding, infant formula supplementation, and autistic disorder: the results of a parent survey.' *International Breastfeeding Journal*, 1: 16–22.

Schulze, A. (2003) 'Creatine deficiency syndromes.' *Molecular and Cellular Biochemistry*, 244: 143–150.

Schulze, A. and Battini, R. (2007) 'Pre-symptomatic treatment of creatine biosynthesis defects.' *Sub-cellular Biochemistry*, 46: 167–181.

Schulze, A., Ebinger, F., Rating, D. and Mayatepek, E. (2001) 'Improving treatment of guanidinoacetate methyltransferase Schulze deficiency: reduction of guanidinoacetic acid in body fluids by arginine restriction and ornithine supplementation.' *Molecular Genetics and Metabolism 74*, 4: 413–419.

Schulze, A., Hess, T., Wevers, R., Mayatepek, E. *et al.* (1997) 'Creatine deficiency syndrome caused by guanidinoacetate methyltransferase deficiency: diagnostic tools for a new inborn error of metabolism.' *Journal of Pediatrics*, 131: 626–631.

Schulze, A., Mayatepek, E. and Rating, D. (2000) 'Improved treatment of guanidinoacetate methyltransferase (GAMT) deficiency.' *Journal of Inherited Metabolic Disease*, 23 (Suppl. 1): 211.

Schumacher, A., Kapranov, P., Kaminsky, Z., Flanagan, J. *et al.* (2006) 'Microarray-based DNA methylation profiling: technology and applications.' *Nucleic Acids Research 34*, 2: 528–542.

Schumann, C.M. and Amaral, D.G. (2006) 'Stereological analysis of amygdala neuron number in autism.' *Journal of Neuroscience*, 26: 7674–7679.

Schwartz, C.E., Tarpey, P.S., Lubs, H.A., Verloes, A. *et al.* (2007) 'The original Lujan syndrome family has a novel missense mutation (p.N1007S) in the MED12 gene.' *Journal of Medical Genetics*, 44: 472–477.

Schwartzman, J.S., Zatz, M., Vasquez, L.R., Gomes, R.R. *et al.* (1999) 'Rett syndrome in a boy with a 47,XXY karyotype' (letter). *American Journal of Human Genetics*, 64: 1781–1785.

Scothorn, D.J. and Butler, M.G. (1997) 'How common is precocious puberty in patients with Williams syndrome?' (letter). *Clinical Dysmorphology*, 6: 91–93.

Scott, A., Micallef, C., Hale, S.L. and Watts, P. (2008) 'Cortical visual impairment in Hypomelanosis of Ito.' *Journal of Pediatric Ophthalmology and Strabismus*, 45: 240–241.

Scottish Intercollegiate Guideline Network (2007) *Assessment, Diagnosis and Clinical Interventions for Children and Young People with Autism Spectrum Disorders: A National Clinical Guideline.* Downloadable as PDF from www.sign.ac.uk.

Scriver, C.R. (2001) 'Garrod's foresight; our hindsight.' *Journal of Inherited Metabolic Disease*, 24: 93–116.

Scriver, C.R., Eisensmith, R.C., Woo, S.L.C. and Kaufman, S. (1994) 'The hyperphenylalaninemias of man and mouse.' *Annual Review of Genetics*, 28: 141–165.

Sebat, J., Lakshmi, B., Malhotra, D., Troge, J. *et al.* (2007) 'Strong association of de novo copy number mutations with autism.' *Science 316*, 5823: 445–449.

Sebesta, I., Krijt, J., Kmoch, S., Hartmannova, H. *et al.* (1997) 'Adenylosuccinase deficiency: clinical and biochemical findings in 5 Czech patients.' *Journal of Inherited Metabolic Diseases*, 20: 343–344.

Sebire, N.J., Snijders, R.J., Brown, R., Southall, T. and Nicolaides, K.H. (1998) 'Detection of sex chromosome abnormalities by nuchal translucency screening at 10–14 weeks.' *Prenatal Diagnosis*, 18: 581–584.

Sedlackova, E. (1955) 'The syndrome of the congenital shortening of the soft palate.' [In Czech.] *Cas Lek Ces*, 94: 1304–1307.

Seidl, R., Cairns, N., Singewald, N., Kaehler, S.T. and Lubec, G. (2001) 'Differences between GABA levels in Alzheimer's disease and Down syndrome with Alzheimer-like neuropathology.' *Naunyn Schmiedeberg's Archives of Pharmacology 363*, 2: 139–145.

Seifert, W., Holder-Espinasse, M., Spranger, S., Hoeltzenbein, M. *et al.* (2006) 'Mutational spectrum of COH1 and clinical heterogeneity in Cohen syndrome' (letter). *Journal of Medical Genetics*, 43: e22.

Seijo-Martínez, M., Navarro, C., Castro del Río, M., Vila, O. et al. (2005) 'L-2-hydroxyglutaric aciduria: clinical, neuroimaging, and neuropathological findings.' *Archives of Neurology*, 62: 666–670.

Sekul, E.A., Moak, J.P., Schultz, R.J., Glaze, D.G. *et al.* (1994) 'Electrocardiographic findings in Rett syndrome: an explanation for sudden death?' *Journal of Pediatrics*, 125: 80–82.

Selicorni, A., Fratoni, A., Pavesi, M.A., Bottigelli, M. *et al.* (2006) 'Thyroid anomalies in Williams syndrome: investigation of 95 patients.' *American Journal of Medical Genetics*, 140A: 1098–1101.

Selicorni, A., Russo, S., Gervasini, C., Castronovo, P. *et al.* (2007) 'Clinical score of 62 Italian patients with Cornelia de Lange syndrome and correlations with the presence and type of NIPBL mutation.' *Clinical Genetics 72*, 2: 98–108.

Seller, M.J., Flinter, F.A., Docherty, Z., Fagg, N. and Newbould, M. (1997) 'Phenotypic diversity in the Smith-Lemli-Opitz syndrome.' *Clinical Dysmorphology*, 6: 69–73.

Sempere, A., Arias, A., Farré, G., García-Villoria, J. et al. (2010) 'Study of inborn errors of metabolism in urine from patients with unexplained mental retardation.' *Journal of Inherited Metabolic Disease*, Jan. 5 [epub ahead of print], doi:10.1007/s10545-009-9004-y.

Seracchioli, R., Bagnoli, A., Colombo, F.M., Missiroli, S. and Venturoli, S. (2001) 'Conservative treatment of recurrent ovarian fibromas in a young patient affected by Gorlin syndrome.' *Human Reproduction*, 16: 1261–1263.

Serajee, F.J., Zhong, H. and Mahbubul Huq, A.H. (2006) 'Association of Reelin gene polymorphisms with autism.' *Genomics 87*, 1: 75–83.

Serajee, F.J., Zhong, H., Nabi, R. and Mahbubul Huq, A.H. (2003) 'The metabotropic glutamate receptor 8 gene at 7q31: partial duplication and possible association with autism.' *Journal of Medical Genetics*, 40: e42.

Sergeyev, A.S. (1975) 'On the mutation rate of neurofibromatosis.' *Humangenetik 28*, 2: 129–138.

Seri, S., Cerquiglini, A., Pisani, F. and Curatolo, P. (1999) 'Autism in tuberous sclerosis: evoked potential evidence for a deficit in auditory sensory processing.' *Clinical Neurophysiology*, 110: 1825–1830.

Seroogy, C.M., Wara, D.W., Bluth, M.H., Dorenbaum, A. *et al.* (1999) 'Cytokine profile of a long-term pediatric HIV survivor with hyper-IgE syndrome and a normal CD4 T-cell count.' *Journal of Allergy and Clinical Immunology 104*, 5: 1045–1051.

Setzer, E.S., Ruiz-Castaneda, N., Severn, C., Ryden, S. and Frias, J.L. (1981) 'Etiologic heterogeneity in the oculoauriculovertebral syndrome.' *Journal of Pediatrics*, 98: 88–90.

Seven, M., Cengiz, M., Tüzgen, S. and Iscan, M.Y. (2001) 'Plasma carnitine levels in children with Down syndrome.' *American Journal of Human Biology 13*, 6: 721–725.

Sever, R.J., Frost, P. and Weinstein, G. (1968) 'Eye changes in ichthyosis.' *Journal of the American Medical Association*, 206: 2283–2286.

Shackleton, C.H.L., Roitman, E., Kratz, L.E. and Kelley, R.I. (1999) 'Equine type estrogens produced by a pregnant woman carrying a Smith-Lemli-Opitz syndrome fetus.' *Journal of Clinical Endocrinology and Metabolism*, 84: 1157–1159.

Shafeghati, Y., Vakili, G. and Entezari, A. (2006) 'L-2-hydroxyglutaric aciduria: a report of six cases and a review of the literature.' *Archives of Iranian Medicine 9*, 2: 165–169.

Shaffer, L.G., Jackson-Cook, C.K., Stasiowski, B.A., Spence, J.E. and Brown, J.A. (1992) 'Parental origin determination in 30 *de novo* Robertsonian translocations.' *American Journal of Medical Genetics*, 43: 957–963.

Shah, A.S., Farmen, S.L., Moninger, T.O., Businga, T.R. et al. (2008) 'Loss of Bardet–Biedl syndrome proteins alters the morphology and function of motile cilia in airway epithelia.', *Proceedings of the National Academy of Science USA, 105*, 9: 3380–3385.

Shah, A. and Frith, U. (1993) 'Why do autistic individuals show superior performance on the block design task?' *Journal of Child Psychology and Psychiatry 34*, 8: 1351–1364.

Shaikh, N.A. and Turner, D.T.L.T. (1988) 'Ehlers-Danlos syndrome presenting with infarction of stomach.' *Journal of the Royal Society of Medicine*, 81: 611.

Shamaly, H., Hartman, C., Pollack, S., Hujerat, M. *et al.* (2007) 'Tissue transglutaminase antibodies are a useful serological marker for the diagnosis of celiac disease in patients with Down syndrome.' *Journal of Pediatric Gastroenterology and Nutrition 44*, 5: 583–586.

Shao, Y., Cuccaro, M.L., Hauser, E.R., Raiford, K.L. *et al.* (2003) 'Fine mapping of autistic disorder to chromosome 15q11–q13 by use of phenotypic subtypes.' *American Journal of Human Genetics*, 72: 539–548.

Shao, Y., Wolpert, C.M., Raiford, K.L., Menold, M.M. *et al.* (2002) 'Genomic screen and follow-up analysis for autistic disorder.' *American Journal of Medical Genetics*, 114: 99–105.

Shapiro, L.J., Weiss, R., Buxman, M.M., Vidgoff, J. and Dimond, R.L. (1978) 'Enzymatic basis of typical X-linked ichthyosis.' *Lancet 312*, 8093: 756–757.

Shaposhnikov, A.M., Khal'chitskii, S.E. and Shvarts, E.I. (1979) ['Disorders of phenylalanine and tyrosine metabolism in Down's syndrome.'] [Article in Russian.] *Voprosy Meditsinskoi Khimii 25*, 1: 15–19.

Sharif, S., Ferner, R., Birch, J.M., Gillespie, J.E. *et al.* (2006) 'Second primary tumors in neurofibromatosis 1 patients treated for optic glioma: substantial risks after radiotherapy.' *Journal of Clinical Oncology*, 24: 2570–2575.

Sharland, M., Burch, M., McKenna, W.M. and Paton, M.A. (1992) 'A clinical study of Noonan syndrome.' *Archives of Disease in Childhood*, 67: 178–183.

Sharma, R., Chandrakantha, E.L. and Mold, B. (2007) 'National autism plan standards for assessment are achievable.' *Child: Care, Health and Development*, 33: 500–501.

Shavelle, R.M., Strauss, D.J. and Pickett, J. (2001) 'Causes of death in autism.' *Journal of Autism and Developmental Disorders*, 31: 569–576.

Shear, C.S., Nyhan, W.L., Kirman, B.H. and Stern, J. (1971) 'Self-mutilative behavior as a feature of the de Lange syndrome.' *The Journal of Pediatrics*, 78: 506–509.

Sheen, V.L. and Walsh, C.A. (2006) 'Periventricular heterotopia: new insights into Ehlers-Danlos syndrome.' *Clinical Medicine and Research 3*, 4: 229–233.

Sheen, V.L., Jansen, A., Chen, M.H., Parrini, E. *et al.* (2005) 'Mutations cause periventricular heterotopia with Ehlers-Danlos syndrome.' *Neurology*, 64: 254–262.

Shen, J.X., Qiu, G.X., Wang, Y.P., Zhao, Y. *et al.* (2005) 'Surgical treatment of scoliosis caused by neurofibromatosis type 1.' *Chinese Medicine and Science Journal*, 20: 88–92.

Shenoy, S., Arnold, S. and Chatila, T. (2000) 'Response to steroid therapy in autism secondary to autoimmune lymphoproliferative syndrome.' *Journal of Pediatrics*, 136: 682–687.

Shereshevskii, N.A. (1925) 'In relation to the question of a connection between congenital abnormalities and endocrinopathies.' Lecture to the Russian Endocrinological Society, 12 November 1925.

Sherman, S.L. (2000) 'Premature ovarian failure in the fragile-X syndrome.' *American Journal of Medical Genetics*, 97: 189–194.

Sherman, S.L., Allen, E.G., Bean, L.H. and Freeman, S.B. (2007) 'Epidemiology of Down syndrome.' *Mental Retardation and Developmental Disabilities Research Reviews 13*, 3: 221–227.

Sherr, E.H. (2003) 'The ARX story (epilepsy, mental retardation, autism, and cerebral malformations): one gene leads to many phenotypes.' *Current Opinion in Pediatrics*, 15: 567–571.

Sherr, E.H., Owen, R., Albertson, D.G., Pinkel, D. *et al.* (2005) 'Genomic microarray analysis identifies candidate loci in patients with corpus callosum anomalies.' *Neurology*, 65: 1496–1498.

Shevell, M., Ashwal, S., Donley, D., Flint, J. *et al.* (2003) 'Practice parameter: evaluation of the child with global developmental delay. Report of the Quality Standards Subcommittee of the American Academy of Neurology and the Practice Committee of the Child Neurology Society.' *Neurology*, 60: 367–380.

Shimizu, T., Takao, A., Ando, M. and Hirayama, A. (1984) 'Conotruncal Face Syndrome: Its Heterogeneity and Association with Thymus Involution.' In: J.J. Nora and A. Takao (eds.) *Congenital Heart Disease: Causes and Processes.* Mount Kisco, NY: Futura Publishing.

Shimojo, Y., Osawa, Y., Fukumizu, M., Hanaoka, S. *et al.* (2001) 'Severe infantile dentatorubral pallidoluysian atrophy with extreme expansion of CAG repeats.' *Neurology,* 56: 277–278.

Shinohe, A., Hashimoto, K., Nakamura, K., Tsujii, M. *et al.* (2006) 'Increased serum levels of glutamate in adult patients with autism.' *Progress in Neuropsychopharmacology and Biological Psychiatry 30,* 8: 1472–1477.

Shonkoff, J.P. and Phillips, D.A. (eds.) (2000) *From Neurons to Neighborhoods: The Science of Early Childhood Development.* Washington, DC: National Academies Press.

Shore, S.M. and Rastelli, L.G. (2006) *Understanding Autism for Dummies.* Hoboken: Wiley.

Shorvon, S. (2005) *Handbook of Epilepsy Treatment* (2nd edn). Oxford: Blackwell Publishing.

Shprintzen, R.J. (1994) 'Velocardiofacial syndrome and DiGeorge sequence' (letter). *Journal of Medical Genetics,* 31: 423–424.

Shprintzen, R.J. (2008) 'Velo-cardio-facial syndrome – 30 years of study.' *Developmental Disabilities Research Reviews,* 14: 3–10.

Shprintzen, R.J., Goldberg, R.B., Young, D. and Wolford, L. (1981) 'The velo-cardio-facial syndrome: a clinical and genetic analysis.' *Pediatrics,* 67: 167–172.

Shuang, M., Liu, J., Jia, M.X., Yang, J.Z. *et al.* (2004) 'Family-based association study between autism and glutamate receptor 6 gene in Chinese Han trios.' *American Journal of Medical Genetics B Neuropsychiatric Genetics,* 131: 48–50.

Shumyatsky, G.P., Tsvetkov, E., Malleret, G., Vronskaya, S. *et al.* (2002) 'Identification of a signaling network in lateral nucleus of amygdala important for inhibiting memory specifically related to learned fear.' *Cell,* 111: 905–918.

Shusta, E.V. (2005) 'Blood–brain barrier genomics, proteomics, and new transporter discovery.' *NeuroRx 2,* 1: 151–161.

Shwayder, T. (2004) 'Disorders of keratinization: diagnosis and management.' *American Journal of Clinical Dermatology 5,* 1: 17–29.

Sicile-Kira, C. (2003) *Autism Spectrum Disorders: The Complete Guide.* London: Vermilion.

Sicouri, S., Timothy, K.W., Zygmunt, A.C., Glass, A. *et al.* (2007) 'Cellular basis for the electrocardiographic and arrhythmic manifestations of Timothy syndrome: effects of ranolazine.' *Heart Rhythm,* 4: 638–647.

Sieg, K.G. (1992) 'Autism and Ehlers-Danlos syndrome.' *Journal of the American Academy of Child and Adolescent Psychiatry,* 31: 173.

Sieg, K.G. (2009) 'Co-occurrence of X-linked congenital adrenal hypoplasia and autistic disorder.' *Journal of Neuropsychiatry and Clinical Neurosciences,* 21: 227–228.

Sikora, D.M., Pettit-Kekel, K., Penfield, J., Merkens, L.S. and Steiner, R.D. (2006) 'The near universal presence of autism spectrum disorders in children with Smith-Lemli-Opitz syndrome.' *American Journal of Medical Genetics A,* 140: 1511–1518.

Sikora, D.M., Ruggiero, M., Petit-Kekel, K, Merkens, L.S. *et al.* (2004) 'Cholesterol supplementation does not improve developmental progress in Smith-Lemli-Opitz syndrome.' *Journal of Pediatrics 144,* 6: 783–791.

Silay, Y.S. and Jankovic, J. (2005) 'Emerging drugs in Tourette syndrome.' *Expert Opinion on Emerging Drugs 10,* 2: 365–380.

Simensen, R.J., Abidi, F., Collins, J.S., Schwartz, C.E. and Stevenson, R.E. (2002) 'Cognitive function in Coffin-Lowry syndrome.' *Clinical Genetics,* 61: 299–304.

Simmonds, H.A. (2003) 'Hereditary xanthinurea.' *Orphanet Enylopaedia* www.orpha.net.

Simon, T.J., Bearden, C.E., Moss, E.M., McDonald-McGinn, D. *et al.* (2002) 'Cognitive development in 22q11.2 deletion syndrome.' *Progress in Pediatric Cardiology* 15: 109–117.

Simon Harvey, A., Leaper, P.M. and Bankier, A. (1991) 'CHARGE association: clinical manifestations and developmental outcome.' *American Journal of Medical Genetics,* 39: 351–356.

Simonyi, A., Schachtman, T.R. and Christoffersen, G.R.J. (2005) 'The role of metabotropic glutamate receptor 5 in learning and memory.' *Drug News Perspectives,* 18: 353–361.

Simopoulos, A.P. and Salem, N. Jr. (1989) 'N-3 fatty acids in eggs from range-fed Greek chickens.' *New England Journal of Medicine,* 321: 1412.

Singer, H.S. (2005) 'Tourette's syndrome: from behaviour to biology.' *Lancet Neurology,* 4: 148–159.

Singh, I., Khan, M., Key, L. and Pai, S. (1998) 'Lovastatin for X-linked adrenoleukodystrophy.', *New England Journal of Medicine, 339,* 10: 702–703.

Sinha, S., Mishra, S., Singh, V., Mittal, R.D. and Mittal, B. (1996) 'High frequency of new mutations in North Indian Duchenne/Becker muscular dystrophy patients.' *Clinical Genetics,* 50: 327–331.

Sisodiya, S.M. (2004) 'Malformations of cortical development: burdens and insights from important causes of human epilepsy.' *The Lancet Neurology 3,* 1: 29–38.

Sivagamasundari, U., Fernando, H., Jardine, P., Rao, J.M. *et al.* (1994) 'The association between Coffin-Lowry syndrome and psychosis: a family study.' *Journal of Intellectual Disability Research,* 38: 469–473.

Skidmore, F.M., Rodriguez, R.L., Fernandez, H.H., Goodman, W.K. *et al.* (2006) 'Lessons learned in deep brain stimulation for movement and neuropsychiatric disorders.' *CNS Spectrums 11,* 7: 521–537.

Skuk, D., Roy, B., Goulet, M., Chapdelaine, P., Bouchard, J.P. *et al.* (2004) 'Dystrophin expression in myofibers of Duchenne muscular dystrophy patients following intramuscular injections of normal myogenic cells.' *Molecular Therapeutics,* 9: 475–482.

Skuse, D.H. (2000) 'Imprinting, the X-chromosome, and the male brain: explaining sex differences in the liability to autism.' *Pediatric Research,* 47: 9–16.

Skuse, D.H. (2007) 'Rethinking the nature of genetic vulnerability to autistic spectrum disorders.' *Trends in Genetics 23,* 8: 387–395.

Skuse, D.H., James, R.S., Bishop, D.V., Coppin, B. *et al.* (1997) 'Evidence from Turner's syndrome of an imprinted X-linked locus affecting cognitive function.' *Nature 387,* 6634: 705–708.

Slack, J.M.W. (2002) 'Conrad Hal Waddington: the last Renaissance biologist?' *Nature Reviews: Genetics,* 3: 889–895.

Slager, R.E., Newton, T.L., Vlangos, C.N., Finucane, B. and Elsea, S.H. (2003) 'Mutations in RAI1 associated with Smith-Magenis syndrome.' *Nature Genetics,* 33: 466–468.

Slavotinek, A. and Biesecker, L.G. (2003) 'Genetic modifiers in human development and malformation syndromes, including chaperone proteins.' *Human Molecular Genetics,* 12 (Review Issue 1): R45–R50, doi: 10.1093/hmg/ddg099.

Slee, J.J., Smart, R.D. and Viljoen, D.L. (1991) 'Deletion of chromosome 13 in Möbius syndrome.' *Journal of Medical Genetics 28,* 6: 413–414.

Slor, H., Batko, S., Khan, S.G., Sobe, T. *et al.* (2000) 'Xeroderma pigmentosum family with a frameshift mutation in the XPC gene: sun protection prolongs life.' *Journal of Investigative Dermatology,* 115: 974–980.

Smalley, S. (1995) 'Autism and tuberous sclerosis.' *Journal of Autism and Developmental Disorders,* 28: 407–414.

Smalley, S.L. (1997) 'Genetic influences in childhood-onset psychiatric disorders: autism and attention-deficit/hyperactivity disorder.' *American Journal of Human Genetics,* 60: 1276–1282.

Smalley, S.L. (1998) 'Autism and tuberous sclerosis.', *Journal of Autism and Developmental Disorders,* 28, 5: 407–414.

Smalley, S.L., Tanguay, P.E., Smith, M. and Gutierrez, G. (1992) 'Autism and tuberous sclerosis.' *Journal of Autism and Developmental Disorders 22,* 3: 339–355.

Smallwood, P.M., Olveczky, B.P., Williams, G.L., Jacobs, G.H. *et al.* (2003) 'Genetically engineered mice with an additional class of cone photoreceptors: implications for the evolution of color vision.' *Proceedings of the National Academy of Science 100,* 20: 11706–11711.

Smeets, H.J., Smits, A.P., Verheij, C.E., Theelen, J.P. *et al.* (1995) 'Normal phenotype in two brothers with a full FMR1 mutation.' *Human Molecular Genetics*, 4: 2103–2108.

Smets, K., Zecic, A. and Willems, J. (2004) 'Ergotamine as a possible cause of Möbius sequence: additional clinical observation.' *Journal of Child Neurology 19*, 5: 398.

Smith, A.C.M., Allanson, J.E., Elsea, S.H., Finucane, B.M. *et al.* (2006) [revision] 'Smith Magenis syndrome.' *GeneReviews*, downloadable from www.ncbi.nlm.nih.gov.

Smith, A.C.M., Gropman, A.L., Bailey-Wilson, J.E., Goker-Alpan, O. *et al.* (2002) 'Hypercholesterolemia in children with Smith-Magenis syndrome: del(17)(p11.2p11.2).' *Genetics in Medicine*, 4: 118–125.

Smith, A.C.M., McGavran, L., Robinson, J., Waldstein, G. *et al.* (1986) 'Interstitial deletion of (17)(p11.2p11.2) in nine patients.' *American Journal of Medical Genetics*, 24: 393–414.

Smith, D.W., Lemli, L. and Opitz, J.M. (1964) 'A newly recognized syndrome of multiple congenital anomalies.' *Journal of Pediatrics*, 64: 210–217.

Smith, G.F. (1966) 'A study of the dermatoglyphs in the de Lange syndrome.' *Journal of Mental Deficiency Research*, 10: 241–254.

Smith, I.M., Nichols, S.L., Issekutz, K. and Blake, K. (2005) 'Behavioral profiles and symptoms of autism in CHARGE syndrome: preliminary Canadian epidemiological data.' *American Journal of Medical Genetics A*, 133: 248–256.

Smith, J.K., Conda, V.E. and Malamud, N. (1958) 'Unusual form of cerebellar ataxia: combined dentate-rubral and pallido-luysian degeneration.' *Neurology*, 8: 205–209.

Smith, J.M. (2003) *Seeds of Deception: Exposing Corporate and Government Lies about the Safety of the Genetically Engineered Foods You're Eating.* Totnes: Green Books.

Smith, J.M., Kirk, E.P.E., Theodosopoulos, G., Marshall, G.M. *et al.* (2002b) 'Germline mutation of the tumour suppressor PTEN in Proteus syndrome.' *Journal of Medical Genetics*, 39: 937–940.

Smith, K.D., Kemp, S., Lelita, T., Braiterman, L.T. *et al.* (1999) 'X-linked adrenoleukodystrophy: Genes, mutations, and phenotypes.' *Neurochemical Research 24*, 4: 521–535.

Smith, M. (2006) *Mental Retardation and Developmental Delay: Genetic and Epigenetic Factors.* Oxford: Oxford University Press.

Smith, M., Escamilla, J.R., Filipek, P., Bocian, M.E. *et al.* (2001) 'Molecular genetic delineation of 2q37.3 deletion in autism and osteodystrophy: report of a case and of new markers for deletion screening by PCR.' *Cytogenetics and Cell Genetics 94*, 1/2: 15–22.

Smith, M., Spence, M.A. and Flodman, P. (2009) 'Nuclear and mitochondrial genome defects in autisms.' *Annals of the New York Academy of Science*, 1151: 102–132.

Smith, M., Woodroffe, A., Smith, R., Holguin, S. *et al.* (2002) 'Molecular genetic delineation of a deletion of chromosome 13q12–q13 in a patient with autism and auditory processing deficits.' *Cytogenetics and Genome Research*, 98: 233–239.

Smith, P.F. (2005) 'Cannabinoids as potential anti-epileptic drugs.' *Current Opinion in Investigational Drugs*, 6: 680–685.

Smith, R. (2006) *The Trouble with Medical Journals.* London: The Royal Society of Medicine Press.

Snape, K.M.G., Fahey, M.C., McGillivray, G., Gupta, P. *et al.* (2006) 'Long-term survival in a child with severe congenital contractural arachnodactyly, autism and severe intellectual disability.' *Clinical Dysmorphology*, 15: 95–99.

Sobin, C., Kiley-Brabeck, K., Daniels, S., Khuri, J. *et al.* (2005) 'Neuropsychological characteristics of children with the 22q11 deletion syndrome: a descriptive analysis.' *Child Neuropsychology*, 11: 39–53.

Soderpalm, A.-C., Magnusson, P., Ahlander, A.-C., Karlsson, J. *et al.* (2007) 'Low bone mineral density and decreased bone turnover in Duchenne muscular dystrophy.' *Neuromuscular Disorders*, 17: 919–928.

Sodhi, M.S. and Sanders-Bush, E. (2004) 'Serotonin and brain development.' *International Review of Neurobiology*, 59: 111–174.

Soljak, M.A., Aftimos, S. and Gluckman, P.D. (1983) 'A new syndrome of short stature, joint limitation and muscle hypertrophy.' *Clinical Genetics*, 23: 441–446.

Solomon, I.L. and Schoen, E.J. (1971) 'Sex-linked ichthyosis in XO gonadal dysgenesis' (letter). *Lancet 227*, 7712: 1304–1305.

Somerville, M.J., Mervis, C.B., Young, E.J., Seo, E.-J. *et al.* (2005) 'Severe expressive-language delay related to duplication of the Williams-Beuren locus.' *New England Journal of Medicine*, 353: 1694–1701.

Sotos, J.F., Dodge, P.R., Muirhead, D., Crawford, J.D. and Talbot, N.B. (1964) 'Cerebral gigantism in childhood: a syndrome of excessively rapid growth with acromegalic features and a nonprogressive neurologic disorder.' *New England Journal of Medicine*, 271: 109–116.

Spaepen, A., Hellemans, H. and Fryns, J.-P. (1994) 'X-linked mental retardation with marfanoid habitus: the eye-catching psychiatric disorders.' *American Journal of Medical Genetics*, 51: 611.

Specchio, N., Balestri, M., Striano, P., Cilio, M.R. *et al.* (2009) 'Efficacy of levetiracetam in the treatment of drug-resistant Rett syndrome.' *Epilepsy Research, 88*, 2–3: 112–117

Speiser, P.W. and White, P.C. (2003) 'Congenital adrenal hyperplasia.' *New England Journal of Medicine*, 349: 776–788.

Speiser, P.W., Dupont, B., Rubinstein, P., Piazza, A. *et al.* (1985) 'High frequency of nonclassical steroid 21-hydroxylase deficiency.' *American Journal of Human Genetics 37*, 4: 650–667.

Spence, S.J. and Schneider, M.T. (2009) 'The role of epilepsy and epileptiform EEGs in autism spectrum disorders.' *Pediatric Research: Articles Ahead of Print*, doi:10.1203/PDR.0b013e31819e7168.

Spencer, K., Tul, N. and Nicolaides, K.H. (2000) 'Maternal serum free beta-hCG and PAPP-A in fetal sex chromosome defects in the first trimester.' *Prenatal Diagnosis*, 20: 390–394.

Spiegel, E.K., Colman, R.F. and Patterson, D. (2006) 'Adenylosuccinate lyase deficiency.' *Molecular Genetics and Metabolism*, 89: 19–31.

Spirito, F., Meneguzzi, G., Danos, O. and Mezzina, M. (2001) 'Cutaneous gene transfer and therapy: the present and the future.' *Journal of Gene Medicine 3*, 1: 21–31.

Splawski, I., Timothy, K.W., Decher, N., Kumar, P. *et al.* (2005) 'Severe arrhythmia disorder caused by cardiac L-type calcium channel mutations.' *Proceedings of the National Academy of Science USA 102*, 23: 8089–8096.

Splawski, I., Timothy, K.W., Priori, S.G., Napolitano, C. and Bloise, R. (2008 update) 'Timothy syndrome.' *GeneReviews*, accessible at www.ncbi.nlm.nih.gov.

Splawski, I., Timothy, K.W., Sharpe, L.M., Decher, N. *et al.* (2004) 'CaV1.2 calcium channel dysfunction causes a multisystem disorder including arrhythmia and autism.' *Cell*, 119: 19–31.

Splawski, I., Yoo, D.S., Stotz, S.C., Cherry, A. *et al.* (2006) 'CACNA1H mutations in autism spectrum disorders.' *Journal of Biological Chemistry 281*, 31: 22085–22091.

Spritz, R.A., Fukai, K., Holmes, S.A. and Luande, J. (1995) 'Frequent intragenic deletion of the P gene in Tanzanian patients with type II oculocutaneous albinism (OCA2).' *American Journal of Human Genetics*, 56: 1320–1323.

Spurek, M., Taylor-Gjevre, R., Van Uum, S. and Khandwala, H.M. (2004) 'Adrenomyeloneuropathy as a cause of primary adrenal insufficiency and spastic paraparesis.' *Canadian Medical Association Journal 171*, 9: 1073–1077.

Stagi, S., Bindi, G., Neri, A.S., Lapi, E. *et al.* (2005) 'Thyroid function and morphology in patients affected by Williams syndrome.' *Clinical Endocrinology*, 63: 456–460.

Stanfield, A.C., McIntosh, A.M., Spencer, M.D., Philip, R. *et al.* (2007) 'Towards a neuroanatomy of autism: a systematic review and meta-analysis of structural magnetic resonance imaging studies.' *European Psychiatry*, doi:10.1016/j.eurpsy.2007.05.006.

Stangle, D.E., Smith, D.R., Beaudin, S.A., Strawderman, M.S. *et al.* (2007) 'Succimer chelation improves learning, attention, and arousal regulation in lead-exposed rats but produces lasting cognitive impairment in the absence of lead exposure.' *Environmental Health Perspectives*, 115: 201–209.

Stanojevic, M., Stipoljev, F., Koprcina, B. and Kurjak, A. (2000) 'Oculoauriculo-vertebral (Goldenhar) spectrum associated with pericentric inversion 9: coincidental findings or etiologic factor?' *Journal of Craniofacial Genetics and Developmental Biology*, 20: 150–154.

Starck, L., Lovgren-Sandblom, A. and Bjorkhem, I. (2002a) 'Cholesterol treatment forever? The first Scandinavian trial of cholesterol supplementation in the cholesterol-synthesis defect Smith-Lemli-Opitz syndrome.' *Journal of Internal Medicine 252*, 4: 314–321.

Starck, L., Lovgren-Sandblom, A. and Bjorkhem, I. (2002b) 'Simvastatin treatment in the SLO syndrome: a safe approach?' *American Journal of Medical Genetics 113*, 2: 183–189.

Starink, T.M., van der Veen, J.P., Arwert, F., de Waal, L.P. *et al.* (1986) 'The Cowden syndrome: a clinical and genetic study in 21 patients.' *Clinical Genetics*, 29: 222–233.

Starr, E.M., Berument, S.K., Tomlins, M., Papanikolaou, K. and Rutter, M. (2005) 'Brief report: autism in individuals with Down syndrome.' *Journal of Autism and Developmental Disorders 35*, 5: 665–673.

Stathopulu, E., Ogilvie, C.M. and Flinter, F.A. (2003) 'Terminal deletion of chromosome 5p in a patient with phenotypical features of Lujan-Fryns syndrome.' *American Journal of Medical Genetics*, 119A: 363–366.

Stefanini, M., Vermeulen, W., Weeda, G., Giliani, S. *et al.* (1993) 'A new nucleotide-excision-repair gene associated with the disorder trichothiodystrophy.' *American Journal of Human Genetics*, 53: 817–821.

Stegink, L.D., Filer, L.J. Jr., Baker, G.L., Bell, E.F. *et al.* (1989) 'Repeated ingestion of aspartame-sweetened beverage: effect on plasma amino acid concentrations in individuals heterozygous for phenylketonuria.' *Metabolism*, 38: 78–84.

Stein, D., Weizman, A., Ring, A. and Barak, Y. (2006) 'Obstetric complications in individuals diagnosed with autism and in healthy controls.' *Comprehensive Psychiatry*, 47: 69–75.

Steinberg, H. (2005) 'Paul Julius Mobius (1853–1907).' *Journal of Neurology*, 252: 624–625.

Steiner, C.E., Guerreiro, M.M. and Marques-de-Faria, A.P. (2003) 'On macrocephaly, epilepsy, autism, specific facial features, and mental retardation.' *American Journal of Medical Genetics A 120*, 4: 564–565.

Steinert, H. (1910) 'Ein neuer fall von atrophischer myotonie: ein nachtag zu meiner arbeit in Bild 37.' *Deutsche Zeitschrift fur Nervenheilkunde*, 39: 168–173.

Steinlin, M., Schmid, M., Landau, K. and Boltshauser, E. (1997) 'Follow-up in children with Joubert syndrome.' *Neuropediatrics*, 28: 204–211.

Steinmann, B., Royce, P. and Superti-Furga, A. (1993) 'The Ehlers-Danlos syndrome.' In P. Royce and B. Steinmann (eds.) *Connective Tissue and its Heritable Disorders*. New York: Wiley-Liss.

Stephenson, J.B., Hoffman, M.C., Russell, A.J. *et al.* (2005) 'The movement disorders of Coffin-Lowry syndrome.' *Brain and Development*, 27: 108–113.

Stern, L., Francoeur, M.J., Primeau, M.N., Sommerville, W., Fombonne, E. and Mazer, B.D. (2005) 'Immune function in autistic children.' *Annals of Allergy, Asthma and Immunology*, 95: 558–565.

Stern, J.S. and Robertson, M.M. (1997) 'Tics associated with autistic and pervasive developmental disorders.' *Neurologic Clinics 15*, 2: 345–355.

Stevens, G., Ramsay, M. and Jenkins, T. (1997) 'Oculocutaneous albinism (OCA2) in sub-Saharan Africa: distribution of the common 2.7-kb P gene deletion mutation.' *Human Genetics*, 99: 523–527.

Stevens, G., van Beukering, J., Jenkins, T. and Ramsay, M. (1995) 'An intragenic deletion of the P gene is the common mutation causing tyrosinase-positive oculocutaneous albinism in southern African Negroids.' *American Journal of Human Genetics*, 56: 586–591.

Stevenson, R.E., Schroer, R.J., Skinner, C., Fender, D. and Simensen, R.J. (1997) 'Autism and macrocephaly.' *Lancet 349*, 9067: 1744–1745.

Stewart, T.L., Irons, M.B., Cowan, J.M. and Bianchi, D.W. (1999) 'Increased incidence of renal anomalies in patients with chromosome 22q11 microdeletion.' *Birth Defects Research A: Clinical and Molecular Teratology 59*, 1: 20–22.

Steyaert, J., Legius, E., Borghgraef, M. and Fryns, J.-P. (2003) 'A distinct neurocognitive phenotype in female fragile-X premutation carriers assessed with visual attention tasks.' *American Journal of Medical Genetics A*, 116: 44–51.

Stiers, P., Swillen, A., De Smedt, B., Lagae, L. *et al.* (2005) 'Atypical neuropsychological profile in a boy with 22q11.2 deletion syndrome.' *Child Neuropsychology*, 11: 87–108.

Stirt, J.A. (1981) 'Anesthetic problems in Rubinstein-Taybi syndrome.' *Anesthesia and Analgesia 60*, 7: 534–536.

Stockfleth, E., Ulrich, C., Hauschild, A., Lischner, S. *et al.* (2002) 'Successful treatment of basal cell carcinomas in a nevoid basal cell carcinoma syndrome with topical 5% imiquimod.' *European Journal of Dermatology*, 12: 569–572.

Stöckler, S., Hanefeld, F. and Frahm, J. (1996) 'Creatine replacement therapy in guanidinoacetate methyltransferase deficiency, a novel inborn error of metabolism.' *Lancet 348*, 9030: 789–790.

Stöckler, S., Holzbach, U., Hanefeld, F., Marquardt, I. *et al.* (1994) 'Creatine deficiency in the brain: a new, treatable inborn error of metabolism.' *Pediatric Research*, 36: 409–413.

Stöckler, S., Schutz, P.W. and Salomons, G.S. (2007) 'Cerebral creatine deficiency syndromes: clinical aspects, treatment and pathophysiology.' *Subcellular Biochemistry*, 46: 149–166.

Stoetzel, C., Laurier, V., Davis, E.E., Muller, J. et al. (2006) 'BBS10 encodes a vertebrate-specific chaperonin-like protein and is a major BBS locus.' *Nature Genetics*, 38: 521–524.

Stoetzel, C., Muller, J., Laurier, V., Davis, E.E. et al. (2007) 'Identification of a novel BBS gene (BBS12) highlights the major role of a vertebrate-specific branch of chaperonin-related proteins in Bardet-Biedl syndrome.' *American Journal of Human Genetics*, 80: 1–11.

Stokke, O., Eldjarn, L., Norum, K., Steen-Johnsen, J. and Halvorsen, S. (1967) 'Methylmalonic acidemia: a new inborn error of metabolism which may cause fatal acidosis in the newborn period.' *Scandinavian Journal of Clinical Investigation*, 20: 213.

Stoll, C. (2001) 'Problems in the diagnosis of fragile-X syndrome in young children are still present.' *American Journal of Medical Genetics*, 100: 110–115.

Stoll, C., Viville, B., Treisser, A. and Gasser, B. (1998) 'A family with dominant oculoauriculovertebral spectrum.' *American Journal of Medical Genetics*, 78: 345–349.

Stone, J.L., Merriman, B., Cantor, R.M., Yonan, A.L. *et al.* (2004) 'Evidence for sex-specific risk alleles in autism spectrum disorder.' *American Journal of Human Genetics*, 75: 1117–1123.

Stone, R.L., Aimi, J., Barshop, B.A., Jaeken, J. *et al.* (1992) 'A mutation in adenylosuccinate lyase associated with mental retardation and autistic features.' *Nature Genetics*, 1: 59–63.

Stos, B., Dembour, G., Ovaert, C., Barrea, C. *et al.* (2004) 'Avantages et risques de la chirurgie cardiaque dans la trisomie 21.' ['Risks and benefits of cardiac surgery in Down's syndrome with congenital heart disease.'] *Archives de pédiatrie*, 11: 1197–1201.

Stover, P.J. (2006) 'Influence of human genetic variation on human nutritional requirements.' *American Journal of Clinical Nutrition*, 83 (Suppl.): 436S–442S.

Stover, P.J. and Garza, C. (2002) 'Bringing individuality to public health recommendations.' *Journal of Nutrition*, 132: 2476S–2480S.

Stratton, R.F., Dobyns, W.B., Greenberg, F., DeSana, J.B. *et al.* (1986) 'Report of six additional patients with new chromosome deletion syndrome.' *American Journal of Medical Genetics*, 24: 421–432.

Straus, S.E., Lenardo, M. and Puck, J.M. (1997) 'The Canale-Smith syndrome' (letter). *New England Journal of Medicine*, 336: 1457.

Straus, S.E., Richardson, W.S., Glasziou, P. and Haynes, R.B. (2005) *Evidence-Based Medicine*. Oxford: Churchill Livingstone.

Strauss, K.A., Puffenberger, E.G., Huentelman, M.J., Gottlieb, S. *et al.* (2006) 'Recessive symptomatic focal epilepsy and mutant contactin-associated protein-like 2.' *New England Journal of Medicine*, 354: 1370–1377.

Stromland, K., Miller, M., Sjogreen, L., Johansson, M. *et al.* (2007) 'Oculo-auriculo-vertebral spectrum: associated anomalies, functional deficits and possible developmental risk factors.' *American Journal of Medical Genetics A, 143A*, 12: 1317–1325.

Strømme, P., Bjørnstad, P.G. and Ramstad, K. (2002a) 'Prevalence estimation of Williams syndrome.' *Journal of Child Neurology 17*, 4: 269–271.

Strømme, P., Mangelsdorf, M.E., Shaw, M.A., Lower, K.M. *et al.* (2002b) 'Mutations in the human ortholog of aristaless cause X-linked mental retardation and epilepsy.' *Nature Genetics*, 30: 441–445.

Strømme, P., Mangelsdorf, M.E., Scheffer, I.E. and Gecz, J. (2002c) 'Infantile spasms, dystonia, and other X-linked phenotypes caused by mutations in Aristaless related homeobox gene, ARX.' *Brain and Development*, 24: 266–268.

Struthers, J.L., Carson, N., McGill, M. and Khalifa, M.M. (2002) 'Molecular screening for Smith-Magenis syndrome among patients with mental retardation of unknown cause' (electronic letter). *Journal of Medical Genetics*, 39: e59. www.jmedgenet.com

Stuart, S.W., King, C.H. and Pai, G.S. (2007) 'Autism spectrum disorder, Klinefelter syndrome, and chromosome 3p21.31 duplication: a case report.' *Medscape General Medicine 9*, 4: 60.

Sturmey, P. (2005) 'Secretin is an ineffective treatment for pervasive developmental disabilities: a review of 15 double-blind randomized controlled trials.' *Research in Developmental Disability 26*, 1: 87–97.

Sullivan, K.E. (2004) 'The clinical, immunological, and molecular spectrum of chromosome 22q11.2 deletion syndrome and DiGeorge syndrome.' *Current Opinion in Allergy and Clinical Immunology*, 4: 505–512.

Sullivan, K.E., McDonald-McGinn, D.M., Driscoll, D.A., Zmijewski, C.M. *et al.* (1997) 'Juvenile rheumatoid arthritis-like polyarthritis in chromosome 22q11.2 deletion syndrome (DiGeorge anomalad/velocardiofacial syndrome/conotruncal anomaly face syndrome).' *Arthritis and Rheumatology*, 40: 430–436.

Sullivan, P.B. (2008a) 'Gastrointestinal disorders in children with neurodevelopmental disabilities.' *Developmental Disabilities Research Reviews*, 14: 128–136.

Sullivan, P.F. (2008b) 'The dice are rolling for schizophrenia genetics.' *Psychological Medicine*, 38: 1693–1696.

Summar, M.L. and Tuchman, M. (2003) 'Urea cycle disorders overview.' *GeneReviews*. Downloadable from http://rarediseasesnetwork.epi.usf.edu.

Summitt, R.L. (1969) 'Familial Goldenhar syndrome.' *Birth Defects Original Articles Series*, V: 106–109.

Sunada, F., Rash, F.C. and Tam, D.A. (1998) 'MRI findings in a patient with partial monosomy 10p.' *Journal of Medical Genetics 35*, 2: 159–161.

Sutera, S., Pandey, J., Esser, E.L., Rosenthal, M.A. *et al.* (2007) 'Predictors of optimal outcome in toddlers diagnosed with autism spectrum disorders.' *Journal of Autism and Developmental Disorders*, 37: 98–107.

Sutherland, G.R., Gecz, J. and Mulley, J.C. (2002) 'Fragile-X and Other Causes of X-linked Mental Retardation.' In D.I. Rimoin, J.M. O'Connor, R.E. Pyeritz and B.R. Korf (eds) *Emery and Rimoin's Principles and Practice of Clinical Genetics*. New York: Churchill Livingstone.

Sutherland, G.R., Gedeon, A., Kornman, L., Donnelly, A. *et al.* (1991) 'Prenatal diagnosis of fragile-X syndrome by direct detection of the unstable DNA sequence.' *New England Journal of Medicine*, 325: 1720–1722.

Sutphen, R., Galan-Gomez, E., Cortada, X., Newkirk, P.N. and Kousseff, B.G. (1995) 'Tracheoesophageal anomalies in oculoauriculovertebral (Goldenhar) spectrum.' *Clinical Genetics*, 48: 66–71.

Sutton, E.J., McInerney-Leo, A., Bondy, C.A., Gollust, S.E., King, D. and Biesecker, B. (2005) 'Turner syndrome: four challenges across the lifespan.' *American Journal of Medical Genetics A, 139A*, 2: 57–66.

Suzuki, H., Hirayama, Y. and Arima, M. (1989) 'Prevalence of Rett syndrome in Tokyo.' *No To Hattatsu*, 21: 430–433.

Svensson, K., Mattsson, R., James, T.C., Wentzel, P. *et al.* (1998) 'The paternal allele of the H19 gene is progressively silenced during early mouse development: the acetylation status of histones may be involved in the generation of variegated expression patterns.' *Development*, 125: 61–69.

Sverd, J. (1991) 'Tourette syndrome and autistic disorder: a significant relationship.' *American Journal of Medical Genetics 39*, 2: 173–179.

Sverd, J., Montero, G. and Gurevich, N. (1993) 'Brief report: cases for an association between Tourette syndrome, autistic disorder, and schizophrenia-like disorder.' *Journal of Autism and Developmental Disorders 23*, 2: 407–413.

Swanson, C.J., Bures, M., Johnson, M.P., Linden, A.-M. *et al.* (2005) 'Metabotropic glutamate receptors as novel target for anxiety and stress disorders.' *Nature Reviews: Drug Discovery*, 4: 131–146.

Swarts, L., Leisegang, F., Owen, E.P. and Henderson, H.E. (2007) 'An OTC deficiency "phenocopy" in association with Klinefelter syndrome.' *Journal of Inherited Metabolic Disease 30*, 1: 101.

Sweeten, T.L., Bowyer, S.L., Posey, D.J., Halberstadt, G.M. and McDougle, C.J. (2003) 'Increased prevalence of familial autoimmunity in probands with pervasive developmental disorders.' *Pediatrics 112*, 5: e420.

Swerdlow, R.H. (2007) 'Treating neurodegeneration by modifying mitochondria: potential solutions to a "complex" problem.' *Antioxidants and Redox Signalling 9*, 10: 1591–1603.

Swillen, A., Glorieux, N., Peeters, M. and Fryns, J.-P. (1995) 'The Coffin-Siris syndrome: data on mental development, language, behavior and social skills in children.' *Clinical Genetics*, 48: 177–182.

Swillen, A., Hellemans, H., Steyaert, J. and Fryns, J.-P. (1996) 'Autism and genetics: high incidence of specific genetic syndromes in 21 autistic adolescents and adults living in two residential homes in Belgium.' *American Journal of Medical Genetics*, 67: 315–316.

Swillen, A., Vandeputte, L., Cracco, J., Maes, B. *et al.* (1999) 'Neuropsychological, learning and psychosocial profile of primary school aged children with the velo-cardio-facial syndrome (22q11 deletion): evidence for a nonverbal learning disability?' *Neuropsychology Development and Cognition C Child Neuropsychology*, 5: 230–241.

Sykes, N.H. and Lamb, J.A. (2007) 'Autism: the quest for the genes.' *Expert Reviews in Molecular Medicine 9*, 24: 1–15, doi:10.1017/S1462399407000452.

Sykut-Cegielska, J., Gradowska, W., Mercimek-Mahmutoglu, S. and Stockler-Ipsiroglu, S. (2004) 'Biochemical and clinical characteristics of creatine deficiency syndromes.' *Acta Biochimica Polonica*, 51: 875–882.

Sylvester, C.L., Drohan, L.A. and Sergott, R.C. (2006) 'Optic-nerve gliomas, chiasmal gliomas and neurofibromatosis type 1.' *Current Opinion in Ophthalmology*, 17: 7–11.

Symons, F.J., Clark, R.D., Hatton, D.D., Skinner, M. and Bailey, D.B. Jr. (2003) 'Self-injurious behavior in young boys with fragile-X syndrome.' *American Journal of Medical Genetics A*, 118: 115–121.

Szeszko, P.R., Betensky, J.D., Mentschel, C., Gunduz-Bruce, H. *et al.* (2006) 'Increased stress and smaller anterior hippocampal volume.' *NeuroReport 7*, 17: 1825–1828.

Szczaluba, K., Nawara, M., Poirier, K., Pilch, J. et al. (2006) 'Genotype–phenotype associations for ARX gene duplication in X-linked mental retardation.' *Neurology*, 67: 2073–2075.

T

Tabak, H.F., Braakman, I. and Distel, B. (1999) 'Peroxisomes: simple in function but complex in maintenance.' *Trends in Cell Biology 9*, 11: 447–453.

Tabin, C.J. and McMahon, A.P. (1997) 'Recent advances in hedgehog signalling.' *Trends in Cell Biology 7*, 11: 442–446.

Tabolacci, E., Pomponi, M.G., Pietrobono, R., Chiurazzi, P. and Neri, G. (2008) 'A unique case of reversion to normal size of a maternal premutation FMR1 allele in a normal boy.' *European Journal of Human Genetics 16*, 2: 209–214.

Takahashi, T.N., Farmer, J.E., Deidrick, K.K., Hsu, B.S., Miles, J.H. and Maria, B.L. (2005) 'Joubert syndrome is not a cause of classical autism.' *American Journal of Medical Genetics A*, 132: 347–351.

Takahashi, Y., Fujiwara, T., Yagi, K. and Seino, M. (1999) 'Photosensitive epilepsies and pathophysiologic mechanisms of the photoparoxysmal response.' *Neurology 53*, 5: 926–932.

Takami, Y., Takeshima, Y., Awano, H., Okizuka, Y. *et al.* (2008) 'High incidence of electrocardiogram abnormalities in young patients with Duchenne muscular dystrophy.' *Pediatric Neurology*, 39: 399–403.

Takano, H., Cancel, G., Ikeuchi, T., Lorenzetti, D. *et al.* (1998) 'Close associations between prevalences of dominantly inherited spinocerebellar ataxias with CAG-repeat expansions and frequencies of large normal CAG alleles in Japanese and Caucasian populations.' *American Journal of Human Genetics 63*, 4: 1060–1066.

Takesada, M., Naruse, H., Nagahata, M., Kazamatsuri, H. *et al.* (1992) 'An Open Clinical Study of Apropterinhydrochloride (R-Tetrahydrobiopterin, R-THBP) in Infantile Autism – Clinical Effects and Long-term Follow-up.' In H. Naruse and E.M. Ornitz (eds.) *Neurobiology of Infantile Autism.* Exerpta Medica, International Congress Series, 965.

Takiyama, Y., Sakoe, K., Amaike, M., Soutome, M. et al. (1999) 'Single sperm analysis of the CAG repeats in the gene for dentatorubral-pallidoluysian atrophy (DRPLA): the instability of the CAG repeats in the DRPLA gene is prominent among the CAG repeat diseases.' *Human Molecular Genetics*, 8: 453–457.

Talebizadeh, Z., Bittel, D.C., Veatch, O.J., Kibiryeva, N. and Butler, M.G. (2005) 'Brief report: non-random X chromosome inactivation in females with autism.' *Journal of Autism and Developmental Disorders 35*, 5: 675–681, doi:10.1007/s10803-005-0011-z.

Talebizadeh, Z., Lam, D.Y., Theodoro, M.F., Bittel, D.C. *et al.* (2006) 'Novel splice isoforms for NLGN3 and NLGN4 with possible implications in autism.' *Journal of Medical Genetics.*) doi:10.1136/jmg.2005.036897.

Tan, W.-H., Baris, H.N., Burrows, P.E., Robson, C.D. *et al.* (2007) 'The spectrum of vascular anomalies in patients with PTEN mutations: implications for diagnosis and management.' *Journal of Medical Genetics*, 44: 594–602.

Tang, P., Park, D.J., Marshall Graves, J.A. and Harley, V.R. (2004) 'ATRX and sex differentiation.' *Trends in Endocrinology and Metabolism*, 15: 339–344.

Tantam, D., Evered, C. and Hersov, L. (1990) 'Asperger's syndrome and ligamentous laxity.' *Journal of the American Academy of Child and Adolescent Psychiatry 29*, 6: 892–896.

Tao, J., Van Esch, H., Hagedorn-Greiwe, M., Hoffinann, K. *et al.* (2004) 'Mutations in the X-linked cyclin-dependent kinase-like 5 (CDKL5/STK9) gene are associated with severe neurodevelopmental retardation.' *American Journal of Human Genetics*, 75: 1149–1154.

Tariverdian, G., Kantner, G. and Vogel, F. (1987) 'A monozygotic twin pair with Rett syndrome.' *Human Genetics*, 75: 88–90.

Tarnopolsky, M.A., Mahoney, D.J., Vajsar, J., Rodriguez, C. *et al.* (2004) 'Creatine monohydrate enhances strength and body composition in Duchenne muscular dystrophy.' *Neurology*, 62: 1771–1777.

Tartaglia, M. and Gelb, B.D. (2005) 'Noonan syndrome and related disorders: genetics and pathogenesis.' *Annual Review of Genomics and Human Genetics*, 6: 45–68.

Tartaglia, M., Cordeddu, V., Chang, H., Shaw, A. *et al.* (2004) 'Paternal germline origin and sex-ratio distortion in transmission of PTPN11 mutations in Noonan syndrome.' *American Journal of Human Genetics*, 75: 492–497.

Tassone, F., Hagerman, R.J., Ikle, D.N., Dyer, P.N. *et al.* (1999) 'FMRP expression as a potential prognostic indicator in fragile-X syndrome.' *American Journal of Medical Genetics*, 84: 250–261.

Tassone, F., Pan, R., Amiri, K., Taylor, A.K. and Hagerman, P.J. (2008) 'A rapid polymerase chain reaction-based screening method for identification of all expanded alleles of the fragile-X (*FMR1*) gene in newborn and high-risk populations.' *Journal of Molecular Diagnosis 10*, 1: 43–49.

Tatton-Brown, K. and Rahman, N. (2004) 'Clinical features of NSD1-positive Sotos syndrome.' *Clinical Dysmorphology*, 13: 199–204.

Tatton-Brown, K. and Rahman, N. (2007) 'Sotos syndrome.' *European Journal of Human Genetics*, 15: 264–271.

Tatton-Brown, K., Douglas, J., Coleman, K., Baujat, G. *et al.* (2005) 'Genotype–phenotype associations in Sotos syndrome: an analysis of 266 individuals with NSD1 aberrations.' *American Journal of Human Genetics*, 77: 193–204.

Tawil, R. (2008) 'Facioscapulohumeral muscular dystrophy.' *Neurotherapeutics*, 5: 601–606.

Tay, C.H. (1971) 'Ichthyosiform erythroderma, hair shaft abnormalities, and mental and growth retardation: a new recessive disorder.' *Archives of Dermatology*, 104: 4–13.

Taylor, D.C., Falconer, M.A., Bruton, C.J. and Corsellis, J.A. (1971) 'Focal dysplasia of the cerebral cortex in epilepsy.' *Journal of Neurology, Neurosurgery and Psychiatry*, 34: 369–387.

Teebi, A.S., Rucquoi, J.K. and Meyn, M.S. (1993) 'Aarskog syndrome: report of a family with review and discussion of nosology.' *American Journal of Medical Genetics*, 46: 501–509.

Teitelbaum, P., Teitelbaum, O., Nye, J., Fryman, J. and Maurer, R.G. (1998) 'Movement analysis in infancy may be useful for early diagnosis of autism.' *Proceedings of the National Academy of Science USA*, 95: 13982–13987.

Teive, H.A., Chien, H.F., Munhoz, R.P. and Barbosa, E.R. (2008) 'Charcot's contribution to the study of Tourette's syndrome.' *Arquivos de Neuropsiquiatrica 66*, 4: 918–921.

Tellier, A.-L., Lyonnet, S., Cormier-Daire, V., de Lonlay, P. *et al.* (1996) 'Increased paternal age in CHARGE association.' *Clinical Genetics*, 50: 548–550.

Telvi, L., Lebbar, A., Del Pino, O., Barbet, J.P. and Chaussain, J.L. (1999) '45,X/46,XY mosaicism: report of 27 cases.' *Pediatrics*, 104: 304–308.

Temple, C.M. and Sanfilippo, P.M. (2003) 'Executive skills in Klinefelter's syndrome.' *Neuropsychologia 41*, 11: 1547–1559.

Temtamy, S.A., Miller, J.D. and Hussels-Maumenee, I. (1975) 'The Coffin-Lowry syndrome: an inherited facio-digital mental retardation syndrome.' *Journal of Pediatrics*, 86: 724–731.

Teriitehau, C., Adamsbaum, C., Merzoug, V., Kalifa, G. *et al.* (2007) 'Subtle brain abnormalities in adrenomyeloneuropathy.' *Journal de Radiologie 88*, 7/8: 957–961.

Tézenas Du Montcel, S., Mendizabai, H., Aymé, S., Levy, A. et al. (1996) 'Prevalence of 22q11 microdeletion.' *Journal of Medical Genetics*, 33: 719.

Thacker, M.J., Hainline, B., St Dennis-Feezle, L., Johnson, N.B. and Pescovitz, O.H. (1998) 'Growth failure in Prader-Willi syndrome is secondary to growth hormone deficiency.' *Hormone Research 49*, 5: 216–220.

Thiel, R.J. and Fowkes, S.W. (2004) 'Down syndrome and epilepsy: a nutritional connection?' *Medical Hypotheses*, 62: 35–44.

Thomas, J.A., Johnson, J., Peterson Kraai, T.L., Wilson, R. *et al.* (2003) 'Genetic and clinical characterization of patients with an interstitial duplication 15q11–q13, emphasizing behavioral phenotype and response to treatment.' *American Journal of Medical Genetics*, 119A: 111–120.

Thomas, N.S., Roberts, S.E. and Browne, C.E. (2003) 'Estimate of the prevalence of chromosome 15q11–q13 duplications.' *American Journal of Medical Genetics A*, 120A, 4: 596–598.

Thomas, P., Bossan, A., Lacour, J.P., Chanalet, S. *et al.* (1996) 'Ehlers-Danlos syndrome with subependymal periventricular heterotopias.' *Neurology*, 46: 1165–1167.

Thomas, P.Q., Dattani, M.T., Brickman, J.M., McNay, D. *et al.* (2001) 'Heterozygous HESX1 mutations associated with isolated congenital pituitary hypoplasia and septo-optic dysplasia.' *Human Molecular Genetics 10*, 1: 39–45.

Thompson, A.J., Tillotson, S., Smith, I., Kendall, B., Moore, S.G. and Brenton, D.P. (1993) 'Brain MRI changes in phenylketonuria: associations with dietary status.' *Brain*, 116: 811–821.

Thöny, B., Auerbach, G. and Blau, N. (2000) Tetrahydrobiopterin biosynthesis, regeneration and functions. *The Biochemical Journal 347*, 1: 1–16.

Tidball, J.G. and Spencer, M.J. (2003) 'Skipping to new gene therapies for muscular dystrophy.' *Nature Medicine*, 9: 997–998.

Tierney, E., Bukelis, I., Thompson, R.E., Ahmed, K. *et al.* (2006) 'Abnormalities of cholesterol metabolism in autism spectrum disorders.' *American Journal of Medical Genetics B Neuropsychiatric Genetics*, 141: 666–668.

Tierney, E., Nwokoro, N.A. and Kelley, R.I. (2000) 'Behavioral phenotype of RSH/Smith-Lemli-Opitz syndrome.' *Mental Retardation and Developmental Disabilities Research Reviews*, 6: 131–134.

Tierney, E., Nwokoro, N.A., Porter, F.D., Freund, L.S. *et al.* (2001) 'Behavior phenotype in the RSH/Smith-Lemli-Opitz syndrome.' *American Journal of Medical Genetics*, 98: 191–200.

Tint, G.S., Irons, M., Elias, E.R., Batta, A.K. *et al.* (1994) 'Defective cholesterol biosynthesis associated with the Smith-Lemli-Opitz syndrome.' *New England Journal of Medicine*, 330: 107–113.

Titomanlio, L., Marzano, M.G., Rossi, E., D'Armiento, M. *et al.* (2001) 'Case of Myhre syndrome with autism and peculiar skin histological findings.' *American Journal of Medical Genetics*, 103: 163–165.

Tobin, J.L. (2008) 'Restoration of renal function in zebrafish models of ciliopathies.' *Pediatric Nephrology*, 23: 2095–2099.

Tolarova, M.M., Harris, J.A., Ordway, D.E. and Vargervik, K. (1997) 'Birth prevalence, mutation rate, sex ratio, parents' age, and ethnicity in Apert syndrome.' *American Journal of Medical Genetics*, 72: 394–398.

Tomaiuolo, F., Di Paola, M., Caravale, B., Vicari, S. *et al.* (2002) 'Morphology and morphometry of the corpus callosum in Williams syndrome: a T1-weighted MRI study.' *Neuroreport 13*, 17: 2281–2284.

Tomas Vila, M. (2004) 'Rendimiento del estudio diagnostico del autismo. La aportacion de la neuroimagen, las pruebas metabolicas y los estudios geneticos.' ['Diagnostic yield in studies of autism. The contribution made by neuroimaging, metabolic tests and genetic studies.'] *Revista de Neurologia*, 38, Suppl. 1: S15–S20.

Tomoda, A., Ikezawa, M., Ohtani, Y., Miike, T. and Kumamoto, T. (1991) 'Progressive myoclonus epilepsy: dentate-rubro-pallido-luysian atrophy (DRPLA) in childhood.' *Brain and Development*, 13: 266–269.

Tonkin, E.T., Wang, T.J., Lisgo, S., Bamshad, M.J. and Strachan, T. (2004) 'NIPBL, encoding a homolog of fungal Scc2-type sister chromatid cohesion proteins and fly Nipped-B, is mutated in Cornelia de Lange syndrome.' *Nature Genetics*, 36: 636–641.

Topçu, M., Aydin, O.F., Yalçunkaya, C., Haliloglu, G. *et al.* (2005) 'L-2-hydroxyglutaric aciduria: a report of 29 patients.' *The Turkish Journal of Pediatrics*, 47: 1–7.

Tordjman, S., Anderson, G.M., Pichard, N., Charbuy, H. and Touitou, Y. (2005) 'Nocturnal excretion of 6-sulphatoxymelatonin in children and adolescents with autistic disorder.' *Biological Psychiatry 57*, 2: 134–138.

Torniero, C., dalla Bernadina, B., Novara, F., Vetro, A. *et al.* (2007) 'Cortical dysplasia of the left temporal lobe might explain severe expressive-receptive language delay in patients with duplication of the Williams-Beuren locus.' *European Journal of Human Genetics 15*, 1: 62–67.

Torres, A.R. (2003) 'Is fever suppression involved in the etiology of autism and neurodevelopmental disorders?' *BMC Pediatrics*, 3: 9. Available at www.biomedcentral.com.

Torrey, E.F., Dhavale, D., Lawlor, J.P. and Yolken, R.H. (2004) 'Autism and head circumference in the first year of life.' *Biological Psychiatry*, 56: 892–894.

Towbin, J.A. (2003) 'A noninvasive means of detecting preclinical cardiomyopathy in Duchenne muscular dystrophy?' *Journal of the American College of Cardiology*, 42: 317–318.

Towbin, J.A., Hejtmancik, J.F., Brink, P., Gelb, B. *et al.* (1993) 'X-linked dilated cardiomyopathy: molecular genetic evidence of linkage to the Duchenne muscular dystrophy (dystrophin) gene at the Xp21 locus.' *Circulation*, 87: 1854–1865.

Towbin, K.E. (2003) 'Strategies for pharmacological treatment of high functioning autism and Asperger syndrome.' *Child and Adolescent Clinics of North America*, 12: 23–45.

Traboulsi, E.I., Koenekoop, R. and Stone, E.M. (2006) 'Lumpers or splitters? The role of molecular diagnosis in Leber congenital amaurosis.' *Ophthalmic Genetics 27*, 4: 113–115.

Traka, M., Goutebroze, L., Denisenko, N., Bessa, M. *et al.* (2003) 'Association of TAG-1 with Caspr2 is essential for the molecular organization of juxtaparanodal regions of myelinated fibers.' *The Journal of Cell Biology 162*, 6: 1161–1172.

Treffert, D. (2006) *Extraordinary People: Understanding Savant Syndrome.* New York: Authors Guild Backprint.

Trefz, F., de Sonneville, L., Matthis, P., Benninger, C., Lanz-Engelert, B. and Bickel, H. (1994) 'Neuropsychological and biochemical investigations in heterozygotes for phenylketonuria during ingestion of high-dose aspartame (a sweetener containing phenylalanine).' *Human Genetics 93*, 4: 369–374.

Trevarthen, C. and Aitken, K.J. (2001) 'Infant intersubjectivity: research, theory, and clinical applications.' Annual research review. *Journal of Child Psychology and Psychiatry*, 42: 3–48.

Trevarthen, C., Aitken, K.J., Vandekerckhove, M., Delafield-Butt, J. and Nagy, E. (2006) 'Collaborative Regulations of Vitality in Early Childhood: Stress in Intimate Relationships and Postnatal Psychopathology.' In D. Cichetti and D.J. Cohen (eds.) *Developmental Psychopathology, Vol. 2.* New York: John Wiley.

Trifilio, M. and Page, T. (2000) 'NAPDD patients exhibit altered electrophoretic mobility of cytosolic 5' nucleotidase.' *Advances in Experimental Medicine and Biology*, 486: 87–90.

Trillingsgaard, A. and Østergaard, O. Jr. (2004) 'Autism in Angelman syndrome: an exploration of comorbidity.' *Autism*, 8: 163–174.

Trip, J., Drost, G.G., van Engelen, B.G.M. and Faber, C.G. (2009) 'Drug treatment for myotonia.' (Review.) *The Cochrane Library*, Issue 1, accessible at www.thecochranelibrary.com.

Tripi, G., Roux, S., Canziani, T., Brilhault, F.B., Barthélémy, C. and Canziania, F. (2007) 'Minor physical anomalies in children with autism spectrum disorder.' *Early Human Development*, doi:10.1016/j.earlhumdev.2007.04.005.

Troger, B., Kutsche, K., Bolz, H., Luttgen, S. *et al.* (2003) 'No mutation in the gene for Noonan syndrome, PTPN11, in 18 patients with Costello syndrome.' *American Journal of Medical Genetics*, 121A: 82–84.

Trovo-Marqui, A.B. and Tajara, E.H. (2006) 'Neurofibromin: a general outlook.' *Clinical Genetics*, 70: 1–13.

Tsankova, N., Renthal, W., Kumar, A. and Nestler, E.J. (2007) 'Epigenetic regulation in psychiatric disorders.' *Nature Reviews: Neuroscience*, 8: 355–367.

Tsao, C.Y. and Mendell, J.R. (2007) 'Autistic disorder in two children with mitochondrial disorders.' *Journal of Child Neurology 22*, 9: 1121–1123.

Tsao, C.Y. and Westman, J.A. (1997) 'Infantile spasms in two children with Williams syndrome.' *American Journal of Medical Genetics 71*, 1: 54–56.

Tsukahara, M., Okamoto, N., Ohashi, H., Kuwajima, K. *et al.* (1998) 'Brachmann-de Lange syndrome and congenital heart disease.' *American Journal of Medical Genetics*, 75: 441–442.

Tuchman, M., McCullough, B.A. and Yudkoff, M. (2000) 'The molecular basis of ornithine transcarbamylase deficiency.' *European Journal of Pediatrics*, 159, Suppl. 3: S196–S198.

Tuchman, R. (2006) 'Autism and epilepsy: what has regression got to do with it?' *Epilepsy Currents 6*, 4: 107–111.

Tuchman, R. and Rapin, I. (2002a) 'Epilepsy in autism.' *Lancet Neurology 1*, 6: 352–358.

Tuchman, R. and Rapin, I. (eds.) (2002b) *Autism: A Neurological Disorder of Early Brain Development.* International Review of Child Neurology Series. Cambridge: MacKeith Press.

Tucker, A.S., Watson, R.P., Lettice, L.A., Yamada, G. and Hill, R.E. (2004) 'Bapx1 regulates patterning in the middle ear: altered regulatory role in the transition from the proximal jaw during vertebrate evolution.' *Development,* 131: 1235–1245.

Tunnessen, W.W. Jr., McMillan, J.A. and Levin, M.B. (1978) 'The Coffin-Siris syndrome.' *American Journal of Diseases of Children,* 132: 393–395.

Turic, D., Langley, K., Mills, S., Stephens, M. *et al.* (2004) 'Follow-up of genetic linkage findings on chromosome 16p13: evidence of association of N-methyl-D aspartate glutamate receptor 2A gene polymorphism with ADHD.' *Molecular Psychiatry,* 9: 169–173.

Turkel, H. and Nusbaum, I. (1985) *Medical Treatment of Down Syndrome and Genetic Diseases* (4th edn). Southfield, MI: Ubiotica.

Türkmen, S., Gillessen-Kaesbach, G., Meinecke, P., Albrecht, B. *et al.* (2003) 'Mutations in NSD1 are responsible for Sotos syndrome, but are not a frequent finding in other overgrowth phenotypes.' *European Journal of Human Genetics,* 11: 858–865.

Turner, G., Partington, M., Kerr, B., Mangelsdorf, M. and Gecz, J. (2002) 'Variable expression of mental retardation, autism, seizures, and dystonic hand movements in two families with an identical ARX gene mutation.' *American Journal of Medical Genetics 112,* 4: 405–411.

Turner, H.H. (1938) 'A syndrome of infantilism, congenital webbed neck, and cubitus valgus.' *Endocrinology,* 23: 566–574.

Turner, J.T., Cohen, M.M. Jr. and Biesecker, L.G. (2004) 'Reassessment of the Proteus syndrome literature: application of diagnostic criteria to published cases.' *American Journal of Medical Genetics A, 130A,* 2: 111–122.

Tutor-Crespo, M.J., Hermida, J. and Tutor, J.C. (2005) 'Effect of antiepileptic drugs on the urinary excretion of porphyrins in non-porphyric subjects.' *Journal of Pharmacological Science,* 99: 323–328.

Twigg, S.J. and Cook, T.M. (2002) 'Anaesthesia in an adult with Rubenstein-Taybi syndrome using the ProSeal laryngeal mask airway.' *British Journal of Anaesthesiology 89,* 5: 786–787.

Tyagi, A. and Harrington, H. (2003) 'Cataplexy in association with Moebius syndrome.' *Journal of Neurology,* 250: 110–111.

Tyler, C.V. Jr., Zyzanski, S.J. and Runser, L. (2004) 'Increased risk of symptomatic gallbladder disease in adults with Down syndrome.' *American Journal of Medical Genetics,* 130A: 351–353.

U

Uhlmann, V., Martin, C.M., Sheils, O., Pilkington, L. et al. (2002) 'Potential viral pathogenic mechanism for new variant inflammatory bowel disease.' *Molecular Pathology,* 55: 84–90.

Ullrich, K., Weglage, J., Schuierer, G., Funders, B. *et al.* (1994) 'Cranial MRI in PKU: evaluation of a critical threshold for blood phenylalanine' (letter). *Neuropediatrics,* 25: 278–279.

Ullrich, O. (1930) 'Über typische Kombinationsbilder multipler Abartungen.' *Zeitschrift für Kinderheilkunde, Berlin,* 49: 271.

Unglaub, W.G. and Goldsmith, G.A. (1955) 'Oral vitamin B12 in the treatment of macrocytic anemias.' *Southern Medical Journal,* 48: 261–269.

Unterrainer, G., Molzer, B., Forss-Petter, S. and Berger, J. (2000) 'Co-expression of mutated and normal adrenoleukodystrophy protein reduces protein function: implications for gene therapy of X-linked adrenoleukodystrophy.' *Human Molecular Genetics 9,* 18: 2609–2616.

Upadhyaya, M., Han, S., Consoli, C., Majounie, E. *et al.* (2004) 'Characterization of the somatic mutational spectrum of the neurofibromatosis type 1 (NF1) gene in neurofibromatosis patients with benign and malignant tumors.' *Human Mutation,* 23: 134–146.

Urban, M. and Hartung, J. (2001) 'Ultrasonographic and clinical appearance of a 22-week-old fetus with Brachmann-de Lange syndrome.' *American Journal of Medical Genetics,* 102: 73–75.

Utsch, B., Sayer, J.A., Attanasio, M., Rodrigues Pereira, R. et al. (2006) 'Identification of the first AHI1 gene mutations in nephronophthisis-associated Joubert syndrome.' *Pediatric Nephrology,* 21: 32–35.

Uyanik, G., Aigner, L., Martin, P., Gross, C. et al. (2003) 'ARX mutations in X-linked lissencephaly with abnormal genitalia.' *Neurology,* 61: 232–235.

Uyanik, O., Dogangun, B., Kayaalp, L., Korkmaz, B. and Dervent, A. (2006) 'Food faddism causing vision loss in an autistic child.' *Child: Care Health and Development 32,* 5: 601–602.

V

Vaccarino, F.M. and Smith, K.M. (2009) 'Increased brain size in autism – what it will take to solve a mystery.' *Biological Psychiatry,* 66: 313–315.

Vajro, P., Strisciuglio, P., Houssin, D., Huault, G. *et al.* (1993) 'Correction of phenylketonuria after liver transplantation in a child with cirrhosis' (letter). *New England Journal of Medicine,* 329: 363.

Valdes-Flores, M., Kofman-Alfaro, S.H., Jimenez-aca, A.L. and Cuevas-Covarrubias, S.A. (2001) 'Carrier identification by FISH analysis in isolated cases of X-linked ichthyosis.' *American Journal of Medical Genetics,* 102: 146–148.

Valdovinos, M.G., Napolitano, D.A., Zarcone, J.R., Hellings, J.A. *et al.* (2002) 'Multimodal evaluation of risperidone for destructive behavior: functional analysis, direct observations, rating scales, and psychiatric impressions.' *Experimental and Clinical Psychopharmacology,* 10: 268–275.

Valente, K.D., Koiffmann, C.P., Fridman, C., Varella, M. *et al.* (2006a) 'Epilepsy in patients with Angelmann syndrome caused by deletion of the chromosome 15q11-13.' *Archives of Neurology,* 63: 122–128.

Valente, E.M., Marsh, S.E., Castori, M., Dixon-Salazar, T. et al. (2005) 'Distinguishing the four genetic causes of Joubert syndrome-related disorders.' *Annals of Neurology,* 57: 513–519.

Valente, E.M., Silhavy, J.L., Brancati, F., Barrano, G. *et al.* (2006b) 'Mutations in CEP290, which encodes a centrosomal protein, cause pleiotropic forms of Joubert syndrome.' *Nature Genetics 38,* 6: 623–625.

Valicenti-McDermott, M., McVicar, K., Rapin, I., Wershil, B.K. *et al.* (2006) 'Frequency of gastrointestinal symptoms in children with autistic spectrum disorders and association with family history of autoimmune disease.' *Journal of Developmental and Behavioral Pediatrics,* 27: 128–136.

Valicenti-McDermott, M.D., McVicar, K., Cohen, H.J., Wershil, B.K. and Shinnar, S. (2008) 'Gastrointestinal symptoms in children with an autism spectrum disorder and language regression.' *Pediatric Neurology,* 39: 392–398.

Valle, D. (2004) '2003 ASHG presidential address: genetics, individuality, and medicine in the 21st century.' *American Journal of Human Genetics,* 74: 374–381.

van Amelsvoort, T., Daly, E., Henry, J., Robertson, D. *et al.* (2004) 'Brain anatomy in adults with velocardiofacial syndrome with and without schizophrenia: preliminary results of a structural magnetic resonance imaging study.' *Archives of General Psychiatry 61,* 11: 1085–1096.

Van Buggenhout, G. and Fryns, J.-P. (2006) 'Lujan-Fryns syndrome (mental retardation, X-linked, marfanoid habitus).' *Orphanet Journal of Rare Diseases* 1: 26, doi:10.1186/1750-1172-1-26.

van Calcar, S.C., Gleason, L.A., Lindh, H., Hoffman, G. *et al.* (2007) '2-methylbutyryl-CoA dehydrogenase deficiency in Hmong infants identified by expanded newborn screen.' *Wisconsin Medical Journal 106,* 1: 12–15.

Vancassel, S., Durand, G., Barthélémy, C., Lejeune, B. et al. (2001) 'Plasma fatty acid levels in autistic children.' *Prostaglandins Leukotrienes and Essential Fatty Acids,* 65: 1–7.

van der Burgt, I., Thoonen, G., Roosenboom, N., Assman-Hulsmans, C. *et al.* (1999) 'Patterns of cognitive functioning in school-aged children with Noonan syndrome associated with variability in phenotypic expression.' *Journal of Pediatrics,* 135: 707–713.

Vanderklish, P.W. and Edelman, G.M. (2005) 'Differential translation and fragile-X syndrome.' *Genes, Brain and Behavior*, 4: 360–384.

van Deutekom, J.C. and van Ommen, G.J. (2003) 'Advances in Duchenne muscular dystrophy gene therapy.' *Nature Reviews Genetics*, 4: 774–783.

van Diggelen, O.P., Schindler, D., Willemsen, R., Boer, M. *et al.* (1988) 'Alpha-N-acetylgalactosaminidase deficiency, a new lysosomal storage disorder.' *Journal of Inherited Metabolic Disease*, 11: 349–357.

Van Dyke, D.L. and Wiktor, A.E. (2006) 'Testing for sex chromosome mosaicism in Turner syndrome.' *International Congress Series*, 1298: 9–12.

van Esch, H., Groenen, P., Fryns, J.-P., van de Ven, W. and Devriendt, K. (1999) 'The phenotypic spectrum of the 10p deletion syndrome versus the classical DiGeorge syndrome.' *Genetic Counselling 10*, 1: 59–65.

van Essen, A.J., Abbs, S., Baiget, M., Bakker, E. *et al.* (1992) 'Parental origin and germline mosaicism of deletions and duplications of the dystrophin gene: a European study.' *Human Genetics 88*, 3: 249–257.

van Essen, A.J., Kneppers, A.L., van der Hout, A.H., Scheffer, H. *et al.* (1997) 'The clinical and molecular genetic approach to Duchenne and Becker muscular dystrophy: an updated protocol.' *Journal of Medical Genetics*, 34: 805–812.

van Essen, A.J., Mulder, I.M., van der Vlies, P., van der Hout, A.H. *et al.* (2003) 'Detection of point mutation in dystrophin gene reveals somatic and germline mosaicism in the mother of a patient with Duchenne muscular dystrophy.' *American Journal of Medical Genetics*, 118A: 296–298.

van Geel, B.M., Assies, J., Haverkort, E.B., Koelman, J.H.T.M. *et al.* (1999) 'Progression of abnormalities in adrenomyeloneuropathy and neurologically asymptomatic X-linked adrenoleukodystrophy despite treatment with "Lorenzo's oil".' *Journal of Neurology, Neurosurgery and Psychiatry*, 67: 290–299.

van Gennip, A.H., Abeling, N.G., Stroomer, A.E., van Lenthe, H. and Bakker, H.D. (1994) 'Clinical and biochemical findings in six patients with pyrimidine degradation defects.' *Journal of Inherited Metabolic Disease*, 17: 130–132.

van Gennip, A.H., Abeling, N.G.G.M., Vreken, P. and van Kuilenburg, A.B.P. (1997) 'Inborn errors of pyrimidine degradation: clinical, biochemical and molecular aspects.' *Journal of Inherited Metabolic Disease 20*, 2: 203–213.

van Haelst, M.M., Hoogeboom, J.J.M., Baujat, G., Bruggenwirth, H.T. *et al.* (2005) 'Familial gigantism caused by an NSD1 mutation.' *American Journal of Medical Genetics*, 139A: 40–44.

van Kuilenburg, A.B. (2006) 'Screening for dihydropyrimidine dehydrogenase deficiency: to do or not to do, that's the question.' *Cancer Investigation* 24, 2: 215–217.

van Kuilenburg, A.B.P., Muller, E.W., Haasjes, J., Meinsma, R. *et al.* (2001) 'Lethal outcome of a patient with a complete dihydropyrimidine dehydrogenase (DPD) deficiency after the administration of 5-fluorouracil: frequency of the common IVS14 + 1G > A mutation causing DPD deficiency.' *Clinical Cancer Research*, 7: 1149–1153.

van Kuilenburg, A.B.P., Stroomer, A.E., Abeling, N.G. and van Gennip, A.H. (2006) 'A pivotal role for beta-aminoisobutyric acid and oxidative stress in dihydropyrimidine dehydrogenase deficiency?' *Nucleosides, Nucleotides and Nucleic Acids 25*, 9–11: 1103–1106.

van Kuilenburg, A.B.P., Stroomer, A.E., Van Lenthe, H., Abeling, N.G. and Van Gennip, A.H. (2004) 'New insights in dihydropyrimidine dehydrogenase deficiency: a pivotal role for beta-aminoisobutyric acid?' *Biochemical Journal 379*, 1: 119–124.

van Kuilenburg, A.B.P., Vreken, P., Abeling, N.G.G.M., Bakker, H.D. *et al.* (1999) 'Genotype and phenotype in patients with dihydropyrimidine dehydrogenase deficiency.' *Human Genetics 104*, 1: 1–9.

Vanli, L., Yilmaz, E., Tokatli, A. and Anlar, B. (2006) 'Phenylketonuria in pediatric neurology practice: a series of 146 cases.' *Journal of Child Neurology*, 21: 987–990.

Van Meekeren, J.A. (1668) *Heel-en Geneeskonstige Aanmerkingen.* Amsterdam.

Van Meter, T.D. and Weaver, D.D. (1996) 'Oculo-auriculo-vertebral spectrum and the CHARGE association: clinical evidence for a common pathogenetic mechanism.' *Clinical Dysmorphology*, 5: 187–196.

van Rijn, S., Swaab, H., Aleman, A. and Kahn, R.S. (2006) 'X chromosomal effects on social cognitive processing and emotion regulation: a study with Klinefelter.' *Schizophrenia Research 84*, 2/3: 194–203.

van Rijn, S., Swaab, H., Aleman, A. and Kahn, R.S. (2008) 'Social behavior and autism traits in a sex chromosomal disorder: Klinefelter (47XXY) syndrome.' *Journal of Autism and Developmental Disorders 38*, 9: 1634–1641.

Van Schaftingen, E., Rzem, R. and Veiga-da-Cunha, M. (2009) 'L-2-hydroxyglutaric aciduria, a disorder of metabolite repair.' *Journal of Inherited Metabolic Disease 32*, 2: 135–142.

Varela, M.C., Kok, F., Otto, P.A. and Koiffmann, C.P. (2004) 'Phenotypic variability in Angelman syndrome: comparison among different deletion classes and between deletion and UPD subjects.' *European Journal of Human Genetics*, 12: 987–992.

Vargas, L., Patino, P.J., Rodriguez, M.F., Forero, C. *et al.* (1999) 'Increase in granulocyte-macrophage-colony-stimulating factor secretion and the respiratory burst with decreased l-selectin expression in hyper-IgE syndrome patients.' *Annals of Allergy, Asthma and Immunology*, 83: 245–251.

Varghese, P.J., Izukawa, T. and Rowe, R.D. (1969) 'Supravalvular aortic stenosis as part of rubella syndrome, with discussion of pathogenesis.' *British Heart Journal*, 31: 59–62.

Varley, C.K. and Crnic, K. (1984) 'Emotional, behavioral, and cognitive status of children with cerebral gigantism.' *Journal of Developmental and Behavioral Pediatrics*, 5: 132–134.

Vatta, S., Cigui, I., Demori, E., Morgutti, M. et al. (1998) 'Fragile X syndrome, mental retardation and macroorchidism.' *Clinical Genetics*, 54: 366–367.

Vaux, K.K., Wojtczak, H., Benirschke, K. and Lyons Jones, K. (2003) 'Vocal cord abnormalities in Williams syndrome: a further manifestation of elastin deficiency.' *American Journal of Medical Genetics*, 119A: 302–304.

Veenstra-Vanderweele, J., Christian, S.L. and Cook, E.H. Jr. (2004) 'Autism as a paradigmatic complex genetic disorder.' *Annual Review of Genomics and Human Genetics*, 5: 379–405.

Vento, A.R., LaBrie, R.A. and Mulliken, J.B. (1991) 'O.M.E.N.S. Classification System.', *Cleft Palate-Craniofacial Journal*, 28, 1: 68–77.

Vergine, G., Mencarelli, F., Diomedi-Camassei, F., Caridi, G. et al. (2008) 'Glomerulocystic kidney disease in Hypomelanosis of Ito.' *Pediatric Nephrology*, 23: 1183–1187.

Veltman, M.W., Craig, E.E. and Bolton, P.F. (2005) 'Autism spectrum disorders in Prader-Willi and Angelman syndromes: a systematic review.' *Psychiatric Genetics 15*, 4: 243–254.

Verhage, J., Habbema, L., Vrensen, G.F., Roord, J.J. and Bleeker-Wagemakers, E.M. (1987) 'A patient with onychotrichodysplasia, neutropenia and normal intelligence.' *Clinical Genetics*, 31: 374–380.

Verhoeven, W.M. and Tuinier, S. (2006) 'Prader-Willi syndrome: atypical psychoses and motor dysfunctions.' *International Review of Neurobiology*, 72: 119–130.

Verkerk, A.J.M.H., Mathews, C.A., Joosse, M., Eussen, B.H.J. *et al.* (2003) 'The Tourette syndrome Association International Consortium for Genetics: CNTNAP2 is disrupted in a family with Gilles de la Tourette syndrome and obsessive compulsive disorder.' *Genomics*, 82: 1–9.

Verkerk, A.J., Pieretti, M., Sutcliffe, J.S., Fu, Y.H. *et al.* (1991) 'Identification of a gene (FMR-1) containing a CGG repeat coincident with a breakpoint cluster region exhibiting length variation in fragile-X syndrome.' *Cell*, 65: 905–914.

Verkman, A.S., Binder, D.K., Bloch, O., Auguste, K. and Papadopoulos, M.C. (2006) 'Three distinct roles of aquaporin-4 in brain function revealed by knockout mice.' *Biochimica et Biophysica Acta, 1758*: 1085–1093.

Verloes, A., Sacré, J.P. and Geubelle, F. (1987) 'Sotos syndrome and fragile-X chromosomes.' *Lancet 330*, 8554: 329.

Vermeulen, W., Bergmann, E., Auriol, J., Rademakers, S. *et al.* (2000) 'Sublimiting concentration of TFIIH transcription/DNA repair factor causes TTD-A trichothiodystrophy disorder.' *Nature Genetics*, 26: 307–313.

Vermeulen, W., Rademakers, S., Jaspers, N.G.J., Appeldoorn, E. et al. (2001) 'A temperature-sensitive disorder in basal transcription and DNA repair in humans.' *Nature Genetics*, 27: 299–303.

Vermot, J., Niederreither, K., Garnier, J.-M., Chambon, P. and Dolle, P. (2003) 'Decreased embryonic retinoic acid synthesis results in a DiGeorge syndrome phenotype in newborn mice.' *Proceedings of the National Academy of Science USA*, 100: 1763–1768.

Verri, A., Maraschio, P., Devriendt, K., Uggetti, C. *et al.* (2004) 'Chromosome 10p deletion in a patient with hypoparathyroidism, severe mental retardation, autism and basal ganglia calcifications.' *Annals of Genetics*, 47: 281–287.

Vervloed, M.P., Hoevenaars-van den Boom, M.A., Knoors, H., van Ravenswaaij, C.M. and Admiraal, R.J. (2006) 'CHARGE syndrome: relations between behavioral characteristics and medical conditions.' *American Journal of Medical Genetics A*, 40: 851–862.

Verzijl, H.T.F.M., Valk, J., de Vries, R. and Padberg, G.W. (2005) 'Radiologic evidence for absence of the facial nerve in Moebius syndrome.' *Neurology*, 64: 849–855.

Verzijl, H.T.F.M., van der Zwaag, B., Cruysberg, J.R.M. and Padberg, G.W. (2003) 'Möbius syndrome redefined: a syndrome of rhombencephalic maldevelopment.' *Neurology*, 61: 327–333.

Viani, F., Romeo, A., Viri, M., Mastrangelo, M. *et al.* (1995) 'Seizure and EEG patterns in Angelman's syndrome.' *Journal of Child Neurology*, 10: 467–471.

Vieira, T.C., Boldarine, V.T. and Abucham, J. (2007) 'Molecular analysis of PROP1, PIT1, HESX1, LHX3, and LHX4 shows high frequency of PROP1 mutations in patients with familial forms of combined pituitary hormone deficiency.' *Arquivos Brasileiros de Endocrinologia & Metabologia*, 51: 1097–1103.

Vilaseca, M.A., Briones, P., Ferrer, I., Campistol, J. *et al.* (1993) 'Controlled diet in phenylketonuria may cause serum carnitine deficiency.' *Journal of Inherited Metabolic Disease 16*, 1: 101–104.

Villard, L., Kpebe, A., Cardoso, C., Chelly, P.J. *et al.* (2000) 'Two affected boys in a Rett syndrome family: clinical and molecular findings.' *Neurology* 55, 8: 1188–1193.

Villard, L., Levy, N., Xiang, F., Kpebe, A. *et al.* (2001) 'Segregation of a totally skewed pattern of X chromosome inactivation in four familial cases of Rett syndrome without MECP2 mutation: implications for the disease.' *Journal of Medical Genetics*, 38: 435–442.

Vincent, J.B., Kolozsvari, D., Roberts, W.S., Bolton, P.F. *et al.* (2004) 'Mutation screening of X-chromosomal neuroligin genes: no mutations in 196 autism probands.' *American Journal of Medical Genetics B Neuropsychiatric Genetics 129*, 1: 82–84.

Vincent, M.-C., Heitz, F., Tricoire, J., Bourrouillou, G. *et al.* (1999) '22q deletion in DGS/VCFS monozygotic twins with discordant phenotypes.' *Genetic Counselling*, 10: 43–49.

Vinken, P. and Bruyn, G. (eds.) *Handbook of Clinical Neurology*. North Holland: Elsevier.

Vinton, A., Fahey, M.C., O'Brien, T.J., Shaw, J. *et al.* (2005) 'Dentatorubral-pallidoluysian atrophy in three generations, with clinical courses from nearly asymptomatic elderly to severe juvenile, in an Australian family of Macedonian descent.' *American Journal of Medical Genetics*, 136A: 201–204.

Virdis, R., Street, M.E., Bandello, M.A., Tripodi, C. *et al.* (2003) 'Growth and pubertal disorders in neurofibromatosis type 1.' *Journal of Pediatric Endocrinology and Metabolism*, 16 (Suppl. 2): 289–292.

Visootsak, J. and Graham, J.M. Jr. (2006) 'Review: Klinefelter syndrome and other sex chromosomal aneuploidies.' *Orphanet Journal of Rare Diseases*, 1: 42, doi:10.1186/1750-1172-1-42, downloadable from: www.OJRD.com.

Vits, L., De Boulle, K., Reyniers, E., Handig, I. *et al.* (1994) 'Apparent regression of the CGG repeat in FMR1 to an allele of normal size.' *Human Genetics*, 94: 523–526.

Vivarelli, R., Grosso, S., Calabrese, F., Farnetani, M. *et al.* (2003) 'Epilepsy in neurofibromatosis 1.' *Journal of Child Neurology*, 18: 338–342.

Vockley, J., Rinaldo, P., Bennett, M.J., Matern, D. and Vladutiu, G.D. (2000) 'Synergistic heterozygosity: disease resulting from multiple partial defects in one or more metabolic pathways.' *Molecular Genetics and Metabolism*, 71: 10–18.

Voit, T., Kramer, H., Thomas, C., Wechsler, W. *et al.* (1991) 'Mypopathy (sic) in Williams-Beuren syndrome.' *European Journal of Pediatrics*, 150: 521–526.

Volkmar, F.R. and Nelson, D.S. (1990) 'Seizure disorders in autism.' *Journal of the American Academy of Child and Adolescent Psychiatry 29*, 1: 127–129.

Vollind, Z.L., Xenophontos, S.L., Cariolou, M.A., Mokone, G.G. *et al.* (2004) 'The ACE gene and endurance performance during the South African ironman triathlons.' *Medicine and Science in Sports and Exercise*, 36: 1314–1320.

von Aster, M., Zachmann, M., Brandeis, D., Wohlrab, G., Richner, M. and Steinhausen, H.C. (1997) 'Psychiatric, neuropediatric, and neuropsychological symptoms in a case of Hypomelanosis of Ito.' *European Child and Adolescent Psychiatry 6*, 4: 227–233.

von Neusser, E. and Wiesel, J. (1910) *Die Erkrankungen der Nebennieren*. Vienna: Holder.

Vostanis, P., Harrington, R., Prendergast, M. and Farndon, P. (1994) 'Case reports of autism with interstitial deletion of chromosome 17 (p11.2 p11.2) and monosomy for chromosome 5 (5pter >5p153).' *Psychiatric Genetics*, 4: 109–111.

Vrolik, W. (1849) *Tabulae ad illustrandam embryogenesin hominis et mammalium, tam naturalem quam abnormem*. Amsterdam: G.M.P. Londinck.

W

Wada, Y., Matsuoka, T., Imai, K., Taniike, M. *et al.* (1998) 'A case of juvenile-type DRPLA with psychomotor retardation since infancy.' *No To Hattatsu*, 30: 543–548.

Waggoner, D. (2007) 'Mechanisms of disease: epigenesis.' *Seminars in Pediatric Neuology*, 14: 7–14.

Wagner, K.R., Hamed, S., Hadley, D.W., Gropman, A.L. *et al.* (2001) 'Gentamicin treatment of Duchenne and Becker muscular dystrophy due to nonsense mutations.' *Annals of Neurology*, 49: 706–711.

Wagstaff, J., Knoll, J.H.M., Fleming, J., Kirkness, E.F. *et al.* (1991) 'Localization of the gene encoding the GABAA receptor β3 subunit to the Angelman/Prader-Willi region of human chromosome 15.' *American Journal of Human Genetics 49*, 2: 330–337.

Wagstaff, J., Knoll, J.H.M., Glatt, K.A., Shugart, Y.Y. *et al.* (1992) 'Maternal but not paternal transmission of 15q11–13-linked nondeletion Angelman syndrome leads to phenotypic expression.' *Nature Genetics*, 1: 291–294.

Wagstaff, J., Shugart, Y.Y. and Lalande, M. (1993) 'Linkage analysis in familial Angelman syndrome.' *American Journal of Human Genetics*, 53: 105–112.

Wainwright, P.E. (2002) 'Dietary essential fatty acids and brain function: a developmental perspective on mechanisms.' *Proceedings of the Nutrition Society*, 61: 61–69.

Waisbren, S.E., Hanley, W., Levy, H.L., Shifrin, H. *et al.* (2000) 'Outcome at age 4 years in offspring of women with maternal phenylketonuria: the maternal PKU collaborative study.' *Journal of the American Medical Association*, 283: 756–762.

Waite, K.A. and Eng, C. (2002) 'Protean PTEN: form and function.' *American Journal of Human Genetics*, 70: 829–844.

Wakabayashi, S. (1979) 'A case of infantile autism associated with Down's syndrome.' *Journal of Autism and Developmental Disorders 9*, 1: 31–36.

Wakefield, A.J., Murch, S.H., Anthony, A., Linnell, J. et al. (1998) 'Ileal-lymphoid-nodular hyperplasia, non-specific colitis, and pervasive developmental disorder in children.' *The Lancet 351*, 9103: 637–641.

Waldman, M., Nicholson, S. and Adilov, N. (2006) 'Does television cause autism?' *National Bureau of Economic Research, Working Paper No.12632*, October 2006, www.nber.org.

Walker, A. and Fitzgerald, M. (2006) *Unstoppable Brilliance*. Dublin: Liberties Press.

Walkup, J.T., LaBuda, M.C., Singer, H.S., Brown, J., Riddle, M.A. and Hurko, O. (1996) 'Family study and segregation analysis of Tourette syndrome: evidence for a mixed model of inheritance.' *American Journal of Human Genetics*, 59: 684–693.

Wallace, D.C. (2005) 'The mitochondrial genome in human adaptive radiation and disease: on the road to therapeutics and performance enhancement.' *Gene*, 354: 169–180.

Wallace, R.A. (2007) 'Clinical audit of gastrointestinal conditions occurring among adults with Down syndrome attending a specialist clinic.' *Journal of Intellectual and Developmental Disability 32*, 1: 45–50.

Wallace, R.H., Hodgson, B.L., Crinton, B.E., Gardiner, R.M. *et al.* (2003) 'Sodium channel 1-subunit mutations in severe myoclonic epilepsy of infancy and infantile spasms.' *Neurology*, 61: 765–769.

Wallace, S.J. (1998) 'Myoclonus and epilepsy in childhood: a review of treatment with valproate, ethosuximide, lamotrigine and zonisamide.' *Epilepsy Research*, 29: 147–154.

Walter, J.H., White, F.J., Hall, S.K., MacDonald, A. *et al.* (2002) 'How practical are recommendations for dietary control in phenylketonuria?' *Lancet 360*, 9326: 55–57.

Walterfang, M.A., O'Donovan, J., Fahey, M.C. and Velakoulis, D. (2007) 'The neuropsychiatry of adrenomyeloneuropathy.' *CNS Spectrums 12*, 9: 696–701.

Walz, K., Paylor, R., Yan, J., Bi, W. and Lupski, J.R. (2006) 'Rai1 duplication causes physical and behavioral phenotypes in a mouse model of dup(17) (p11.2p11.2).' *The Journal of Clinical Investigation*, 116: 3035–3041.

Walzer, S., Bashir, A.S. and Silbert, A.R. (1990) 'Cognitive and behavioral factors in the learning disabilities of 47,XXY and 47,XYY boys.' *Birth Defects Original Articles Series*, 26: 45–58.

Wanders, R.J.A. (1999) 'Peroxisomal disorders: clinical, biochemical, and molecular aspects.' *Neurochemical Research 24*, 4: 565–580.

Wanders, R.J.A., Vreken, P., Ferdinandusse, S., Jansen, G.A. *et al.* (2001) 'Peroxisomal fatty acid α- and β-oxidation in humans: enzymology, peroxisomal metabolite transporters and peroxisomal diseases.' *Biochemical Society Transactions 29*, 2: 250–267.

Wang, A.M., Schindler, D., Bishop, D.F., Lemieux, R.U. and Desnick, R.J. (1988) 'Schindler disease: biochemical and molecular characterization of a new neuroaxonal dystrophy due to alpha-N-acetylgalactosaminidase deficiency' (abstract). *American Journal of Human Genetics*, 43: A99.

Wang, P.P., Hesselink, J.R., Jernigan, T.L., Doherty, S. and Bellugi, U. (1992) 'Specific neurobehavioral profile of Williams' syndrome is associated with neocerebellar hemispheric preservation.' *Neurology 42*, 10: 1999–2002.

Wang, P.P., Solot, C., Moss, E.M., Gerdes, M. *et al.* (1998) 'Developmental presentation of 22q11.2 deletion (DiGeorge/velocardiofacial syndrome).' *Journal of Developmental and Behavioral Pediatrics*, 19: 342–345.

Wang, R., Martinez-Frias, M.L. and Graham, J.M. Jr. (2002) 'Infants of diabetic mothers are at increased risk for the oculo-auriculo-vertebral sequence: a case-based and case-control approach.' *Journal of Pediatrics*, 141: 611–617.

Wang, Y.C., Lin, M.L., Lin, S.J. *et al.* (1997) 'Novel point mutation within intron 10 of FMR-1 gene causing fragile-X syndrome.' *Human Mutation*, 10: 393–399.

Wardle, M., Majounie, E., Williams, N.M., Rosser, A.E. *et al.* (2007) 'Dentatorubral pallidoluysian atrophy in South Wales.' *Journal of Neurology, Neurosurgery and Psychiatry 79*, 7: 804–807.

Warwick, T.C., Griffith, J., Reyes, B., Legesse, B. and Evans, M. (2007) 'Effects of vagus nerve stimulation in a patient with temporal lobe epilepsy and Asperger syndrome: case report and review of the literature.' *Epilepsy and Behavior 10*, 2: 344–347, doi:10.1016/j.yebeh.2007.01.001.

Wasdell, M.B., Jan, J.E., Bomben, M.M., Freeman, R.D. *et al.* (2008) 'A placebo-controlled melatonin study of circadian rhythm sleep disorders in children with neurodevelopmental disabilities.' *Journal of Pineal Research*, 44: 57–64.

Wassif, C.A., Maslen, C., Kachilele-Linjewile, S., Lin, D. *et al.* (1998) 'Mutations in the human sterol delta-7-reductase gene at 11q12-13 cause Smith-Lemli-Opitz syndrome.' *American Journal of Human Genetics*, 63: 55–62.

Wassink, T.H., Piven, J., Vieland, V.J., Jenkins, L. *et al.* (2005) 'Evaluation of the chromosome 2q37.3 gene CENTG2 as an autism susceptibility gene.' *American Journal of Medical Genetics B Neuropsychiatric Genetics*, 136: 36–44.

Wasternack, C. (1980) 'Degradation of pyrimidines and pyrimidine analogs – pathways and mutual influences.' *Pharmacology and Therapeutics*, 8: 629–651.

Watson, L.R., Baranek, G.T., Crais, E.R., Reznick, J.S. *et al.* (2007) 'The First Year Inventory: retrospective parent responses to a questionnaire designed to identify one-year-olds at risk for autism.' *Journal of Autism and Developmental Disorders*, 37: 49–61.

Waye, J.S., Nakamura, L.M., Eng, B., Hunnisett, L. *et al.* (2002) 'Smith-Lemli-Opitz syndrome: carrier frequency and spectrum of DHCR7 mutations in Canada.' *Journal of Medical Genetics*, 39: E31.

Weaver, I.C.G., Meaney, M.J. and Szyf, M. (2006) 'Maternal care effects on the hippocampal transcriptome and anxiety-mediated behaviors in the offspring that are reversible in adulthood.' *Proceedings of the National Academy of Science USA 103*, 9: 3480–3485. www.pnas.org

Weaver, R.G. Jr., Martin, T. and Zanolli, M.D. (1991) 'The ocular changes of incontinentia pigmenti achromians (Hypomelanosis of Ito).' *Journal of Pediatrics, Ophthalmology and Strabismus 28*, 3: 160–163.

Weaving, L.S., Christodoulou, J., Williamson, S.L., Friend, K.L. *et al.* (2004) 'Mutations of CDKL5 cause a severe neurodevelopmental disorder with infantile spasms and mental retardation.' *American Journal of Human Genetics*, 75: 1079–1093.

Weaving, L.S., Ellaway, C.J., Gecz, J. and Christodoulou, J. (2005) 'Rett syndrome: clinical review and genetic update.' *Journal of Medical Genetics*, 42: 1–7.

Weaving, L.S., Williamson, S.L., Bennetts, B., Davis, M. *et al.* (2003) 'Effects of MECP2 mutation type, location and X-inactivation in modulating Rett syndrome phenotype.' *American Journal of Medical Genetics*, 118A: 103–114.

Wechsler, J., Greene, M., McDevitt, M.A., Anastasi, J. *et al.* (2002) 'Acquired mutations in GATA1 in the megakaryoblastic leukemia of Down syndrome.' *Nature Genetics*, 32: 148–152.

Weech, A.A. (1927) 'Combined acrocephaly and syndactylism occurring in mother and daughter: a case report.' *Bulletin of Johns Hopkins Hospital*, 40: 73–76.

Weeda, G., Eveno, E., Donker, I., Vermeulen, W. *et al.* (1997) 'A mutation in the XPB/ERCC3 DNA repair transcription gene, associated with trichothiodystrophy.' *American Journal of Human Genetics*, 60: 320–329.

Weglage, J., Pietsch, M., Denecke, J., Sprinz, A. *et al.* (1999) 'Regression of neuropsychological deficits in early-treated phenylketonurics during adolescence.' *Journal of Inherited Metabolic Disease*, 22: 693–705.

Wei, X., McLeod, H.L., McMurrough, J., Gonzalez, F.J. and Fernandez-Salguero, P. (1996) 'Molecular basis of the human dihydropyrimidine dehydrogenase deficiency and 5-fluorouracil toxicity.' *Journal of Clinical Investigation*, 98: 610–615.

Weiler, I.J. and Greenough, W.T. (1999) 'Synaptic synthesis of the fragile-X protein: possible involvement in synapse maturation and elimination.' *American Journal of Medical Genetics*, 83: 248–252.

Weinzimer, S.A., McDonald-McGinn, D.M., Driscoll, D.A., Emanuel, B.S. *et al.* (1998) 'Growth hormone deficiency in patients with 22q11.2 deletion: expanding the phenotype.' *Pediatrics*, 101: 929–932.

Weise, P., Koch, R., Shaw, K.N. and Rosenfeld, M.J. (1974) 'The use of 5-HTP in the treatment of Down's syndrome.' *Pediatrics 54*, 2: 165–168.

Weiskop, S., Richdale, A. and Matthews, J. (2005) 'Behavioural treatment to reduce sleep problems in children with autism or fragile-X syndrome.' *Developmental Medicine and Child Neurology 47*, 2: 94–104.

Weiss, L.A., Arking, D.E., Gene Discovery Project of Johns Hopkins and the Autism Consortium, Daly, M.J. et al. (2009) 'A genome-wide linkage and association scan reveals novel loci for autism.' *Nature*, 461: 802–808.

Weiss, L.A., Escayg, A., Kearney, J.A., Trudeau, M. *et al.* (2003) 'Sodium channels SCN1A, SCN2A and SCN3A in familial autism.' *Molecular Psychiatry*, 8: 186–194.

Weiss, L.A., Shen, Y., Korn, J.M., Arking, D.E. *et al.* (2008) 'Association between microdeletion and microduplication at 16p11.2 and autism.' *New England Journal of Medicine*, 358: 667–675.

Weissman, J.R., Kelley, R.I., Bauman, M.L., Cohen, B.H. *et al.* (2008) 'Mitochondrial disease in autism spectrum disorder patients: a cohort analysis.' *PLoS ONE 3*, 11: e3815, doi:10.1371/journal.pone.0003815.

Welch, E.M., Barton, E.R., Zhuo, J., Tomizawa, Y. *et al.* (2007) 'PTC124 targets genetic disorders caused by nonsense mutations.' *Nature 447*, 7140: 87–91.

Welch, J.P. (1974) 'Elucidation of a "new" pleiotropic connective tissue disorder.' *Birth Defects Original Articles Series X*, 10: 138–146.

Welch, M.G., Ludwig, R.J., Opler, M. and Ruggiero, D.A. (2006) 'Secretin's role in the cerebellum: A larger biological context and implications for developmental disorders.' *The Cerebellum*, 5: 2–6.

Wells, R.S. and Jennings, M.C. (1967) 'X-linked ichthyosis and ichthyosis vulgaris: clinical and genetic distinctions in a second series of families.' *Journal of the American Medical Association*, 202: 485–488.

Wells, R.S. and Kerr, C.B. (1965) 'Genetic classification of ichthyosis.' *Archives of Dermatology 92*, 1: 1–6.

Welt, C.K., Smith, P.C. and Taylor, A.E. (2004) 'Evidence of early ovarian aging in fragile-X premutation carriers.' *Journal of Clinical Endocrinology and Metabolism*, 89: 4569–4574.

Werner, E. and Dawson, G. (2006) 'Validation of the phenomenon of autistic regression using home videotapes.' *Archives of General Psychiatry*, 62: 889–895.

Wessel, A., Pankau, R., Kececioglu, D., Ruschewski, W. and Bursch, J.H. (1994) 'Three decades of follow-up of aortic and pulmonary vascular lesions in the Williams-Beuren syndrome.' *American Journal of Medical Genetics*, 52: 297–301.

Westaway, S.K., Gregory, A. and Hayflick, S.J. (2007) 'Mutations in PLA2G6 and the riddle of Schindler disease' (correspondence). *Journal of Medical Genetics*, 44: e64.

Westmark, C.J. and Malter, J.S. (2007) 'FMRP mediates mGluR5-dependent translation of amyloid precursor protein.' *PLoS Biology 5*, 3: e52 doi:10.1371/journal.pbio.0050052.

Wheeler, P.G., Quigley, C.A., Sadeghi-Nejad, A. and Weaver, D.D. (2000) 'Hypogonadism and CHARGE association.' *American Journal of Medical Genetics*, 94: 228–231.

White, J.F. (2003) 'Intestinal pathophysiology in autism.' *Experimental Biology and Medicine*, 228: 639–649.

Whiteford, M.L., Doig, W.B., Raine, P.A.M., Hollman, A.S. and Tolmie, J.L. (2001) 'A new case of Myhre syndrome.' *Clinical Dysmorphology*, 10: 135–140.

Whiteley, P., Dodou, K., Todd, L. and Shattock, P. (2004) 'Body mass index of children from the United Kingdom diagnosed with pervasive developmental disorders.' *Pediatrics International*, 46: 531–533.

Whiteley, P., Waring, R., Williams, L., Klovrza, L. *et al.* (2006) 'Spot urinary creatinine excretion in pervasive developmental disorders.' *Pediatrics International*, 48: 292–297.

Whittington, J.E., Holland, A.J., Webb, T., Butler, J. *et al.* (2001) 'Population prevalence and estimated birth incidence and mortality rate for people with Prader-Willi syndrome in one UK health region.' *Journal of Medical Genetics 38*, 11: 792–798.

Wicksell, R.K., Kihlgren, M., Melin, L. and Eeg-Olofsson, O. (2004) 'Specific cognitive deficits are common in children with Duchenne muscular dystrophy.' *Developmental Medicine and Child Neurology*, 46: 154–159.

Widemann, B.C., Salzer, W.L., Arceci, R.J., Blaney, S.M. et al. (2006) 'Phase I trial and pharmacokinetic study of the farnesyltransferase inhibitor tipifarnib in children with refractory solid tumors or neurofibromatosis type I and plexiform neurofibromas.' *Journal of Clinical Oncology*, 24: 507–516.

Wieacker, P., Davies, K.E., Mevorah, B. and Ropers, H.H. (1983) 'Linkage studies in a family with X-linked recessive ichthyosis employing a cloned DNA sequence from the distal short arm of the X chromosome.' *Human Genetics*, 63: 113–116.

Wieczorek, D., Ludwig, M., Boehringer, S., Hein, P. *et al.* (2007) 'Reproduction abnormalities and twin pregnancies in parents of sporadic patients with oculo-auriculo-vertebral spectrum/Goldenhar syndrome.' *Human Genetics*, 121: 369–376.

Wiedemann, H.R., Burgio, G.R., Aldenhoff, P., Kunze, J. et al. (1983) 'The Proteus syndrome: partial gigantism of the hands and/or feet, nevi, hemihypertrophy, subcutaneous tumors, macrocephaly or other skull anomalies and possible accelerated growth and visceral affections.' *European Journal of Pediatrics*, 140: 5–12.

Wier, M.L., Yoshida, C.K., Odouli, R., Grether, J.K. and Croen, L.A. (2006) 'Congenital anomalies associated with autism spectrum disorders.' *Developmental Medicine and Child Neurology*, 48: 500–507.

Wiggins, L.D., Baio, J. and Rice, C. (2006) 'Examination of the time between first evaluation and first autism spectrum diagnosis in a population-based sample.' *Developmental and Behavioural Pediatrics*, 27: s79–s87.

Wiley, S., Swayne, S., Rubinstein, J.H., Lanphear, N.E. and Stevens, C.A. (2003) 'Rubinstein-Taybi syndrome medical guidelines.' *American Journal of Medical Genetics A, 119A*, 2: 101–110.

Willems, P.J. (2008) 'Bottlenecks in molecular testing for rare genetic diseases.' *Human Mutation 29*, 6: 772–775.

Willemsen, R., Smits, A., Mohkamsing, S., van Beerendonk, H. *et al.* (1997) 'Rapid antibody test for diagnosing fragile-X syndrome: a validation of the technique.' *Human Genetics*, 99: 308–311.

Williams, C.A. and Frias, J.L. (1982) 'The Angelman ("happy puppet") syndrome.' *American Journal of Medical Genetics*, 11: 453–460.

Williams, C.A., Beaudet, A.L., Clayton-Smith, J., Knoll, J.H. *et al.* (2006) 'Angelman syndrome 2005: updated consensus for diagnostic criteria.' *American Journal of Medical Genetics*, 140A: 413–418.

Williams, C.A., Lossie, A. and Driscoll, D. (2001) 'Angelman syndrome: mimicking conditions and phenotypes.' *American Journal of Medical Genetics*, 101: 59–64.

Williams, J.C., Barratt-Boyes, B.G. and Lowe, J.B. (1961) 'Supravalvular aortic stenosis.' *Circulation*, 24: 1311–1318.

Williams, M.S. (2003) 'Can genomics deliver on the promise of improved outcomes and reduced costs? Background and recommendations for health insurers.' *Disease Management and Health Outcomes 11*, 5: 277–290.

Williams, M.S. (2006) 'Neuropsychological evaluation in Lujan-Fryns syndrome: commentary and clinical report.' *American Journal of Medical Genetics*, 140A: 2812–2815.

Williams, P.G. and Hersh, J.H. (1998) 'Brief report: the association of neurofibromatosis type 1 and autism.' *Journal of Autism and Developmental Disorders 28*, 6: 567–571.

Williams, R.A., Mamotte, C.D.S. and Burnett, J.R. (2008) 'Phenylketonuria: an inborn error of phenylalanine metabolism.' *The Clinical Biochemist Review*, 29: 31–41.

Williams, R.J. (1956) *Biochemical Individuality*. Chichester: John Wiley Publishing.

Williams, T.A., Mars, A.E., Buyske, S.G., Stenroos, E.S. *et al.* (2007) 'Risk of autistic disorder in affected offspring of mothers with a glutathione s-transferase p1 haplotype.' *Archives of Pediatric and Adolescent Medicine*, 161: 356–361.

Willmore, L.J., Abelson, M.B., Ben-Menachem, E., Pellock, J.M. and Shields, W.D. (2009) 'Vigabatrin: 2008 update.' *Epilepsia 50*, 2: 163–173.

Wilson, D.I., Burn, J., Scambler, P. and Goodship, J. (1993) 'DiGeorge syndrome, part of CATCH 22.' *Journal of Medical Genetics*, 30: 852–856.

Wilson, H.L., Wong, A.C.C., Shaw, S.R., Tse, W.-Y. *et al.* (2003) 'Molecular characterization of the 22q13 deletion syndrome supports the role of haploinsufficiency of SHANK3/PROSAP2 in the major neurological symptoms.' *Journal of Medical Genetics*, 40: 575–584.

Wilson, L.C., Leverton, K., Oude Luttikhuis, M.E.M., Oley, C.A. *et al.* (1995) 'Brachydactyly and mental retardation: an Albright hereditary osteodystrophy-like syndrome localized to 2q37.' *American Journal of Human Genetics*, 56: 400–407.

Wimmer, K., Yao, S., Claes, K., Kehrer-Sawatzki, H. et al. (2006) 'Spectrum of si genes chromosomes.' *Cancer*, 45: 265–276.

Winter, M., Pankau, R., Amm, M., Gosch, A. and Wessel, A. (1996) 'The spectrum of ocular features in the Williams-Beuren syndrome.' *Clinical Genetics*, 49: 28–31.

Wintour, E.M. and Henry, B.A. (2006) 'Glycerol transport: an additional target for obesity therapy?' *TRENDS in Endocrinology and Metabolism 17*, 3: 77–78.

Wisbeck, J.M., Huffman, L.C., Freund, L., Gunnar, M.R. *et al.* (2000) 'Cortisol and social stressors in children with fragile-X: a pilot study.' *Journal of Developmental and Behavioral Pediatrics*, 21: 278–282.

Wisniewski, K.E., Kida, E., Connell, F. and Zhong, N. (2000) 'Neuronal ceroid lipofuscinoses: research update.' *Neurological Sciences*, 21 (Suppl. 3): S49–56.

Wisniewski, K.E., Wisniewski, H.M. and Wen, G.Y. (1985) 'Occurrence of neuropathological changes and dementia of Alzheimer's disease in Down's syndrome.' *Annals of Neurology*, 17: 278–282.

Witkin, H.A., Mednick, S.A., Schulsinger, F., Bakkestrom, E. *et al.* (1976) 'Criminality in XYY and XXY men.' *Science 193*, 4253: 547–555.

Witsch-Baumgartner, M., Ciara, E., Loffler, J., Menzel, H.J. *et al.* (2001) 'Frequency gradients of DHCR7 mutations in patients with Smith-Lemli-Opitz syndrome in Europe: evidence for different origins of common mutations.' *European Journal of Human Genetics*, 9: 45–50.

Witsch-Baumgartner, M., Gruber, M., Kraft, H.G., Rossi, M. et al. (2004) 'Maternal apo E genotype is a modifier of the Smith-Lemli-Opitz syndrome.' *Journal of Medical Genetics*, 41: 577–584.

Witsch-Baumgartner, M., Schwentner, I., Gruber, M., Benlian, P. *et al.* (2008) 'Age and origin of major Smith-Lemli-Opitz syndrome (SLOS) mutations in European populations.' *Journal of Medical Genetics 45*, 4: 200–209.

Wittine, L.M., Josephson, K.D. and Williams, M.S. (1999) 'Aortic root dilation in apparent Lujan-Fryns syndrome.' *American Journal of Medical Genetics*, 86: 405–409.

Wiznitzer, M. (2004) 'Autism and tuberous sclerosis.' *Journal of Child Neurology*, 19: 675–679.

Wiznitzer, M., Rapin, I. and Van de Water, T.R. (1987) 'Neurologic findings in children with ear malformation.' *International Journal of Pediatric Otolaryngology*, 13: 41–55.

Wolfe, D.E., Schindler, D. and Desnick, R.J. (1995) 'Neuroaxonal dystrophy in infantile alpha-N-acetylgalactosaminidase deficiency.' *Journal of Neurological Science*, 132: 44–56.

Wolff, S. (2004) 'The history of autism.', *European Child and Adolescent Psychiatry, 13*, 4: 201–208.

Wolff, M., Casse-Perrot, C. and Dravet, C. (2006) 'Severe myoclonic epilepsy of infants (Dravet syndrome): natural history and neuropsychological findings.' *Epilepsia*, 47 (Suppl. 2): 45–48.

Wolkenstein, P., Durand-Zaleski, I., Moreno, J.C., Zeller, J. *et al.* (2000) 'Cost evaluation of the medical management of neurofibromatosis 1: a prospective study on 201 patients.' *British Journal of Dermatology*, 142: 1166–1170.

Wolkenstein, P., Rodriguez, D., Ferkal, S., Gravier, H. *et al.* (2008) 'Impact of neurofibromatosis 1 upon quality of life in childhood: a cross-sectional study of 79 cases.' *British Journal of Dermatology*, doi:10.1111/j.1365-2133.2008.08949.x.

Wolpert, C.M., Menold, M.M., Bass, M.P., Qumsiyeh, M.B. *et al.* (2000) 'Three probands with autistic disorder and isodicentric chromosome 15.' *American Journal of Medical Genetics (Neuropsychiatric Genetics)*, 96: 365–372.

Wolters, P.L., Gropman, A.L., Martin, S.C., Smith, M.R. *et al.* (2009) 'Neurodevelopment of children under 3 years of age with Smith-Magenis syndrome.' *Pediatric Neurology 41*, 4: 250–258.

Wong, V. and Khong, P.L. (2006) 'Tuberous sclerosis complex: correlation of magnetic resonance imaging (MRI) findings with comorbidities.' *Journal of Child Neurology 21*, 2: 99–105.

Wong, V., Hui L.H., Lee, W.C., Leung, L.S. *et al.* (2004) 'A modified screening tool for autism (Checklist for Autism in Toddlers [CHAT–23]) for Chinese children.' *Pediatrics 114*, 2: e166–176.

Wong, W.S. and Nielsen, R. (2004) 'Detecting selection in non-coding regions of nucleotide sequences.' *Genetics*, 167: 949–958.

Woodin, M., Wang, P.P., Aleman, D., McDonald-McGinn, D. *et al.* (2001) 'Neuropsychological profile of children and adolescents with the 22q11.2 microdeletion.', *Genetics in Medicine, 3*, 1: 34–39.

Woo, S.L.C., Lidsky, A.S., Guttler, F., Thirumalachary, C. and Robson, K.J.H. (1984) 'Prenatal diagnosis of classical phenylketonuria by gene mapping.', *Journal of the American Medical Association, 251*: 1998-2002.

Wooten, N., Bakalov, V.K., Hill, S. and Bondy, C.A. (2008) 'Reduced abdominal adiposity and improved glucose tolerance in GH-treated girls with Turner syndrome.' *Journal of Clinical Endocrinology and Metabolism 93*, 6: 2109–2114.

Wraith, J.E. (2001) 'Ornithine carbamoyltransferase deficiency.' *Archives of Disease in Childhood 84*, 1: 84–88.

Wright, B., Brzozowski, A.M., Calvert, E., Farnworth, H. *et al.* (2005) 'Is the presence of urinary indolyl-3-acryloylglycine associated with autism spectrum disorder?', *Developmental Medicine and Child Neurology, 47*, 3: 190–192.

Wu, H.Y., Rusnack, S.L., Bellah, R.D., Plachter, N. *et al.* (2002) 'Genitourinary malformations in chromosome 22q11.2 deletion.' *Journal of Urology*, 168: 2564–2565.

Wu, J.Y., Kuban, K.C., Allred, E., Shapiro, F. and Darras, B.T. (2005) 'Association of Duchenne muscular dystrophy with autism spectrum disorder.' *Journal of Child Neurology*, 20: 790–795.

Wu, S., Jia, M., Ruan, Y., Liu, J. *et al.* (2005b) 'Positive association of the oxytocin receptor gene (OXTR) with autism in the Chinese Han Population.' *Biological Psychiatry*, 58: 74–77.

Wyrobek, A.J., Eskenaz, B., Young, S., Arnheim, N. *et al.* (2006) 'Advancing age has differential effects on DNA damage, chromatin integrity, gene mutations, and aneuploidies in sperm.' *Proceedings of the National Academy of Science 103*, 25: 9601–9606.

Wyse, R.K.H., Al-Mahdawi, S., Burn, J. and Blake, K. (1993) 'Congenital heart disease in CHARGE association.' *Pediatric Cardiology 14*, 2: 75–81.

X

Xekouki, P., Fryssira, H., Maniati-Christidi, M., Amenta, S. *et al.* (2005) 'Growth hormone deficiency in a child with Williams-Beuren syndrome: the response to growth hormone therapy.' *Journal of Pediatric Endocrinology and Metabolism 18*, 2: 205–207.

Xi, C.Y., Ma, H.W., Lu, Y., Zhao, Y.J. *et al.* (2007) 'MeCP2 gene mutation analysis in autistic boys with developmental regression.' *Psychiatric Genetics 17*, 2: 113–116.

Xiong, N., Ji, C., Li, Y., He, Z. *et al.* (2007) 'The physical status of children with autism in China.' *Research in Developmental Disabilities*, doi:10.1016/j.ridd.2007.11.001.

Y

Yagi, H., Furutani, Y., Hamada, H., Sasaki, T. *et al.* (2003) 'Role of TBX1 in human del22q11.2 syndrome.' *Lancet 362*, 9393: 1366–1373.

Yakoub, M., Dulac, O., Jambaqué, I., Chiron, C. and Plouin, P. (1992) 'Early diagnosis of severe myoclonic epilepsy in infancy.' *Brain and Development 14*, 5: 299–303.

Yam, W.K.L., Wu, N.S.P., Lo, I.F.M., Ko, C.H. *et al.* (2004) 'Dentatorubral-pallidoluysian atrophy in two Chinese families in Hong Kong.' *Hong Kong Medical Journal 10*, 4: 53–56.

Yamagata, T., Aradhya, S., Mori, M., Inoue, K. *et al.* (2002) 'The human secretin gene: fine structure in 11p15.5 and sequence variation in patients with autism.' *Genome 80*, 2: 185–194.

Yamaguchi, S., Brailey, L.L., Morizono, H., Bale, A.E. and Tuchman, M. (2006) 'Mutations and polymorphisms in the human ornithine transcarbamylase (OTC) gene.' *Human Mutation*, 27: 626–632.

Yamamoto, T., Kuramoto, H. and Kadowaki, M. (2007) 'Downregulation in aquaporin 4 and aquaporin 8 expression of the colon associated with the induction of allergic diarrhea in a mouse model of food allergy.' *Life Sciences*, 81: 115–120.

Yang, M.S. and Gill, M. (2007) 'A review of gene linkage, association and expression studies in autism and an assessment of convergent evidence.' *International Journal of Developmental Neuroscience*, 25: 69–85.

Yang, P. and Tsai, J.H. (2004) 'Occurrence of priapism with risperidone-paroxetine combination in an autistic child.' *Journal of Child and Adolescent Psychopharmacology 14*, 3: 342–343.

Yang, Y., Guo, J., Liu, Z., Tang, S. *et al.* (2006a) 'A locus for autosomal dominant accessory auricular anomaly maps to 14q11.2–q12.' *Human Genetics*, 120: 144–147

Yang, Y., Sun, F., Song, J., Hasegawa, Y. *et al.* (2006b) 'Clinical and biochemical studies on Chinese patients with methylmalonic aciduria.' *Journal of Child Neurology*, 21: 1020–1024.

Yatsenko, S.A., Yatsenko, A.N., Szigeti, K., Craigen, W.J. *et al.* (2004) 'Interstitial deletion of 10p and atrial septal defect in DiGeorge 2 syndrome.' *Clinical Genetics 66*, 2: 128–136.

Yau, E.K.C., Shek, C.C., Chan, K.Y. and Chan, A.Y.W. (2004) 'Dihydropyrimidine dehydrogenase deficiency: a baby boy with ocular abnormalities, neonatal seizure and global developmental delay.' *Hong Kong Journal of Paediatrics* [new series], 9: 167–170.

Yazaki, M., Yoshida, K., Nakamura, A., Koyama, J. *et al.* (1999) 'Clinical characteristics of aged Becker muscular dystrophy patients with onset after 30 years.' *European Neurology*, 42: 145–149.

Yik, W.Y., Steinberg, S.J., Moser, A.B., Moser, H.W. and Hacia, J.G. (2009) 'Identification of novel mutations and sequence variation in the Zellweger syndrome spectrum of peroxisome biogenesis disorders.' *Human Mutation 30*, 3: E467–E480 doi:10.1002/humu.20932.

Yilmaz, K. (2009) 'Riboflavin treatment in a case with 1-2-hydroxyglutaric aciduria.' *European Journal of Pediatric Neurology*, 13: 57–60.

Ylisaukko-oja, T., Alarcon, M., Cantor, R.M., Auranen, M. *et al.* (2006) 'Search for autism loci by combined analysis of Autism Genetic Resource Exchange and Finnish families.' *Annals of Neurology 59*, 1: 145–155.

Ylisaukko-oja, T., Nieminen-von Wendt, T., Kempas, E., Sarenius, S. *et al.* (2004) 'Genome-wide scan for loci of Asperger syndrome.' *Molecular Psychiatry*, 9: 161–168.

Ylisaukko-oja, T., Rehnström, K., Auranen, M., Vanhala, R. *et al.* (2005) 'Analysis of four neuroligin genes as candidates for autism.' *European Journal of Human Genetics 13*, 12: 1285–1292.

Yonan, A.L., Alarcon, M., Cheng, R., Magnusson, P.K. *et al.* (2003) 'A genomewide screen of 345 families for autism-susceptibility loci.' *American Journal of Human Genetics*, 73: 886–897.

Yorifuji, T., Muroi, J., Uematsu, A., Tanaka, K. *et al.* (1998) 'X-inactivation pattern in the liver of a manifesting female with ornithine transcarbamylase (OTC) deficiency.' *Clinical Genetics*, 54: 349–353.

Yoshimura, I., Sasaki, A., Akimoto, H. and Yoshimura, N. (1989) ['A case of congenital myotonic dystrophy with infantile autism.'] [Article in Japanese.] *No To Hattatsu*, 21: 379–384.

Yovich, J.L., Stanger, J.D., Grauaug, A.A., Lunay, G.G. *et al.* (1985) 'Fetal abnormality (Goldenhar syndrome) occurring in one of triplet infants derived from in vitro fertilization with possible monozygotic twinning.' *Journal of In Vitro Fertilization and Embryo Transfer*, 2: 27–32.

Yu, H. and Patel, S.B. (2005) 'Recent insights into the Smith-Lemli-Opitz syndrome.' *Clinical Genetics 68*, 5: 383–391.

Yussman, S.M., Ryan, S.A., Auinger, P. and Weitzman, M. (2004) 'Visits to complementary and alternative medicine providers by children and adolescents in the United States.' *Ambulatory Pediatrics 4*, 5: 429–435.

Z

Zacharin, M. (2007) 'The spectrum of McCune Albright syndrome.' *Pediatric Endocrinology Reviews 4*, Suppl. 4: 412–418.

Zafeiriou, D.I., Ververi, A., Salomons, G.S., Vargiami, E. *et al.* (2007) 'L-2-hydroxyglutaric aciduria presenting with severe autistic features.' *Brain and Development 30*, 4: 305–307, doi:10.1016/j.braindev.2007.09.005.

Zafeiriou, D.I., Ververi, A. and Vargiami, E. (2006) 'Childhood autism and associated comorbidities.' *Brain and Development 29*, 5: 257–272.

Zana, M., Janka, Z. and Kalman, J. (2007) 'Oxidative stress: A bridge between Down's syndrome and Alzheimer's disease.' *Neurobiology of Aging*, 28: 648–676.

Zannolli, R., Micheli, V., Mazzei, M.A., Sacco, P. *et al.* (2003) 'Hereditary xanthinuria type II associated with mental delay, autism, cortical renal cysts, nephrocalcinosis, osteopenia, and hair and teeth defects.' *Journal of Medical Genetics*, 40: 121, www.jmedgenet.com – doi:10.1136/jmg.40.11. e121.

Zapella, M. (1990) 'Autistic features in children affected by cerebral gigantism. *Brain Dysfunction*, 3: 241–244.

Zapella, M. (1993) 'Autism and Hypomelanosis of Ito in twins.' *Developmental Medicine and Child Neurology*, 35: 826–832.

Zapella, M. (1997) 'The preserved speech variant of the Rett complex: a report of 8 cases.' *European Child and Adolescent Psychiatry 6*, 1: 23–25.

Zapella, M., Gillberg, C. and Ehlers, S. (1998) 'The preserved speech variant: a subgroup of the Rett complex. A clinical report of 30 cases.' *Journal of Autism and Developmental Disorders 28*, 6: 519–526.

Zapella, M., Meloni, I., Longo, I., Hayek, G. and Renieri, A. (2001) 'Preserved speech variants of the Rett syndrome: molecular and clinical analysis.' *American Journal of Medical Genetics*, 104: 14–22.

Zarnescu, D.C., Jin, P., Betschinger, J., Nakamoto, M. *et al.* (2005a) 'Fragile-X protein functions with lgl and the PAR complex in flies and mice.' *Developmental Cell*, 8: 43–52.

Zarnescu, D.C., Shan, G., Warren, S.T. and Jin, P. (2005b) 'Come FLY with us: toward understanding fragile-X syndrome.' *Genes, Brain and Behavior 4*, 6: 385–392.

Zatz, M., Rapaport, D., Vainzof, M., Passos-Bueno, M.R. *et al.* (1991) 'Serum creatine-kinase (CK) and pyruvate-kinase (PK) activities in Duchenne (DMD) as compared with Becker (BMD) muscular dystrophy.' *Journal of Neurological Science*, 102: 190–196.

Zbuk, K.M., Stein, J.L. and Eng, C. (2006) '*PTEN* hamartoma tumor syndrome (PHTS).' *GeneReviews*, accessible at www.ncbi.nlm.nih.gov.

Zeev, B.B., Yaron, Y., Schanen, N.C., Wolf, H. *et al.* (2002) 'Rett syndrome: clinical manifestations in males with *MECP2* mutations.' *Journal of Child Neurology*, 17: 20–24.

Zettersten, E., Man, M.-Q., Sato, J., Denda, M. *et al.* (1998) 'Recessive X-linked ichthyosis: role of cholesterol-sulfate accumulation in the barrier abnormality.' *Journal of Investigative Dermatology*, 111: 784–790.

Zhou, J., Kong, H., Hua, X., Xiao, M. *et al.* (2008) 'Altered blood–brain barrier integrity in adult aquaporin-4 knockout mice.' *NeuroReport*, 19: 1–5.

Zhou, X., Hampel, H., Thiele, H., Gorlin, R.J. *et al.* (2001) 'Association of germline mutation in the PTEN tumour suppressor gene and Proteus and Proteus-like syndromes.' *Lancet* 358, 9277: 210–211.

Zhou, X.P., Marsh, D.J., Hampel, H., Mulliken, J.B. *et al.* (2000) 'Germline and germline mosaic mutations associated with a Proteus-like syndrome of hemihypertrophy, lower limb asymmetry, arterio-venous malformations and lipomatosis.' *Human Molecular Genetics*, 9: 765–768.

Zhou, X.P., Waite, K.A., Pilarski, R., Hampel, H. *et al.* (2003) 'Germline PTEN promoter mutations and deletions in Cowden/Bannayan-Riley-Ruvalcaba syndrome result in aberrant PTEN protein and dysregulation of the phosphoinositol-3kinase/Akt pathway.' *American Journal of Human Genetics*, 73: 404–411.

Zigman, A.F., Lavine, J.E., Jones, M.C., Boland, C.R. and Carethers, J.M. (1997) 'Localization of the Bannayan-Riley-Ruvalcaba syndrome gene to chromosome 10q23.' *Gastroenterology*, 113: 1433–1437.

Zimmerman, A.W., Connors, S.L., Matteson, K.J., Lee, L.-C. *et al.* (2007) 'Maternal antibrain antibodies in autism.' *Brain, Behavior, and Immunity*, 21: 351–357.

Zimmerman, A.W., Jyonouchi, H., Comi, A.M., Connors, S.L. *et al.* (2005) 'Cerebrospinal fluid and serum markers of inflammation in autism.' *Pediatric Neurology*, 33: 195–201.

Zimmermann, N., Acosta, A.M.B.F., Kohlhase, J. and Bartsch, O. (2007) 'Confirmation of EP300 gene mutations as a rare cause of Rubinstein-Taybi syndrome.' *European Journal of Human Genetics*, 15: 837–842.

Zingerevich, C., GreissHess, L., Lemons-Chitwood, K., Harris, S.W. *et al.* (2009) 'Motor abilities of children diagnosed with fragile-X syndrome with and without autism.' *Journal of Intellectual Disability Research 53*, 1: 11–18.

Zinn, A.R., Roeltgen, D., Stefanatos, G., Ramos, P. *et al.* (2007) 'A Turner syndrome neurocognitive phenotype maps to Xp22.3.' *Behavioral and Brain Functions*, 3: 24 doi:10.1186/1744-9081-3-24.

Zipursky, A., Peeters, M. and Poon, A. (1987) 'Megakaryoblastic leukemia and Down syndrome – A Review.' In E.E. McCoy and C.J. Epstein: *Oncology and Immunology of Down Syndrome*. New York: Alan R. Liss.

Ziter, F.A., Wiser, W.C. and Robinson, A. (1977) 'Three-generation pedigree of a Möbius syndrome variant with chromosome translocation.' *Archives of Neurology 34*, 7: 437–442.

Zittoun, J. (1995) 'Congenital errors of folate metabolism.' *Bailliere's Clinical Haematology 8*, 3: 603–616.

Zittoun, J. (2001) ['Biermer's disease.'] [Article in French.] *Revue Pratique 51*, 14: 1542–1546.

Zizka, J., Elias, P. and Jakubec, J. (2001) 'Spontaneous regression of low-grade astrocytomas: an underrecognized condition?' *European Radiology*, 11: 2638–2640.

Zoghbi, H.Y., Ledbetter, D.H., Schultz, R., Percy, A.K. and Glaze, D.G. (1990) 'A de novo X3 translocation in Rett syndrome.' *American Journal of Medical Genetics*, 35: 148–151.

Zoller, M.E., Rembeck, B. and Backman, L. (1997) 'Neuropsychological deficits in adults with neurofibromatosis type 1.' *Acta Neurologica Scandinavica*, 95: 225–232.

Zonana, J., Davis, D. and Rimoin, D.L. (1975) 'Multiple lipomas, hemangiomas and macrocephaly – an autosomal dominant hamartomatous syndrome' (abstract). *American Journal of Human Genetics*, 27: 97A.

Zonana, J., Rimoin, D.L. and Davis, D.C. (1976) 'Macrocephaly with multiple lipomas and hemangiomas.' *Journal of Pediatrics*, 89: 600–603.

Zschocke, J., Graham, C.A., Stewart, F.J., Carson, D.J. and Nevin, N.C. (1994) 'Non-phenylketonuria hyperphenylalaninaemia in Northern Ireland: frequent mutation allows screening and early diagnosis.' *Human Mutation*, 4: 114–118.

Zucconi, M., Ferini-Strambi, L., Erminio, C., Pestalozza, G. and Smirne, S. (1993) 'Obstructive sleep apnea in the Rubinstein-Taybi syndrome.' *Respiration 60*, 2: 127–132.

Zwaigenbaum, L. and Tarnopolsky, M. (2003) 'Two children with muscular dystrophies ascertained due to referral for diagnosis of autism.' *Journal of Autism and Developmental Disorders*, 33: 193–199.

Zweier, C., Thiel, C.T., Dufke, A., Crow, Y.J. *et al.* (2005) 'Clinical and mutational spectrum of Mowat-Wilson syndrome.' *European Journal of Medical Genetics*, 48: 97–111.

Further reading

There are many excellent books on genetics, biology and their relevance to everyday human life which provide far greater coverage of elements of this extensive field than is possible here. For those who require an easy introduction, I recommend these simple but well-written books:

Chiu, L.S. (2006) *When a Gene Makes You Smell Like a Fish...and Other Tales about the Genes in Your Body.* New York: Oxford University Press.
Moalem, S. (2007) *Survival of the Sickest: A Medical Maverick Discovers Why We Need Disease.* London: HarperCollins.

The following are particularly commended to those who wish to read further in areas relevant to the neurobiology of ASD:

Allis, C.D., Jenuwein, T., Reinberg, D. and Caparros, M.-L. (eds.) (2006) *Epigenetics.* Cold Spring Harbour: Cold Spring Harbour Press.
Arbib, M.A. (2006) *Action to Language via the Mirror Neuron System.* Cambridge: Cambridge University Press.
Baxter, P. (ed.) (2001) *Vitamin Responsive Conditions in Paediatric Neurology.* Cambridge: MacKeith Press.
Berthoz, A., Andres, C., Barthelemy, C., Massion, J. and Roge, B. (eds.) (2005) *L'Autisme: De la recherche a la pratique.* Paris: Odile Jacob.
Butler, M.G. and Meaney, F.J. (eds.) (2005) *Genetics of Developmental Disabilities.* Boca Raton: Taylor and Francis.
Cassidy, S.B. and Allanson, J.E. (eds.) (2005) *Management of Genetic Syndromes* (2nd edn.). Hoboken, New Jersey: John Wiley and Sons.
Charman, T. and Stone, W. (eds.) (2006) *Social and Communication Development in Autism Spectrum Disorders: Early Identification, Diagnosis, and Intervention.* New York: Guilford Press.
Cicchetti, D. and Cohen, D.J. (eds.) (2006) *Developmental Psychopathology* (3 vols.; 2nd edn). Hoboken, New Jersey: John Wiley and Sons.
Cohen, M. Jr., Neri, G. and Weksberg, R. (2002) *Overgrowth Syndromes.* New York: Oxford University Press.
Coleman, M. (ed.) (2005) *The Neurology of Autism.* Oxford: Oxford University Press.
Dhossche, D.M. (ed.) (2005) *GABA in Autism and Related Disorders.* New York: Academic Press.
Doerfler, W. and Bohm, P. (eds.) (2006) *DNA Methylation: Development, Genetic Disease and Cancer.* Berlin: Springer.
Fisch, G.S. and Flint, J.M.D. (eds.) (2006) *Transgenic and Knockout Models of Neuropsychiatric Disorders.* Tolowa, New Jersey: Humana Press.
Gluckman, P. and Hanson, M. (2005) *The Fetal Matrix: Evolution, Development and Disease.* Cambridge: Cambridge University Press.
Hagerman, R. (1999) *Neurodevelopmental Disorders: Diagnosis and Treatment.* Oxford: Oxford University Press.
Harris, J.C. (1995) *Developmental Neuropsychiatry* (2 vols.). New York: Oxford University Press.
Harris, J.C. (2006) *Intellectual Disability: Understanding its Development, Causes, Classification, Evaluation, and Treatment.* New York: Oxford University Press.
Hurst, J.A., Firth, H.V. and Hall, J.G. (eds.) (2005) *Oxford Desk Reference Clinical Genetics.* Oxford: Oxford University Press.
Jones, K. (2005) *Smith's Recognizable Patterns of Human Malformation* (6th edn). Amsterdam: Saunders (Elsevier).
McKinlay Gardner, R.J. and Sutherland, G.R. (2003) *Chromosome Abnormalities and Genetic Counselling.* Oxford: Oxford University Press.
Moldin, S.O. and Rubenstein, J.L.R. (eds.) (2006) *Understanding Autism: From Basic Neuroscience to Treatment.* Boca Raton: Taylor and Francis.
Nyhan, W.L., Barshop, B.A. and Ozand, P.T. (2006) *Atlas of Metabolic Diseases* (2nd edn). London: Chapman and Hall.
Oldstone, M.B.A. (ed.) (2005) *Molecular Mimicry: Infection Inducing Autoimmune Disease.* New York: Springer.
Ozonoff, S., Rogers, S.J. and Hendren, R.L. (eds.) (2003) *Autism Spectrum Disorders: A Research Review for Practitioners.* Washington: American Psychiatric Publishing.
Peres, J.M., Gonzalez, P.M., Comi, M.L. and Nieto, C. (eds.) (2007) *New Developments in Autism: The Future is Today.* London: Jessica Kingsley Publishers.
Reilley, P.R. (2006) *The Strongest Boy in the World: How Genetic Information is Reshaping Our Lives.* New York: Cold Spring Harbour Laboratory Press.
Rogers, S.J. and Williams, J.H.G. (eds.) (2006) *Imitation and the Social Mind: Autism and Typical Development.* New York: Guilford Press.
Romer, D. and Walker, E.F. (2007) *Adolescent Psychopathology and the Developing Brain.* New York: Oxford University Press.
Runge, M.S. and Patterson, C. (eds.) (2006) *Principles of Molecular Medicine* (2nd edn). Tolowa, New Jersey: Humana Press.
Smith, M. (2006) *Mental Retardation and Developmental Delay: Genetic and Epigenetic Factors.* Oxford: Oxford University Press.
Stamenov, M.I. and Gallese, V. (eds.) (2002) *Mirror Neurons and the Evolution of Brain and Language.* Amsterdam: John Benjamins.
Tager-Flussberg, H. (ed.) (1999) *Neurodevelopmental Disorders.* Cambridge, Massachusetts: MIT Press.
Tuchman, R. and Rapin, I. (eds.) (2006) *Autism: A Neurological Disorder of Early Brain Development.* Cambridge: Cambridge University Press.
Volkmar, F.R., Paul, R., Klin, A. and Cohen, D. (eds.) (2005) *Handbook of Autism and Developmental Disorders* (2 vols.; 3rd edn). Hoboken, New Jersey: John Wiley and Sons.

the baby signing book

the
baby signing
book

Includes **350** ASL Signs
for Babies & Toddlers

Sara Bingham

B.A. (Linguistics), B.A. (Psychology), Honors Diploma
(Communicative Disorders Assistant)

Illustrated by Jamie Villanueva

Robert
ROSE

To my husband, Angelo, our two children,
and all the families WeeHands has taught.
Thank you all.

Disclaimer
This book is a general guide only and should never be a substitute for the skill, knowledge, and experience of a qualified medical professional dealing with the facts, circumstances, and symptoms of a particular case.

    The nutritional, medical, and health information presented in this book is based on the research, training, and professional experience of the author, and is true and complete to the best of her knowledge. However, this book is intended only as an informative guide for those wishing to know more about health, nutrition, and medicine; it is not intended to replace or countermand the advice given by the reader's personal physician. Because each person and situation is unique, the author and the publisher urge the reader to check with a qualified health-care professional before using any procedure where there is a question as to its appropriateness. A physician should be consulted before beginning any exercise program. The author and the publisher are not responsible for any adverse effects or consequences resulting from the use of the information in this book. It is the responsibility of the reader to consult a physician or other qualified health-care professional regarding his or her personal care.

Library and Archives Canada Cataloguing in Publication

Bingham, Sara
   The baby signing book: includes 350 ASL signs for babies & toddlers / Sara Bingham.

Includes index.
ISBN 978-0-7788-0163-4

1. Nonverbal communication in infants. 2. Interpersonal communication in infants.
3. American Sign Language. 4. Sign language. I. Title.

BF720.C65B55 2007   419'.70832   C2007-903028-9

Design and page composition: Joseph Gisini / PageWave Graphics Inc.
Illustrator: Jamie Villanueva
Cover photograph: © Larry Williams/zefa/Corbis
Editor: Bob Hilderley, Senior Editor, Health
Copyeditor: Sue Sumeraj
Proofreader: Sheila Wawanash
Indexer: Gillian Watts

The publisher acknowledges the financial support of the Government of Canada through the Book Publishing Industry Development Program.

Published by Robert Rose Inc.,
120 Eglinton Ave. E., Suite 800, Toronto, Ontario Canada M4P 1E2
Tel: (416) 322-6552 Fax: (416) 322-6936

Printed and bound in Canada.

1 2 3 4 5 6 7 8 9 TCP 15 14 13 12 11 10 09 08 07

Contents

Preface

LIKE MANY PARENTS WHO SIGN WITH THEIR baby, my initial motivation for teaching my son American Sign Language (ASL) vocabulary was to give him a way to express his wants and needs before he was able to speak. Joshua started signing at 9 months of age, and by the time he was 18 months old, he could use at least 80 words, a combination of spoken words and signs. He was able to communicate his needs and wants. He could request a cookie by signing COOKIE. He could ask for more fruit cocktail by signing FRUIT. He could even ask to have the family minivan cooled down in the middle of a heat wave by pointing to the dashboard and signing COLD WIND — a better phrase, really, than air conditioner! Joshua's ability to make clear requests using signs delighted my husband and me.

What truly impressed us, though, was Joshua's ability to comment on his world and share his experiences with us. I have a clear memory of one cloudy, chilly, windy, miserable spring day when I took Joshua for a walk and he was able to sign about the weather. We were walking along the streets in a new housing development — no houses up, but the streets were paved — with nothing to block the wind. It was cold! I just wanted to get our walk over with and go home. What brought me back to the moment was when Joshua pulled on my jacket and signed WIND. A few seconds later, he signed CLOUD. He was marveling at the weather — not simply making a request, but sharing a moment with me. I could tell from his face that it was a remarkable experience for him as well.

I am often asked why I started signing with my children. Before having children, I worked with the Toronto Preschool Speech and Language Services. Alongside speech-language pathologists and other professionals, I worked with children with Down syndrome, autism, and other developmental delays. These children had difficulty communicating, and we used sign language and pictures to help facilitate their language development. Our therapy included helping parents learn to use sign language and pictures with their children.

Because of my work, I knew the benefits of using ASL with children who are non-verbal or beginning communicators. Together, we learned to sign songs and nursery rhymes. After